AYS REMAIN

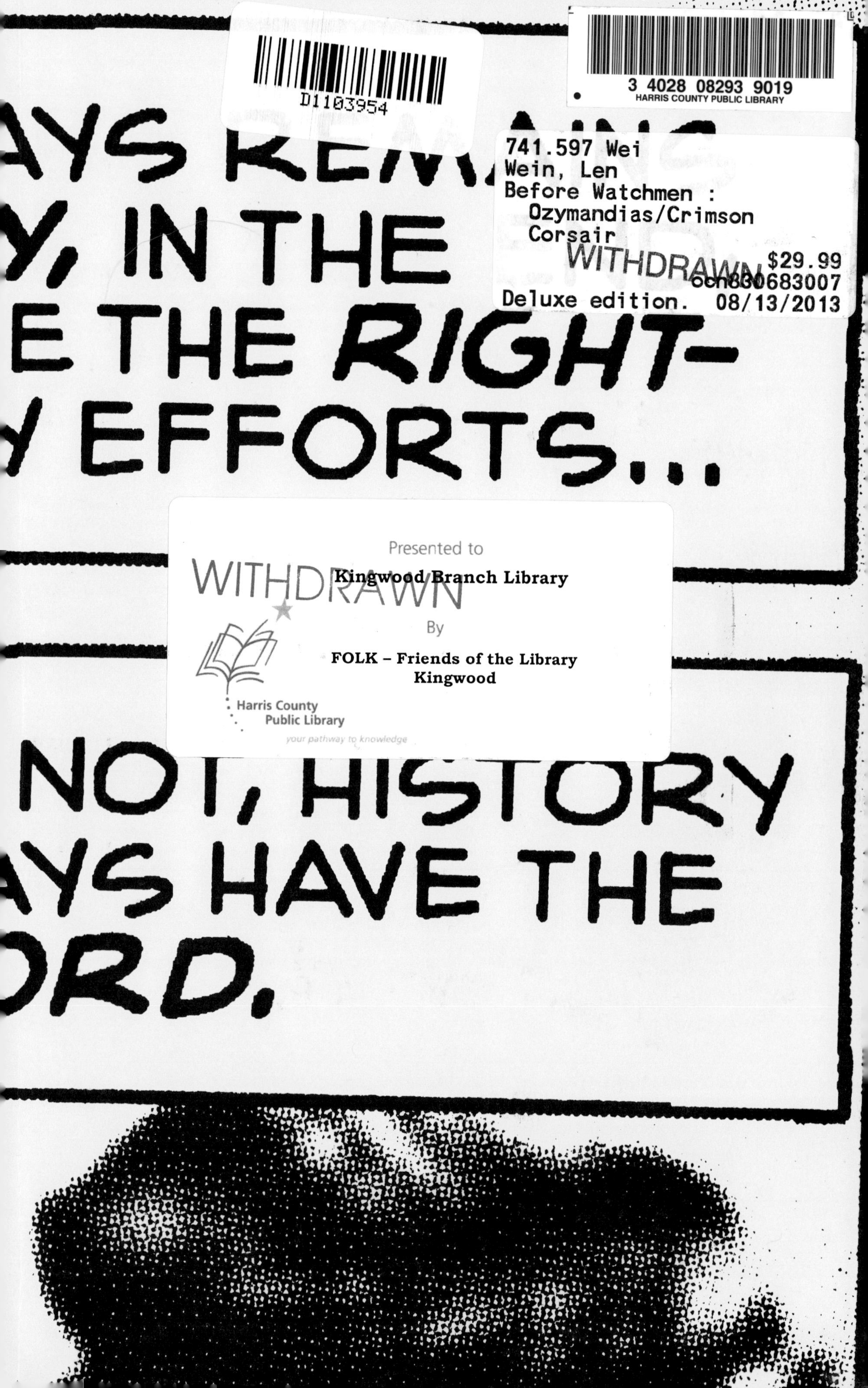

Y, IN THE

E THE *RIGHT-*

Y EFFORTS...

NOT, HISTORY

AYS HAVE THE

ORD.

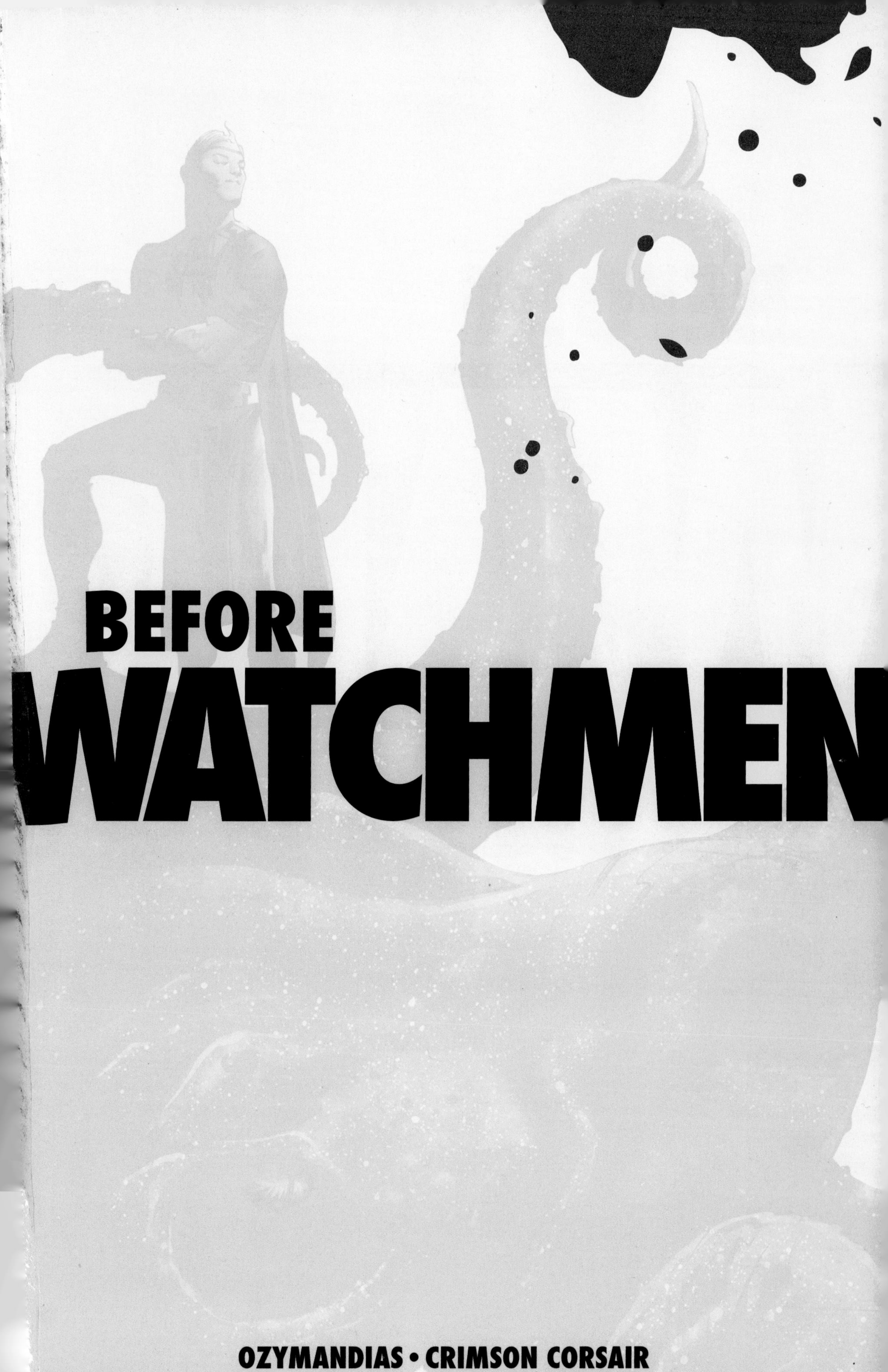

BEFORE WATCHMEN

OZYMANDIAS • CRIMSON CORSAIR

BEFORE

WATC

HMEN

OZYMANDIAS • CRIMSON CORSAIR

LEN WEIN
JOHN HIGGINS
writers

JAE LEE JOHN HIGGINS
STEVE RUDE
artists

JUNE CHUNG JOHN HIGGINS
GLEN WHITMORE
colorists

JOHN WORKMAN SAL CIPRIANO
STEVE RUDE
letterers

JAE LEE and **JOHN HIGGINS** with **JUNE CHUNG**
cover artists

Watchmen created by
ALAN MOORE and **DAVE GIBBONS**

MARK CHIARELLO WILL DENNIS Editors – Original Series
CHRIS CONROY MARK DOYLE WIL MOSS Associate Editors – Original Series
CAMILLA ZHANG Assistant Editor – Original Series
PETER HAMBOUSSI Editor
RACHEL PINNELAS Assistant Editor
ROBBIN BROSTERMAN Design Director – Books
ROBBIE BIEDERMAN Publication Design

BOB HARRAS Senior VP – Editor-in-Chief, DC Comics

DIANE NELSON President
DAN DIDIO and JIM LEE Co-Publishers
GEOFF JOHNS Chief Creative Officer
JOHN ROOD Executive VP – Sales, Marketing & Business Development
AMY GENKINS Senior VP – Business & Legal Affairs
NAIRI GARDINER Senior VP – Finance
JEFF BOISON VP – Publishing Planning
MARK CHIARELLO VP – Art Direction & Design
JOHN CUNNINGHAM VP – Marketing
TERRI CUNNINGHAM VP – Editorial Administration
ALISON GILL Senior VP – Manufacturing & Operations
HANK KANALZ Senior VP – Vertigo & Integrated Publishing
JAY KOGAN VP – Business & Legal Affairs, Publishing
JACK MAHAN VP – Business Affairs, Talent
NICK NAPOLITANO VP – Manufacturing Administration
SUE POHJA VP – Book Sales
COURTNEY SIMMONS Senior VP – Publicity
BOB WAYNE Senior VP – Sales

Cover design by CHIP KIDD

BEFORE WATCHMEN: OZYMANDIAS/CRIMSON CORSAIR
Published by DC Comics. Cover and compilation Copyright © 2013 DC Comics. All Rights Reserved.
Originally published in single magazine form in BEFORE WATCHMEN: OZYMANDIAS 1-6, BEFORE WATCHMEN: DOLLAR BILL 1,
BEFORE WATCHMEN: MINUTEMEN 1-5, BEFORE WATCHMEN: SILK SPECTRE 1-4, BEFORE WATCHMEN: COMEDIAN 1-4,
BEFORE WATCHMEN: NITE OWL 1-3, BEFORE WATCHMEN: RORSCHACH 1-3, BEFORE WATCHMEN: DR. MANHATTAN 1-3,
BEFORE WATCHMEN: MOLOCH 1-2. Copyright © 2012, 2013 DC Comics. All Rights Reserved. All characters, their distinctive likenesses
and related elements featured in this publication are trademarks of DC Comics. The stories, characters and incidents featured in this
publication are entirely fictional. DC Comics does not read or accept unsolicited ideas, stories or artwork.

DC Comics, 1700 Broadway, New York, NY 10019. A Warner Bros. Entertainment Company.
Printed by RR Donnelley, Salem, VA, USA. 5/24/13. First Printing.
ISBN: 978-1-4012-3895-7

SUSTAINABLE FORESTRY INITIATIVE
Certified Chain of Custody
At Least 20% Certified Forest Content
www.sfiprogram.org
SFI-01042
APPLIES TO TEXT STOCK ONLY

Library of Congress Cataloging-in-Publication Data

Wein, Len, author.
  Before Watchmen : Ozymandias/Crimson Corsair / Len Wein, Jae Lee, John Higgins.
    pages cm. — (Before Watchmen)
  "Originally published in single magazine form in Before Watchmen: Ozymandias 1-6,
Before Watchmen: Dollar Bill 1, Before Watchmen: Night Owl 1-4, Before Watchmen: Dr. Manhattan 1-4,
Before Watchmen: Comedian 1-6, Before Watchmen: Rorschach 1-4, Before Watchmen: Moloch 1-2,
Before Watchmen: Minutemen 1-6 and Before Watchmen: Silk Spectre 1-4."
  ISBN 978-1-4012-3895-7
1. Graphic novels. I. Lee, Jae, 1972- illustrator. II. Higgins, John, 1949- illustrator. III. Title. IV.
Title: Ozymandias/Crimson Corsair.
  PN6728.W386W46 2013
  741.5'973—DC23
                        2013009153

BEFORE WATCHMEN

OZYMANDIAS
writer – LEN WEIN   artist – JAE LEE
colorist – JUNE CHUNG   letterer – JOHN WORKMAN

THE CURSE OF THE CRIMSON CORSAIR
writers – LEN WEIN and JOHN HIGGINS
artist – JOHN HIGGINS   letterer – SAL CIPRIANO

DOLLAR BILL
writer – LEN WEIN   artist – STEVE RUDE
colorist – GLEN WHITMORE   letterer – STEVE RUDE

To my darling wife Christine,
for making me realize who I truly am.

LEN WEIN

John has a number of creative people to thank for help and support on *Curse of the Crimson Corsair*, first and foremost Sally Jane Hurst for colour and for working with me on all the seven-day weeks.

Mike Carroll, for dialogue coaching when needed, and the wisdom he has on oblique storytelling.

Sam Hart and Juliano Oliveira for the Mayan (Tupi Guarani) dialogue.

And all the people involved in the *Before Watchmen* series for the supreme artistry they brought to it, and particularly my editorial buddies for their professionalism, patience and direction when needed.

Finally, a major thank-you to the creators of the *Watchmen*, Dave Gibbons and Alan Moore, without whom none of this would have been possible.

JOHN HIGGINS

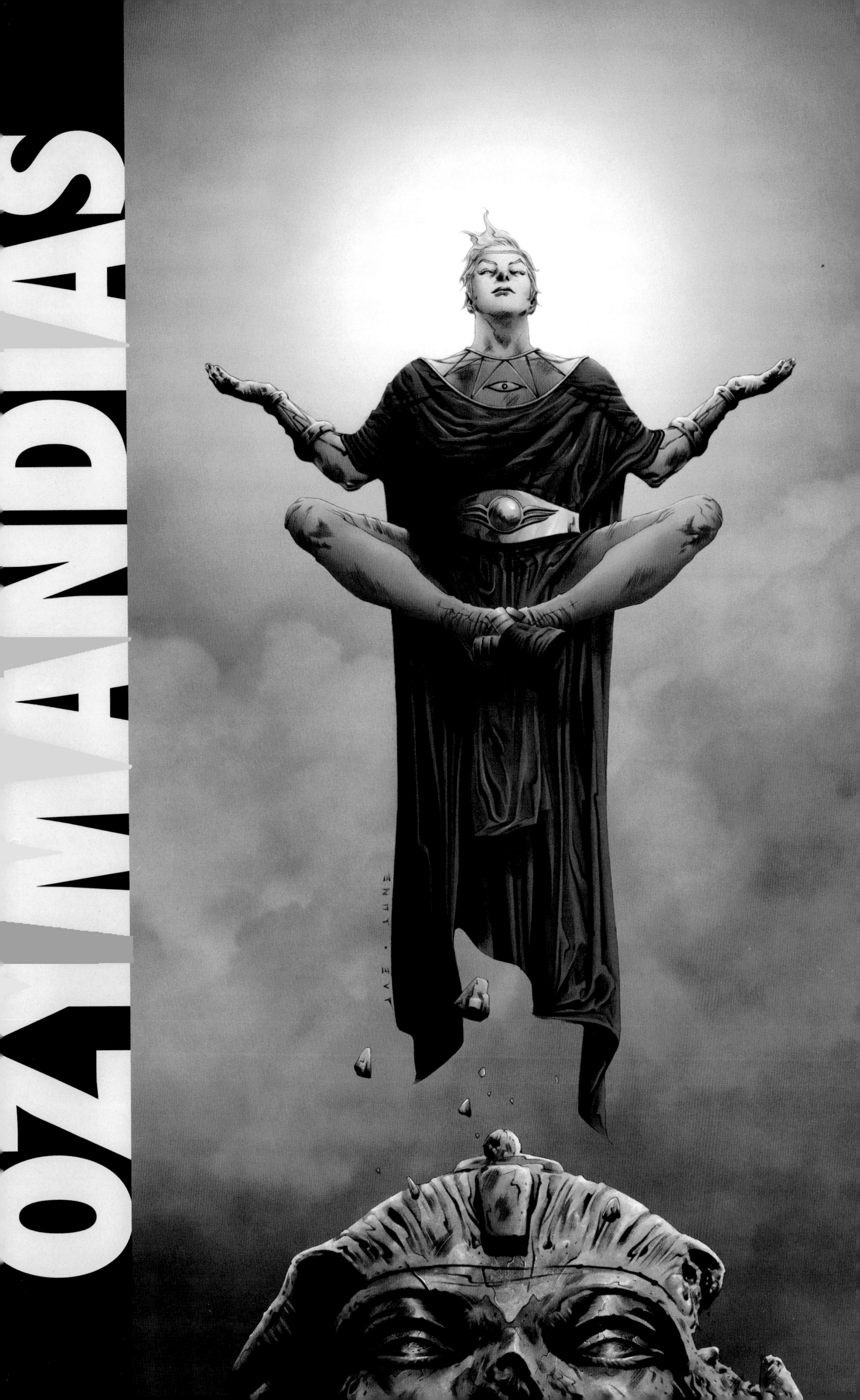
OZYMANDIAS

OZYMANDIAS

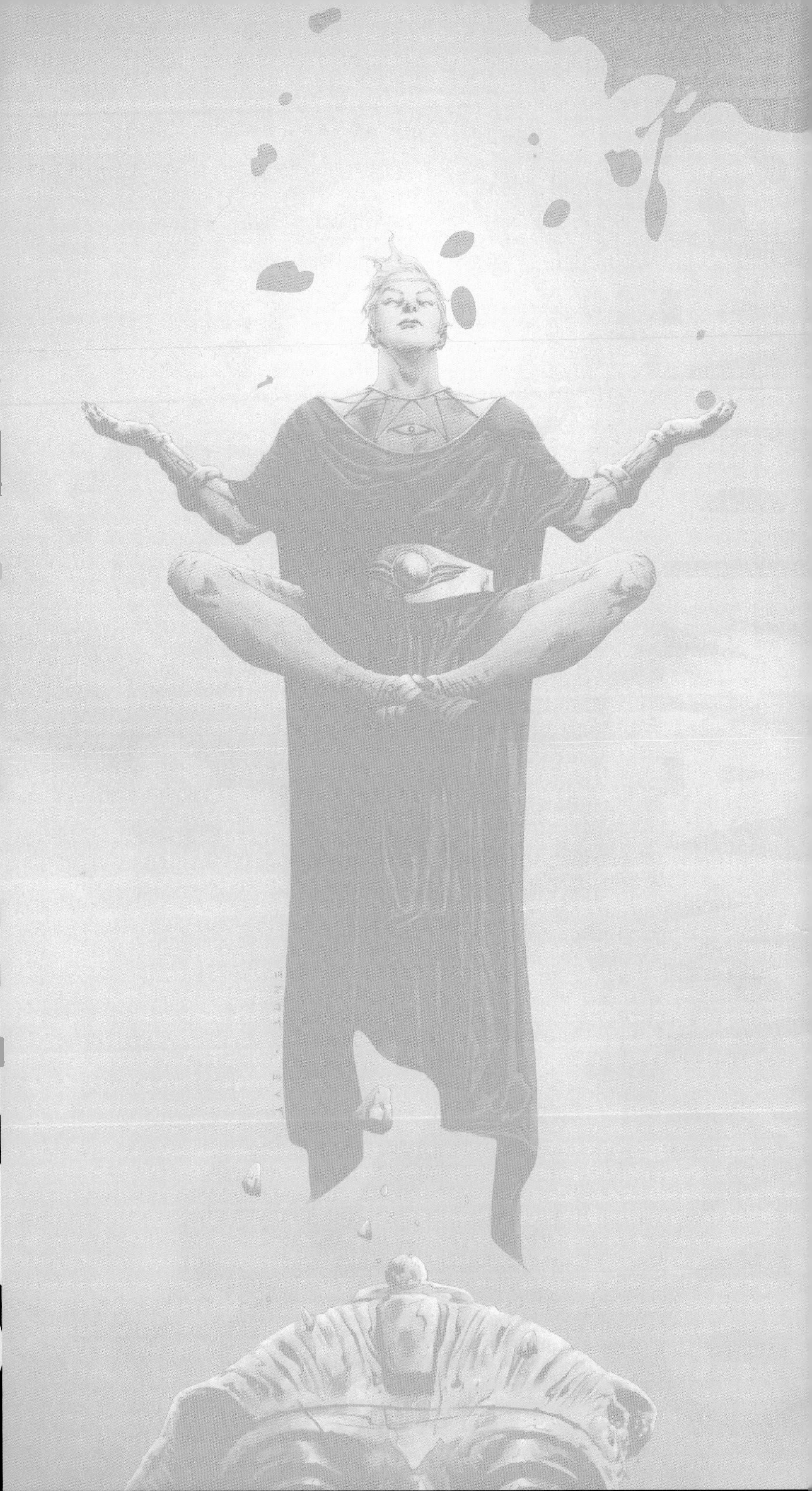

"I HAVE GOALS TO ACHIEVE. DREAMS TO MAKE COME TRUE."

I MET A TRAVELER...!

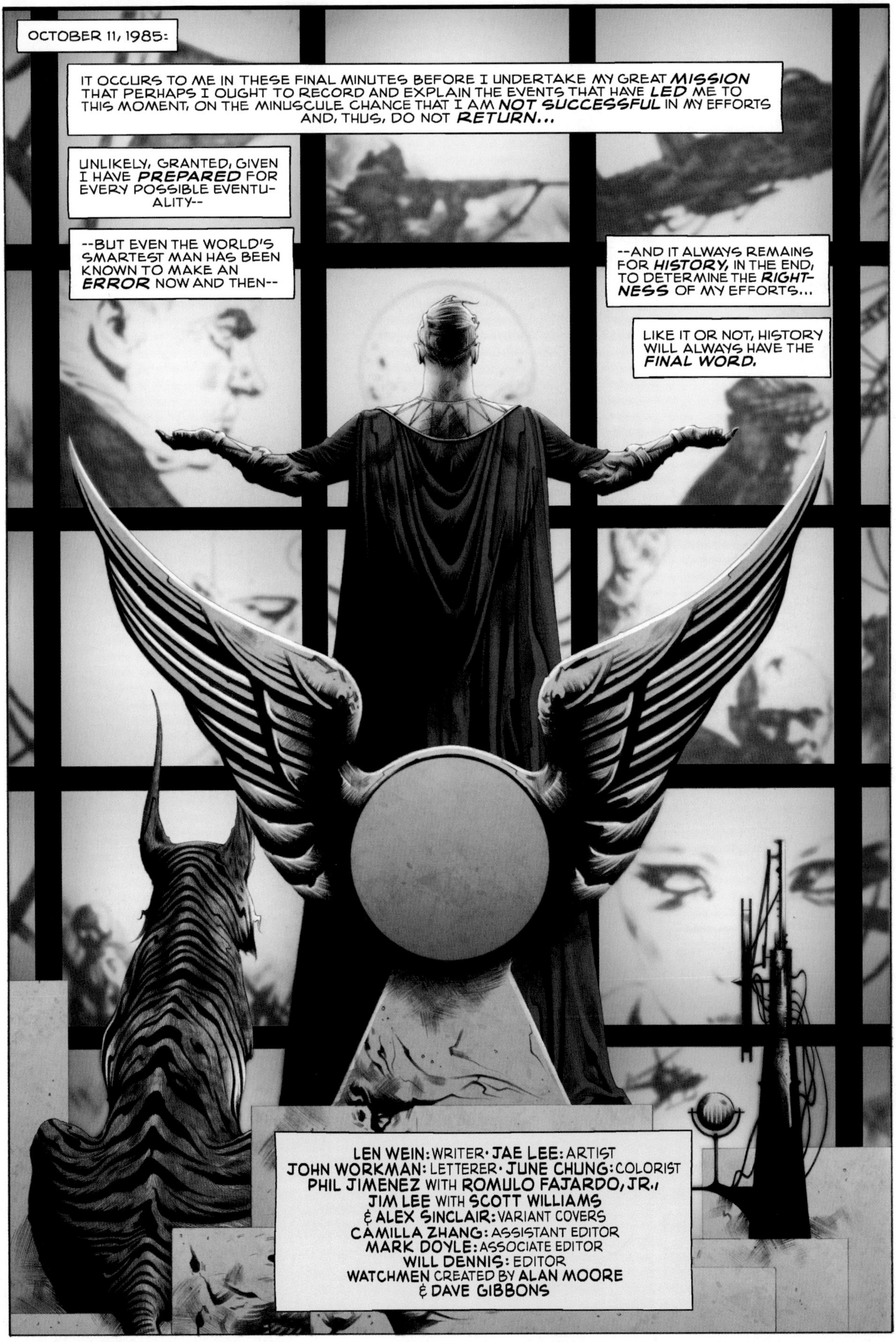
OCTOBER 11, 1985:
IT OCCURS TO ME IN THESE FINAL MINUTES BEFORE I UNDERTAKE MY GREAT MISSION THAT PERHAPS I OUGHT TO RECORD AND EXPLAIN THE EVENTS THAT HAVE LED ME TO THIS MOMENT, ON THE MINUSCULE CHANCE THAT I AM NOT SUCCESSFUL IN MY EFFORTS AND, THUS, DO NOT RETURN...
UNLIKELY, GRANTED, GIVEN I HAVE PREPARED FOR EVERY POSSIBLE EVENTUALITY--
--BUT EVEN THE WORLD'S SMARTEST MAN HAS BEEN KNOWN TO MAKE AN ERROR NOW AND THEN--
--AND IT ALWAYS REMAINS FOR HISTORY, IN THE END, TO DETERMINE THE RIGHTNESS OF MY EFFORTS...
LIKE IT OR NOT, HISTORY WILL ALWAYS HAVE THE FINAL WORD.
LEN WEIN: WRITER • JAE LEE: ARTIST
JOHN WORKMAN: LETTERER • JUNE CHUNG: COLORIST
PHIL JIMENEZ WITH ROMULO FAJARDO, JR.,
JIM LEE WITH SCOTT WILLIAMS
& ALEX SINCLAIR: VARIANT COVERS
CAMILLA ZHANG: ASSISTANT EDITOR
MARK DOYLE: ASSOCIATE EDITOR
WILL DENNIS: EDITOR
WATCHMEN CREATED BY ALAN MOORE
& DAVE GIBBONS

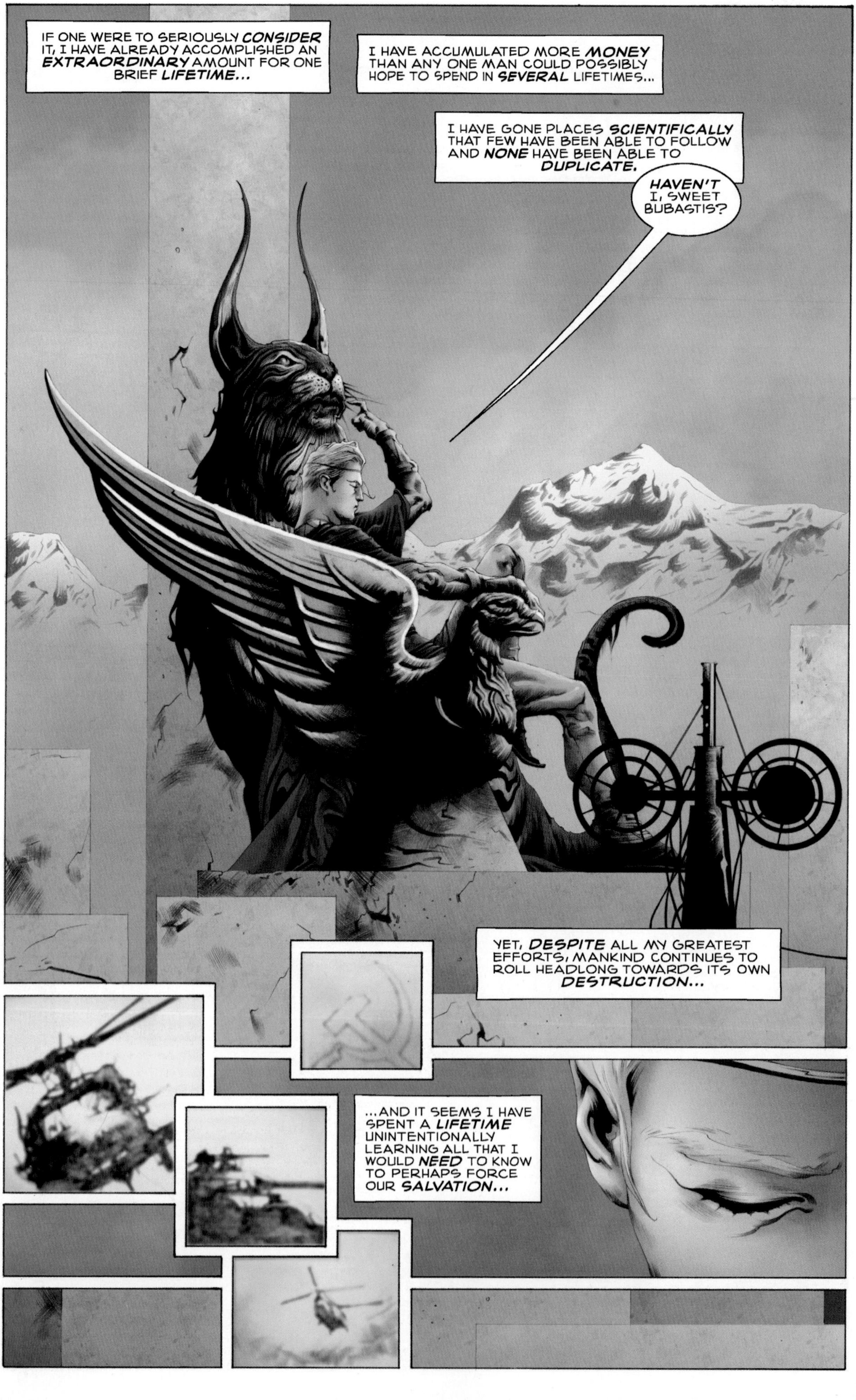
IF ONE WERE TO SERIOUSLY CONSIDER IT, I HAVE ALREADY ACCOMPLISHED AN EXTRAORDINARY AMOUNT FOR ONE BRIEF LIFETIME...
I HAVE ACCUMULATED MORE MONEY THAN ANY ONE MAN COULD POSSIBLY HOPE TO SPEND IN SEVERAL LIFETIMES...
I HAVE GONE PLACES SCIENTIFICALLY THAT FEW HAVE BEEN ABLE TO FOLLOW AND NONE HAVE BEEN ABLE TO DUPLICATE.
HAVEN'T I, SWEET BUBASTIS?
YET, DESPITE ALL MY GREATEST EFFORTS, MANKIND CONTINUES TO ROLL HEADLONG TOWARDS ITS OWN DESTRUCTION...
...AND IT SEEMS I HAVE SPENT A LIFETIME UNINTENTIONALLY LEARNING ALL THAT I WOULD NEED TO KNOW TO PERHAPS FORCE OUR SALVATION...

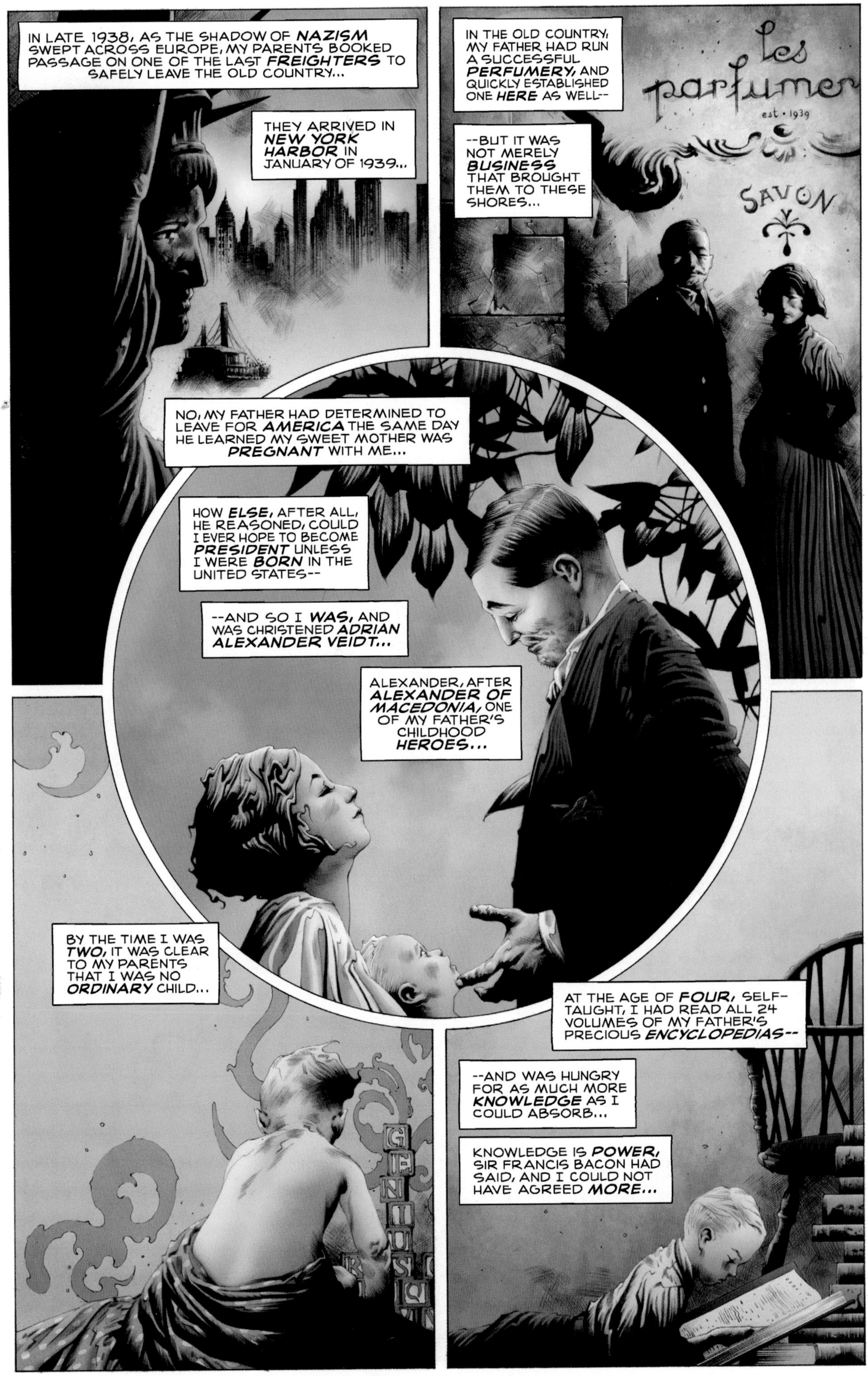
IN LATE 1938, AS THE SHADOW OF NAZISM SWEPT ACROSS EUROPE, MY PARENTS BOOKED PASSAGE ON ONE OF THE LAST FREIGHTERS TO SAFELY LEAVE THE OLD COUNTRY...
THEY ARRIVED IN NEW YORK HARBOR IN JANUARY OF 1939...
IN THE OLD COUNTRY, MY FATHER HAD RUN A SUCCESSFUL PERFUMERY, AND QUICKLY ESTABLISHED ONE HERE AS WELL--
--BUT IT WAS NOT MERELY BUSINESS THAT BROUGHT THEM TO THESE SHORES...
Les parfumer
est • 1939
SAVON
NO, MY FATHER HAD DETERMINED TO LEAVE FOR AMERICA THE SAME DAY HE LEARNED MY SWEET MOTHER WAS PREGNANT WITH ME...
HOW ELSE, AFTER ALL, HE REASONED, COULD I EVER HOPE TO BECOME PRESIDENT UNLESS I WERE BORN IN THE UNITED STATES--
--AND SO I WAS, AND WAS CHRISTENED ADRIAN ALEXANDER VEIDT...
ALEXANDER, AFTER ALEXANDER OF MACEDONIA, ONE OF MY FATHER'S CHILDHOOD HEROES...
BY THE TIME I WAS TWO, IT WAS CLEAR TO MY PARENTS THAT I WAS NO ORDINARY CHILD...
GENIUS
AT THE AGE OF FOUR, SELF-TAUGHT, I HAD READ ALL 24 VOLUMES OF MY FATHER'S PRECIOUS ENCYCLOPEDIAS--
--AND WAS HUNGRY FOR AS MUCH MORE KNOWLEDGE AS I COULD ABSORB...
KNOWLEDGE IS POWER, SIR FRANCIS BACON HAD SAID, AND I COULD NOT HAVE AGREED MORE...

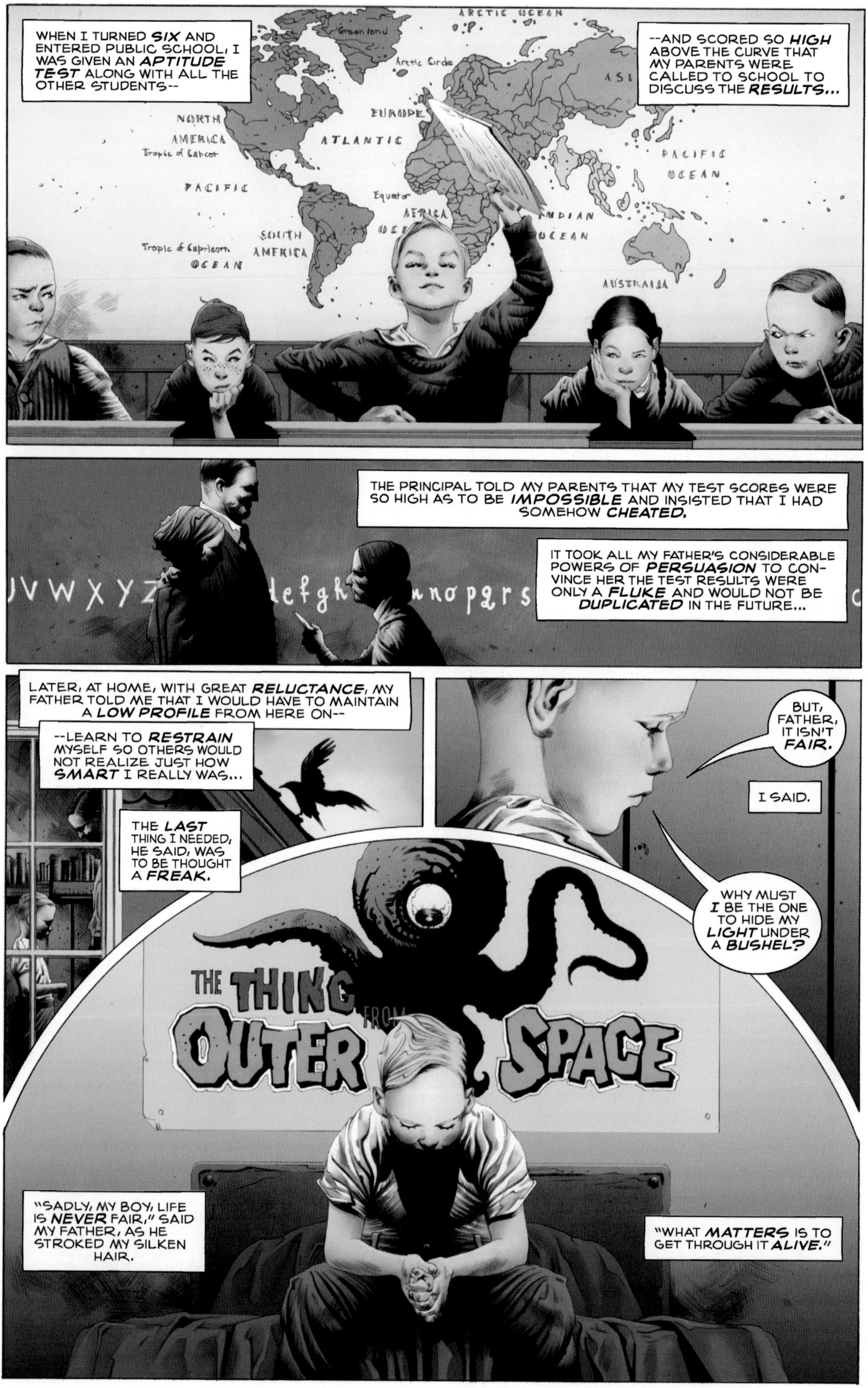
WHEN I TURNED SIX AND ENTERED PUBLIC SCHOOL, I WAS GIVEN AN APTITUDE TEST ALONG WITH ALL THE OTHER STUDENTS--
--AND SCORED SO HIGH ABOVE THE CURVE THAT MY PARENTS WERE CALLED TO SCHOOL TO DISCUSS THE RESULTS...
THE PRINCIPAL TOLD MY PARENTS THAT MY TEST SCORES WERE SO HIGH AS TO BE IMPOSSIBLE AND INSISTED THAT I HAD SOMEHOW CHEATED.
IT TOOK ALL MY FATHER'S CONSIDERABLE POWERS OF PERSUASION TO CONVINCE HER THE TEST RESULTS WERE ONLY A FLUKE AND WOULD NOT BE DUPLICATED IN THE FUTURE...
LATER, AT HOME, WITH GREAT RELUCTANCE, MY FATHER TOLD ME THAT I WOULD HAVE TO MAINTAIN A LOW PROFILE FROM HERE ON--
--LEARN TO RESTRAIN MYSELF SO OTHERS WOULD NOT REALIZE JUST HOW SMART I REALLY WAS...
THE LAST THING I NEEDED, HE SAID, WAS TO BE THOUGHT A FREAK.
BUT, FATHER, IT ISN'T FAIR.
I SAID.
WHY MUST I BE THE ONE TO HIDE MY LIGHT UNDER A BUSHEL?
THE THING FROM OUTER SPACE
"SADLY, MY BOY, LIFE IS NEVER FAIR," SAID MY FATHER, AS HE STROKED MY SILKEN HAIR.
"WHAT MATTERS IS TO GET THROUGH IT ALIVE."

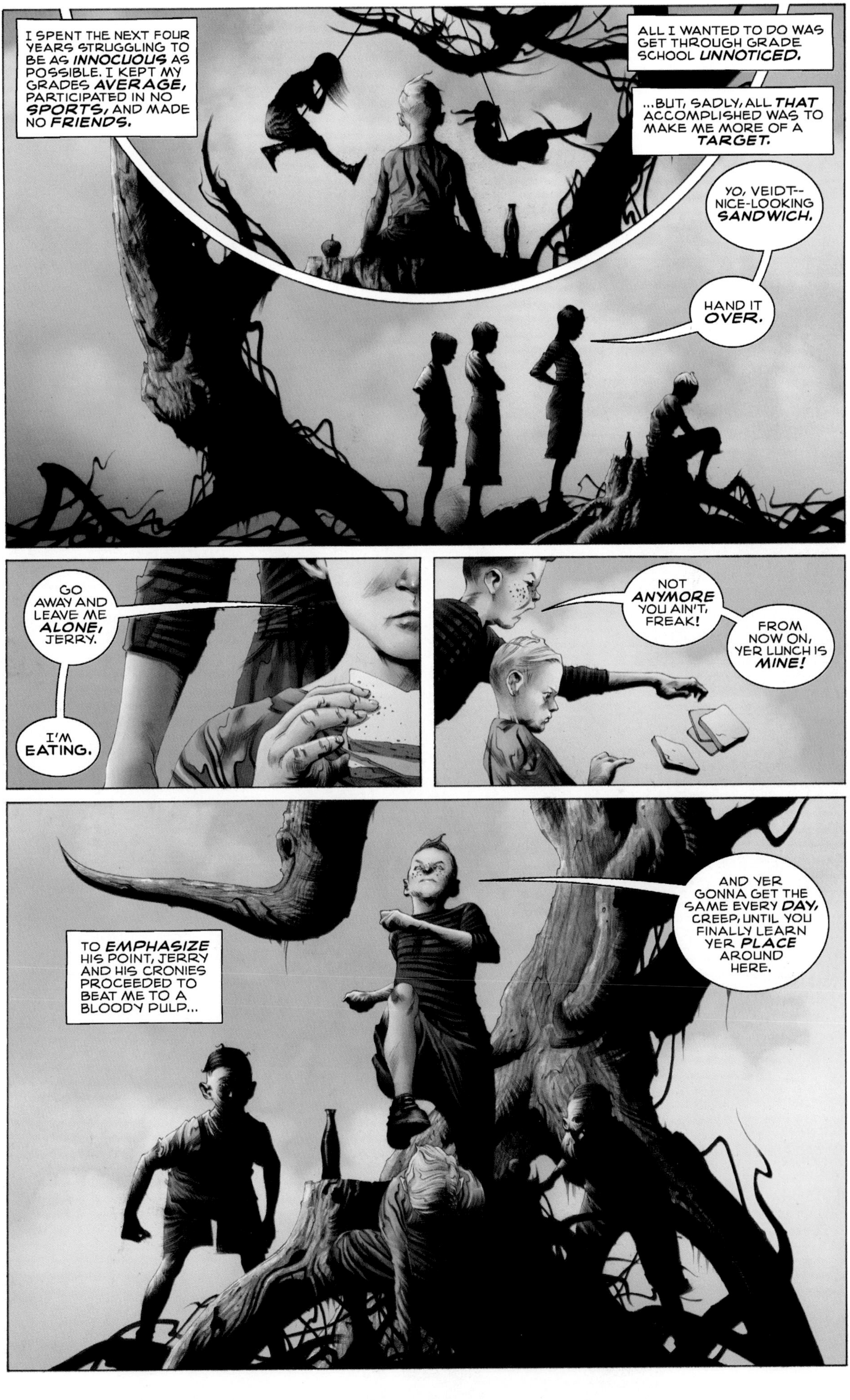
I SPENT THE NEXT FOUR YEARS STRUGGLING TO BE AS INNOCUOUS AS POSSIBLE. I KEPT MY GRADES AVERAGE, PARTICIPATED IN NO SPORTS, AND MADE NO FRIENDS.
ALL I WANTED TO DO WAS GET THROUGH GRADE SCHOOL UNNOTICED.
...BUT, SADLY, ALL THAT ACCOMPLISHED WAS TO MAKE ME MORE OF A TARGET.
YO, VEIDT-- NICE-LOOKING SANDWICH.
HAND IT OVER.
GO AWAY AND LEAVE ME ALONE, JERRY.
I'M EATING.
NOT ANYMORE YOU AIN'T, FREAK!
FROM NOW ON, YER LUNCH IS MINE!
AND YER GONNA GET THE SAME EVERY DAY, CREEP, UNTIL YOU FINALLY LEARN YER PLACE AROUND HERE.
TO EMPHASIZE HIS POINT, JERRY AND HIS CRONIES PROCEEDED TO BEAT ME TO A BLOODY PULP...

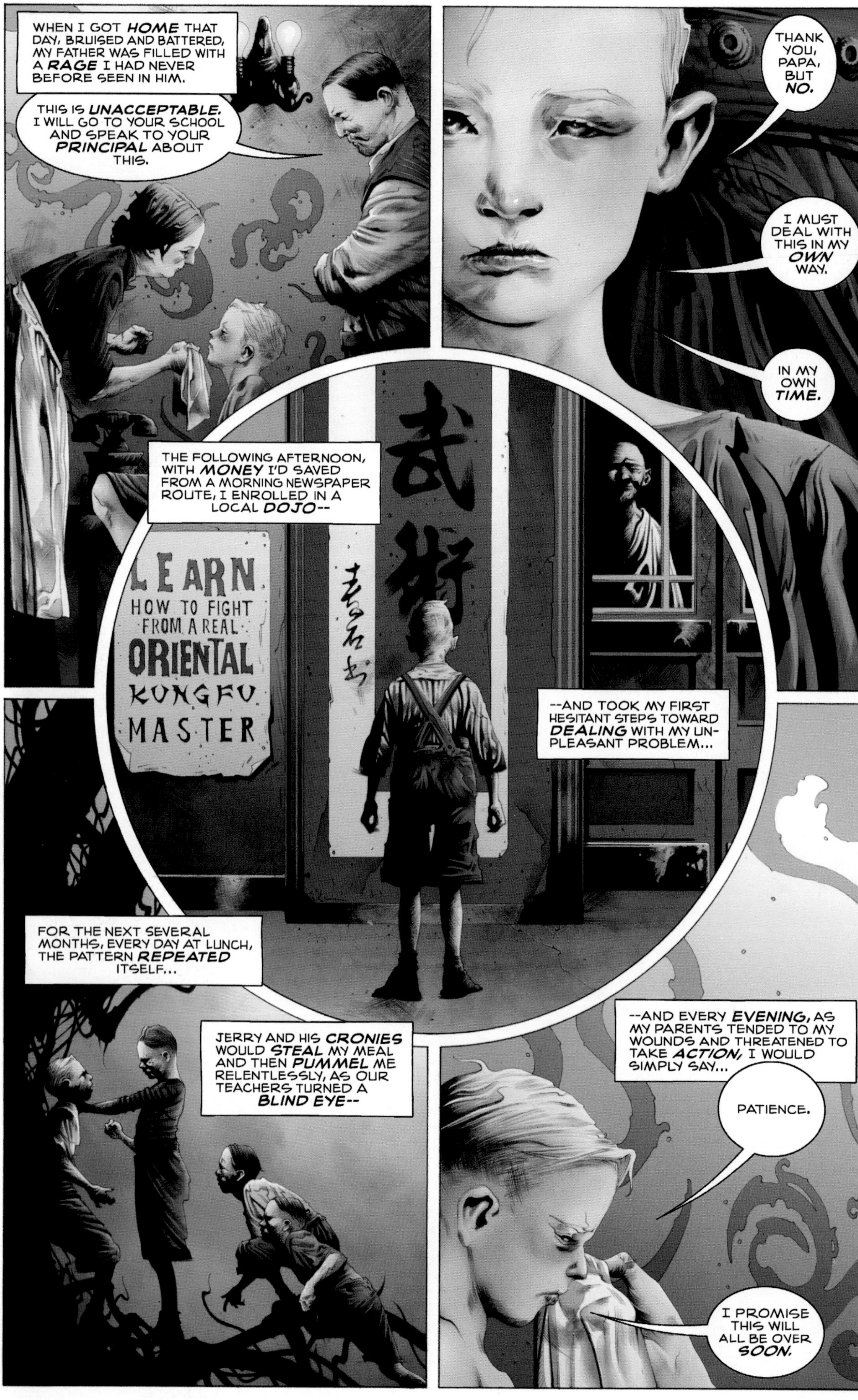

WHEN I GOT HOME THAT DAY, BRUISED AND BATTERED, MY FATHER WAS FILLED WITH A RAGE I HAD NEVER BEFORE SEEN IN HIM.
THIS IS UNACCEPTABLE. I WILL GO TO YOUR SCHOOL AND SPEAK TO YOUR PRINCIPAL ABOUT THIS.
THANK YOU, PAPA, BUT NO.
I MUST DEAL WITH THIS IN MY OWN WAY.
IN MY OWN TIME.
THE FOLLOWING AFTERNOON, WITH MONEY I'D SAVED FROM A MORNING NEWSPAPER ROUTE, I ENROLLED IN A LOCAL DOJO--
武術
LEARN HOW TO FIGHT FROM A REAL ORIENTAL KUNGFU MASTER
--AND TOOK MY FIRST HESITANT STEPS TOWARD DEALING WITH MY UNPLEASANT PROBLEM...
FOR THE NEXT SEVERAL MONTHS, EVERY DAY AT LUNCH, THE PATTERN REPEATED ITSELF...
JERRY AND HIS CRONIES WOULD STEAL MY MEAL AND THEN PUMMEL ME RELENTLESSLY, AS OUR TEACHERS TURNED A BLIND EYE--
--AND EVERY EVENING, AS MY PARENTS TENDED TO MY WOUNDS AND THREATENED TO TAKE ACTION, I WOULD SIMPLY SAY...
PATIENCE.
I PROMISE THIS WILL ALL BE OVER SOON.

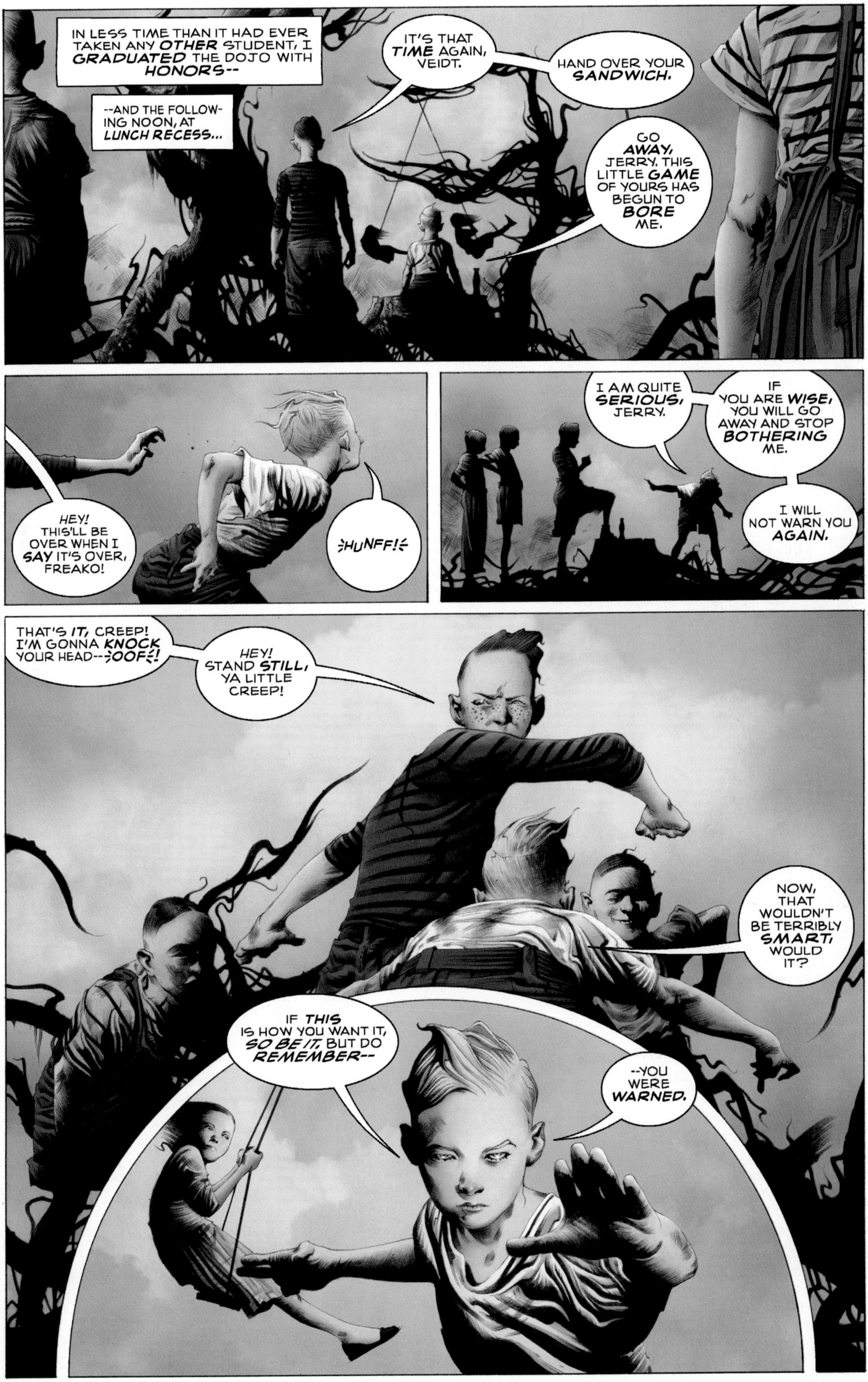
IN LESS TIME THAN IT HAD EVER TAKEN ANY OTHER STUDENT, I GRADUATED THE DOJO WITH HONORS--
--AND THE FOLLOWING NOON, AT LUNCH RECESS...
IT'S THAT TIME AGAIN, VEIDT.
HAND OVER YOUR SANDWICH.
GO AWAY, JERRY. THIS LITTLE GAME OF YOURS HAS BEGUN TO BORE ME.
HEY! THIS'LL BE OVER WHEN I SAY IT'S OVER, FREAKO!
HUNFF!
I AM QUITE SERIOUS, JERRY.
IF YOU ARE WISE, YOU WILL GO AWAY AND STOP BOTHERING ME.
I WILL NOT WARN YOU AGAIN.
THAT'S IT, CREEP! I'M GONNA KNOCK YOUR HEAD--OOF!
HEY! STAND STILL, YA LITTLE CREEP!
NOW, THAT WOULDN'T BE TERRIBLY SMART, WOULD IT?
IF THIS IS HOW YOU WANT IT, SO BE IT, BUT DO REMEMBER--
--YOU WERE WARNED.

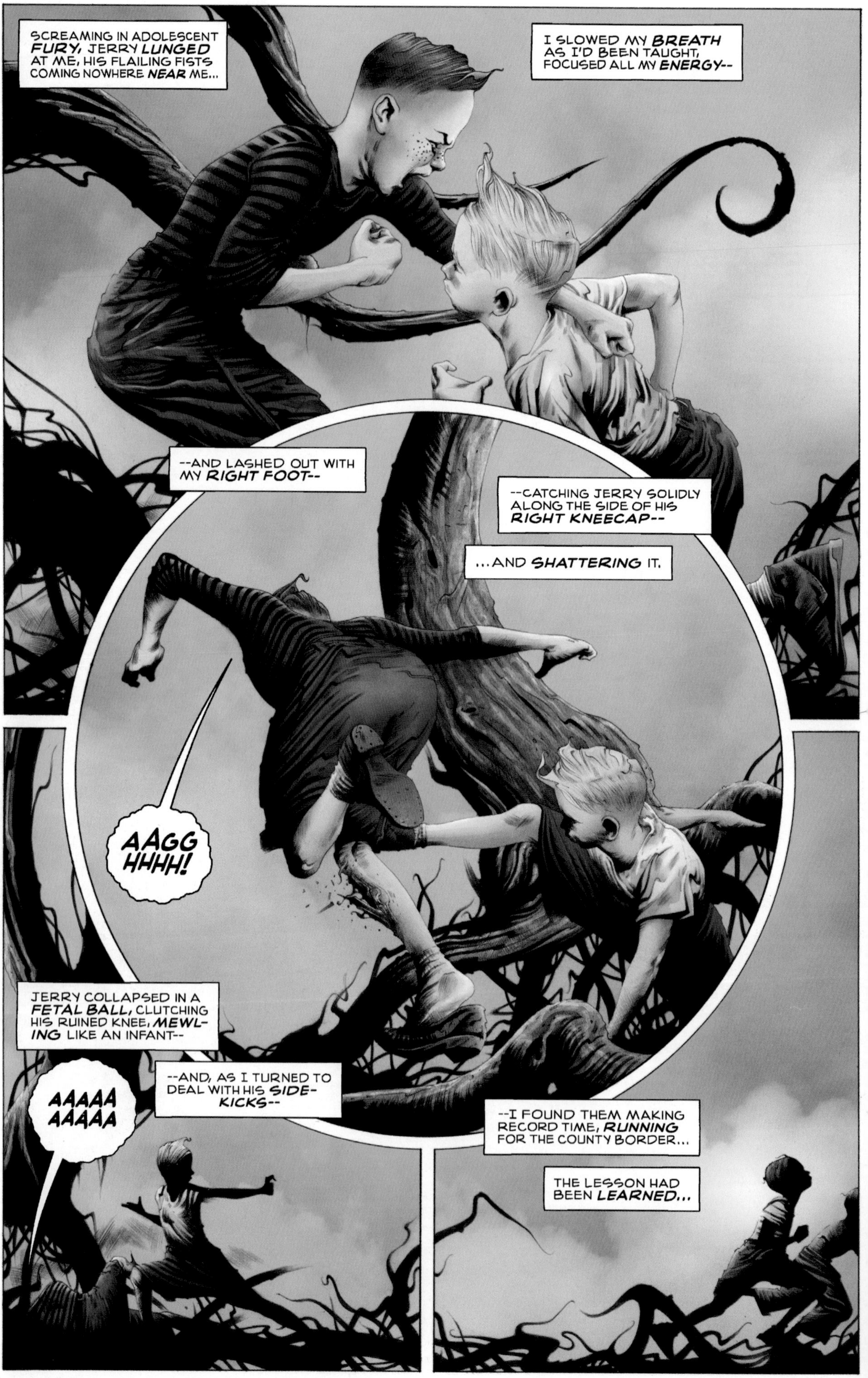

SCREAMING IN ADOLESCENT FURY, JERRY LUNGED AT ME, HIS FLAILING FISTS COMING NOWHERE NEAR ME...
I SLOWED MY BREATH AS I'D BEEN TAUGHT, FOCUSED ALL MY ENERGY--
--AND LASHED OUT WITH MY RIGHT FOOT--
--CATCHING JERRY SOLIDLY ALONG THE SIDE OF HIS RIGHT KNEECAP--
...AND SHATTERING IT.
AAGG HHHH!
JERRY COLLAPSED IN A FETAL BALL, CLUTCHING HIS RUINED KNEE, MEWL-ING LIKE AN INFANT--
AAAAA AAAAA
--AND, AS I TURNED TO DEAL WITH HIS SIDE-KICKS--
--I FOUND THEM MAKING RECORD TIME, RUNNING FOR THE COUNTY BORDER...
THE LESSON HAD BEEN LEARNED...

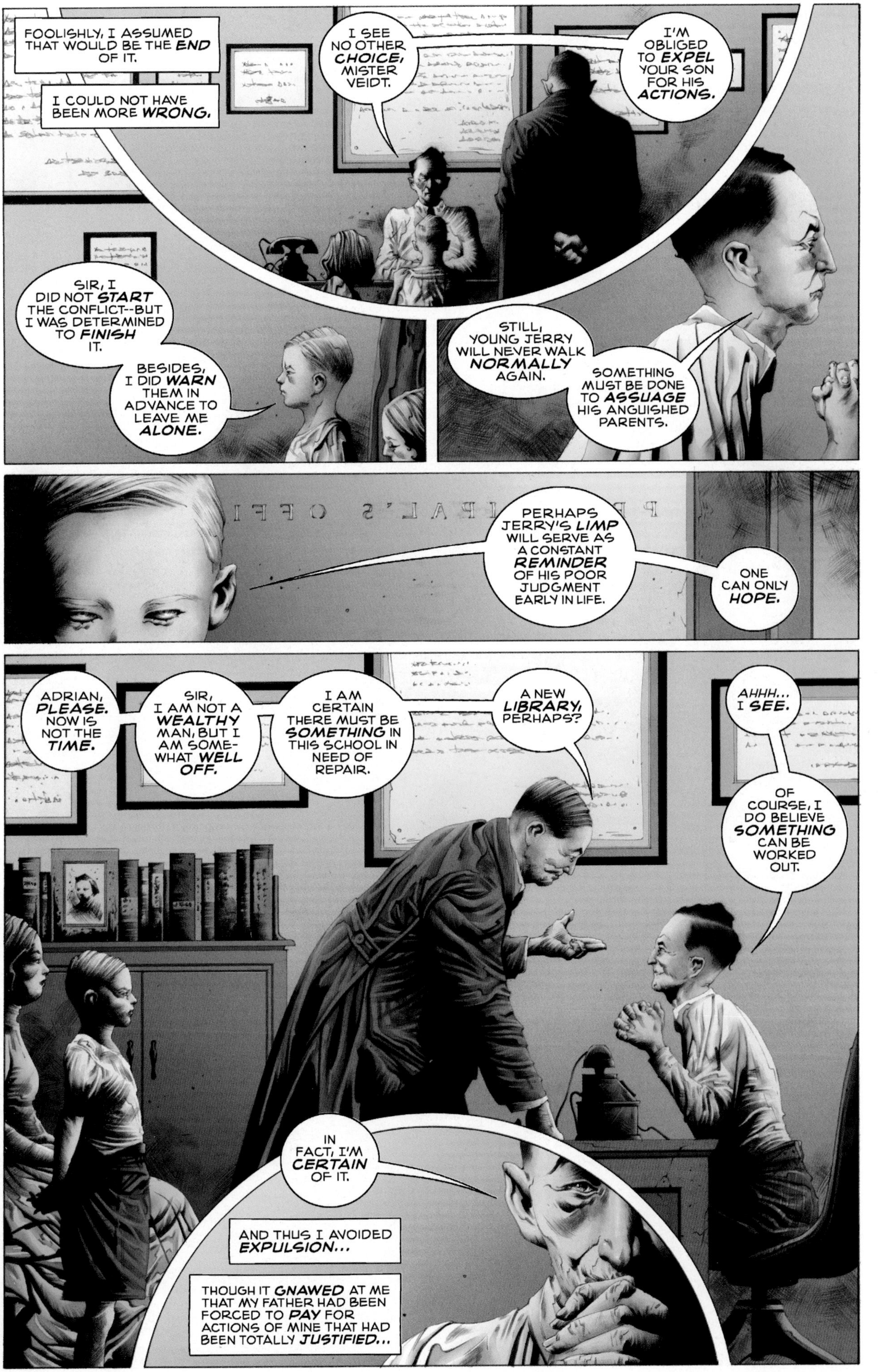
FOOLISHLY, I ASSUMED THAT WOULD BE THE END OF IT.
I COULD NOT HAVE BEEN MORE WRONG.
I SEE NO OTHER CHOICE, MISTER VEIDT.
I'M OBLIGED TO EXPEL YOUR SON FOR HIS ACTIONS.
SIR, I DID NOT START THE CONFLICT--BUT I WAS DETERMINED TO FINISH IT.
BESIDES, I DID WARN THEM IN ADVANCE TO LEAVE ME ALONE.
STILL, YOUNG JERRY WILL NEVER WALK NORMALLY AGAIN.
SOMETHING MUST BE DONE TO ASSUAGE HIS ANGUISHED PARENTS.
PERHAPS JERRY'S LIMP WILL SERVE AS A CONSTANT REMINDER OF HIS POOR JUDGMENT EARLY IN LIFE.
ONE CAN ONLY HOPE.
ADRIAN, PLEASE. NOW IS NOT THE TIME.
SIR, I AM NOT A WEALTHY MAN, BUT I AM SOMEWHAT WELL OFF.
I AM CERTAIN THERE MUST BE SOMETHING IN THIS SCHOOL IN NEED OF REPAIR.
A NEW LIBRARY, PERHAPS?
AHHH... I SEE.
OF COURSE, I DO BELIEVE SOMETHING CAN BE WORKED OUT.
IN FACT, I'M CERTAIN OF IT.
AND THUS I AVOIDED EXPULSION...
THOUGH IT GNAWED AT ME THAT MY FATHER HAD BEEN FORCED TO PAY FOR ACTIONS OF MINE THAT HAD BEEN TOTALLY JUSTIFIED...

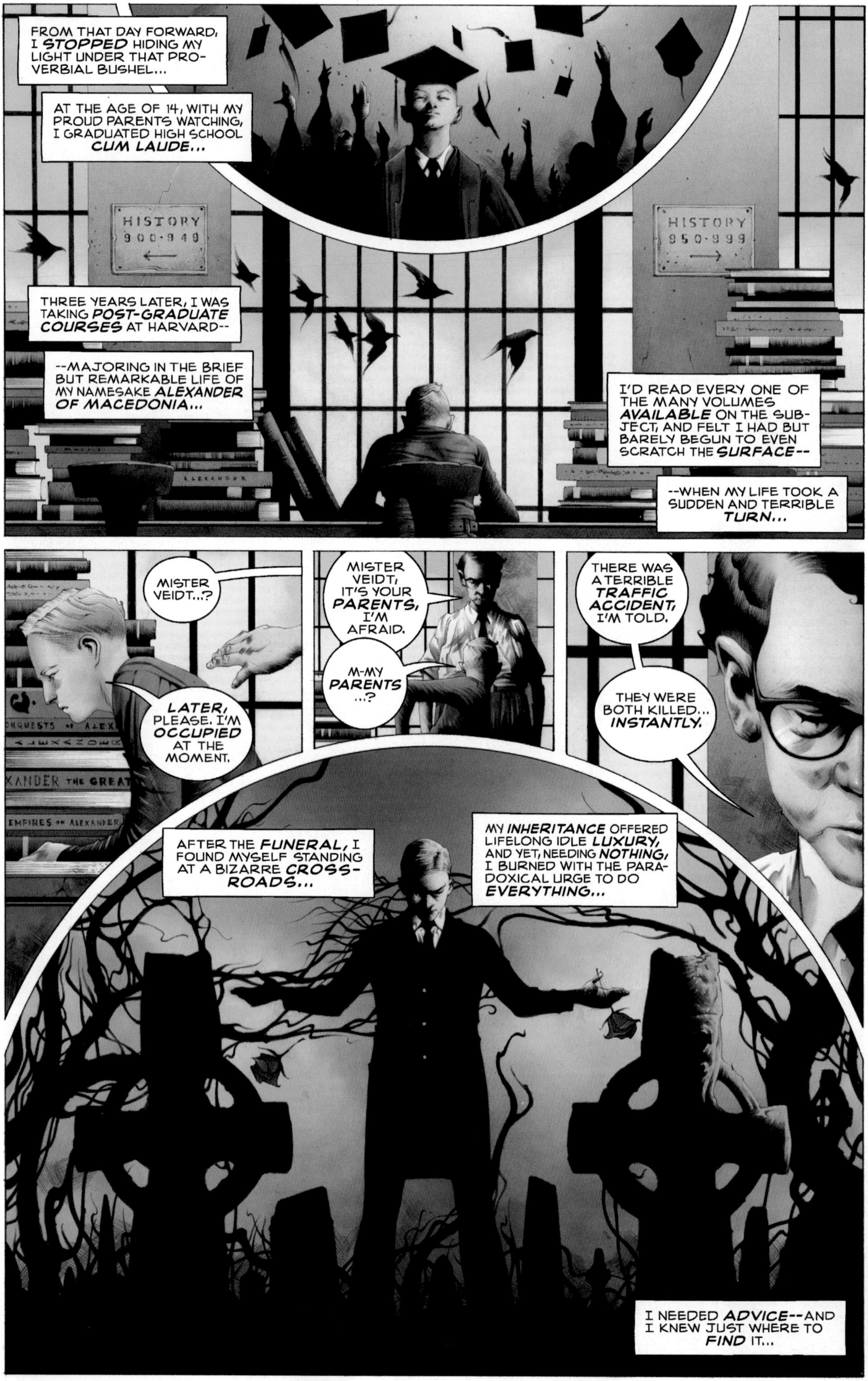
FROM THAT DAY FORWARD, I STOPPED HIDING MY LIGHT UNDER THAT PROVERBIAL BUSHEL...
AT THE AGE OF 14, WITH MY PROUD PARENTS WATCHING, I GRADUATED HIGH SCHOOL CUM LAUDE...
HISTORY 900-949
HISTORY 950-999
THREE YEARS LATER, I WAS TAKING POST-GRADUATE COURSES AT HARVARD--
--MAJORING IN THE BRIEF BUT REMARKABLE LIFE OF MY NAMESAKE ALEXANDER OF MACEDONIA...
I'D READ EVERY ONE OF THE MANY VOLUMES AVAILABLE ON THE SUBJECT, AND FELT I HAD BUT BARELY BEGUN TO EVEN SCRATCH THE SURFACE--
--WHEN MY LIFE TOOK A SUDDEN AND TERRIBLE TURN...
MISTER VEIDT...?
LATER, PLEASE. I'M OCCUPIED AT THE MOMENT.
CONQUESTS OF ALEX
XANDER THE GREAT
EMPIRES OF ALEXANDER
MISTER VEIDT, IT'S YOUR PARENTS, I'M AFRAID.
M-MY PARENTS ...?
THERE WAS A TERRIBLE TRAFFIC ACCIDENT, I'M TOLD.
THEY WERE BOTH KILLED... INSTANTLY.
AFTER THE FUNERAL, I FOUND MYSELF STANDING AT A BIZARRE CROSSROADS...
MY INHERITANCE OFFERED LIFELONG IDLE LUXURY, AND YET, NEEDING NOTHING, I BURNED WITH THE PARADOXICAL URGE TO DO EVERYTHING...
I NEEDED ADVICE--AND I KNEW JUST WHERE TO FIND IT...

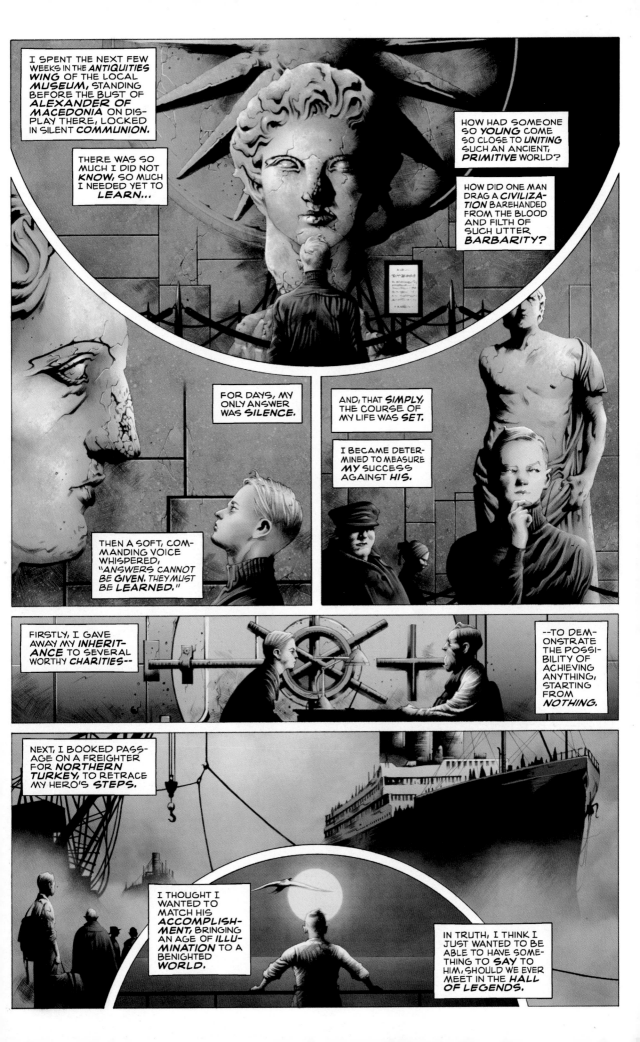

I SPENT THE NEXT FEW WEEKS IN THE *ANTIQUITIES WING* OF THE LOCAL *MUSEUM*, STANDING BEFORE THE BUST OF *ALEXANDER OF MACEDONIA* ON DISPLAY THERE, LOCKED IN SILENT *COMMUNION*.

THERE WAS SO MUCH I DID NOT *KNOW*, SO MUCH I NEEDED YET TO *LEARN*...

HOW HAD SOMEONE SO *YOUNG* COME SO CLOSE TO *UNITING* SUCH AN ANCIENT, *PRIMITIVE* WORLD?

HOW DID ONE MAN DRAG A *CIVILIZATION* BAREHANDED FROM THE BLOOD AND FILTH OF SUCH UTTER *BARBARITY*?

FOR DAYS, MY ONLY ANSWER WAS *SILENCE*.

THEN A SOFT, COMMANDING VOICE WHISPERED, *"ANSWERS CANNOT BE GIVEN. THEY MUST BE LEARNED."*

AND, THAT *SIMPLY*, THE COURSE OF MY LIFE WAS *SET*.

I BECAME DETERMINED TO MEASURE *MY* SUCCESS AGAINST *HIS*.

FIRSTLY, I GAVE AWAY MY *INHERITANCE* TO SEVERAL WORTHY *CHARITIES*--

--TO DEMONSTRATE THE POSSIBILITY OF ACHIEVING ANYTHING, STARTING FROM *NOTHING*.

NEXT, I BOOKED PASSAGE ON A FREIGHTER FOR *NORTHERN TURKEY*, TO RETRACE MY HERO'S *STEPS*.

I THOUGHT I WANTED TO MATCH HIS *ACCOMPLISHMENT*, BRINGING AN AGE OF *ILLUMINATION* TO A *BENIGHTED* WORLD.

IN TRUTH, I THINK I JUST WANTED TO BE ABLE TO HAVE SOMETHING TO *SAY* TO HIM, SHOULD WE EVER MEET IN THE *HALL OF LEGENDS*.

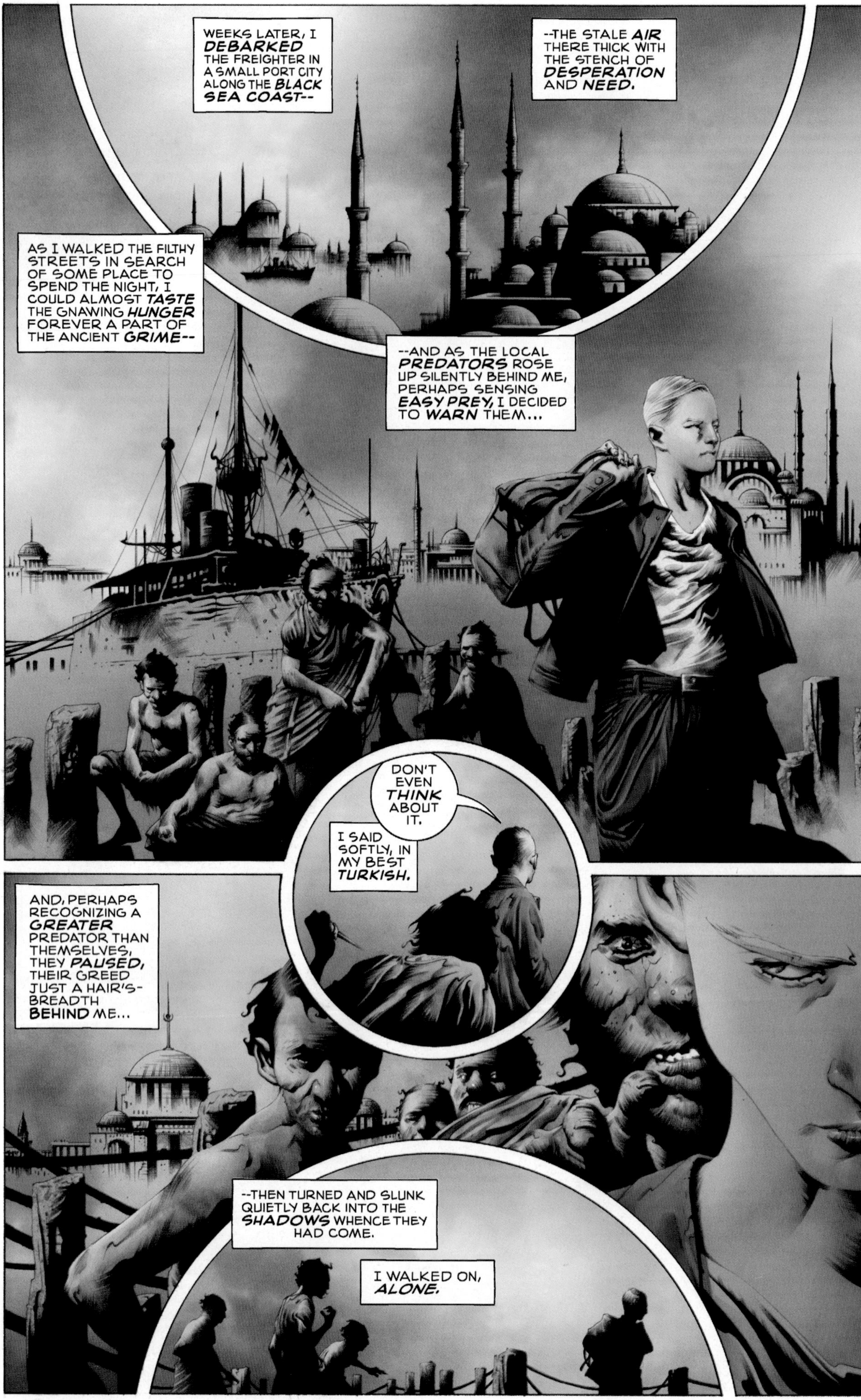
WEEKS LATER, I DEBARKED THE FREIGHTER IN A SMALL PORT CITY ALONG THE BLACK SEA COAST--
--THE STALE AIR THERE THICK WITH THE STENCH OF DESPERATION AND NEED.
AS I WALKED THE FILTHY STREETS IN SEARCH OF SOME PLACE TO SPEND THE NIGHT, I COULD ALMOST TASTE THE GNAWING HUNGER FOREVER A PART OF THE ANCIENT GRIME--
--AND AS THE LOCAL PREDATORS ROSE UP SILENTLY BEHIND ME, PERHAPS SENSING EASY PREY, I DECIDED TO WARN THEM...
DON'T EVEN THINK ABOUT IT.
I SAID SOFTLY, IN MY BEST TURKISH.
AND, PERHAPS RECOGNIZING A GREATER PREDATOR THAN THEMSELVES, THEY PAUSED, THEIR GREED JUST A HAIR'S-BREADTH BEHIND ME...
--THEN TURNED AND SLUNK QUIETLY BACK INTO THE SHADOWS WHENCE THEY HAD COME.
I WALKED ON, ALONE.

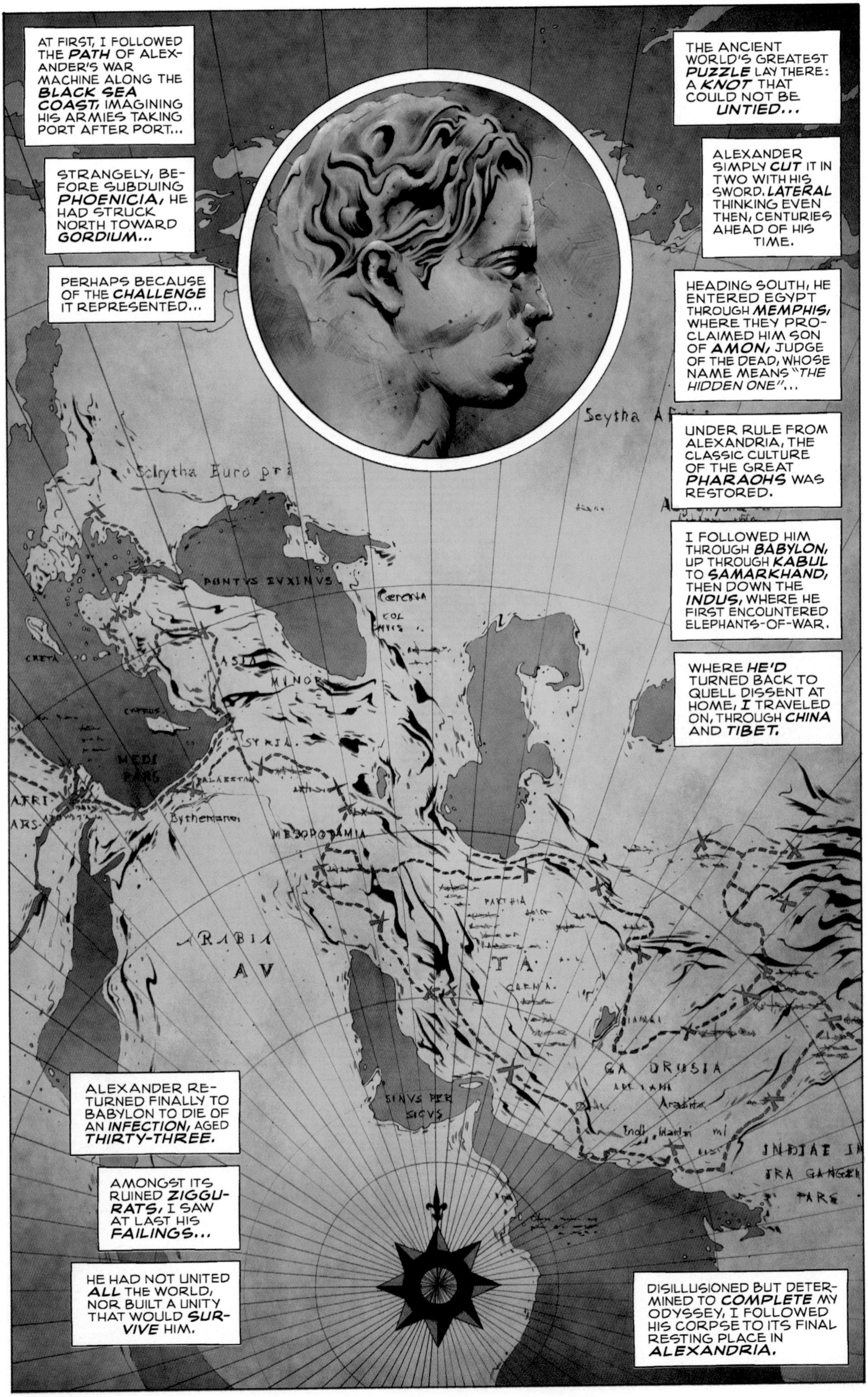
AT FIRST, I FOLLOWED THE PATH OF ALEXANDER'S WAR MACHINE ALONG THE BLACK SEA COAST, IMAGINING HIS ARMIES TAKING PORT AFTER PORT...
STRANGELY, BEFORE SUBDUING PHOENICIA, HE HAD STRUCK NORTH TOWARD GORDIUM...
PERHAPS BECAUSE OF THE CHALLENGE IT REPRESENTED...
THE ANCIENT WORLD'S GREATEST PUZZLE LAY THERE: A KNOT THAT COULD NOT BE UNTIED...
ALEXANDER SIMPLY CUT IT IN TWO WITH HIS SWORD. LATERAL THINKING EVEN THEN, CENTURIES AHEAD OF HIS TIME.
HEADING SOUTH, HE ENTERED EGYPT THROUGH MEMPHIS, WHERE THEY PROCLAIMED HIM SON OF AMON, JUDGE OF THE DEAD, WHOSE NAME MEANS "THE HIDDEN ONE"...
UNDER RULE FROM ALEXANDRIA, THE CLASSIC CULTURE OF THE GREAT PHARAOHS WAS RESTORED.
I FOLLOWED HIM THROUGH BABYLON, UP THROUGH KABUL TO SAMARKHAND, THEN DOWN THE INDUS, WHERE HE FIRST ENCOUNTERED ELEPHANTS-OF-WAR.
WHERE HE'D TURNED BACK TO QUELL DISSENT AT HOME, I TRAVELED ON, THROUGH CHINA AND TIBET.
ALEXANDER RETURNED FINALLY TO BABYLON TO DIE OF AN INFECTION, AGED THIRTY-THREE.
AMONGST ITS RUINED ZIGGURATS, I SAW AT LAST HIS FAILINGS...
HE HAD NOT UNITED ALL THE WORLD, NOR BUILT A UNITY THAT WOULD SURVIVE HIM.
DISILLUSIONED BUT DETERMINED TO COMPLETE MY ODYSSEY, I FOLLOWED HIS CORPSE TO ITS FINAL RESTING PLACE IN ALEXANDRIA.
PONTVS EVXINVS
CRETA
ASIA
MINOR
CYPRUS
SYRIA
MESOPOTAMIA
ARABIA
PARTHIA
SINVS PER SICVS

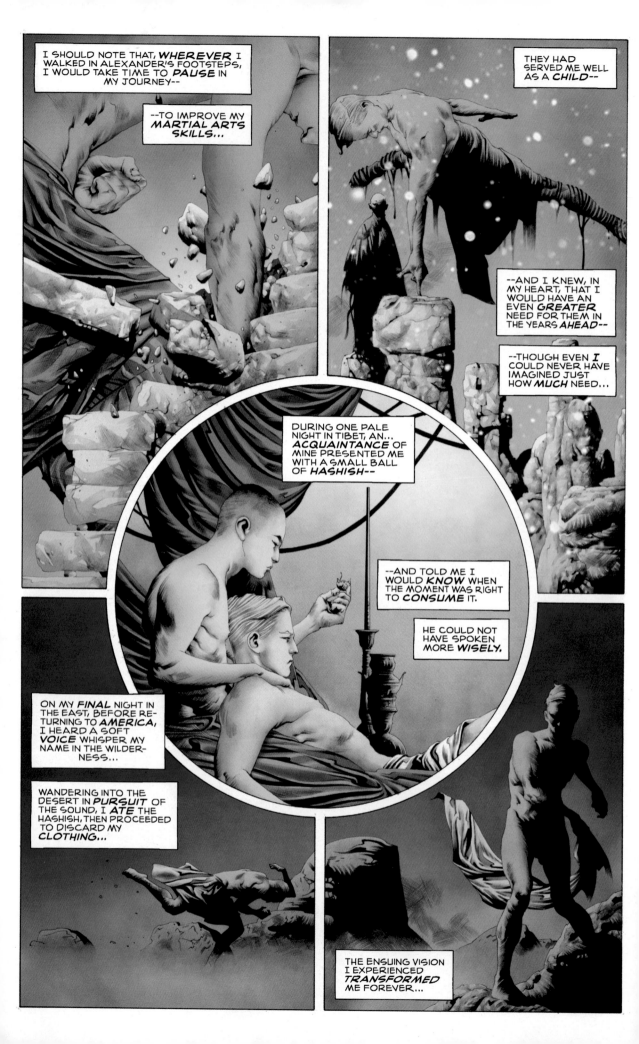

I SHOULD NOTE THAT, *WHEREVER* I WALKED IN ALEXANDER'S FOOTSTEPS, I WOULD TAKE TIME TO *PAUSE* IN MY JOURNEY--

--TO IMPROVE MY *MARTIAL ARTS* SKILLS...

THEY HAD SERVED ME WELL AS A *CHILD*--

--AND I KNEW, IN MY HEART, THAT I WOULD HAVE AN EVEN *GREATER* NEED FOR THEM IN THE YEARS *AHEAD*--

--THOUGH EVEN *I* COULD NEVER HAVE IMAGINED JUST HOW *MUCH* NEED...

DURING ONE PALE NIGHT IN TIBET, AN... *ACQUAINTANCE* OF MINE PRESENTED ME WITH A SMALL BALL OF *HASHISH*--

--AND TOLD ME I WOULD *KNOW* WHEN THE MOMENT WAS RIGHT TO *CONSUME* IT.

HE COULD NOT HAVE SPOKEN MORE *WISELY*.

ON MY *FINAL* NIGHT IN THE EAST, BEFORE RE-TURNING TO *AMERICA*, I HEARD A SOFT *VOICE* WHISPER MY NAME IN THE WILDER-NESS...

WANDERING INTO THE DESERT IN *PURSUIT* OF THE SOUND, I *ATE* THE HASHISH, THEN PROCEEDED TO DISCARD MY *CLOTHING*...

THE ENSUING VISION I EXPERIENCED *TRANSFORMED* ME FOREVER...

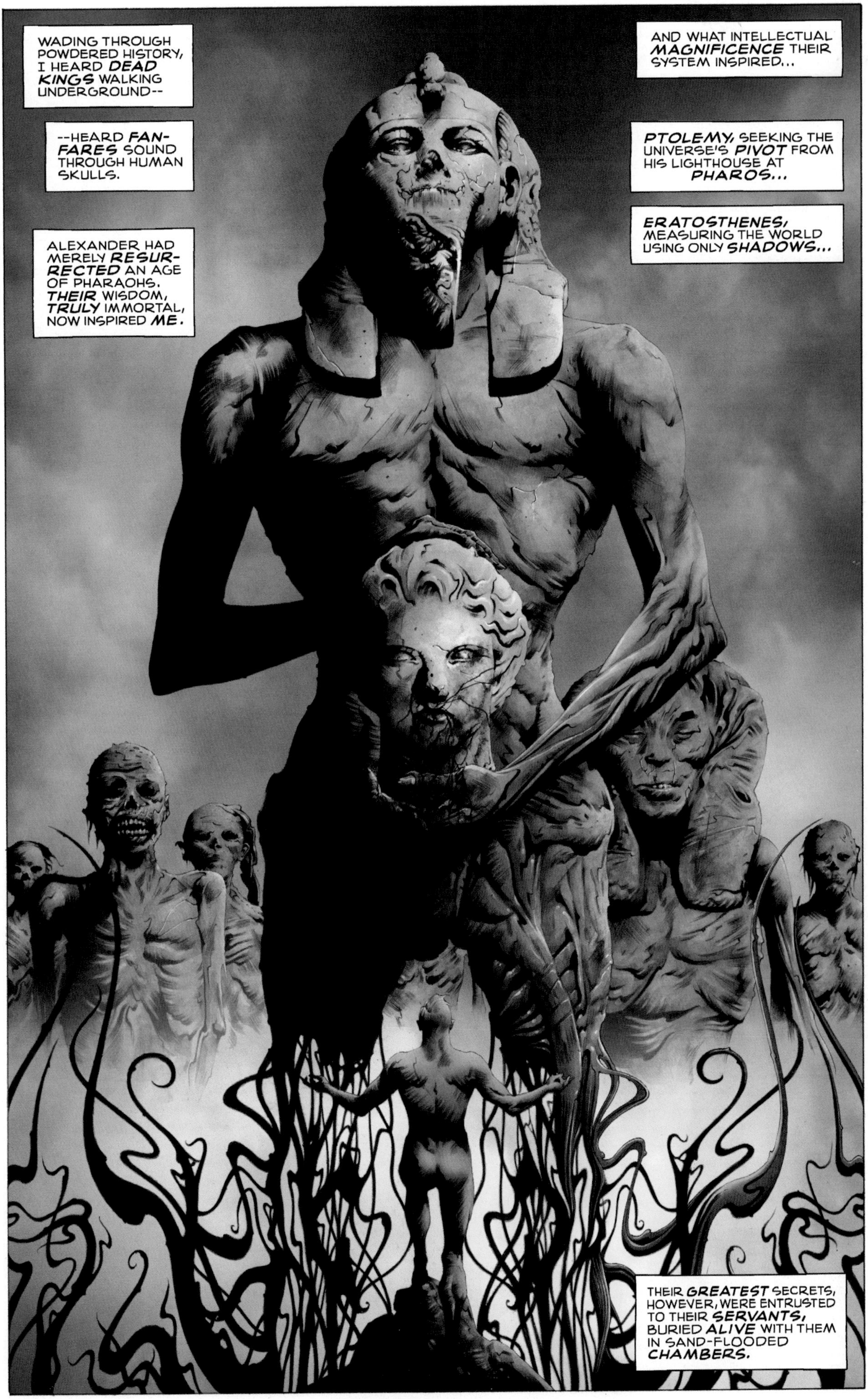
WADING THROUGH POWDERED HISTORY, I HEARD DEAD KINGS WALKING UNDERGROUND--
--HEARD FANFARES SOUND THROUGH HUMAN SKULLS.
ALEXANDER HAD MERELY RESURRECTED AN AGE OF PHARAOHS. THEIR WISDOM, TRULY IMMORTAL, NOW INSPIRED ME.
AND WHAT INTELLECTUAL MAGNIFICENCE THEIR SYSTEM INSPIRED...
PTOLEMY, SEEKING THE UNIVERSE'S PIVOT FROM HIS LIGHTHOUSE AT PHAROS...
ERATOSTHENES, MEASURING THE WORLD USING ONLY SHADOWS...
THEIR GREATEST SECRETS, HOWEVER, WERE ENTRUSTED TO THEIR SERVANTS, BURIED ALIVE WITH THEM IN SAND-FLOODED CHAMBERS.

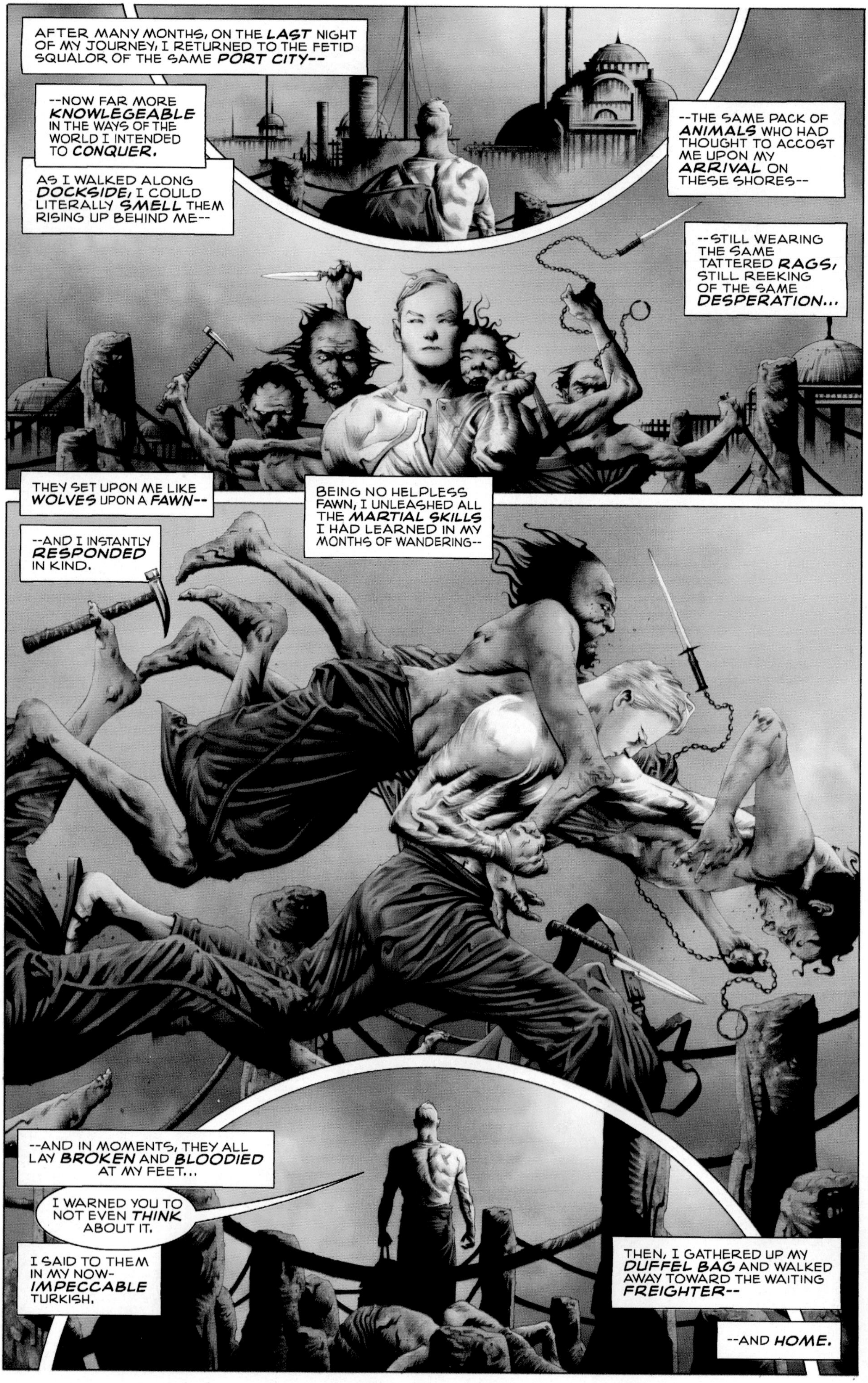
AFTER MANY MONTHS, ON THE LAST NIGHT OF MY JOURNEY, I RETURNED TO THE FETID SQUALOR OF THE SAME PORT CITY--
--NOW FAR MORE KNOWLEGEABLE IN THE WAYS OF THE WORLD I INTENDED TO CONQUER.
AS I WALKED ALONG DOCKSIDE, I COULD LITERALLY SMELL THEM RISING UP BEHIND ME--
--THE SAME PACK OF ANIMALS WHO HAD THOUGHT TO ACCOST ME UPON MY ARRIVAL ON THESE SHORES--
--STILL WEARING THE SAME TATTERED RAGS, STILL REEKING OF THE SAME DESPERATION...
THEY SET UPON ME LIKE WOLVES UPON A FAWN--
--AND I INSTANTLY RESPONDED IN KIND.
BEING NO HELPLESS FAWN, I UNLEASHED ALL THE MARTIAL SKILLS I HAD LEARNED IN MY MONTHS OF WANDERING--
--AND IN MOMENTS, THEY ALL LAY BROKEN AND BLOODIED AT MY FEET...
I WARNED YOU TO NOT EVEN THINK ABOUT IT.
I SAID TO THEM IN MY NOW-IMPECCABLE TURKISH.
THEN, I GATHERED UP MY DUFFEL BAG AND WALKED AWAY TOWARD THE WAITING FREIGHTER--
--AND HOME.

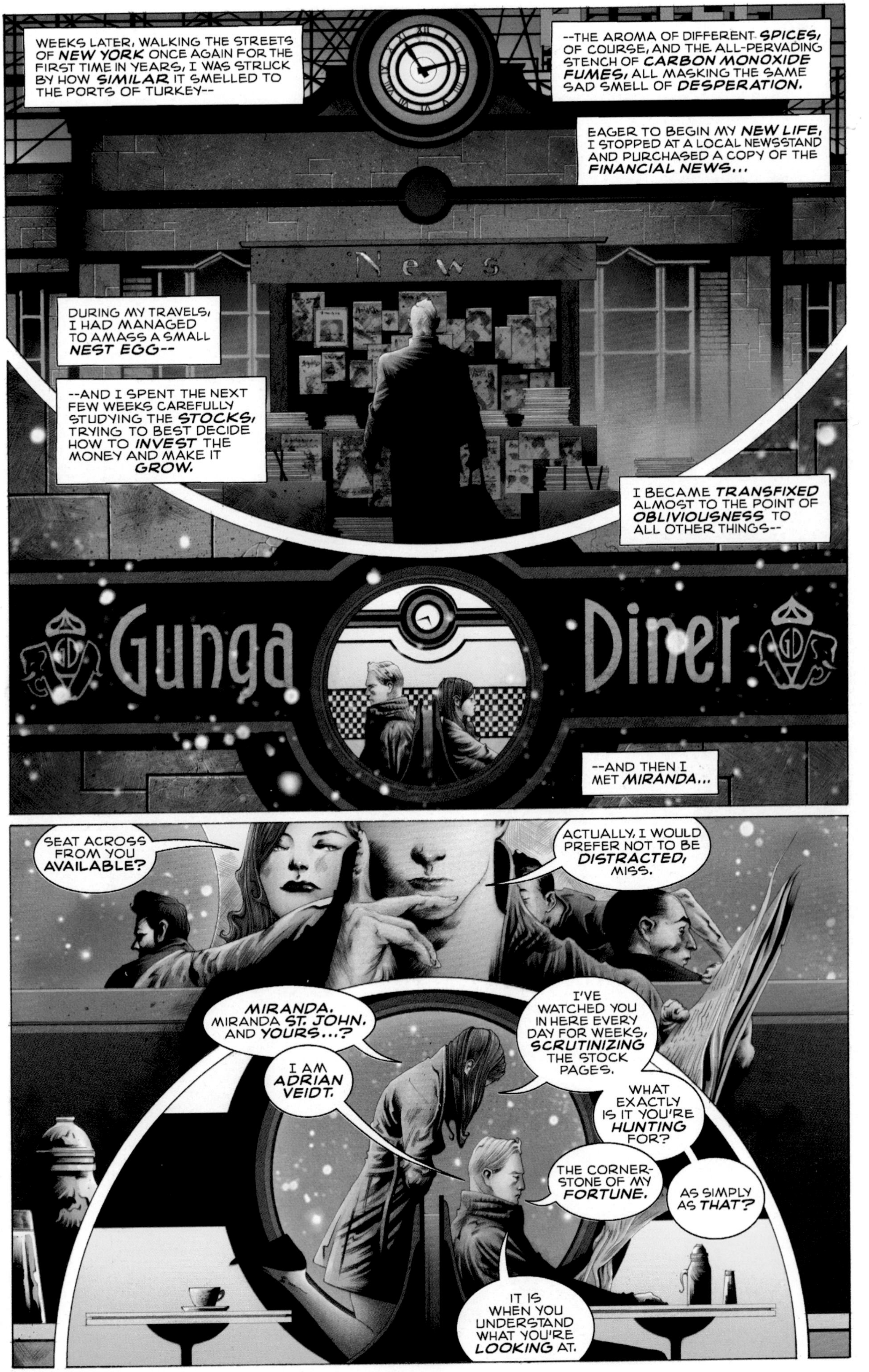
WEEKS LATER, WALKING THE STREETS OF NEW YORK ONCE AGAIN FOR THE FIRST TIME IN YEARS, I WAS STRUCK BY HOW SIMILAR IT SMELLED TO THE PORTS OF TURKEY--
--THE AROMA OF DIFFERENT SPICES, OF COURSE, AND THE ALL-PERVADING STENCH OF CARBON MONOXIDE FUMES, ALL MASKING THE SAME SAD SMELL OF DESPERATION.
EAGER TO BEGIN MY NEW LIFE, I STOPPED AT A LOCAL NEWSSTAND AND PURCHASED A COPY OF THE FINANCIAL NEWS...
News
DURING MY TRAVELS, I HAD MANAGED TO AMASS A SMALL NEST EGG--
--AND I SPENT THE NEXT FEW WEEKS CAREFULLY STUDYING THE STOCKS, TRYING TO BEST DECIDE HOW TO INVEST THE MONEY AND MAKE IT GROW.
I BECAME TRANSFIXED ALMOST TO THE POINT OF OBLIVIOUSNESS TO ALL OTHER THINGS--
Gunga Diner
--AND THEN I MET MIRANDA...
SEAT ACROSS FROM YOU AVAILABLE?
ACTUALLY, I WOULD PREFER NOT TO BE DISTRACTED, MISS.
MIRANDA. MIRANDA ST. JOHN. AND YOURS...?
I AM ADRIAN VEIDT.
I'VE WATCHED YOU IN HERE EVERY DAY FOR WEEKS, SCRUTINIZING THE STOCK PAGES.
WHAT EXACTLY IS IT YOU'RE HUNTING FOR?
THE CORNER-STONE OF MY FORTUNE.
AS SIMPLY AS THAT?
IT IS WHEN YOU UNDERSTAND WHAT YOU'RE LOOKING AT.

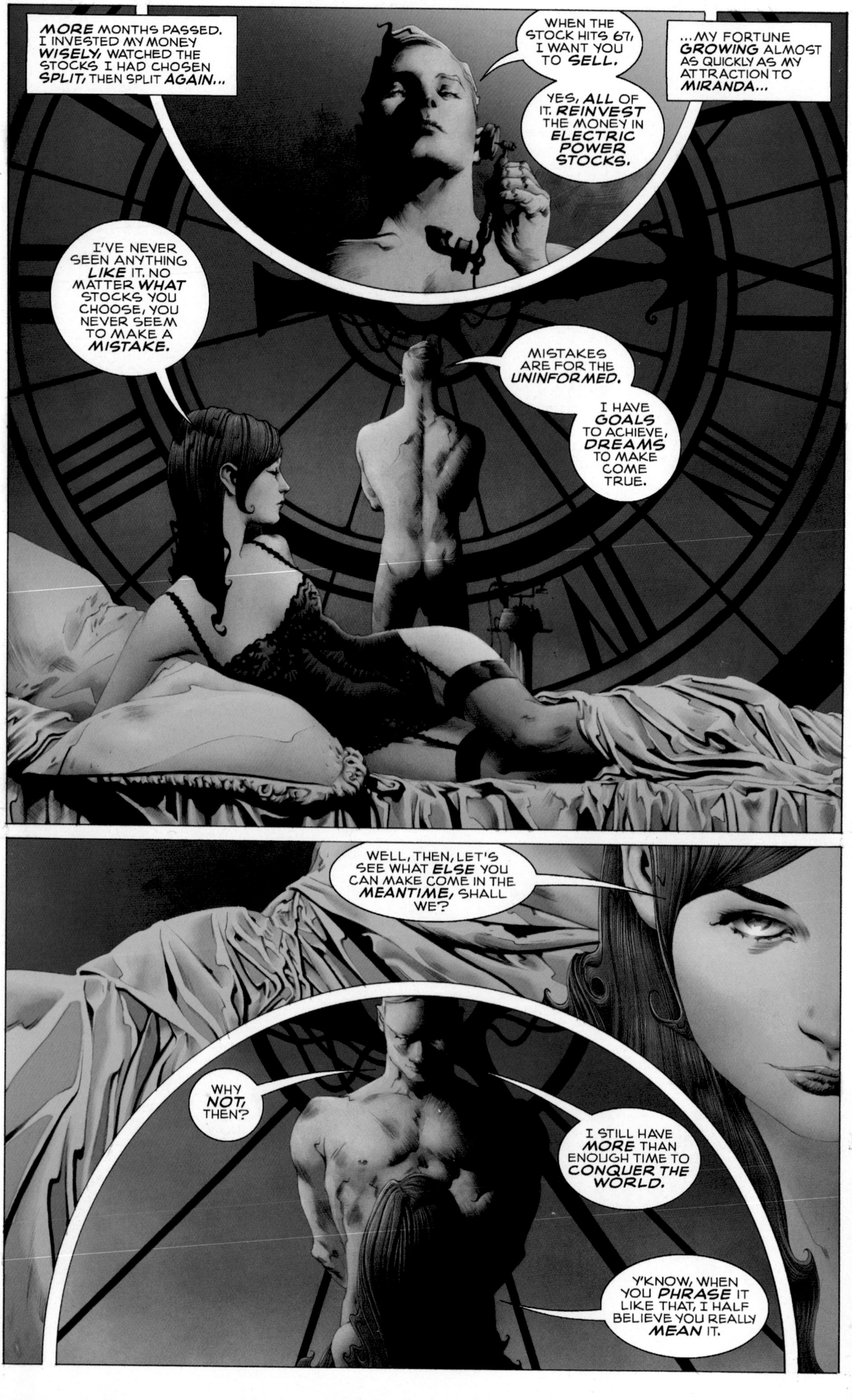
MORE MONTHS PASSED. I INVESTED MY MONEY WISELY, WATCHED THE STOCKS I HAD CHOSEN SPLIT, THEN SPLIT AGAIN...
WHEN THE STOCK HITS 67, I WANT YOU TO SELL.
YES, ALL OF IT. REINVEST THE MONEY IN ELECTRIC POWER STOCKS.
...MY FORTUNE GROWING ALMOST AS QUICKLY AS MY ATTRACTION TO MIRANDA...
I'VE NEVER SEEN ANYTHING LIKE IT. NO MATTER WHAT STOCKS YOU CHOOSE, YOU NEVER SEEM TO MAKE A MISTAKE.
MISTAKES ARE FOR THE UNINFORMED.
I HAVE GOALS TO ACHIEVE, DREAMS TO MAKE COME TRUE.
WELL, THEN, LET'S SEE WHAT ELSE YOU CAN MAKE COME IN THE MEANTIME, SHALL WE?
WHY NOT, THEN?
I STILL HAVE MORE THAN ENOUGH TIME TO CONQUER THE WORLD.
Y'KNOW, WHEN YOU PHRASE IT LIKE THAT, I HALF BELIEVE YOU REALLY MEAN IT.

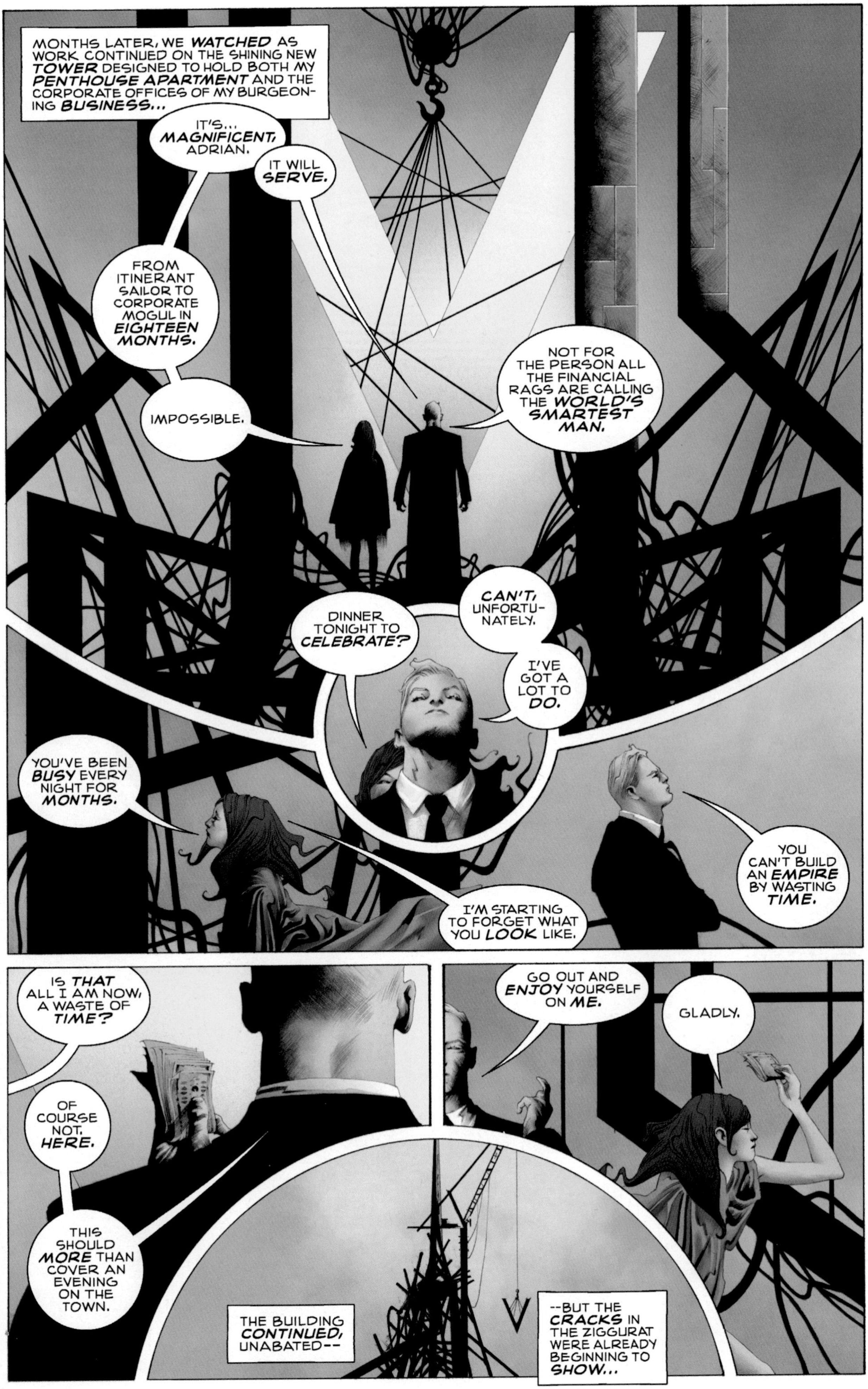
MONTHS LATER, WE WATCHED AS WORK CONTINUED ON THE SHINING NEW TOWER DESIGNED TO HOLD BOTH MY PENTHOUSE APARTMENT AND THE CORPORATE OFFICES OF MY BURGEONING BUSINESS...
IT'S... MAGNIFICENT, ADRIAN.
IT WILL SERVE.
FROM ITINERANT SAILOR TO CORPORATE MOGUL IN EIGHTEEN MONTHS.
IMPOSSIBLE.
NOT FOR THE PERSON ALL THE FINANCIAL RAGS ARE CALLING THE WORLD'S SMARTEST MAN.
DINNER TONIGHT TO CELEBRATE?
CAN'T, UNFORTUNATELY.
I'VE GOT A LOT TO DO.
YOU'VE BEEN BUSY EVERY NIGHT FOR MONTHS.
I'M STARTING TO FORGET WHAT YOU LOOK LIKE.
YOU CAN'T BUILD AN EMPIRE BY WASTING TIME.
IS THAT ALL I AM NOW, A WASTE OF TIME?
OF COURSE NOT. HERE.
THIS SHOULD MORE THAN COVER AN EVENING ON THE TOWN.
GO OUT AND ENJOY YOURSELF ON ME.
GLADLY.
THE BUILDING CONTINUED, UNABATED--
--BUT THE CRACKS IN THE ZIGGURAT WERE ALREADY BEGINNING TO SHOW...

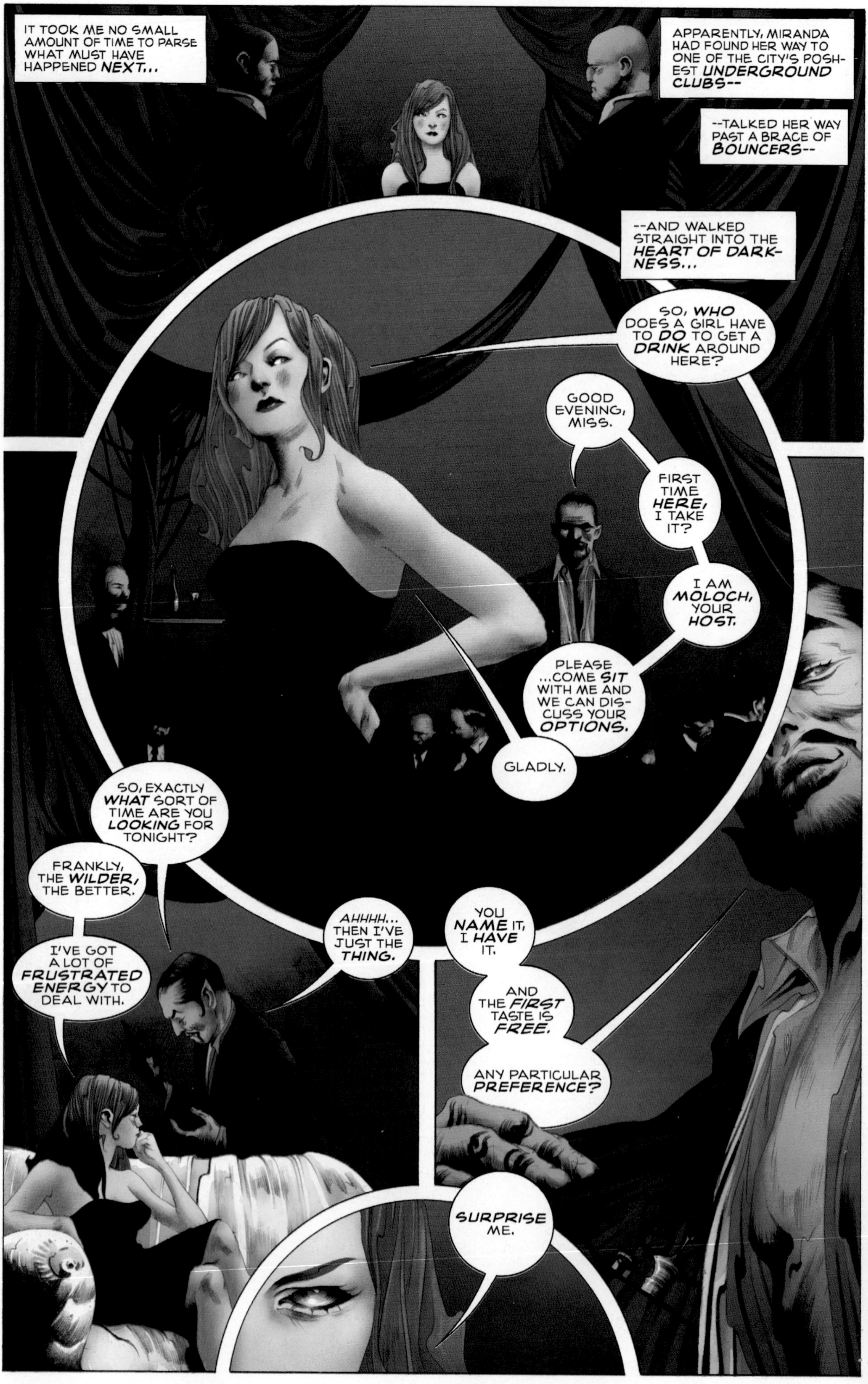
IT TOOK ME NO SMALL AMOUNT OF TIME TO PARSE WHAT MUST HAVE HAPPENED NEXT...
APPARENTLY, MIRANDA HAD FOUND HER WAY TO ONE OF THE CITY'S POSH-EST UNDERGROUND CLUBS--
--TALKED HER WAY PAST A BRACE OF BOUNCERS--
--AND WALKED STRAIGHT INTO THE HEART OF DARK-NESS...
SO, WHO DOES A GIRL HAVE TO DO TO GET A DRINK AROUND HERE?
GOOD EVENING, MISS.
FIRST TIME HERE, I TAKE IT?
I AM MOLOCH, YOUR HOST.
PLEASE ...COME SIT WITH ME AND WE CAN DIS-CUSS YOUR OPTIONS.
GLADLY.
SO, EXACTLY WHAT SORT OF TIME ARE YOU LOOKING FOR TONIGHT?
FRANKLY, THE WILDER, THE BETTER.
I'VE GOT A LOT OF FRUSTRATED ENERGY TO DEAL WITH.
AHHHH... THEN I'VE JUST THE THING.
YOU NAME IT, I HAVE IT.
AND THE FIRST TASTE IS FREE.
ANY PARTICULAR PREFERENCE?
SURPRISE ME.

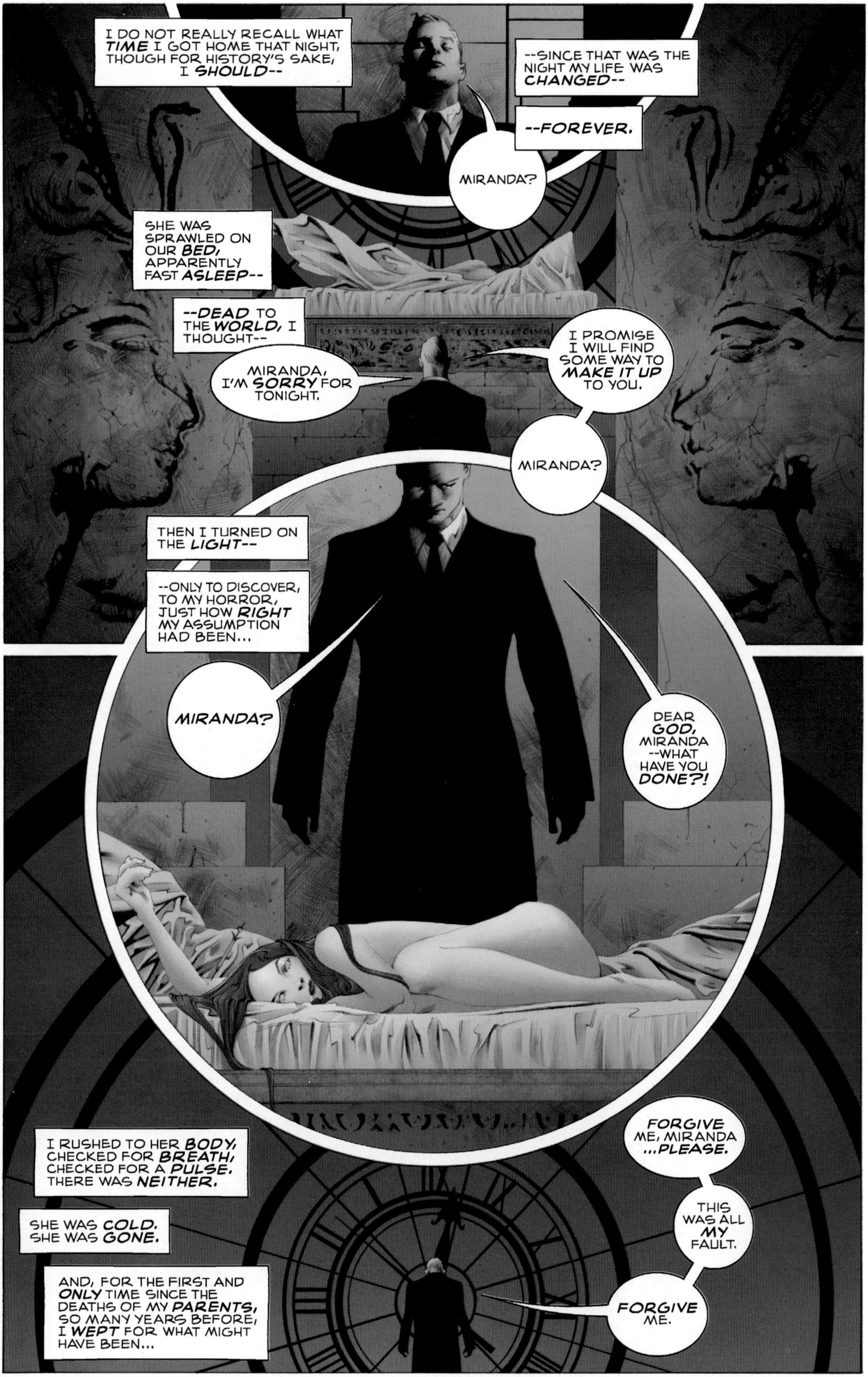
I DO NOT REALLY RECALL WHAT TIME I GOT HOME THAT NIGHT, THOUGH FOR HISTORY'S SAKE, I SHOULD--
--SINCE THAT WAS THE NIGHT MY LIFE WAS CHANGED--
--FOREVER.
MIRANDA?
SHE WAS SPRAWLED ON OUR BED, APPARENTLY FAST ASLEEP--
--DEAD TO THE WORLD, I THOUGHT--
MIRANDA, I'M SORRY FOR TONIGHT.
I PROMISE I WILL FIND SOME WAY TO MAKE IT UP TO YOU.
MIRANDA?
THEN I TURNED ON THE LIGHT--
--ONLY TO DISCOVER, TO MY HORROR, JUST HOW RIGHT MY ASSUMPTION HAD BEEN...
MIRANDA?
DEAR GOD, MIRANDA --WHAT HAVE YOU DONE?!
I RUSHED TO HER BODY, CHECKED FOR BREATH, CHECKED FOR A PULSE. THERE WAS NEITHER.
SHE WAS COLD. SHE WAS GONE.
AND, FOR THE FIRST AND ONLY TIME SINCE THE DEATHS OF MY PARENTS, SO MANY YEARS BEFORE, I WEPT FOR WHAT MIGHT HAVE BEEN...
FORGIVE ME, MIRANDA ...PLEASE.
THIS WAS ALL MY FAULT.
FORGIVE ME.

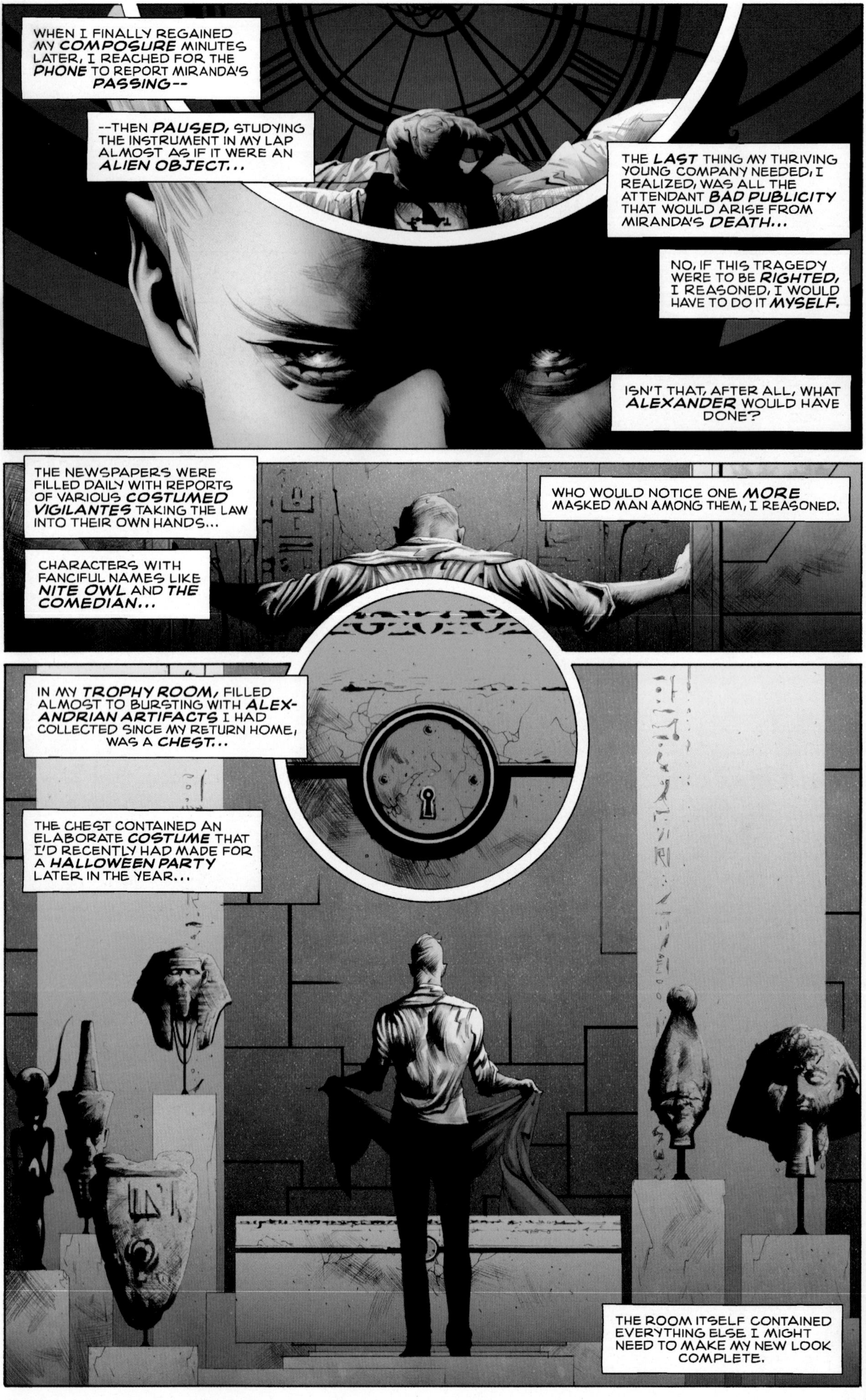
WHEN I FINALLY REGAINED MY COMPOSURE MINUTES LATER, I REACHED FOR THE PHONE TO REPORT MIRANDA'S PASSING--
--THEN PAUSED, STUDYING THE INSTRUMENT IN MY LAP ALMOST AS IF IT WERE AN ALIEN OBJECT...
THE LAST THING MY THRIVING YOUNG COMPANY NEEDED, I REALIZED, WAS ALL THE ATTENDANT BAD PUBLICITY THAT WOULD ARISE FROM MIRANDA'S DEATH...
NO, IF THIS TRAGEDY WERE TO BE RIGHTED, I REASONED, I WOULD HAVE TO DO IT MYSELF.
ISN'T THAT, AFTER ALL, WHAT ALEXANDER WOULD HAVE DONE?
THE NEWSPAPERS WERE FILLED DAILY WITH REPORTS OF VARIOUS COSTUMED VIGILANTES TAKING THE LAW INTO THEIR OWN HANDS...
CHARACTERS WITH FANCIFUL NAMES LIKE NITE OWL AND THE COMEDIAN...
WHO WOULD NOTICE ONE MORE MASKED MAN AMONG THEM, I REASONED.
IN MY TROPHY ROOM, FILLED ALMOST TO BURSTING WITH ALEX-ANDRIAN ARTIFACTS I HAD COLLECTED SINCE MY RETURN HOME, WAS A CHEST...
THE CHEST CONTAINED AN ELABORATE COSTUME THAT I'D RECENTLY HAD MADE FOR A HALLOWEEN PARTY LATER IN THE YEAR...
THE ROOM ITSELF CONTAINED EVERYTHING ELSE I MIGHT NEED TO MAKE MY NEW LOOK COMPLETE.

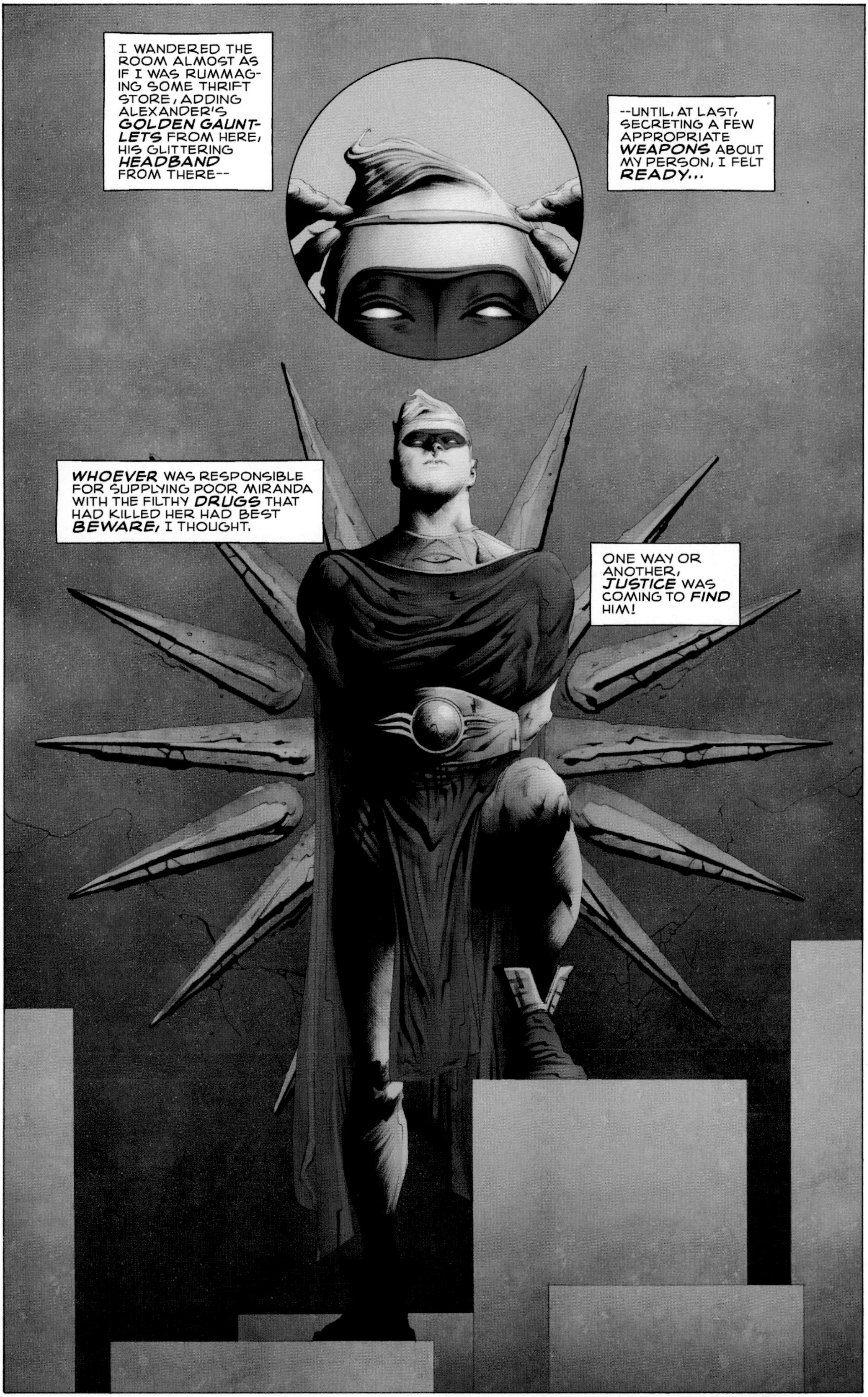
I WANDERED THE ROOM ALMOST AS IF I WAS RUMMAGING SOME THRIFT STORE, ADDING ALEXANDER'S GOLDEN GAUNTLETS FROM HERE, HIS GLITTERING HEADBAND FROM THERE--
--UNTIL, AT LAST, SECRETING A FEW APPROPRIATE WEAPONS ABOUT MY PERSON, I FELT READY...
WHOEVER WAS RESPONSIBLE FOR SUPPLYING POOR MIRANDA WITH THE FILTHY DRUGS THAT HAD KILLED HER HAD BEST BEWARE, I THOUGHT.
ONE WAY OR ANOTHER, JUSTICE WAS COMING TO FIND HIM!

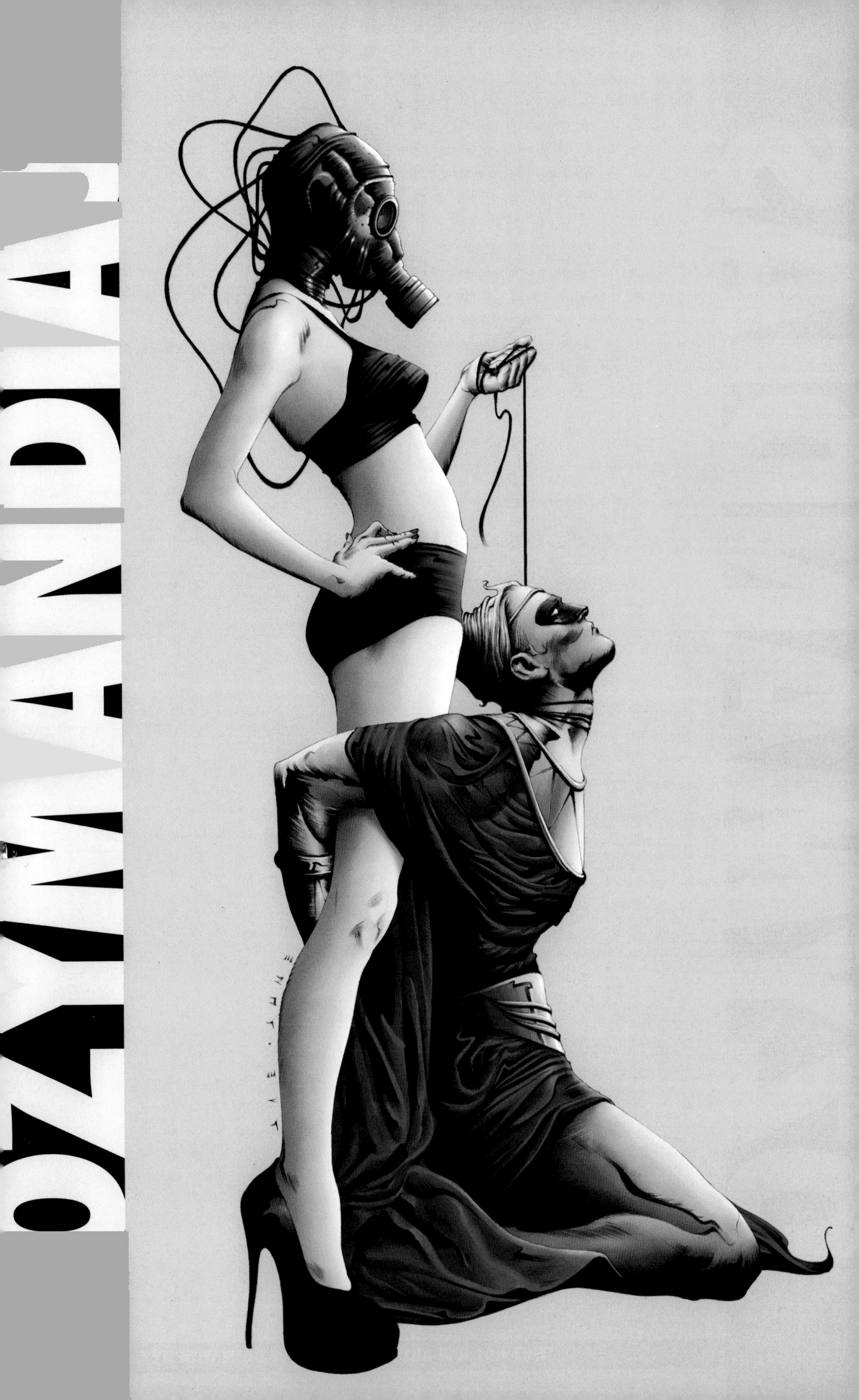

OZYMANDIAS

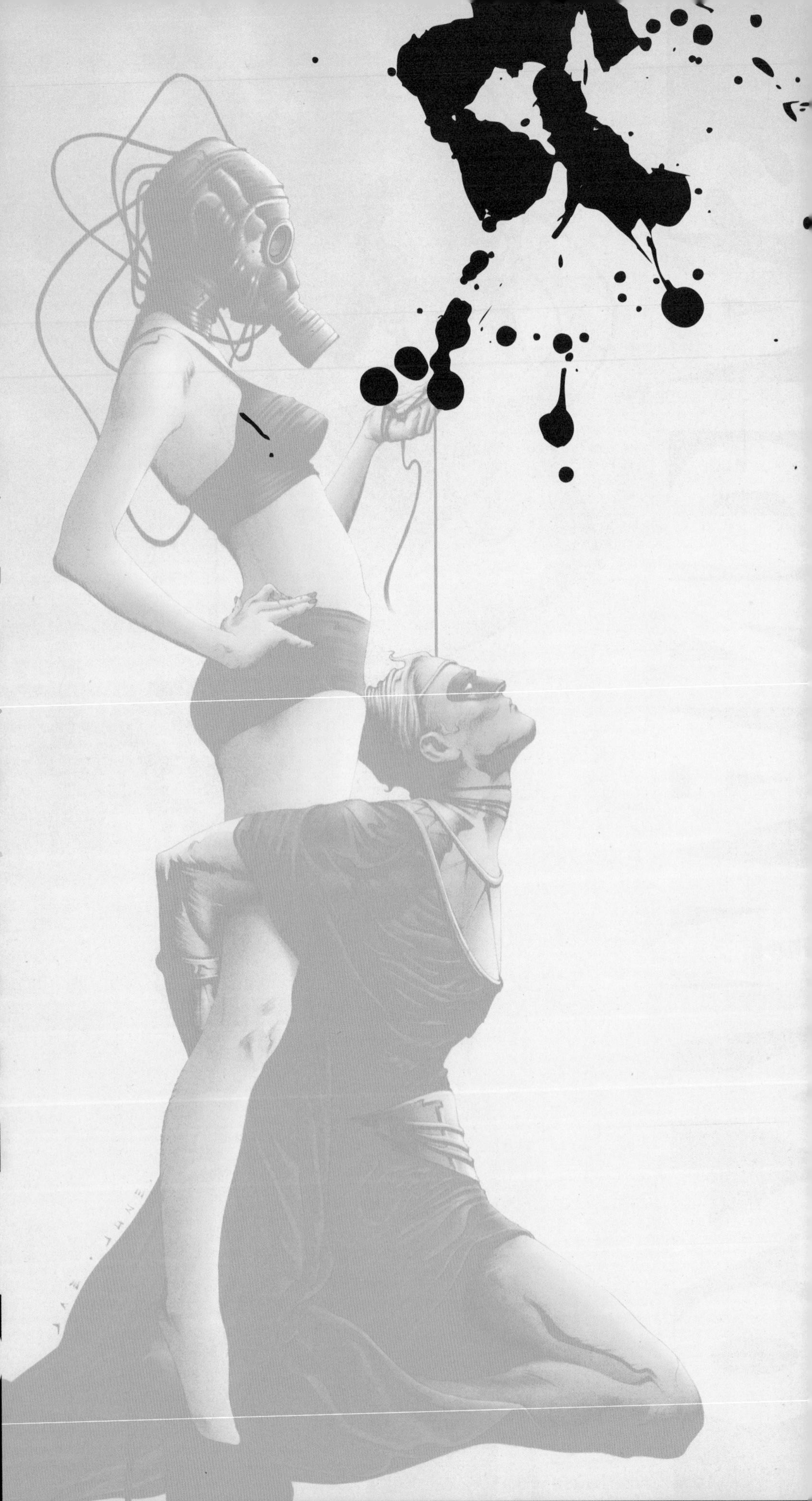

"WHY NOT JUST KILL ME NOW AND BE DONE WITH IT?"

THE HAND THAT MOCKED THEM...!

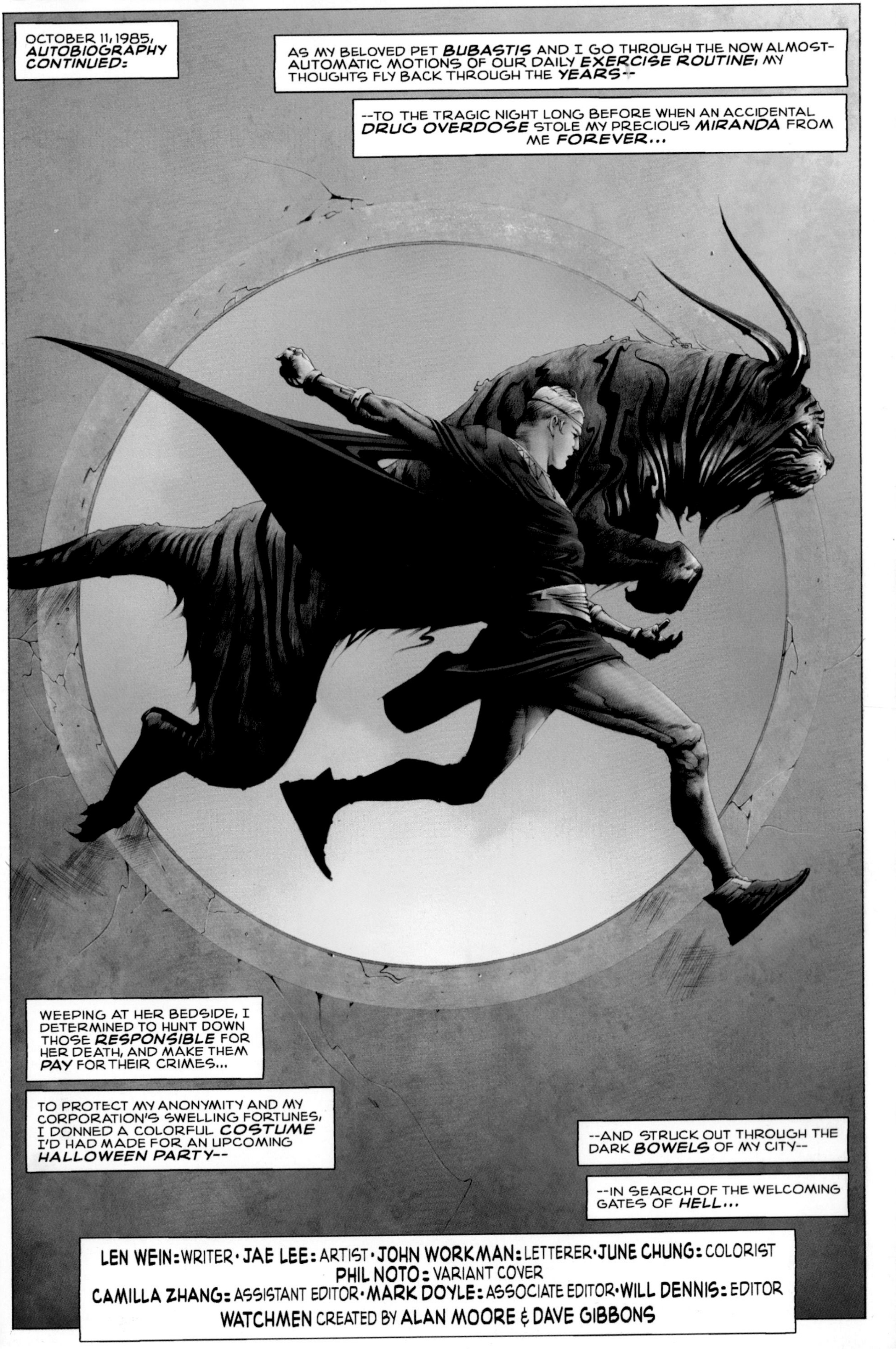

OCTOBER 11, 1985, AUTOBIOGRAPHY CONTINUED:
AS MY BELOVED PET BUBASTIS AND I GO THROUGH THE NOW ALMOST-AUTOMATIC MOTIONS OF OUR DAILY EXERCISE ROUTINE, MY THOUGHTS FLY BACK THROUGH THE YEARS--
--TO THE TRAGIC NIGHT LONG BEFORE WHEN AN ACCIDENTAL DRUG OVERDOSE STOLE MY PRECIOUS MIRANDA FROM ME FOREVER...
WEEPING AT HER BEDSIDE, I DETERMINED TO HUNT DOWN THOSE RESPONSIBLE FOR HER DEATH, AND MAKE THEM PAY FOR THEIR CRIMES...
TO PROTECT MY ANONYMITY AND MY CORPORATION'S SWELLING FORTUNES, I DONNED A COLORFUL COSTUME I'D HAD MADE FOR AN UPCOMING HALLOWEEN PARTY--
--AND STRUCK OUT THROUGH THE DARK BOWELS OF MY CITY--
--IN SEARCH OF THE WELCOMING GATES OF HELL...
LEN WEIN: WRITER • JAE LEE: ARTIST • JOHN WORKMAN: LETTERER • JUNE CHUNG: COLORIST
PHIL NOTO: VARIANT COVER
CAMILLA ZHANG: ASSISTANT EDITOR • MARK DOYLE: ASSOCIATE EDITOR • WILL DENNIS: EDITOR
WATCHMEN CREATED BY ALAN MOORE & DAVE GIBBONS

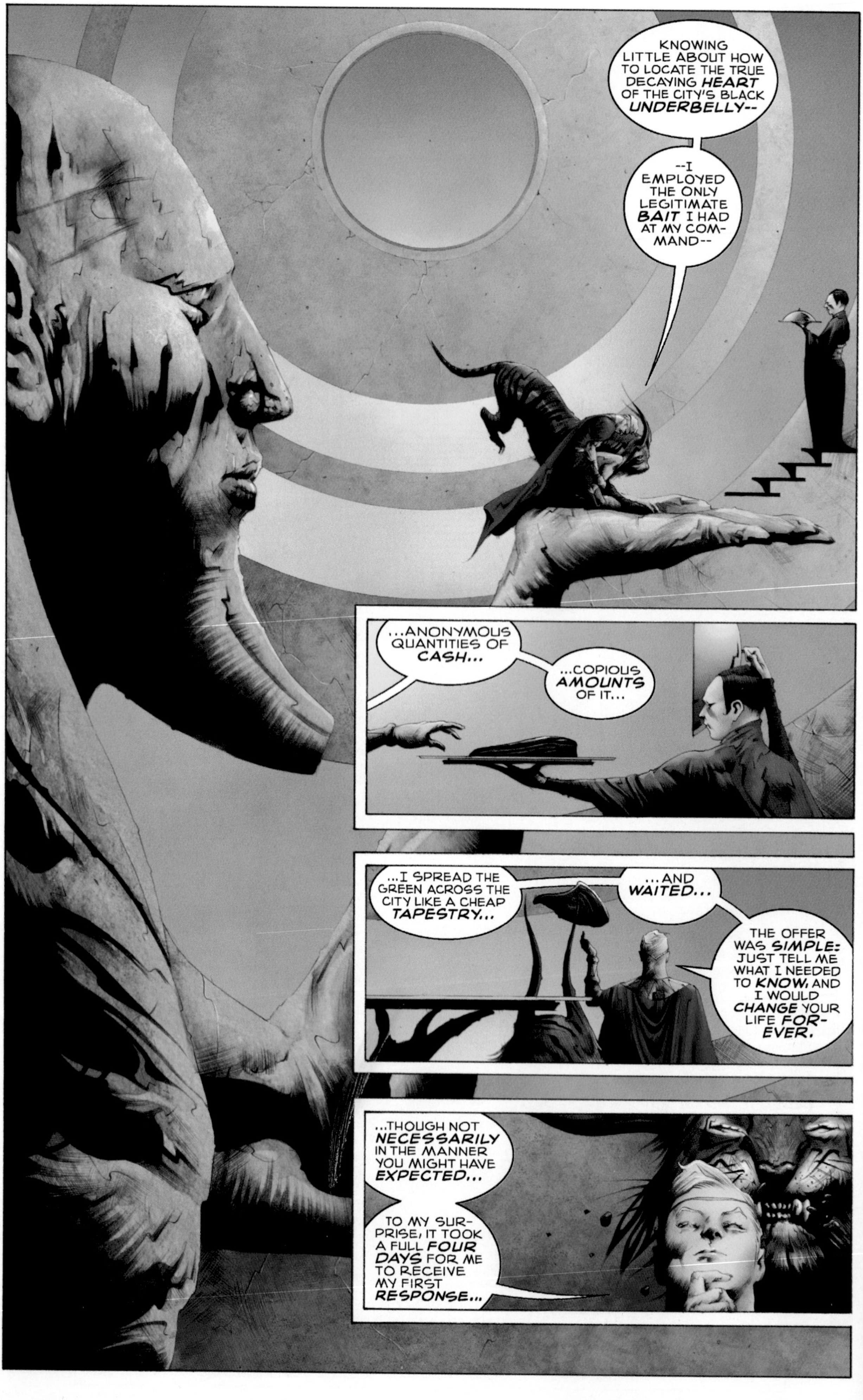
KNOWING LITTLE ABOUT HOW TO LOCATE THE TRUE DECAYING HEART OF THE CITY'S BLACK UNDERBELLY--
--I EMPLOYED THE ONLY LEGITIMATE BAIT I HAD AT MY COMMAND--
...ANONYMOUS QUANTITIES OF CASH...
...COPIOUS AMOUNTS OF IT...
...I SPREAD THE GREEN ACROSS THE CITY LIKE A CHEAP TAPESTRY...
...AND WAITED...
THE OFFER WAS SIMPLE: JUST TELL ME WHAT I NEEDED TO KNOW, AND I WOULD CHANGE YOUR LIFE FOREVER.
...THOUGH NOT NECESSARILY IN THE MANNER YOU MIGHT HAVE EXPECTED...
TO MY SURPRISE, IT TOOK A FULL FOUR DAYS FOR ME TO RECEIVE MY FIRST RESPONSE...

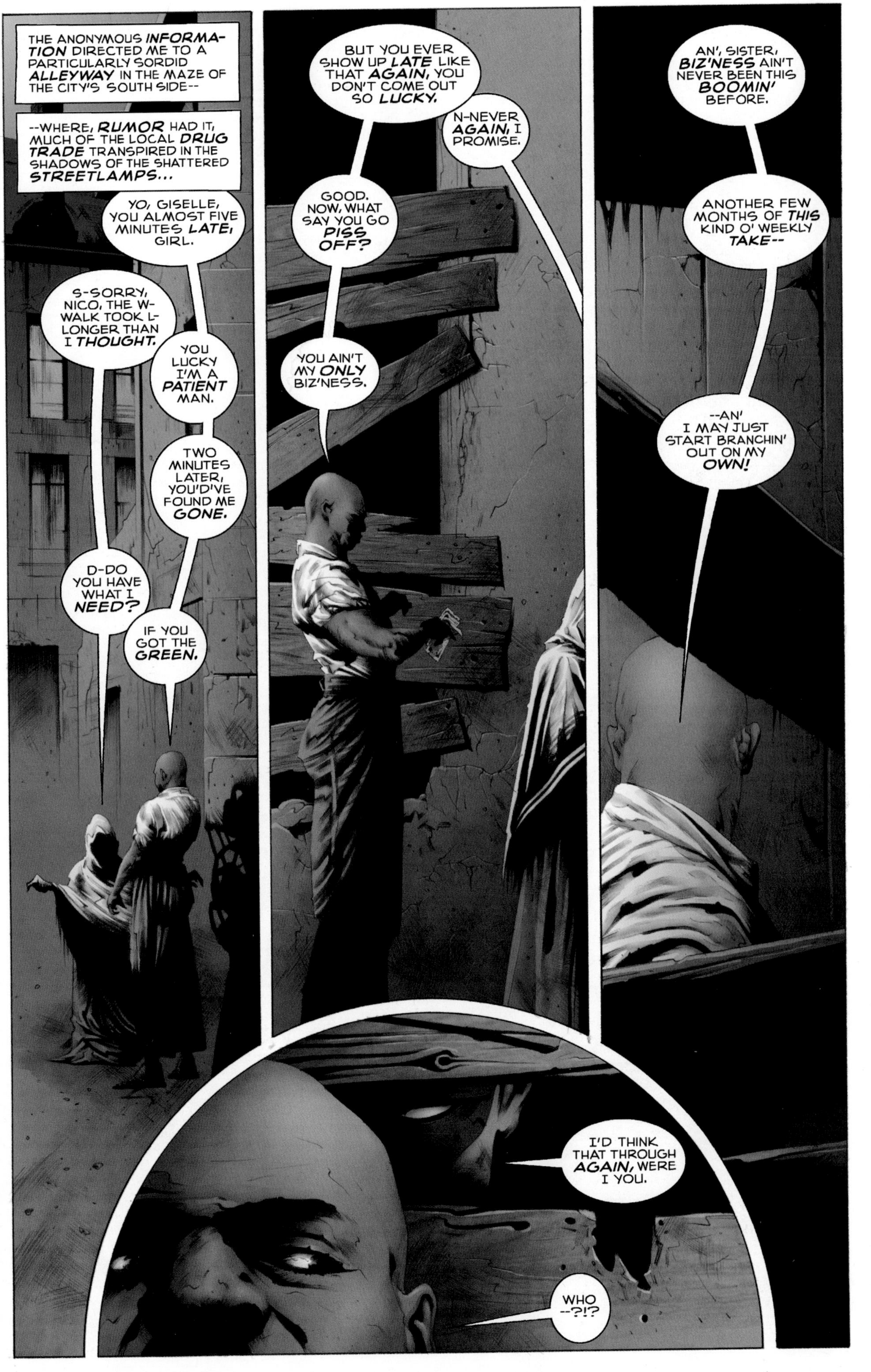

THE ANONYMOUS INFORMATION DIRECTED ME TO A PARTICULARLY SORDID ALLEYWAY IN THE MAZE OF THE CITY'S SOUTH SIDE--
--WHERE, RUMOR HAD IT, MUCH OF THE LOCAL DRUG TRADE TRANSPIRED IN THE SHADOWS OF THE SHATTERED STREETLAMPS...
YO, GISELLE, YOU ALMOST FIVE MINUTES LATE, GIRL.
S-SORRY, NICO, THE W-WALK TOOK L-LONGER THAN I THOUGHT.
YOU LUCKY I'M A PATIENT MAN.
TWO MINUTES LATER, YOU'D'VE FOUND ME GONE.
D-DO YOU HAVE WHAT I NEED?
IF YOU GOT THE GREEN.
BUT YOU EVER SHOW UP LATE LIKE THAT AGAIN, YOU DON'T COME OUT SO LUCKY.
N-NEVER AGAIN, I PROMISE.
GOOD. NOW, WHAT SAY YOU GO PISS OFF?
YOU AIN'T MY ONLY BIZ'NESS.
AN', SISTER, BIZ'NESS AIN'T NEVER BEEN THIS BOOMIN' BEFORE.
ANOTHER FEW MONTHS OF THIS KIND O' WEEKLY TAKE--
--AN' I MAY JUST START BRANCHIN' OUT ON MY OWN!
I'D THINK THAT THROUGH AGAIN, WERE I YOU.
WHO --?!?

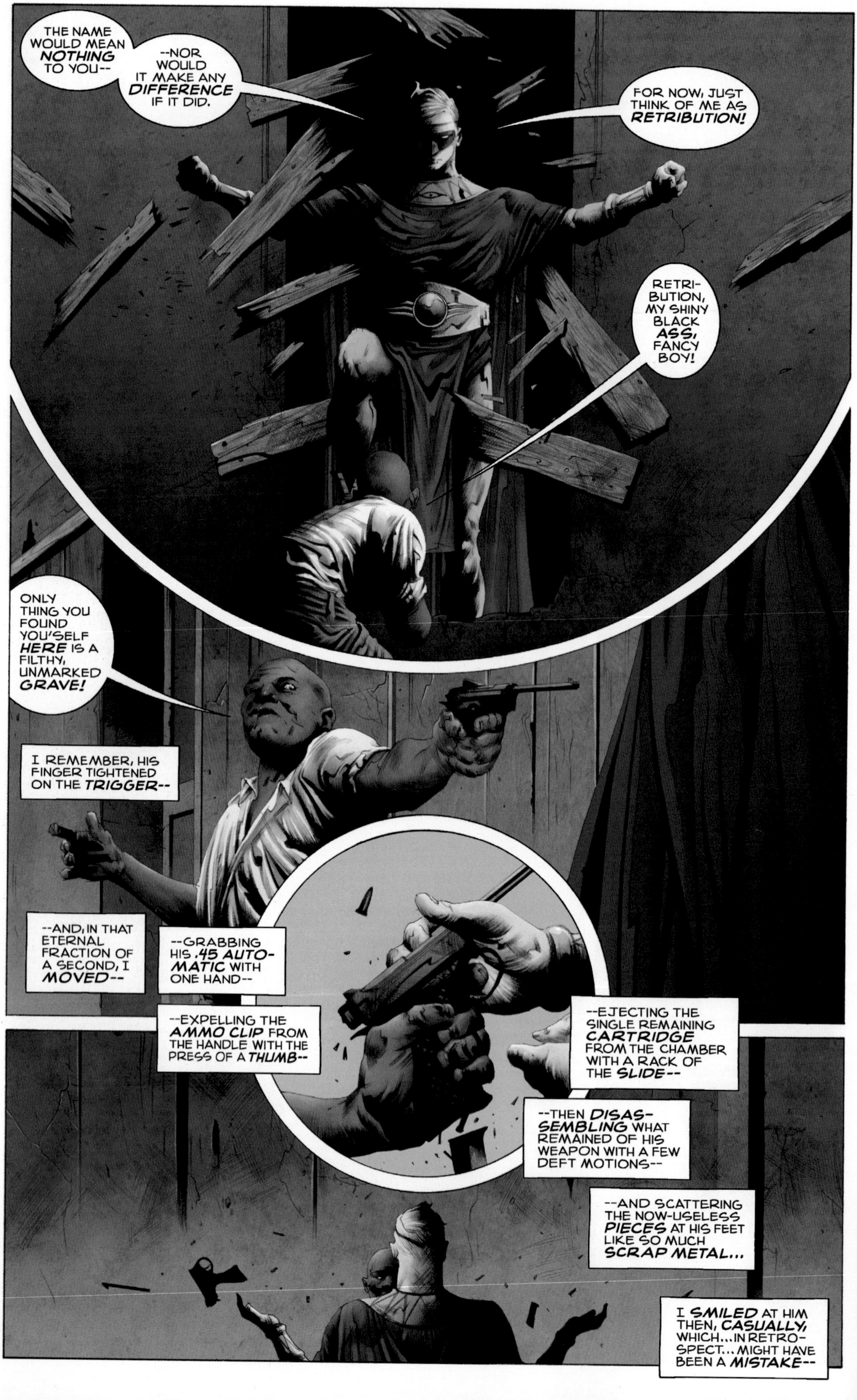
THE NAME WOULD MEAN NOTHING TO YOU--
--NOR WOULD IT MAKE ANY DIFFERENCE IF IT DID.
FOR NOW, JUST THINK OF ME AS RETRIBUTION!
RETRIBUTION, MY SHINY BLACK ASS, FANCY BOY!
ONLY THING YOU FOUND YOU'SELF HERE IS A FILTHY, UNMARKED GRAVE!
I REMEMBER, HIS FINGER TIGHTENED ON THE TRIGGER--
--AND, IN THAT ETERNAL FRACTION OF A SECOND, I MOVED--
--GRABBING HIS .45 AUTOMATIC WITH ONE HAND--
--EXPELLING THE AMMO CLIP FROM THE HANDLE WITH THE PRESS OF A THUMB--
--EJECTING THE SINGLE REMAINING CARTRIDGE FROM THE CHAMBER WITH A RACK OF THE SLIDE--
--THEN DISASSEMBLING WHAT REMAINED OF HIS WEAPON WITH A FEW DEFT MOTIONS--
--AND SCATTERING THE NOW-USELESS PIECES AT HIS FEET LIKE SO MUCH SCRAP METAL...
I SMILED AT HIM THEN, CASUALLY, WHICH... IN RETROSPECT... MIGHT HAVE BEEN A MISTAKE--

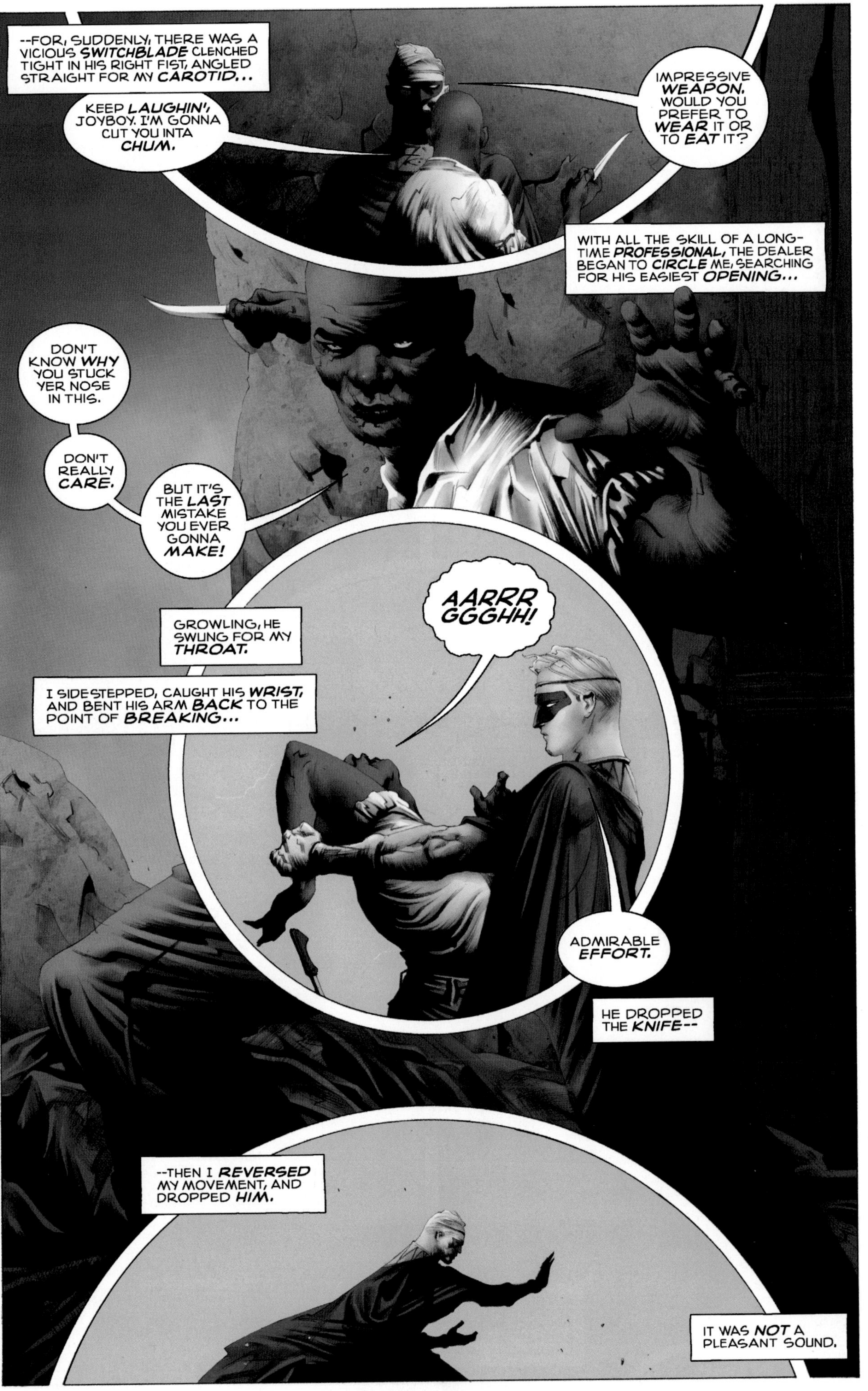
--FOR, SUDDENLY, THERE WAS A VICIOUS SWITCHBLADE CLENCHED TIGHT IN HIS RIGHT FIST, ANGLED STRAIGHT FOR MY CAROTID...
KEEP LAUGHIN', JOYBOY. I'M GONNA CUT YOU INTA CHUM.
IMPRESSIVE WEAPON. WOULD YOU PREFER TO WEAR IT OR TO EAT IT?
WITH ALL THE SKILL OF A LONG-TIME PROFESSIONAL, THE DEALER BEGAN TO CIRCLE ME, SEARCHING FOR HIS EASIEST OPENING...
DON'T KNOW WHY YOU STUCK YER NOSE IN THIS.
DON'T REALLY CARE.
BUT IT'S THE LAST MISTAKE YOU EVER GONNA MAKE!
GROWLING, HE SWUNG FOR MY THROAT.
AARRR GGGHH!
I SIDESTEPPED, CAUGHT HIS WRIST, AND BENT HIS ARM BACK TO THE POINT OF BREAKING...
ADMIRABLE EFFORT.
HE DROPPED THE KNIFE--
--THEN I REVERSED MY MOVEMENT, AND DROPPED HIM.
IT WAS NOT A PLEASANT SOUND.

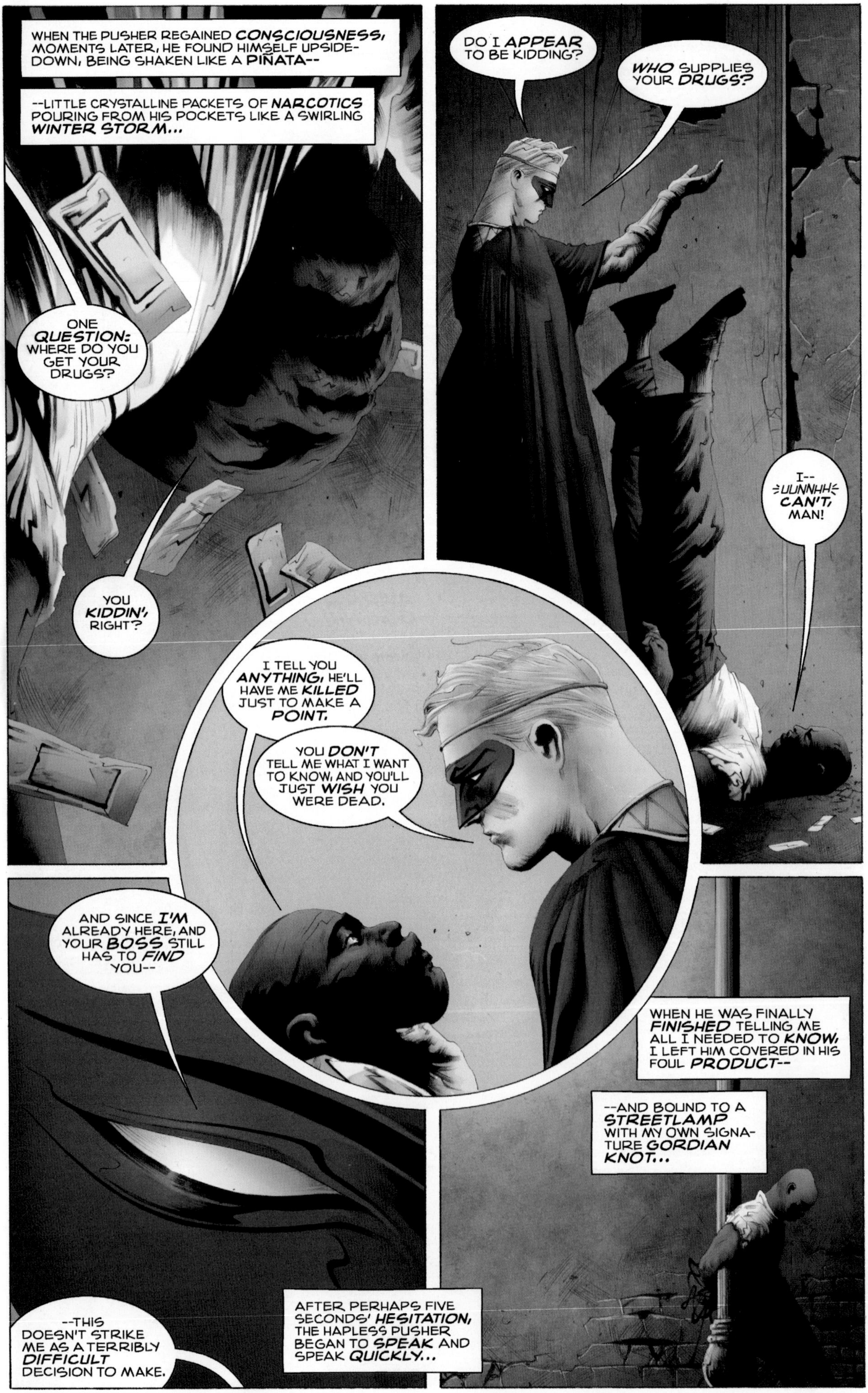
WHEN THE PUSHER REGAINED CONSCIOUSNESS, MOMENTS LATER, HE FOUND HIMSELF UPSIDE-DOWN, BEING SHAKEN LIKE A PIÑATA--
--LITTLE CRYSTALLINE PACKETS OF NARCOTICS POURING FROM HIS POCKETS LIKE A SWIRLING WINTER STORM...
ONE QUESTION: WHERE DO YOU GET YOUR DRUGS?
YOU KIDDIN', RIGHT?
DO I APPEAR TO BE KIDDING?
WHO SUPPLIES YOUR DRUGS?
I-- UUNNHH CAN'T, MAN!
I TELL YOU ANYTHING, HE'LL HAVE ME KILLED JUST TO MAKE A POINT.
YOU DON'T TELL ME WHAT I WANT TO KNOW, AND YOU'LL JUST WISH YOU WERE DEAD.
AND SINCE I'M ALREADY HERE, AND YOUR BOSS STILL HAS TO FIND YOU--
--THIS DOESN'T STRIKE ME AS A TERRIBLY DIFFICULT DECISION TO MAKE.
AFTER PERHAPS FIVE SECONDS' HESITATION, THE HAPLESS PUSHER BEGAN TO SPEAK AND SPEAK QUICKLY...
WHEN HE WAS FINALLY FINISHED TELLING ME ALL I NEEDED TO KNOW, I LEFT HIM COVERED IN HIS FOUL PRODUCT--
--AND BOUND TO A STREETLAMP WITH MY OWN SIGNATURE GORDIAN KNOT...

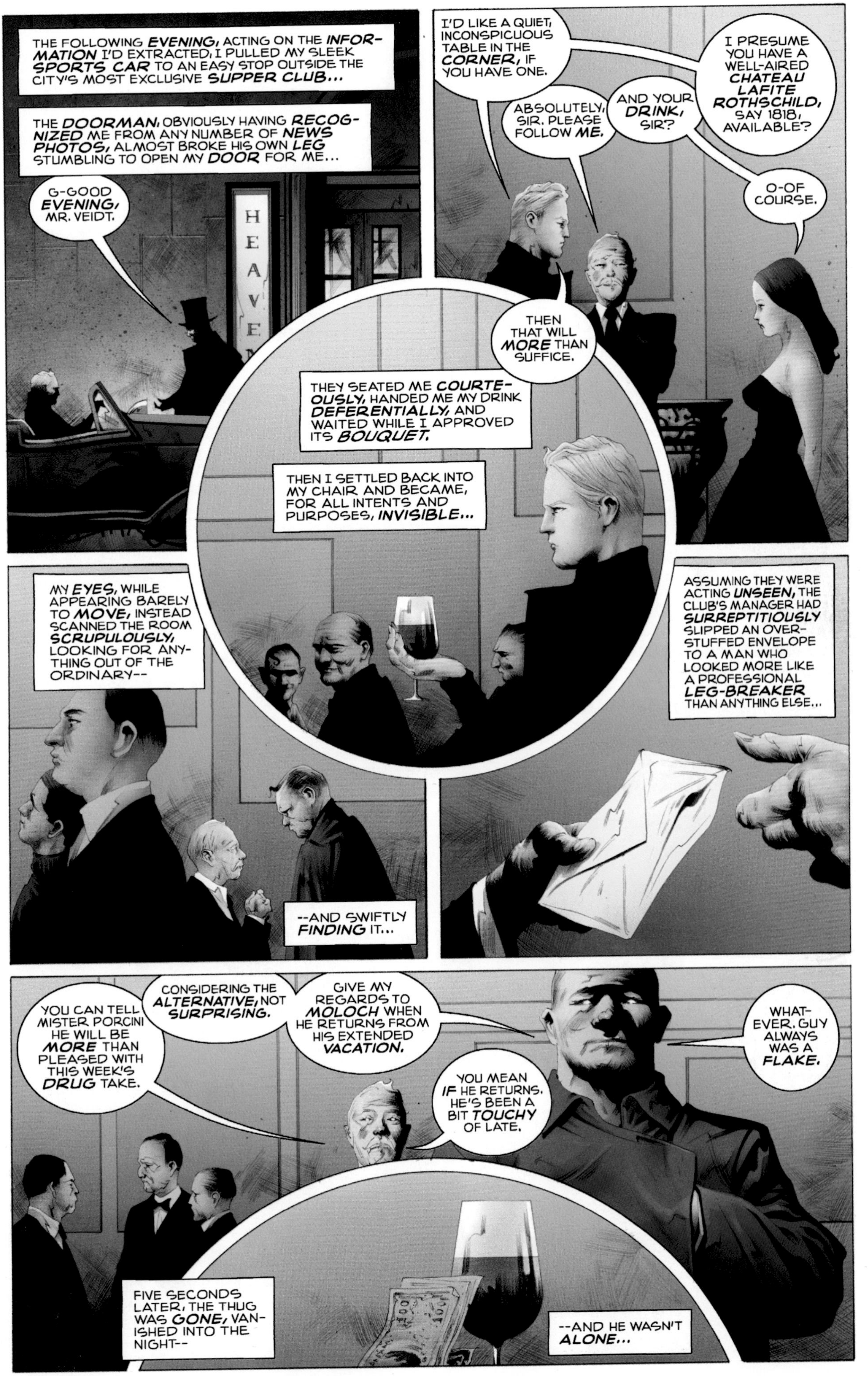
THE FOLLOWING EVENING, ACTING ON THE INFORMATION I'D EXTRACTED, I PULLED MY SLEEK SPORTS CAR TO AN EASY STOP OUTSIDE THE CITY'S MOST EXCLUSIVE SUPPER CLUB...
THE DOORMAN, OBVIOUSLY HAVING RECOGNIZED ME FROM ANY NUMBER OF NEWS PHOTOS, ALMOST BROKE HIS OWN LEG STUMBLING TO OPEN MY DOOR FOR ME...
G-GOOD EVENING, MR. VEIDT.
HEAVEN
I'D LIKE A QUIET, INCONSPICUOUS TABLE IN THE CORNER, IF YOU HAVE ONE.
ABSOLUTELY, SIR. PLEASE FOLLOW ME.
AND YOUR DRINK, SIR?
I PRESUME YOU HAVE A WELL-AIRED CHATEAU LAFITE ROTHSCHILD, SAY 1818, AVAILABLE?
O-OF COURSE.
THEN THAT WILL MORE THAN SUFFICE.
THEY SEATED ME COURTEOUSLY, HANDED ME MY DRINK DEFERENTIALLY, AND WAITED WHILE I APPROVED ITS BOUQUET.
THEN I SETTLED BACK INTO MY CHAIR AND BECAME, FOR ALL INTENTS AND PURPOSES, INVISIBLE...
MY EYES, WHILE APPEARING BARELY TO MOVE, INSTEAD SCANNED THE ROOM SCRUPULOUSLY, LOOKING FOR ANYTHING OUT OF THE ORDINARY--
--AND SWIFTLY FINDING IT...
ASSUMING THEY WERE ACTING UNSEEN, THE CLUB'S MANAGER HAD SURREPTITIOUSLY SLIPPED AN OVER-STUFFED ENVELOPE TO A MAN WHO LOOKED MORE LIKE A PROFESSIONAL LEG-BREAKER THAN ANYTHING ELSE...
YOU CAN TELL MISTER PORCINI HE WILL BE MORE THAN PLEASED WITH THIS WEEK'S DRUG TAKE.
CONSIDERING THE ALTERNATIVE, NOT SURPRISING.
GIVE MY REGARDS TO MOLOCH WHEN HE RETURNS FROM HIS EXTENDED VACATION.
YOU MEAN IF HE RETURNS. HE'S BEEN A BIT TOUCHY OF LATE.
WHAT-EVER. GUY ALWAYS WAS A FLAKE.
FIVE SECONDS LATER, THE THUG WAS GONE, VANISHED INTO THE NIGHT--
--AND HE WASN'T ALONE...

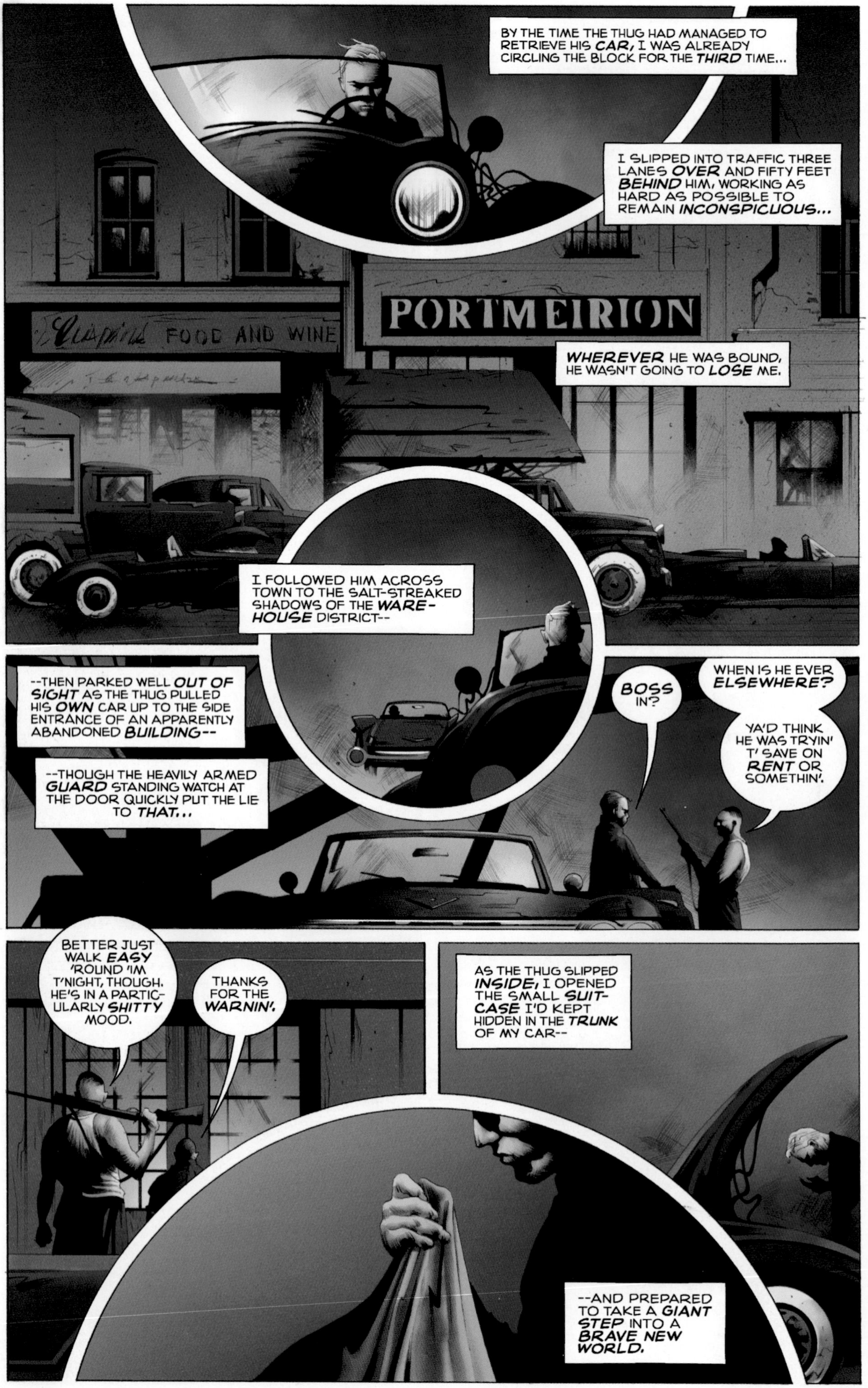
BY THE TIME THE THUG HAD MANAGED TO RETRIEVE HIS CAR, I WAS ALREADY CIRCLING THE BLOCK FOR THE THIRD TIME...
I SLIPPED INTO TRAFFIC THREE LANES OVER AND FIFTY FEET BEHIND HIM, WORKING AS HARD AS POSSIBLE TO REMAIN INCONSPICUOUS...
FOOD AND WINE
PORTMEIRION
WHEREVER HE WAS BOUND, HE WASN'T GOING TO LOSE ME.
I FOLLOWED HIM ACROSS TOWN TO THE SALT-STREAKED SHADOWS OF THE WARE-HOUSE DISTRICT--
--THEN PARKED WELL OUT OF SIGHT AS THE THUG PULLED HIS OWN CAR UP TO THE SIDE ENTRANCE OF AN APPARENTLY ABANDONED BUILDING--
--THOUGH THE HEAVILY ARMED GUARD STANDING WATCH AT THE DOOR QUICKLY PUT THE LIE TO THAT...
BOSS IN?
WHEN IS HE EVER ELSEWHERE?
YA'D THINK HE WAS TRYIN' T' SAVE ON RENT OR SOMETHIN'.
BETTER JUST WALK EASY 'ROUND 'IM T'NIGHT, THOUGH. HE'S IN A PARTIC-ULARLY SHITTY MOOD.
THANKS FOR THE WARNIN'.
AS THE THUG SLIPPED INSIDE, I OPENED THE SMALL SUIT-CASE I'D KEPT HIDDEN IN THE TRUNK OF MY CAR--
--AND PREPARED TO TAKE A GIANT STEP INTO A BRAVE NEW WORLD.

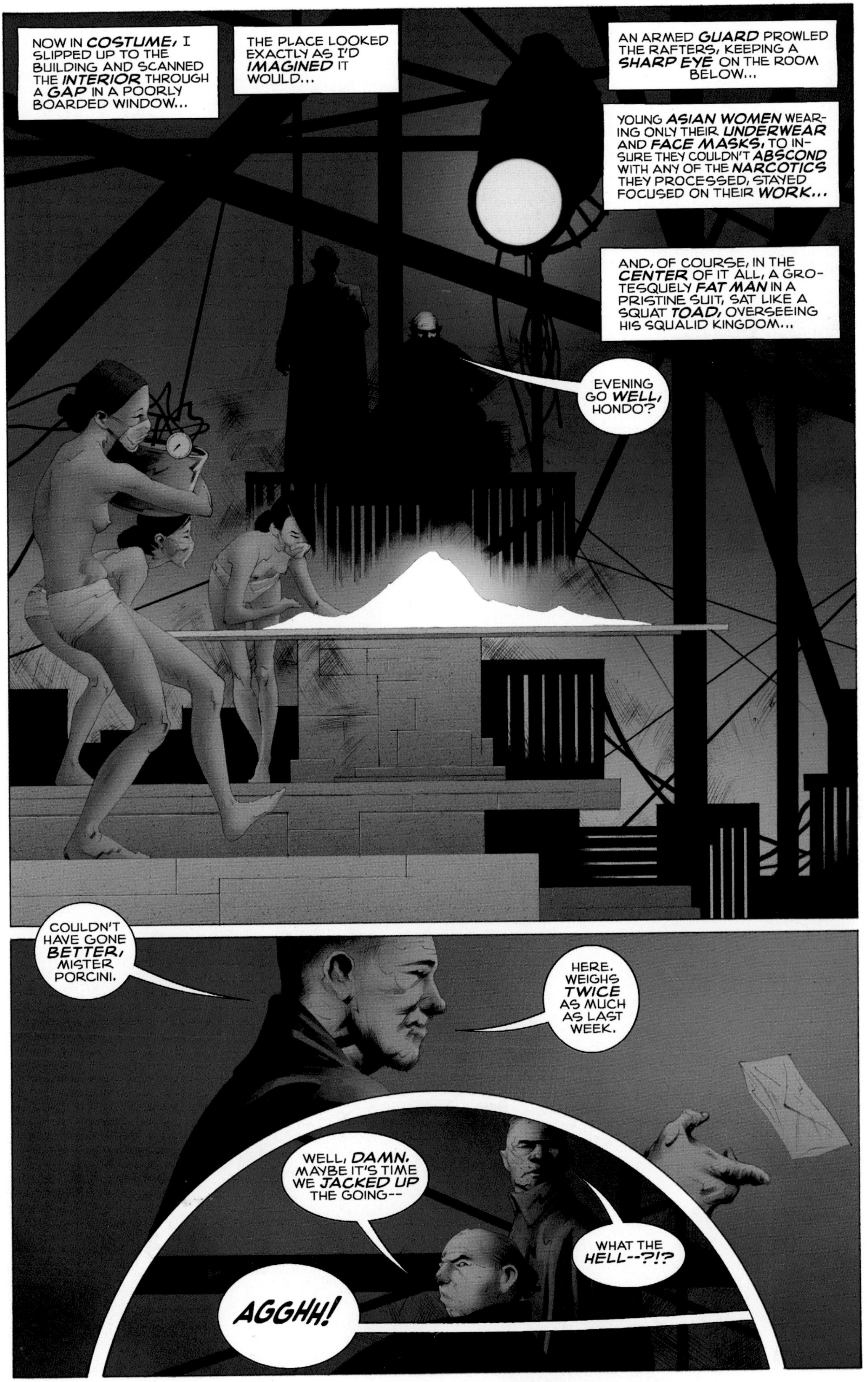
NOW IN COSTUME, I SLIPPED UP TO THE BUILDING AND SCANNED THE INTERIOR THROUGH A GAP IN A POORLY BOARDED WINDOW...
THE PLACE LOOKED EXACTLY AS I'D IMAGINED IT WOULD...
AN ARMED GUARD PROWLED THE RAFTERS, KEEPING A SHARP EYE ON THE ROOM BELOW...
YOUNG ASIAN WOMEN WEARING ONLY THEIR UNDERWEAR AND FACE MASKS, TO INSURE THEY COULDN'T ABSCOND WITH ANY OF THE NARCOTICS THEY PROCESSED, STAYED FOCUSED ON THEIR WORK...
AND, OF COURSE, IN THE CENTER OF IT ALL, A GROTESQUELY FAT MAN IN A PRISTINE SUIT, SAT LIKE A SQUAT TOAD, OVERSEEING HIS SQUALID KINGDOM...
EVENING GO WELL, HONDO?
COULDN'T HAVE GONE BETTER, MISTER PORCINI.
HERE. WEIGHS TWICE AS MUCH AS LAST WEEK.
WELL, DAMN. MAYBE IT'S TIME WE JACKED UP THE GOING--
WHAT THE HELL--?!?
AGGHH!

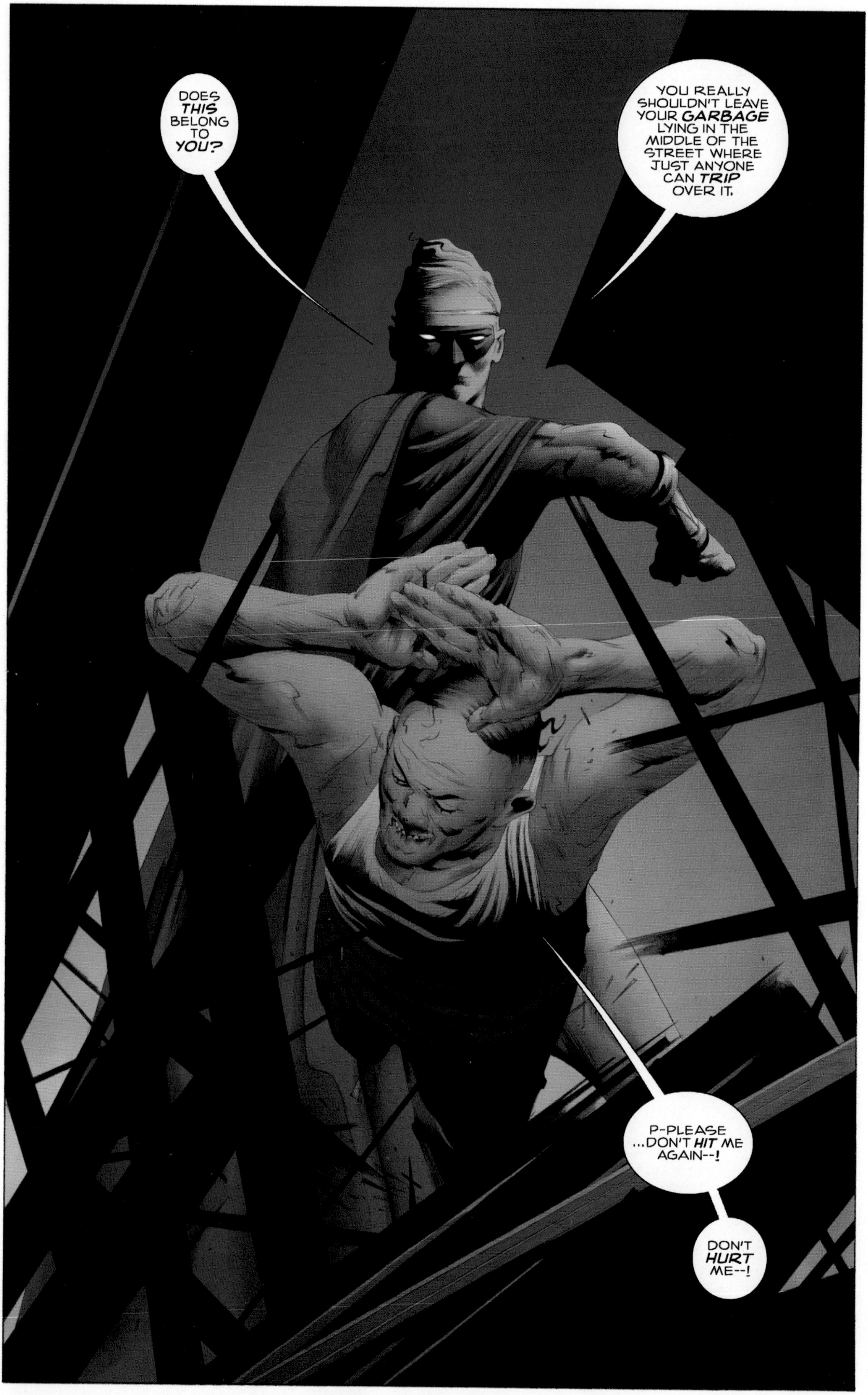
DOES THIS BELONG TO YOU?
YOU REALLY SHOULDN'T LEAVE YOUR GARBAGE LYING IN THE MIDDLE OF THE STREET WHERE JUST ANYONE CAN TRIP OVER IT.
P-PLEASE ...DON'T HIT ME AGAIN--!
DON'T HURT ME--!

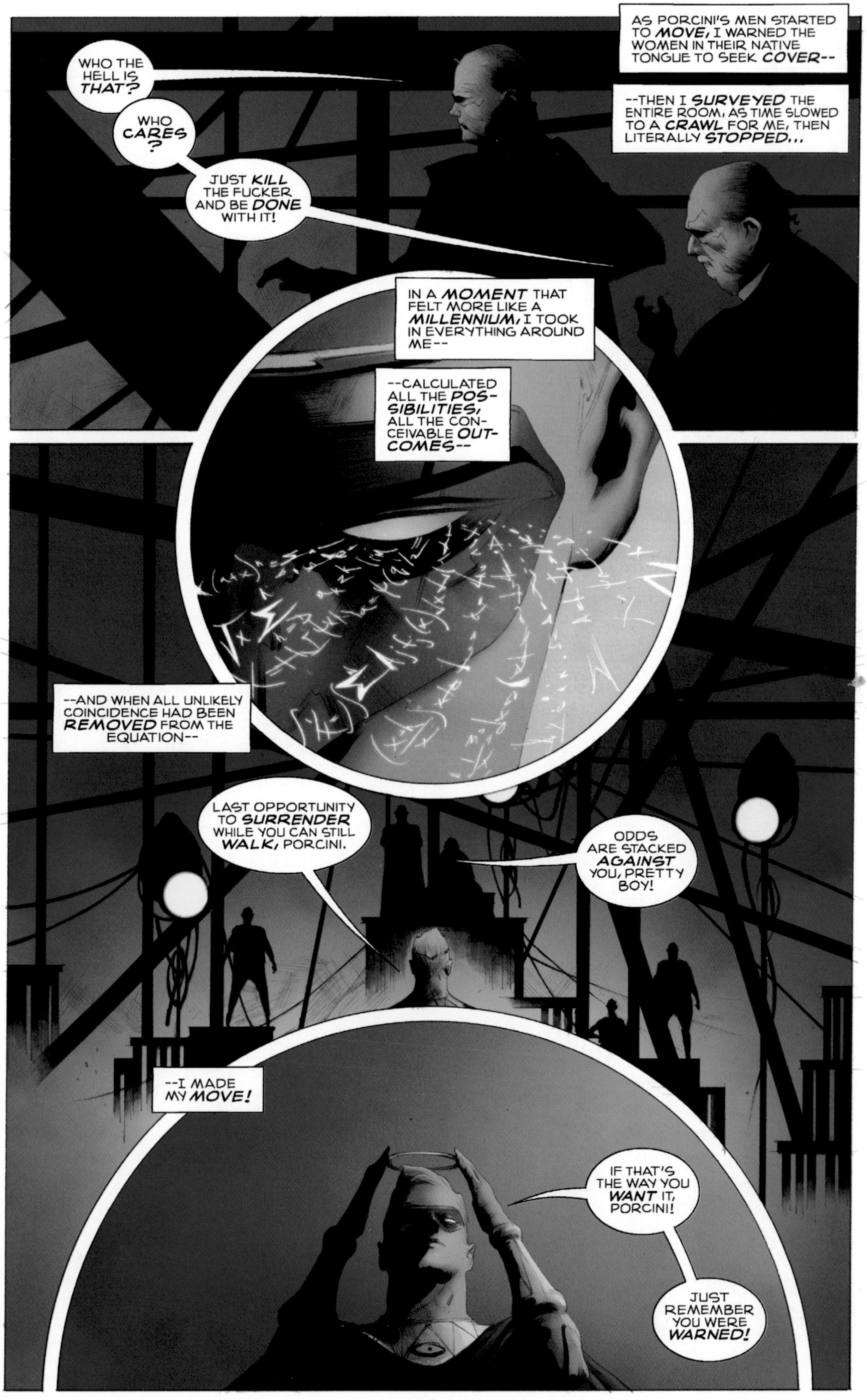
AS PORCINI'S MEN STARTED TO MOVE, I WARNED THE WOMEN IN THEIR NATIVE TONGUE TO SEEK COVER--
WHO THE HELL IS THAT?
WHO CARES?
JUST KILL THE FUCKER AND BE DONE WITH IT!
--THEN I SURVEYED THE ENTIRE ROOM, AS TIME SLOWED TO A CRAWL FOR ME, THEN LITERALLY STOPPED...
IN A MOMENT THAT FELT MORE LIKE A MILLENNIUM, I TOOK IN EVERYTHING AROUND ME--
--CALCULATED ALL THE POSSIBILITIES, ALL THE CONCEIVABLE OUTCOMES--
--AND WHEN ALL UNLIKELY COINCIDENCE HAD BEEN REMOVED FROM THE EQUATION--
LAST OPPORTUNITY TO SURRENDER WHILE YOU CAN STILL WALK, PORCINI.
ODDS ARE STACKED AGAINST YOU, PRETTY BOY!
--I MADE MY MOVE!
IF THAT'S THE WAY YOU WANT IT, PORCINI!
JUST REMEMBER YOU WERE WARNED!

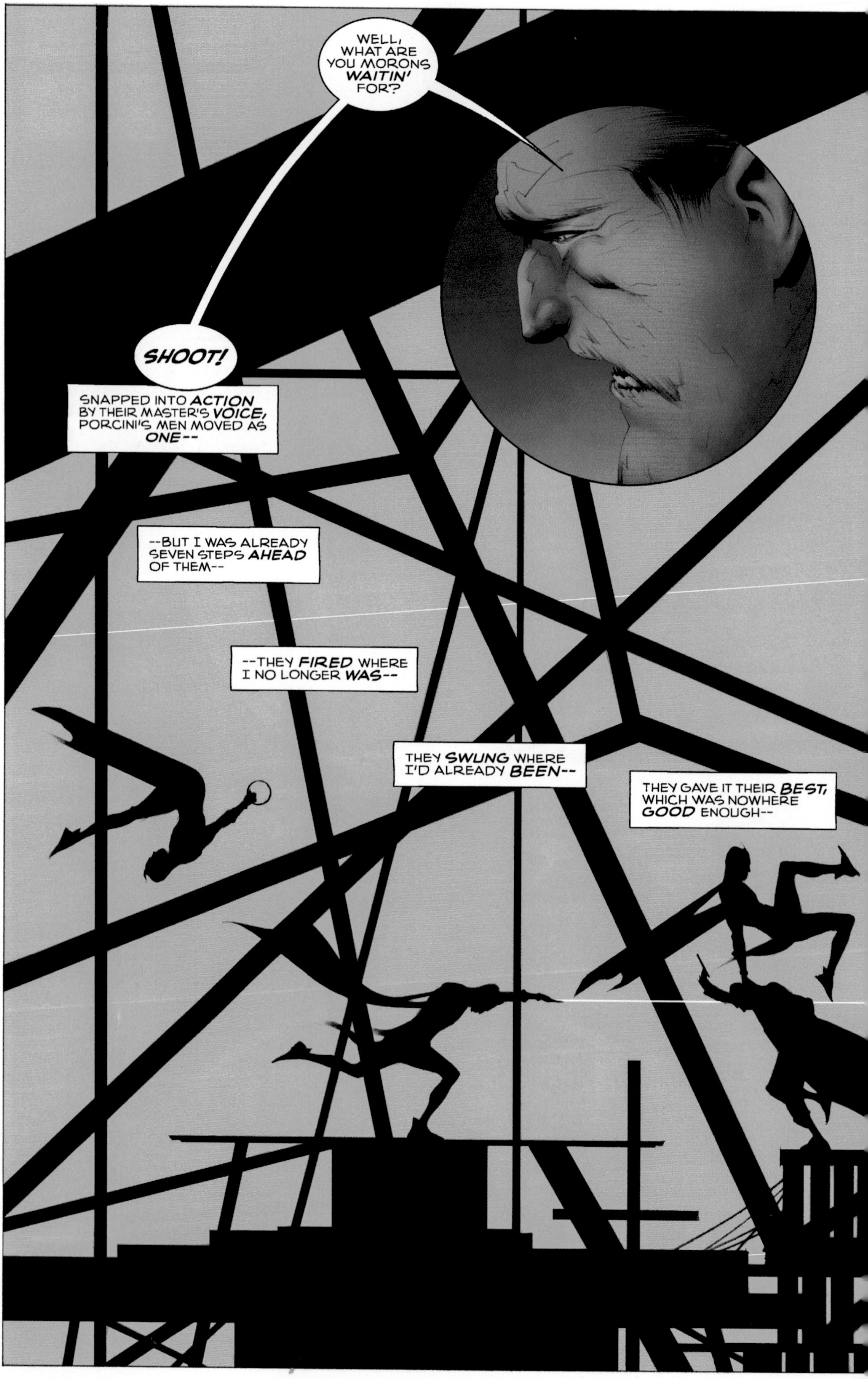
WELL, WHAT ARE YOU MORONS WAITIN' FOR?
SHOOT!
SNAPPED INTO ACTION BY THEIR MASTER'S VOICE, PORCINI'S MEN MOVED AS ONE--
--BUT I WAS ALREADY SEVEN STEPS AHEAD OF THEM--
--THEY FIRED WHERE I NO LONGER WAS--
THEY SWUNG WHERE I'D ALREADY BEEN--
THEY GAVE IT THEIR BEST, WHICH WAS NOWHERE GOOD ENOUGH--

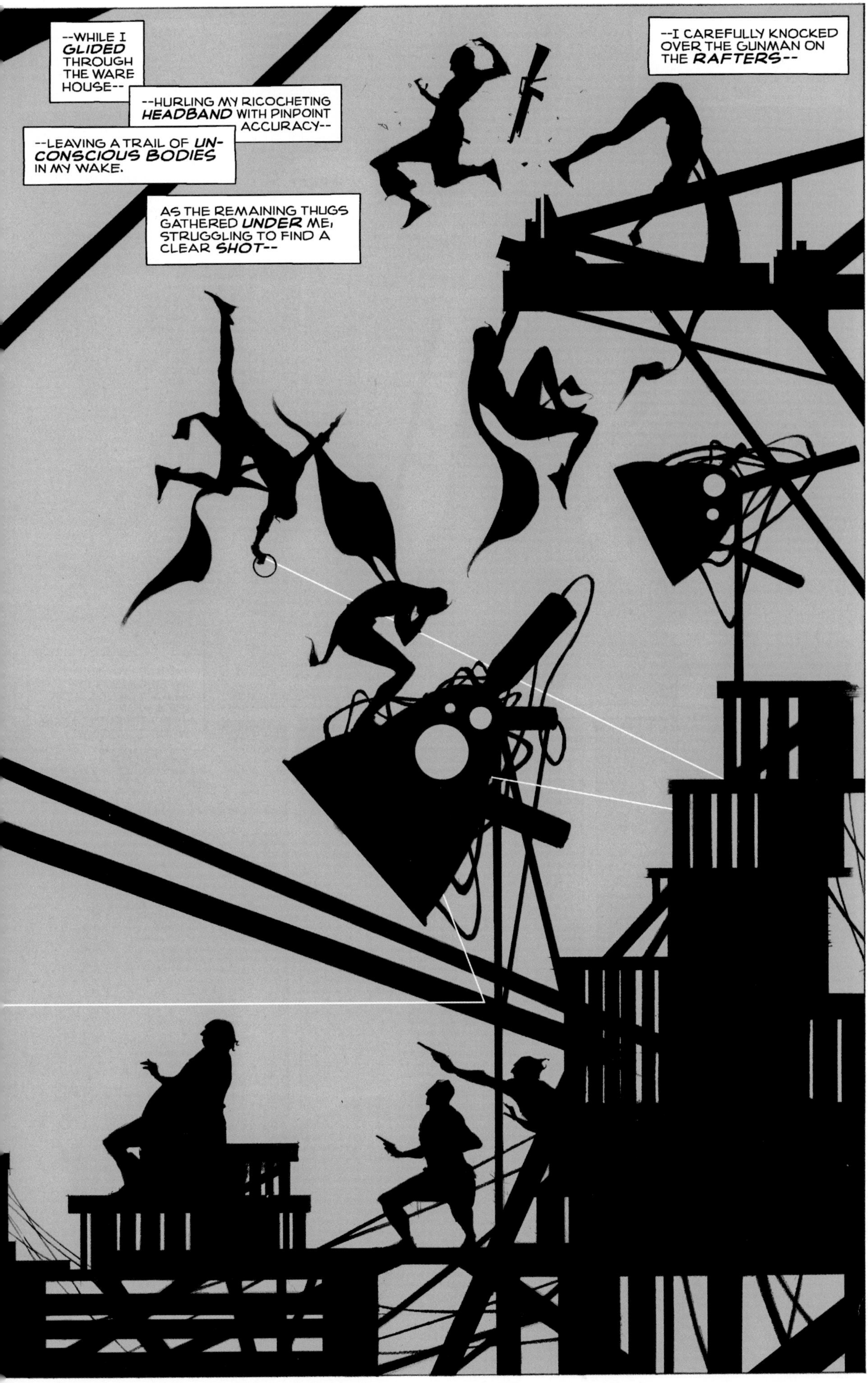
--WHILE I GLIDED THROUGH THE WARE HOUSE--
--HURLING MY RICOCHETING HEADBAND WITH PINPOINT ACCURACY--
--LEAVING A TRAIL OF UNCONSCIOUS BODIES IN MY WAKE.
AS THE REMAINING THUGS GATHERED UNDER ME, STRUGGLING TO FIND A CLEAR SHOT--
--I CAREFULLY KNOCKED OVER THE GUNMAN ON THE RAFTERS--

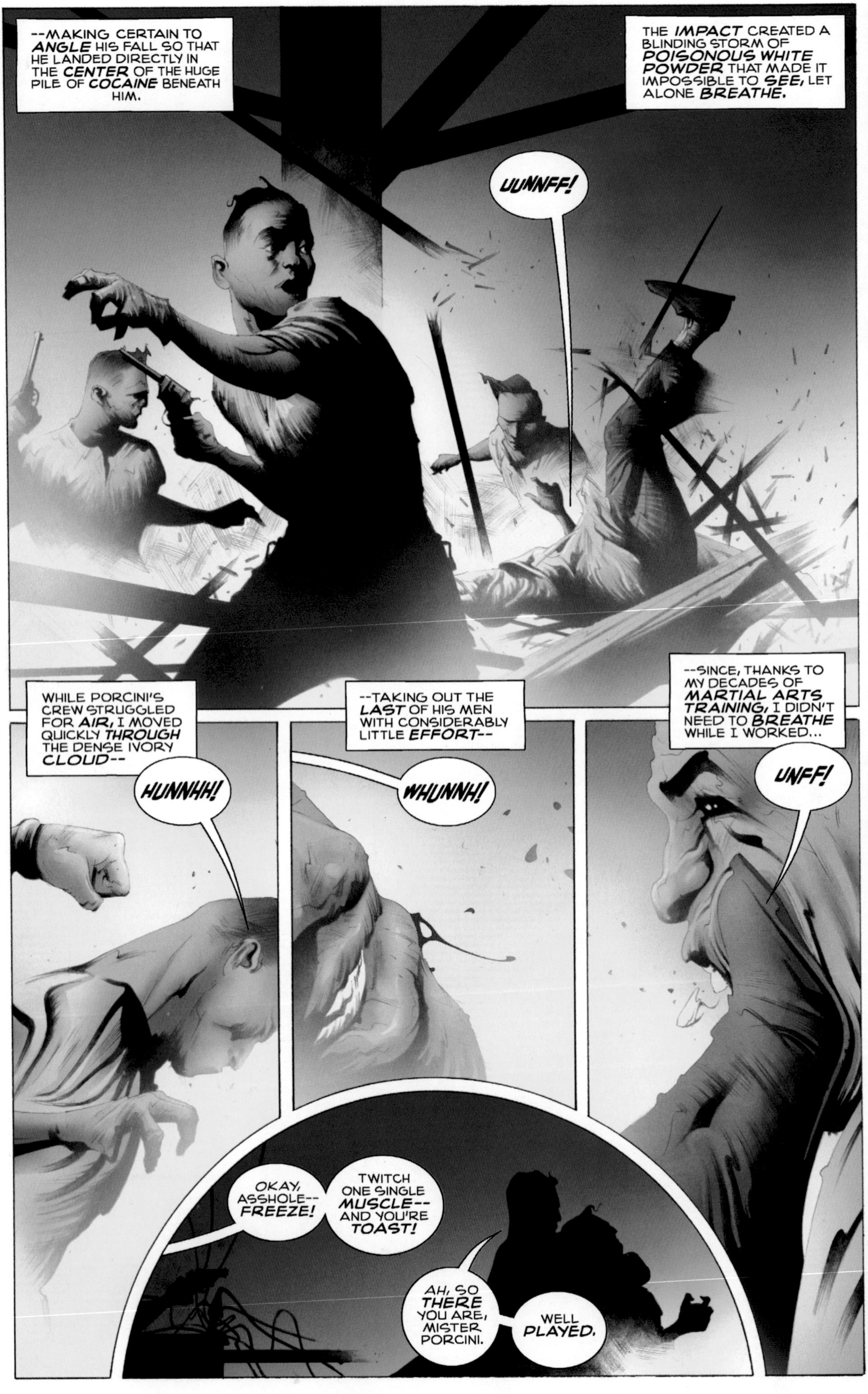
--MAKING CERTAIN TO ANGLE HIS FALL SO THAT HE LANDED DIRECTLY IN THE CENTER OF THE HUGE PILE OF COCAINE BENEATH HIM.
THE IMPACT CREATED A BLINDING STORM OF POISONOUS WHITE POWDER THAT MADE IT IMPOSSIBLE TO SEE, LET ALONE BREATHE.
UUNNFF!
WHILE PORCINI'S CREW STRUGGLED FOR AIR, I MOVED QUICKLY THROUGH THE DENSE IVORY CLOUD--
HUNNHH!
--TAKING OUT THE LAST OF HIS MEN WITH CONSIDERABLY LITTLE EFFORT--
WHUNNH!
--SINCE, THANKS TO MY DECADES OF MARTIAL ARTS TRAINING, I DIDN'T NEED TO BREATHE WHILE I WORKED...
UNFF!
OKAY, ASSHOLE-- FREEZE!
TWITCH ONE SINGLE MUSCLE-- AND YOU'RE TOAST!
AH, SO THERE YOU ARE, MISTER PORCINI.
WELL PLAYED.

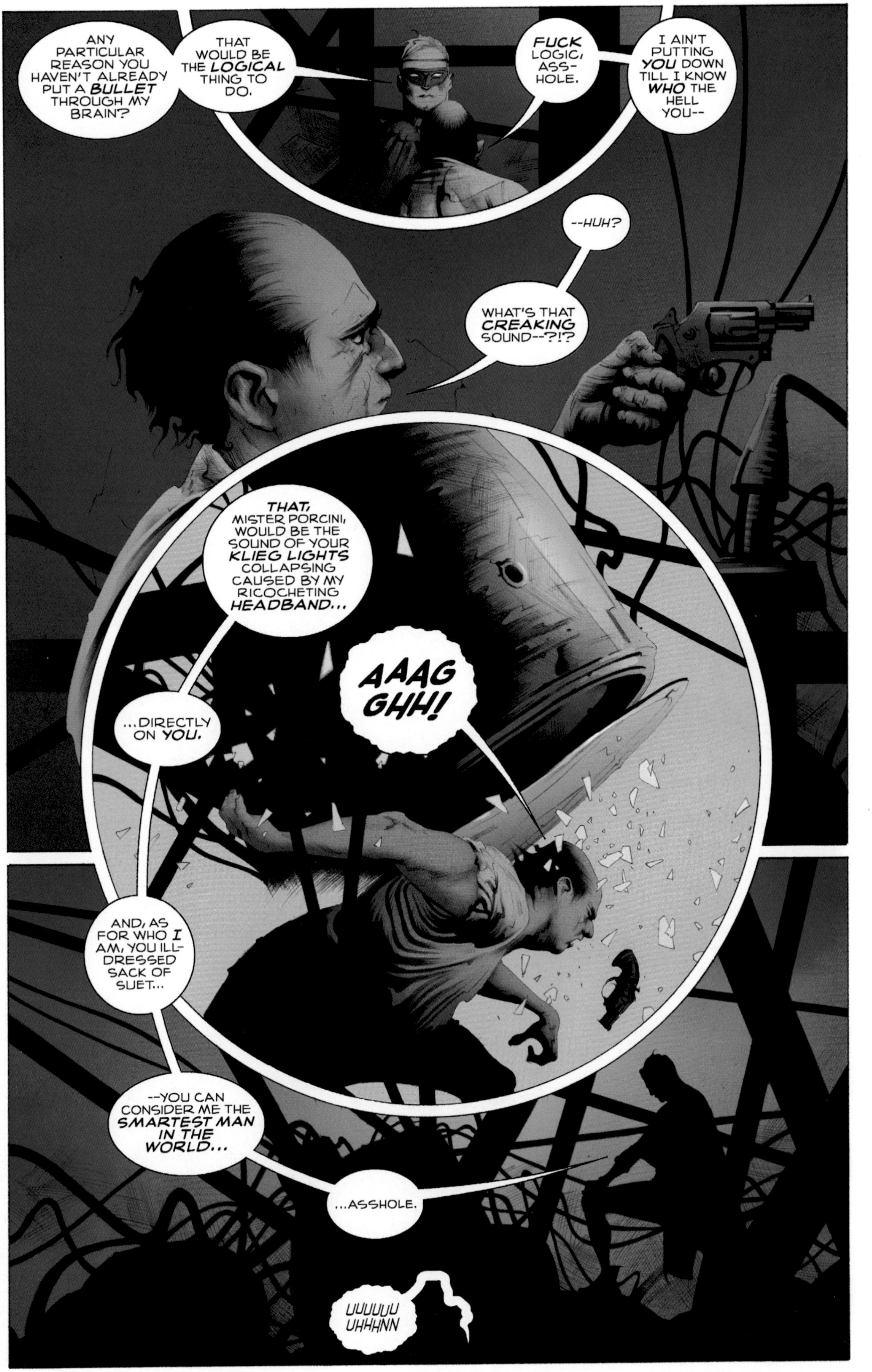
ANY PARTICULAR REASON YOU HAVEN'T ALREADY PUT A BULLET THROUGH MY BRAIN?
THAT WOULD BE THE LOGICAL THING TO DO.
FUCK LOGIC, ASS-HOLE.
I AIN'T PUTTING YOU DOWN TILL I KNOW WHO THE HELL YOU--
--HUH?
WHAT'S THAT CREAKING SOUND--?!?
THAT, MISTER PORCINI, WOULD BE THE SOUND OF YOUR KLIEG LIGHTS COLLAPSING CAUSED BY MY RICOCHETING HEADBAND...
...DIRECTLY ON YOU.
AAAG GHH!
AND, AS FOR WHO I AM, YOU ILL-DRESSED SACK OF SUET...
--YOU CAN CONSIDER ME THE SMARTEST MAN IN THE WORLD...
...ASSHOLE.
UUUUUU UHHHNN

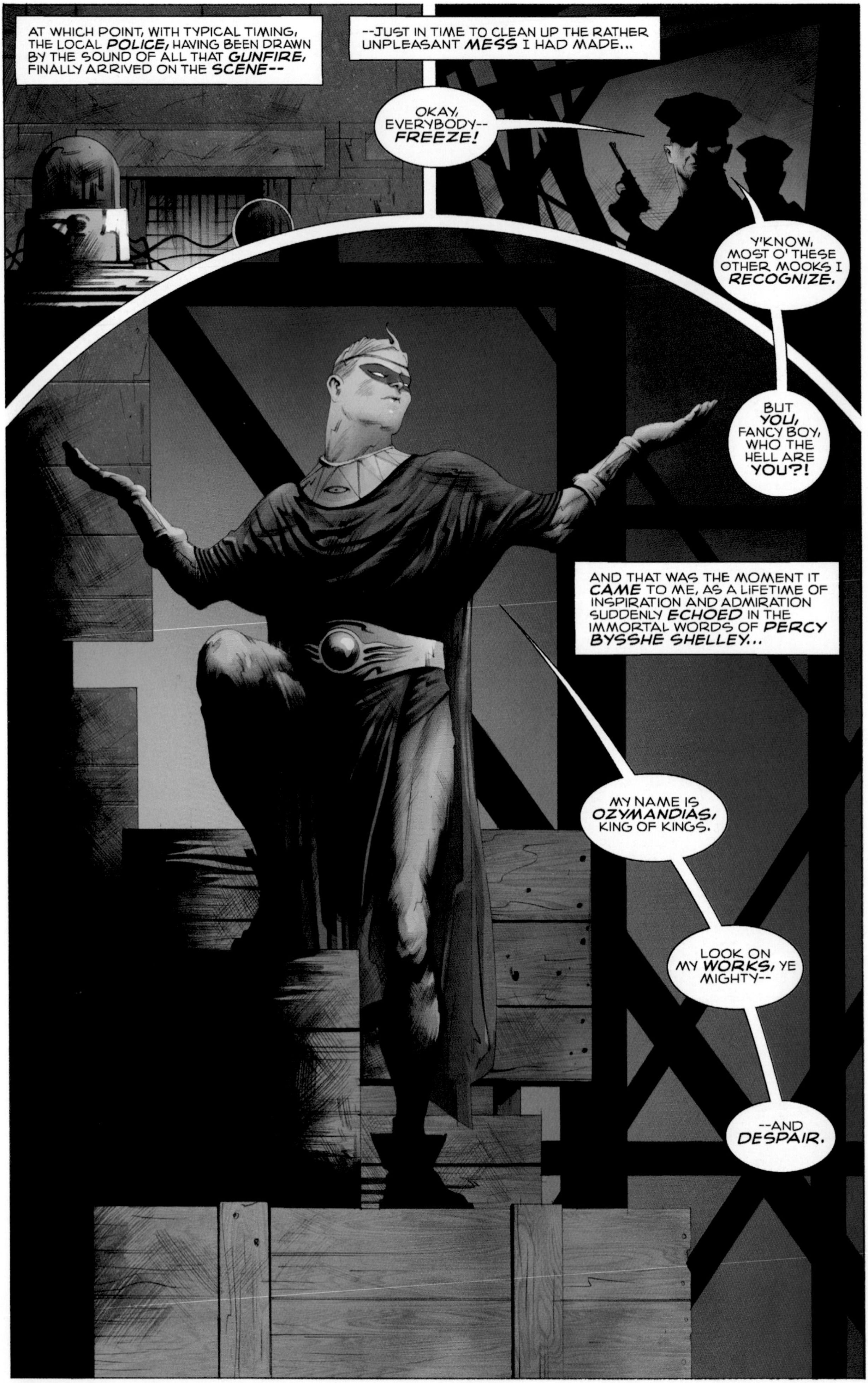
AT WHICH POINT, WITH TYPICAL TIMING, THE LOCAL POLICE, HAVING BEEN DRAWN BY THE SOUND OF ALL THAT GUNFIRE, FINALLY ARRIVED ON THE SCENE--
--JUST IN TIME TO CLEAN UP THE RATHER UNPLEASANT MESS I HAD MADE...
OKAY, EVERYBODY-- FREEZE!
Y'KNOW, MOST O' THESE OTHER MOOKS I RECOGNIZE.
BUT YOU, FANCY BOY, WHO THE HELL ARE YOU?!
AND THAT WAS THE MOMENT IT CAME TO ME, AS A LIFETIME OF INSPIRATION AND ADMIRATION SUDDENLY ECHOED IN THE IMMORTAL WORDS OF PERCY BYSSHE SHELLEY...
MY NAME IS OZYMANDIAS, KING OF KINGS.
LOOK ON MY WORKS, YE MIGHTY--
--AND DESPAIR.

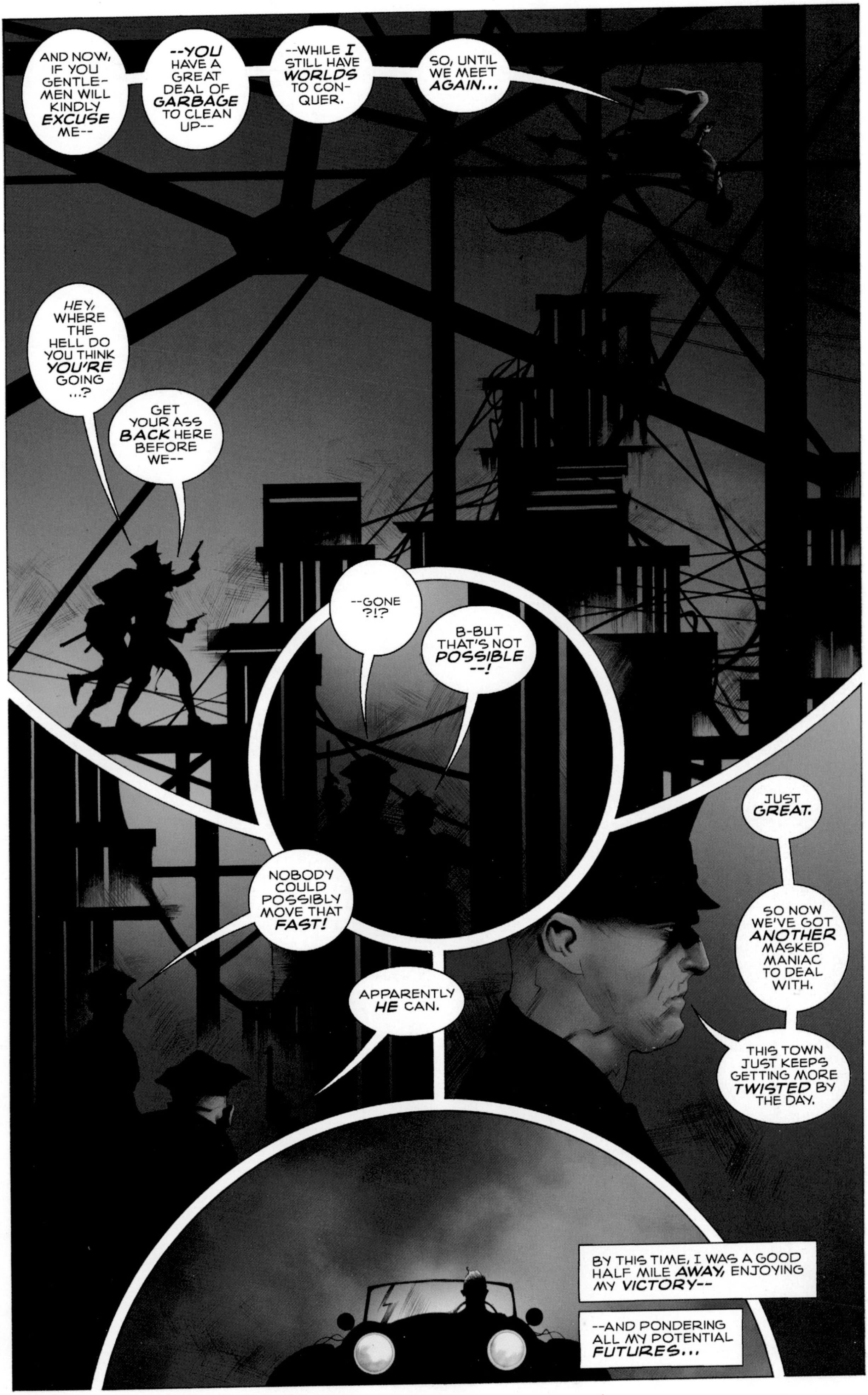
AND NOW, IF YOU GENTLE-MEN WILL KINDLY EXCUSE ME--
--YOU HAVE A GREAT DEAL OF GARBAGE TO CLEAN UP--
--WHILE I STILL HAVE WORLDS TO CON-QUER.
SO, UNTIL WE MEET AGAIN...
HEY, WHERE THE HELL DO YOU THINK YOU'RE GOING ...?
GET YOUR ASS BACK HERE BEFORE WE--
--GONE ?!?
B-BUT THAT'S NOT POSSIBLE --!
NOBODY COULD POSSIBLY MOVE THAT FAST!
APPARENTLY HE CAN.
JUST GREAT.
SO NOW WE'VE GOT ANOTHER MASKED MANIAC TO DEAL WITH.
THIS TOWN JUST KEEPS GETTING MORE TWISTED BY THE DAY.
BY THIS TIME, I WAS A GOOD HALF MILE AWAY, ENJOYING MY VICTORY--
--AND PONDERING ALL MY POTENTIAL FUTURES...

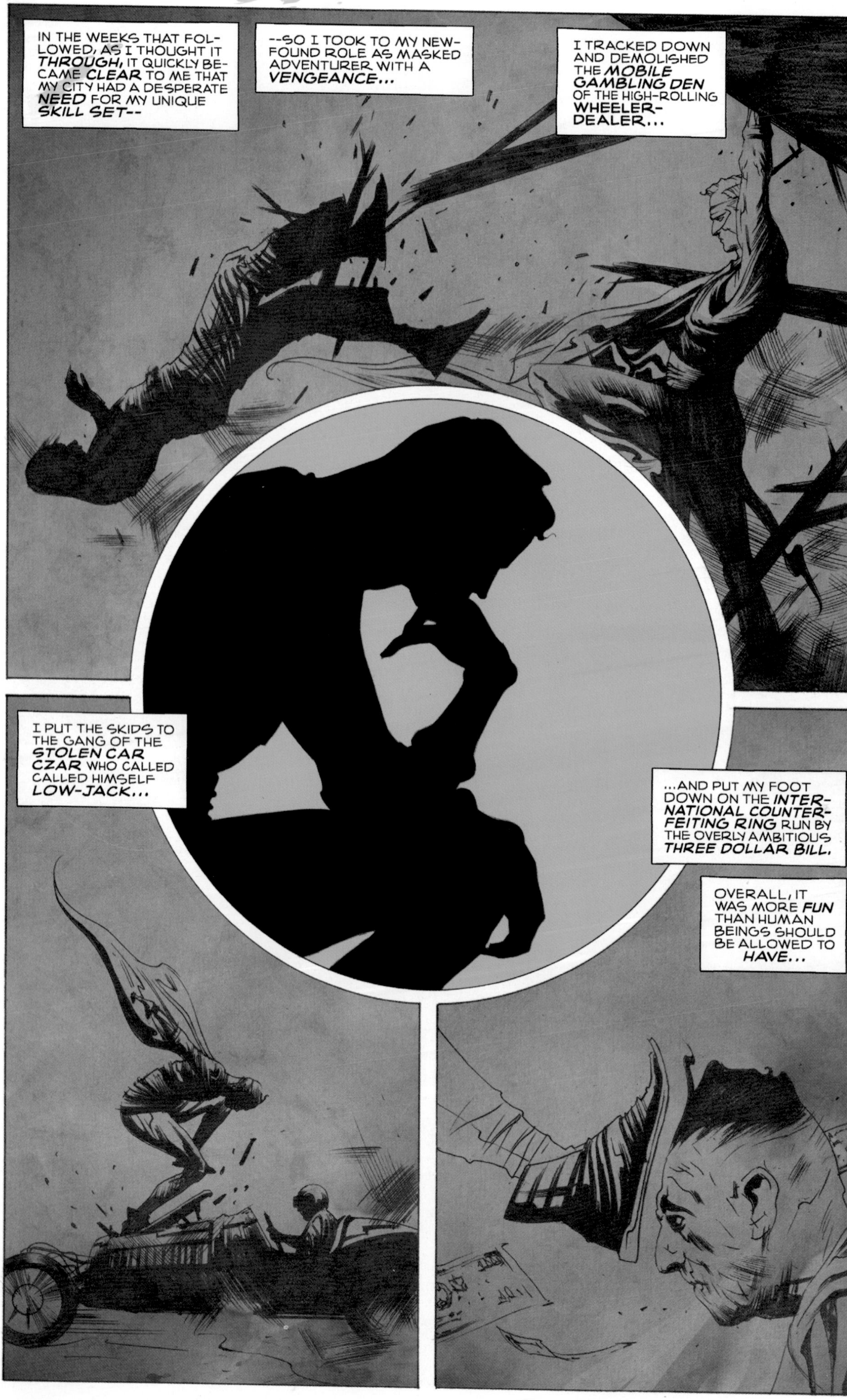
IN THE WEEKS THAT FOLLOWED, AS I THOUGHT IT THROUGH, IT QUICKLY BECAME CLEAR TO ME THAT MY CITY HAD A DESPERATE NEED FOR MY UNIQUE SKILL SET--
--SO I TOOK TO MY NEW-FOUND ROLE AS MASKED ADVENTURER WITH A VENGEANCE...
I TRACKED DOWN AND DEMOLISHED THE MOBILE GAMBLING DEN OF THE HIGH-ROLLING WHEELER-DEALER...
I PUT THE SKIDS TO THE GANG OF THE STOLEN CAR CZAR WHO CALLED CALLED HIMSELF LOW-JACK...
...AND PUT MY FOOT DOWN ON THE INTERNATIONAL COUNTERFEITING RING RUN BY THE OVERLY AMBITIOUS THREE DOLLAR BILL.
OVERALL, IT WAS MORE FUN THAN HUMAN BEINGS SHOULD BE ALLOWED TO HAVE...

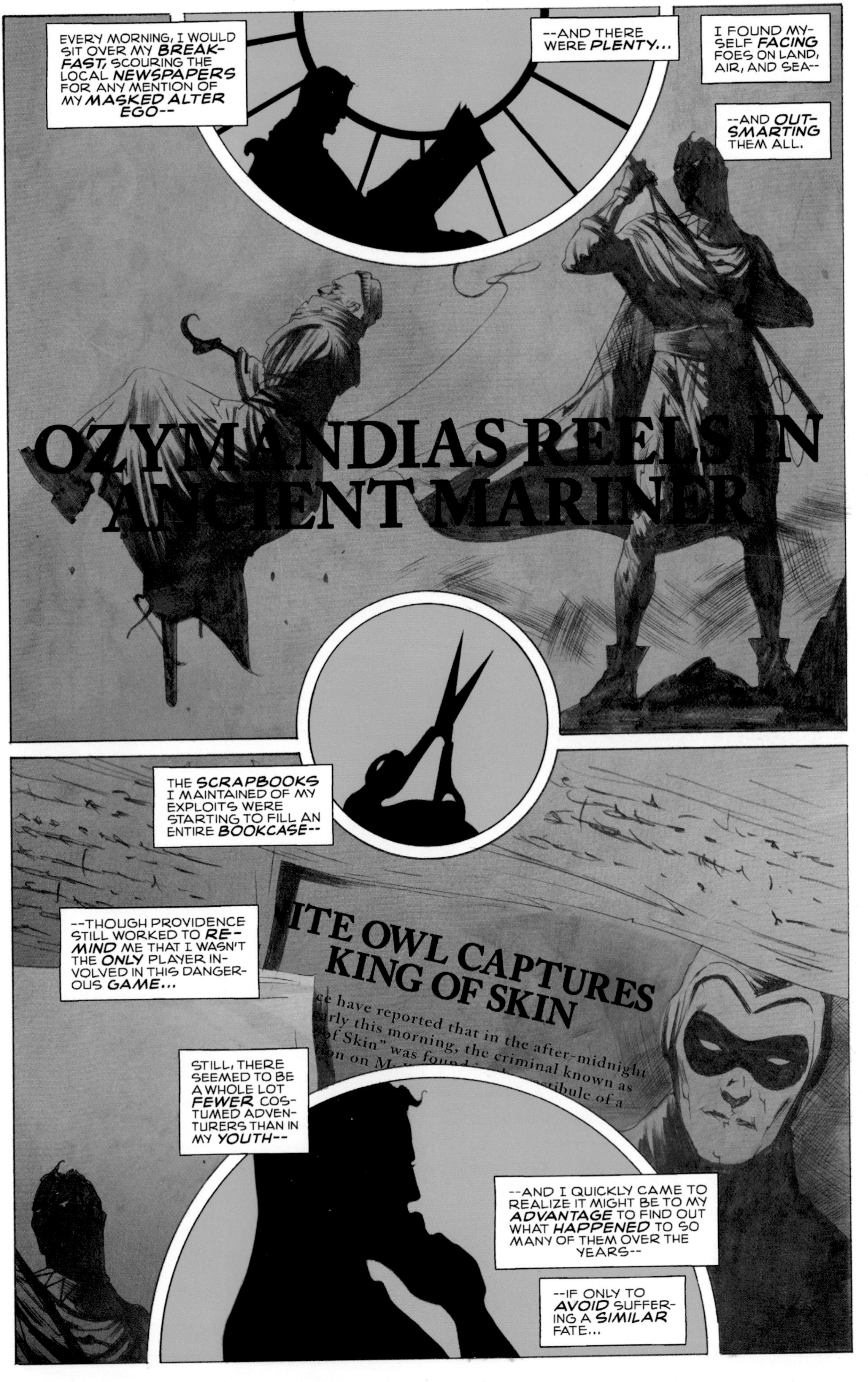
EVERY MORNING, I WOULD SIT OVER MY BREAKFAST, SCOURING THE LOCAL NEWSPAPERS FOR ANY MENTION OF MY MASKED ALTER EGO--
--AND THERE WERE PLENTY...
I FOUND MYSELF FACING FOES ON LAND, AIR, AND SEA--
--AND OUTSMARTING THEM ALL.
OZYMANDIAS REELS IN ANCIENT MARINER
THE SCRAPBOOKS I MAINTAINED OF MY EXPLOITS WERE STARTING TO FILL AN ENTIRE BOOKCASE--
--THOUGH PROVIDENCE STILL WORKED TO REMIND ME THAT I WASN'T THE ONLY PLAYER INVOLVED IN THIS DANGEROUS GAME...
ITE OWL CAPTURES KING OF SKIN
ce have reported that in the after-midnight
arly this morning, the criminal known as
of Skin" was found
STILL, THERE SEEMED TO BE A WHOLE LOT FEWER COSTUMED ADVENTURERS THAN IN MY YOUTH--
--AND I QUICKLY CAME TO REALIZE IT MIGHT BE TO MY ADVANTAGE TO FIND OUT WHAT HAPPENED TO SO MANY OF THEM OVER THE YEARS--
--IF ONLY TO AVOID SUFFERING A SIMILAR FATE...

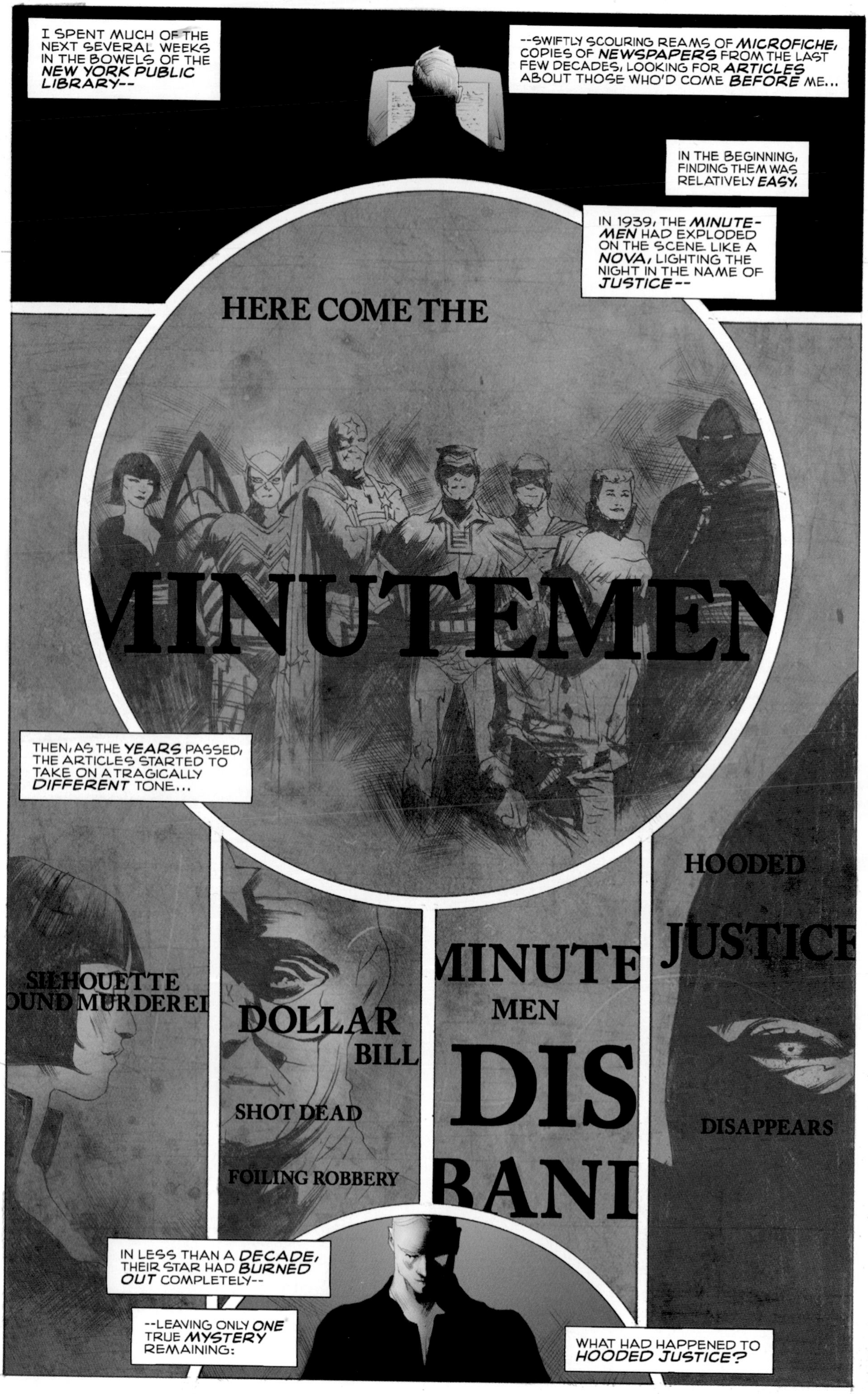
I SPENT MUCH OF THE NEXT SEVERAL WEEKS IN THE BOWELS OF THE NEW YORK PUBLIC LIBRARY--
--SWIFTLY SCOURING REAMS OF MICROFICHE, COPIES OF NEWSPAPERS FROM THE LAST FEW DECADES, LOOKING FOR ARTICLES ABOUT THOSE WHO'D COME BEFORE ME...
IN THE BEGINNING, FINDING THEM WAS RELATIVELY EASY.
IN 1939, THE MINUTEMEN HAD EXPLODED ON THE SCENE LIKE A NOVA, LIGHTING THE NIGHT IN THE NAME OF JUSTICE--
HERE COME THE
MINUTEMEN
THEN, AS THE YEARS PASSED, THE ARTICLES STARTED TO TAKE ON A TRAGICALLY DIFFERENT TONE...
SILHOUETTE
OUND MURDEREI
DOLLAR
BILL
SHOT DEAD
FOILING ROBBERY
MINUTE
MEN
DIS
BANI
HOODED
JUSTICE
DISAPPEARS
IN LESS THAN A DECADE, THEIR STAR HAD BURNED OUT COMPLETELY--
--LEAVING ONLY ONE TRUE MYSTERY REMAINING:
WHAT HAD HAPPENED TO HOODED JUSTICE?

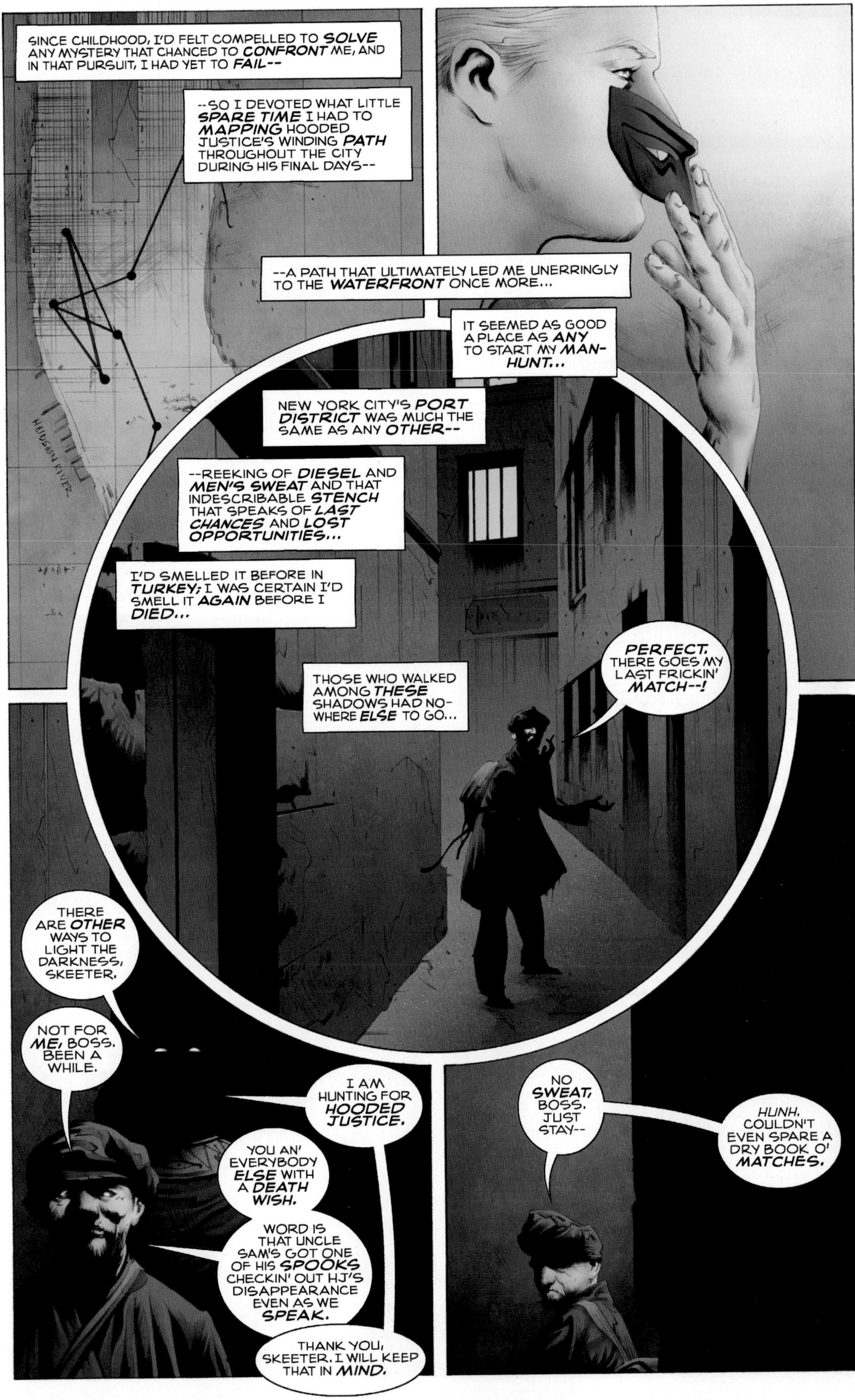
SINCE CHILDHOOD, I'D FELT COMPELLED TO SOLVE ANY MYSTERY THAT CHANCED TO CONFRONT ME, AND IN THAT PURSUIT, I HAD YET TO FAIL--
--SO I DEVOTED WHAT LITTLE SPARE TIME I HAD TO MAPPING HOODED JUSTICE'S WINDING PATH THROUGHOUT THE CITY DURING HIS FINAL DAYS--
HUDSON RIVER
--A PATH THAT ULTIMATELY LED ME UNERRINGLY TO THE WATERFRONT ONCE MORE...
IT SEEMED AS GOOD A PLACE AS ANY TO START MY MAN-HUNT...
NEW YORK CITY'S PORT DISTRICT WAS MUCH THE SAME AS ANY OTHER--
--REEKING OF DIESEL AND MEN'S SWEAT AND THAT INDESCRIBABLE STENCH THAT SPEAKS OF LAST CHANCES AND LOST OPPORTUNITIES...
I'D SMELLED IT BEFORE IN TURKEY; I WAS CERTAIN I'D SMELL IT AGAIN BEFORE I DIED...
THOSE WHO WALKED AMONG THESE SHADOWS HAD NO-WHERE ELSE TO GO...
PERFECT. THERE GOES MY LAST FRICKIN' MATCH--!
THERE ARE OTHER WAYS TO LIGHT THE DARKNESS, SKEETER.
NOT FOR ME, BOSS. BEEN A WHILE.
I AM HUNTING FOR HOODED JUSTICE.
YOU AN' EVERYBODY ELSE WITH A DEATH WISH.
WORD IS THAT UNCLE SAM'S GOT ONE OF HIS SPOOKS CHECKIN' OUT HJ'S DISAPPEARANCE EVEN AS WE SPEAK.
THANK YOU, SKEETER. I WILL KEEP THAT IN MIND.
NO SWEAT, BOSS. JUST STAY--
HUNH. COULDN'T EVEN SPARE A DRY BOOK O' MATCHES.

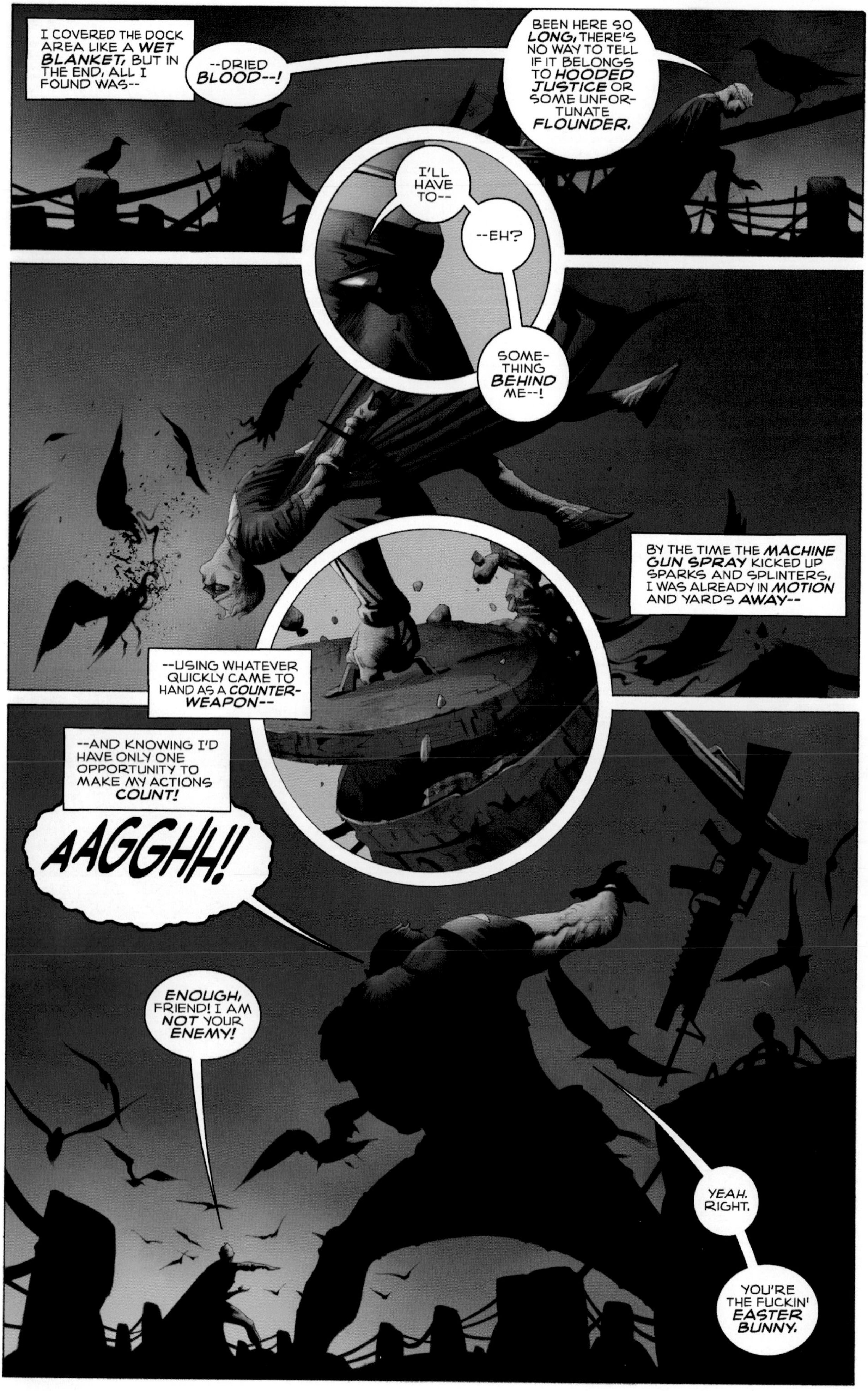

I COVERED THE DOCK AREA LIKE A WET BLANKET, BUT IN THE END, ALL I FOUND WAS--
--DRIED BLOOD--!
BEEN HERE SO LONG, THERE'S NO WAY TO TELL IF IT BELONGS TO HOODED JUSTICE OR SOME UNFORTUNATE FLOUNDER.
I'LL HAVE TO--
--EH?
SOME-THING BEHIND ME--!
BY THE TIME THE MACHINE GUN SPRAY KICKED UP SPARKS AND SPLINTERS, I WAS ALREADY IN MOTION AND YARDS AWAY--
--USING WHATEVER QUICKLY CAME TO HAND AS A COUNTER-WEAPON--
--AND KNOWING I'D HAVE ONLY ONE OPPORTUNITY TO MAKE MY ACTIONS COUNT!
AAGGHH!
ENOUGH, FRIEND! I AM NOT YOUR ENEMY!
YEAH. RIGHT.
YOU'RE THE FUCKIN' EASTER BUNNY.

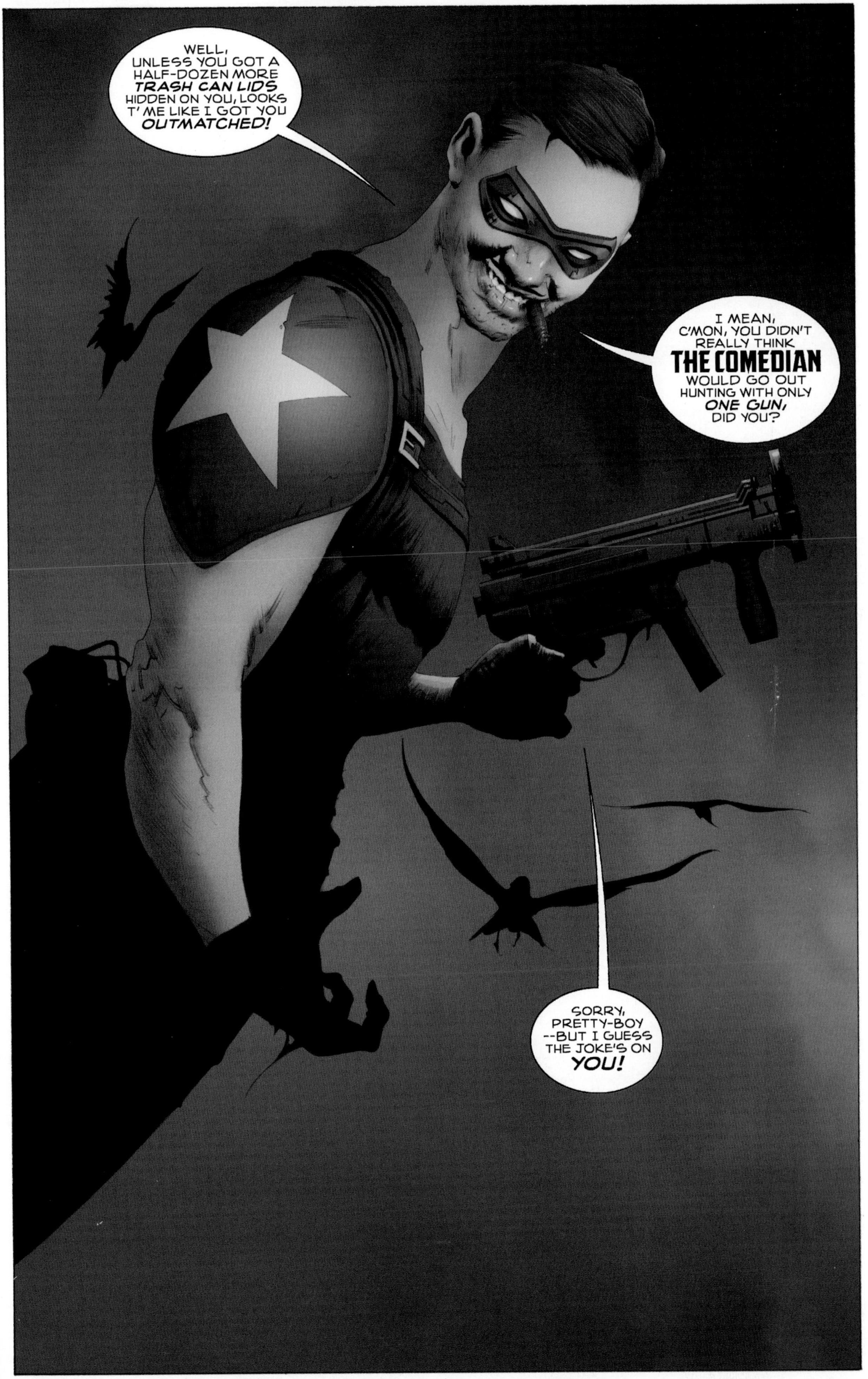
WELL, UNLESS YOU GOT A HALF-DOZEN MORE TRASH CAN LIDS HIDDEN ON YOU, LOOKS T' ME LIKE I GOT YOU OUTMATCHED!
I MEAN, C'MON, YOU DIDN'T REALLY THINK THE COMEDIAN WOULD GO OUT HUNTING WITH ONLY ONE GUN, DID YOU?
SORRY, PRETTY-BOY --BUT I GUESS THE JOKE'S ON YOU!

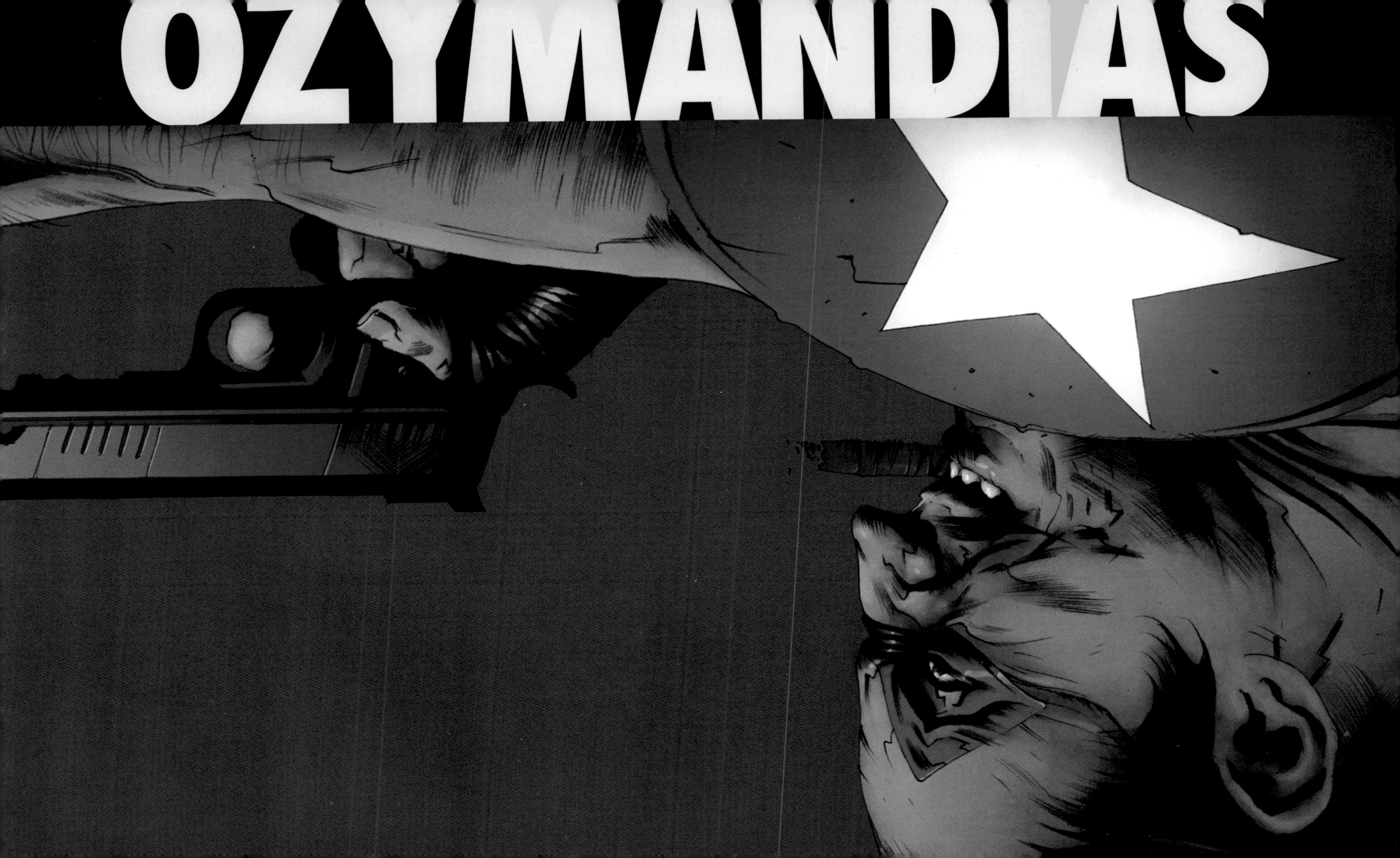
OZYMANDIAS

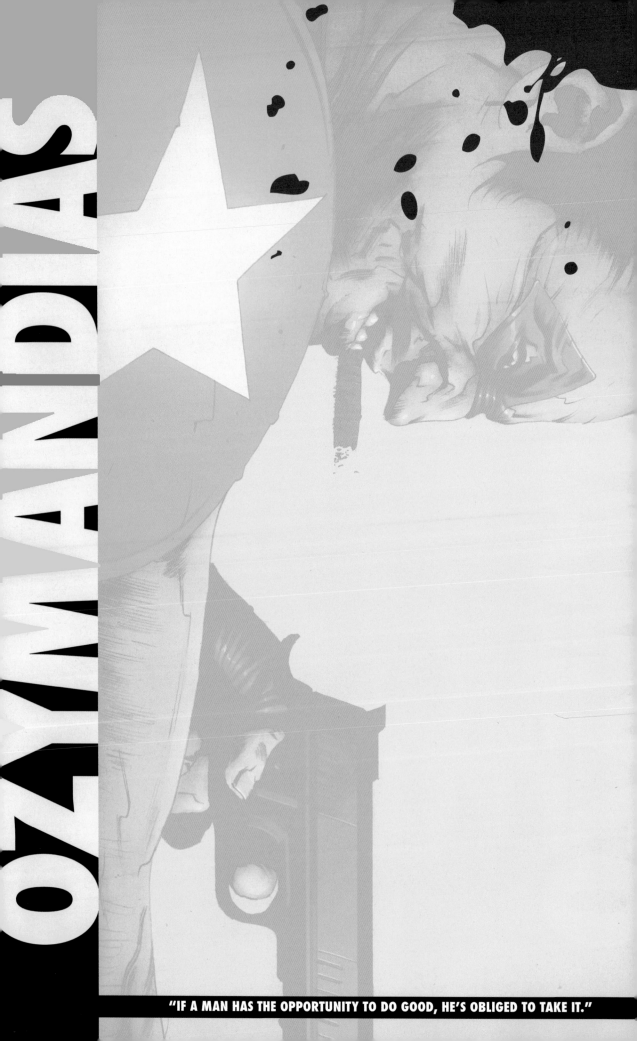

OZYMANDIAS

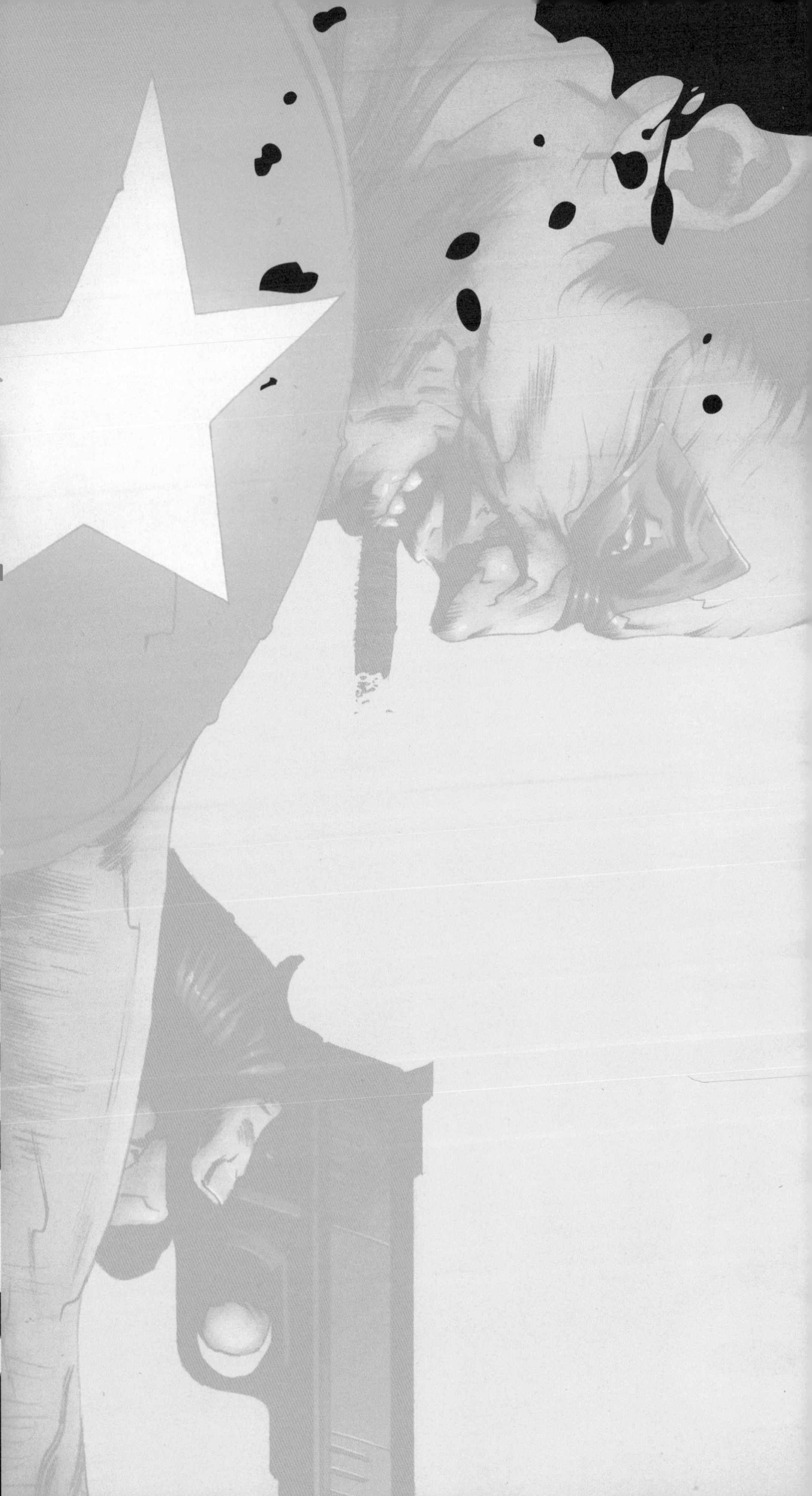

"IF A MAN HAS THE OPPORTUNITY TO DO GOOD, HE'S OBLIGED TO TAKE IT."

THE HEART THAT FED...!

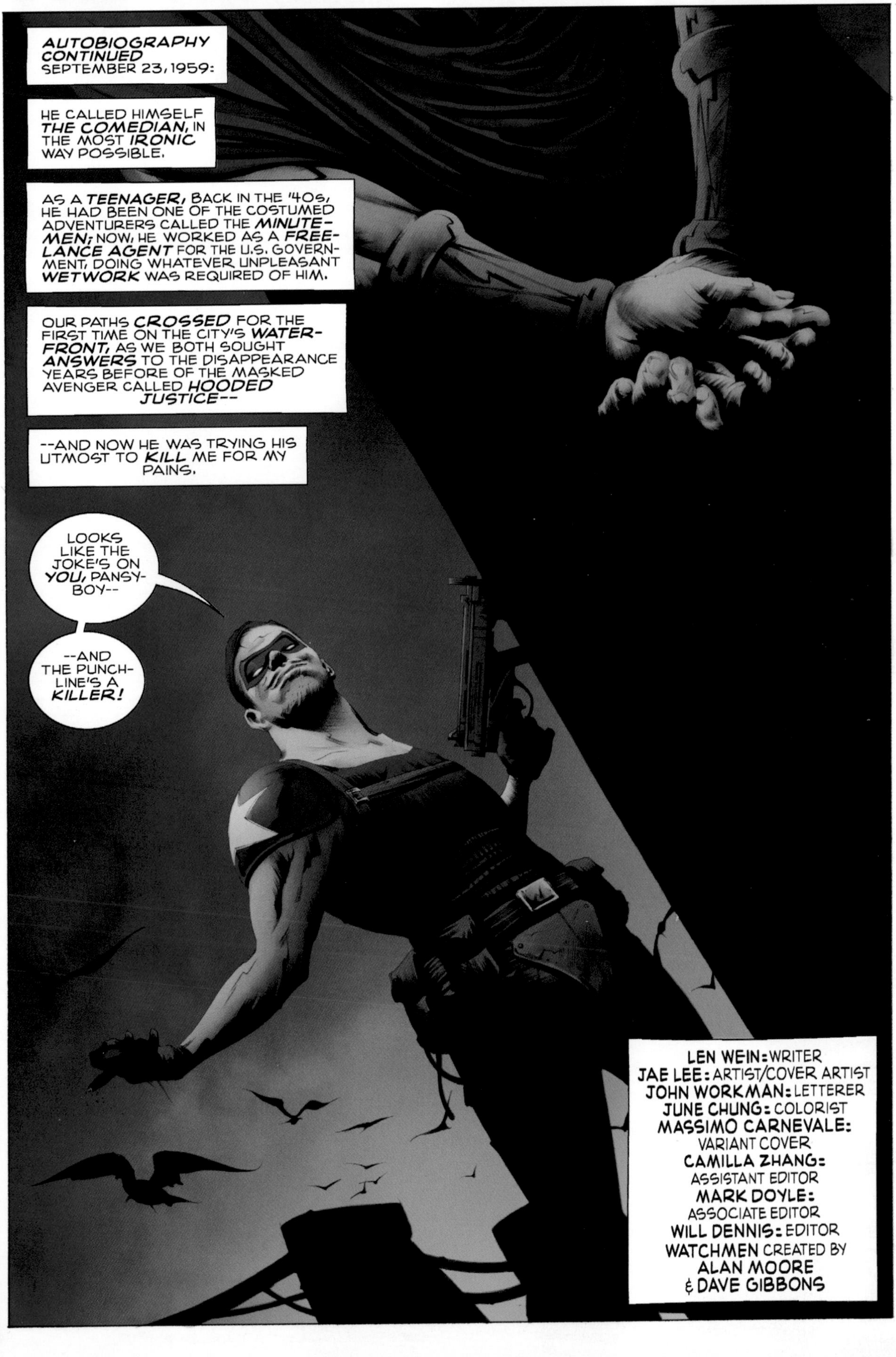

AUTOBIOGRAPHY CONTINUED SEPTEMBER 23, 1959:
HE CALLED HIMSELF THE COMEDIAN, IN THE MOST IRONIC WAY POSSIBLE.
AS A TEENAGER, BACK IN THE '40s, HE HAD BEEN ONE OF THE COSTUMED ADVENTURERS CALLED THE MINUTEMEN; NOW, HE WORKED AS A FREE-LANCE AGENT FOR THE U.S. GOVERNMENT, DOING WHATEVER UNPLEASANT WETWORK WAS REQUIRED OF HIM.
OUR PATHS CROSSED FOR THE FIRST TIME ON THE CITY'S WATERFRONT, AS WE BOTH SOUGHT ANSWERS TO THE DISAPPEARANCE YEARS BEFORE OF THE MASKED AVENGER CALLED HOODED JUSTICE--
--AND NOW HE WAS TRYING HIS UTMOST TO KILL ME FOR MY PAINS.
LOOKS LIKE THE JOKE'S ON YOU, PANSY-BOY--
--AND THE PUNCH-LINE'S A KILLER!
LEN WEIN: WRITER
JAE LEE: ARTIST/COVER ARTIST
JOHN WORKMAN: LETTERER
JUNE CHUNG: COLORIST
MASSIMO CARNEVALE: VARIANT COVER
CAMILLA ZHANG: ASSISTANT EDITOR
MARK DOYLE: ASSOCIATE EDITOR
WILL DENNIS: EDITOR
WATCHMEN CREATED BY ALAN MOORE & DAVE GIBBONS

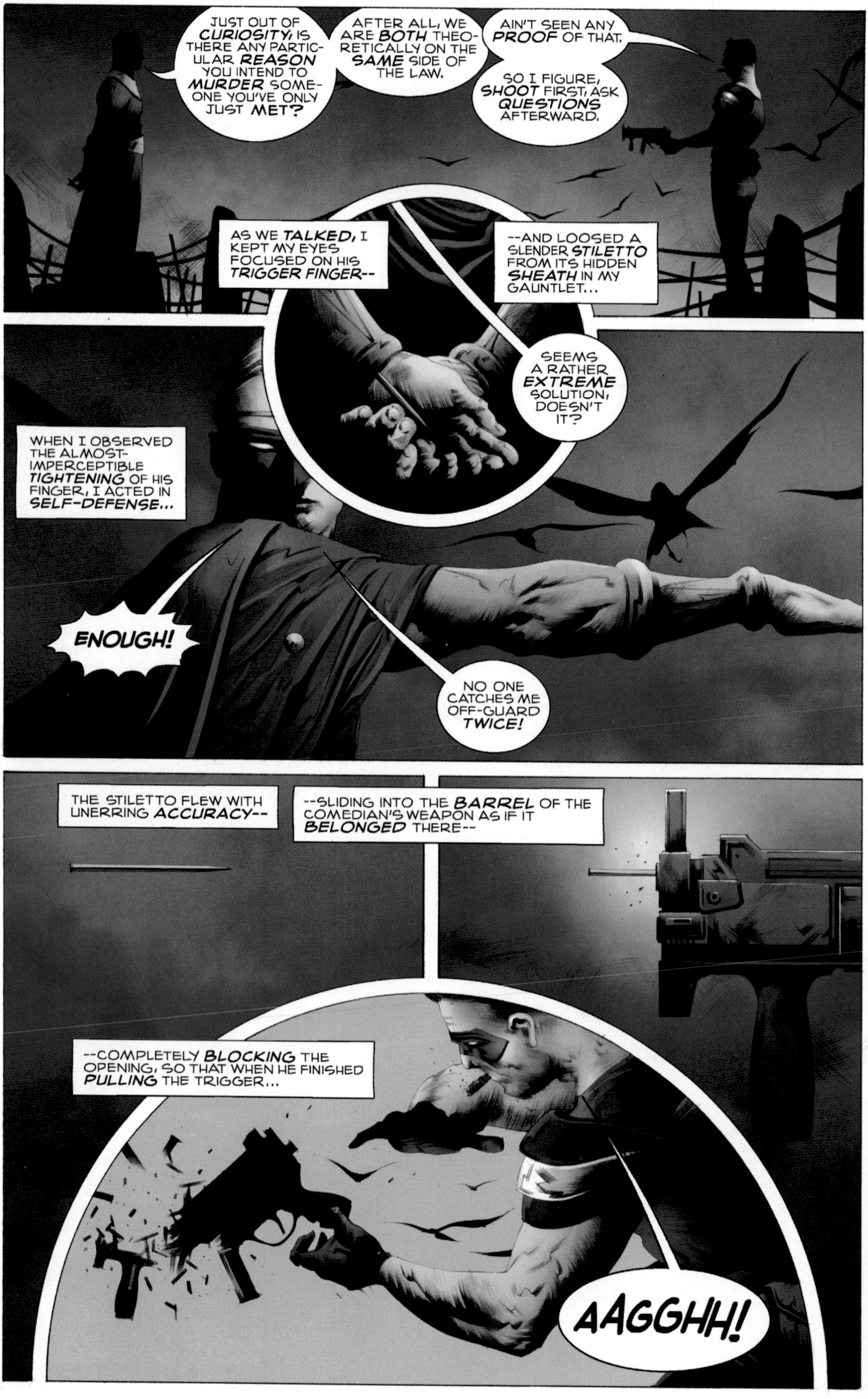
JUST OUT OF CURIOSITY, IS THERE ANY PARTICULAR REASON YOU INTEND TO MURDER SOMEONE YOU'VE ONLY JUST MET?
AFTER ALL, WE ARE BOTH THEORETICALLY ON THE SAME SIDE OF THE LAW.
AIN'T SEEN ANY PROOF OF THAT.
SO I FIGURE, SHOOT FIRST, ASK QUESTIONS AFTERWARD.
AS WE TALKED, I KEPT MY EYES FOCUSED ON HIS TRIGGER FINGER--
--AND LOOSED A SLENDER STILETTO FROM ITS HIDDEN SHEATH IN MY GAUNTLET...
SEEMS A RATHER EXTREME SOLUTION, DOESN'T IT?
WHEN I OBSERVED THE ALMOST-IMPERCEPTIBLE TIGHTENING OF HIS FINGER, I ACTED IN SELF-DEFENSE...
ENOUGH!
NO ONE CATCHES ME OFF-GUARD TWICE!
THE STILETTO FLEW WITH UNERRING ACCURACY--
--SLIDING INTO THE BARREL OF THE COMEDIAN'S WEAPON AS IF IT BELONGED THERE--
--COMPLETELY BLOCKING THE OPENING, SO THAT WHEN HE FINISHED PULLING THE TRIGGER...
AAGGHH!

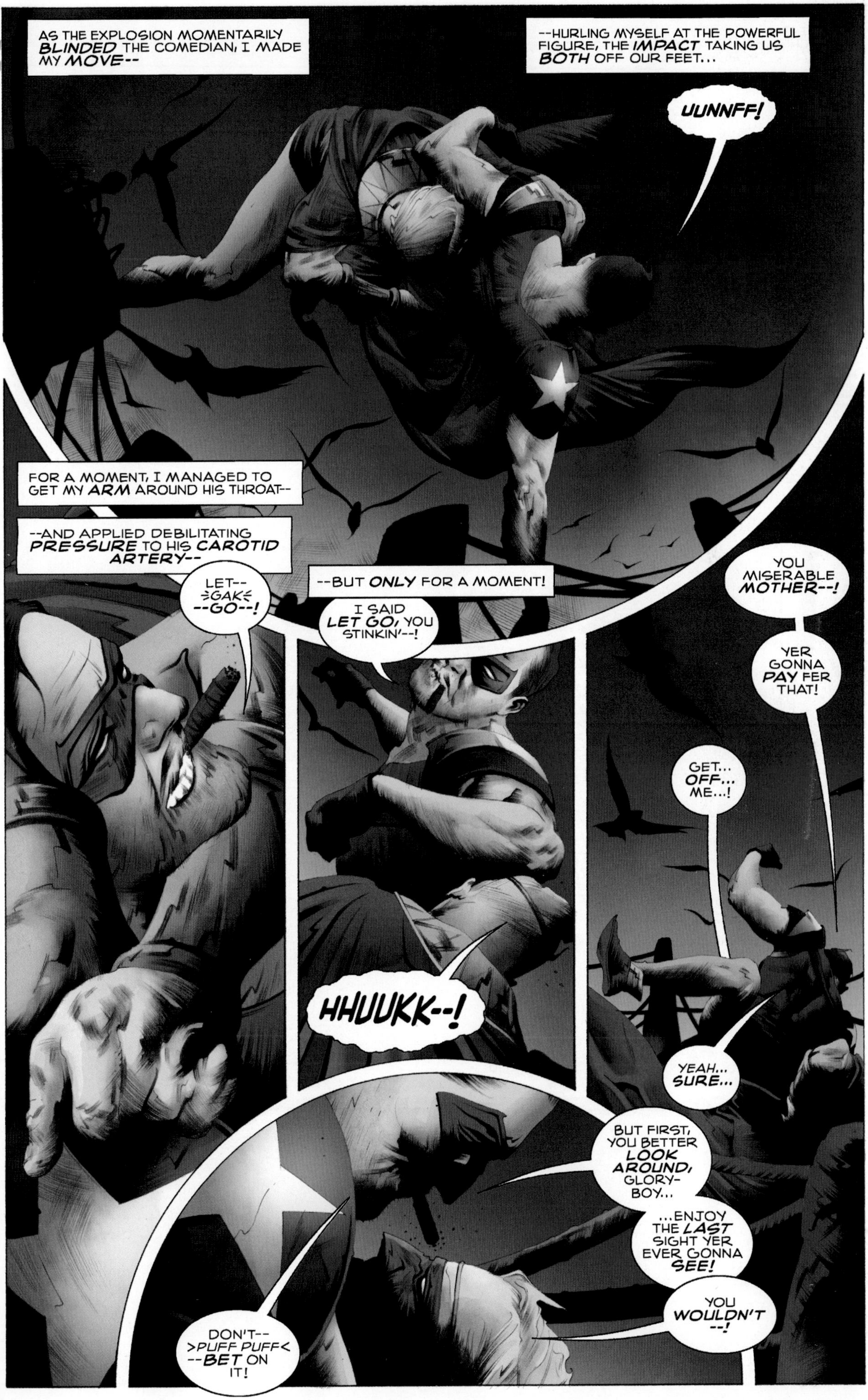

AS THE EXPLOSION MOMENTARILY BLINDED THE COMEDIAN, I MADE MY MOVE--
--HURLING MYSELF AT THE POWERFUL FIGURE, THE IMPACT TAKING US BOTH OFF OUR FEET...
UUNNFF!
FOR A MOMENT, I MANAGED TO GET MY ARM AROUND HIS THROAT--
--AND APPLIED DEBILITATING PRESSURE TO HIS CAROTID ARTERY--
LET-- GAK --GO--!
--BUT ONLY FOR A MOMENT!
I SAID LET GO, YOU STINKIN'--!
HHUUKK--!
YOU MISERABLE MOTHER--!
YER GONNA PAY FER THAT!
GET... OFF... ME...!
YEAH... SURE...
BUT FIRST, YOU BETTER LOOK AROUND, GLORY-BOY...
...ENJOY THE LAST SIGHT YER EVER GONNA SEE!
YOU WOULDN'T --!
DON'T-- >PUFF PUFF< --BET ON IT!

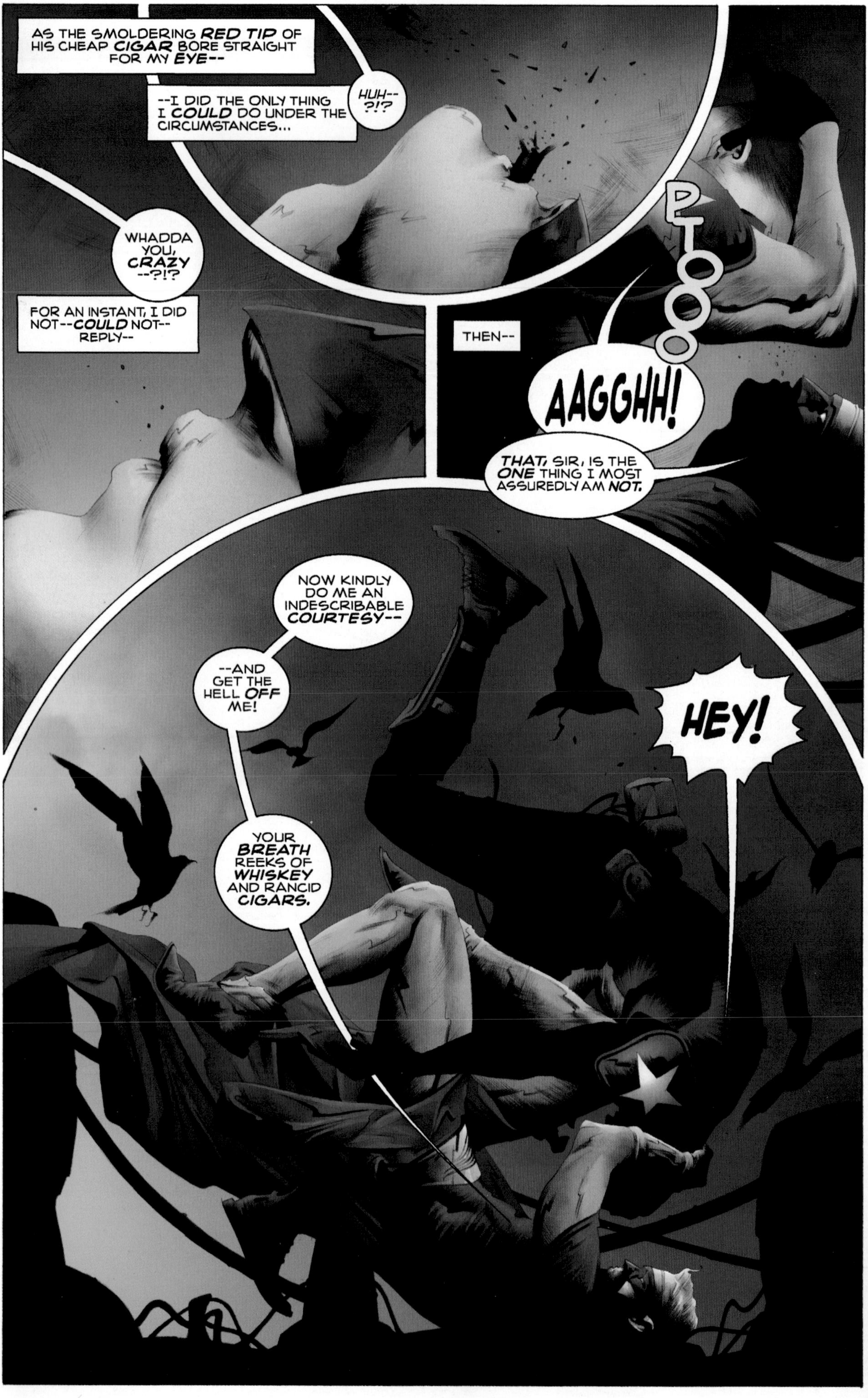

AS THE SMOLDERING RED TIP OF HIS CHEAP CIGAR BORE STRAIGHT FOR MY EYE--
--I DID THE ONLY THING I COULD DO UNDER THE CIRCUMSTANCES...
HUH-- ?!?
PTOOO
WHADDA YOU, CRAZY --?!?
FOR AN INSTANT, I DID NOT--COULD NOT--REPLY--
THEN--
AAGGHH!
THAT, SIR, IS THE ONE THING I MOST ASSUREDLY AM NOT.
NOW KINDLY DO ME AN INDESCRIBABLE COURTESY--
--AND GET THE HELL OFF ME!
YOUR BREATH REEKS OF WHISKEY AND RANCID CIGARS.
HEY!

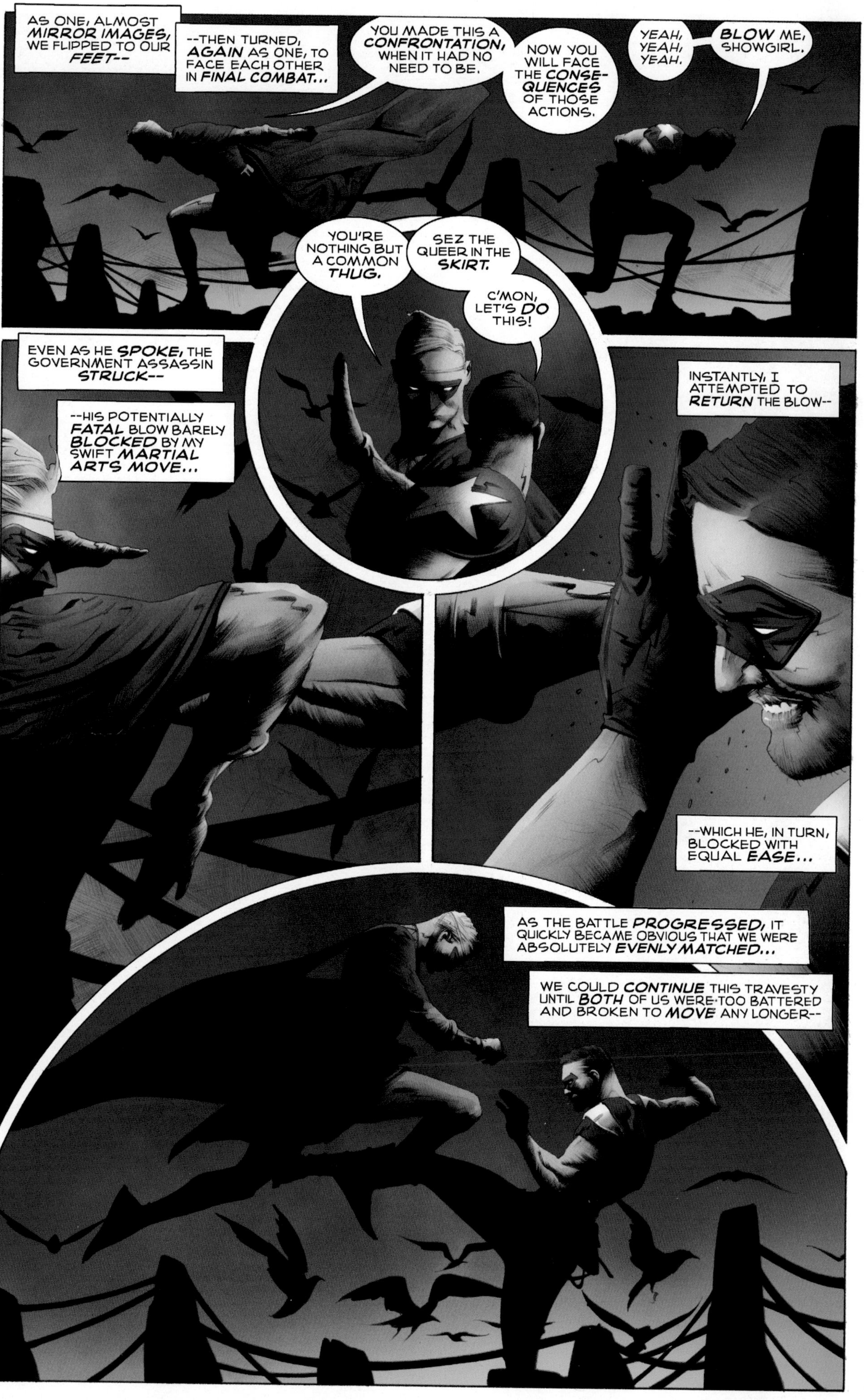
AS ONE, ALMOST MIRROR IMAGES, WE FLIPPED TO OUR FEET--
--THEN TURNED, AGAIN AS ONE, TO FACE EACH OTHER IN FINAL COMBAT...
YOU MADE THIS A CONFRONTATION, WHEN IT HAD NO NEED TO BE.
NOW YOU WILL FACE THE CONSEQUENCES OF THOSE ACTIONS.
YEAH, YEAH, YEAH.
BLOW ME, SHOWGIRL.
YOU'RE NOTHING BUT A COMMON THUG.
SEZ THE QUEER IN THE SKIRT.
C'MON, LET'S DO THIS!
EVEN AS HE SPOKE, THE GOVERNMENT ASSASSIN STRUCK--
--HIS POTENTIALLY FATAL BLOW BARELY BLOCKED BY MY SWIFT MARTIAL ARTS MOVE...
INSTANTLY, I ATTEMPTED TO RETURN THE BLOW--
--WHICH HE, IN TURN, BLOCKED WITH EQUAL EASE...
AS THE BATTLE PROGRESSED, IT QUICKLY BECAME OBVIOUS THAT WE WERE ABSOLUTELY EVENLY MATCHED...
WE COULD CONTINUE THIS TRAVESTY UNTIL BOTH OF US WERE TOO BATTERED AND BROKEN TO MOVE ANY LONGER--

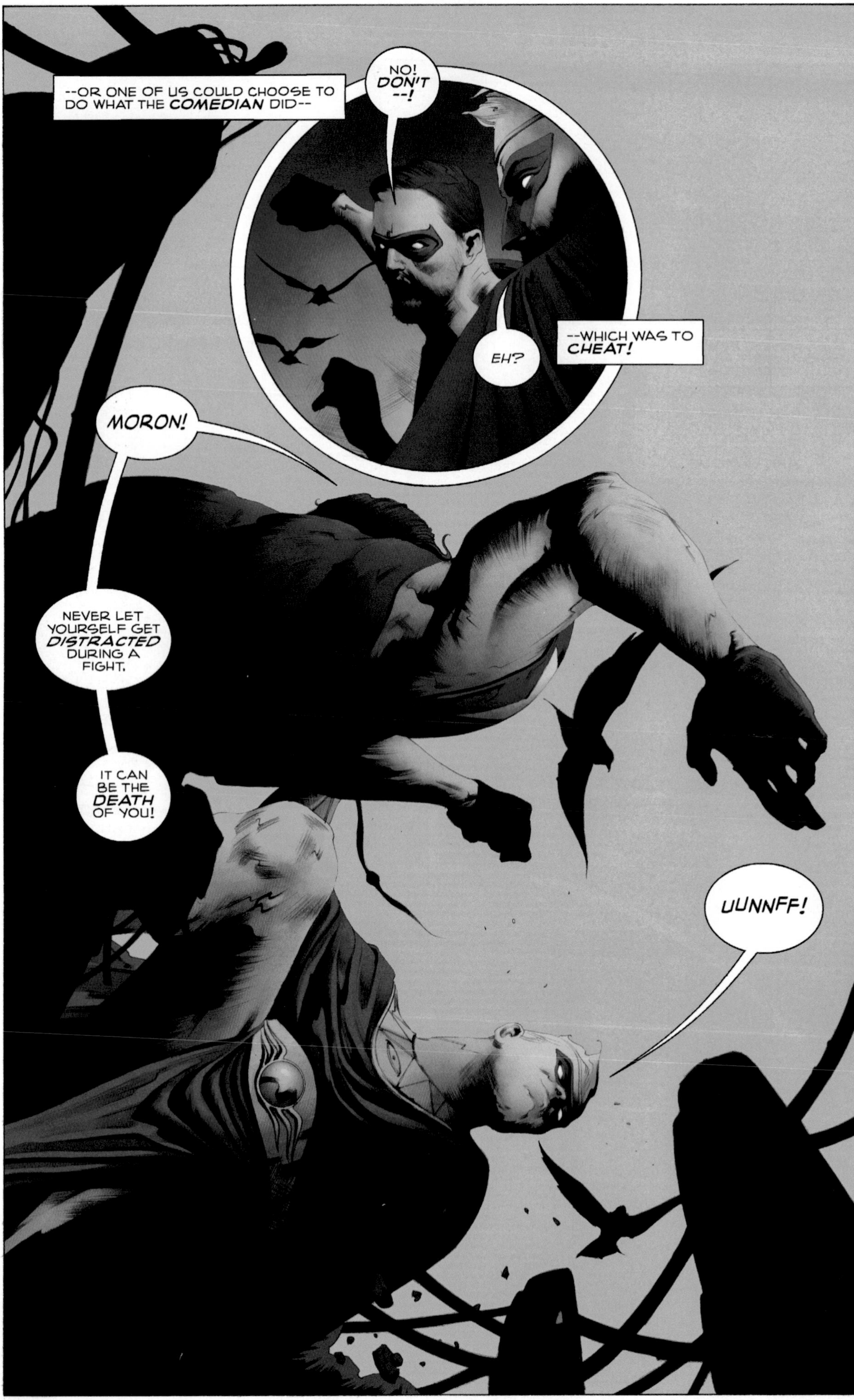
--OR ONE OF US COULD CHOOSE TO DO WHAT THE COMEDIAN DID--
NO! DON'T --!
EH?
--WHICH WAS TO CHEAT!
MORON!
NEVER LET YOURSELF GET DISTRACTED DURING A FIGHT.
IT CAN BE THE DEATH OF YOU!
UUNNFF!

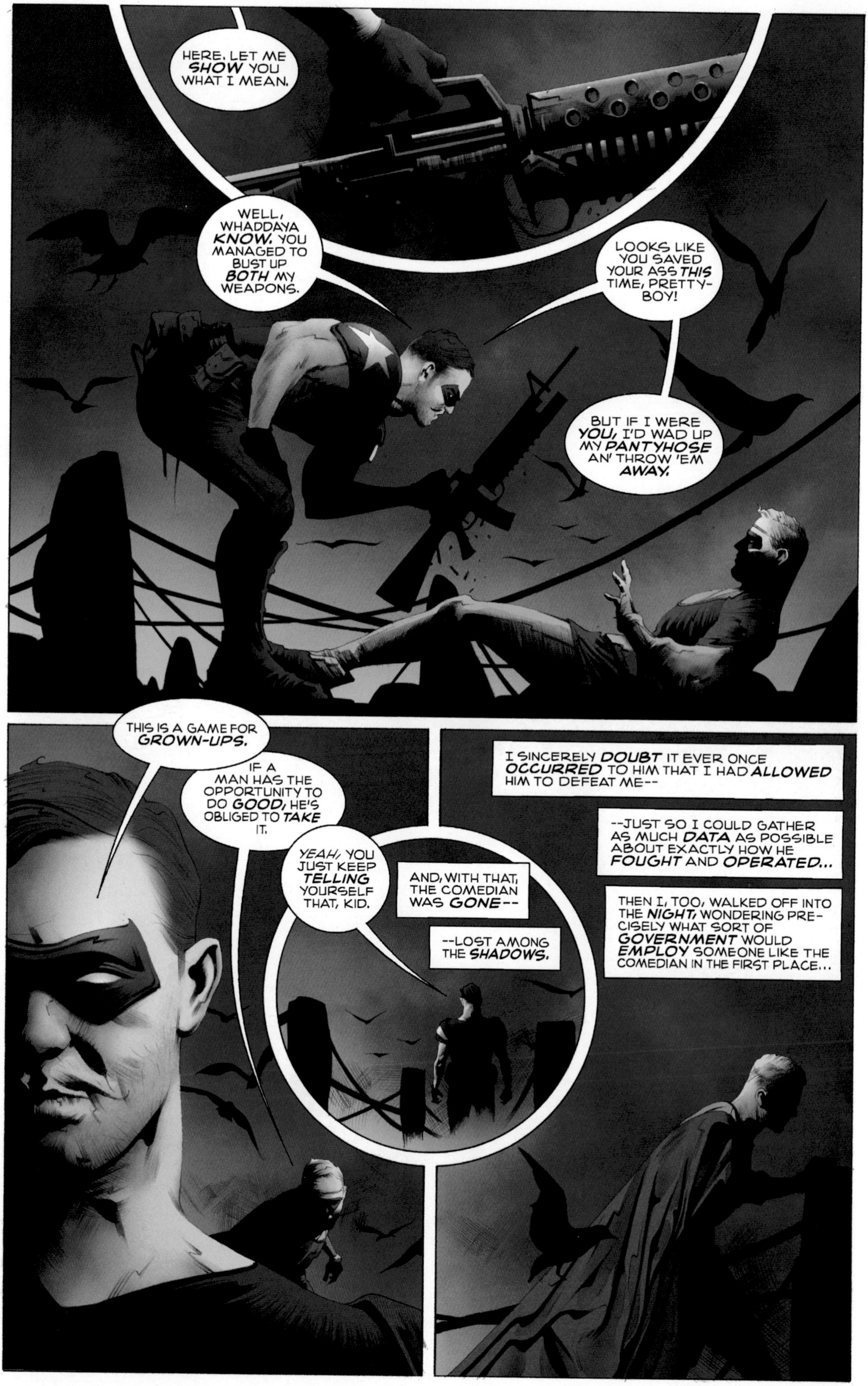
HERE. LET ME SHOW YOU WHAT I MEAN.
WELL, WHADDAYA KNOW. YOU MANAGED TO BUST UP BOTH MY WEAPONS.
LOOKS LIKE YOU SAVED YOUR ASS THIS TIME, PRETTY-BOY!
BUT IF I WERE YOU, I'D WAD UP MY PANTYHOSE AN' THROW 'EM AWAY.
THIS IS A GAME FOR GROWN-UPS.
IF A MAN HAS THE OPPORTUNITY TO DO GOOD, HE'S OBLIGED TO TAKE IT.
YEAH, YOU JUST KEEP TELLING YOURSELF THAT, KID.
AND, WITH THAT, THE COMEDIAN WAS GONE--
--LOST AMONG THE SHADOWS.
I SINCERELY DOUBT IT EVER ONCE OCCURRED TO HIM THAT I HAD ALLOWED HIM TO DEFEAT ME--
--JUST SO I COULD GATHER AS MUCH DATA AS POSSIBLE ABOUT EXACTLY HOW HE FOUGHT AND OPERATED...
THEN I, TOO, WALKED OFF INTO THE NIGHT, WONDERING PRECISELY WHAT SORT OF GOVERNMENT WOULD EMPLOY SOMEONE LIKE THE COMEDIAN IN THE FIRST PLACE...

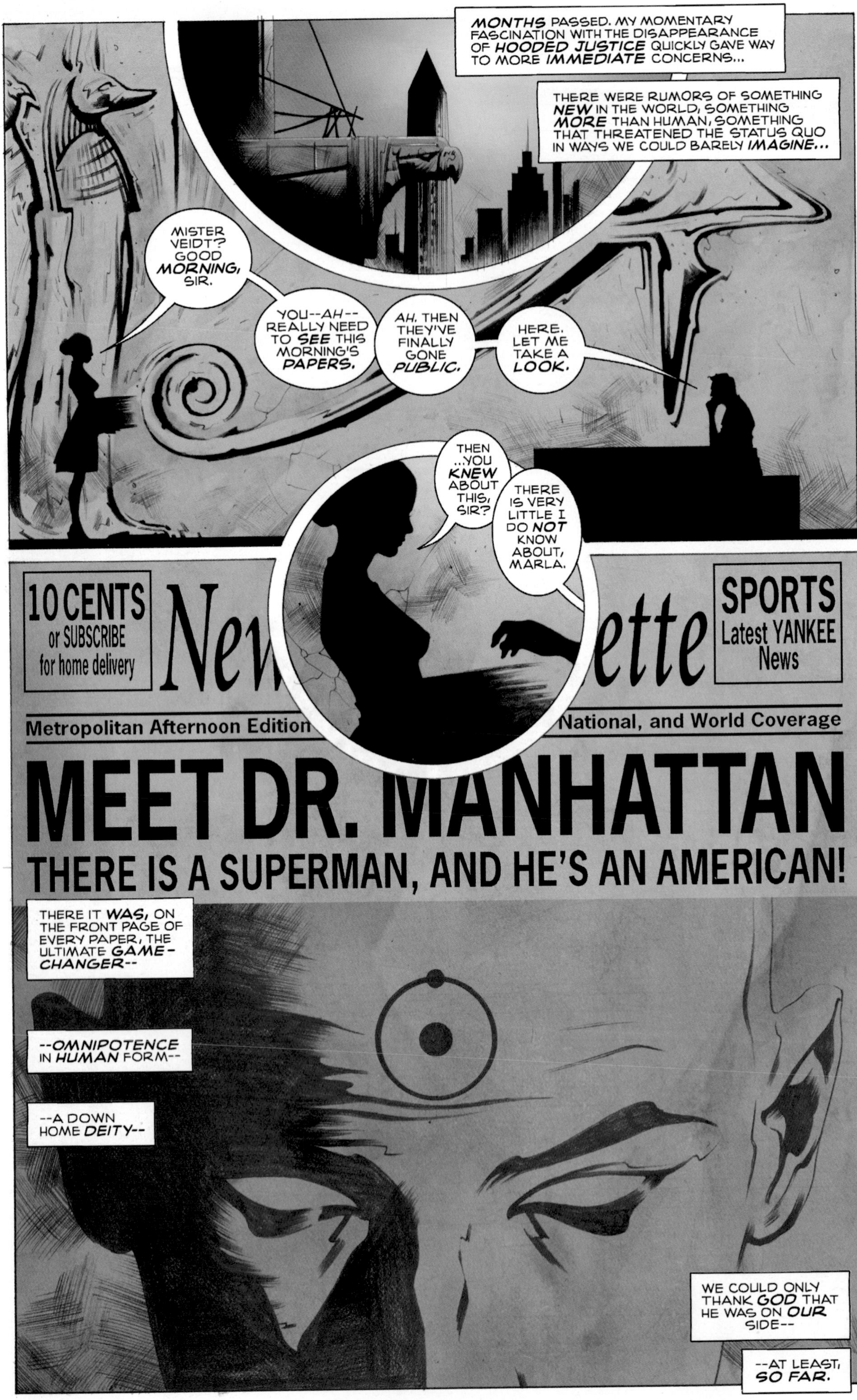
MONTHS PASSED. MY MOMENTARY FASCINATION WITH THE DISAPPEARANCE OF HOODED JUSTICE QUICKLY GAVE WAY TO MORE IMMEDIATE CONCERNS...
THERE WERE RUMORS OF SOMETHING NEW IN THE WORLD, SOMETHING MORE THAN HUMAN, SOMETHING THAT THREATENED THE STATUS QUO IN WAYS WE COULD BARELY IMAGINE...
MISTER VEIDT? GOOD MORNING, SIR.
YOU--AH--REALLY NEED TO SEE THIS MORNING'S PAPERS.
AH. THEN THEY'VE FINALLY GONE PUBLIC.
HERE. LET ME TAKE A LOOK.
THEN ...YOU KNEW ABOUT THIS, SIR?
THERE IS VERY LITTLE I DO NOT KNOW ABOUT, MARLA.
10 CENTS or SUBSCRIBE for home delivery
New ette
SPORTS Latest YANKEE News
Metropolitan Afternoon Edition
National, and World Coverage
MEET DR. MANHATTAN
THERE IS A SUPERMAN, AND HE'S AN AMERICAN!
THERE IT WAS, ON THE FRONT PAGE OF EVERY PAPER, THE ULTIMATE GAME-CHANGER--
--OMNIPOTENCE IN HUMAN FORM--
--A DOWN HOME DEITY--
WE COULD ONLY THANK GOD THAT HE WAS ON OUR SIDE--
--AT LEAST, SO FAR.

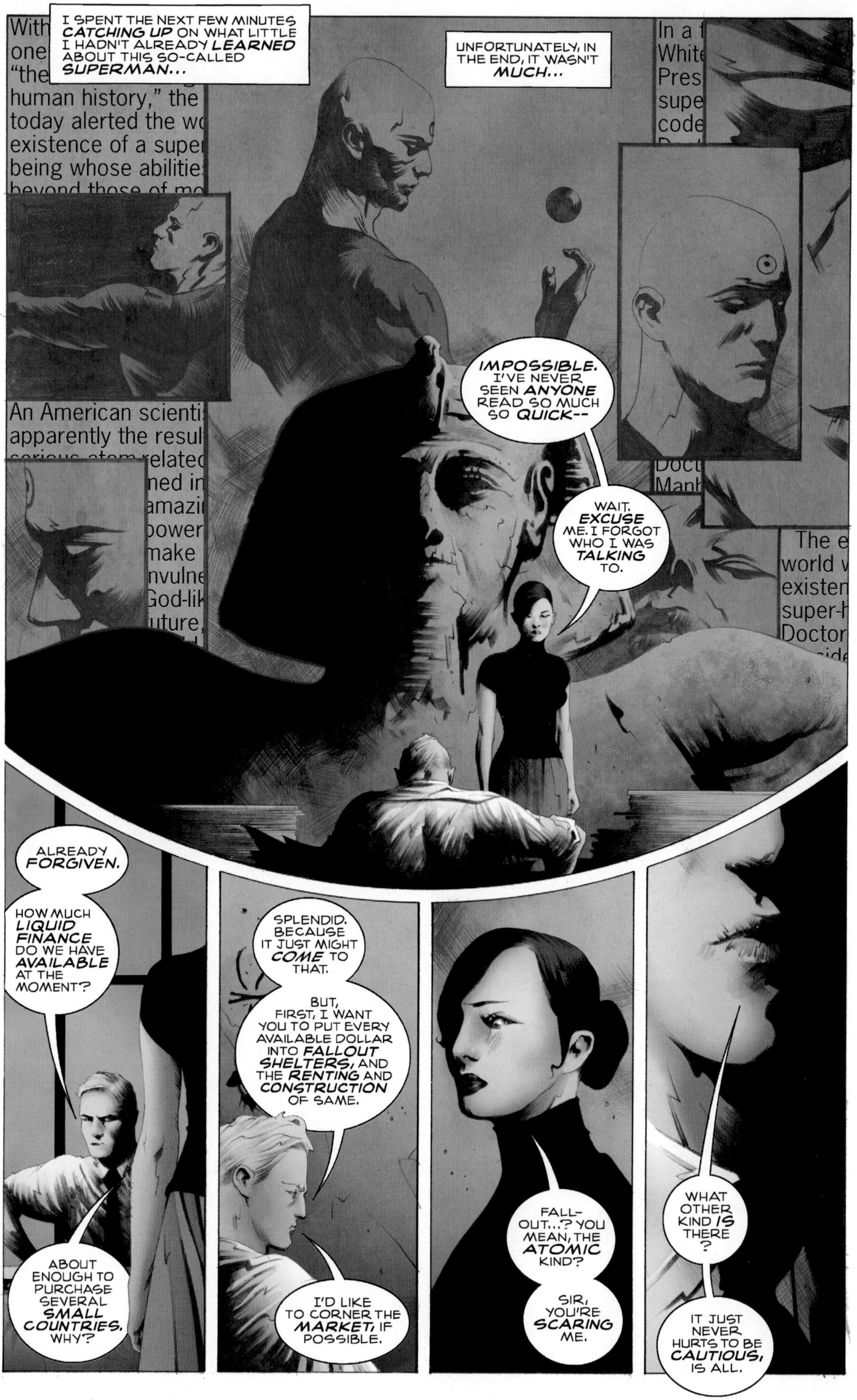

I SPENT THE NEXT FEW MINUTES CATCHING UP ON WHAT LITTLE I HADN'T ALREADY LEARNED ABOUT THIS SO-CALLED SUPERMAN...
UNFORTUNATELY, IN THE END, IT WASN'T MUCH...
IMPOSSIBLE. I'VE NEVER SEEN ANYONE READ SO MUCH SO QUICK--
WAIT. EXCUSE ME. I FORGOT WHO I WAS TALKING TO.
ALREADY FORGIVEN.
HOW MUCH LIQUID FINANCE DO WE HAVE AVAILABLE AT THE MOMENT?
ABOUT ENOUGH TO PURCHASE SEVERAL SMALL COUNTRIES. WHY?
SPLENDID. BECAUSE IT JUST MIGHT COME TO THAT.
BUT, FIRST, I WANT YOU TO PUT EVERY AVAILABLE DOLLAR INTO FALLOUT SHELTERS, AND THE RENTING AND CONSTRUCTION OF SAME.
I'D LIKE TO CORNER THE MARKET, IF POSSIBLE.
FALL-OUT...? YOU MEAN, THE ATOMIC KIND?
SIR, YOU'RE SCARING ME.
WHAT OTHER KIND IS THERE?
IT JUST NEVER HURTS TO BE CAUTIOUS, IS ALL.

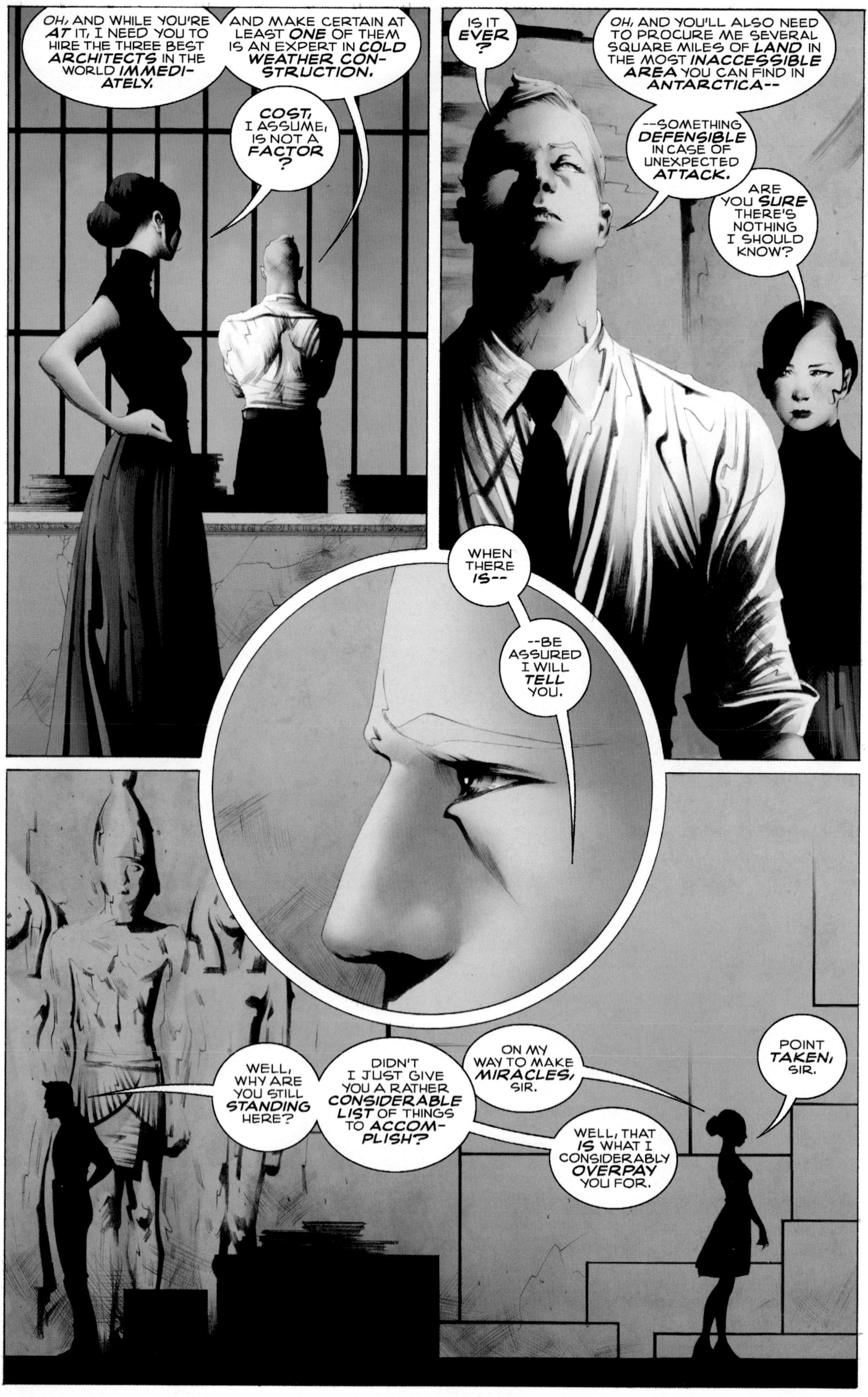
OH, AND WHILE YOU'RE AT IT, I NEED YOU TO HIRE THE THREE BEST ARCHITECTS IN THE WORLD IMMEDIATELY.
AND MAKE CERTAIN AT LEAST ONE OF THEM IS AN EXPERT IN COLD WEATHER CONSTRUCTION.
COST, I ASSUME, IS NOT A FACTOR?
IS IT EVER?
OH, AND YOU'LL ALSO NEED TO PROCURE ME SEVERAL SQUARE MILES OF LAND IN THE MOST INACCESSIBLE AREA YOU CAN FIND IN ANTARCTICA--
--SOMETHING DEFENSIBLE IN CASE OF UNEXPECTED ATTACK.
ARE YOU SURE THERE'S NOTHING I SHOULD KNOW?
WHEN THERE IS--
--BE ASSURED I WILL TELL YOU.
WELL, WHY ARE YOU STILL STANDING HERE?
DIDN'T I JUST GIVE YOU A RATHER CONSIDERABLE LIST OF THINGS TO ACCOMPLISH?
ON MY WAY TO MAKE MIRACLES, SIR.
WELL, THAT IS WHAT I CONSIDERABLY OVERPAY YOU FOR.
POINT TAKEN, SIR.

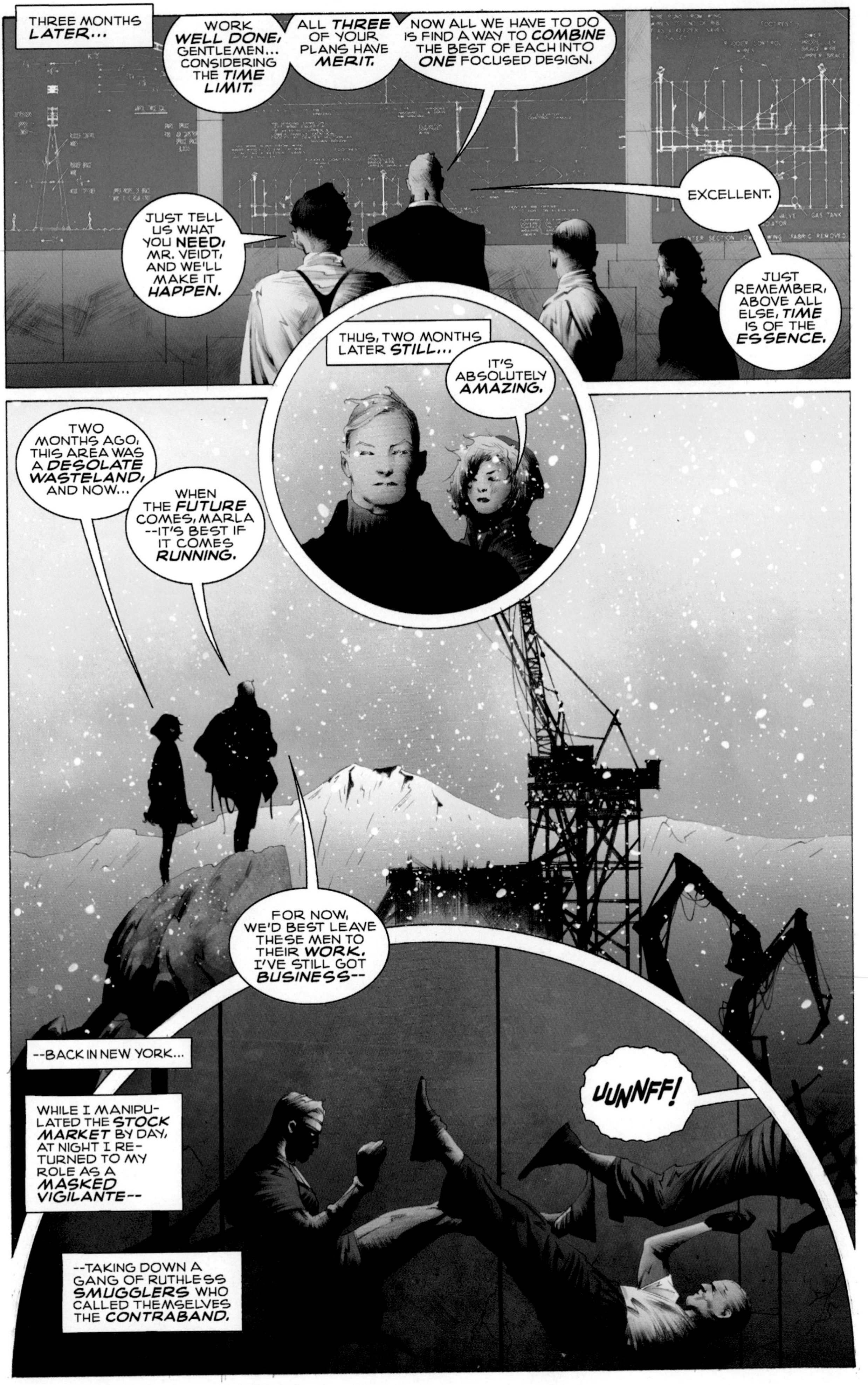
THREE MONTHS LATER...
WORK WELL DONE, GENTLEMEN... CONSIDERING THE TIME LIMIT.
ALL THREE OF YOUR PLANS HAVE MERIT.
NOW ALL WE HAVE TO DO IS FIND A WAY TO COMBINE THE BEST OF EACH INTO ONE FOCUSED DESIGN.
JUST TELL US WHAT YOU NEED, MR. VEIDT, AND WE'LL MAKE IT HAPPEN.
EXCELLENT.
JUST REMEMBER, ABOVE ALL ELSE, TIME IS OF THE ESSENCE.
THUS, TWO MONTHS LATER STILL...
IT'S ABSOLUTELY AMAZING.
TWO MONTHS AGO, THIS AREA WAS A DESOLATE WASTELAND, AND NOW...
WHEN THE FUTURE COMES, MARLA --IT'S BEST IF IT COMES RUNNING.
FOR NOW, WE'D BEST LEAVE THESE MEN TO THEIR WORK. I'VE STILL GOT BUSINESS--
--BACK IN NEW YORK...
WHILE I MANIPULATED THE STOCK MARKET BY DAY, AT NIGHT I RETURNED TO MY ROLE AS A MASKED VIGILANTE--
UUNNFF!
--TAKING DOWN A GANG OF RUTHLESS SMUGGLERS WHO CALLED THEMSELVES THE CONTRABAND.

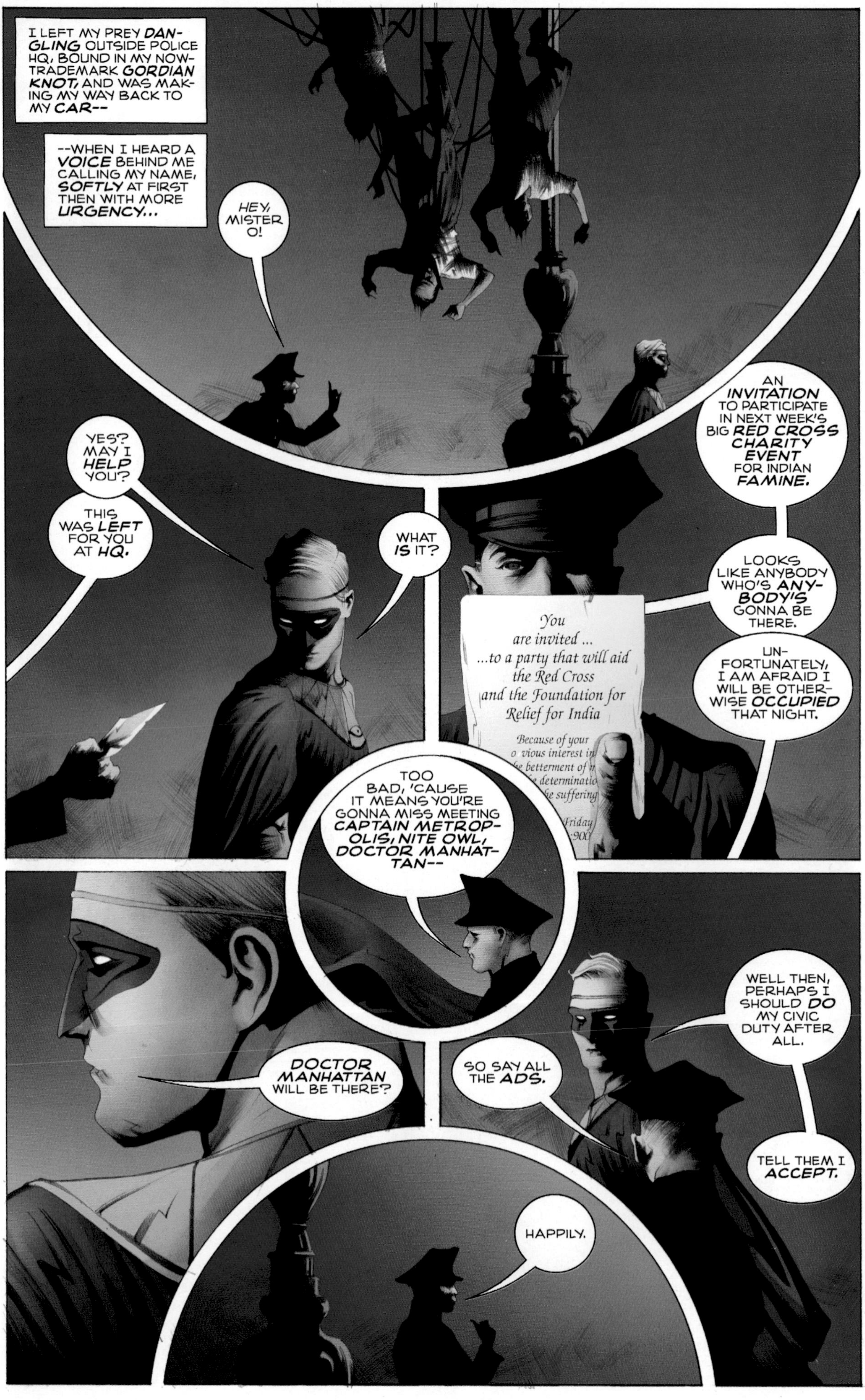
I LEFT MY PREY DANGLING OUTSIDE POLICE HQ, BOUND IN MY NOW-TRADEMARK GORDIAN KNOT, AND WAS MAKING MY WAY BACK TO MY CAR--
--WHEN I HEARD A VOICE BEHIND ME CALLING MY NAME, SOFTLY AT FIRST THEN WITH MORE URGENCY...
HEY, MISTER O!
YES? MAY I HELP YOU?
THIS WAS LEFT FOR YOU AT HQ.
WHAT IS IT?
AN INVITATION TO PARTICIPATE IN NEXT WEEK'S BIG RED CROSS CHARITY EVENT FOR INDIAN FAMINE.
You are invited ... ...to a party that will aid the Red Cross and the Foundation for Relief for India
LOOKS LIKE ANYBODY WHO'S ANY-BODY'S GONNA BE THERE.
UN-FORTUNATELY, I AM AFRAID I WILL BE OTHER-WISE OCCUPIED THAT NIGHT.
TOO BAD, 'CAUSE IT MEANS YOU'RE GONNA MISS MEETING CAPTAIN METROPOLIS, NITE OWL, DOCTOR MANHATTAN--
DOCTOR MANHATTAN WILL BE THERE?
SO SAY ALL THE ADS.
WELL THEN, PERHAPS I SHOULD DO MY CIVIC DUTY AFTER ALL.
TELL THEM I ACCEPT.
HAPPILY.

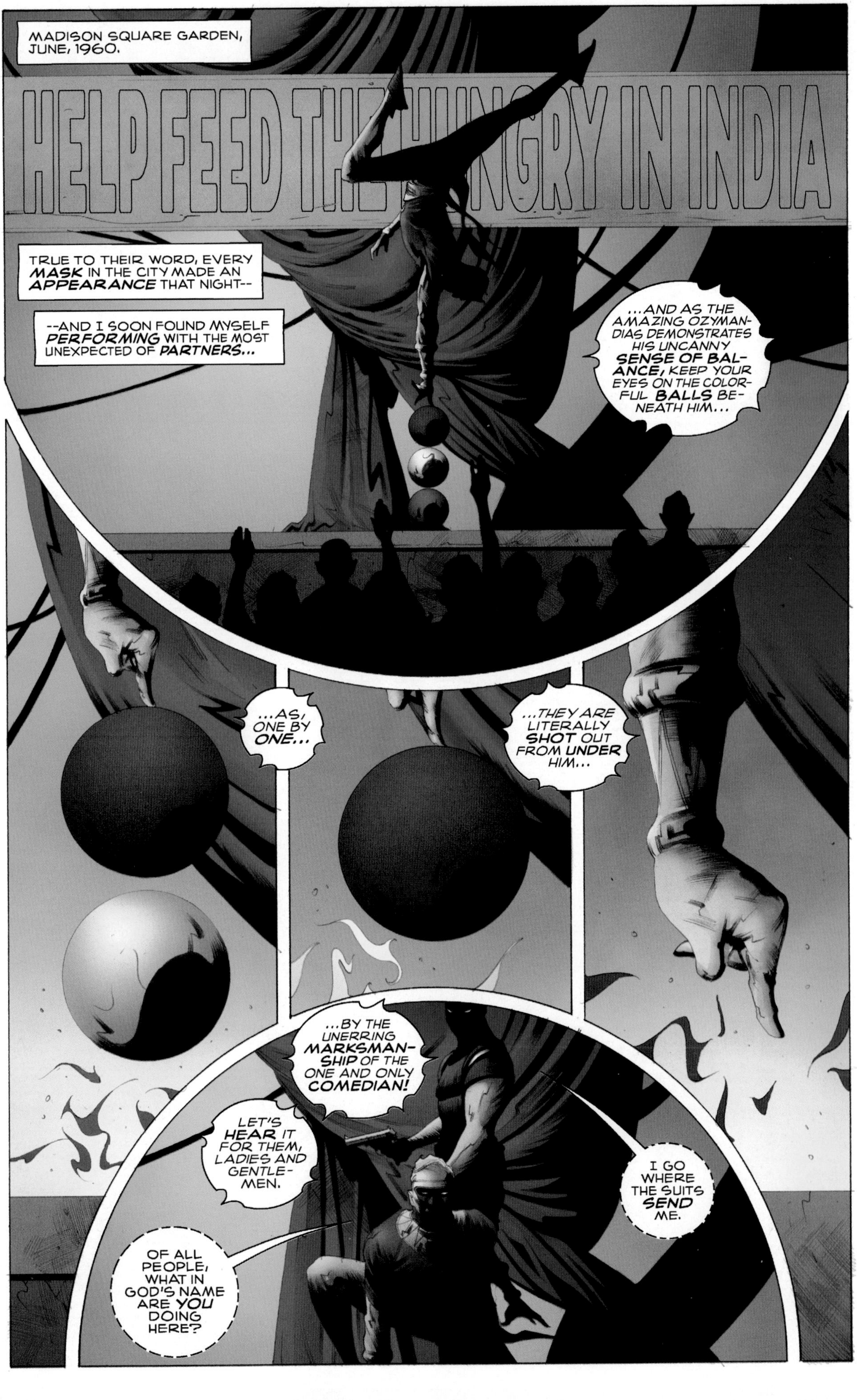

MADISON SQUARE GARDEN, JUNE, 1960.
HELP FEED THE HUNGRY IN INDIA
TRUE TO THEIR WORD, EVERY MASK IN THE CITY MADE AN APPEARANCE THAT NIGHT--
--AND I SOON FOUND MYSELF PERFORMING WITH THE MOST UNEXPECTED OF PARTNERS...
...AND AS THE AMAZING OZYMANDIAS DEMONSTRATES HIS UNCANNY SENSE OF BALANCE, KEEP YOUR EYES ON THE COLORFUL BALLS BENEATH HIM...
...AS, ONE BY ONE...
...THEY ARE LITERALLY SHOT OUT FROM UNDER HIM...
...BY THE UNERRING MARKSMANSHIP OF THE ONE AND ONLY COMEDIAN!
LET'S HEAR IT FOR THEM, LADIES AND GENTLEMEN.
I GO WHERE THE SUITS SEND ME.
OF ALL PEOPLE, WHAT IN GOD'S NAME ARE YOU DOING HERE?

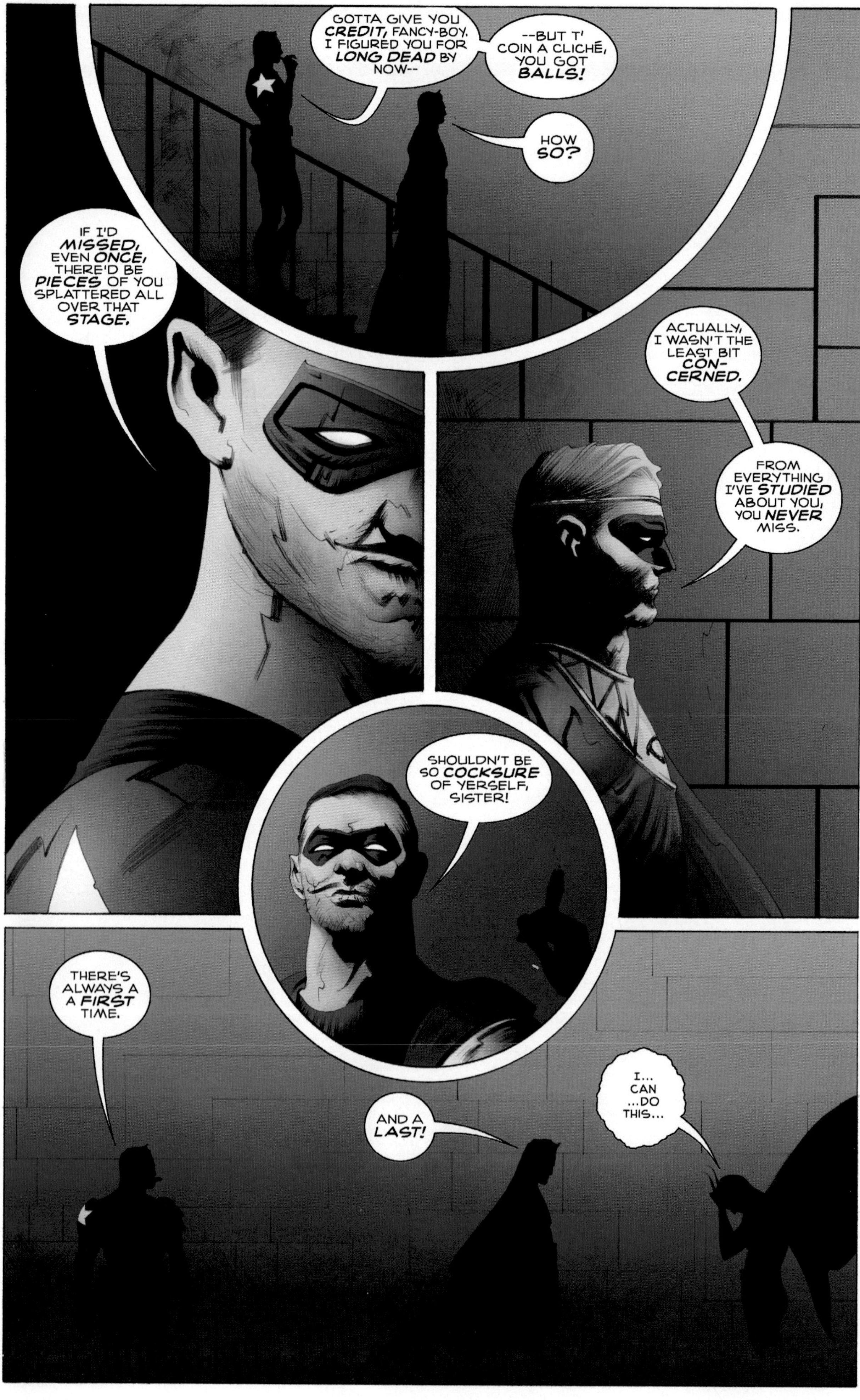
GOTTA GIVE YOU CREDIT, FANCY-BOY. I FIGURED YOU FOR LONG DEAD BY NOW--
--BUT T' COIN A CLICHÉ, YOU GOT BALLS!
HOW SO?
IF I'D MISSED, EVEN ONCE, THERE'D BE PIECES OF YOU SPLATTERED ALL OVER THAT STAGE.
ACTUALLY, I WASN'T THE LEAST BIT CON-CERNED.
FROM EVERYTHING I'VE STUDIED ABOUT YOU, YOU NEVER MISS.
SHOULDN'T BE SO COCKSURE OF YERSELF, SISTER!
THERE'S ALWAYS A A FIRST TIME.
AND A LAST!
I... CAN ...DO THIS...

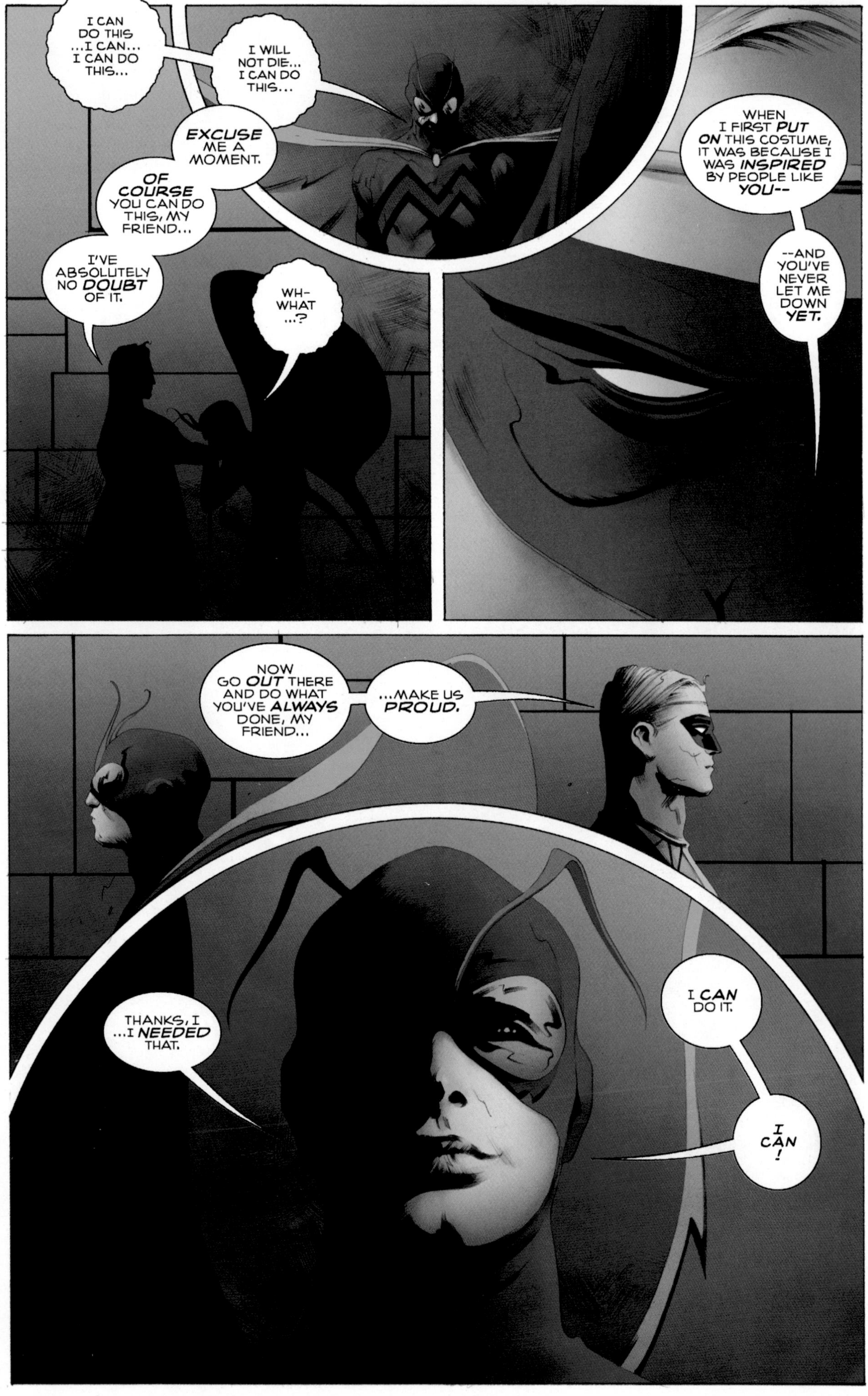
I CAN DO THIS ...I CAN... I CAN DO THIS...
I WILL NOT DIE... I CAN DO THIS...
EXCUSE ME A MOMENT.
OF COURSE YOU CAN DO THIS, MY FRIEND...
I'VE ABSOLUTELY NO DOUBT OF IT.
WH-WHAT ...?
WHEN I FIRST PUT ON THIS COSTUME, IT WAS BECAUSE I WAS INSPIRED BY PEOPLE LIKE YOU--
--AND YOU'VE NEVER LET ME DOWN YET.
NOW GO OUT THERE AND DO WHAT YOU'VE ALWAYS DONE, MY FRIEND...
...MAKE US PROUD.
THANKS, I ...I NEEDED THAT.
I CAN DO IT.
I CAN!

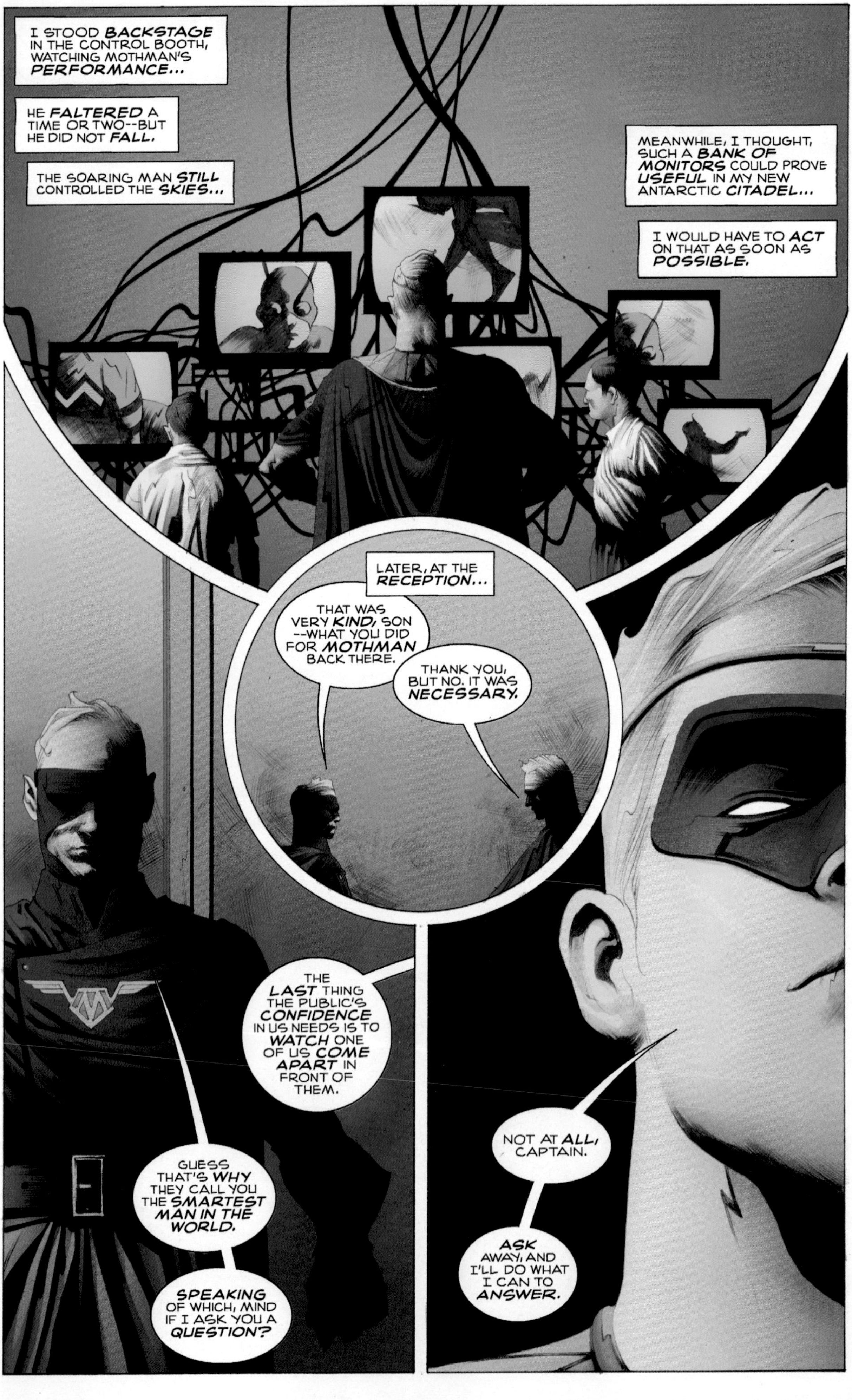
I STOOD BACKSTAGE IN THE CONTROL BOOTH, WATCHING MOTHMAN'S PERFORMANCE...
HE FALTERED A TIME OR TWO--BUT HE DID NOT FALL.
THE SOARING MAN STILL CONTROLLED THE SKIES...
MEANWHILE, I THOUGHT, SUCH A BANK OF MONITORS COULD PROVE USEFUL IN MY NEW ANTARCTIC CITADEL...
I WOULD HAVE TO ACT ON THAT AS SOON AS POSSIBLE.
LATER, AT THE RECEPTION...
THAT WAS VERY KIND, SON --WHAT YOU DID FOR MOTHMAN BACK THERE.
THANK YOU, BUT NO. IT WAS NECESSARY.
THE LAST THING THE PUBLIC'S CONFIDENCE IN US NEEDS IS TO WATCH ONE OF US COME APART IN FRONT OF THEM.
GUESS THAT'S WHY THEY CALL YOU THE SMARTEST MAN IN THE WORLD.
SPEAKING OF WHICH, MIND IF I ASK YOU A QUESTION?
NOT AT ALL, CAPTAIN.
ASK AWAY, AND I'LL DO WHAT I CAN TO ANSWER.

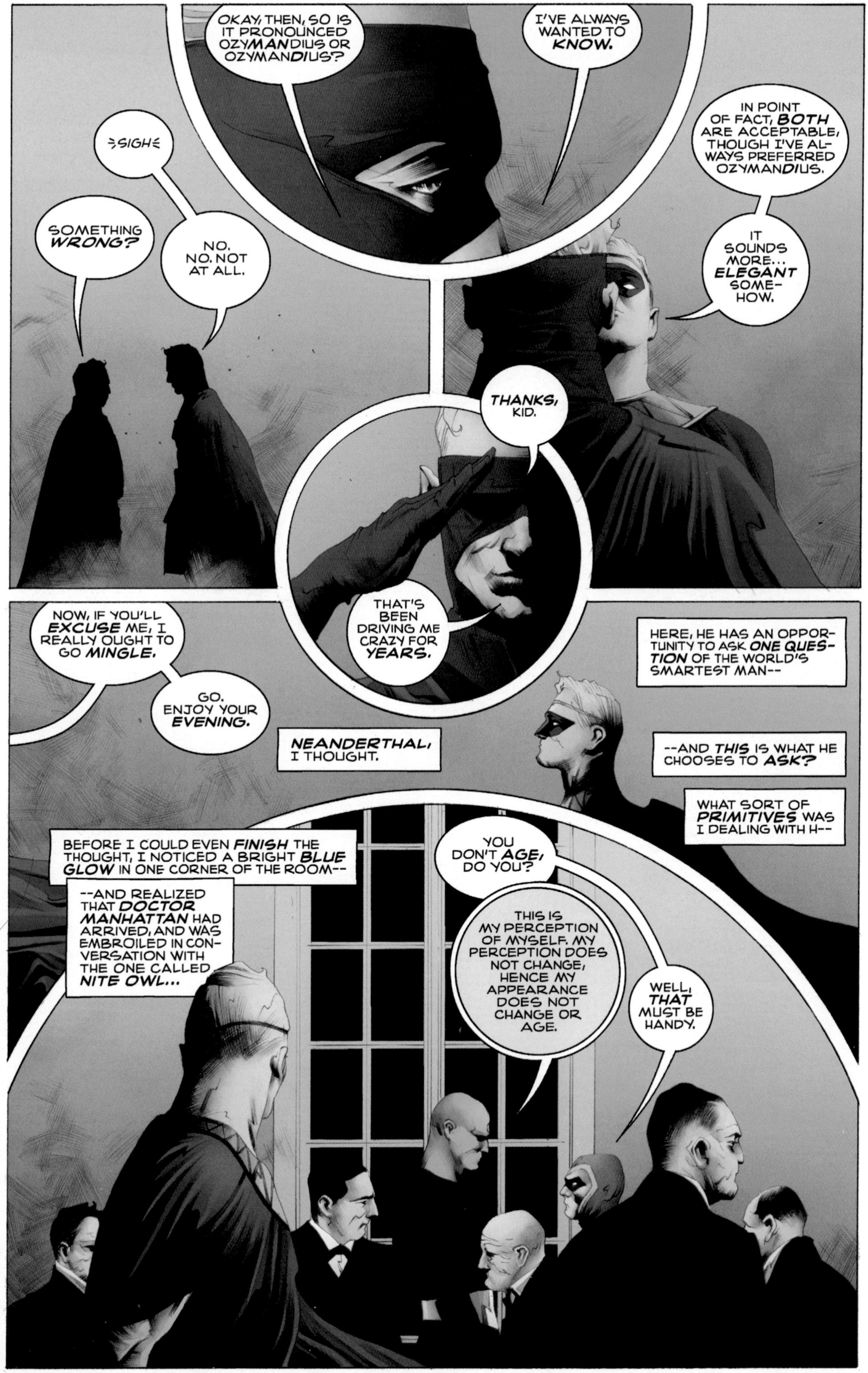
OKAY, THEN, SO IS IT PRONOUNCED OZYMANDIUS OR OZYMANDIUS?
I'VE ALWAYS WANTED TO KNOW.
SIGH
SOMETHING WRONG?
NO. NO. NOT AT ALL.
IN POINT OF FACT, BOTH ARE ACCEPTABLE, THOUGH I'VE ALWAYS PREFERRED OZYMANDIUS.
IT SOUNDS MORE... ELEGANT SOMEHOW.
THANKS, KID.
THAT'S BEEN DRIVING ME CRAZY FOR YEARS.
NOW, IF YOU'LL EXCUSE ME, I REALLY OUGHT TO GO MINGLE.
GO. ENJOY YOUR EVENING.
NEANDERTHAL, I THOUGHT.
HERE, HE HAS AN OPPORTUNITY TO ASK ONE QUESTION OF THE WORLD'S SMARTEST MAN--
--AND THIS IS WHAT HE CHOOSES TO ASK?
WHAT SORT OF PRIMITIVES WAS I DEALING WITH H--
BEFORE I COULD EVEN FINISH THE THOUGHT, I NOTICED A BRIGHT BLUE GLOW IN ONE CORNER OF THE ROOM--
--AND REALIZED THAT DOCTOR MANHATTAN HAD ARRIVED, AND WAS EMBROILED IN CONVERSATION WITH THE ONE CALLED NITE OWL...
YOU DON'T AGE, DO YOU?
THIS IS MY PERCEPTION OF MYSELF. MY PERCEPTION DOES NOT CHANGE, HENCE MY APPEARANCE DOES NOT CHANGE OR AGE.
WELL, THAT MUST BE HANDY.

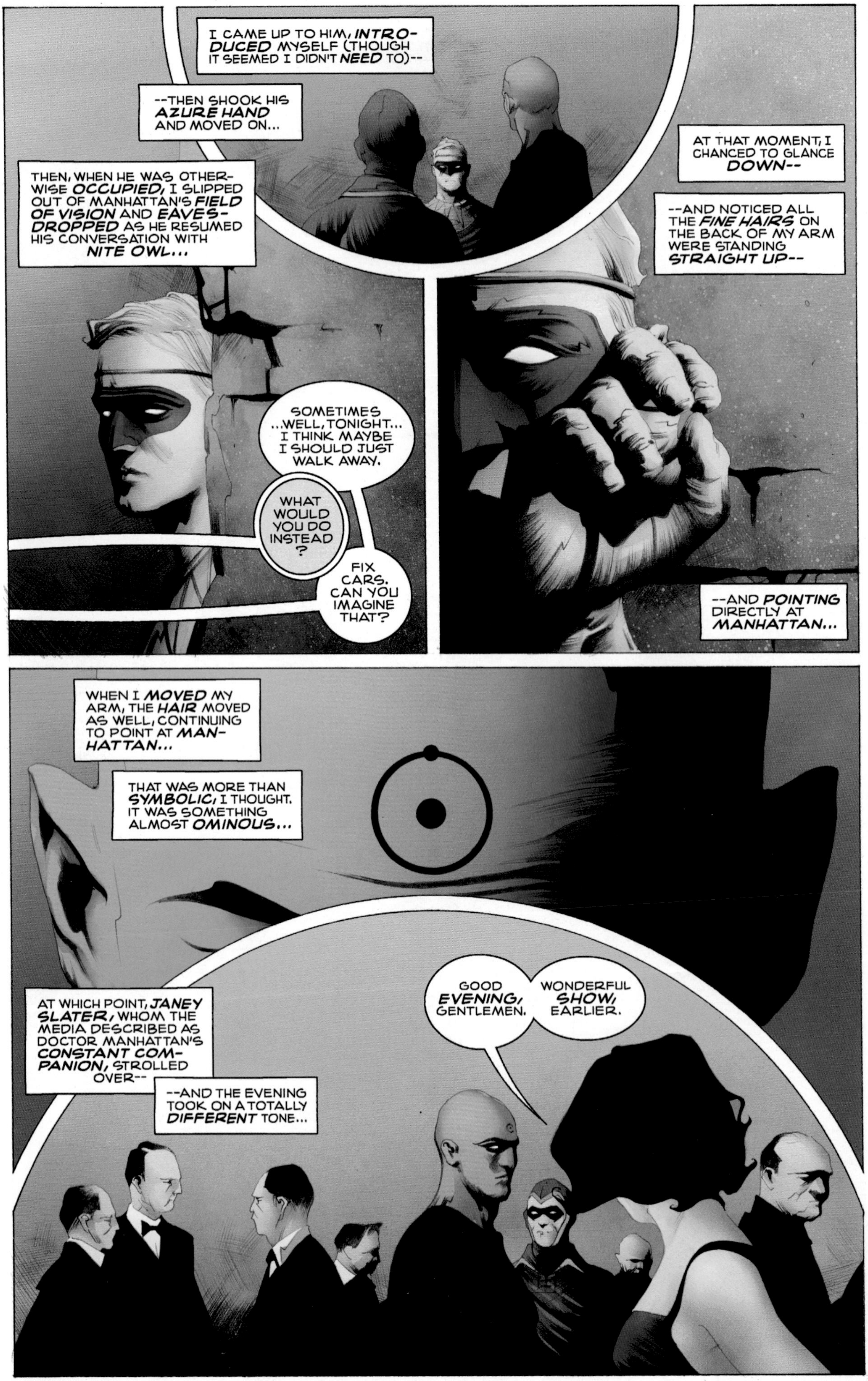
I CAME UP TO HIM, INTRODUCED MYSELF (THOUGH IT SEEMED I DIDN'T NEED TO)--
--THEN SHOOK HIS AZURE HAND AND MOVED ON...
THEN, WHEN HE WAS OTHERWISE OCCUPIED, I SLIPPED OUT OF MANHATTAN'S FIELD OF VISION AND EAVES-DROPPED AS HE RESUMED HIS CONVERSATION WITH NITE OWL...
AT THAT MOMENT, I CHANCED TO GLANCE DOWN--
--AND NOTICED ALL THE FINE HAIRS ON THE BACK OF MY ARM WERE STANDING STRAIGHT UP--
SOMETIMES ...WELL, TONIGHT... I THINK MAYBE I SHOULD JUST WALK AWAY.
WHAT WOULD YOU DO INSTEAD?
FIX CARS. CAN YOU IMAGINE THAT?
--AND POINTING DIRECTLY AT MANHATTAN...
WHEN I MOVED MY ARM, THE HAIR MOVED AS WELL, CONTINUING TO POINT AT MANHATTAN...
THAT WAS MORE THAN SYMBOLIC, I THOUGHT. IT WAS SOMETHING ALMOST OMINOUS...
AT WHICH POINT, JANEY SLATER, WHOM THE MEDIA DESCRIBED AS DOCTOR MANHATTAN'S CONSTANT COMPANION, STROLLED OVER--
--AND THE EVENING TOOK ON A TOTALLY DIFFERENT TONE...
GOOD EVENING, GENTLEMEN.
WONDERFUL SHOW, EARLIER.

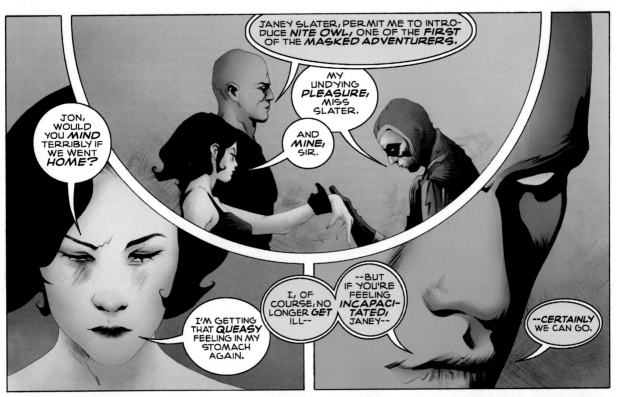

JANEY SLATER, PERMIT ME TO INTRODUCE *NITE OWL*, ONE OF THE *FIRST* OF THE *MASKED ADVENTURERS*.

MY UNDYING *PLEASURE*, MISS SLATER.

AND *MINE*, SIR.

JON, WOULD YOU *MIND* TERRIBLY IF WE WENT *HOME*?

I, OF COURSE, NO LONGER *GET* ILL—

I'M GETTING THAT *QUEASY* FEELING IN MY STOMACH AGAIN.

—BUT IF YOU'RE FEELING *INCAPACITATED*, JANEY—

—CERTAINLY WE CAN GO.

NITE OWL, IT WAS AN HONOR TO *SEE* YOU AGAIN, SIR.

I HOPE OUR PATHS WILL *CROSS* AGAIN SOON.

WHO *KNOWS*, DOC? YOU CAN NEVER *TELL*.

WELL, ACTUALLY, I *CAN*.

JON, STOP *SHOWING OFF*.

IT WAS NICE TO *MEET* YOU, NITE OWL. HAVE A *LOVELY* NIGHT.

AND *YOU*, AS WELL, MR. *OZYMANDIAS*. DO *ENJOY* THE REST OF YOUR EVENING.

I SHALL SEE YOU AGAIN *SOON*.

AND, IN A *BLUE FLASH*, THEY WERE *GONE*—

—LEAVING ME EVEN MORE *UNNERVED* THAN BEFORE.

ALL THE TIME I'D BEEN *HIDING*, HE HAD *KNOWN* I WAS THERE.

JUST WHAT SORT OF CREATURE *WAS* THIS DOCTOR MANHATTAN *ANYWAY*?

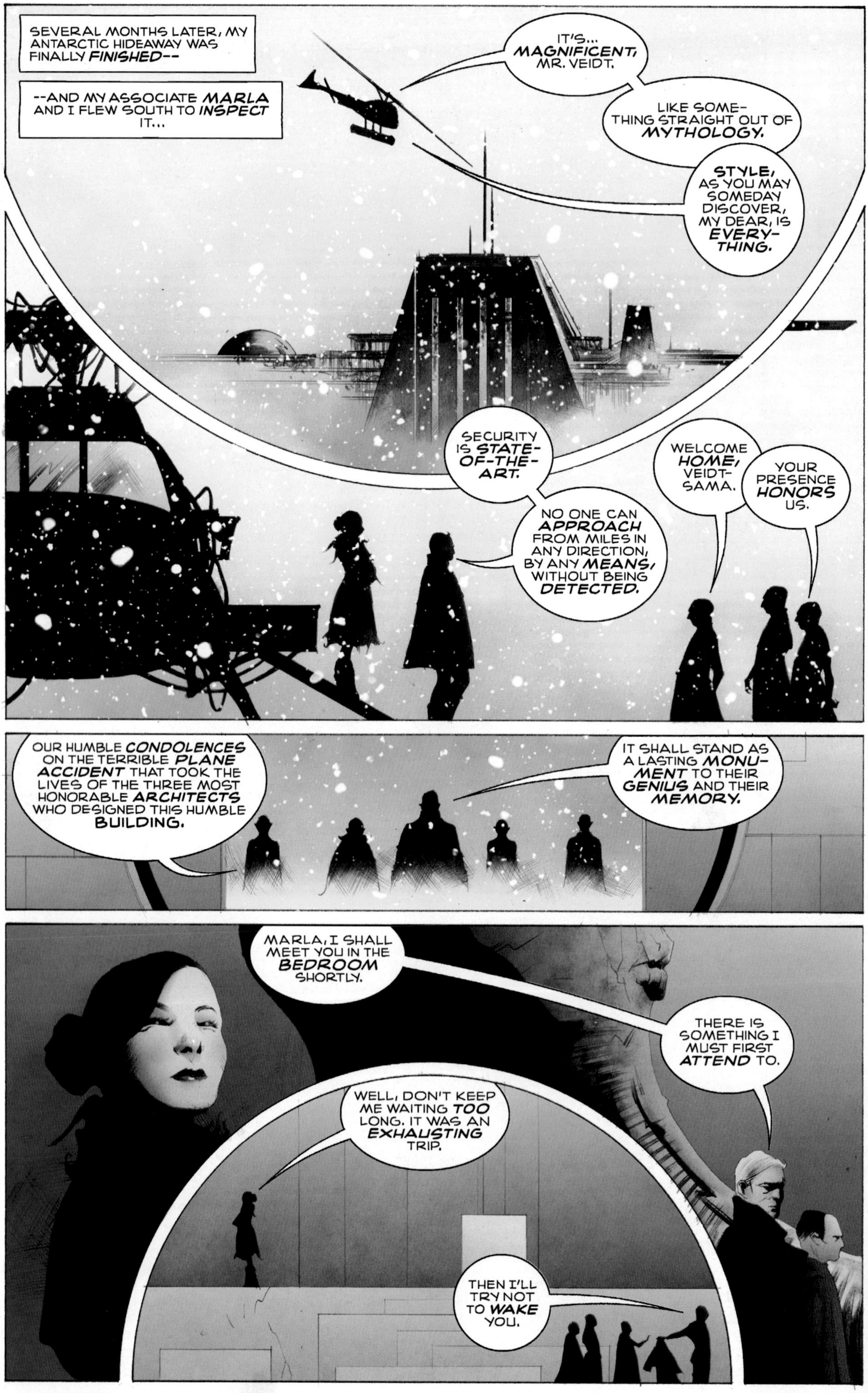
SEVERAL MONTHS LATER, MY ANTARCTIC HIDEAWAY WAS FINALLY FINISHED--
--AND MY ASSOCIATE MARLA AND I FLEW SOUTH TO INSPECT IT...
IT'S... MAGNIFICENT, MR. VEIDT.
LIKE SOME-THING STRAIGHT OUT OF MYTHOLOGY.
STYLE, AS YOU MAY SOMEDAY DISCOVER, MY DEAR, IS EVERY-THING.
SECURITY IS STATE-OF-THE-ART.
NO ONE CAN APPROACH FROM MILES IN ANY DIRECTION, BY ANY MEANS, WITHOUT BEING DETECTED.
WELCOME HOME, VEIDT-SAMA.
YOUR PRESENCE HONORS US.
OUR HUMBLE CONDOLENCES ON THE TERRIBLE PLANE ACCIDENT THAT TOOK THE LIVES OF THE THREE MOST HONORABLE ARCHITECTS WHO DESIGNED THIS HUMBLE BUILDING.
IT SHALL STAND AS A LASTING MONU-MENT TO THEIR GENIUS AND THEIR MEMORY.
MARLA, I SHALL MEET YOU IN THE BEDROOM SHORTLY.
THERE IS SOMETHING I MUST FIRST ATTEND TO.
WELL, DON'T KEEP ME WAITING TOO LONG. IT WAS AN EXHAUSTING TRIP.
THEN I'LL TRY NOT TO WAKE YOU.

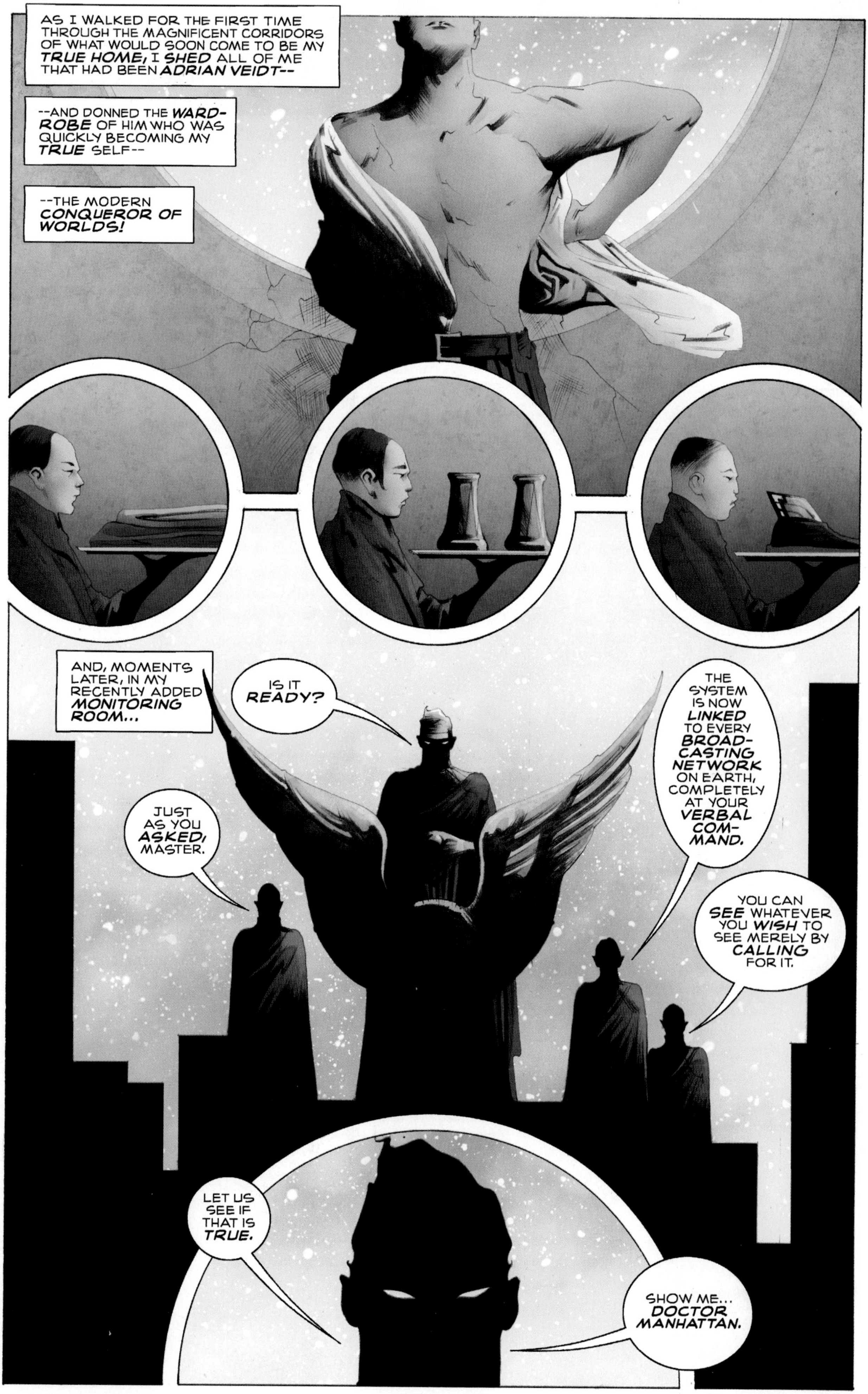
AS I WALKED FOR THE FIRST TIME THROUGH THE MAGNIFICENT CORRIDORS OF WHAT WOULD SOON COME TO BE MY TRUE HOME, I SHED ALL OF ME THAT HAD BEEN ADRIAN VEIDT--
--AND DONNED THE WARD-ROBE OF HIM WHO WAS QUICKLY BECOMING MY TRUE SELF--
--THE MODERN CONQUEROR OF WORLDS!
AND, MOMENTS LATER, IN MY RECENTLY ADDED MONITORING ROOM...
IS IT READY?
JUST AS YOU ASKED, MASTER.
THE SYSTEM IS NOW LINKED TO EVERY BROAD-CASTING NETWORK ON EARTH, COMPLETELY AT YOUR VERBAL COM-MAND.
YOU CAN SEE WHATEVER YOU WISH TO SEE MERELY BY CALLING FOR IT.
LET US SEE IF THAT IS TRUE.
SHOW ME... DOCTOR MANHATTAN.

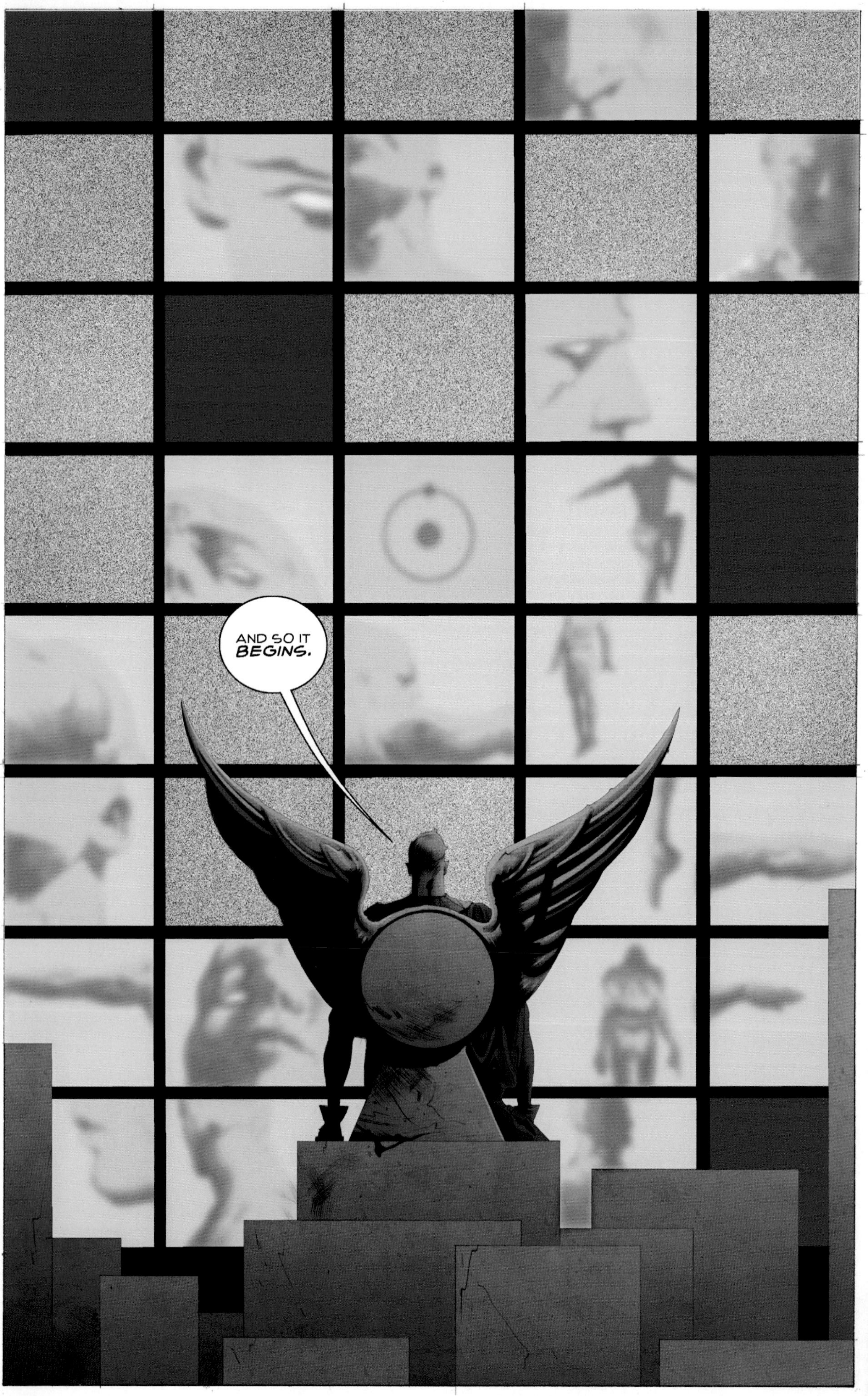
AND SO IT BEGINS.

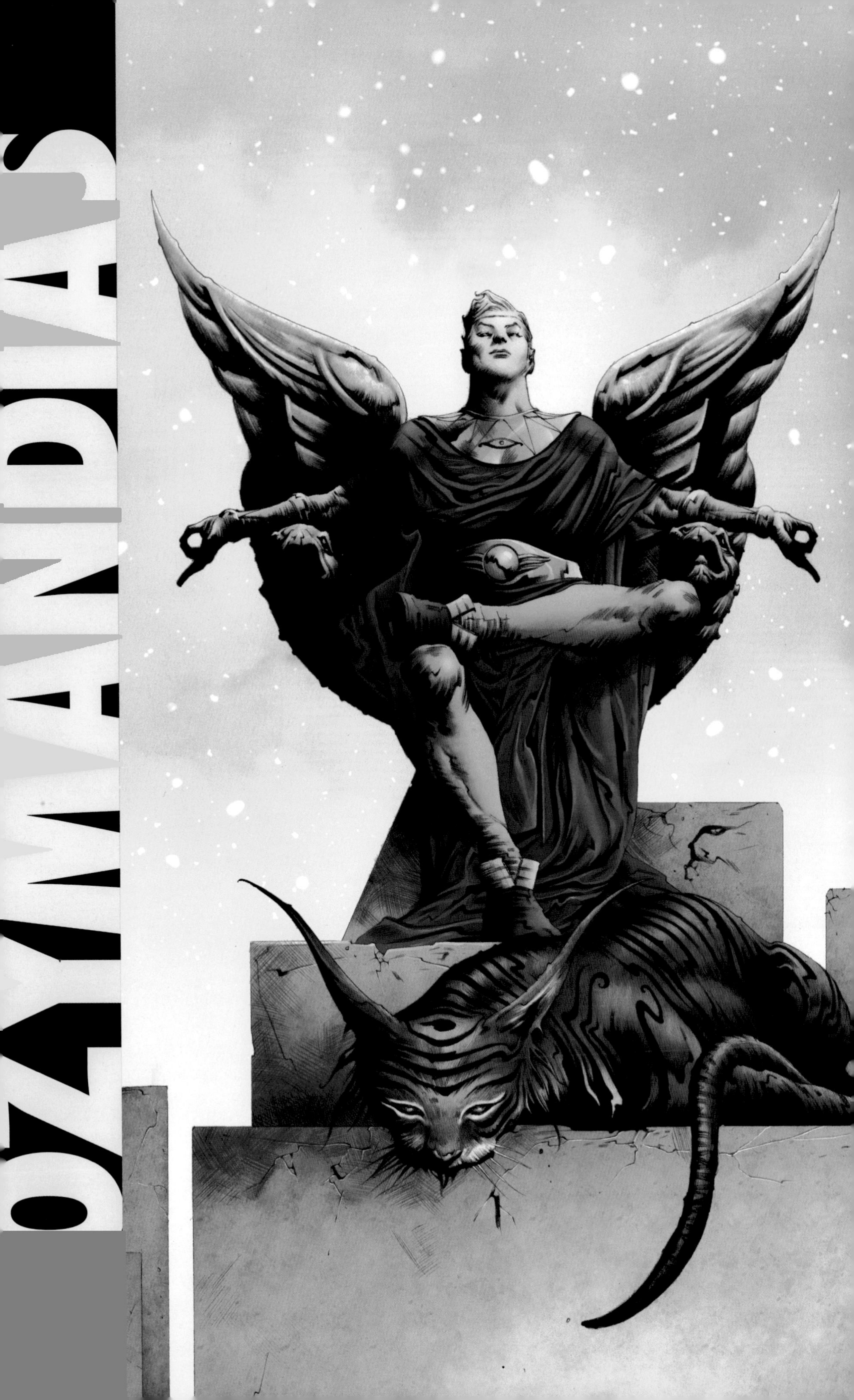
OZYMANDIAS

OZYMANDIAS

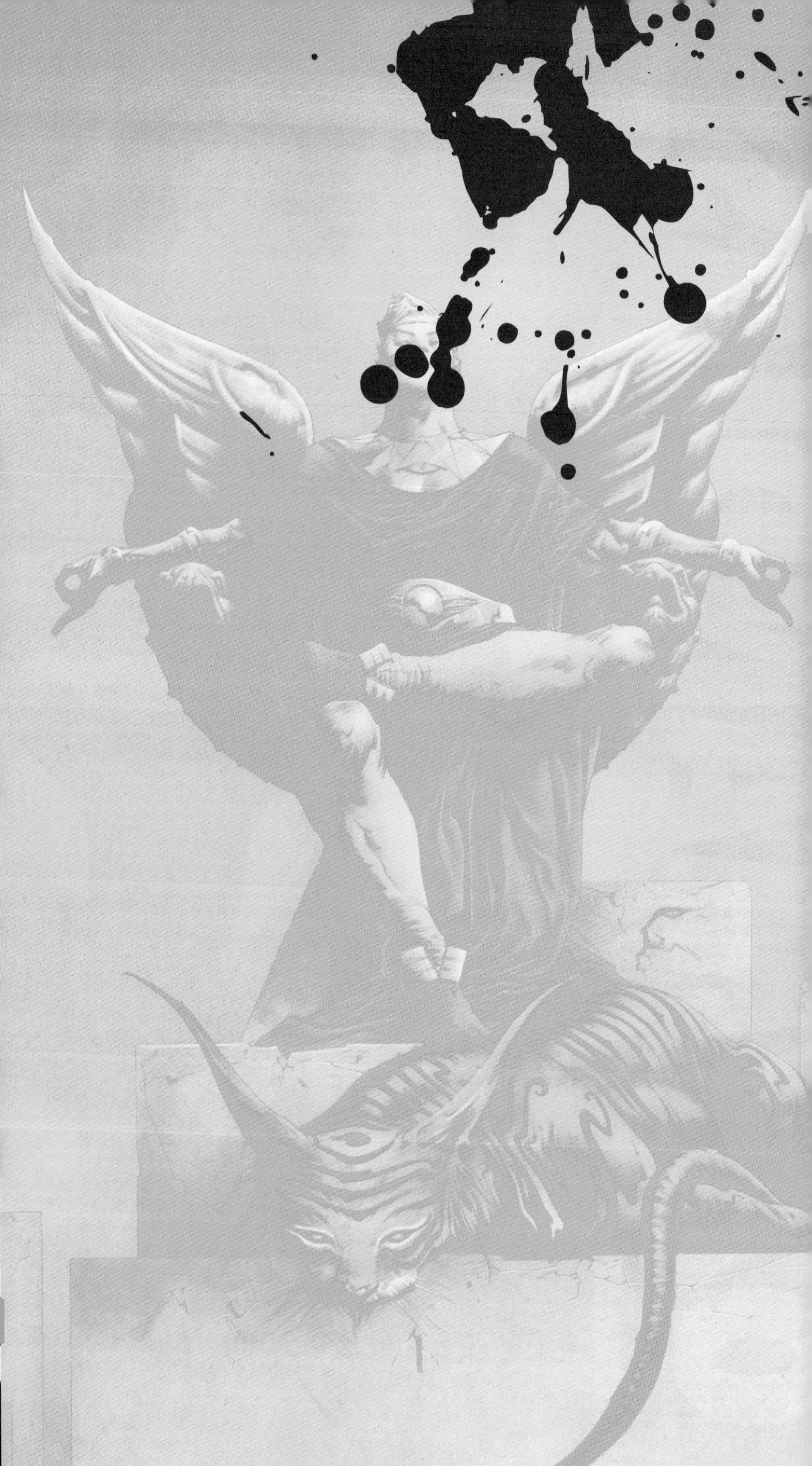

"IT WAS SOMEBODY TIDYING UP LOOSE ENDS..."

SHATTERED VISAGE...!

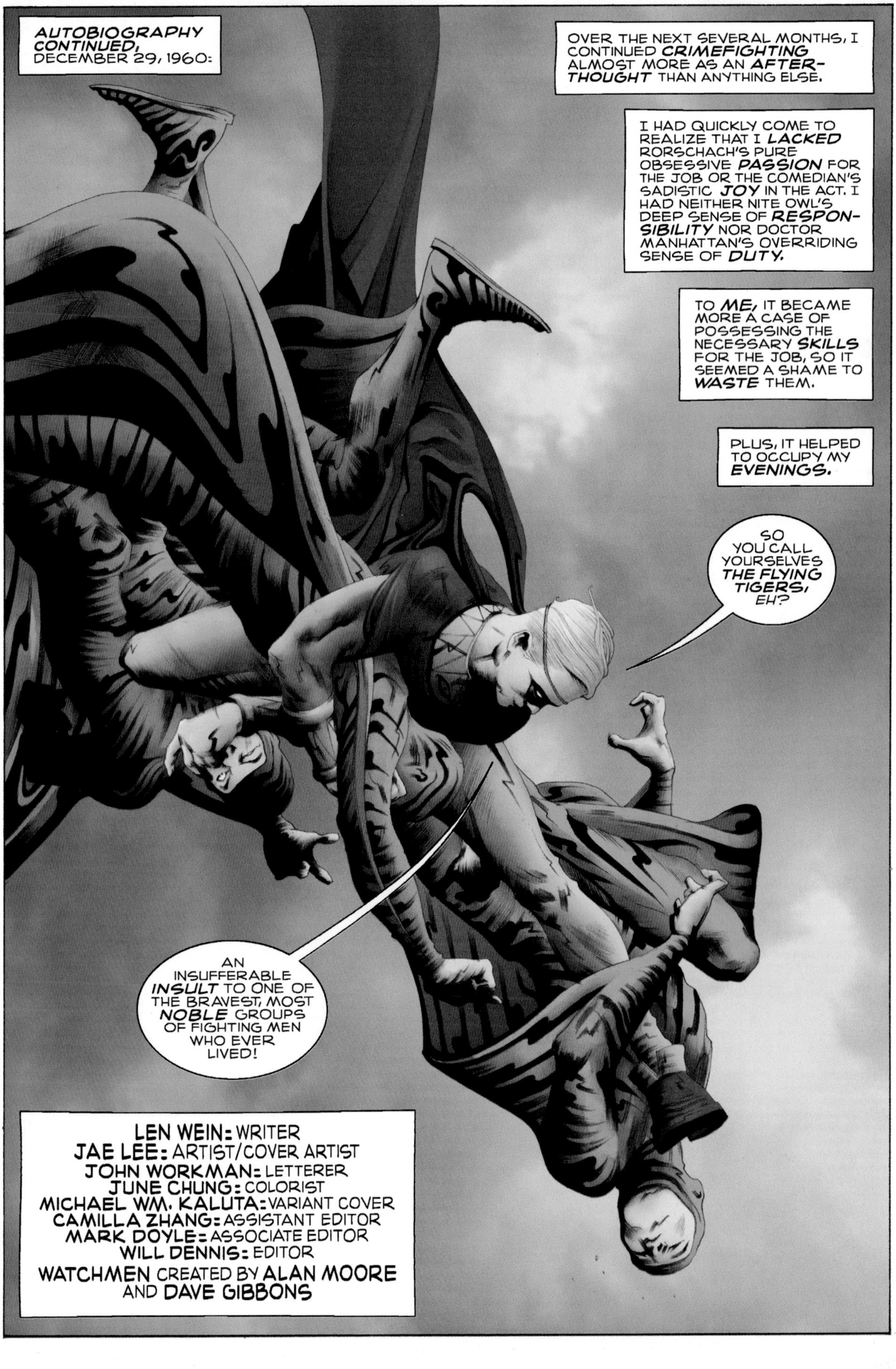
AUTOBIOGRAPHY CONTINUED, DECEMBER 29, 1960:
OVER THE NEXT SEVERAL MONTHS, I CONTINUED CRIMEFIGHTING ALMOST MORE AS AN AFTERTHOUGHT THAN ANYTHING ELSE.
I HAD QUICKLY COME TO REALIZE THAT I LACKED RORSCHACH'S PURE OBSESSIVE PASSION FOR THE JOB OR THE COMEDIAN'S SADISTIC JOY IN THE ACT. I HAD NEITHER NITE OWL'S DEEP SENSE OF RESPONSIBILITY NOR DOCTOR MANHATTAN'S OVERRIDING SENSE OF DUTY.
TO ME, IT BECAME MORE A CASE OF POSSESSING THE NECESSARY SKILLS FOR THE JOB, SO IT SEEMED A SHAME TO WASTE THEM.
PLUS, IT HELPED TO OCCUPY MY EVENINGS.
SO YOU CALL YOURSELVES THE FLYING TIGERS, EH?
AN INSUFFERABLE INSULT TO ONE OF THE BRAVEST, MOST NOBLE GROUPS OF FIGHTING MEN WHO EVER LIVED!

LEN WEIN: WRITER
JAE LEE: ARTIST/COVER ARTIST
JOHN WORKMAN: LETTERER
JUNE CHUNG: COLORIST
MICHAEL WM. KALUTA: VARIANT COVER
CAMILLA ZHANG: ASSISTANT EDITOR
MARK DOYLE: ASSOCIATE EDITOR
WILL DENNIS: EDITOR
WATCHMEN CREATED BY ALAN MOORE AND DAVE GIBBONS

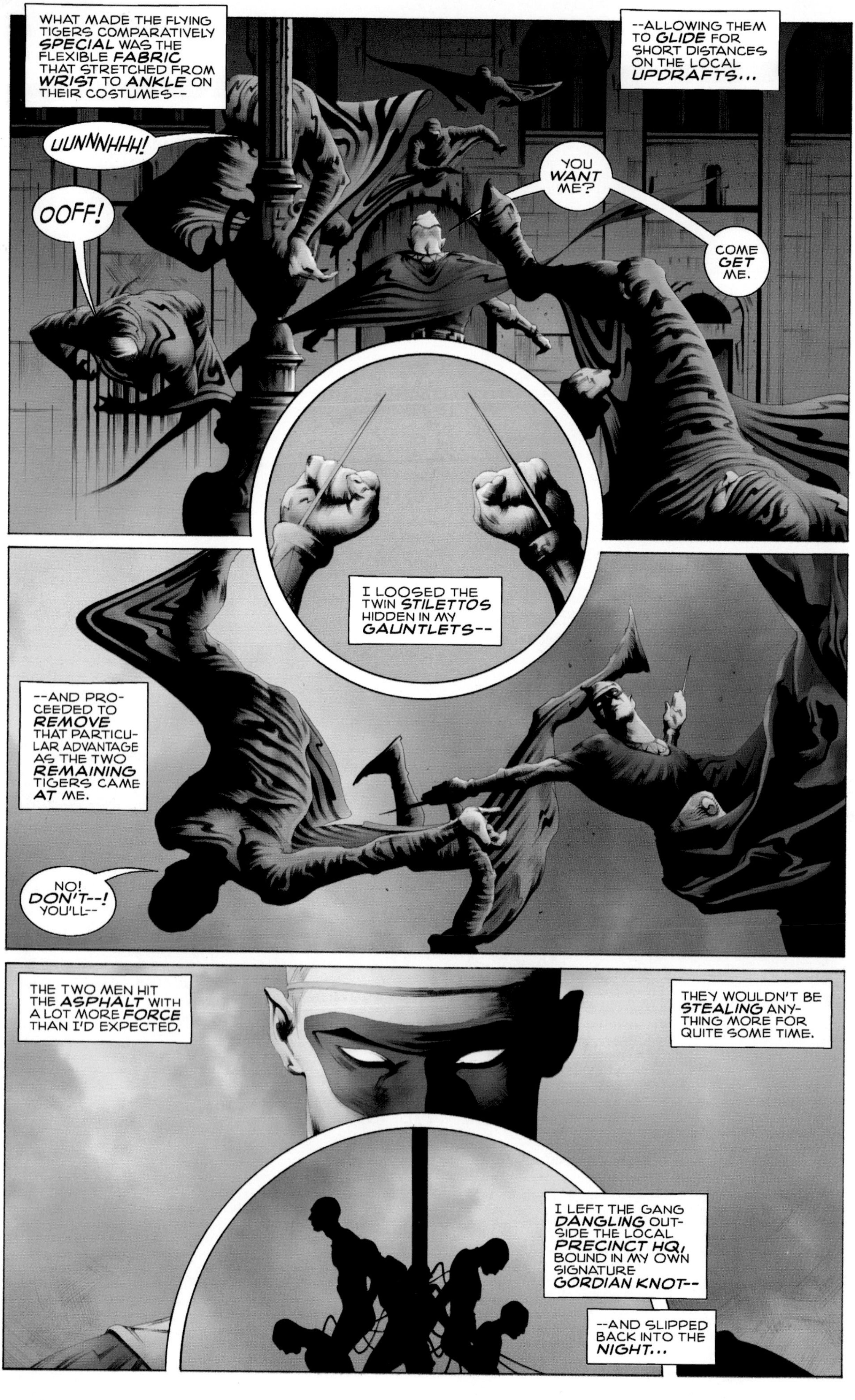
WHAT MADE THE FLYING TIGERS COMPARATIVELY SPECIAL WAS THE FLEXIBLE FABRIC THAT STRETCHED FROM WRIST TO ANKLE ON THEIR COSTUMES--
--ALLOWING THEM TO GLIDE FOR SHORT DISTANCES ON THE LOCAL UPDRAFTS...
UUNNNHHH!
OOFF!
YOU WANT ME?
COME GET ME.
I LOOSED THE TWIN STILETTOS HIDDEN IN MY GAUNTLETS--
--AND PROCEEDED TO REMOVE THAT PARTICULAR ADVANTAGE AS THE TWO REMAINING TIGERS CAME AT ME.
NO! DON'T--! YOU'LL--
THE TWO MEN HIT THE ASPHALT WITH A LOT MORE FORCE THAN I'D EXPECTED.
THEY WOULDN'T BE STEALING ANYTHING MORE FOR QUITE SOME TIME.
I LEFT THE GANG DANGLING OUTSIDE THE LOCAL PRECINCT HQ, BOUND IN MY OWN SIGNATURE GORDIAN KNOT--
--AND SLIPPED BACK INTO THE NIGHT...

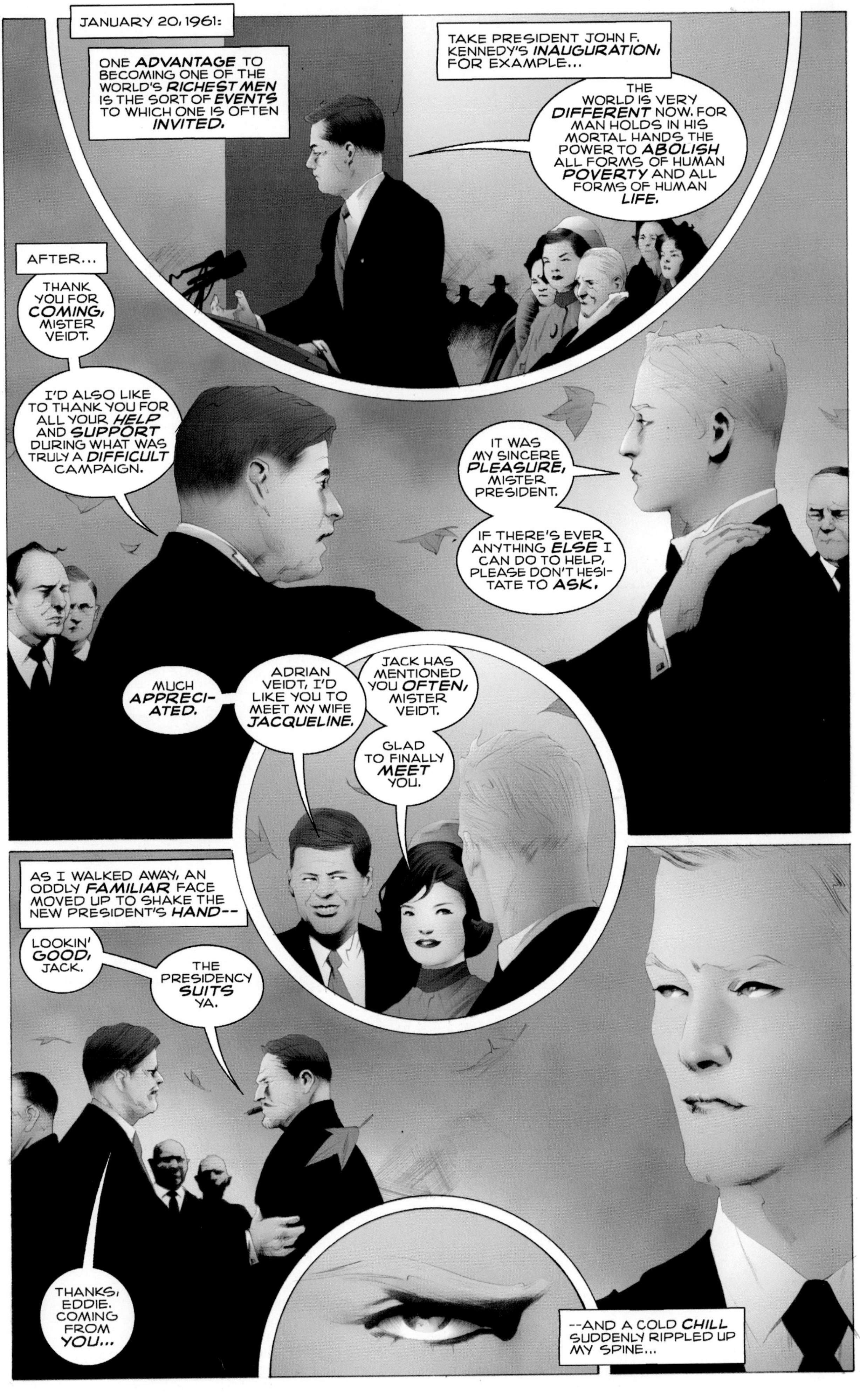
JANUARY 20, 1961:
ONE ADVANTAGE TO BECOMING ONE OF THE WORLD'S RICHEST MEN IS THE SORT OF EVENTS TO WHICH ONE IS OFTEN INVITED.
TAKE PRESIDENT JOHN F. KENNEDY'S INAUGURATION, FOR EXAMPLE...
THE WORLD IS VERY DIFFERENT NOW. FOR MAN HOLDS IN HIS MORTAL HANDS THE POWER TO ABOLISH ALL FORMS OF HUMAN POVERTY AND ALL FORMS OF HUMAN LIFE.
AFTER...
THANK YOU FOR COMING, MISTER VEIDT.
I'D ALSO LIKE TO THANK YOU FOR ALL YOUR HELP AND SUPPORT DURING WHAT WAS TRULY A DIFFICULT CAMPAIGN.
IT WAS MY SINCERE PLEASURE, MISTER PRESIDENT.
IF THERE'S EVER ANYTHING ELSE I CAN DO TO HELP, PLEASE DON'T HESITATE TO ASK.
MUCH APPRECIATED.
ADRIAN VEIDT, I'D LIKE YOU TO MEET MY WIFE JACQUELINE.
JACK HAS MENTIONED YOU OFTEN, MISTER VEIDT.
GLAD TO FINALLY MEET YOU.
AS I WALKED AWAY, AN ODDLY FAMILIAR FACE MOVED UP TO SHAKE THE NEW PRESIDENT'S HAND--
LOOKIN' GOOD, JACK.
THE PRESIDENCY SUITS YA.
THANKS, EDDIE. COMING FROM YOU...
--AND A COLD CHILL SUDDENLY RIPPLED UP MY SPINE...

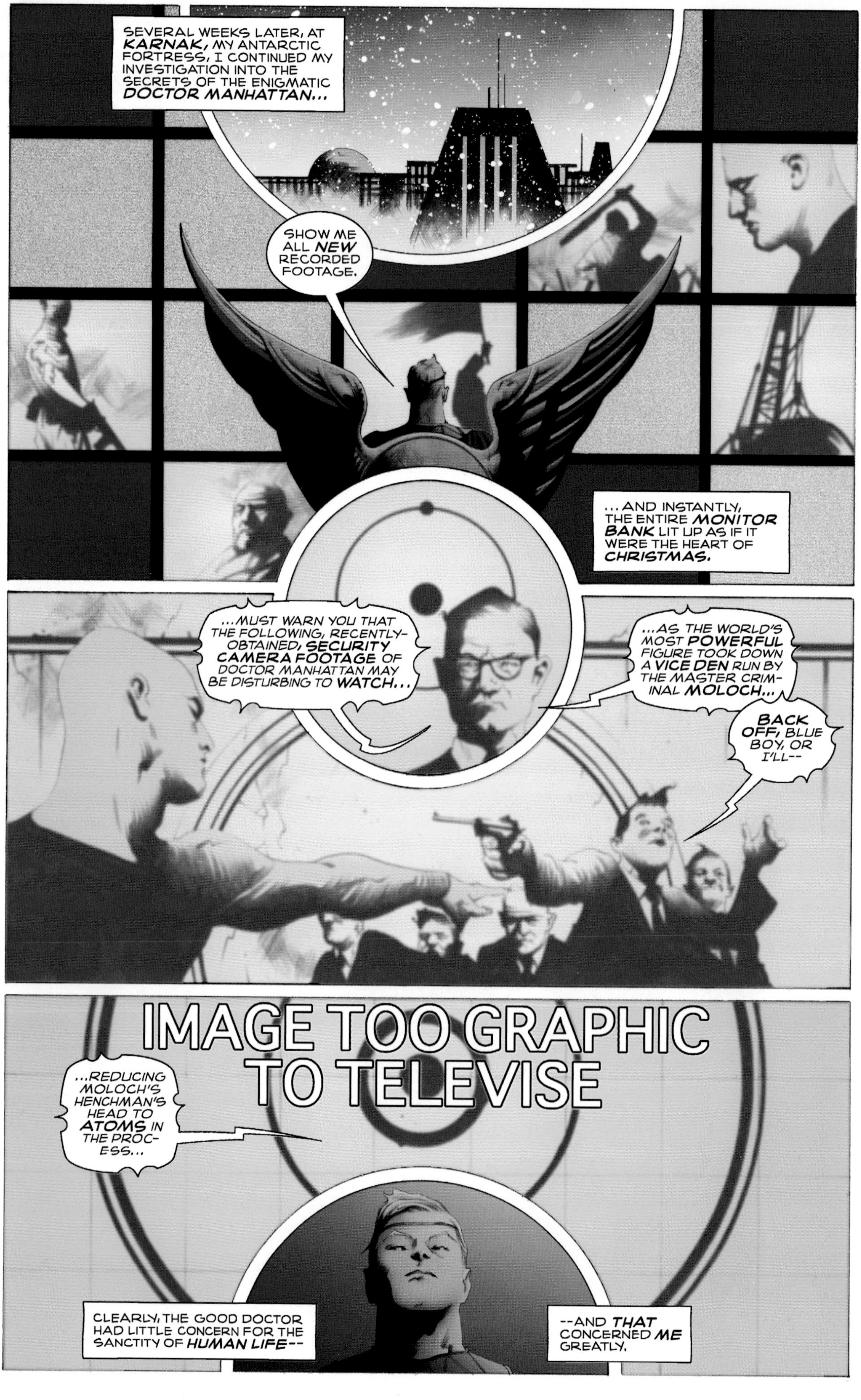

SEVERAL WEEKS LATER, AT KARNAK, MY ANTARCTIC FORTRESS, I CONTINUED MY INVESTIGATION INTO THE SECRETS OF THE ENIGMATIC DOCTOR MANHATTAN...
SHOW ME ALL NEW RECORDED FOOTAGE.
...AND INSTANTLY, THE ENTIRE MONITOR BANK LIT UP AS IF IT WERE THE HEART OF CHRISTMAS.
...MUST WARN YOU THAT THE FOLLOWING, RECENTLY-OBTAINED, SECURITY CAMERA FOOTAGE OF DOCTOR MANHATTAN MAY BE DISTURBING TO WATCH...
...AS THE WORLD'S MOST POWERFUL FIGURE TOOK DOWN A VICE DEN RUN BY THE MASTER CRIMINAL MOLOCH...
BACK OFF, BLUE BOY, OR I'LL--
IMAGE TOO GRAPHIC TO TELEVISE
...REDUCING MOLOCH'S HENCHMAN'S HEAD TO ATOMS IN THE PROCESS...
CLEARLY, THE GOOD DOCTOR HAD LITTLE CONCERN FOR THE SANCTITY OF HUMAN LIFE--
--AND THAT CONCERNED ME GREATLY.

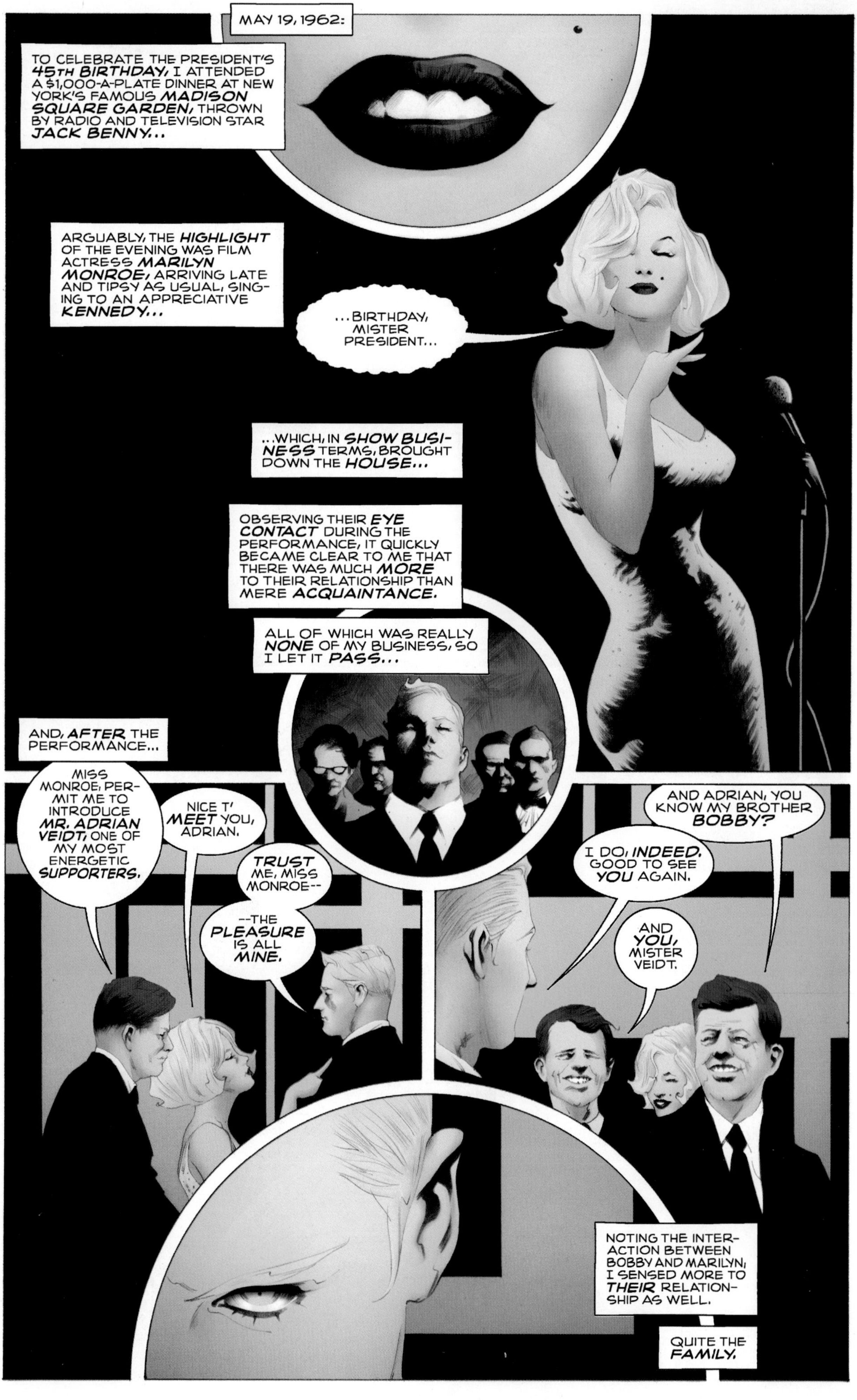
MAY 19, 1962:
TO CELEBRATE THE PRESIDENT'S 45TH BIRTHDAY, I ATTENDED A $1,000-A-PLATE DINNER AT NEW YORK'S FAMOUS MADISON SQUARE GARDEN, THROWN BY RADIO AND TELEVISION STAR JACK BENNY...
ARGUABLY, THE HIGHLIGHT OF THE EVENING WAS FILM ACTRESS MARILYN MONROE, ARRIVING LATE AND TIPSY AS USUAL, SINGING TO AN APPRECIATIVE KENNEDY...
...BIRTHDAY, MISTER PRESIDENT...
...WHICH, IN SHOW BUSINESS TERMS, BROUGHT DOWN THE HOUSE...
OBSERVING THEIR EYE CONTACT DURING THE PERFORMANCE, IT QUICKLY BECAME CLEAR TO ME THAT THERE WAS MUCH MORE TO THEIR RELATIONSHIP THAN MERE ACQUAINTANCE.
ALL OF WHICH WAS REALLY NONE OF MY BUSINESS, SO I LET IT PASS...
AND, AFTER THE PERFORMANCE...
MISS MONROE, PERMIT ME TO INTRODUCE MR. ADRIAN VEIDT, ONE OF MY MOST ENERGETIC SUPPORTERS.
NICE T' MEET YOU, ADRIAN.
TRUST ME, MISS MONROE--
--THE PLEASURE IS ALL MINE.
AND ADRIAN, YOU KNOW MY BROTHER BOBBY?
I DO, INDEED. GOOD TO SEE YOU AGAIN.
AND YOU, MISTER VEIDT.
NOTING THE INTERACTION BETWEEN BOBBY AND MARILYN, I SENSED MORE TO THEIR RELATIONSHIP AS WELL.
QUITE THE FAMILY.

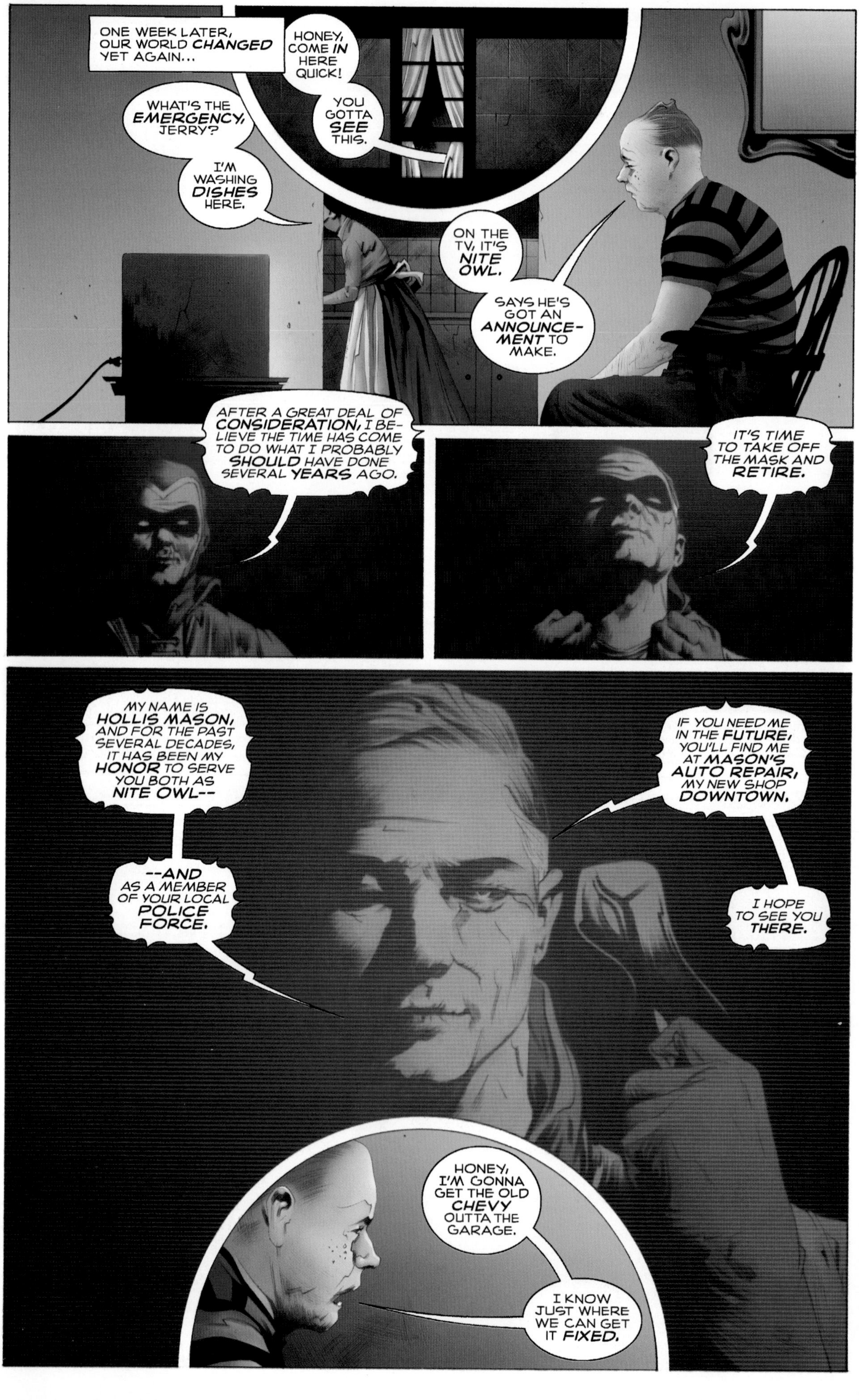
ONE WEEK LATER, OUR WORLD CHANGED YET AGAIN...
HONEY, COME IN HERE QUICK!
YOU GOTTA SEE THIS.
WHAT'S THE EMERGENCY, JERRY?
I'M WASHING DISHES HERE.
ON THE TV, IT'S NITE OWL.
SAYS HE'S GOT AN ANNOUNCEMENT TO MAKE.
AFTER A GREAT DEAL OF CONSIDERATION, I BELIEVE THE TIME HAS COME TO DO WHAT I PROBABLY SHOULD HAVE DONE SEVERAL YEARS AGO.
IT'S TIME TO TAKE OFF THE MASK AND RETIRE.
MY NAME IS HOLLIS MASON, AND FOR THE PAST SEVERAL DECADES, IT HAS BEEN MY HONOR TO SERVE YOU BOTH AS NITE OWL--
--AND AS A MEMBER OF YOUR LOCAL POLICE FORCE.
IF YOU NEED ME IN THE FUTURE, YOU'LL FIND ME AT MASON'S AUTO REPAIR, MY NEW SHOP DOWNTOWN.
I HOPE TO SEE YOU THERE.
HONEY, I'M GONNA GET THE OLD CHEVY OUTTA THE GARAGE.
I KNOW JUST WHERE WE CAN GET IT FIXED.

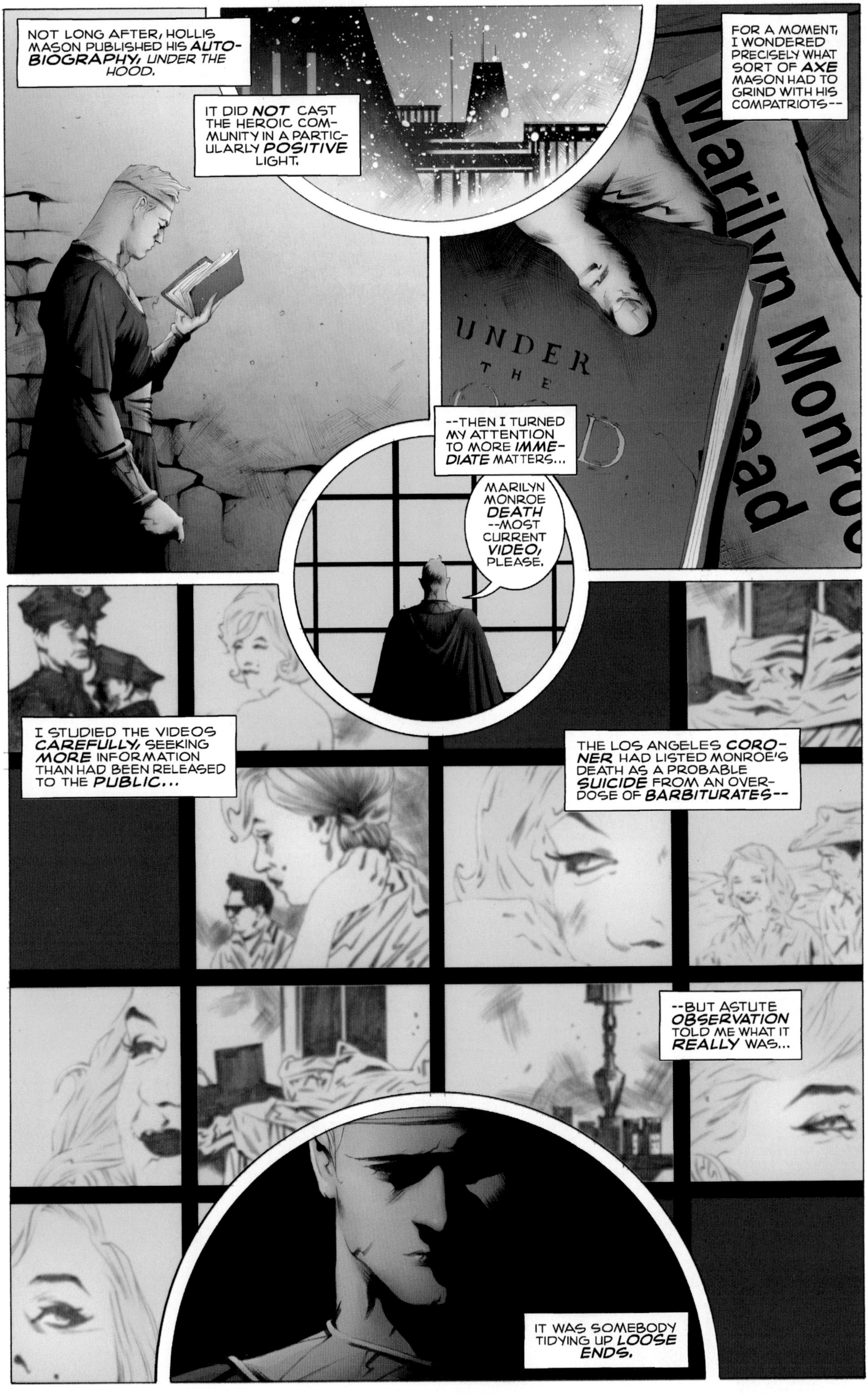
NOT LONG AFTER, HOLLIS MASON PUBLISHED HIS AUTO-BIOGRAPHY, UNDER THE HOOD.
IT DID NOT CAST THE HEROIC COM-MUNITY IN A PARTIC-ULARLY POSITIVE LIGHT.
FOR A MOMENT, I WONDERED PRECISELY WHAT SORT OF AXE MASON HAD TO GRIND WITH HIS COMPATRIOTS--
Marilyn Monroe Dead
UNDER THE
--THEN I TURNED MY ATTENTION TO MORE IMME-DIATE MATTERS...
MARILYN MONROE DEATH --MOST CURRENT VIDEO, PLEASE.
I STUDIED THE VIDEOS CAREFULLY, SEEKING MORE INFORMATION THAN HAD BEEN RELEASED TO THE PUBLIC...
THE LOS ANGELES CORO-NER HAD LISTED MONROE'S DEATH AS A PROBABLE SUICIDE FROM AN OVER-DOSE OF BARBITURATES--
--BUT ASTUTE OBSERVATION TOLD ME WHAT IT REALLY WAS...
IT WAS SOMEBODY TIDYING UP LOOSE ENDS.

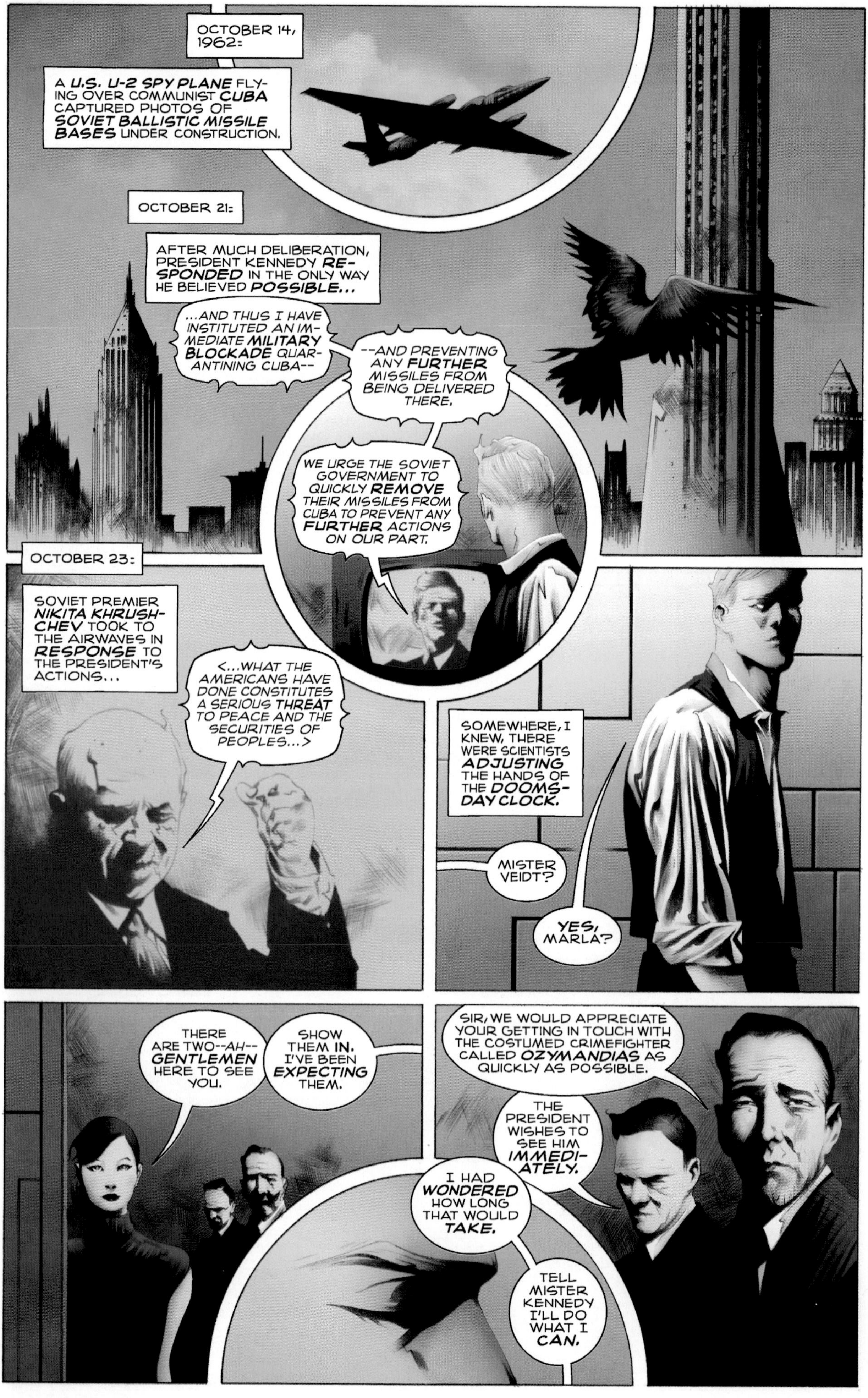
OCTOBER 14, 1962:
A U.S. U-2 SPY PLANE FLYING OVER COMMUNIST CUBA CAPTURED PHOTOS OF SOVIET BALLISTIC MISSILE BASES UNDER CONSTRUCTION.
OCTOBER 21:
AFTER MUCH DELIBERATION, PRESIDENT KENNEDY RESPONDED IN THE ONLY WAY HE BELIEVED POSSIBLE...
...AND THUS I HAVE INSTITUTED AN IMMEDIATE MILITARY BLOCKADE QUARANTINING CUBA--
--AND PREVENTING ANY FURTHER MISSILES FROM BEING DELIVERED THERE.
WE URGE THE SOVIET GOVERNMENT TO QUICKLY REMOVE THEIR MISSILES FROM CUBA TO PREVENT ANY FURTHER ACTIONS ON OUR PART.
OCTOBER 23:
SOVIET PREMIER NIKITA KHRUSHCHEV TOOK TO THE AIRWAVES IN RESPONSE TO THE PRESIDENT'S ACTIONS...
<...WHAT THE AMERICANS HAVE DONE CONSTITUTES A SERIOUS THREAT TO PEACE AND THE SECURITIES OF PEOPLES...>
SOMEWHERE, I KNEW, THERE WERE SCIENTISTS ADJUSTING THE HANDS OF THE DOOMSDAY CLOCK.
MISTER VEIDT?
YES, MARLA?
THERE ARE TWO--AH--GENTLEMEN HERE TO SEE YOU.
SHOW THEM IN. I'VE BEEN EXPECTING THEM.
SIR, WE WOULD APPRECIATE YOUR GETTING IN TOUCH WITH THE COSTUMED CRIMEFIGHTER CALLED OZYMANDIAS AS QUICKLY AS POSSIBLE.
THE PRESIDENT WISHES TO SEE HIM IMMEDIATELY.
I HAD WONDERED HOW LONG THAT WOULD TAKE.
TELL MISTER KENNEDY I'LL DO WHAT I CAN.

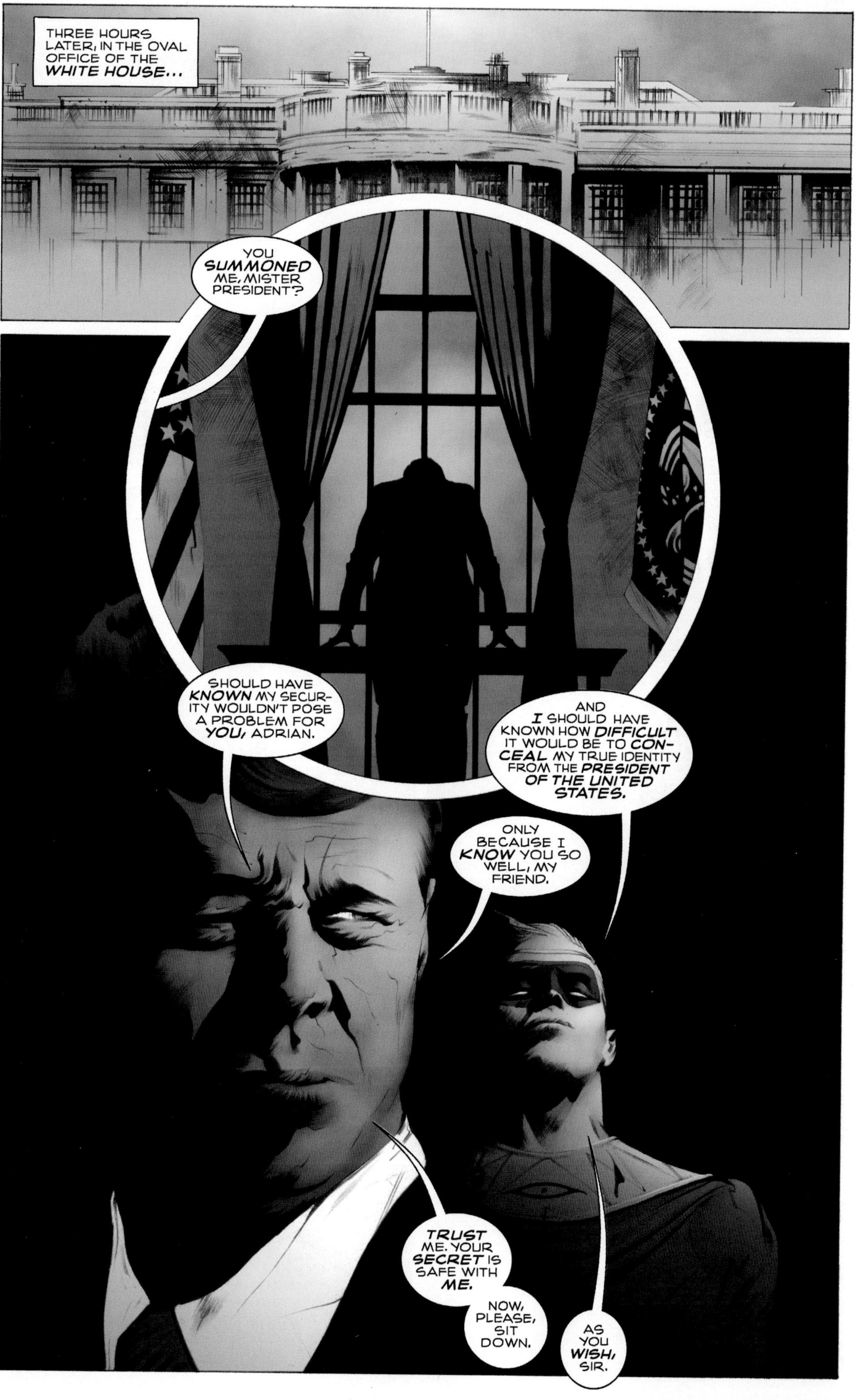
THREE HOURS LATER, IN THE OVAL OFFICE OF THE WHITE HOUSE...
YOU SUMMONED ME, MISTER PRESIDENT?
SHOULD HAVE KNOWN MY SECURITY WOULDN'T POSE A PROBLEM FOR YOU, ADRIAN.
AND I SHOULD HAVE KNOWN HOW DIFFICULT IT WOULD BE TO CONCEAL MY TRUE IDENTITY FROM THE PRESIDENT OF THE UNITED STATES.
ONLY BECAUSE I KNOW YOU SO WELL, MY FRIEND.
TRUST ME. YOUR SECRET IS SAFE WITH ME.
NOW, PLEASE, SIT DOWN.
AS YOU WISH, SIR.

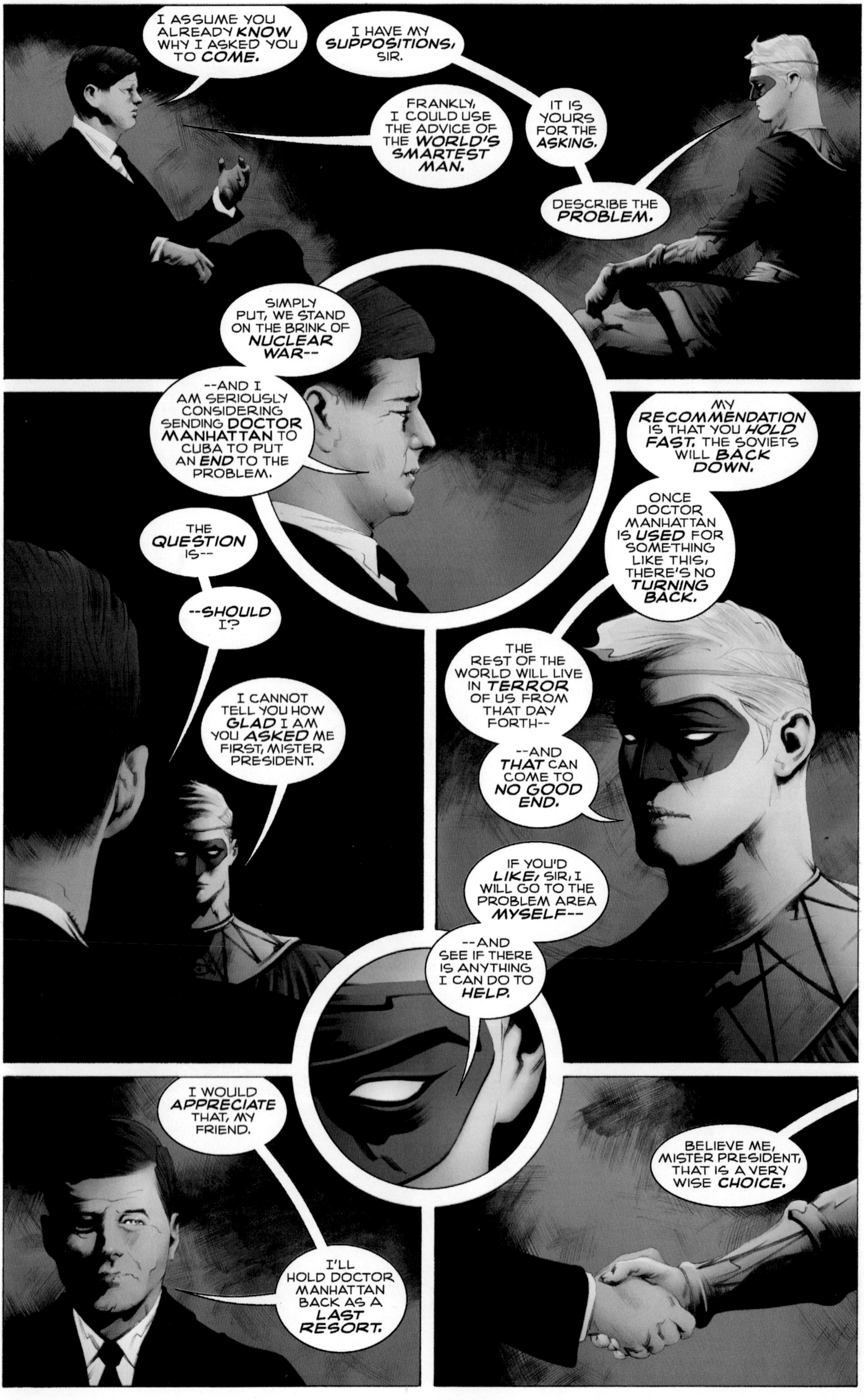
I ASSUME YOU ALREADY KNOW WHY I ASKED YOU TO COME.
I HAVE MY SUPPOSITIONS, SIR.
FRANKLY, I COULD USE THE ADVICE OF THE WORLD'S SMARTEST MAN.
IT IS YOURS FOR THE ASKING.
DESCRIBE THE PROBLEM.
SIMPLY PUT, WE STAND ON THE BRINK OF NUCLEAR WAR--
--AND I AM SERIOUSLY CONSIDERING SENDING DOCTOR MANHATTAN TO CUBA TO PUT AN END TO THE PROBLEM.
THE QUESTION IS--
--SHOULD I?
I CANNOT TELL YOU HOW GLAD I AM YOU ASKED ME FIRST, MISTER PRESIDENT.
MY RECOMMENDATION IS THAT YOU HOLD FAST. THE SOVIETS WILL BACK DOWN.
ONCE DOCTOR MANHATTAN IS USED FOR SOMETHING LIKE THIS, THERE'S NO TURNING BACK.
THE REST OF THE WORLD WILL LIVE IN TERROR OF US FROM THAT DAY FORTH--
--AND THAT CAN COME TO NO GOOD END.
IF YOU'D LIKE, SIR, I WILL GO TO THE PROBLEM AREA MYSELF--
--AND SEE IF THERE IS ANYTHING I CAN DO TO HELP.
I WOULD APPRECIATE THAT, MY FRIEND.
I'LL HOLD DOCTOR MANHATTAN BACK AS A LAST RESORT.
BELIEVE ME, MISTER PRESIDENT, THAT IS A VERY WISE CHOICE.

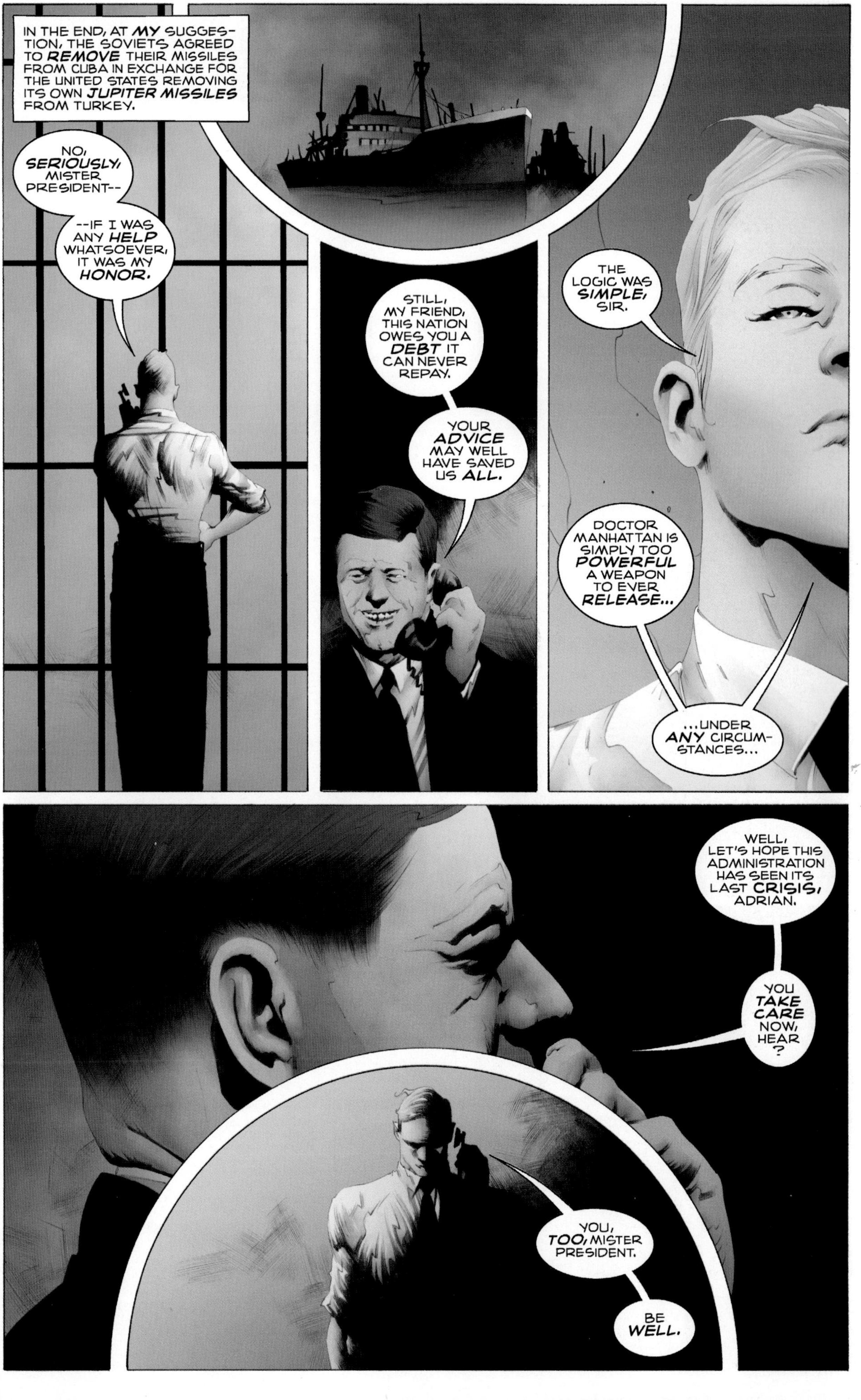
IN THE END, AT MY SUGGESTION, THE SOVIETS AGREED TO REMOVE THEIR MISSILES FROM CUBA IN EXCHANGE FOR THE UNITED STATES REMOVING ITS OWN JUPITER MISSILES FROM TURKEY.
NO, SERIOUSLY, MISTER PRESIDENT--
--IF I WAS ANY HELP WHATSOEVER, IT WAS MY HONOR.
STILL, MY FRIEND, THIS NATION OWES YOU A DEBT IT CAN NEVER REPAY.
YOUR ADVICE MAY WELL HAVE SAVED US ALL.
THE LOGIC WAS SIMPLE, SIR.
DOCTOR MANHATTAN IS SIMPLY TOO POWERFUL A WEAPON TO EVER RELEASE...
...UNDER ANY CIRCUMSTANCES...
WELL, LET'S HOPE THIS ADMINISTRATION HAS SEEN ITS LAST CRISIS, ADRIAN.
YOU TAKE CARE NOW, HEAR?
YOU, TOO, MISTER PRESIDENT.
BE WELL.

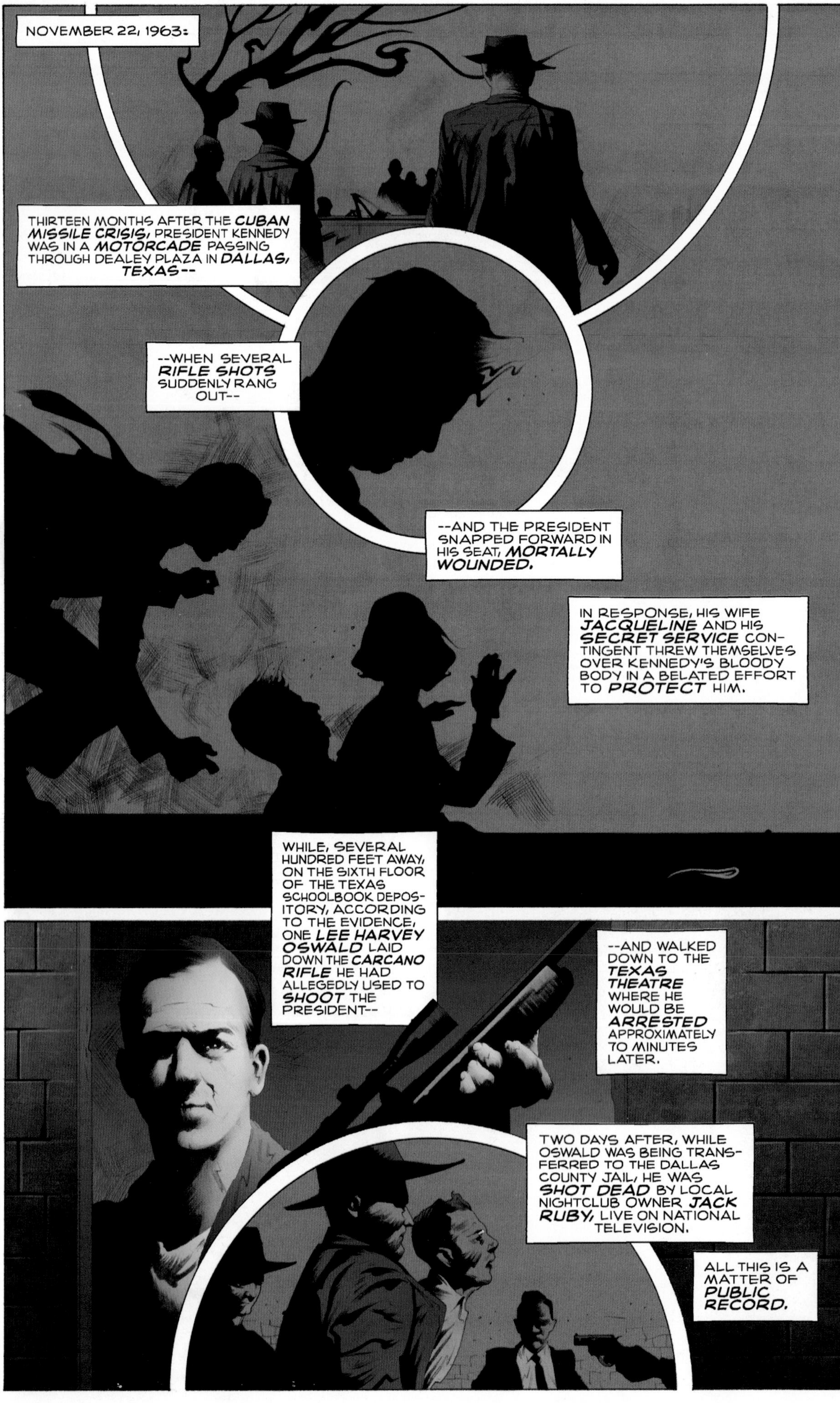
NOVEMBER 22, 1963:
THIRTEEN MONTHS AFTER THE CUBAN MISSILE CRISIS, PRESIDENT KENNEDY WAS IN A MOTORCADE PASSING THROUGH DEALEY PLAZA IN DALLAS, TEXAS--
--WHEN SEVERAL RIFLE SHOTS SUDDENLY RANG OUT--
--AND THE PRESIDENT SNAPPED FORWARD IN HIS SEAT, MORTALLY WOUNDED.
IN RESPONSE, HIS WIFE JACQUELINE AND HIS SECRET SERVICE CONTINGENT THREW THEMSELVES OVER KENNEDY'S BLOODY BODY IN A BELATED EFFORT TO PROTECT HIM.
WHILE, SEVERAL HUNDRED FEET AWAY, ON THE SIXTH FLOOR OF THE TEXAS SCHOOLBOOK DEPOSITORY, ACCORDING TO THE EVIDENCE, ONE LEE HARVEY OSWALD LAID DOWN THE CARCANO RIFLE HE HAD ALLEGEDLY USED TO SHOOT THE PRESIDENT--
--AND WALKED DOWN TO THE TEXAS THEATRE WHERE HE WOULD BE ARRESTED APPROXIMATELY 70 MINUTES LATER.
TWO DAYS AFTER, WHILE OSWALD WAS BEING TRANSFERRED TO THE DALLAS COUNTY JAIL, HE WAS SHOT DEAD BY LOCAL NIGHTCLUB OWNER JACK RUBY, LIVE ON NATIONAL TELEVISION.
ALL THIS IS A MATTER OF PUBLIC RECORD.

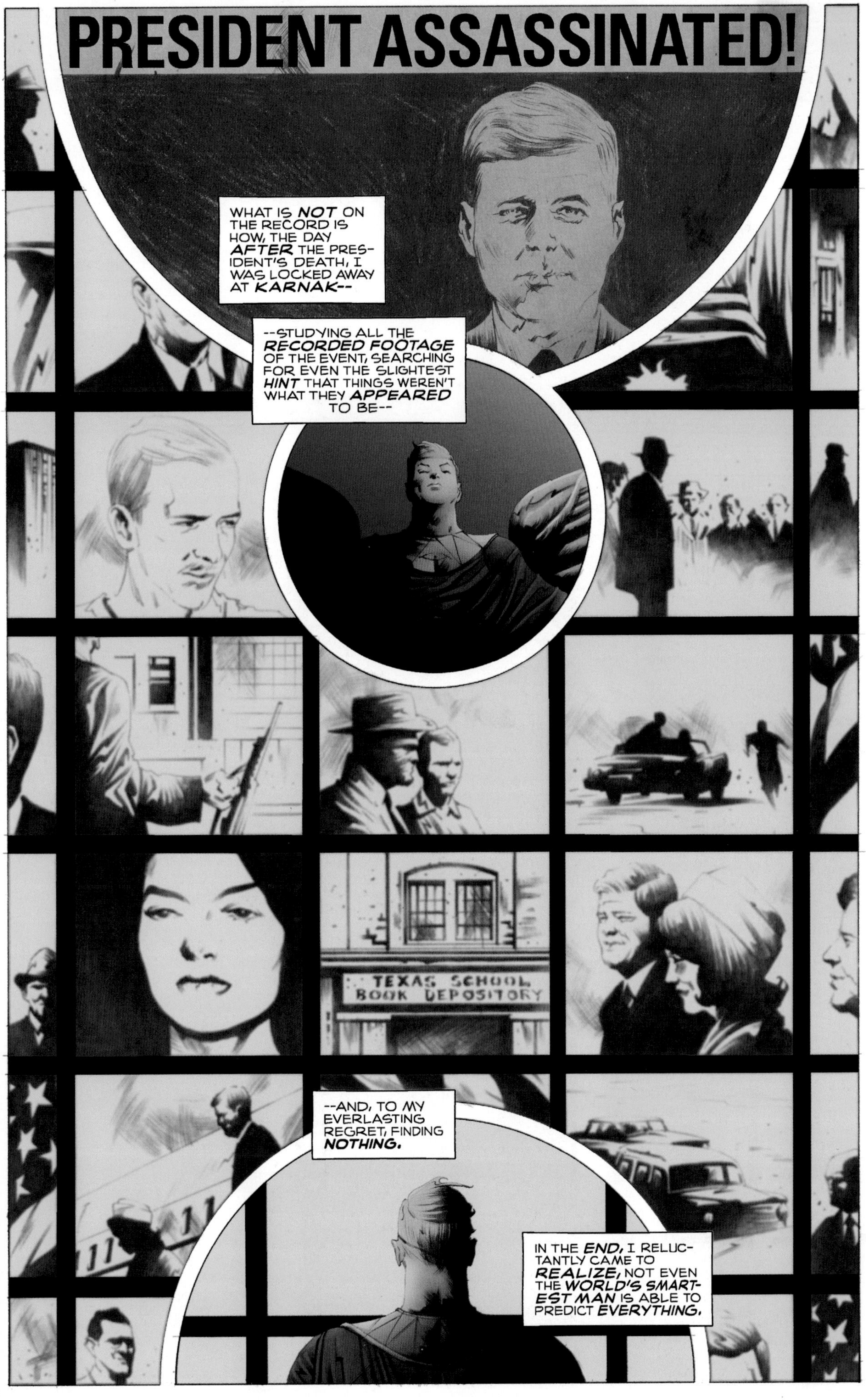
PRESIDENT ASSASSINATED!
WHAT IS NOT ON THE RECORD IS HOW, THE DAY AFTER THE PRESIDENT'S DEATH, I WAS LOCKED AWAY AT KARNAK--
--STUDYING ALL THE RECORDED FOOTAGE OF THE EVENT, SEARCHING FOR EVEN THE SLIGHTEST HINT THAT THINGS WEREN'T WHAT THEY APPEARED TO BE--
TEXAS SCHOOL BOOK DEPOSITORY
--AND, TO MY EVERLASTING REGRET, FINDING NOTHING.
IN THE END, I RELUCTANTLY CAME TO REALIZE, NOT EVEN THE WORLD'S SMARTEST MAN IS ABLE TO PREDICT EVERYTHING.

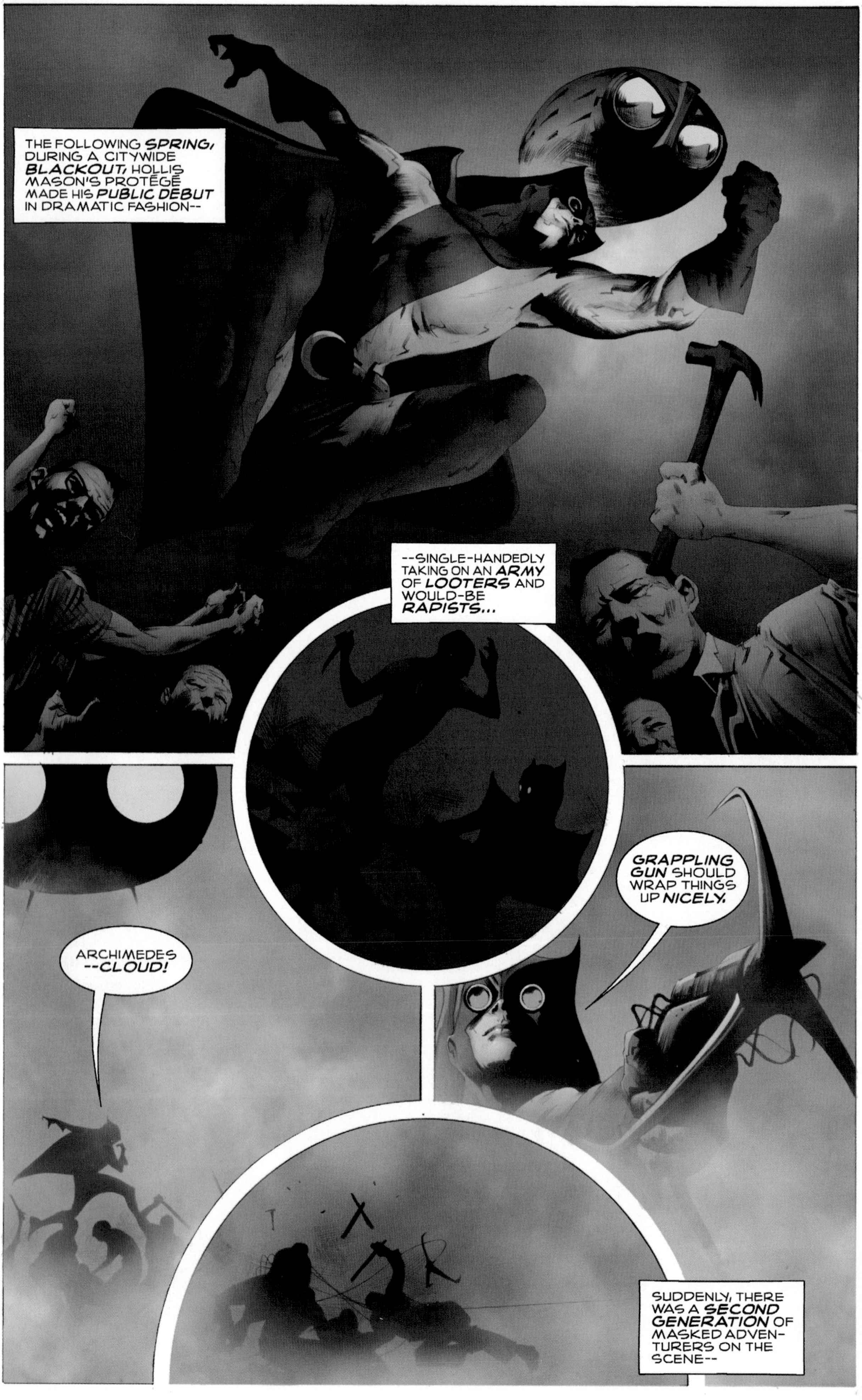
THE FOLLOWING SPRING, DURING A CITYWIDE BLACKOUT, HOLLIS MASON'S PROTÉGÉ MADE HIS PUBLIC DEBUT IN DRAMATIC FASHION--
--SINGLE-HANDEDLY TAKING ON AN ARMY OF LOOTERS AND WOULD-BE RAPISTS...
ARCHIMEDES --CLOUD!
GRAPPLING GUN SHOULD WRAP THINGS UP NICELY.
SUDDENLY, THERE WAS A SECOND GENERATION OF MASKED ADVEN-TURERS ON THE SCENE--

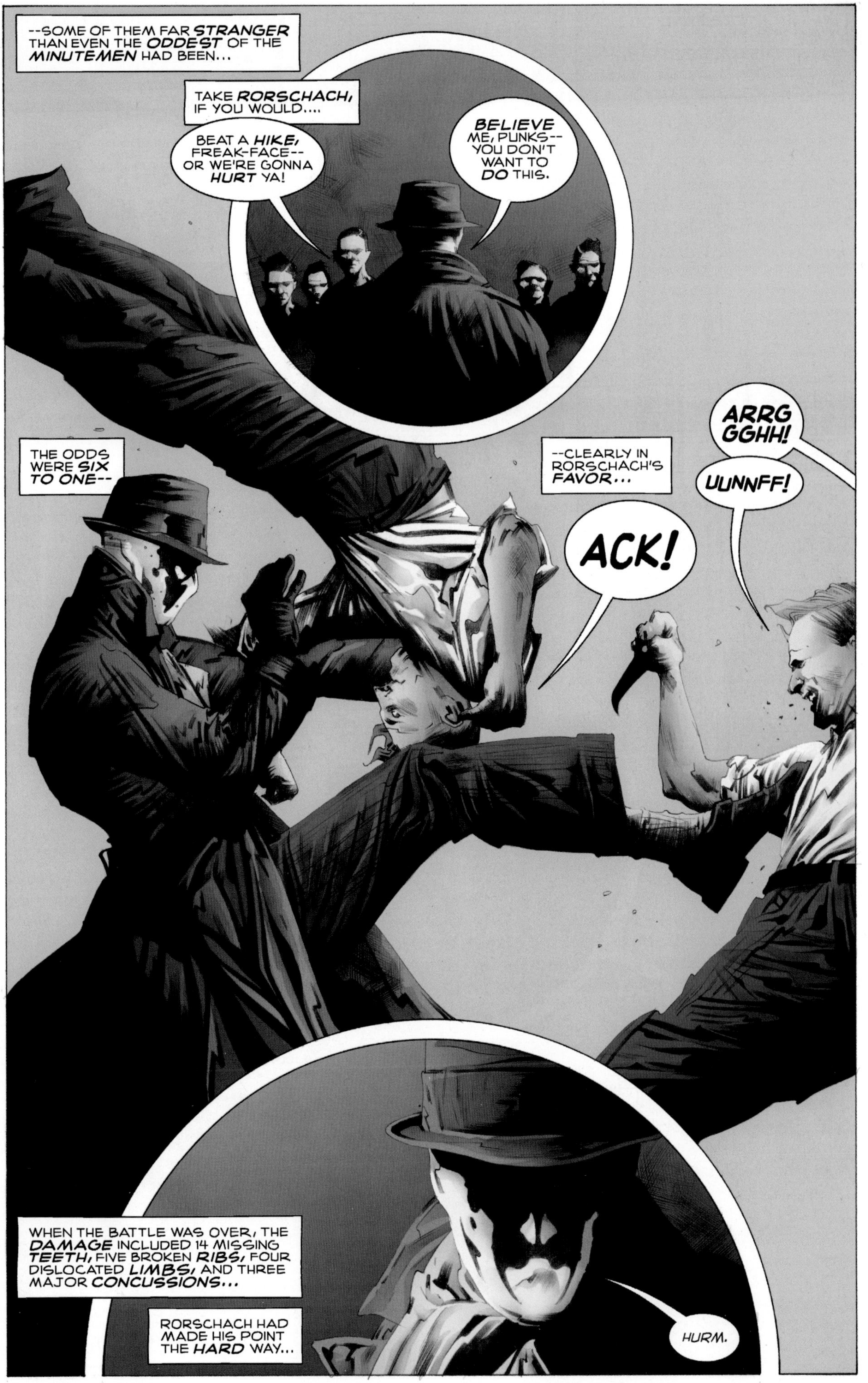
--SOME OF THEM FAR STRANGER THAN EVEN THE ODDEST OF THE MINUTEMEN HAD BEEN...
TAKE RORSCHACH, IF YOU WOULD....
BEAT A HIKE, FREAK-FACE-- OR WE'RE GONNA HURT YA!
BELIEVE ME, PUNKS-- YOU DON'T WANT TO DO THIS.
THE ODDS WERE SIX TO ONE--
--CLEARLY IN RORSCHACH'S FAVOR...
ARRG GGHH!
UUNNFF!
ACK!
WHEN THE BATTLE WAS OVER, THE DAMAGE INCLUDED 14 MISSING TEETH, FIVE BROKEN RIBS, FOUR DISLOCATED LIMBS, AND THREE MAJOR CONCUSSIONS...
RORSCHACH HAD MADE HIS POINT THE HARD WAY...
HURM.

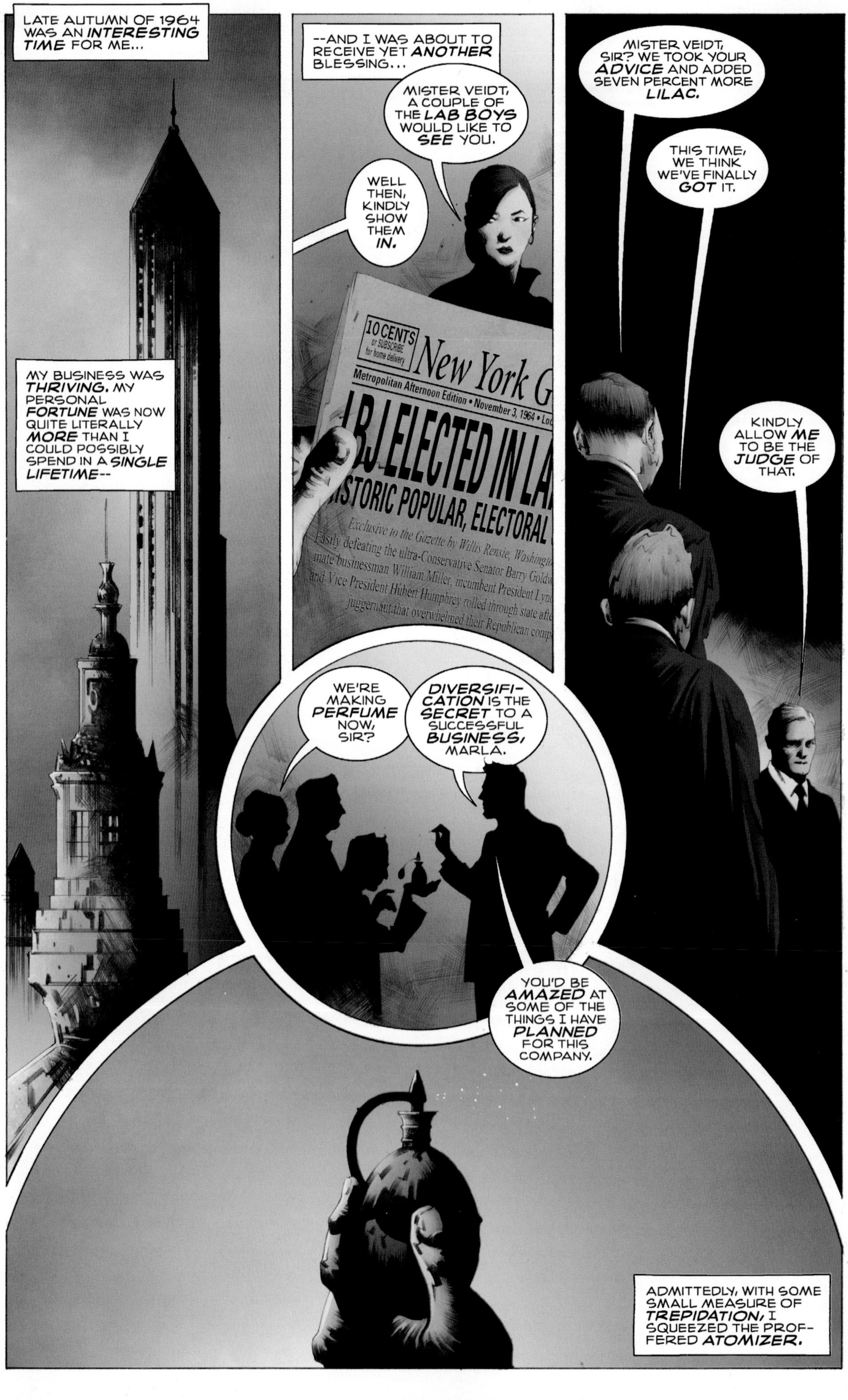

LATE AUTUMN OF 1964 WAS AN INTERESTING TIME FOR ME...
MY BUSINESS WAS THRIVING. MY PERSONAL FORTUNE WAS NOW QUITE LITERALLY MORE THAN I COULD POSSIBLY SPEND IN A SINGLE LIFETIME--
--AND I WAS ABOUT TO RECEIVE YET ANOTHER BLESSING...
MISTER VEIDT, A COUPLE OF THE LAB BOYS WOULD LIKE TO SEE YOU.
WELL THEN, KINDLY SHOW THEM IN.
10 CENTS or SUBSCRIBE for home delivery
Metropolitan Afternoon Edition • November 3, 1964
Exclusive to the Gazette by Willis Rensie
Easily defeating the ultra-Conservative Senator Barry
inate businessman William Miller, incumbent President
and Vice President Hubert Humphrey rolled through state
juggernaut that overwhelmed their Republican
MISTER VEIDT, SIR? WE TOOK YOUR ADVICE AND ADDED SEVEN PERCENT MORE LILAC.
THIS TIME, WE THINK WE'VE FINALLY GOT IT.
KINDLY ALLOW ME TO BE THE JUDGE OF THAT.
WE'RE MAKING PERFUME NOW, SIR?
DIVERSIFICATION IS THE SECRET TO A SUCCESSFUL BUSINESS, MARLA.
YOU'D BE AMAZED AT SOME OF THE THINGS I HAVE PLANNED FOR THIS COMPANY.
ADMITTEDLY, WITH SOME SMALL MEASURE OF TREPIDATION, I SQUEEZED THE PROFFERED ATOMIZER.

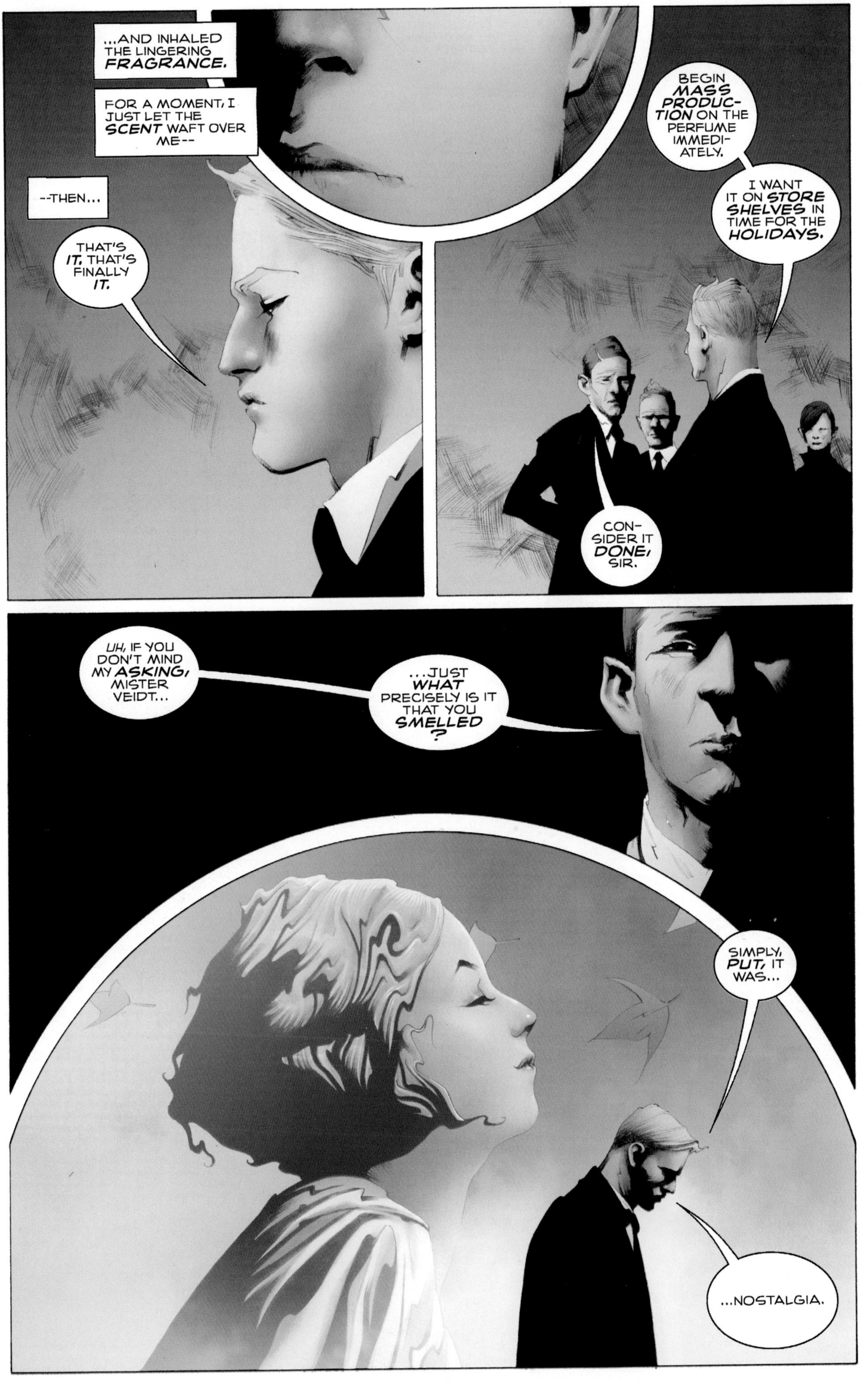
...AND INHALED THE LINGERING FRAGRANCE.
FOR A MOMENT, I JUST LET THE SCENT WAFT OVER ME--
--THEN...
THAT'S IT. THAT'S FINALLY IT.
BEGIN MASS PRODUCTION ON THE PERFUME IMMEDIATELY.
I WANT IT ON STORE SHELVES IN TIME FOR THE HOLIDAYS.
CONSIDER IT DONE, SIR.
UH, IF YOU DON'T MIND MY ASKING, MISTER VEIDT...
...JUST WHAT PRECISELY IS IT THAT YOU SMELLED?
SIMPLY, PUT, IT WAS...
...NOSTALGIA.

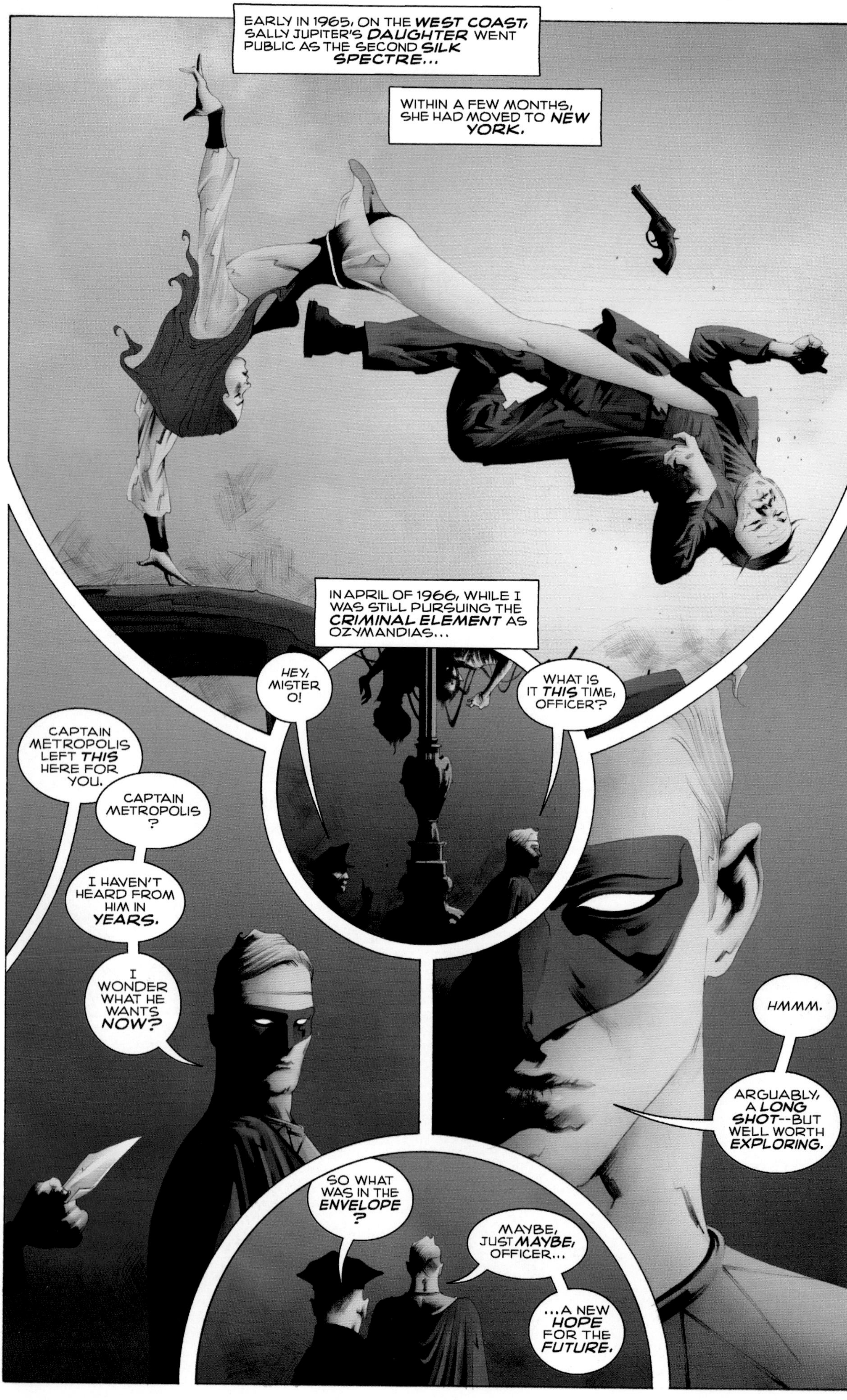

EARLY IN 1965, ON THE WEST COAST, SALLY JUPITER'S DAUGHTER WENT PUBLIC AS THE SECOND SILK SPECTRE...
WITHIN A FEW MONTHS, SHE HAD MOVED TO NEW YORK.
IN APRIL OF 1966, WHILE I WAS STILL PURSUING THE CRIMINAL ELEMENT AS OZYMANDIAS...
HEY, MISTER O!
WHAT IS IT THIS TIME, OFFICER?
CAPTAIN METROPOLIS LEFT THIS HERE FOR YOU.
CAPTAIN METROPOLIS?
I HAVEN'T HEARD FROM HIM IN YEARS.
I WONDER WHAT HE WANTS NOW?
HMMM.
ARGUABLY, A LONG SHOT--BUT WELL WORTH EXPLORING.
SO WHAT WAS IN THE ENVELOPE?
MAYBE, JUST MAYBE, OFFICER...
...A NEW HOPE FOR THE FUTURE.

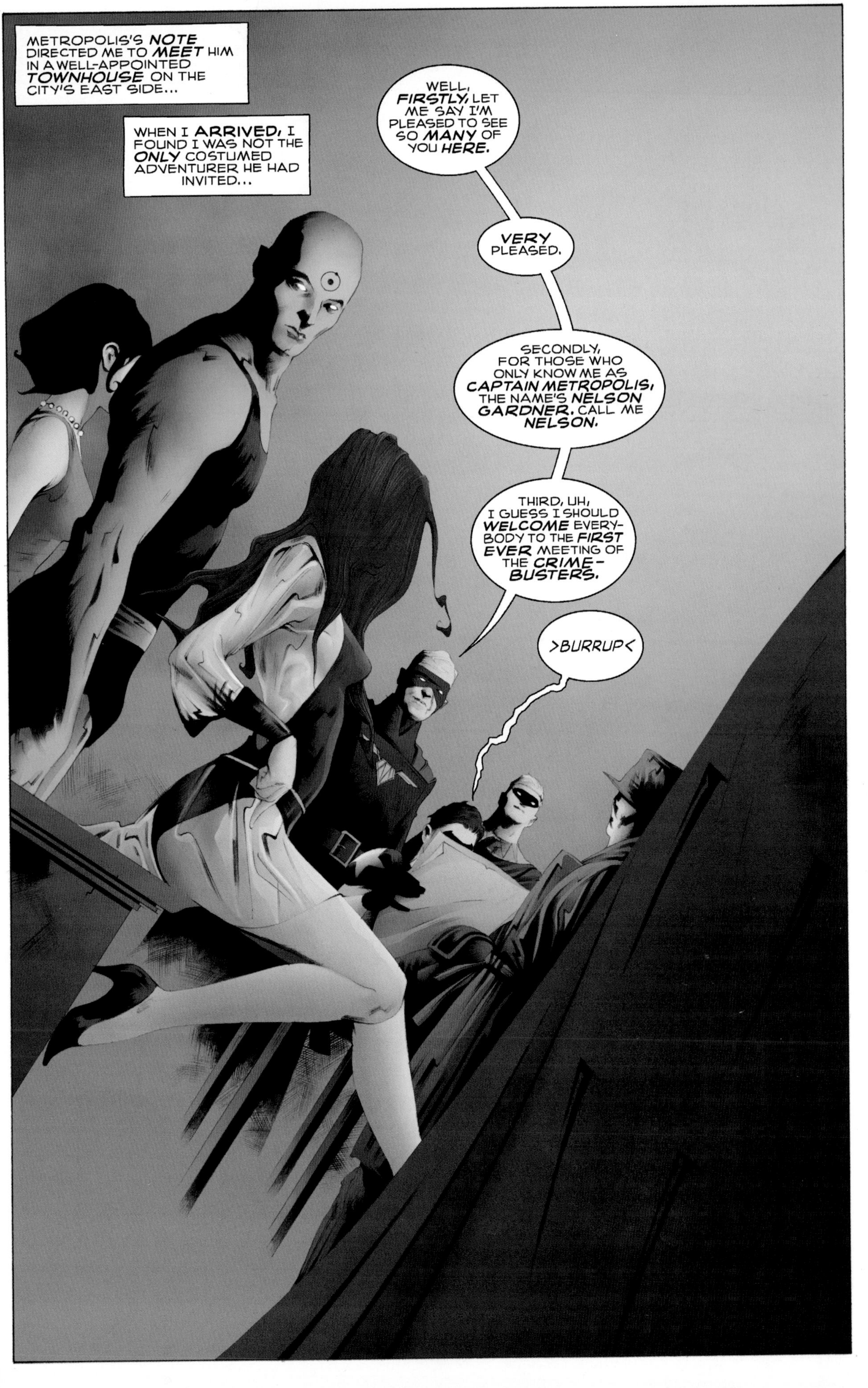
METROPOLIS'S NOTE DIRECTED ME TO MEET HIM IN A WELL-APPOINTED TOWNHOUSE ON THE CITY'S EAST SIDE...
WHEN I ARRIVED, I FOUND I WAS NOT THE ONLY COSTUMED ADVENTURER HE HAD INVITED...
WELL, FIRSTLY, LET ME SAY I'M PLEASED TO SEE SO MANY OF YOU HERE.
VERY PLEASED.
SECONDLY, FOR THOSE WHO ONLY KNOW ME AS CAPTAIN METROPOLIS, THE NAME'S NELSON GARDNER. CALL ME NELSON.
THIRD, UH, I GUESS I SHOULD WELCOME EVERY-BODY TO THE FIRST EVER MEETING OF THE CRIME-BUSTERS.
>BURRUP<

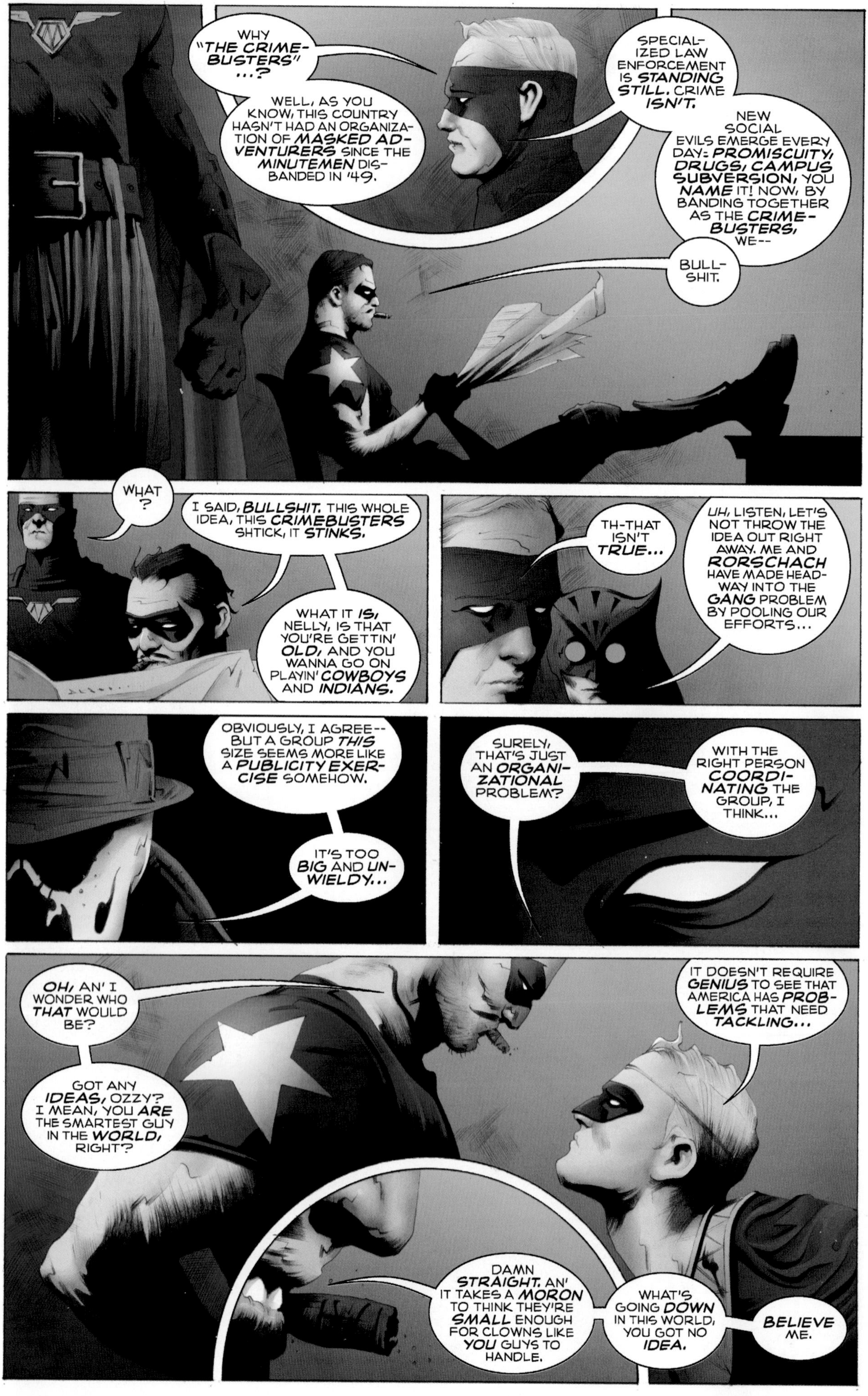

WHY "THE CRIME-BUSTERS" ...?
WELL, AS YOU KNOW, THIS COUNTRY HASN'T HAD AN ORGANIZATION OF MASKED ADVENTURERS SINCE THE MINUTEMEN DISBANDED IN '49.
SPECIALIZED LAW ENFORCEMENT IS STANDING STILL. CRIME ISN'T.
NEW SOCIAL EVILS EMERGE EVERY DAY: PROMISCUITY, DRUGS, CAMPUS SUBVERSION, YOU NAME IT! NOW, BY BANDING TOGETHER AS THE CRIME-BUSTERS, WE--
BULLSHIT.
WHAT?
I SAID, BULLSHIT. THIS WHOLE IDEA, THIS CRIMEBUSTERS SHTICK, IT STINKS.
WHAT IT IS, NELLY, IS THAT YOU'RE GETTIN' OLD, AND YOU WANNA GO ON PLAYIN' COWBOYS AND INDIANS.
TH-THAT ISN'T TRUE...
UH, LISTEN, LET'S NOT THROW THE IDEA OUT RIGHT AWAY. ME AND RORSCHACH HAVE MADE HEADWAY INTO THE GANG PROBLEM BY POOLING OUR EFFORTS...
OBVIOUSLY, I AGREE-- BUT A GROUP THIS SIZE SEEMS MORE LIKE A PUBLICITY EXERCISE SOMEHOW.
IT'S TOO BIG AND UNWIELDY...
SURELY, THAT'S JUST AN ORGANIZATIONAL PROBLEM?
WITH THE RIGHT PERSON COORDINATING THE GROUP, I THINK...
OH, AN' I WONDER WHO THAT WOULD BE?
GOT ANY IDEAS, OZZY? I MEAN, YOU ARE THE SMARTEST GUY IN THE WORLD, RIGHT?
IT DOESN'T REQUIRE GENIUS TO SEE THAT AMERICA HAS PROBLEMS THAT NEED TACKLING...
DAMN STRAIGHT. AN' IT TAKES A MORON TO THINK THEY'RE SMALL ENOUGH FOR CLOWNS LIKE YOU GUYS TO HANDLE.
WHAT'S GOING DOWN IN THIS WORLD, YOU GOT NO IDEA.
BELIEVE ME.

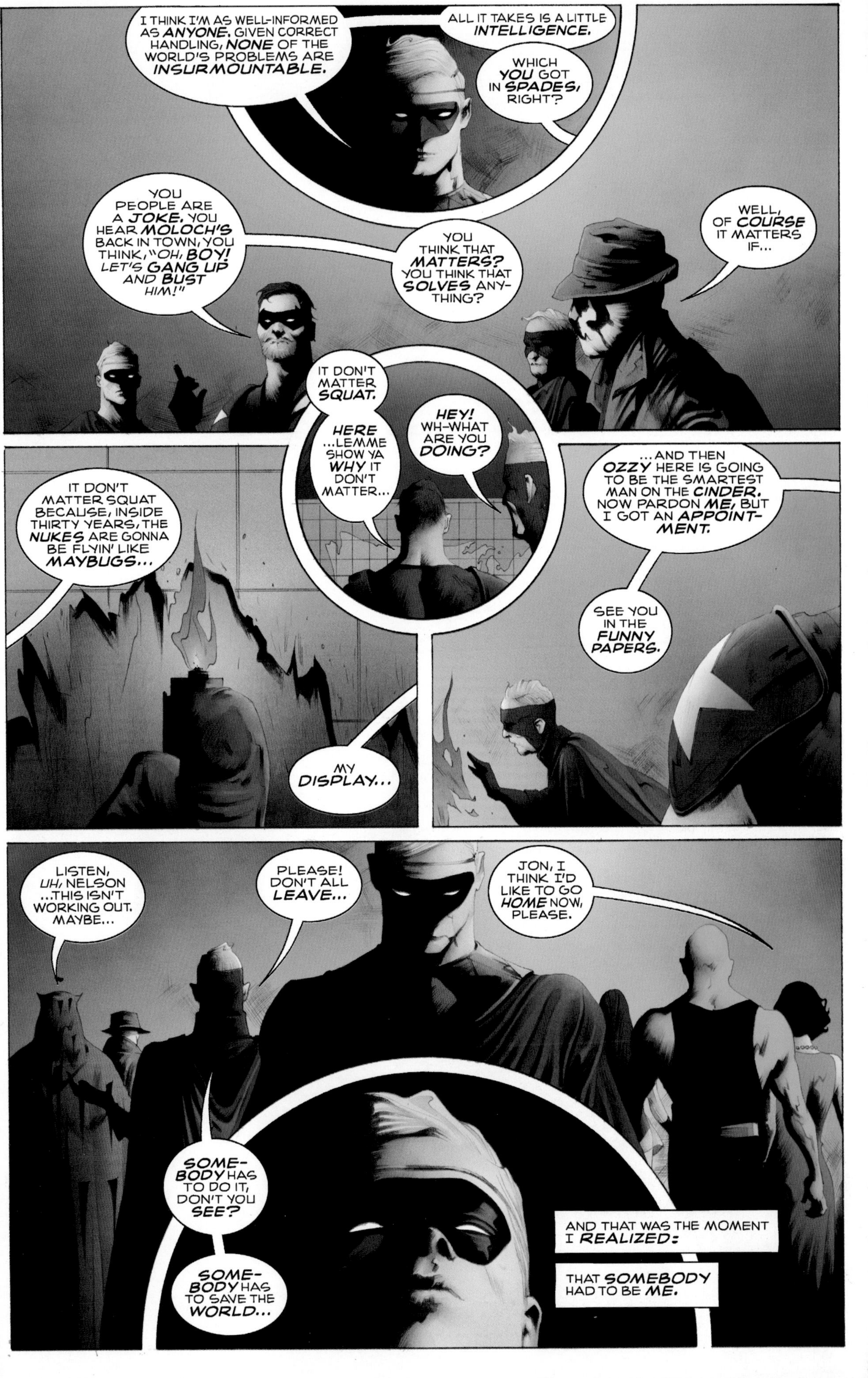
I THINK I'M AS WELL-INFORMED AS ANYONE. GIVEN CORRECT HANDLING, NONE OF THE WORLD'S PROBLEMS ARE INSURMOUNTABLE.
ALL IT TAKES IS A LITTLE INTELLIGENCE.
WHICH YOU GOT IN SPADES, RIGHT?
YOU PEOPLE ARE A JOKE. YOU HEAR MOLOCH'S BACK IN TOWN, YOU THINK, "OH, BOY! LET'S GANG UP AND BUST HIM!"
YOU THINK THAT MATTERS? YOU THINK THAT SOLVES ANY-THING?
WELL, OF COURSE IT MATTERS IF...
IT DON'T MATTER SQUAT.
HERE ...LEMME SHOW YA WHY IT DON'T MATTER...
HEY! WH-WHAT ARE YOU DOING?
IT DON'T MATTER SQUAT BECAUSE, INSIDE THIRTY YEARS, THE NUKES ARE GONNA BE FLYIN' LIKE MAYBUGS...
MY DISPLAY...
...AND THEN OZZY HERE IS GOING TO BE THE SMARTEST MAN ON THE CINDER. NOW PARDON ME, BUT I GOT AN APPOINT-MENT.
SEE YOU IN THE FUNNY PAPERS.
LISTEN, UH, NELSON ...THIS ISN'T WORKING OUT. MAYBE...
PLEASE! DON'T ALL LEAVE...
JON, I THINK I'D LIKE TO GO HOME NOW, PLEASE.
SOME-BODY HAS TO DO IT, DON'T YOU SEE?
SOME-BODY HAS TO SAVE THE WORLD...
AND THAT WAS THE MOMENT I REALIZED:
THAT SOMEBODY HAD TO BE ME.

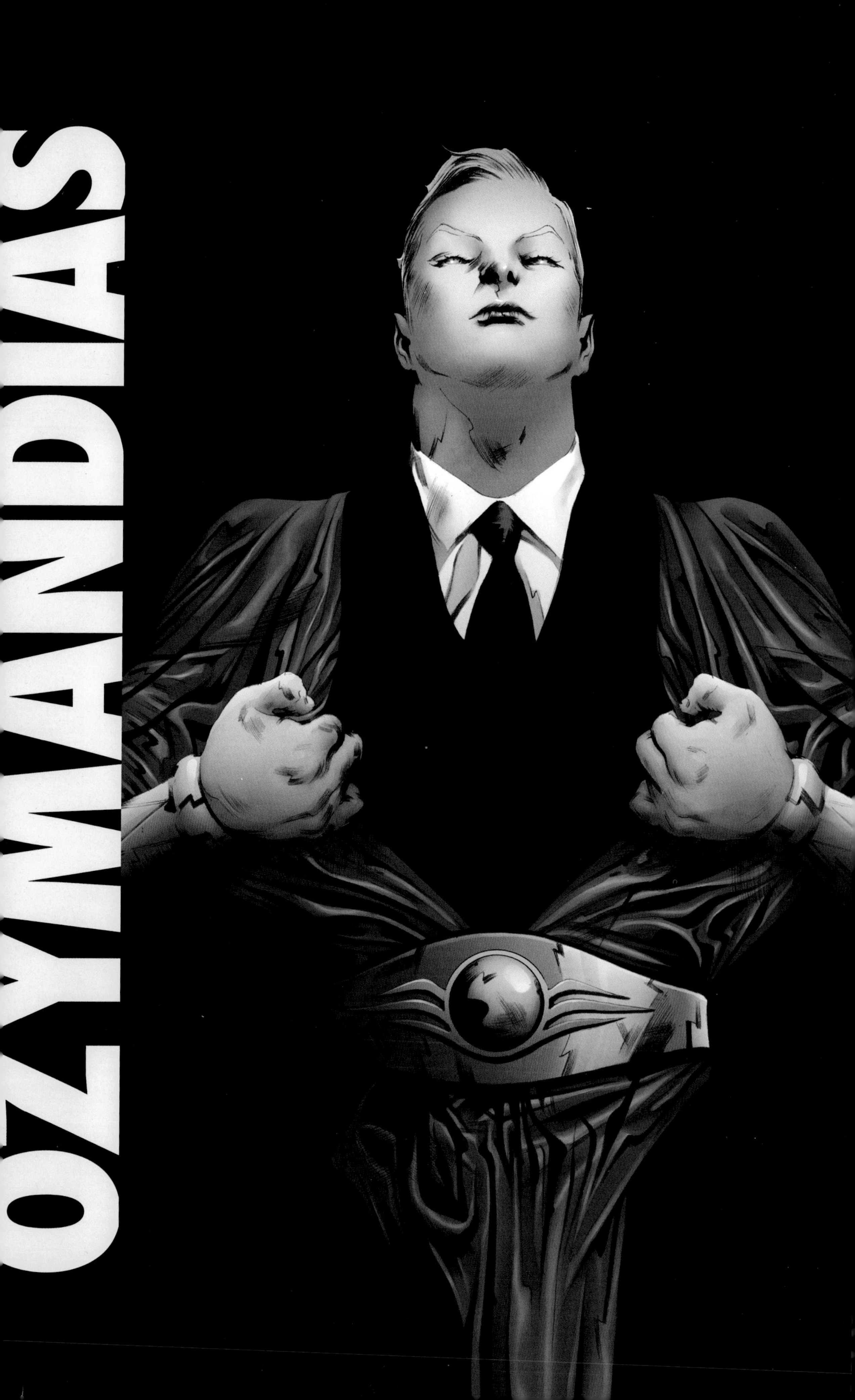
OZYMANDIAS

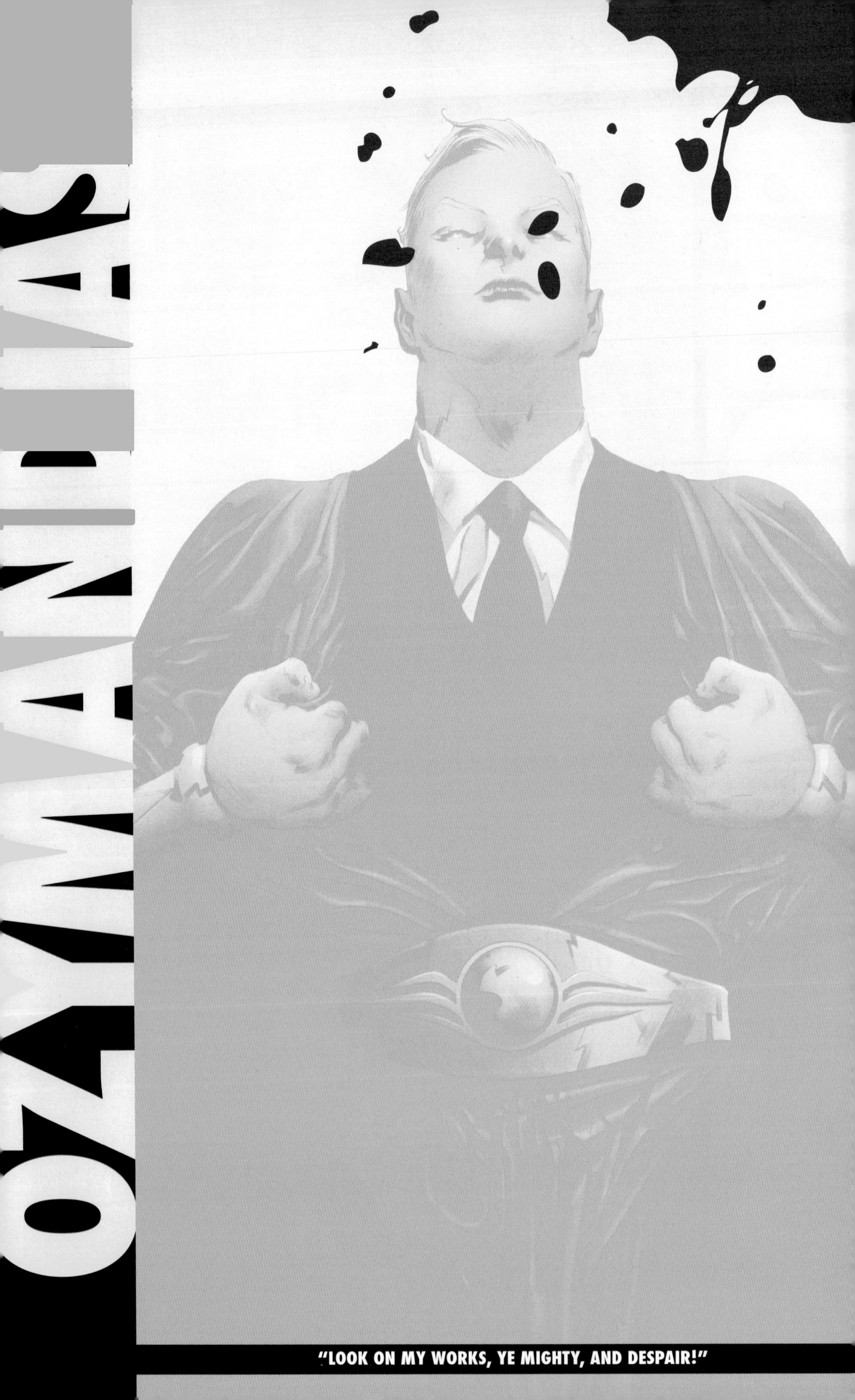
OZYMANDIAS
"LOOK ON MY WORKS, YE MIGHTY, AND DESPAIR!"

THESE LIFELESS THINGS...!

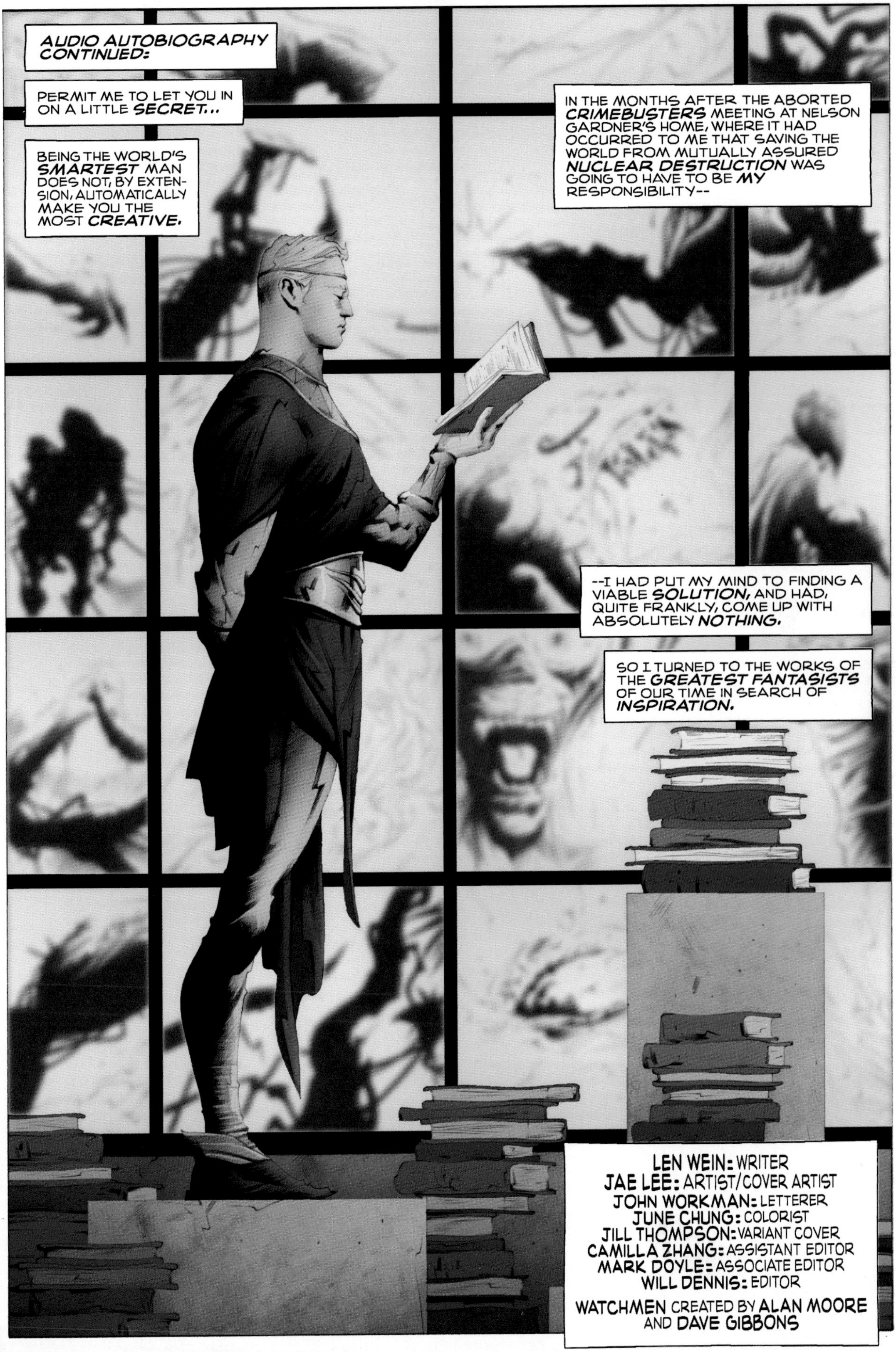

AUDIO AUTOBIOGRAPHY CONTINUED:
PERMIT ME TO LET YOU IN ON A LITTLE SECRET...
BEING THE WORLD'S SMARTEST MAN DOES NOT, BY EXTENSION, AUTOMATICALLY MAKE YOU THE MOST CREATIVE.
IN THE MONTHS AFTER THE ABORTED CRIMEBUSTERS MEETING AT NELSON GARDNER'S HOME, WHERE IT HAD OCCURRED TO ME THAT SAVING THE WORLD FROM MUTUALLY ASSURED NUCLEAR DESTRUCTION WAS GOING TO HAVE TO BE MY RESPONSIBILITY--
--I HAD PUT MY MIND TO FINDING A VIABLE SOLUTION, AND HAD, QUITE FRANKLY, COME UP WITH ABSOLUTELY NOTHING.
SO I TURNED TO THE WORKS OF THE GREATEST FANTASISTS OF OUR TIME IN SEARCH OF INSPIRATION.
LEN WEIN: WRITER
JAE LEE: ARTIST/COVER ARTIST
JOHN WORKMAN: LETTERER
JUNE CHUNG: COLORIST
JILL THOMPSON: VARIANT COVER
CAMILLA ZHANG: ASSISTANT EDITOR
MARK DOYLE: ASSOCIATE EDITOR
WILL DENNIS: EDITOR
WATCHMEN CREATED BY ALAN MOORE AND DAVE GIBBONS

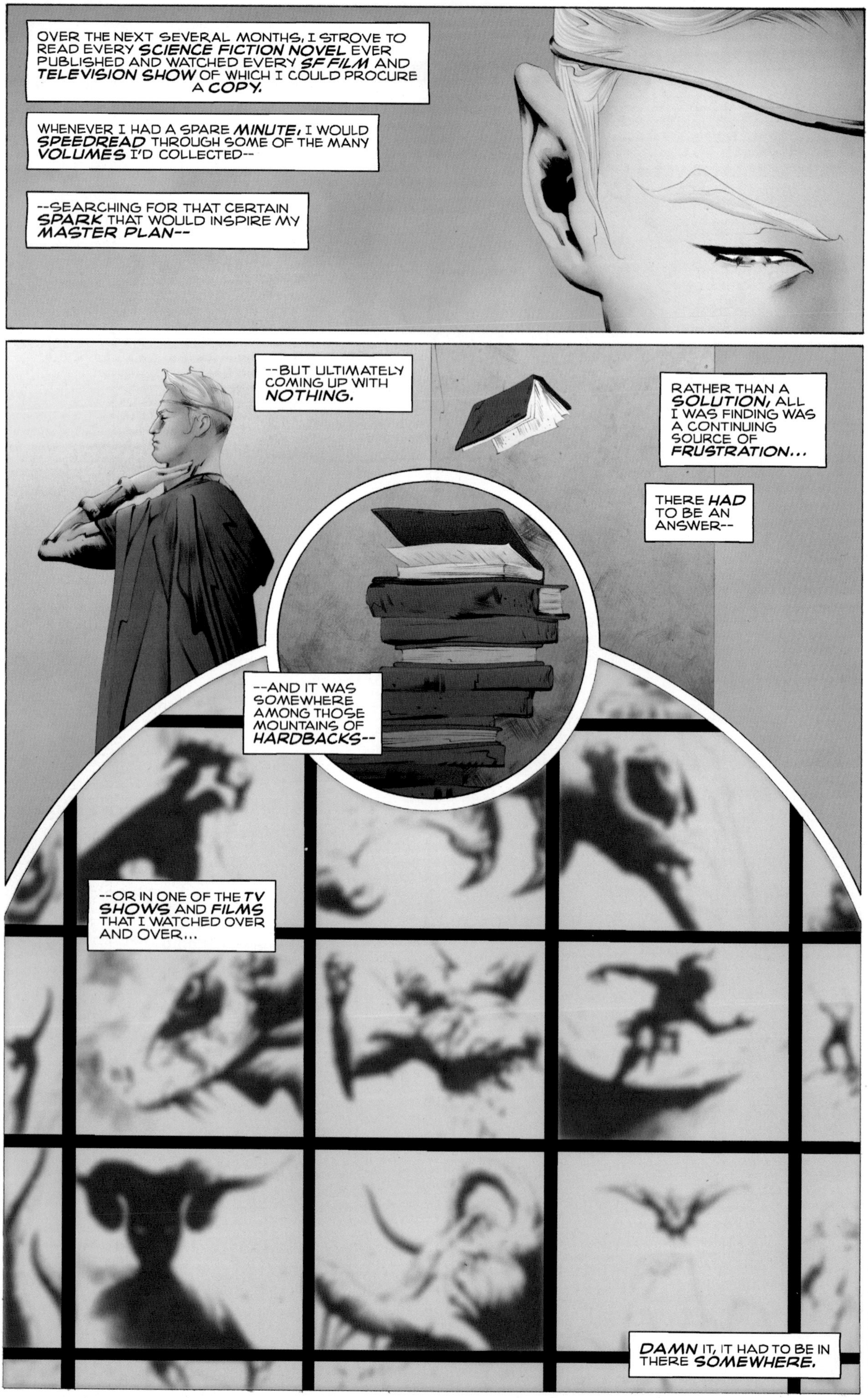
OVER THE NEXT SEVERAL MONTHS, I STROVE TO READ EVERY SCIENCE FICTION NOVEL EVER PUBLISHED AND WATCHED EVERY SF FILM AND TELEVISION SHOW OF WHICH I COULD PROCURE A COPY.
WHENEVER I HAD A SPARE MINUTE, I WOULD SPEEDREAD THROUGH SOME OF THE MANY VOLUMES I'D COLLECTED--
--SEARCHING FOR THAT CERTAIN SPARK THAT WOULD INSPIRE MY MASTER PLAN--
--BUT ULTIMATELY COMING UP WITH NOTHING.
RATHER THAN A SOLUTION, ALL I WAS FINDING WAS A CONTINUING SOURCE OF FRUSTRATION...
THERE HAD TO BE AN ANSWER--
--AND IT WAS SOMEWHERE AMONG THOSE MOUNTAINS OF HARDBACKS--
--OR IN ONE OF THE TV SHOWS AND FILMS THAT I WATCHED OVER AND OVER...
DAMN IT, IT HAD TO BE IN THERE SOMEWHERE.

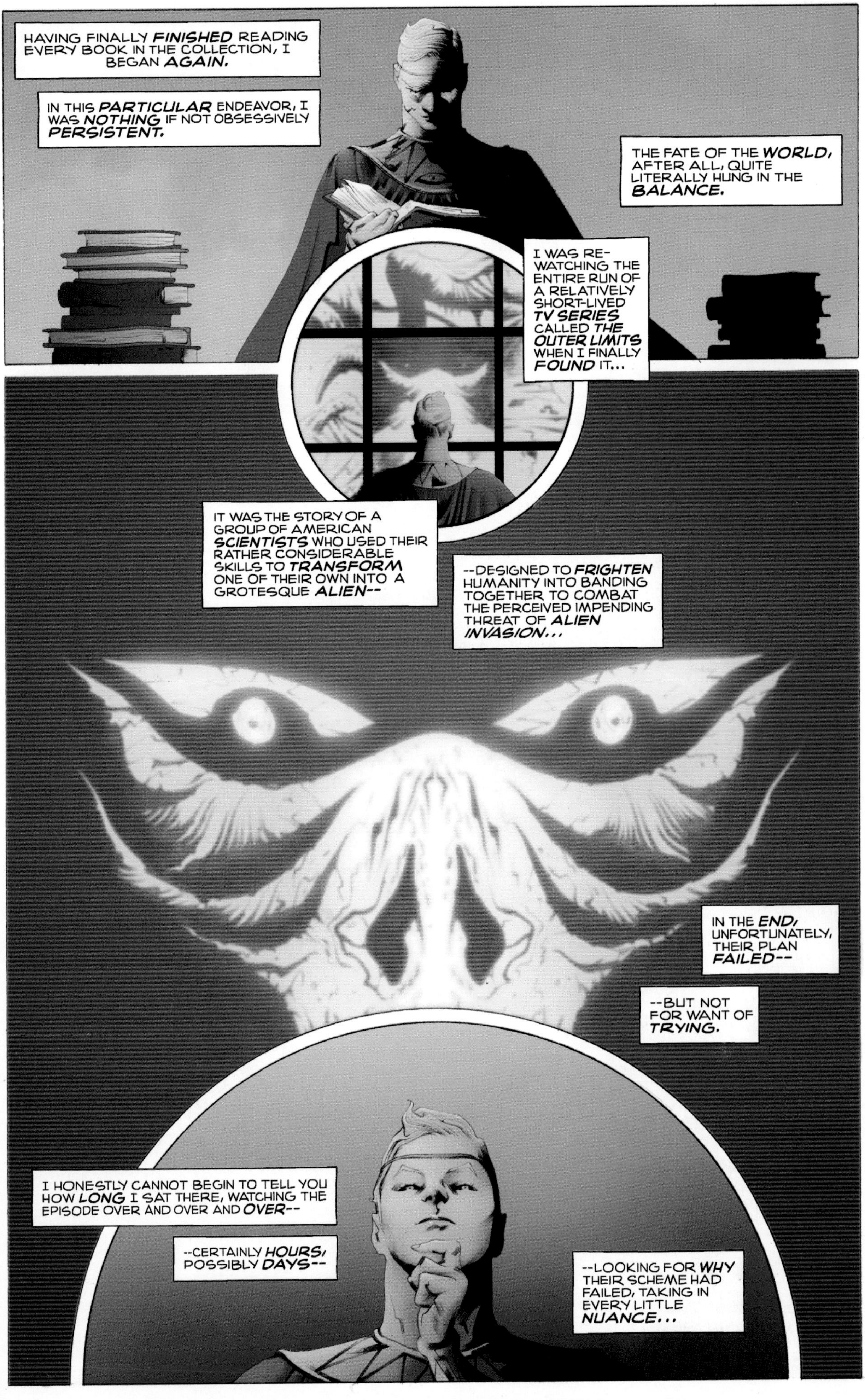
HAVING FINALLY FINISHED READING EVERY BOOK IN THE COLLECTION, I BEGAN AGAIN.
IN THIS PARTICULAR ENDEAVOR, I WAS NOTHING IF NOT OBSESSIVELY PERSISTENT.
THE FATE OF THE WORLD, AFTER ALL, QUITE LITERALLY HUNG IN THE BALANCE.
I WAS RE-WATCHING THE ENTIRE RUN OF A RELATIVELY SHORT-LIVED TV SERIES CALLED THE OUTER LIMITS WHEN I FINALLY FOUND IT...
IT WAS THE STORY OF A GROUP OF AMERICAN SCIENTISTS WHO USED THEIR RATHER CONSIDERABLE SKILLS TO TRANSFORM ONE OF THEIR OWN INTO A GROTESQUE ALIEN--
--DESIGNED TO FRIGHTEN HUMANITY INTO BANDING TOGETHER TO COMBAT THE PERCEIVED IMPENDING THREAT OF ALIEN INVASION...
IN THE END, UNFORTUNATELY, THEIR PLAN FAILED--
--BUT NOT FOR WANT OF TRYING.
I HONESTLY CANNOT BEGIN TO TELL YOU HOW LONG I SAT THERE, WATCHING THE EPISODE OVER AND OVER AND OVER--
--CERTAINLY HOURS, POSSIBLY DAYS--
--LOOKING FOR WHY THEIR SCHEME HAD FAILED, TAKING IN EVERY LITTLE NUANCE...

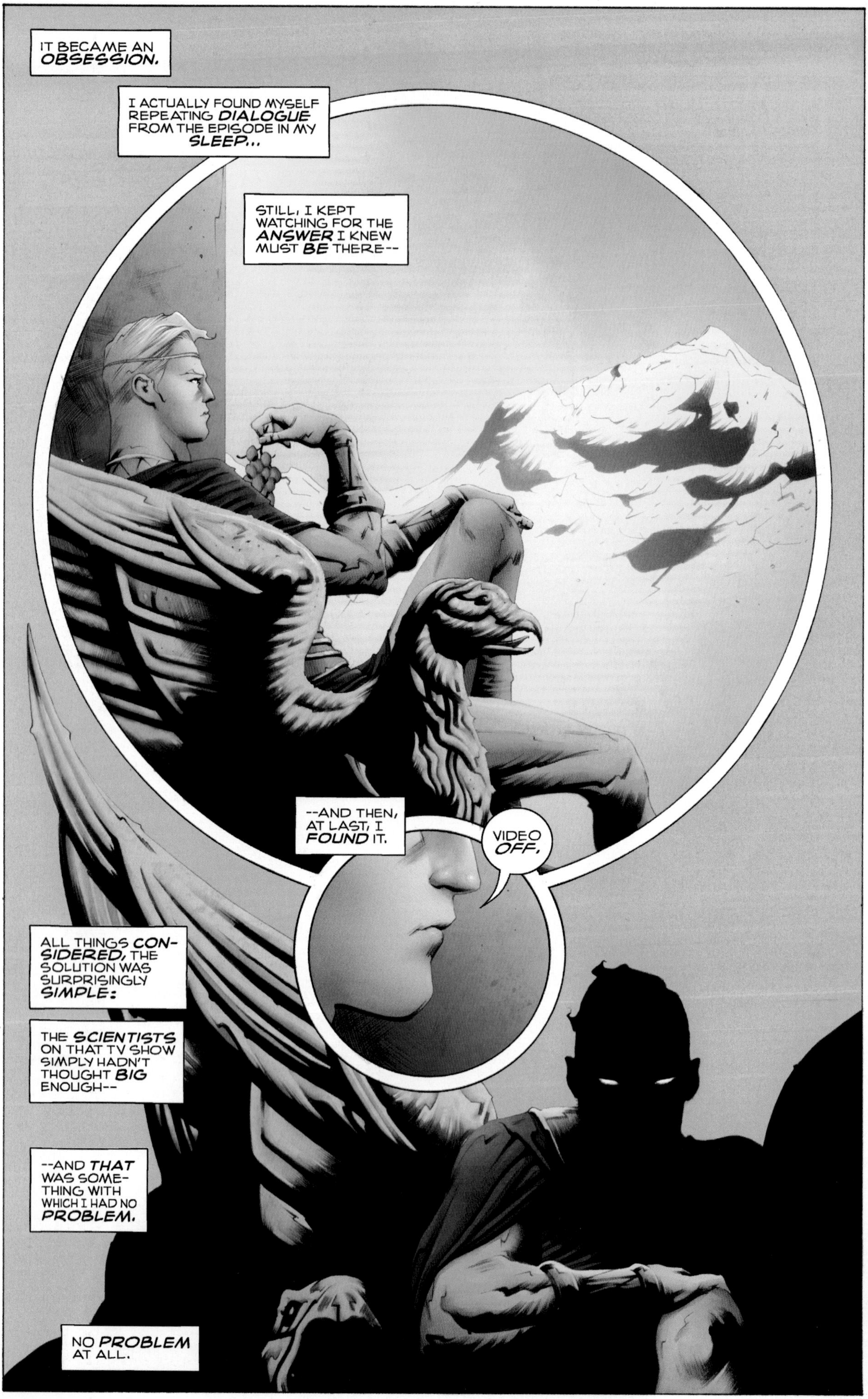
IT BECAME AN OBSESSION.
I ACTUALLY FOUND MYSELF REPEATING DIALOGUE FROM THE EPISODE IN MY SLEEP...
STILL, I KEPT WATCHING FOR THE ANSWER I KNEW MUST BE THERE--
--AND THEN, AT LAST, I FOUND IT.
VIDEO OFF.
ALL THINGS CONSIDERED, THE SOLUTION WAS SURPRISINGLY SIMPLE:
THE SCIENTISTS ON THAT TV SHOW SIMPLY HADN'T THOUGHT BIG ENOUGH--
--AND THAT WAS SOMETHING WITH WHICH I HAD NO PROBLEM.
NO PROBLEM AT ALL.

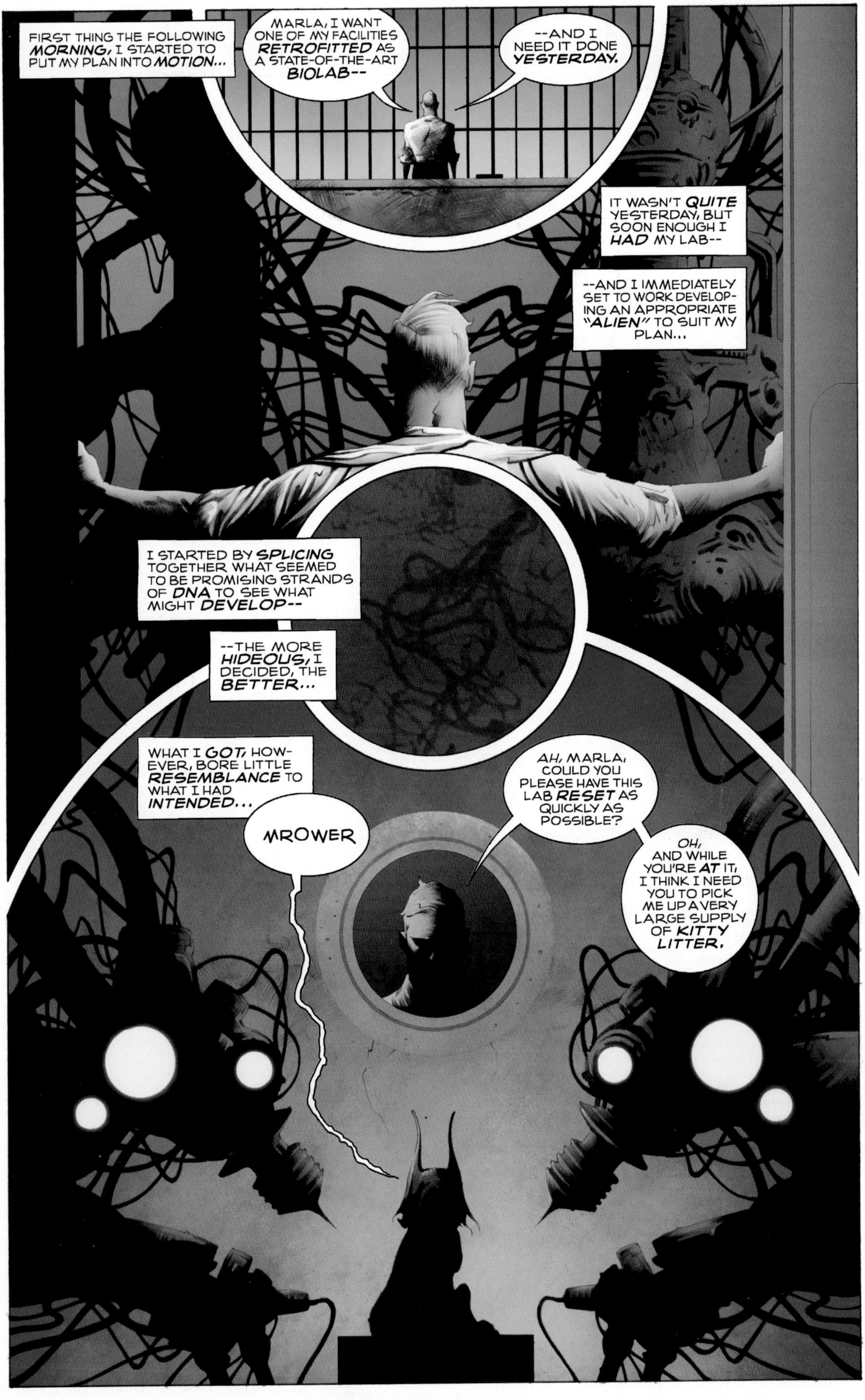
FIRST THING THE FOLLOWING MORNING, I STARTED TO PUT MY PLAN INTO MOTION...
MARLA, I WANT ONE OF MY FACILITIES RETROFITTED AS A STATE-OF-THE-ART BIOLAB--
--AND I NEED IT DONE YESTERDAY.
IT WASN'T QUITE YESTERDAY, BUT SOON ENOUGH I HAD MY LAB--
--AND I IMMEDIATELY SET TO WORK DEVELOPING AN APPROPRIATE "ALIEN" TO SUIT MY PLAN...
I STARTED BY SPLICING TOGETHER WHAT SEEMED TO BE PROMISING STRANDS OF DNA TO SEE WHAT MIGHT DEVELOP--
--THE MORE HIDEOUS, I DECIDED, THE BETTER...
WHAT I GOT, HOWEVER, BORE LITTLE RESEMBLANCE TO WHAT I HAD INTENDED...
MROWER
AH, MARLA, COULD YOU PLEASE HAVE THIS LAB RESET AS QUICKLY AS POSSIBLE?
OH, AND WHILE YOU'RE AT IT, I THINK I NEED YOU TO PICK ME UP A VERY LARGE SUPPLY OF KITTY LITTER.

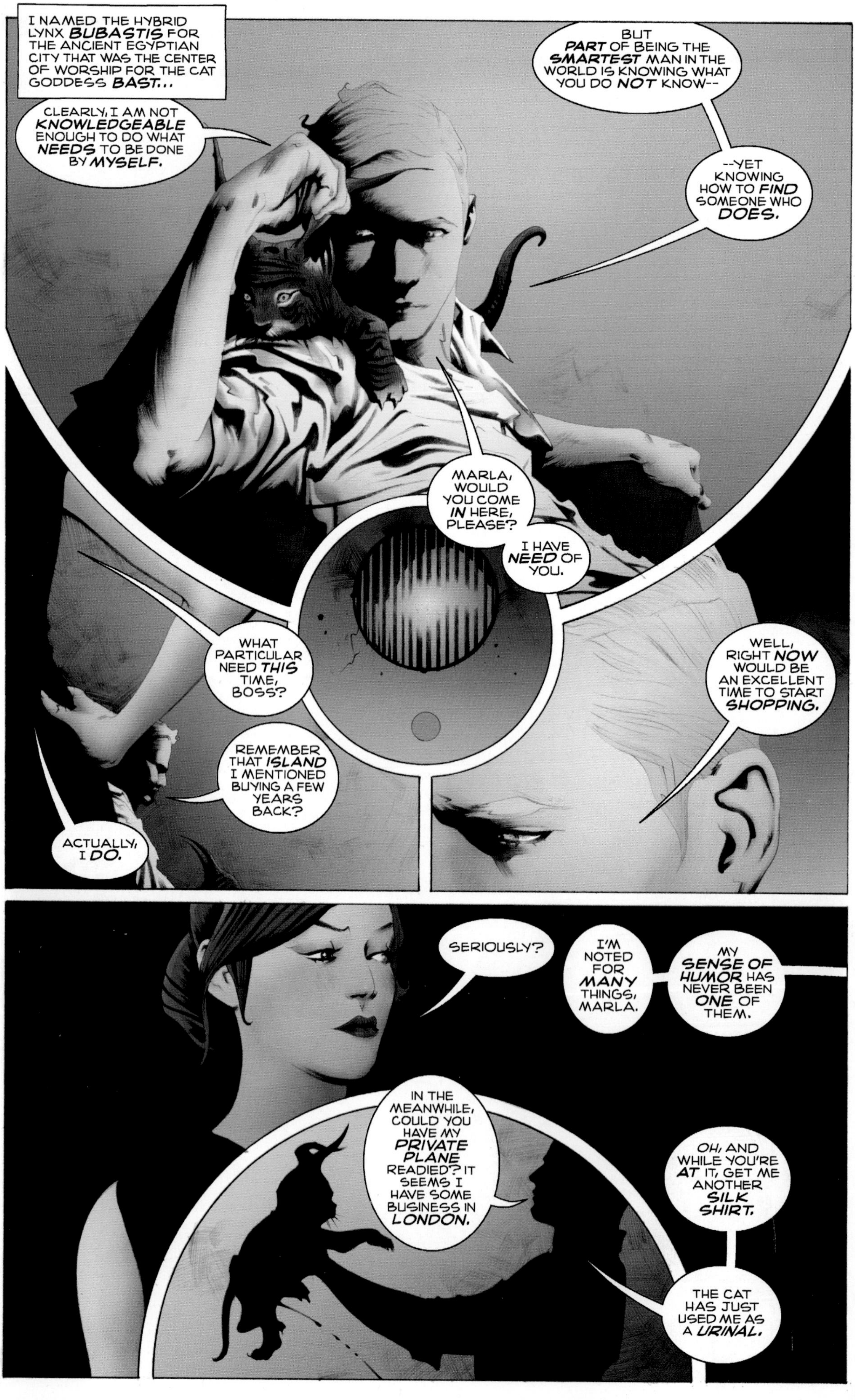

I NAMED THE HYBRID LYNX BUBASTIS FOR THE ANCIENT EGYPTIAN CITY THAT WAS THE CENTER OF WORSHIP FOR THE CAT GODDESS BAST...
CLEARLY, I AM NOT KNOWLEDGEABLE ENOUGH TO DO WHAT NEEDS TO BE DONE BY MYSELF.
BUT PART OF BEING THE SMARTEST MAN IN THE WORLD IS KNOWING WHAT YOU DO NOT KNOW--
--YET KNOWING HOW TO FIND SOMEONE WHO DOES.
MARLA, WOULD YOU COME IN HERE, PLEASE?
I HAVE NEED OF YOU.
WHAT PARTICULAR NEED THIS TIME, BOSS?
WELL, RIGHT NOW WOULD BE AN EXCELLENT TIME TO START SHOPPING.
REMEMBER THAT ISLAND I MENTIONED BUYING A FEW YEARS BACK?
ACTUALLY, I DO.
SERIOUSLY?
I'M NOTED FOR MANY THINGS, MARLA.
MY SENSE OF HUMOR HAS NEVER BEEN ONE OF THEM.
IN THE MEANWHILE, COULD YOU HAVE MY PRIVATE PLANE READIED? IT SEEMS I HAVE SOME BUSINESS IN LONDON.
OH, AND WHILE YOU'RE AT IT, GET ME ANOTHER SILK SHIRT.
THE CAT HAS JUST USED ME AS A URINAL.

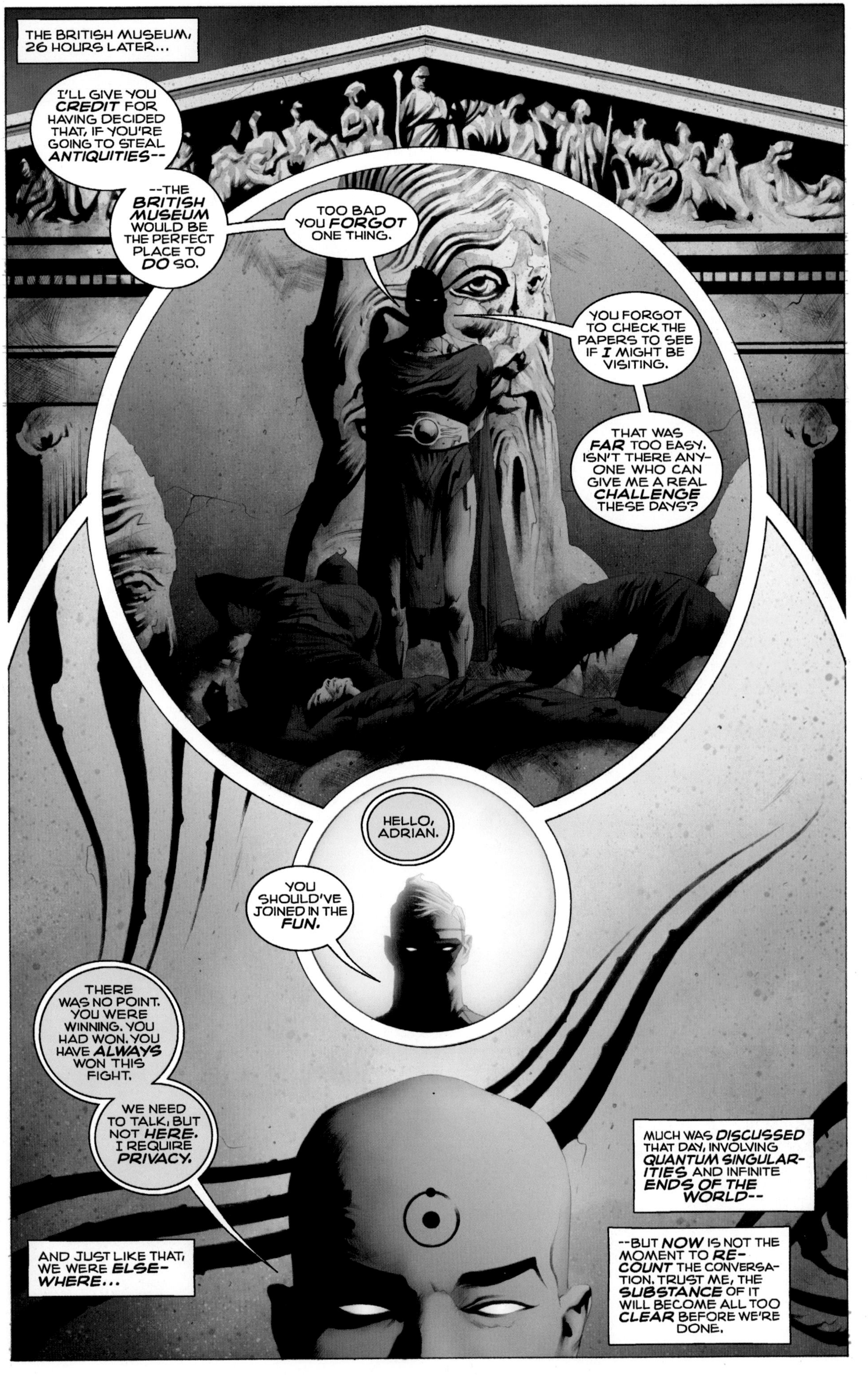
THE BRITISH MUSEUM, 26 HOURS LATER...
I'LL GIVE YOU CREDIT FOR HAVING DECIDED THAT, IF YOU'RE GOING TO STEAL ANTIQUITIES--
--THE BRITISH MUSEUM WOULD BE THE PERFECT PLACE TO DO SO.
TOO BAD YOU FORGOT ONE THING.
YOU FORGOT TO CHECK THE PAPERS TO SEE IF I MIGHT BE VISITING.
THAT WAS FAR TOO EASY. ISN'T THERE ANY-ONE WHO CAN GIVE ME A REAL CHALLENGE THESE DAYS?
HELLO, ADRIAN.
YOU SHOULD'VE JOINED IN THE FUN.
THERE WAS NO POINT. YOU WERE WINNING. YOU HAD WON. YOU HAVE ALWAYS WON THIS FIGHT.
WE NEED TO TALK, BUT NOT HERE. I REQUIRE PRIVACY.
MUCH WAS DISCUSSED THAT DAY, INVOLVING QUANTUM SINGULAR-ITIES AND INFINITE ENDS OF THE WORLD--
AND JUST LIKE THAT, WE WERE ELSE-WHERE...
--BUT NOW IS NOT THE MOMENT TO RE-COUNT THE CONVERSA-TION. TRUST ME, THE SUBSTANCE OF IT WILL BECOME ALL TOO CLEAR BEFORE WE'RE DONE.

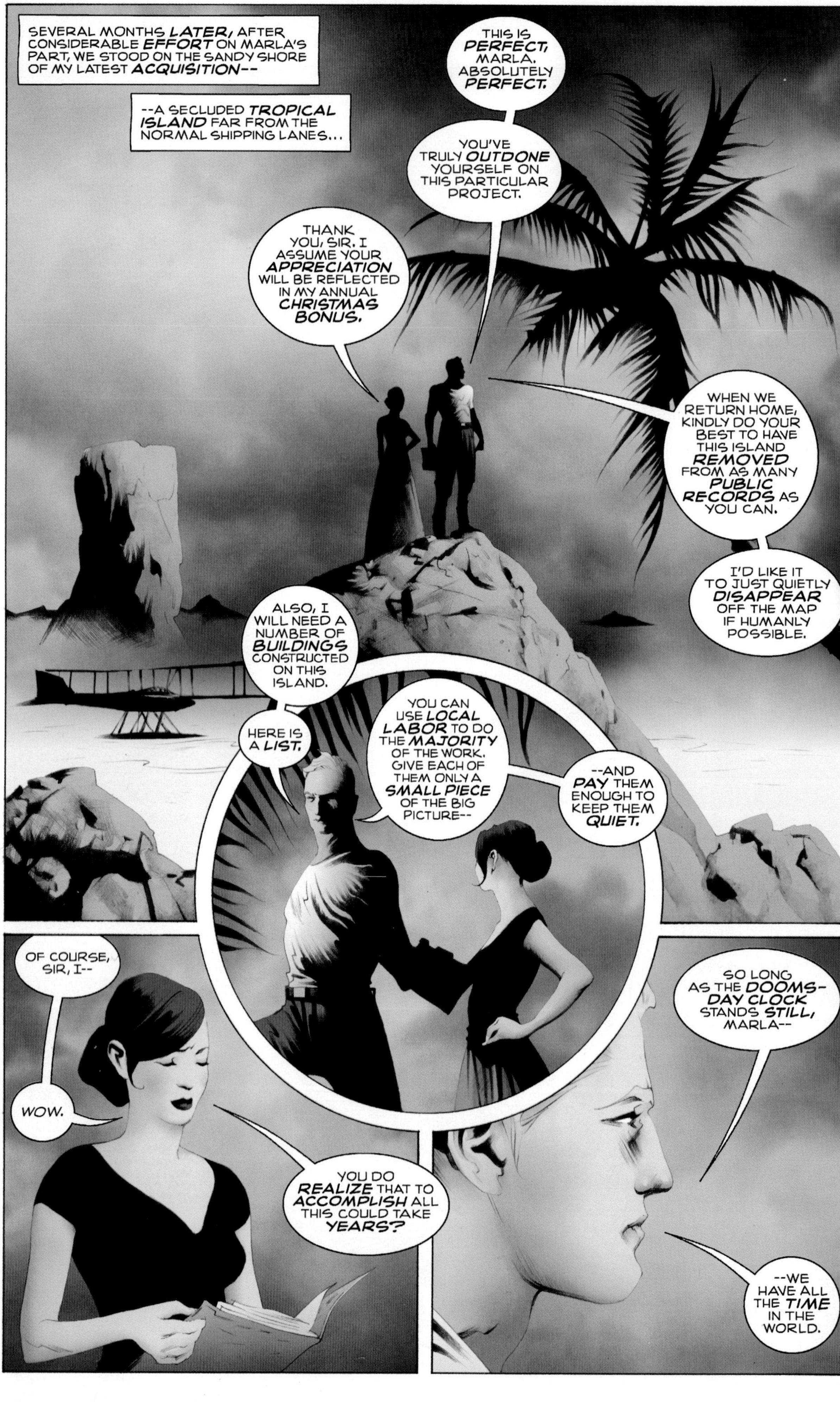
SEVERAL MONTHS LATER, AFTER CONSIDERABLE EFFORT ON MARLA'S PART, WE STOOD ON THE SANDY SHORE OF MY LATEST ACQUISITION--
--A SECLUDED TROPICAL ISLAND FAR FROM THE NORMAL SHIPPING LANES...
THIS IS PERFECT, MARLA. ABSOLUTELY PERFECT.
YOU'VE TRULY OUTDONE YOURSELF ON THIS PARTICULAR PROJECT.
THANK YOU, SIR. I ASSUME YOUR APPRECIATION WILL BE REFLECTED IN MY ANNUAL CHRISTMAS BONUS.
WHEN WE RETURN HOME, KINDLY DO YOUR BEST TO HAVE THIS ISLAND REMOVED FROM AS MANY PUBLIC RECORDS AS YOU CAN.
I'D LIKE IT TO JUST QUIETLY DISAPPEAR OFF THE MAP IF HUMANLY POSSIBLE.
ALSO, I WILL NEED A NUMBER OF BUILDINGS CONSTRUCTED ON THIS ISLAND.
HERE IS A LIST.
YOU CAN USE LOCAL LABOR TO DO THE MAJORITY OF THE WORK. GIVE EACH OF THEM ONLY A SMALL PIECE OF THE BIG PICTURE--
--AND PAY THEM ENOUGH TO KEEP THEM QUIET.
OF COURSE, SIR, I--
WOW.
YOU DO REALIZE THAT TO ACCOMPLISH ALL THIS COULD TAKE YEARS?
SO LONG AS THE DOOMSDAY CLOCK STANDS STILL, MARLA--
--WE HAVE ALL THE TIME IN THE WORLD.

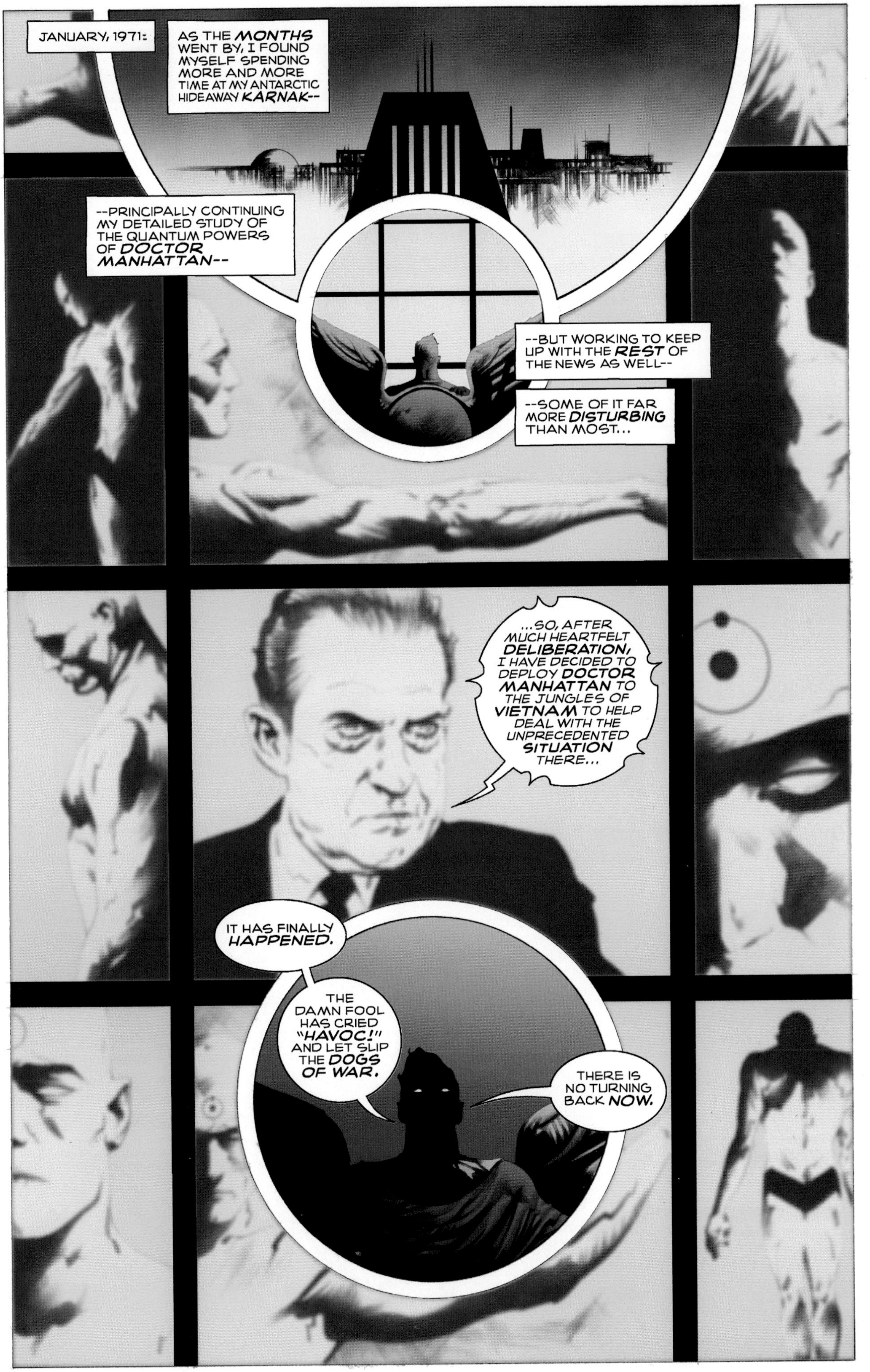
JANUARY, 1971:
AS THE MONTHS WENT BY, I FOUND MYSELF SPENDING MORE AND MORE TIME AT MY ANTARCTIC HIDEAWAY KARNAK--
--PRINCIPALLY CONTINUING MY DETAILED STUDY OF THE QUANTUM POWERS OF DOCTOR MANHATTAN--
--BUT WORKING TO KEEP UP WITH THE REST OF THE NEWS AS WELL--
--SOME OF IT FAR MORE DISTURBING THAN MOST...
...SO, AFTER MUCH HEARTFELT DELIBERATION, I HAVE DECIDED TO DEPLOY DOCTOR MANHATTAN TO THE JUNGLES OF VIETNAM TO HELP DEAL WITH THE UNPRECEDENTED SITUATION THERE...
IT HAS FINALLY HAPPENED.
THE DAMN FOOL HAS CRIED "HAVOC!" AND LET SLIP THE DOGS OF WAR.
THERE IS NO TURNING BACK NOW.

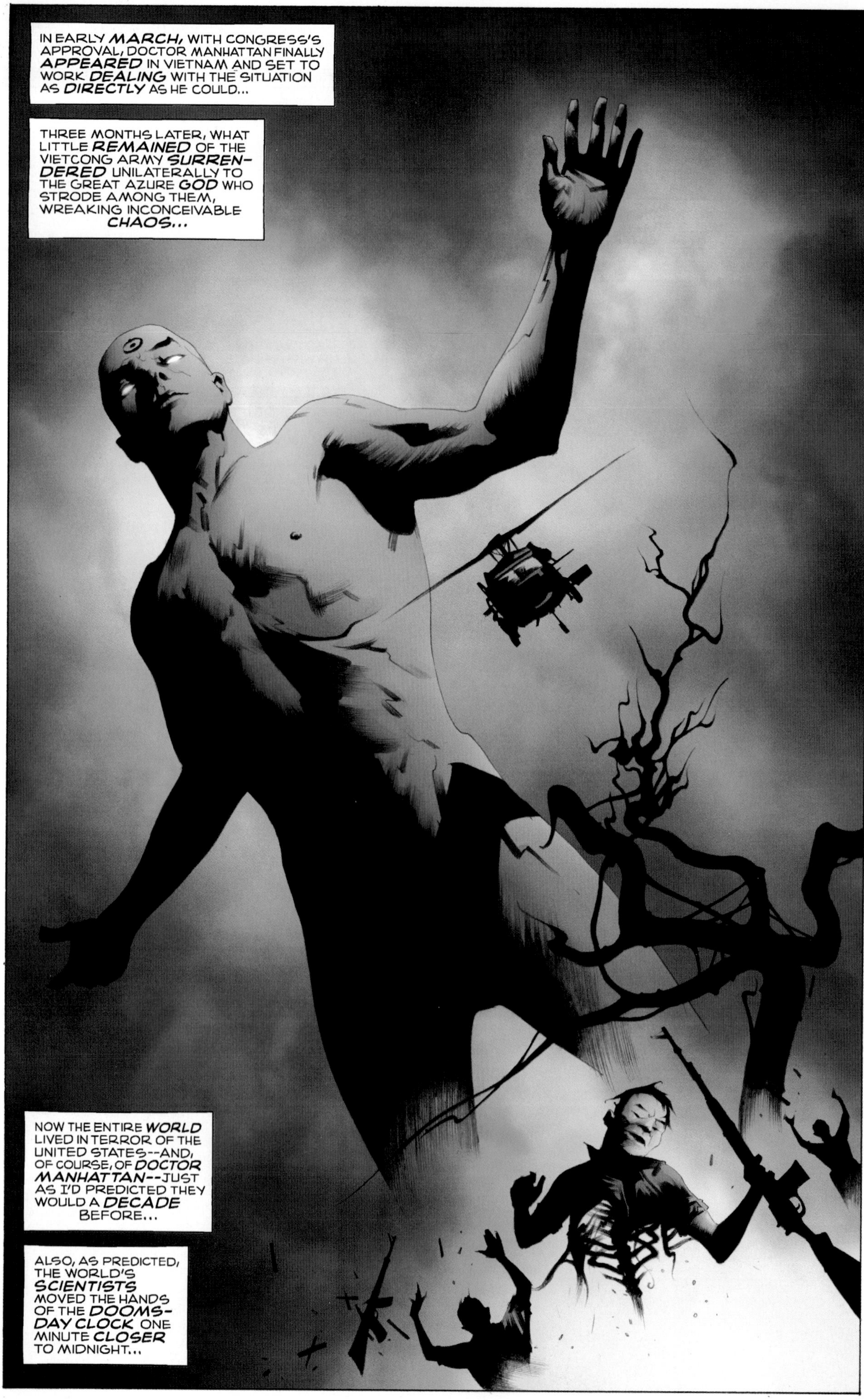
IN EARLY **MARCH,** WITH CONGRESS'S APPROVAL, DOCTOR MANHATTAN FINALLY **APPEARED** IN VIETNAM AND SET TO WORK **DEALING** WITH THE SITUATION AS **DIRECTLY** AS HE COULD...
THREE MONTHS LATER, WHAT LITTLE **REMAINED** OF THE VIETCONG ARMY **SURRENDERED** UNILATERALLY TO THE GREAT AZURE **GOD** WHO STRODE AMONG THEM, WREAKING INCONCEIVABLE **CHAOS...**
NOW THE ENTIRE **WORLD** LIVED IN TERROR OF THE UNITED STATES--AND, OF COURSE, OF **DOCTOR MANHATTAN**--JUST AS I'D PREDICTED THEY WOULD A **DECADE** BEFORE...
ALSO, AS PREDICTED, THE WORLD'S **SCIENTISTS** MOVED THE HANDS OF THE **DOOMSDAY CLOCK** ONE MINUTE **CLOSER** TO MIDNIGHT...

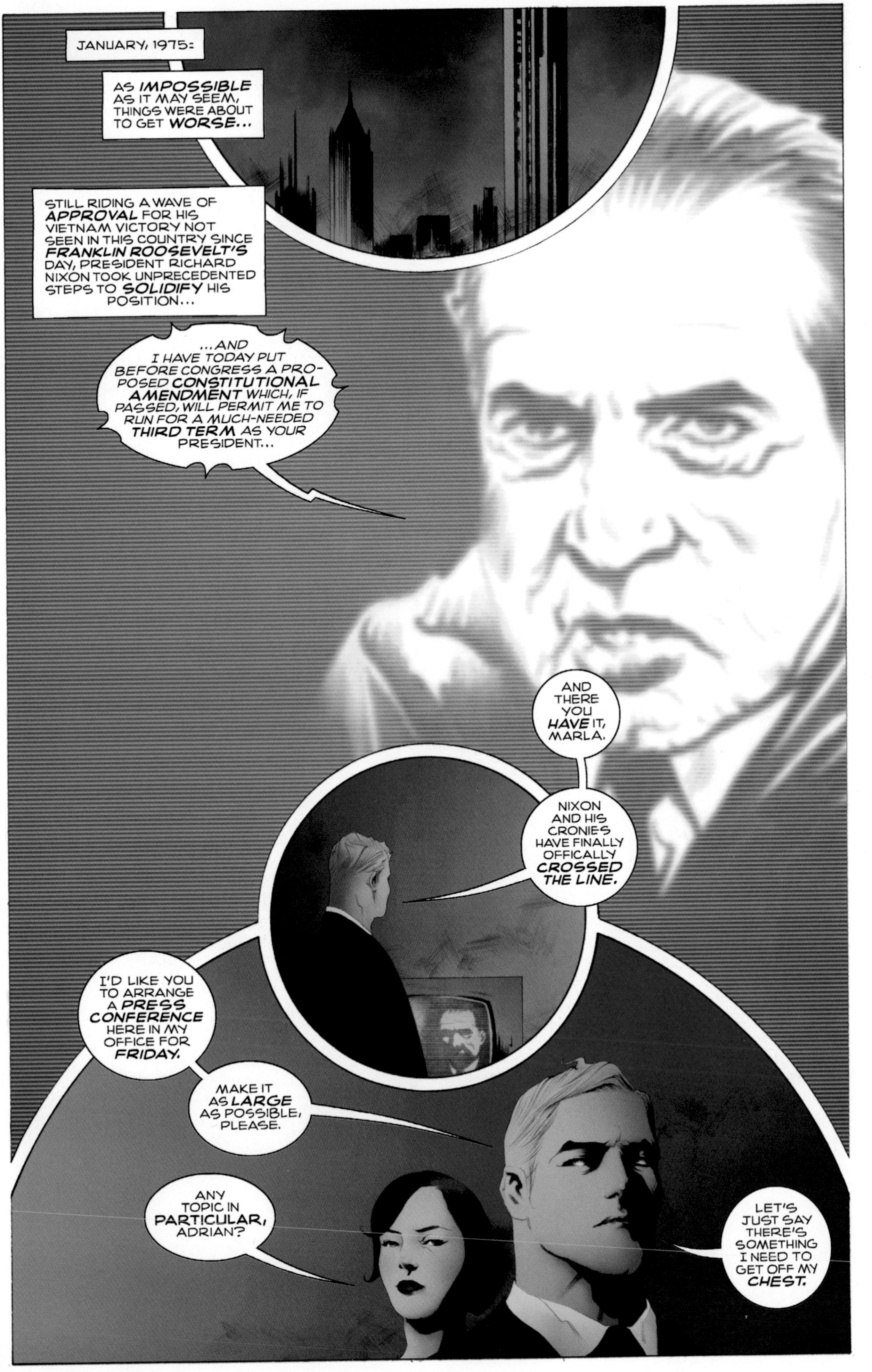

JANUARY, 1975:
AS IMPOSSIBLE AS IT MAY SEEM, THINGS WERE ABOUT TO GET WORSE...
STILL RIDING A WAVE OF APPROVAL FOR HIS VIETNAM VICTORY NOT SEEN IN THIS COUNTRY SINCE FRANKLIN ROOSEVELT'S DAY, PRESIDENT RICHARD NIXON TOOK UNPRECEDENTED STEPS TO SOLIDIFY HIS POSITION...
...AND I HAVE TODAY PUT BEFORE CONGRESS A PROPOSED CONSTITUTIONAL AMENDMENT WHICH, IF PASSED, WILL PERMIT ME TO RUN FOR A MUCH-NEEDED THIRD TERM AS YOUR PRESIDENT...
AND THERE YOU HAVE IT, MARLA.
NIXON AND HIS CRONIES HAVE FINALLY OFFICALLY CROSSED THE LINE.
I'D LIKE YOU TO ARRANGE A PRESS CONFERENCE HERE IN MY OFFICE FOR FRIDAY.
MAKE IT AS LARGE AS POSSIBLE, PLEASE.
ANY TOPIC IN PARTICULAR, ADRIAN?
LET'S JUST SAY THERE'S SOMETHING I NEED TO GET OFF MY CHEST.

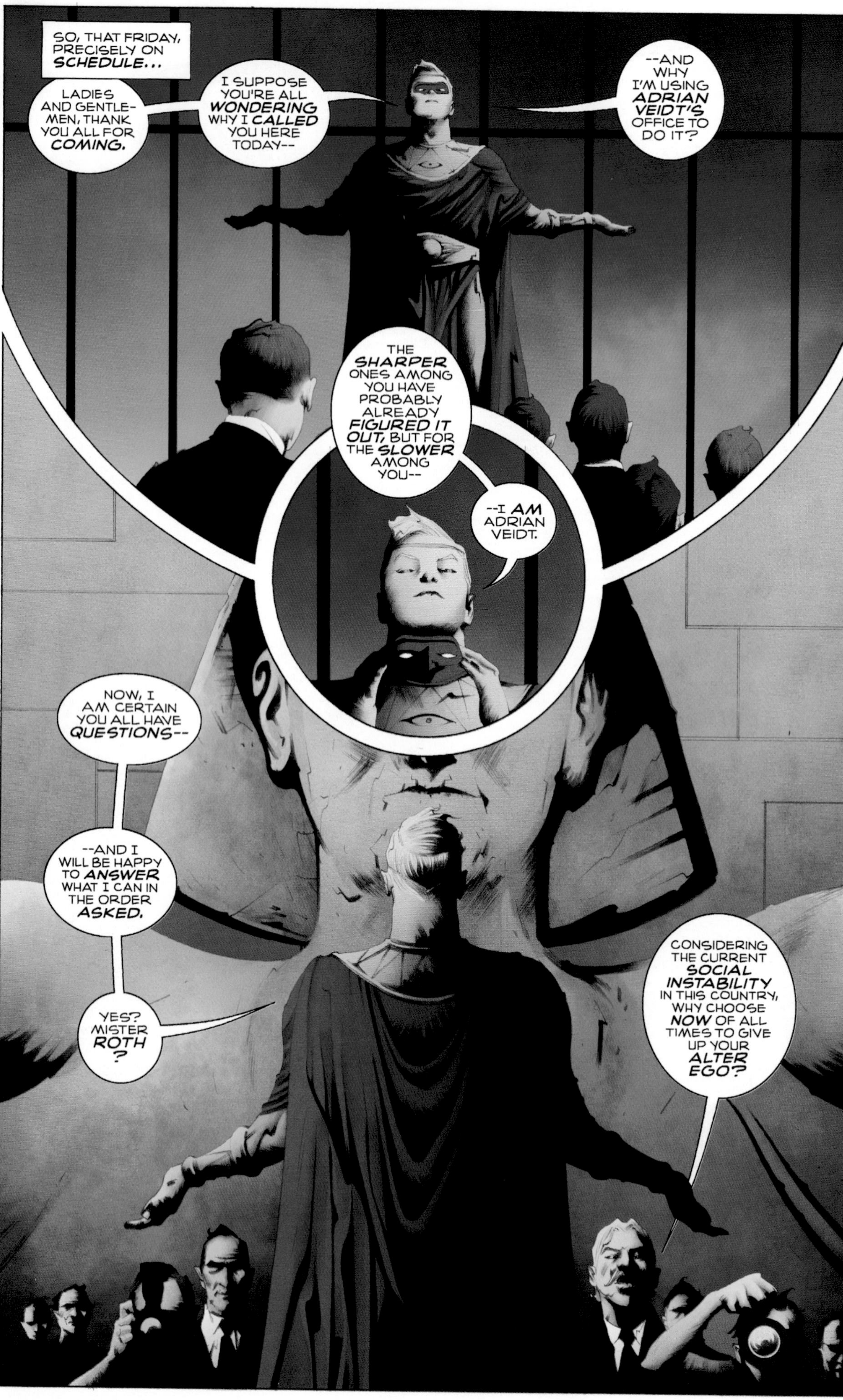
SO, THAT FRIDAY, PRECISELY ON SCHEDULE...
LADIES AND GENTLE-MEN, THANK YOU ALL FOR COMING.
I SUPPOSE YOU'RE ALL WONDERING WHY I CALLED YOU HERE TODAY--
--AND WHY I'M USING ADRIAN VEIDT'S OFFICE TO DO IT?
THE SHARPER ONES AMONG YOU HAVE PROBABLY ALREADY FIGURED IT OUT, BUT FOR THE SLOWER AMONG YOU--
--I AM ADRIAN VEIDT.
NOW, I AM CERTAIN YOU ALL HAVE QUESTIONS--
--AND I WILL BE HAPPY TO ANSWER WHAT I CAN IN THE ORDER ASKED.
YES? MISTER ROTH?
CONSIDERING THE CURRENT SOCIAL INSTABILITY IN THIS COUNTRY, WHY CHOOSE NOW OF ALL TIMES TO GIVE UP YOUR ALTER EGO?

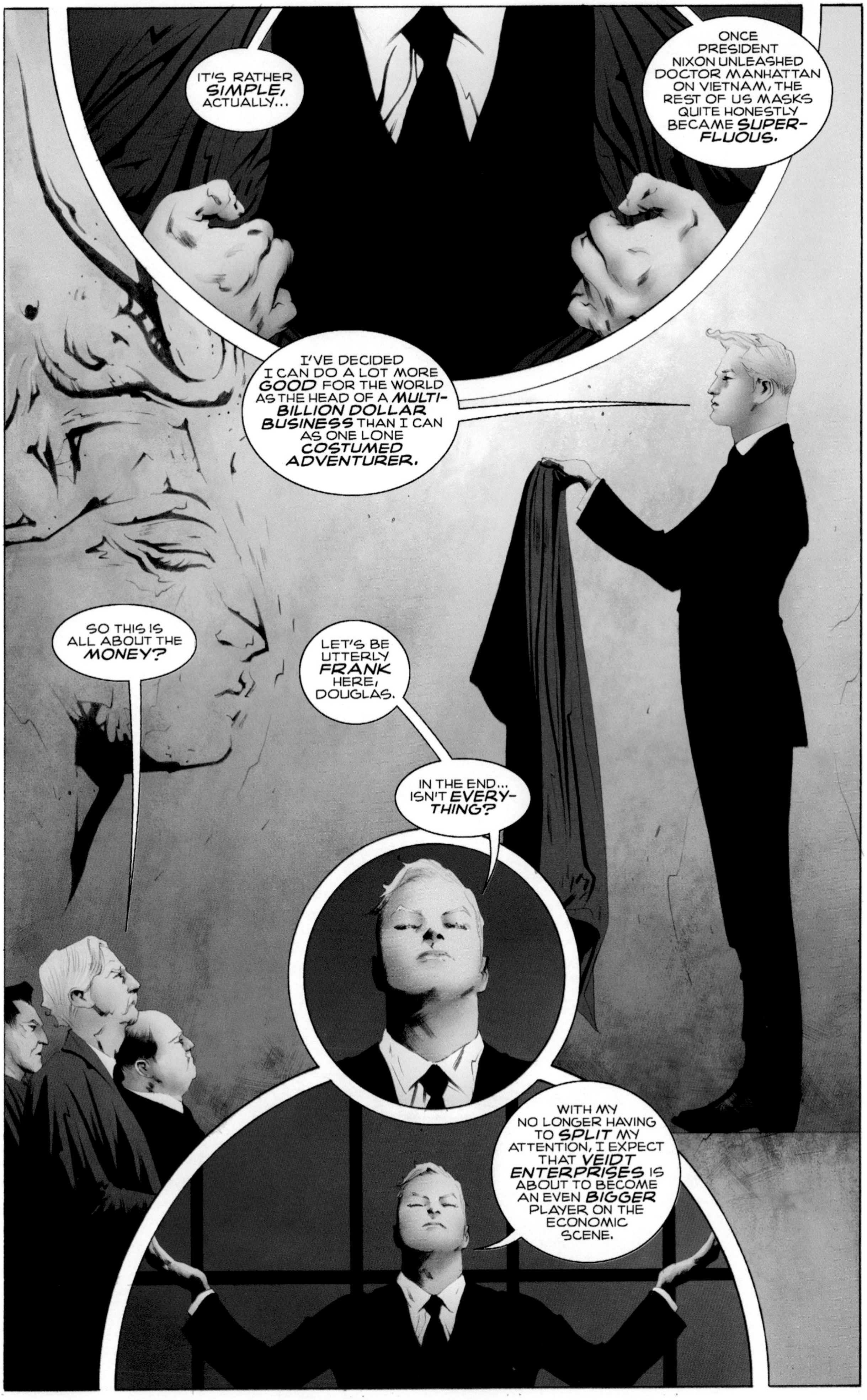
IT'S RATHER SIMPLE, ACTUALLY...
ONCE PRESIDENT NIXON UNLEASHED DOCTOR MANHATTAN ON VIETNAM, THE REST OF US MASKS QUITE HONESTLY BECAME SUPER-FLUOUS.
I'VE DECIDED I CAN DO A LOT MORE GOOD FOR THE WORLD AS THE HEAD OF A MULTI-BILLION DOLLAR BUSINESS THAN I CAN AS ONE LONE COSTUMED ADVENTURER.
SO THIS IS ALL ABOUT THE MONEY?
LET'S BE UTTERLY FRANK HERE, DOUGLAS.
IN THE END... ISN'T EVERY-THING?
WITH MY NO LONGER HAVING TO SPLIT MY ATTENTION, I EXPECT THAT VEIDT ENTERPRISES IS ABOUT TO BECOME AN EVEN BIGGER PLAYER ON THE ECONOMIC SCENE.

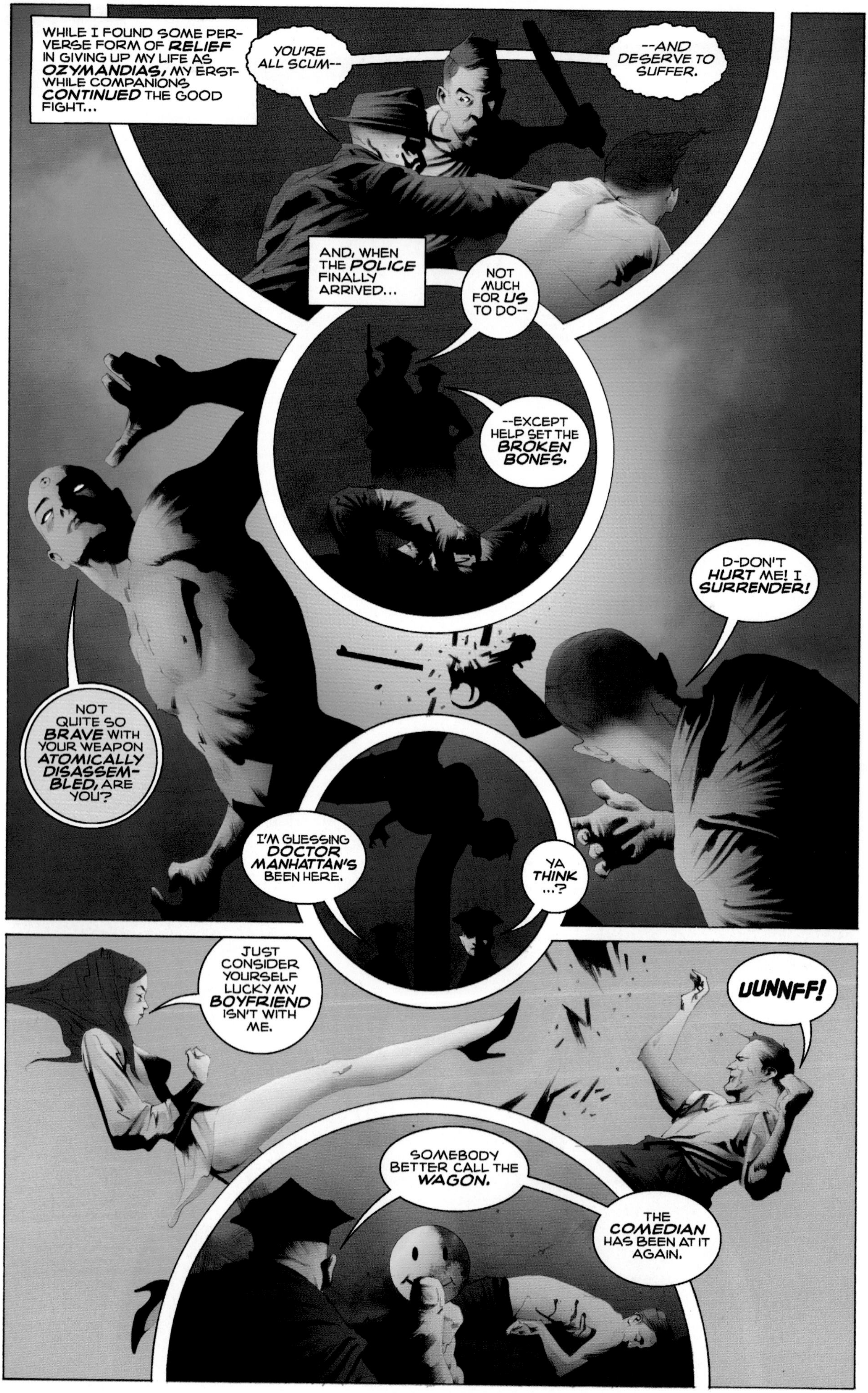
WHILE I FOUND SOME PERVERSE FORM OF RELIEF IN GIVING UP MY LIFE AS OZYMANDIAS, MY ERSTWHILE COMPANIONS CONTINUED THE GOOD FIGHT...
YOU'RE ALL SCUM--
--AND DESERVE TO SUFFER.
AND, WHEN THE POLICE FINALLY ARRIVED...
NOT MUCH FOR US TO DO--
--EXCEPT HELP SET THE BROKEN BONES.
D-DON'T HURT ME! I SURRENDER!
NOT QUITE SO BRAVE WITH YOUR WEAPON ATOMICALLY DISASSEMBLED, ARE YOU?
I'M GUESSING DOCTOR MANHATTAN'S BEEN HERE.
YA THINK ...?
JUST CONSIDER YOURSELF LUCKY MY BOYFRIEND ISN'T WITH ME.
UUNNFF!
SOMEBODY BETTER CALL THE WAGON.
THE COMEDIAN HAS BEEN AT IT AGAIN.

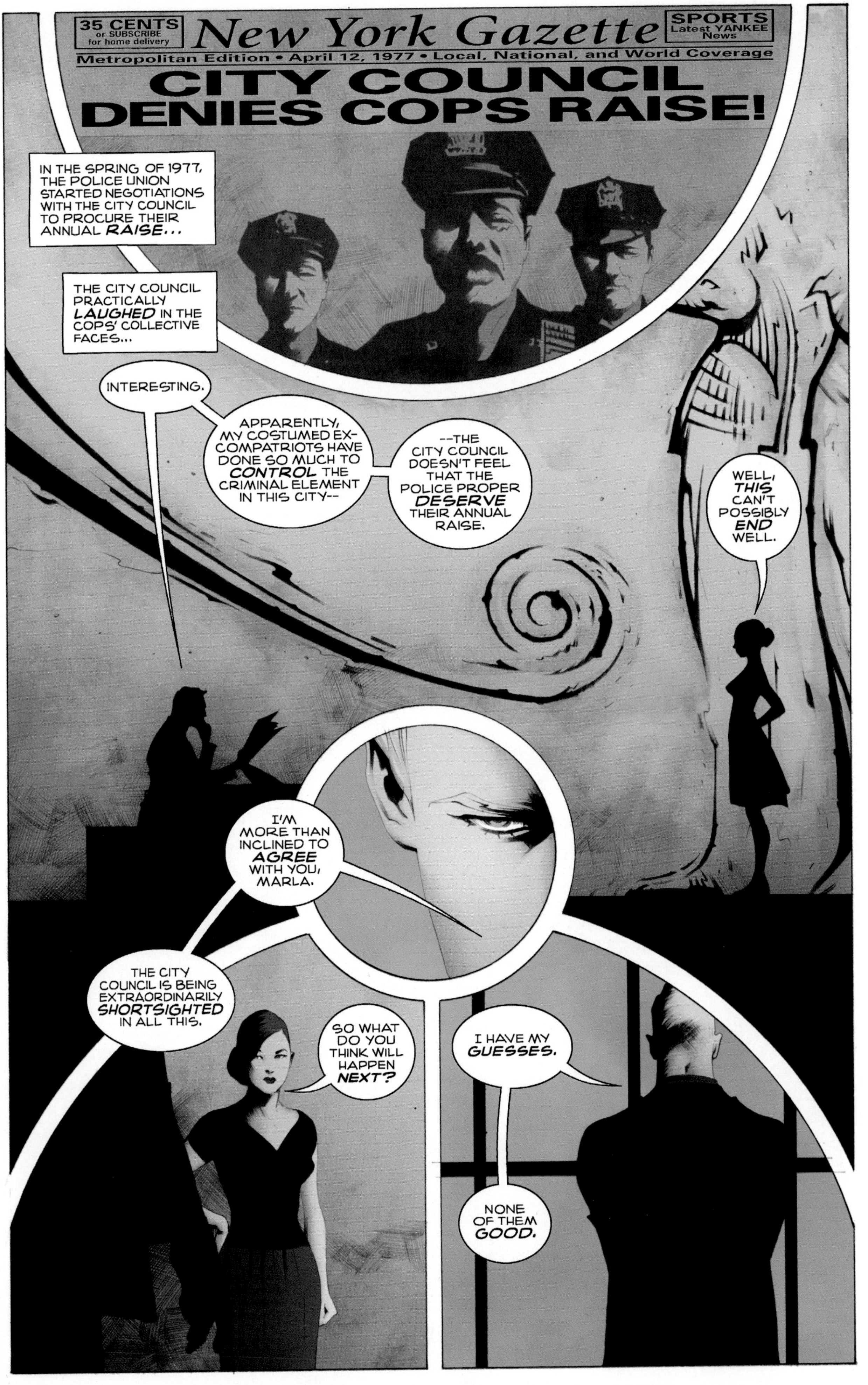
35 CENTS or SUBSCRIBE for home delivery
New York Gazette
SPORTS Latest YANKEE News
Metropolitan Edition • April 12, 1977 • Local, National, and World Coverage
CITY COUNCIL DENIES COPS RAISE!
IN THE SPRING OF 1977, THE POLICE UNION STARTED NEGOTIATIONS WITH THE CITY COUNCIL TO PROCURE THEIR ANNUAL RAISE...
THE CITY COUNCIL PRACTICALLY LAUGHED IN THE COPS' COLLECTIVE FACES...
INTERESTING.
APPARENTLY, MY COSTUMED EX-COMPATRIOTS HAVE DONE SO MUCH TO CONTROL THE CRIMINAL ELEMENT IN THIS CITY--
--THE CITY COUNCIL DOESN'T FEEL THAT THE POLICE PROPER DESERVE THEIR ANNUAL RAISE.
WELL, THIS CAN'T POSSIBLY END WELL.
I'M MORE THAN INCLINED TO AGREE WITH YOU, MARLA.
THE CITY COUNCIL IS BEING EXTRAORDINARILY SHORTSIGHTED IN ALL THIS.
SO WHAT DO YOU THINK WILL HAPPEN NEXT?
I HAVE MY GUESSES.
NONE OF THEM GOOD.

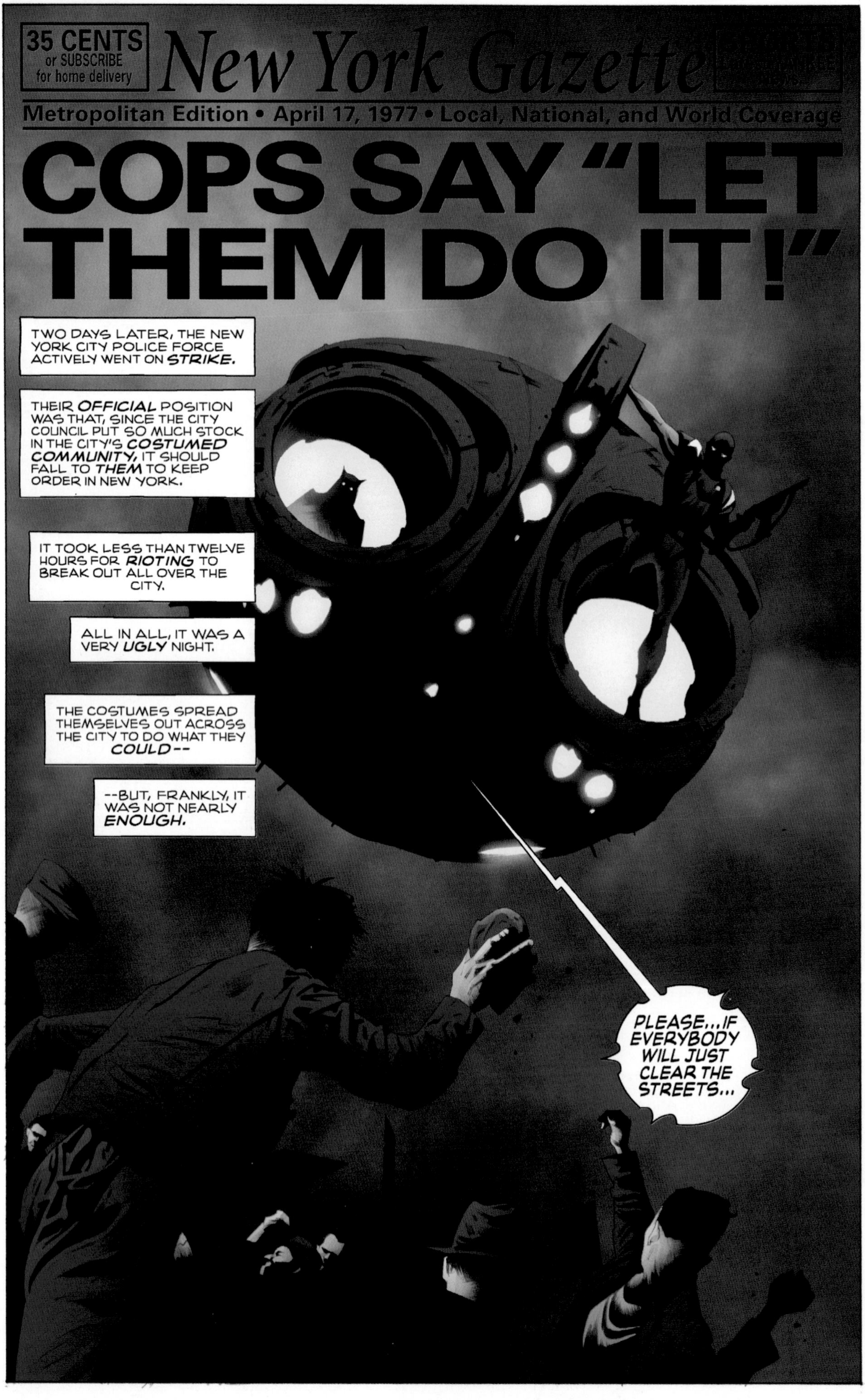
35 CENTS or SUBSCRIBE for home delivery
New York Gazette
Metropolitan Edition • April 17, 1977 • Local, National, and World Coverage
COPS SAY "LET THEM DO IT!"
TWO DAYS LATER, THE NEW YORK CITY POLICE FORCE ACTIVELY WENT ON STRIKE.
THEIR OFFICIAL POSITION WAS THAT, SINCE THE CITY COUNCIL PUT SO MUCH STOCK IN THE CITY'S COSTUMED COMMUNITY, IT SHOULD FALL TO THEM TO KEEP ORDER IN NEW YORK.
IT TOOK LESS THAN TWELVE HOURS FOR RIOTING TO BREAK OUT ALL OVER THE CITY.
ALL IN ALL, IT WAS A VERY UGLY NIGHT.
THE COSTUMES SPREAD THEMSELVES OUT ACROSS THE CITY TO DO WHAT THEY COULD--
--BUT, FRANKLY, IT WAS NOT NEARLY ENOUGH.
PLEASE...IF EVERYBODY WILL JUST CLEAR THE STREETS...

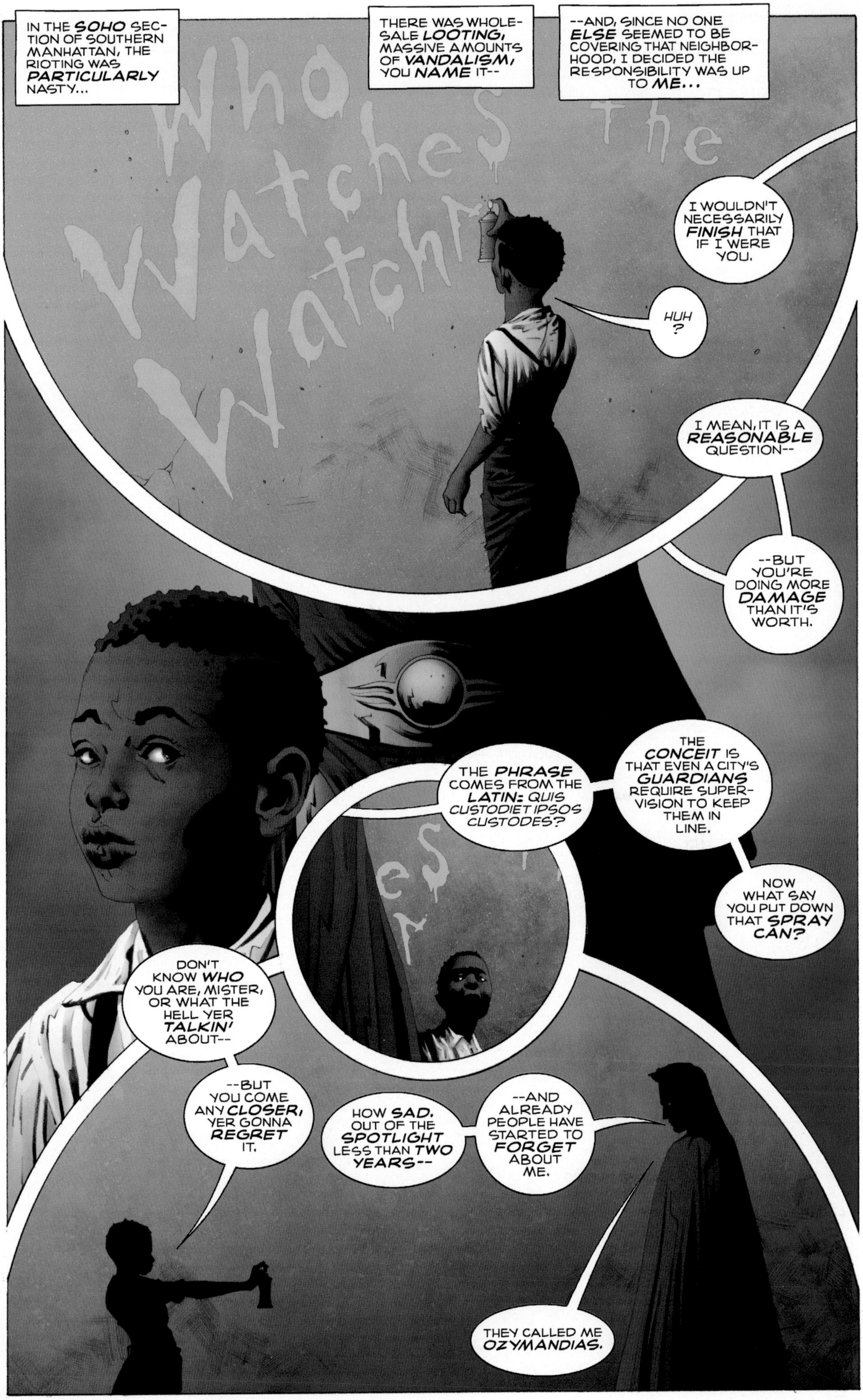
IN THE SOHO SECTION OF SOUTHERN MANHATTAN, THE RIOTING WAS PARTICULARLY NASTY...
THERE WAS WHOLESALE LOOTING, MASSIVE AMOUNTS OF VANDALISM, YOU NAME IT--
--AND, SINCE NO ONE ELSE SEEMED TO BE COVERING THAT NEIGHBORHOOD, I DECIDED THE RESPONSIBILITY WAS UP TO ME...
Who Watches the Watchm
I WOULDN'T NECESSARILY FINISH THAT IF I WERE YOU.
HUH?
I MEAN, IT IS A REASONABLE QUESTION--
--BUT YOU'RE DOING MORE DAMAGE THAN IT'S WORTH.
THE PHRASE COMES FROM THE LATIN: QUIS CUSTODIET IPSOS CUSTODES?
THE CONCEIT IS THAT EVEN A CITY'S GUARDIANS REQUIRE SUPERVISION TO KEEP THEM IN LINE.
NOW WHAT SAY YOU PUT DOWN THAT SPRAY CAN?
DON'T KNOW WHO YOU ARE, MISTER, OR WHAT THE HELL YER TALKIN' ABOUT--
--BUT YOU COME ANY CLOSER, YER GONNA REGRET IT.
HOW SAD. OUT OF THE SPOTLIGHT LESS THAN TWO YEARS--
--AND ALREADY PEOPLE HAVE STARTED TO FORGET ABOUT ME.
THEY CALLED ME OZYMANDIAS.

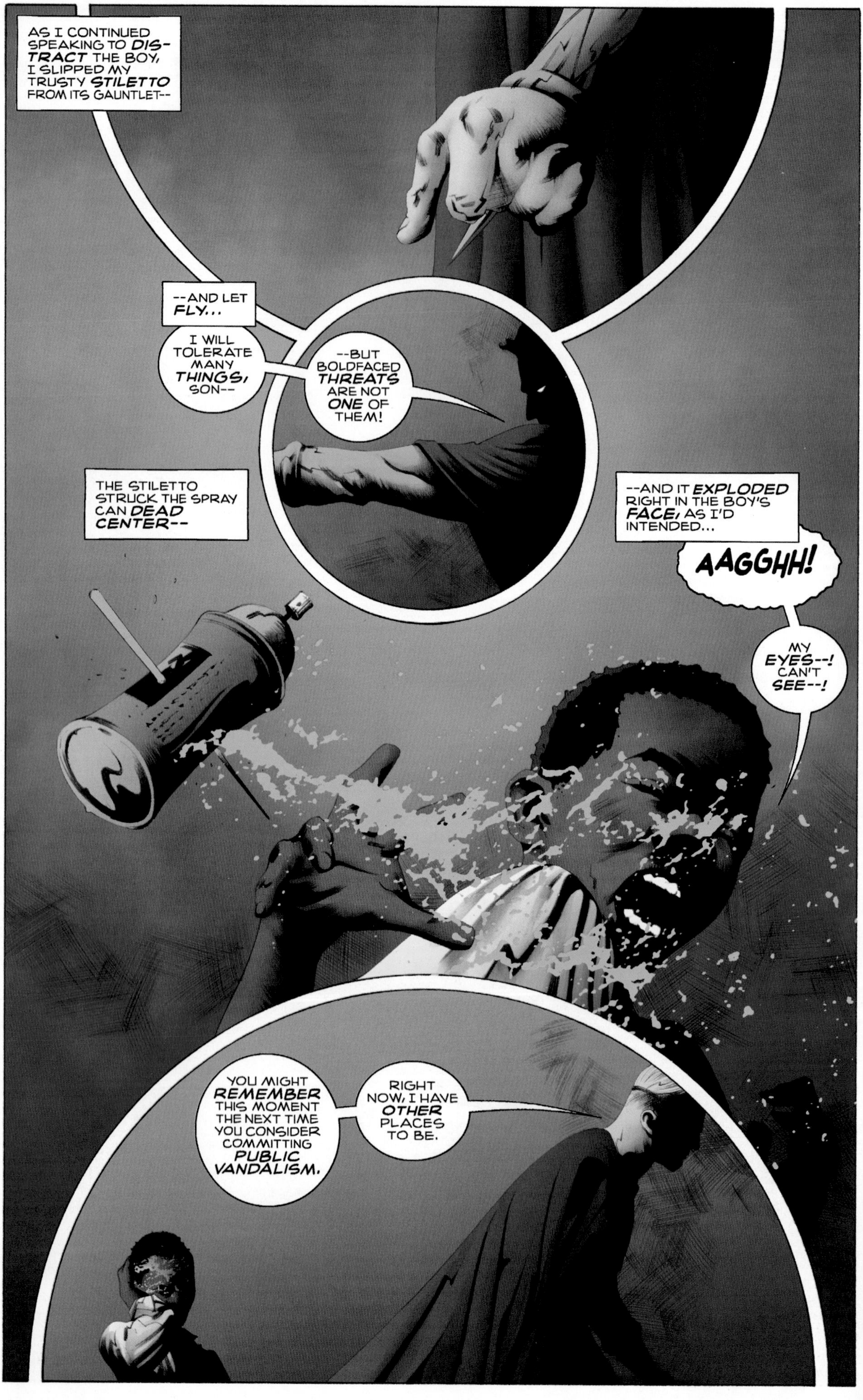
AS I CONTINUED SPEAKING TO DISTRACT THE BOY, I SLIPPED MY TRUSTY STILETTO FROM ITS GAUNTLET--
--AND LET FLY...
I WILL TOLERATE MANY THINGS, SON--
--BUT BOLDFACED THREATS ARE NOT ONE OF THEM!
THE STILETTO STRUCK THE SPRAY CAN DEAD CENTER--
--AND IT EXPLODED RIGHT IN THE BOY'S FACE, AS I'D INTENDED...
AAGGHH!
MY EYES--! CAN'T SEE--!
YOU MIGHT REMEMBER THIS MOMENT THE NEXT TIME YOU CONSIDER COMMITTING PUBLIC VANDALISM.
RIGHT NOW, I HAVE OTHER PLACES TO BE.

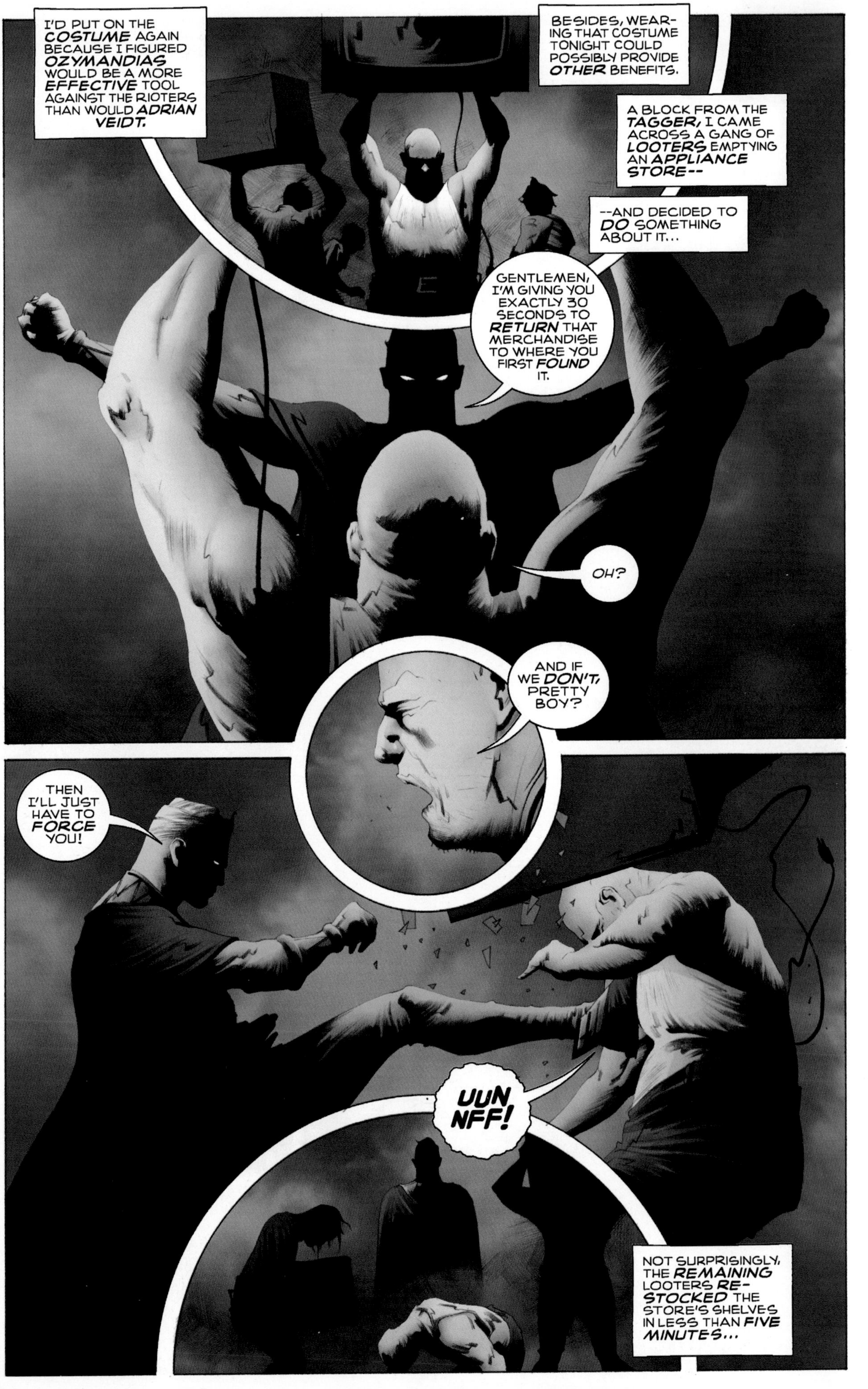
I'D PUT ON THE COSTUME AGAIN BECAUSE I FIGURED OZYMANDIAS WOULD BE A MORE EFFECTIVE TOOL AGAINST THE RIOTERS THAN WOULD ADRIAN VEIDT.
BESIDES, WEARING THAT COSTUME TONIGHT COULD POSSIBLY PROVIDE OTHER BENEFITS.
A BLOCK FROM THE TAGGER, I CAME ACROSS A GANG OF LOOTERS EMPTYING AN APPLIANCE STORE--
--AND DECIDED TO DO SOMETHING ABOUT IT...
GENTLEMEN, I'M GIVING YOU EXACTLY 30 SECONDS TO RETURN THAT MERCHANDISE TO WHERE YOU FIRST FOUND IT.
OH?
AND IF WE DON'T, PRETTY BOY?
THEN I'LL JUST HAVE TO FORCE YOU!
UUN NFF!
NOT SURPRISINGLY, THE REMAINING LOOTERS RE-STOCKED THE STORE'S SHELVES IN LESS THAN FIVE MINUTES...

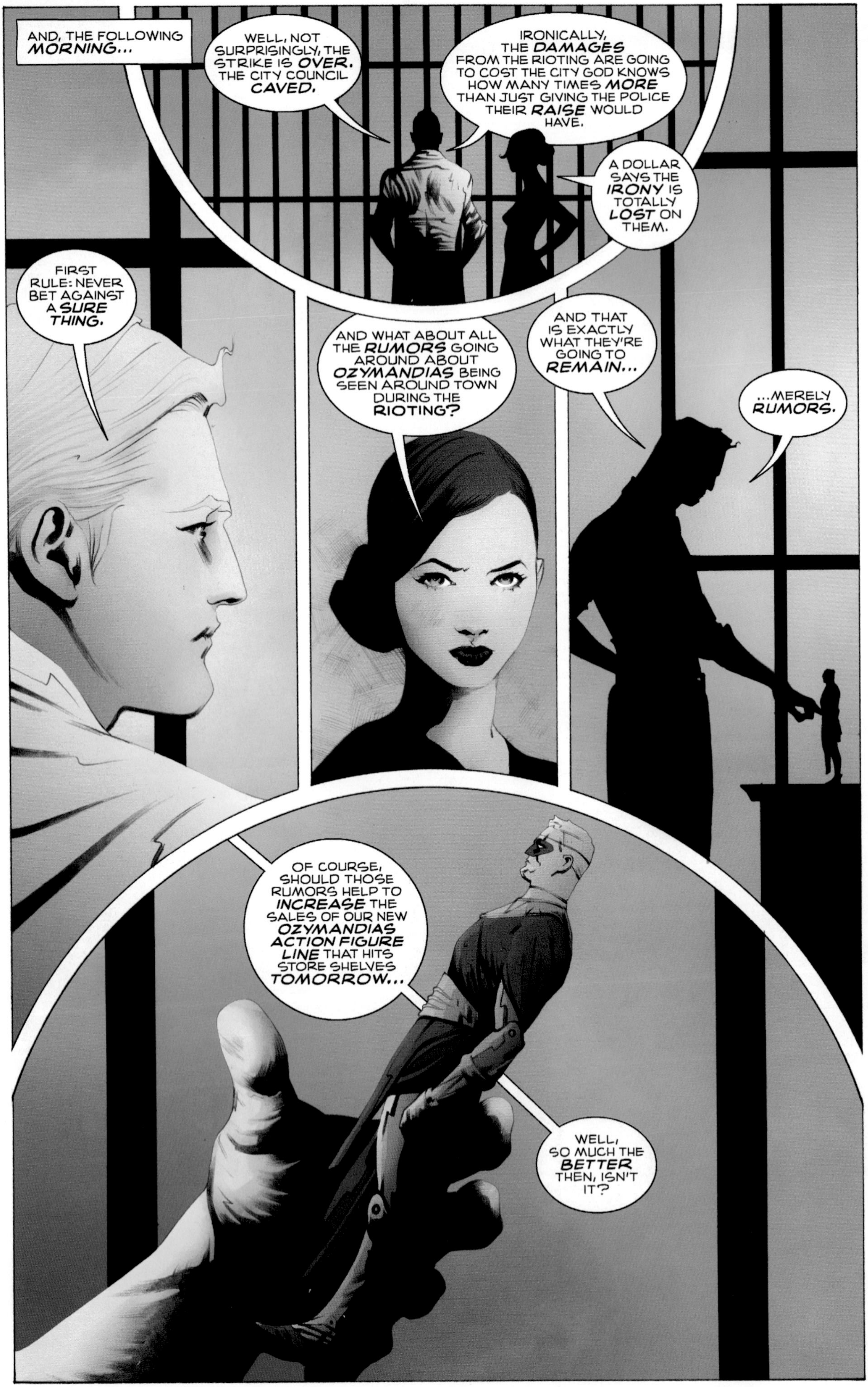
AND, THE FOLLOWING MORNING...
WELL, NOT SURPRISINGLY, THE STRIKE IS OVER. THE CITY COUNCIL CAVED.
IRONICALLY, THE DAMAGES FROM THE RIOTING ARE GOING TO COST THE CITY GOD KNOWS HOW MANY TIMES MORE THAN JUST GIVING THE POLICE THEIR RAISE WOULD HAVE.
A DOLLAR SAYS THE IRONY IS TOTALLY LOST ON THEM.
FIRST RULE: NEVER BET AGAINST A SURE THING.
AND WHAT ABOUT ALL THE RUMORS GOING AROUND ABOUT OZYMANDIAS BEING SEEN AROUND TOWN DURING THE RIOTING?
AND THAT IS EXACTLY WHAT THEY'RE GOING TO REMAIN...
...MERELY RUMORS.
OF COURSE, SHOULD THOSE RUMORS HELP TO INCREASE THE SALES OF OUR NEW OZYMANDIAS ACTION FIGURE LINE THAT HITS STORE SHELVES TOMORROW...
WELL, SO MUCH THE BETTER THEN, ISN'T IT?

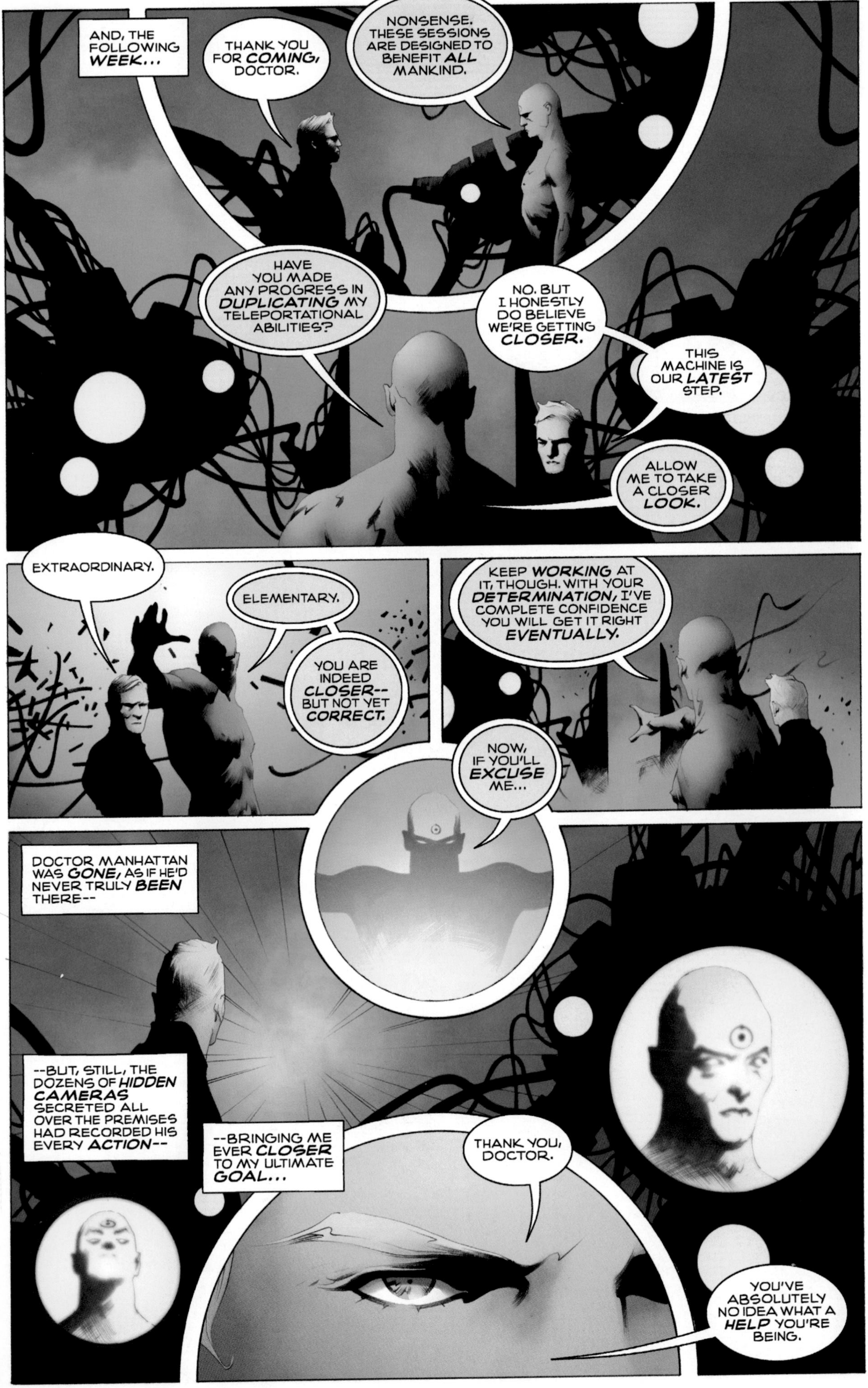
AND, THE FOLLOWING WEEK...
THANK YOU FOR COMING, DOCTOR.
NONSENSE. THESE SESSIONS ARE DESIGNED TO BENEFIT ALL MANKIND.
HAVE YOU MADE ANY PROGRESS IN DUPLICATING MY TELEPORTATIONAL ABILITIES?
NO. BUT I HONESTLY DO BELIEVE WE'RE GETTING CLOSER.
THIS MACHINE IS OUR LATEST STEP.
ALLOW ME TO TAKE A CLOSER LOOK.
EXTRAORDINARY.
ELEMENTARY.
YOU ARE INDEED CLOSER-- BUT NOT YET CORRECT.
KEEP WORKING AT IT, THOUGH. WITH YOUR DETERMINATION, I'VE COMPLETE CONFIDENCE YOU WILL GET IT RIGHT EVENTUALLY.
NOW, IF YOU'LL EXCUSE ME...
DOCTOR MANHATTAN WAS GONE, AS IF HE'D NEVER TRULY BEEN THERE--
--BUT, STILL, THE DOZENS OF HIDDEN CAMERAS SECRETED ALL OVER THE PREMISES HAD RECORDED HIS EVERY ACTION--
--BRINGING ME EVER CLOSER TO MY ULTIMATE GOAL...
THANK YOU, DOCTOR.
YOU'VE ABSOLUTELY NO IDEA WHAT A HELP YOU'RE BEING.

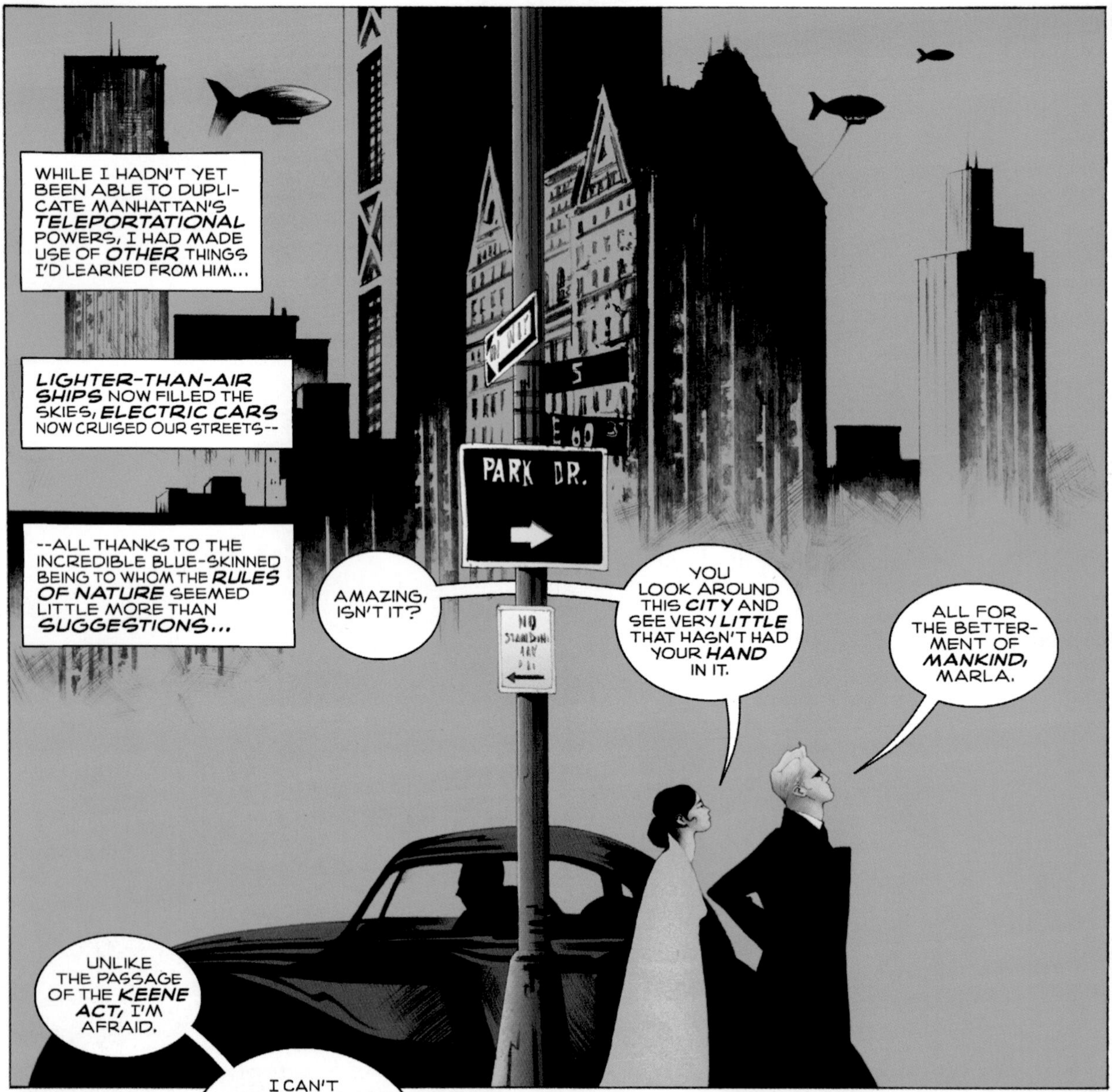
WHILE I HADN'T YET BEEN ABLE TO DUPLICATE MANHATTAN'S TELEPORTATIONAL POWERS, I HAD MADE USE OF OTHER THINGS I'D LEARNED FROM HIM...
LIGHTER-THAN-AIR SHIPS NOW FILLED THE SKIES, ELECTRIC CARS NOW CRUISED OUR STREETS--
--ALL THANKS TO THE INCREDIBLE BLUE-SKINNED BEING TO WHOM THE RULES OF NATURE SEEMED LITTLE MORE THAN SUGGESTIONS...
PARK DR.
AMAZING, ISN'T IT?
YOU LOOK AROUND THIS CITY AND SEE VERY LITTLE THAT HASN'T HAD YOUR HAND IN IT.
ALL FOR THE BETTERMENT OF MANKIND, MARLA.
UNLIKE THE PASSAGE OF THE KEENE ACT, I'M AFRAID.

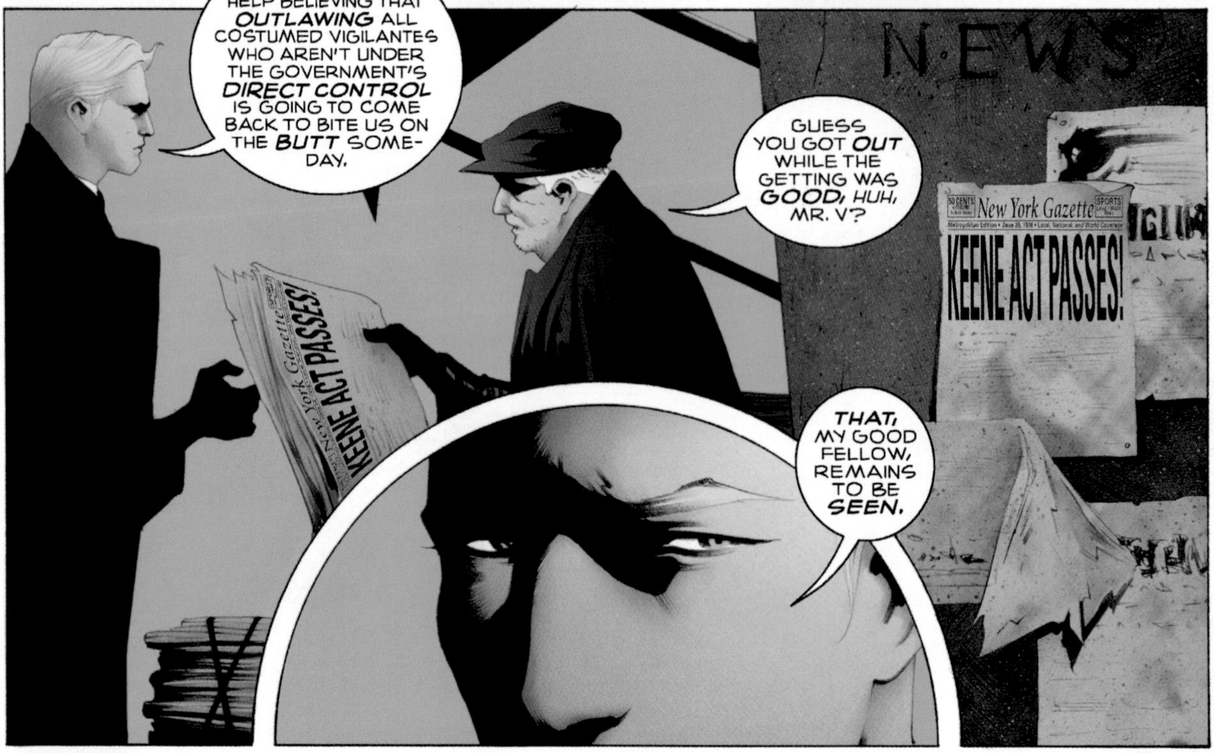
I CAN'T HELP BELIEVING THAT OUTLAWING ALL COSTUMED VIGILANTES WHO AREN'T UNDER THE GOVERNMENT'S DIRECT CONTROL IS GOING TO COME BACK TO BITE US ON THE BUTT SOMEDAY.
NEWS
GUESS YOU GOT OUT WHILE THE GETTING WAS GOOD, HUH, MR. V?
New York Gazette
KEENE ACT PASSES!
THAT, MY GOOD FELLOW, REMAINS TO BE SEEN.

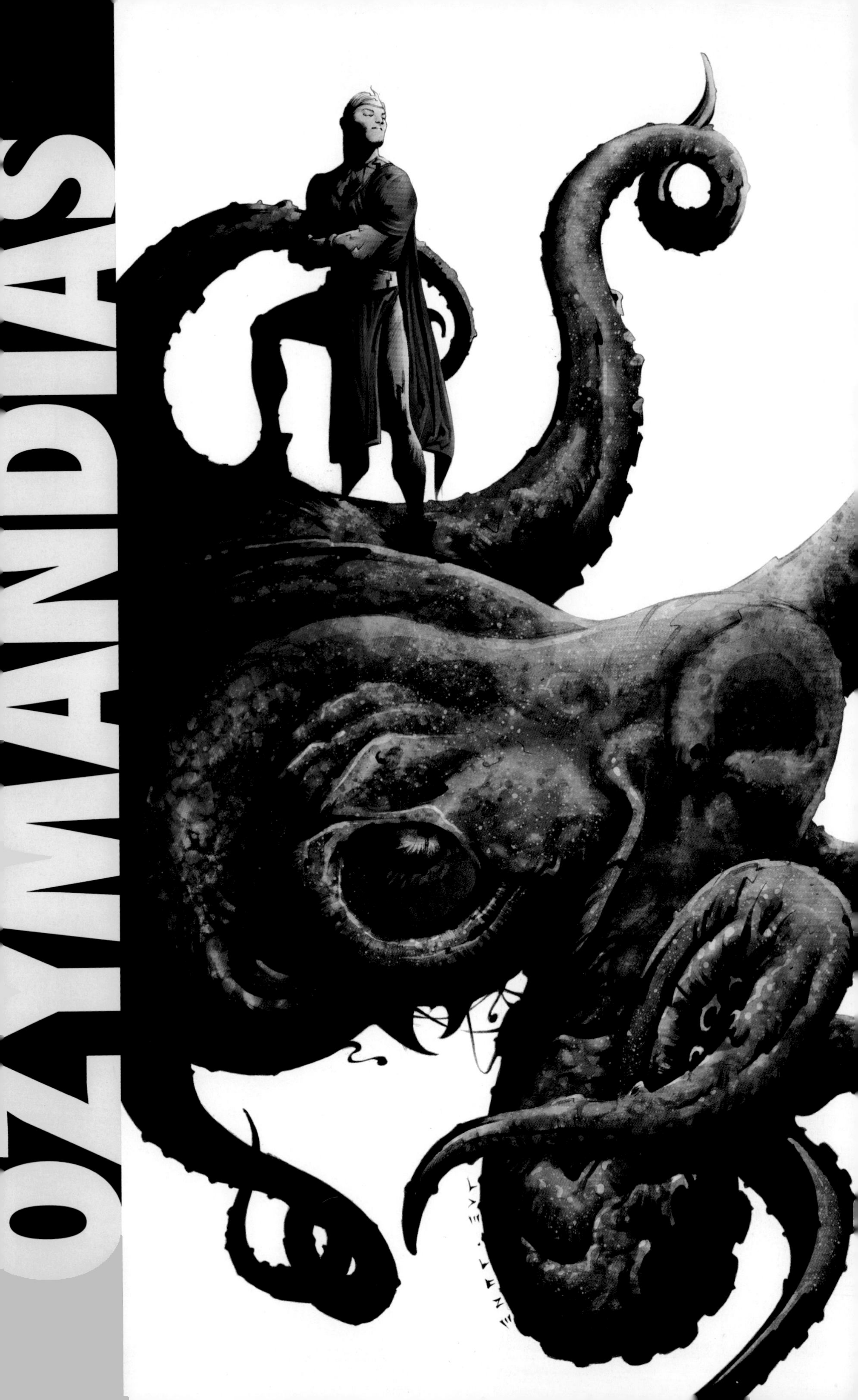
OZYMANDIAS

OZYMANDIAS

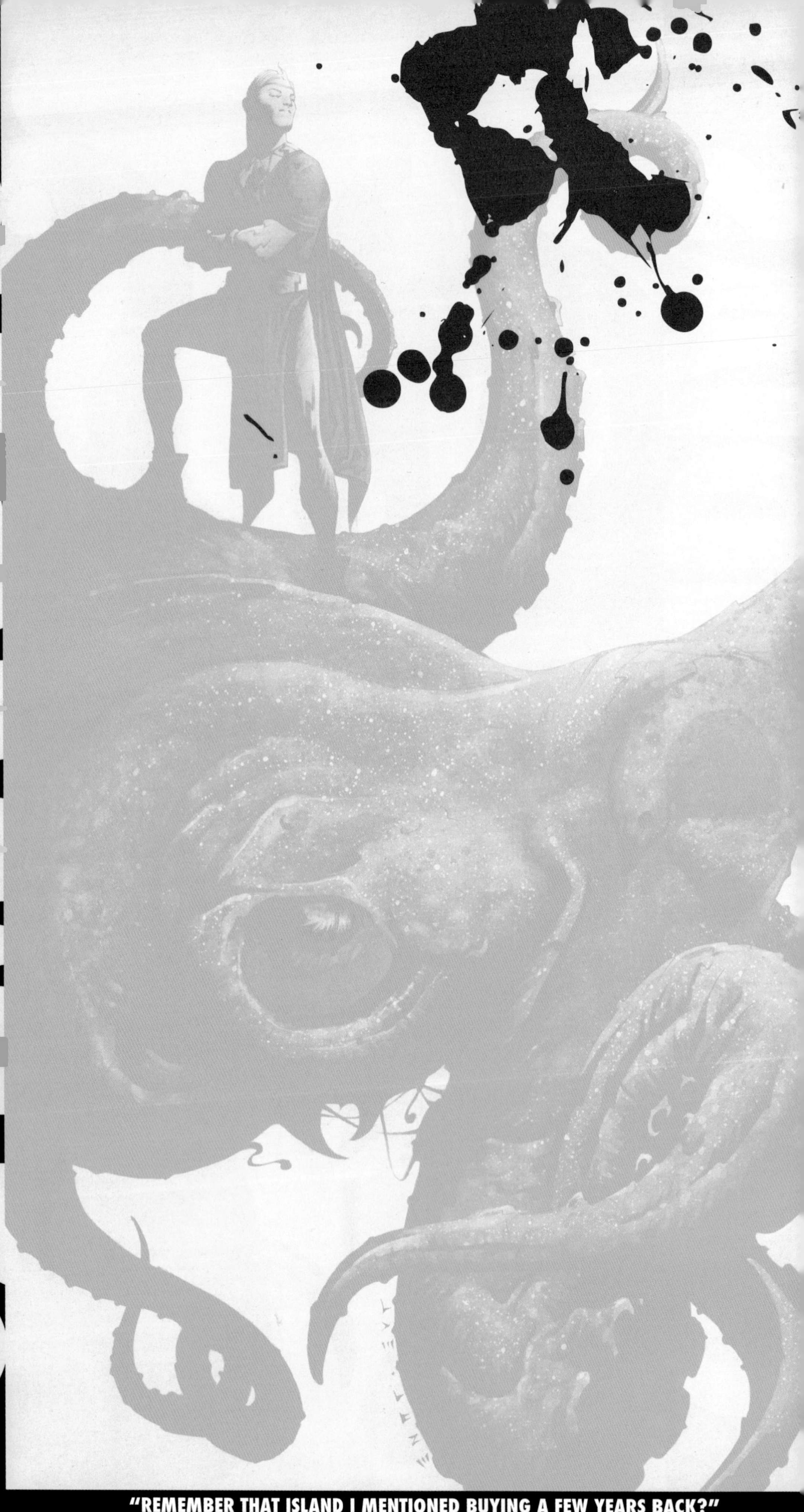

"REMEMBER THAT ISLAND I MENTIONED BUYING A FEW YEARS BACK?"

NOTHING BESIDE REMAINS

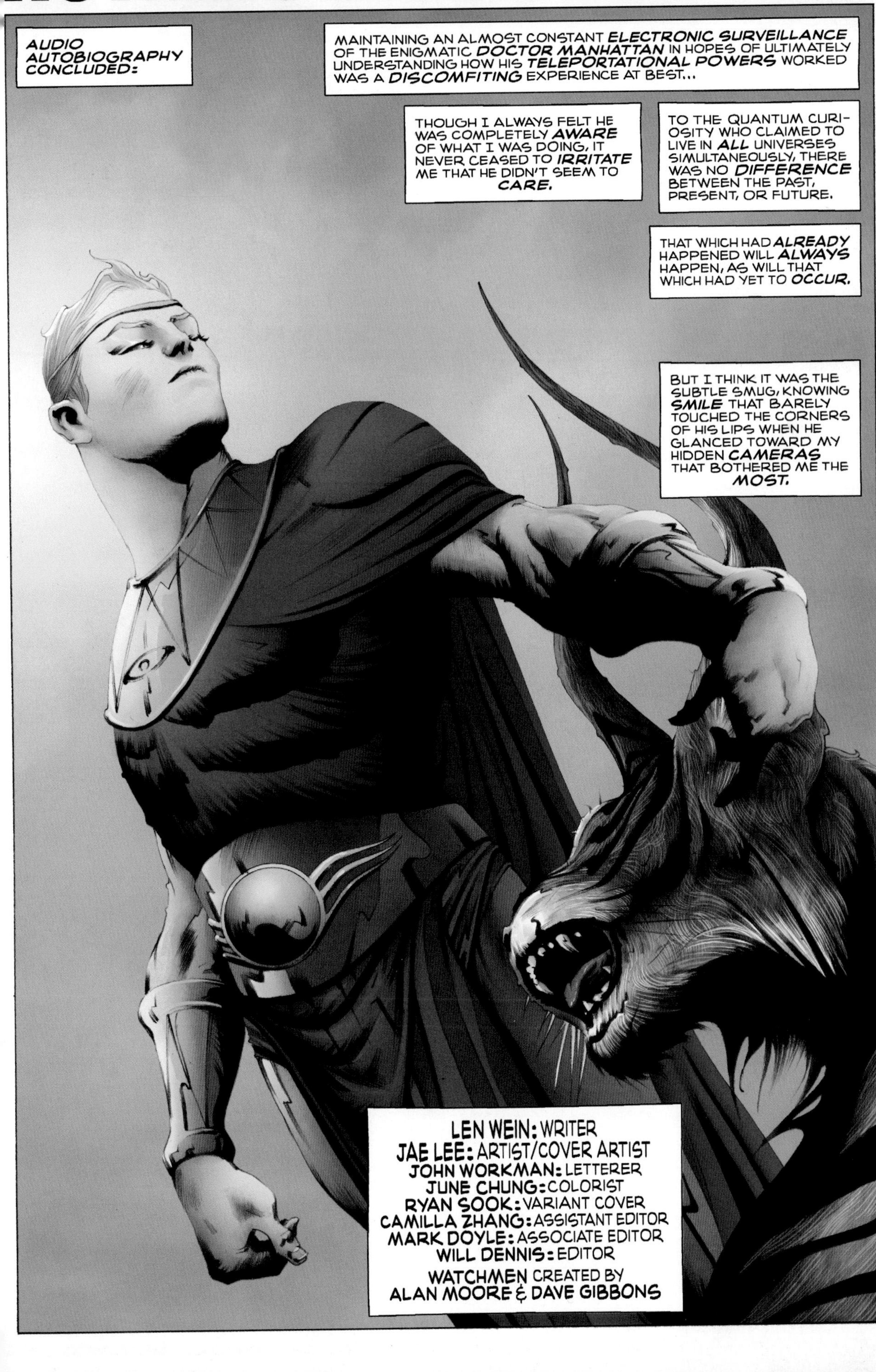

AUDIO AUTOBIOGRAPHY CONCLUDED:
MAINTAINING AN ALMOST CONSTANT ELECTRONIC SURVEILLANCE OF THE ENIGMATIC DOCTOR MANHATTAN IN HOPES OF ULTIMATELY UNDERSTANDING HOW HIS TELEPORTATIONAL POWERS WORKED WAS A DISCOMFITING EXPERIENCE AT BEST...
THOUGH I ALWAYS FELT HE WAS COMPLETELY AWARE OF WHAT I WAS DOING, IT NEVER CEASED TO IRRITATE ME THAT HE DIDN'T SEEM TO CARE.
TO THE QUANTUM CURIOSITY WHO CLAIMED TO LIVE IN ALL UNIVERSES SIMULTANEOUSLY, THERE WAS NO DIFFERENCE BETWEEN THE PAST, PRESENT, OR FUTURE.
THAT WHICH HAD ALREADY HAPPENED WILL ALWAYS HAPPEN, AS WILL THAT WHICH HAD YET TO OCCUR.
BUT I THINK IT WAS THE SUBTLE SMUG, KNOWING SMILE THAT BARELY TOUCHED THE CORNERS OF HIS LIPS WHEN HE GLANCED TOWARD MY HIDDEN CAMERAS THAT BOTHERED ME THE MOST.
LEN WEIN: WRITER
JAE LEE: ARTIST/COVER ARTIST
JOHN WORKMAN: LETTERER
JUNE CHUNG: COLORIST
RYAN SOOK: VARIANT COVER
CAMILLA ZHANG: ASSISTANT EDITOR
MARK DOYLE: ASSOCIATE EDITOR
WILL DENNIS: EDITOR
WATCHMEN CREATED BY ALAN MOORE & DAVE GIBBONS

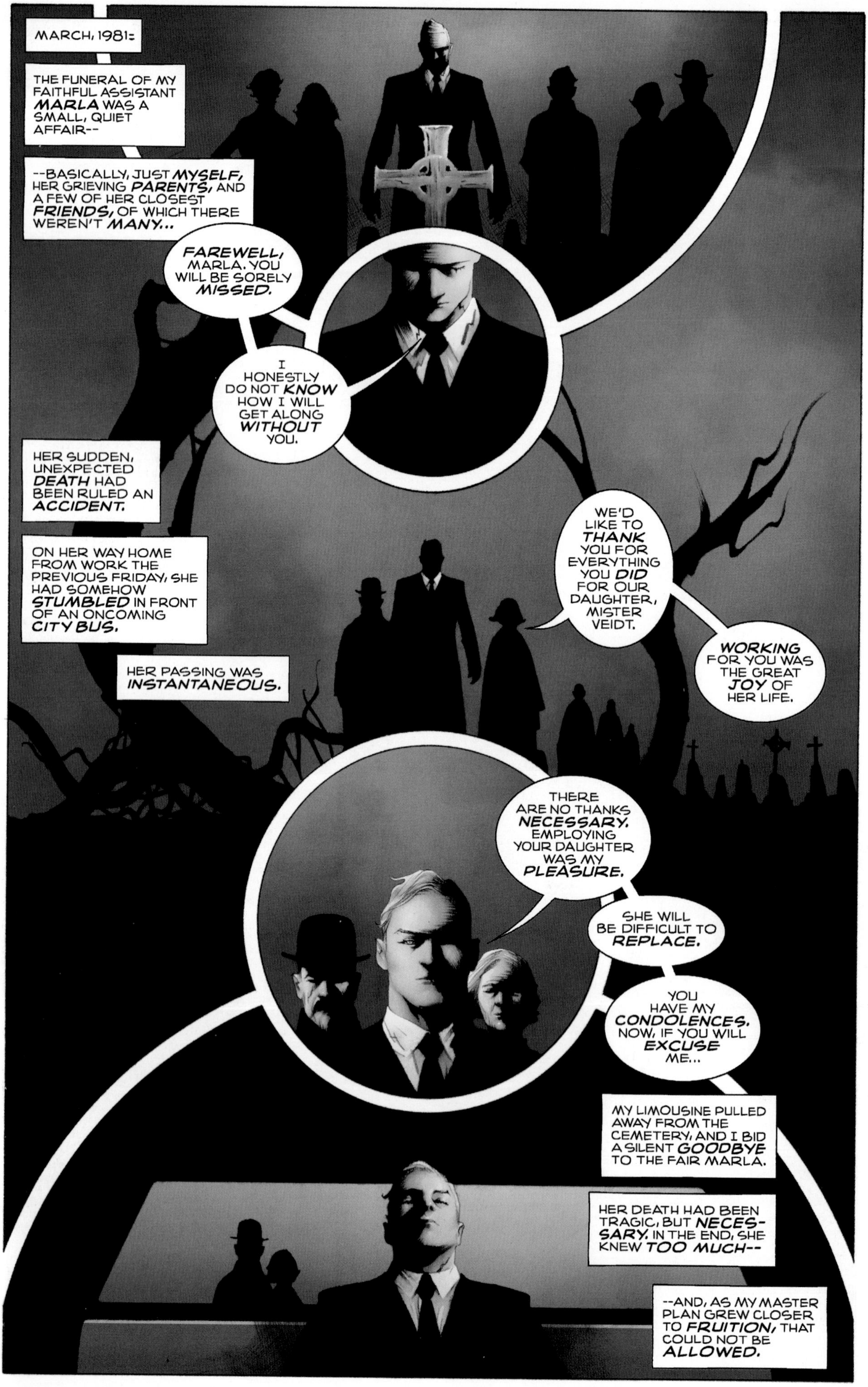
MARCH, 1981:
THE FUNERAL OF MY FAITHFUL ASSISTANT MARLA WAS A SMALL, QUIET AFFAIR--
--BASICALLY, JUST MYSELF, HER GRIEVING PARENTS, AND A FEW OF HER CLOSEST FRIENDS, OF WHICH THERE WEREN'T MANY...
FAREWELL, MARLA. YOU WILL BE SORELY MISSED.
I HONESTLY DO NOT KNOW HOW I WILL GET ALONG WITHOUT YOU.
HER SUDDEN, UNEXPECTED DEATH HAD BEEN RULED AN ACCIDENT.
ON HER WAY HOME FROM WORK THE PREVIOUS FRIDAY, SHE HAD SOMEHOW STUMBLED IN FRONT OF AN ONCOMING CITY BUS.
HER PASSING WAS INSTANTANEOUS.
WE'D LIKE TO THANK YOU FOR EVERYTHING YOU DID FOR OUR DAUGHTER, MISTER VEIDT.
WORKING FOR YOU WAS THE GREAT JOY OF HER LIFE.
THERE ARE NO THANKS NECESSARY. EMPLOYING YOUR DAUGHTER WAS MY PLEASURE.
SHE WILL BE DIFFICULT TO REPLACE.
YOU HAVE MY CONDOLENCES. NOW, IF YOU WILL EXCUSE ME...
MY LIMOUSINE PULLED AWAY FROM THE CEMETERY, AND I BID A SILENT GOODBYE TO THE FAIR MARLA.
HER DEATH HAD BEEN TRAGIC, BUT NECES-SARY. IN THE END, SHE KNEW TOO MUCH--
--AND, AS MY MASTER PLAN GREW CLOSER TO FRUITION, THAT COULD NOT BE ALLOWED.

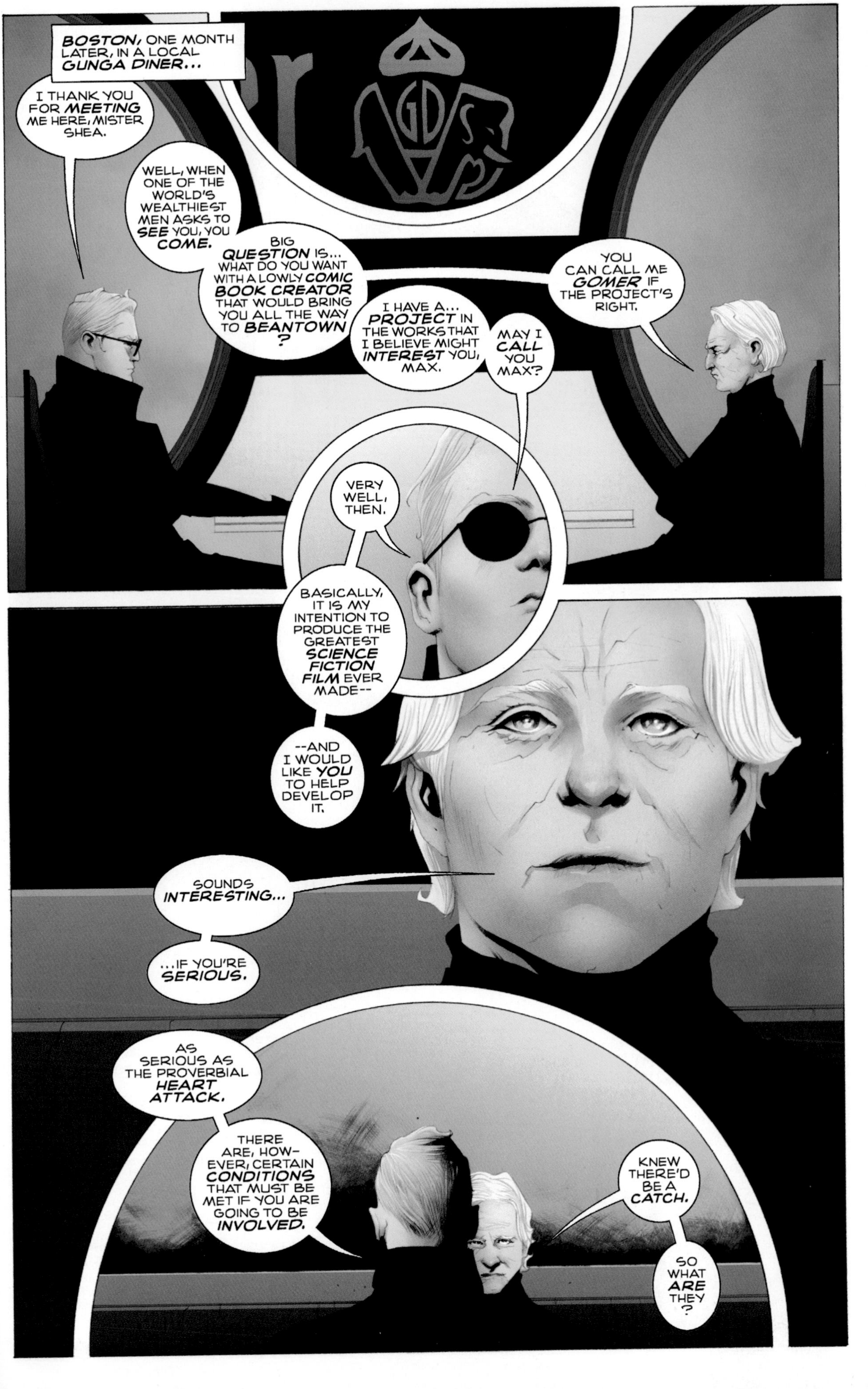
BOSTON, ONE MONTH LATER, IN A LOCAL GUNGA DINER...
I THANK YOU FOR MEETING ME HERE, MISTER SHEA.
WELL, WHEN ONE OF THE WORLD'S WEALTHIEST MEN ASKS TO SEE YOU, YOU COME.
BIG QUESTION IS... WHAT DO YOU WANT WITH A LOWLY COMIC BOOK CREATOR THAT WOULD BRING YOU ALL THE WAY TO BEANTOWN?
I HAVE A... PROJECT IN THE WORKS THAT I BELIEVE MIGHT INTEREST YOU, MAX.
MAY I CALL YOU MAX?
YOU CAN CALL ME GOMER IF THE PROJECT'S RIGHT.
VERY WELL, THEN.
BASICALLY, IT IS MY INTENTION TO PRODUCE THE GREATEST SCIENCE FICTION FILM EVER MADE--
--AND I WOULD LIKE YOU TO HELP DEVELOP IT.
SOUNDS INTERESTING...
...IF YOU'RE SERIOUS.
AS SERIOUS AS THE PROVERBIAL HEART ATTACK.
THERE ARE, HOW-EVER, CERTAIN CONDITIONS THAT MUST BE MET IF YOU ARE GOING TO BE INVOLVED.
KNEW THERE'D BE A CATCH.
SO WHAT ARE THEY?

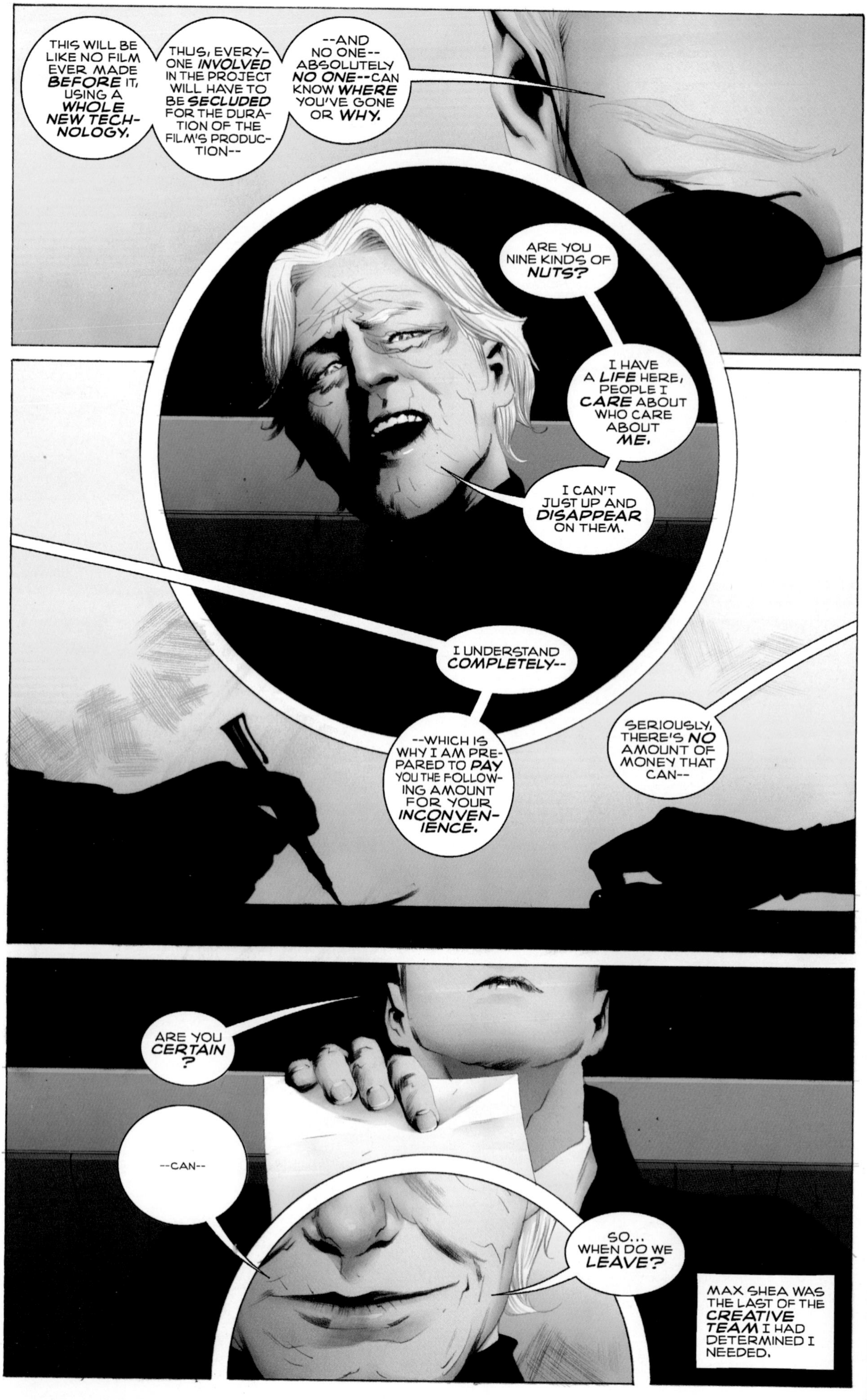
THIS WILL BE LIKE NO FILM EVER MADE BEFORE IT, USING A WHOLE NEW TECHNOLOGY.
THUS, EVERYONE INVOLVED IN THE PROJECT WILL HAVE TO BE SECLUDED FOR THE DURATION OF THE FILM'S PRODUCTION--
--AND NO ONE--ABSOLUTELY NO ONE--CAN KNOW WHERE YOU'VE GONE OR WHY.
ARE YOU NINE KINDS OF NUTS?
I HAVE A LIFE HERE, PEOPLE I CARE ABOUT WHO CARE ABOUT ME.
I CAN'T JUST UP AND DISAPPEAR ON THEM.
I UNDERSTAND COMPLETELY--
--WHICH IS WHY I AM PREPARED TO PAY YOU THE FOLLOWING AMOUNT FOR YOUR INCONVENIENCE.
SERIOUSLY, THERE'S NO AMOUNT OF MONEY THAT CAN--
ARE YOU CERTAIN?
--CAN--
SO... WHEN DO WE LEAVE?
MAX SHEA WAS THE LAST OF THE CREATIVE TEAM I HAD DETERMINED I NEEDED.

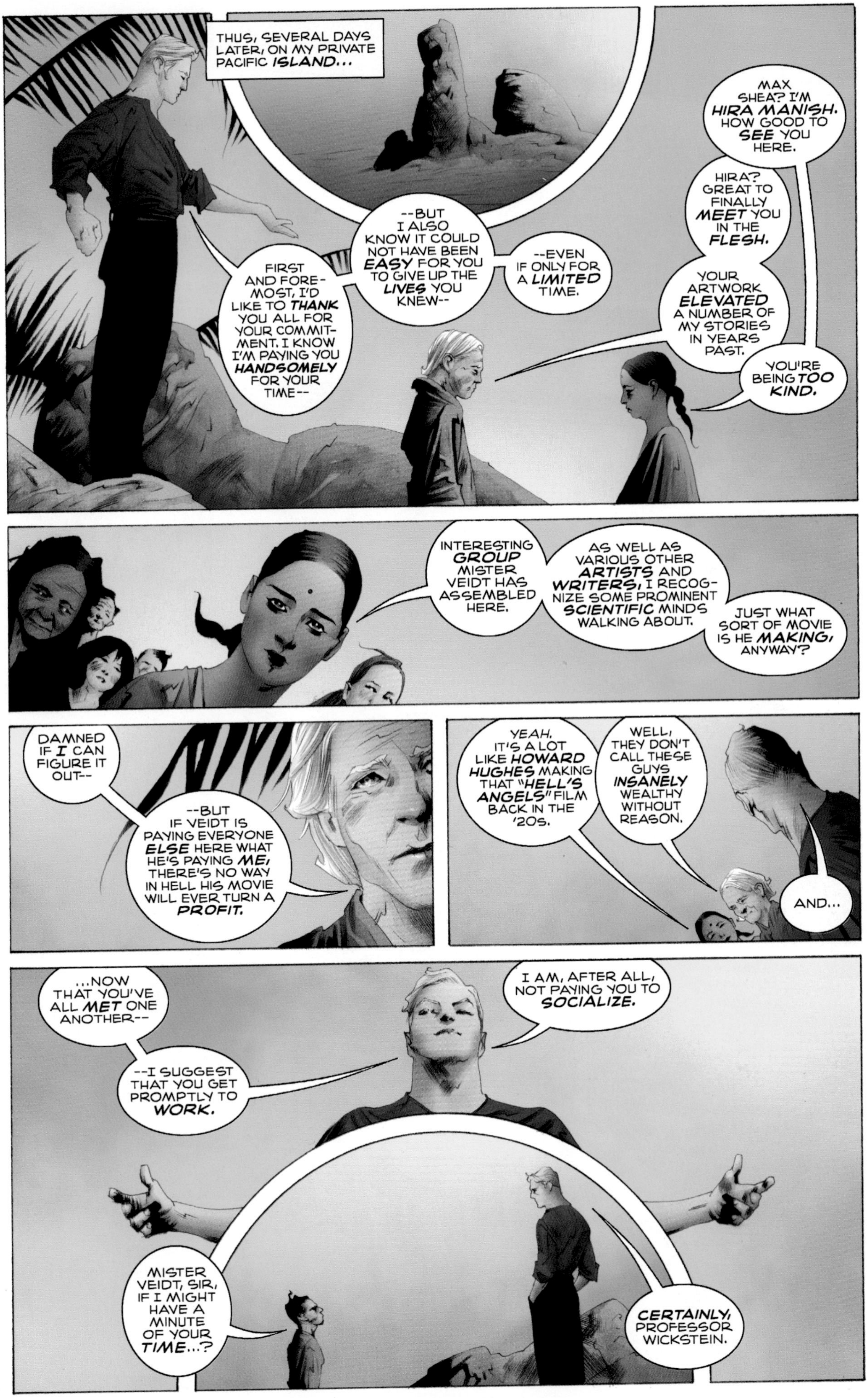
THUS, SEVERAL DAYS LATER, ON MY PRIVATE PACIFIC ISLAND...
FIRST AND FORE-MOST, I'D LIKE TO THANK YOU ALL FOR YOUR COMMIT-MENT. I KNOW I'M PAYING YOU HANDSOMELY FOR YOUR TIME--
--BUT I ALSO KNOW IT COULD NOT HAVE BEEN EASY FOR YOU TO GIVE UP THE LIVES YOU KNEW--
--EVEN IF ONLY FOR A LIMITED TIME.
MAX SHEA? I'M HIRA MANISH. HOW GOOD TO SEE YOU HERE.
HIRA? GREAT TO FINALLY MEET YOU IN THE FLESH.
YOUR ARTWORK ELEVATED A NUMBER OF MY STORIES IN YEARS PAST.
YOU'RE BEING TOO KIND.
INTERESTING GROUP MISTER VEIDT HAS ASSEMBLED HERE.
AS WELL AS VARIOUS OTHER ARTISTS AND WRITERS, I RECOG-NIZE SOME PROMINENT SCIENTIFIC MINDS WALKING ABOUT.
JUST WHAT SORT OF MOVIE IS HE MAKING, ANYWAY?
DAMNED IF I CAN FIGURE IT OUT--
--BUT IF VEIDT IS PAYING EVERYONE ELSE HERE WHAT HE'S PAYING ME, THERE'S NO WAY IN HELL HIS MOVIE WILL EVER TURN A PROFIT.
YEAH. IT'S A LOT LIKE HOWARD HUGHES MAKING THAT "HELL'S ANGELS" FILM BACK IN THE '20S.
WELL, THEY DON'T CALL THESE GUYS INSANELY WEALTHY WITHOUT REASON.
AND...
...NOW THAT YOU'VE ALL MET ONE ANOTHER--
--I SUGGEST THAT YOU GET PROMPTLY TO WORK.
I AM, AFTER ALL, NOT PAYING YOU TO SOCIALIZE.
MISTER VEIDT, SIR, IF I MIGHT HAVE A MINUTE OF YOUR TIME...?
CERTAINLY, PROFESSOR WICKSTEIN.

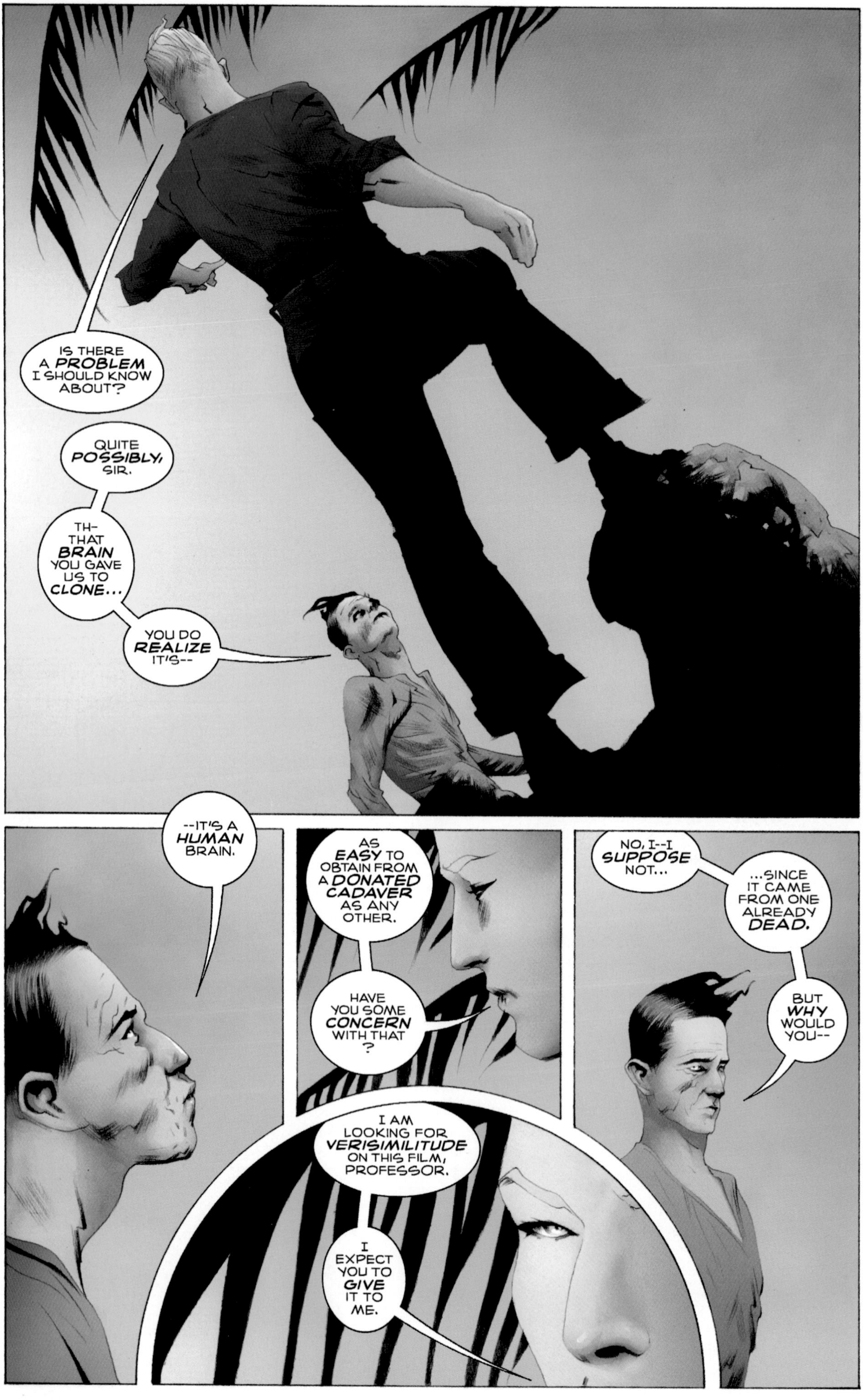
IS THERE A PROBLEM I SHOULD KNOW ABOUT?
QUITE POSSIBLY, SIR.
TH-THAT BRAIN YOU GAVE US TO CLONE...
YOU DO REALIZE IT'S--
--IT'S A HUMAN BRAIN.
AS EASY TO OBTAIN FROM A DONATED CADAVER AS ANY OTHER.
HAVE YOU SOME CONCERN WITH THAT?
NO, I--I SUPPOSE NOT...
...SINCE IT CAME FROM ONE ALREADY DEAD.
BUT WHY WOULD YOU--
I AM LOOKING FOR VERISIMILITUDE ON THIS FILM, PROFESSOR.
I EXPECT YOU TO GIVE IT TO ME.

LEAVING MY ASSEMBLED *"FILM CREW"* TO THEIR DESIGNATED TASKS, I RE-TURNED TO *NEW YORK*--

--AND MY SO-CALLED *"NORMAL"* LIFE...

YOU WANTED COPIES OF ALL THE MORNING *PAPERS,* MISTER *VEIDT?*

YES, TODAY AND *EVERY* DAY ...*YVONNE,* WAS IT?

YES, SIR.

AND THANK YOU AGAIN FOR THE OPPORTUNITY TO BE YOUR *ASSISTANT.*

JUST REMEMBER YOU HAVE EXCEPTIONAL *SHOES* TO FILL.

MY *PREVIOUS* ASSISTANT... MARLA... WAS AN *EXTRAORDINARY* YOUNG WOMAN.

SO YOU'VE *TOLD* ME *SEVERAL TIMES* ALREADY, SIR.

WELL, *THIS* IS DISTRESSING.

WHAT IS, SIR?

THIS *HEADLINE* IN THE GAZETTE...

I'VE BEEN *ANTICIPATING* THIS.

New York Gazette

News

...olitan Edition • April 28, 1981 • Local, National, and World Coverage

SCIENTISTS MOVE DOOMSDAY CLOCK ONE MINUTE CLOSER TO MIDNIGHT!

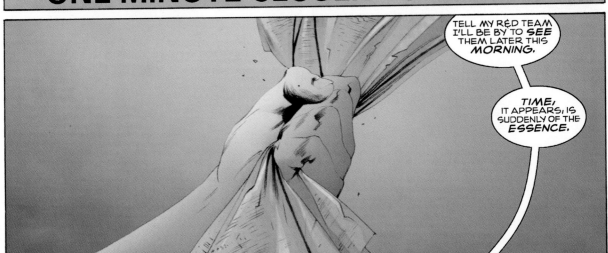

TELL MY *RED* TEAM I'LL BE BY TO *SEE* THEM LATER THIS *MORNING.*

TIME, IT APPEARS, IS SUDDENLY OF THE *ESSENCE.*

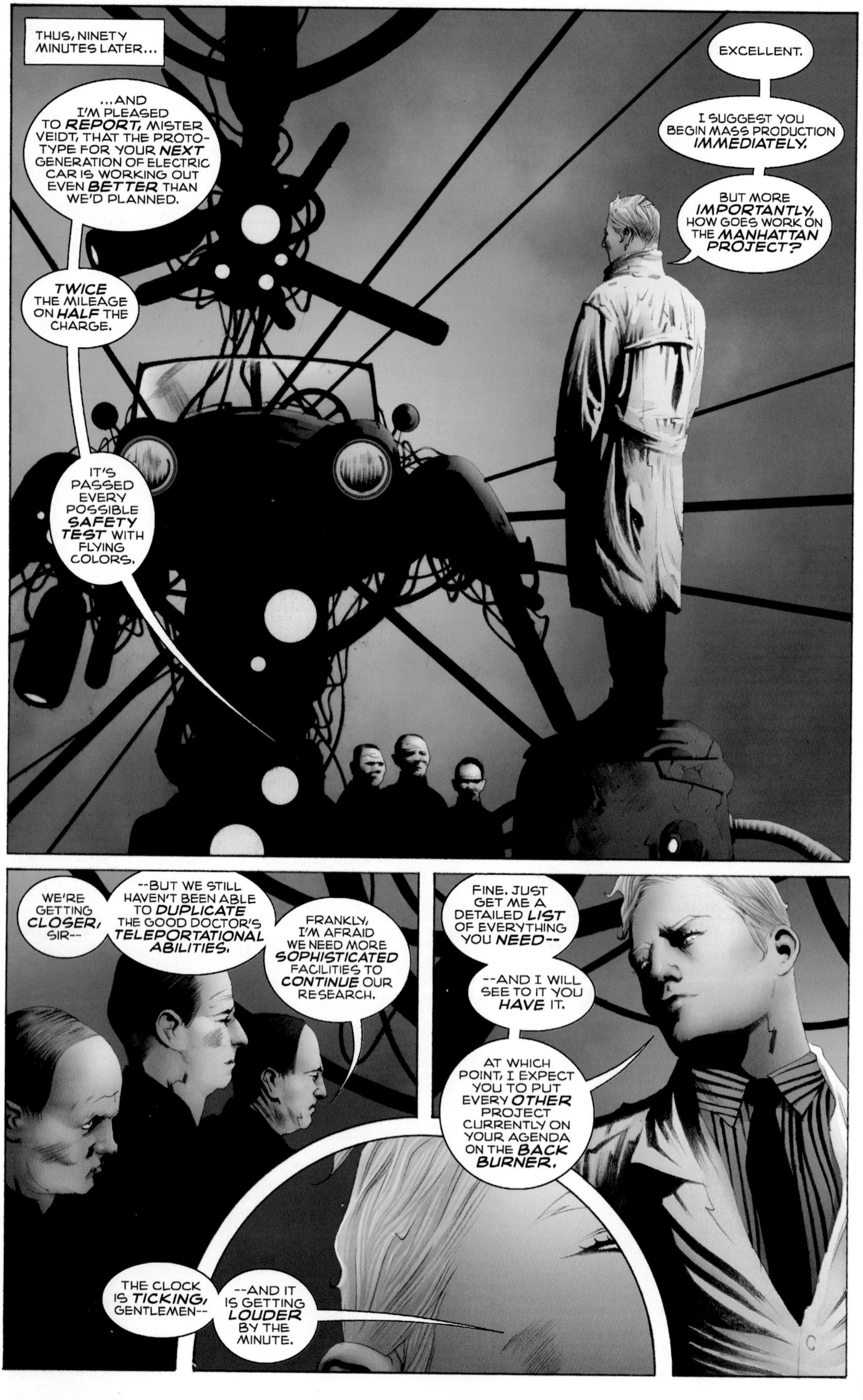
THUS, NINETY MINUTES LATER...
...AND I'M PLEASED TO REPORT, MISTER VEIDT, THAT THE PROTOTYPE FOR YOUR NEXT GENERATION OF ELECTRIC CAR IS WORKING OUT EVEN BETTER THAN WE'D PLANNED.
TWICE THE MILEAGE ON HALF THE CHARGE.
IT'S PASSED EVERY POSSIBLE SAFETY TEST WITH FLYING COLORS.
EXCELLENT.
I SUGGEST YOU BEGIN MASS PRODUCTION IMMEDIATELY.
BUT MORE IMPORTANTLY, HOW GOES WORK ON THE MANHATTAN PROJECT?
WE'RE GETTING CLOSER, SIR--
--BUT WE STILL HAVEN'T BEEN ABLE TO DUPLICATE THE GOOD DOCTOR'S TELEPORTATIONAL ABILITIES.
FRANKLY, I'M AFRAID WE NEED MORE SOPHISTICATED FACILITIES TO CONTINUE OUR RESEARCH.
FINE. JUST GET ME A DETAILED LIST OF EVERYTHING YOU NEED--
--AND I WILL SEE TO IT YOU HAVE IT.
AT WHICH POINT, I EXPECT YOU TO PUT EVERY OTHER PROJECT CURRENTLY ON YOUR AGENDA ON THE BACK BURNER.
THE CLOCK IS TICKING, GENTLEMEN--
--AND IT IS GETTING LOUDER BY THE MINUTE.

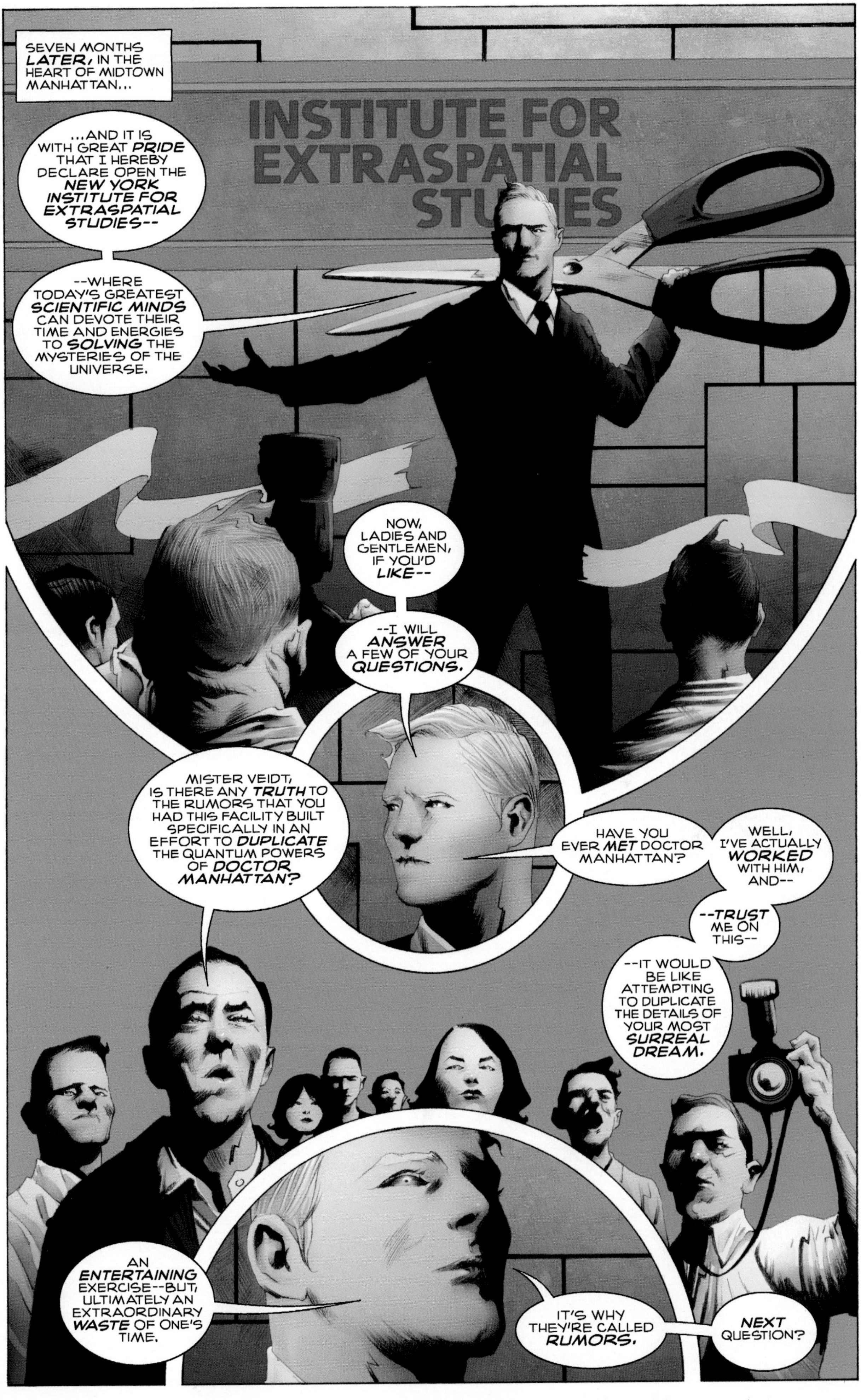
SEVEN MONTHS LATER, IN THE HEART OF MIDTOWN MANHATTAN...
INSTITUTE FOR EXTRASPATIAL STUDIES
...AND IT IS WITH GREAT PRIDE THAT I HEREBY DECLARE OPEN THE NEW YORK INSTITUTE FOR EXTRASPATIAL STUDIES--
--WHERE TODAY'S GREATEST SCIENTIFIC MINDS CAN DEVOTE THEIR TIME AND ENERGIES TO SOLVING THE MYSTERIES OF THE UNIVERSE.
NOW, LADIES AND GENTLEMEN, IF YOU'D LIKE--
--I WILL ANSWER A FEW OF YOUR QUESTIONS.
MISTER VEIDT, IS THERE ANY TRUTH TO THE RUMORS THAT YOU HAD THIS FACILITY BUILT SPECIFICALLY IN AN EFFORT TO DUPLICATE THE QUANTUM POWERS OF DOCTOR MANHATTAN?
HAVE YOU EVER MET DOCTOR MANHATTAN?
WELL, I'VE ACTUALLY WORKED WITH HIM, AND--
--TRUST ME ON THIS--
--IT WOULD BE LIKE ATTEMPTING TO DUPLICATE THE DETAILS OF YOUR MOST SURREAL DREAM.
AN ENTERTAINING EXERCISE--BUT, ULTIMATELY AN EXTRAORDINARY WASTE OF ONE'S TIME.
IT'S WHY THEY'RE CALLED RUMORS.
NEXT QUESTION?

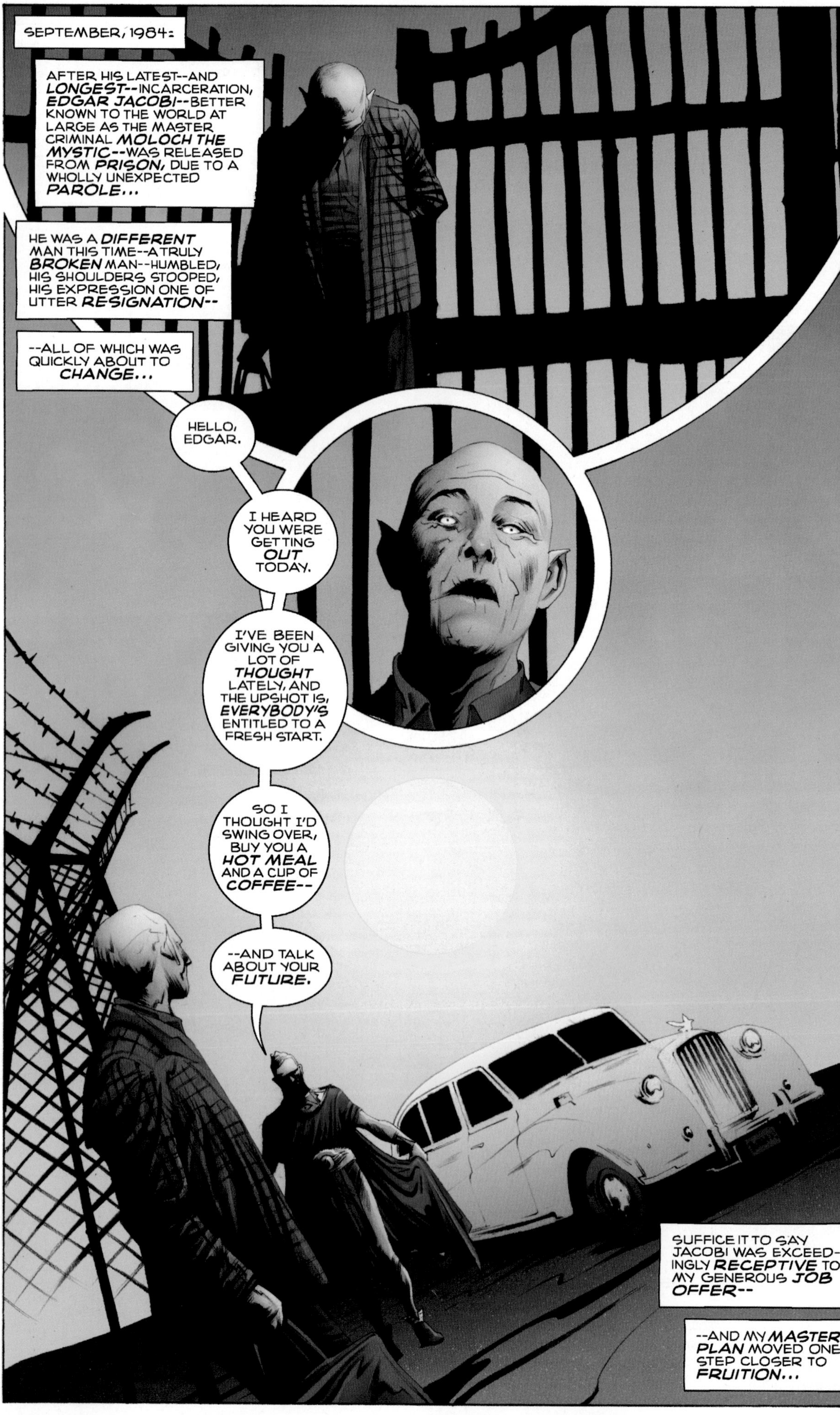
SEPTEMBER, 1984:
AFTER HIS LATEST--AND LONGEST--INCARCERATION, EDGAR JACOBI--BETTER KNOWN TO THE WORLD AT LARGE AS THE MASTER CRIMINAL MOLOCH THE MYSTIC--WAS RELEASED FROM PRISON, DUE TO A WHOLLY UNEXPECTED PAROLE...
HE WAS A DIFFERENT MAN THIS TIME--A TRULY BROKEN MAN--HUMBLED, HIS SHOULDERS STOOPED, HIS EXPRESSION ONE OF UTTER RESIGNATION--
--ALL OF WHICH WAS QUICKLY ABOUT TO CHANGE...
HELLO, EDGAR.
I HEARD YOU WERE GETTING OUT TODAY.
I'VE BEEN GIVING YOU A LOT OF THOUGHT LATELY, AND THE UPSHOT IS, EVERYBODY'S ENTITLED TO A FRESH START.
SO I THOUGHT I'D SWING OVER, BUY YOU A HOT MEAL AND A CUP OF COFFEE--
--AND TALK ABOUT YOUR FUTURE.
SUFFICE IT TO SAY JACOBI WAS EXCEEDINGLY RECEPTIVE TO MY GENEROUS JOB OFFER--
--AND MY MASTER PLAN MOVED ONE STEP CLOSER TO FRUITION...

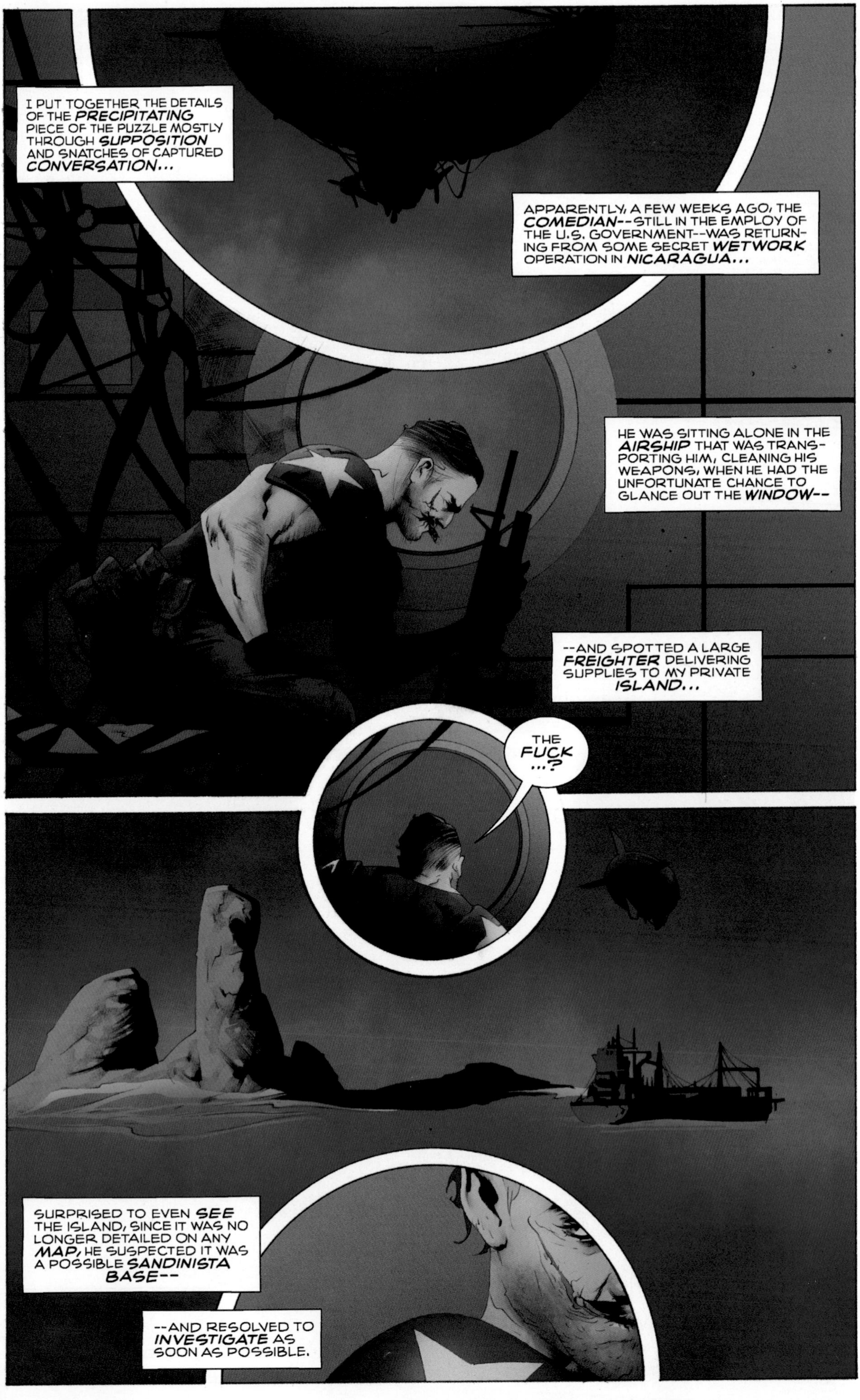

I PUT TOGETHER THE DETAILS OF THE PRECIPITATING PIECE OF THE PUZZLE MOSTLY THROUGH SUPPOSITION AND SNATCHES OF CAPTURED CONVERSATION...
APPARENTLY, A FEW WEEKS AGO, THE COMEDIAN--STILL IN THE EMPLOY OF THE U.S. GOVERNMENT--WAS RETURNING FROM SOME SECRET WETWORK OPERATION IN NICARAGUA...
HE WAS SITTING ALONE IN THE AIRSHIP THAT WAS TRANSPORTING HIM, CLEANING HIS WEAPONS, WHEN HE HAD THE UNFORTUNATE CHANCE TO GLANCE OUT THE WINDOW--
--AND SPOTTED A LARGE FREIGHTER DELIVERING SUPPLIES TO MY PRIVATE ISLAND...
THE FUCK ...?
SURPRISED TO EVEN SEE THE ISLAND, SINCE IT WAS NO LONGER DETAILED ON ANY MAP, HE SUSPECTED IT WAS A POSSIBLE SANDINISTA BASE--
--AND RESOLVED TO INVESTIGATE AS SOON AS POSSIBLE.

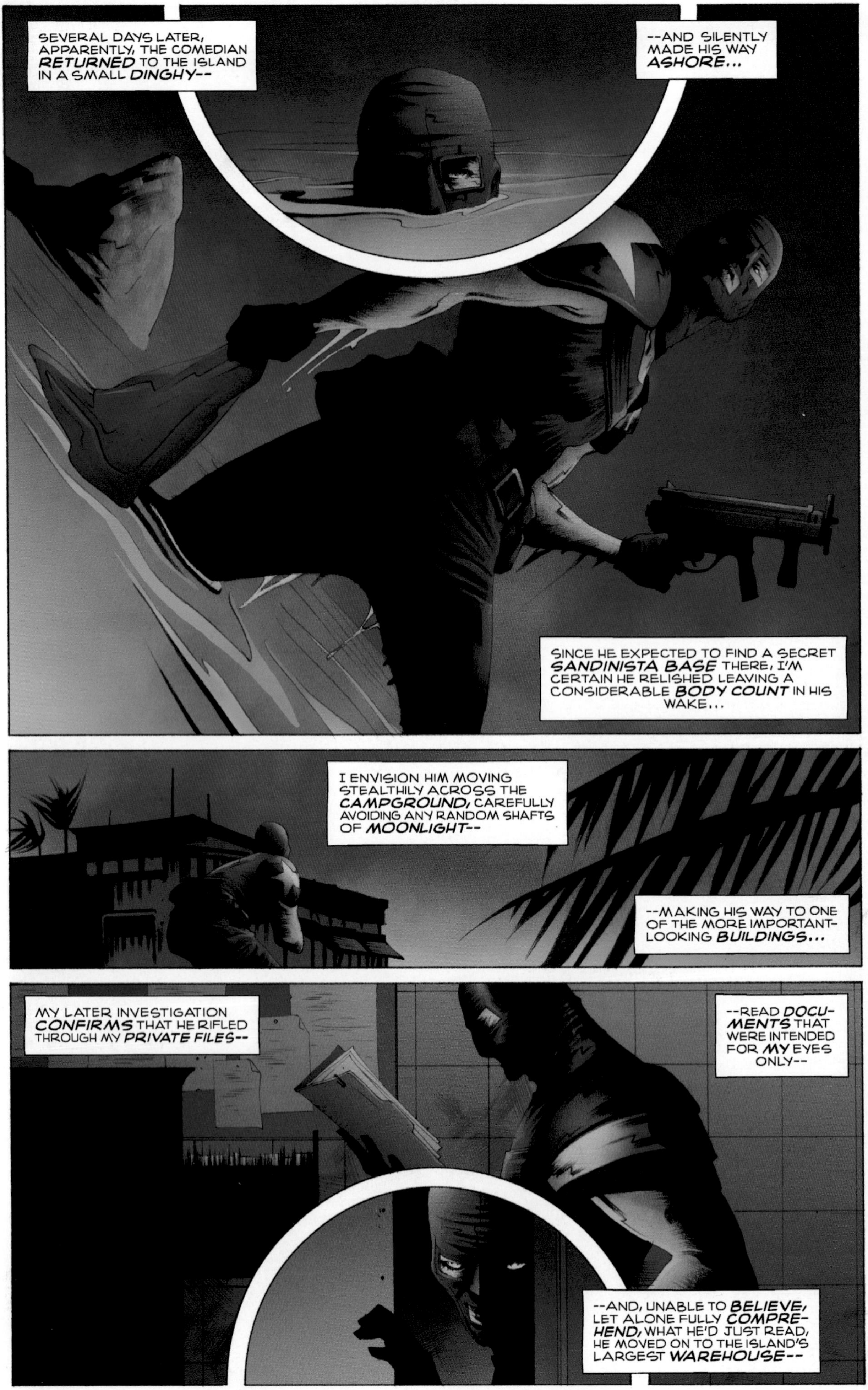
SEVERAL DAYS LATER, APPARENTLY, THE COMEDIAN RETURNED TO THE ISLAND IN A SMALL DINGHY--
--AND SILENTLY MADE HIS WAY ASHORE...
SINCE HE EXPECTED TO FIND A SECRET SANDINISTA BASE THERE, I'M CERTAIN HE RELISHED LEAVING A CONSIDERABLE BODY COUNT IN HIS WAKE...
I ENVISION HIM MOVING STEALTHILY ACROSS THE CAMPGROUND, CAREFULLY AVOIDING ANY RANDOM SHAFTS OF MOONLIGHT--
--MAKING HIS WAY TO ONE OF THE MORE IMPORTANT-LOOKING BUILDINGS...
MY LATER INVESTIGATION CONFIRMS THAT HE RIFLED THROUGH MY PRIVATE FILES--
--READ DOCUMENTS THAT WERE INTENDED FOR MY EYES ONLY--
--AND, UNABLE TO BELIEVE, LET ALONE FULLY COMPREHEND, WHAT HE'D JUST READ, HE MOVED ON TO THE ISLAND'S LARGEST WAREHOUSE--

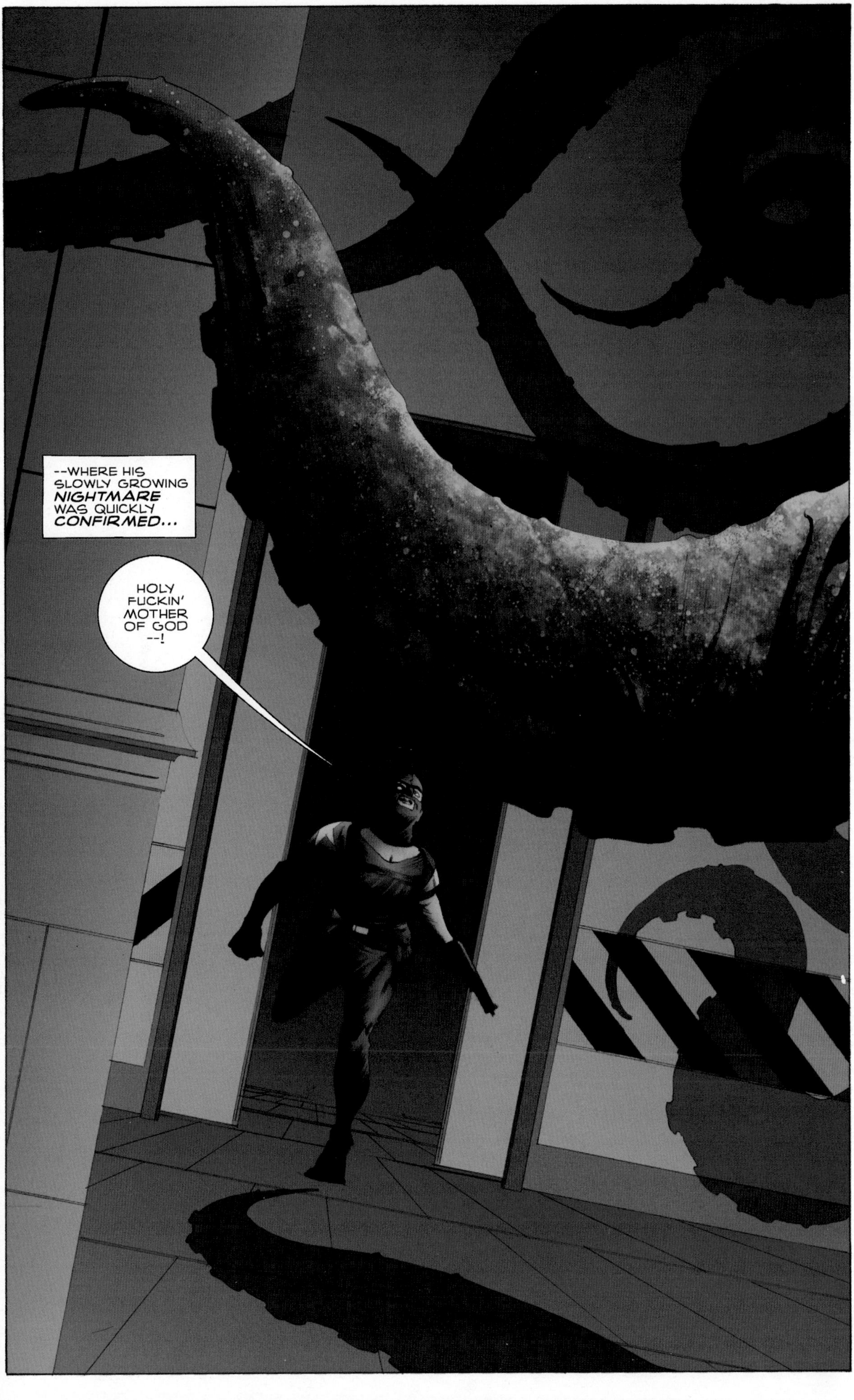

--WHERE HIS SLOWLY GROWING ***NIGHTMARE*** WAS QUICKLY ***CONFIRMED...***
HOLY FUCKIN' MOTHER OF GOD --!

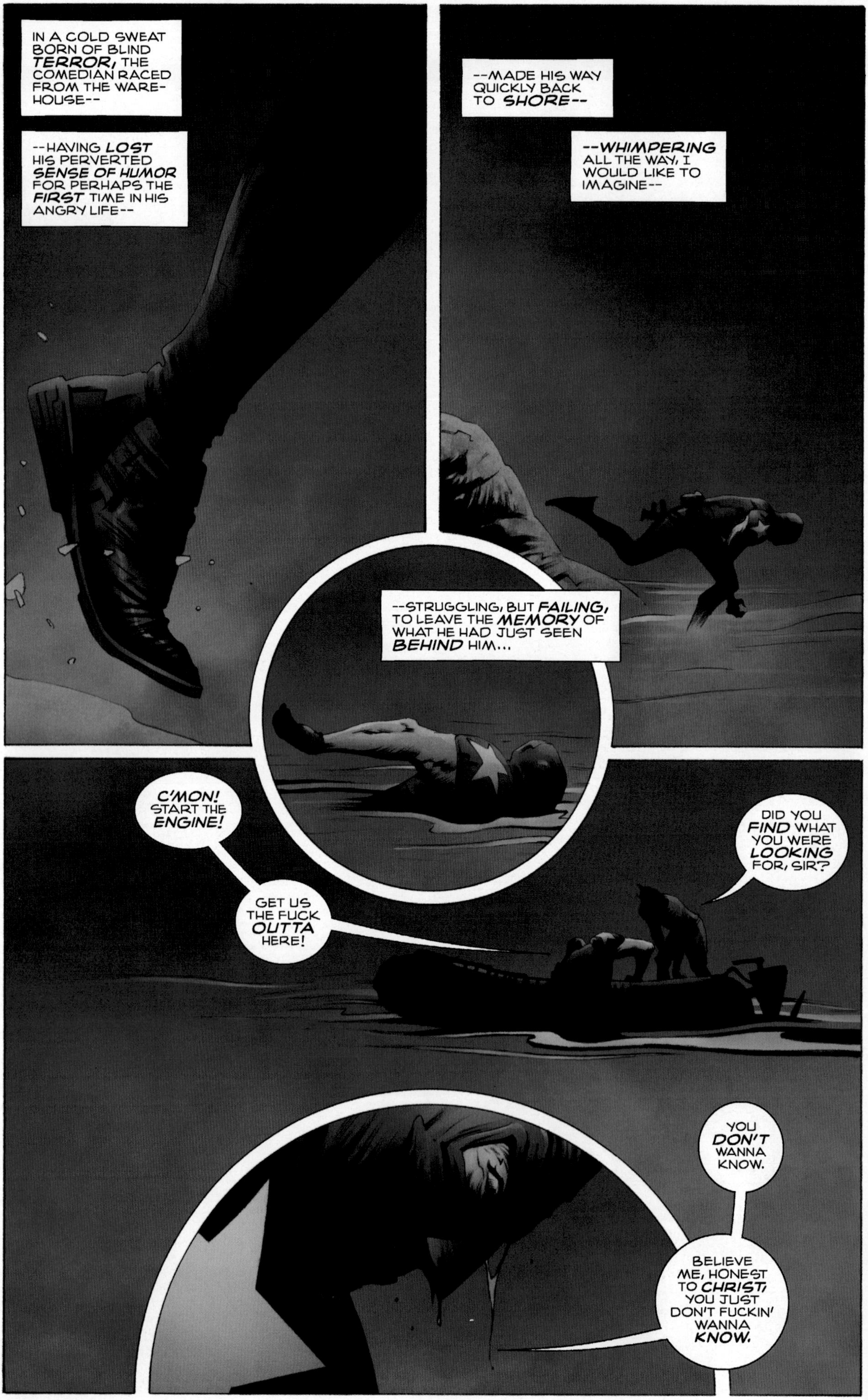
IN A COLD SWEAT BORN OF BLIND TERROR, THE COMEDIAN RACED FROM THE WAREHOUSE--
--HAVING LOST HIS PERVERTED SENSE OF HUMOR FOR PERHAPS THE FIRST TIME IN HIS ANGRY LIFE--
--MADE HIS WAY QUICKLY BACK TO SHORE--
--WHIMPERING ALL THE WAY, I WOULD LIKE TO IMAGINE--
--STRUGGLING, BUT FAILING, TO LEAVE THE MEMORY OF WHAT HE HAD JUST SEEN BEHIND HIM...
C'MON! START THE ENGINE!
GET US THE FUCK OUTTA HERE!
DID YOU FIND WHAT YOU WERE LOOKING FOR, SIR?
YOU DON'T WANNA KNOW.
BELIEVE ME, HONEST TO CHRIST, YOU JUST DON'T FUCKIN' WANNA KNOW.

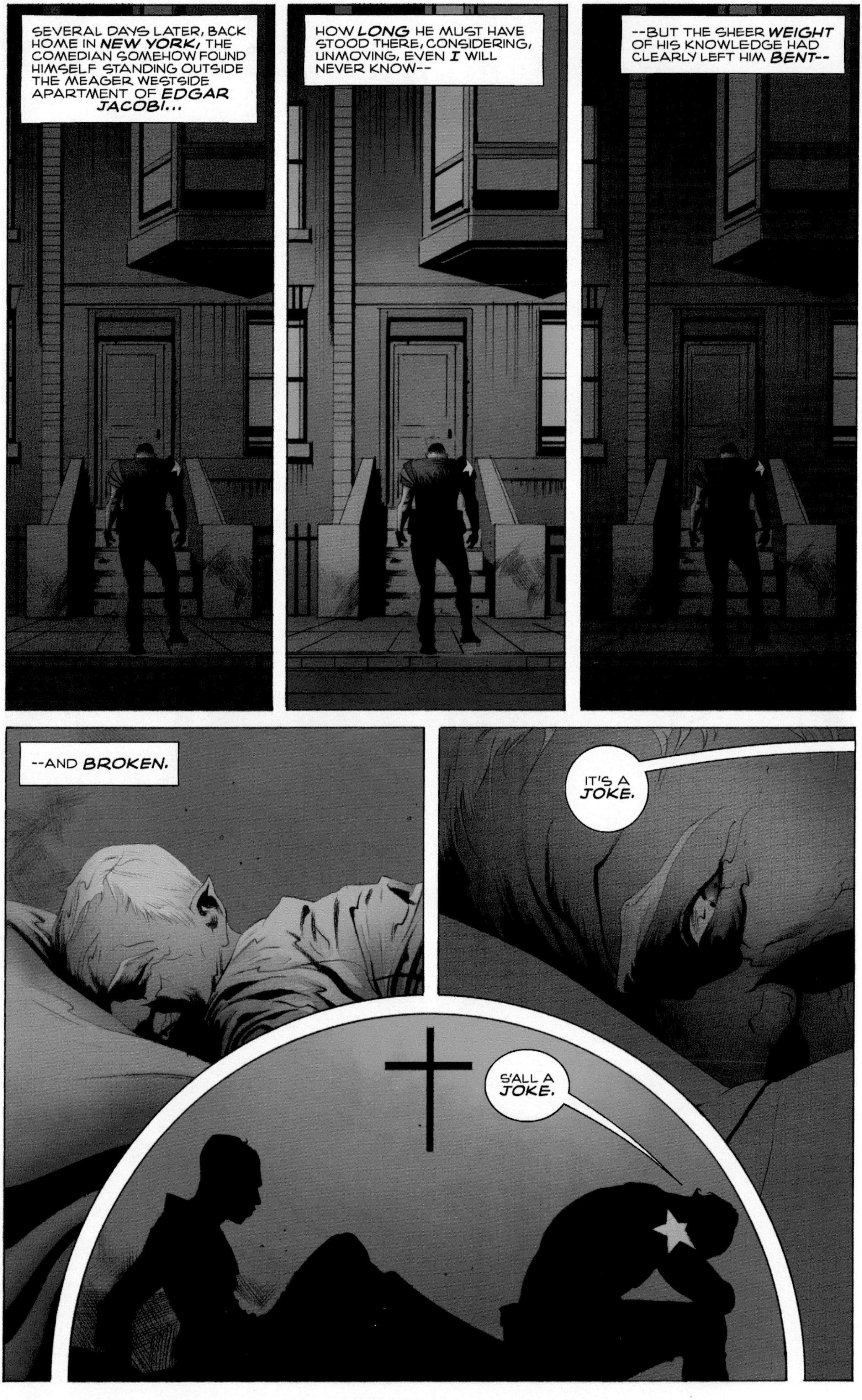
SEVERAL DAYS LATER, BACK HOME IN NEW YORK, THE COMEDIAN SOMEHOW FOUND HIMSELF STANDING OUTSIDE THE MEAGER WESTSIDE APARTMENT OF EDGAR JACOBI...
HOW LONG HE MUST HAVE STOOD THERE, CONSIDERING, UNMOVING, EVEN I WILL NEVER KNOW--
--BUT THE SHEER WEIGHT OF HIS KNOWLEDGE HAD CLEARLY LEFT HIM BENT--
--AND BROKEN.
IT'S A JOKE.
S'ALL A JOKE.

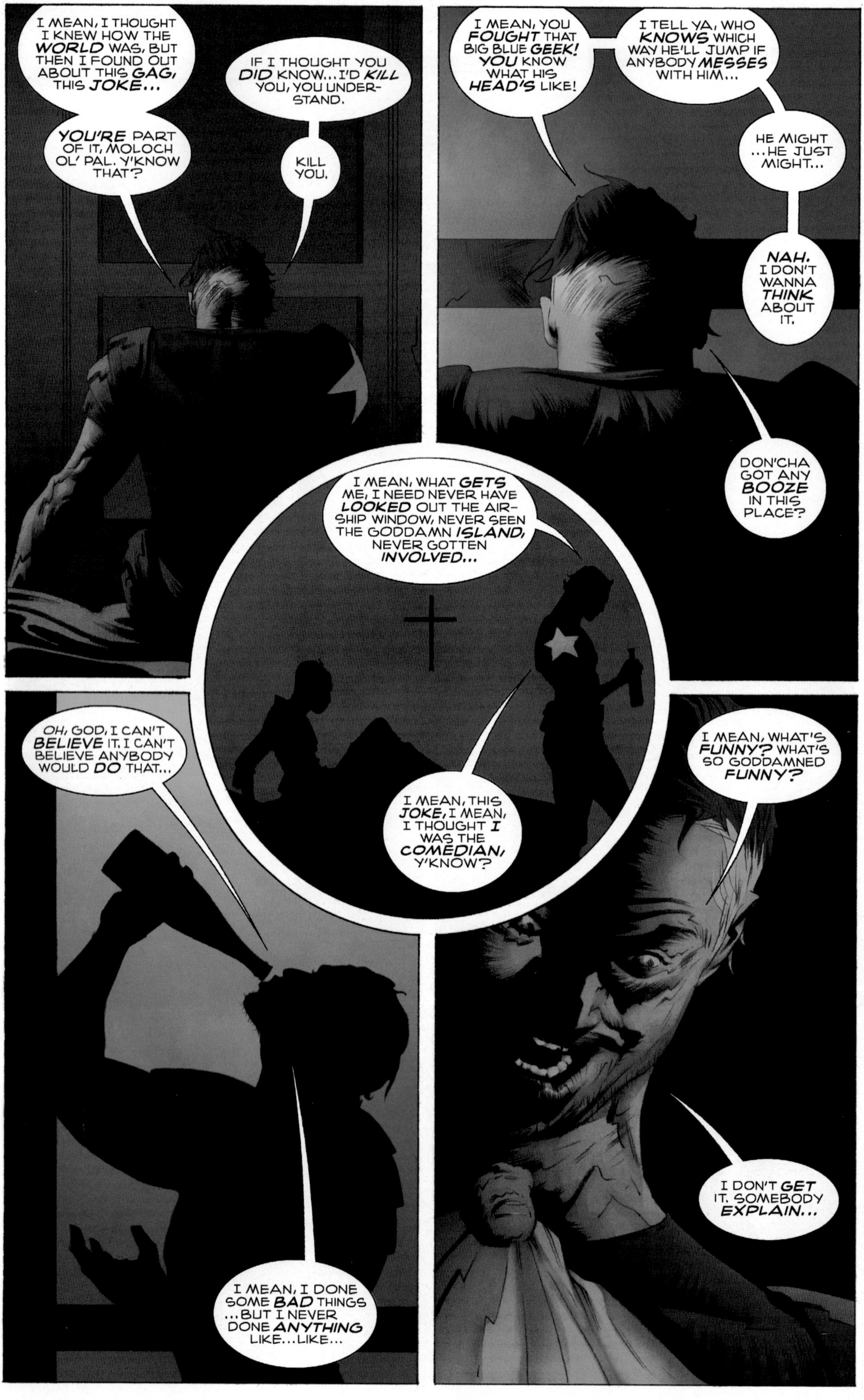
I MEAN, I THOUGHT I KNEW HOW THE WORLD WAS, BUT THEN I FOUND OUT ABOUT THIS GAG, THIS JOKE...
YOU'RE PART OF IT, MOLOCH OL' PAL. Y'KNOW THAT?
IF I THOUGHT YOU DID KNOW...I'D KILL YOU, YOU UNDER-STAND.
KILL YOU.
I MEAN, YOU FOUGHT THAT BIG BLUE GEEK! YOU KNOW WHAT HIS HEAD'S LIKE!
I TELL YA, WHO KNOWS WHICH WAY HE'LL JUMP IF ANYBODY MESSES WITH HIM...
HE MIGHT ...HE JUST MIGHT...
NAH. I DON'T WANNA THINK ABOUT IT.
DON'CHA GOT ANY BOOZE IN THIS PLACE?
I MEAN, WHAT GETS ME, I NEED NEVER HAVE LOOKED OUT THE AIR-SHIP WINDOW, NEVER SEEN THE GODDAMN ISLAND, NEVER GOTTEN INVOLVED...
I MEAN, THIS JOKE, I MEAN, I THOUGHT I WAS THE COMEDIAN, Y'KNOW?
OH, GOD, I CAN'T BELIEVE IT. I CAN'T BELIEVE ANYBODY WOULD DO THAT...
I MEAN, I DONE SOME BAD THINGS ...BUT I NEVER DONE ANYTHING LIKE...LIKE...
I MEAN, WHAT'S FUNNY? WHAT'S SO GODDAMNED FUNNY?
I DON'T GET IT. SOMEBODY EXPLAIN...

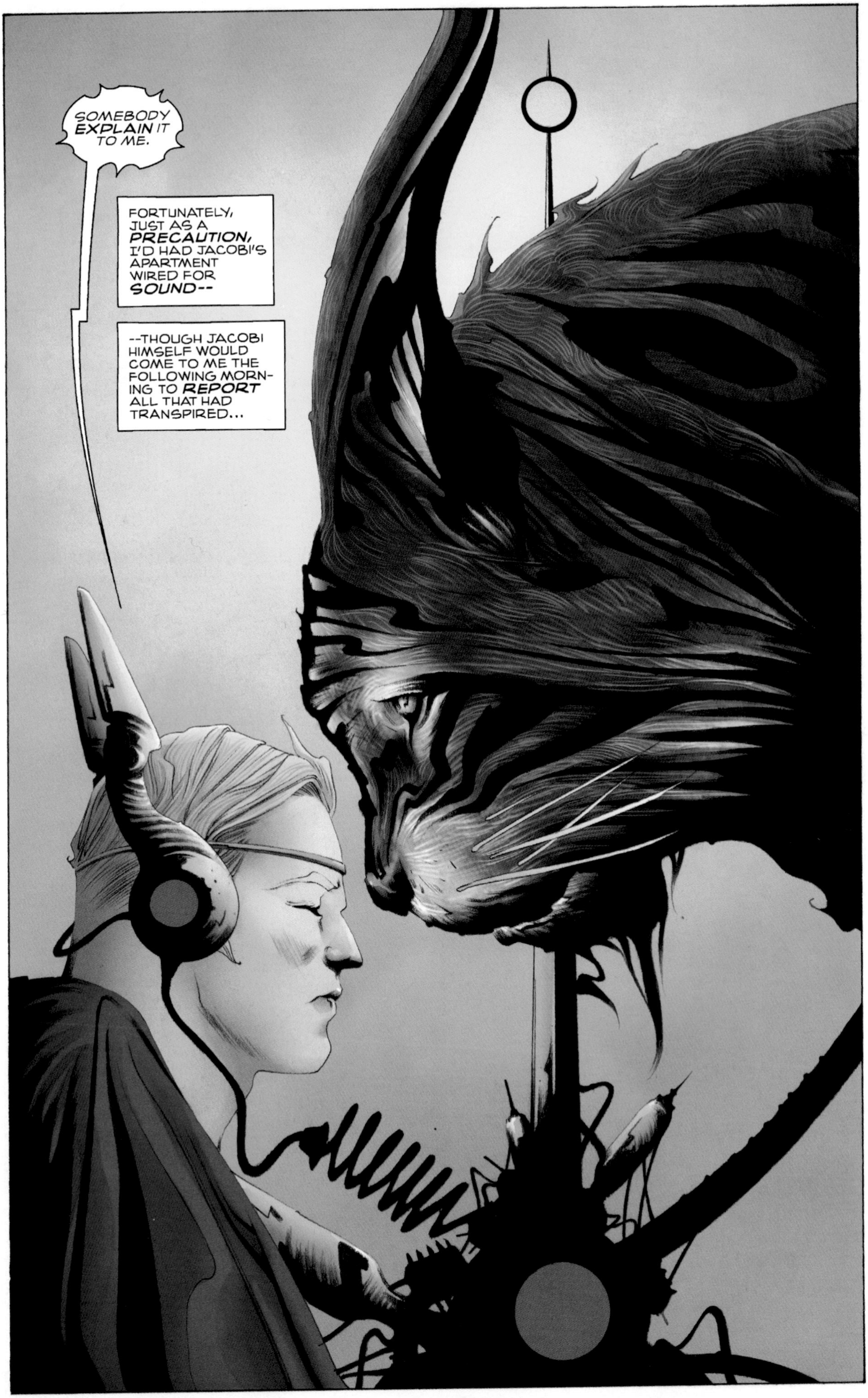
SOMEBODY EXPLAIN IT TO ME.
FORTUNATELY, JUST AS A PRECAUTION, I'D HAD JACOBI'S APARTMENT WIRED FOR SOUND--
--THOUGH JACOBI HIMSELF WOULD COME TO ME THE FOLLOWING MORNING TO REPORT ALL THAT HAD TRANSPIRED...

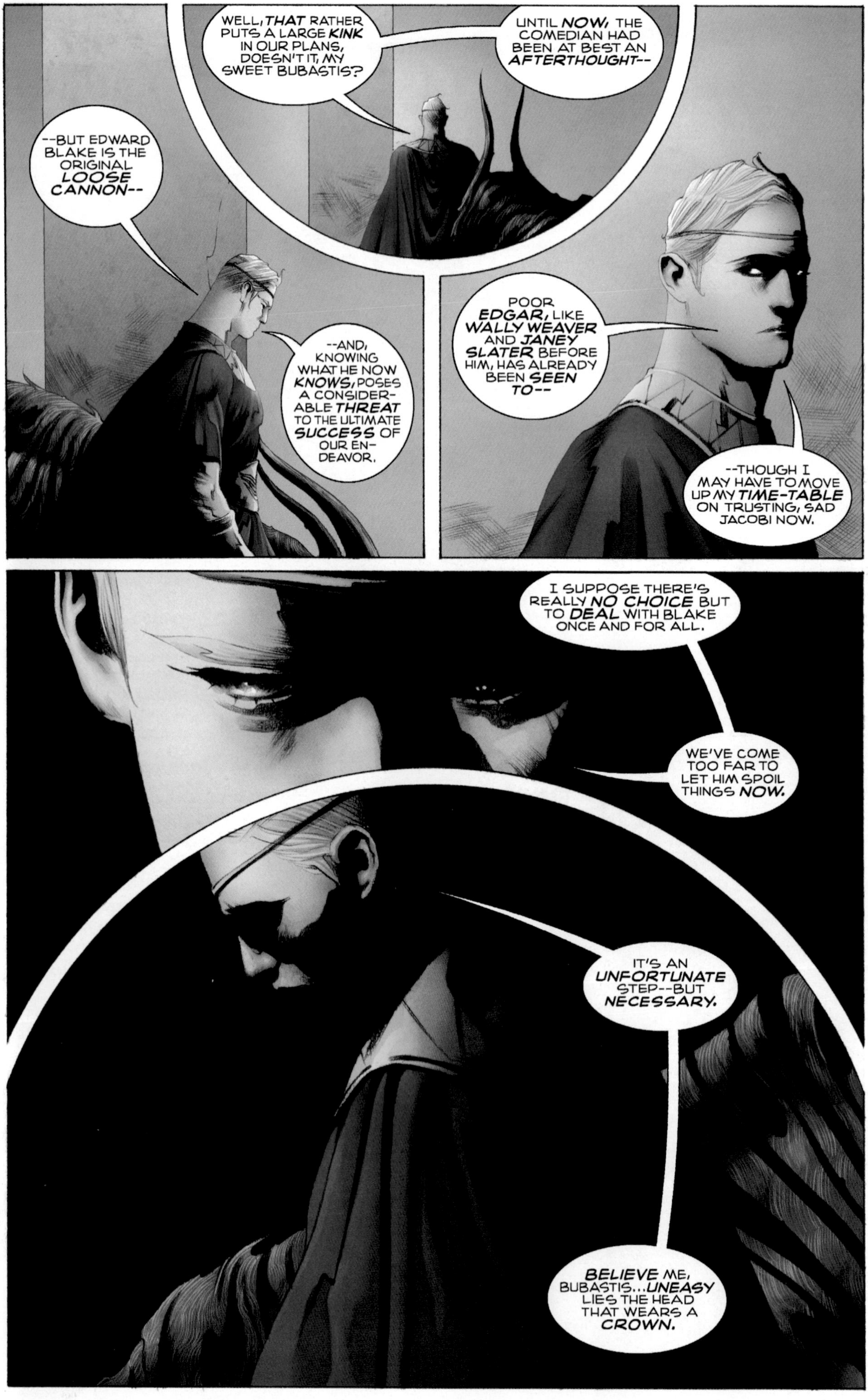
WELL, THAT RATHER PUTS A LARGE KINK IN OUR PLANS, DOESN'T IT, MY SWEET BUBASTIS?
UNTIL NOW, THE COMEDIAN HAD BEEN AT BEST AN AFTERTHOUGHT--
--BUT EDWARD BLAKE IS THE ORIGINAL LOOSE CANNON--
--AND, KNOWING WHAT HE NOW KNOWS, POSES A CONSIDER-ABLE THREAT TO THE ULTIMATE SUCCESS OF OUR EN-DEAVOR.
POOR EDGAR, LIKE WALLY WEAVER AND JANEY SLATER BEFORE HIM, HAS ALREADY BEEN SEEN TO--
--THOUGH I MAY HAVE TO MOVE UP MY TIME-TABLE ON TRUSTING, SAD JACOBI NOW.
I SUPPOSE THERE'S REALLY NO CHOICE BUT TO DEAL WITH BLAKE ONCE AND FOR ALL.
WE'VE COME TOO FAR TO LET HIM SPOIL THINGS NOW.
IT'S AN UNFORTUNATE STEP--BUT NECESSARY.
BELIEVE ME, BUBASTIS...UNEASY LIES THE HEAD THAT WEARS A CROWN.

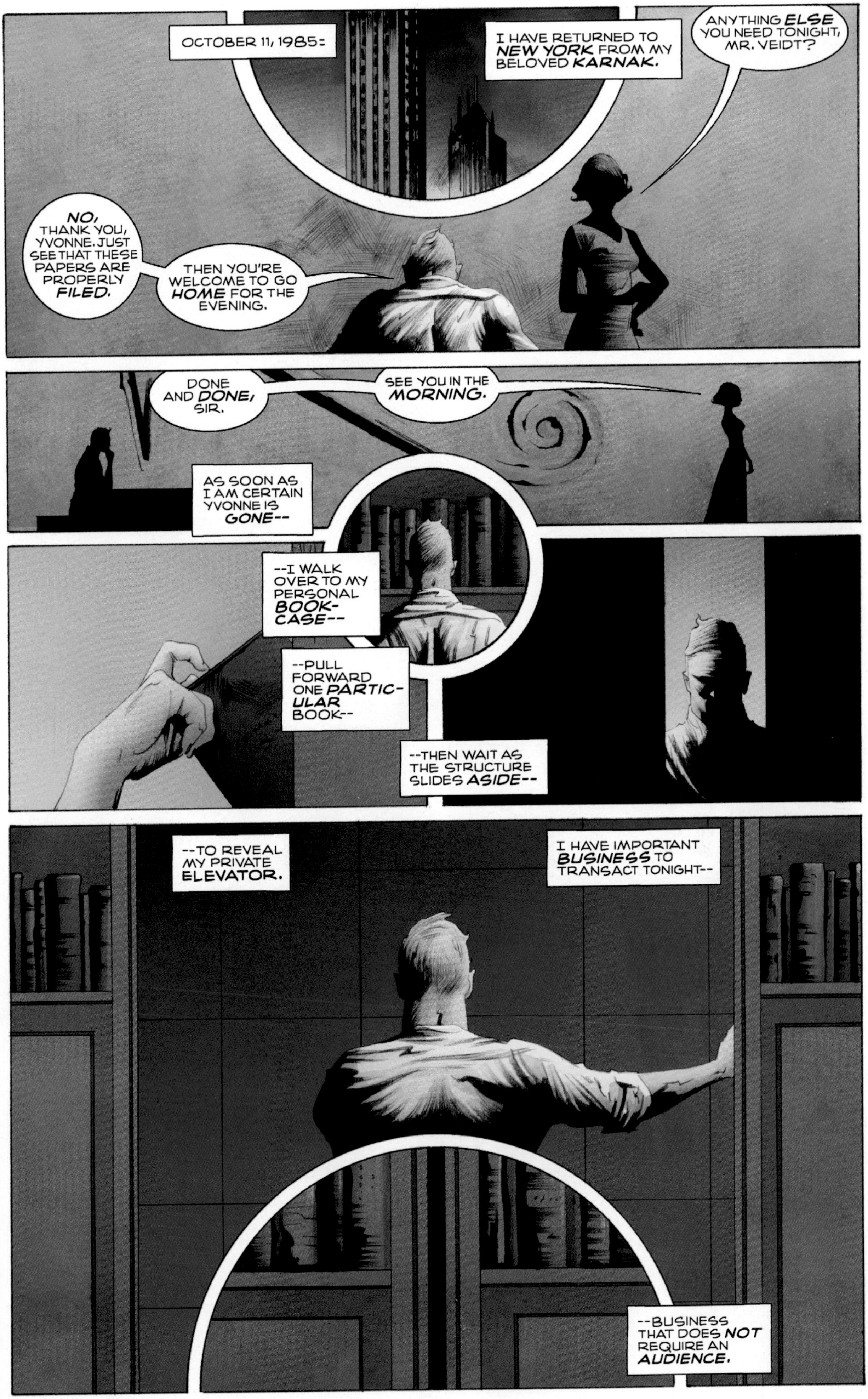

OCTOBER 11, 1985:
I HAVE RETURNED TO NEW YORK FROM MY BELOVED KARNAK.
ANYTHING ELSE YOU NEED TONIGHT, MR. VEIDT?
NO, THANK YOU, YVONNE. JUST SEE THAT THESE PAPERS ARE PROPERLY FILED.
THEN YOU'RE WELCOME TO GO HOME FOR THE EVENING.
DONE AND DONE, SIR.
SEE YOU IN THE MORNING.
AS SOON AS I AM CERTAIN YVONNE IS GONE--
--I WALK OVER TO MY PERSONAL BOOK-CASE--
--PULL FORWARD ONE PARTICULAR BOOK--
--THEN WAIT AS THE STRUCTURE SLIDES ASIDE--
--TO REVEAL MY PRIVATE ELEVATOR.
I HAVE IMPORTANT BUSINESS TO TRANSACT TONIGHT--
--BUSINESS THAT DOES NOT REQUIRE AN AUDIENCE.

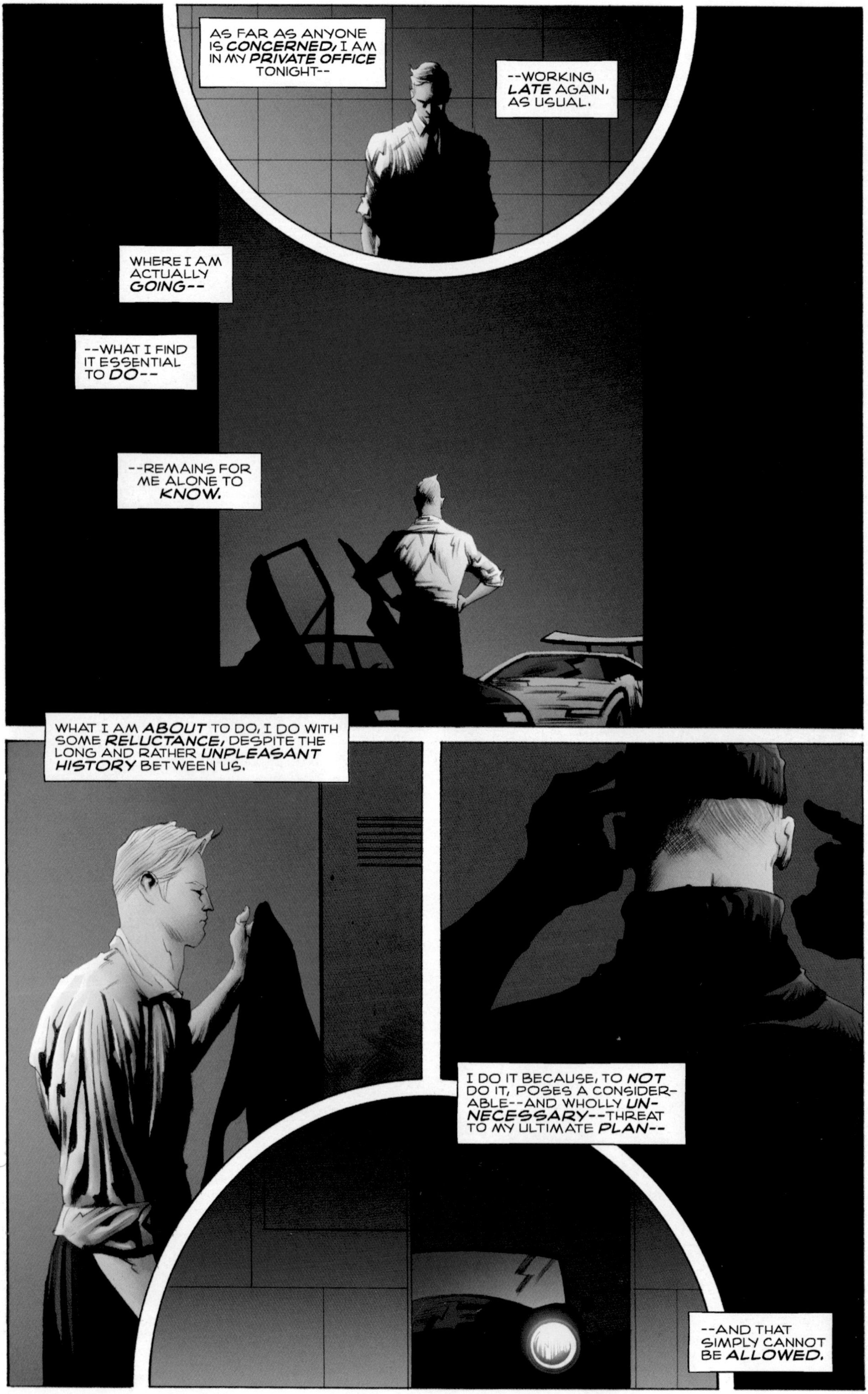

AS FAR AS ANYONE IS CONCERNED, I AM IN MY PRIVATE OFFICE TONIGHT--
--WORKING LATE AGAIN, AS USUAL.
WHERE I AM ACTUALLY GOING--
--WHAT I FIND IT ESSENTIAL TO DO--
--REMAINS FOR ME ALONE TO KNOW.
WHAT I AM ABOUT TO DO, I DO WITH SOME RELUCTANCE, DESPITE THE LONG AND RATHER UNPLEASANT HISTORY BETWEEN US.
I DO IT BECAUSE, TO NOT DO IT, POSES A CONSIDERABLE--AND WHOLLY UNNECESSARY--THREAT TO MY ULTIMATE PLAN--
--AND THAT SIMPLY CANNOT BE ALLOWED.

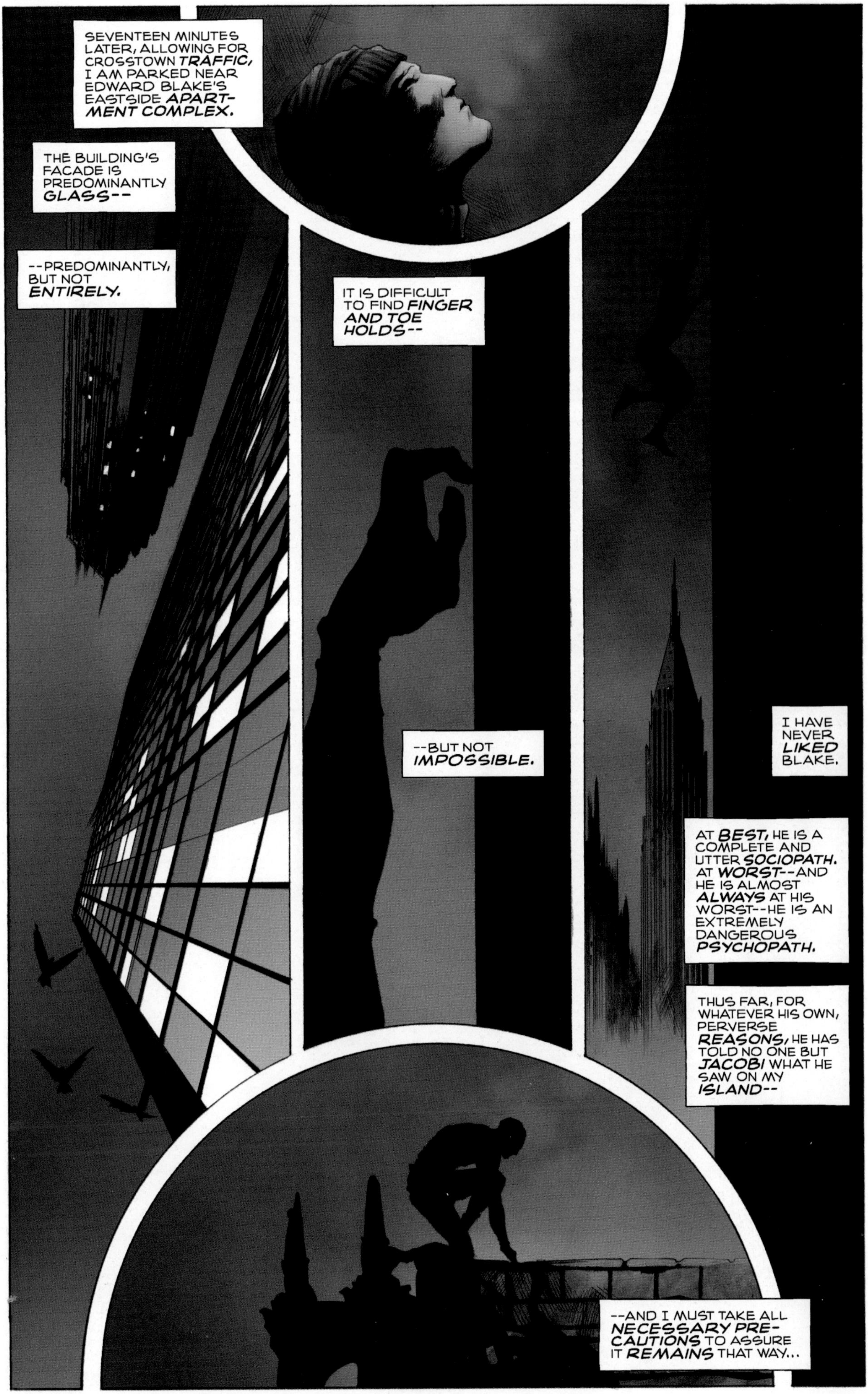
SEVENTEEN MINUTES LATER, ALLOWING FOR CROSSTOWN TRAFFIC, I AM PARKED NEAR EDWARD BLAKE'S EASTSIDE APARTMENT COMPLEX.
THE BUILDING'S FACADE IS PREDOMINANTLY GLASS--
--PREDOMINANTLY, BUT NOT ENTIRELY.
IT IS DIFFICULT TO FIND FINGER AND TOE HOLDS--
--BUT NOT IMPOSSIBLE.
I HAVE NEVER LIKED BLAKE.
AT BEST, HE IS A COMPLETE AND UTTER SOCIOPATH. AT WORST--AND HE IS ALMOST ALWAYS AT HIS WORST--HE IS AN EXTREMELY DANGEROUS PSYCHOPATH.
THUS FAR, FOR WHATEVER HIS OWN, PERVERSE REASONS, HE HAS TOLD NO ONE BUT JACOBI WHAT HE SAW ON MY ISLAND--
--AND I MUST TAKE ALL NECESSARY PRECAUTIONS TO ASSURE IT REMAINS THAT WAY...

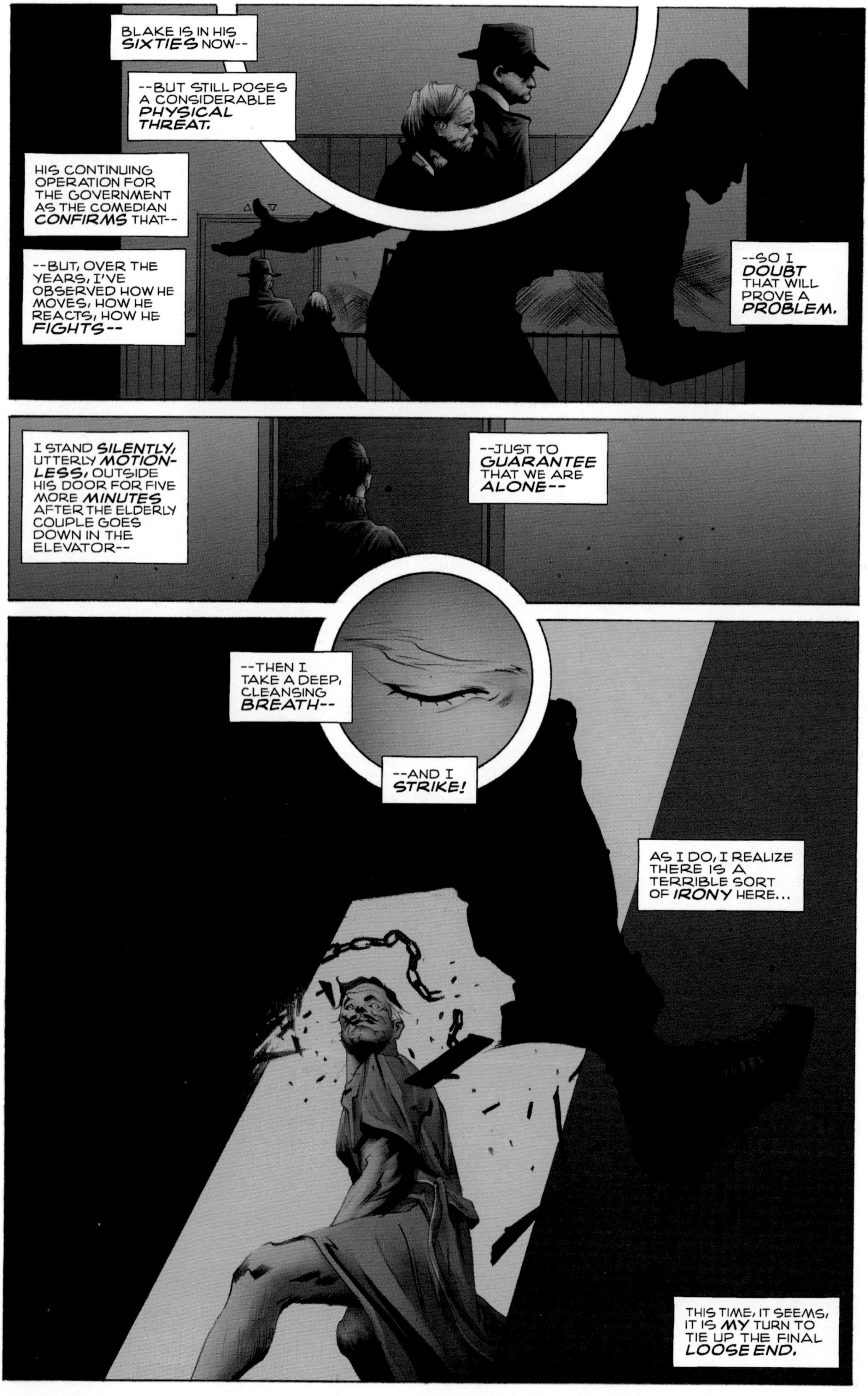
BLAKE IS IN HIS SIXTIES NOW--
--BUT STILL POSES A CONSIDERABLE PHYSICAL THREAT.
HIS CONTINUING OPERATION FOR THE GOVERNMENT AS THE COMEDIAN CONFIRMS THAT--
--BUT, OVER THE YEARS, I'VE OBSERVED HOW HE MOVES, HOW HE REACTS, HOW HE FIGHTS--
--SO I DOUBT THAT WILL PROVE A PROBLEM.
I STAND SILENTLY, UTTERLY MOTIONLESS, OUTSIDE HIS DOOR FOR FIVE MORE MINUTES AFTER THE ELDERLY COUPLE GOES DOWN IN THE ELEVATOR--
--JUST TO GUARANTEE THAT WE ARE ALONE--
--THEN I TAKE A DEEP, CLEANSING BREATH--
--AND I STRIKE!
AS I DO, I REALIZE THERE IS A TERRIBLE SORT OF IRONY HERE...
THIS TIME, IT SEEMS, IT IS MY TURN TO TIE UP THE FINAL LOOSE END.

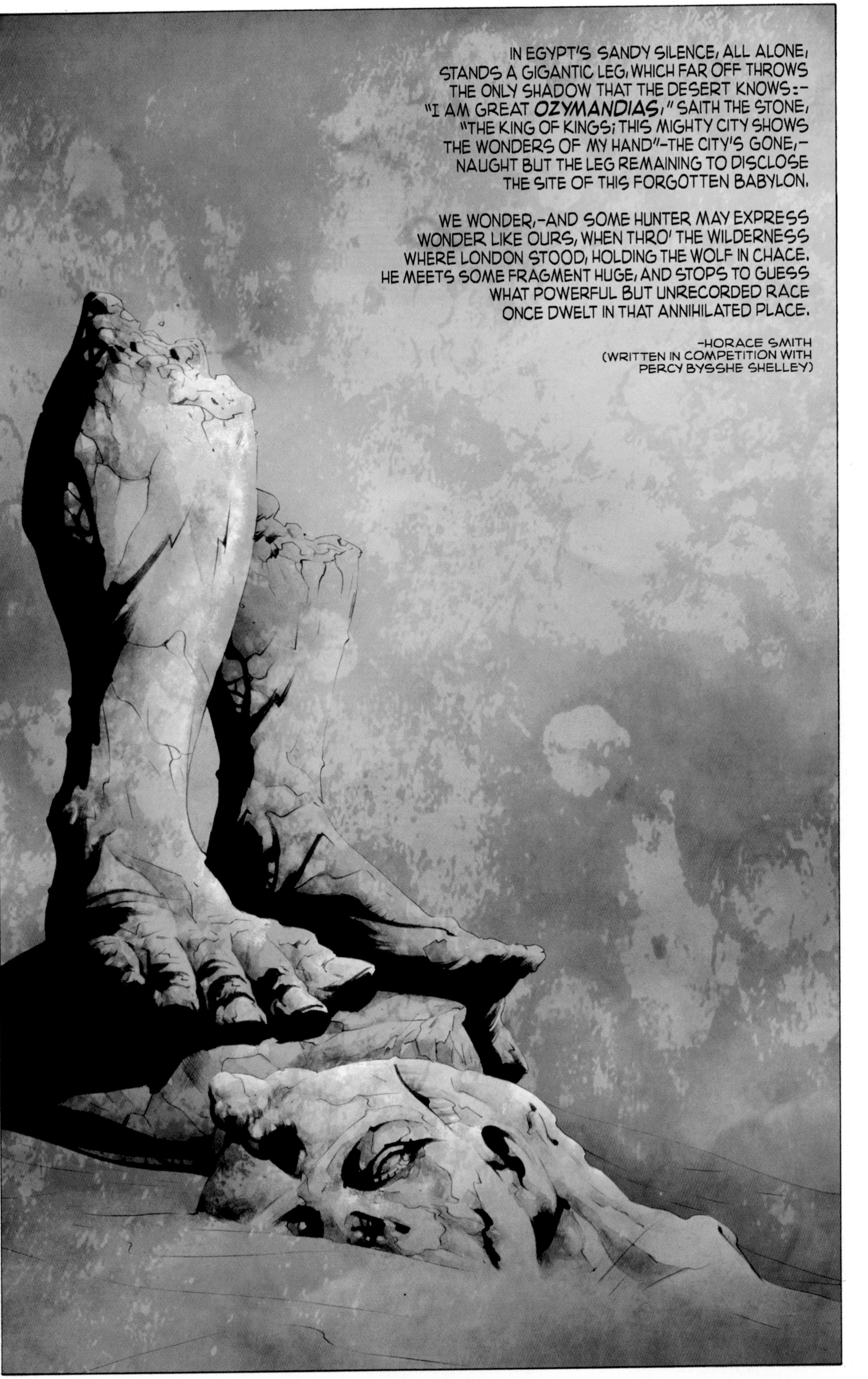
IN EGYPT'S SANDY SILENCE, ALL ALONE,
STANDS A GIGANTIC LEG, WHICH FAR OFF THROWS
THE ONLY SHADOW THAT THE DESERT KNOWS:-
"I AM GREAT OZYMANDIAS," SAITH THE STONE,
"THE KING OF KINGS; THIS MIGHTY CITY SHOWS
THE WONDERS OF MY HAND"-THE CITY'S GONE,-
NAUGHT BUT THE LEG REMAINING TO DISCLOSE
THE SITE OF THIS FORGOTTEN BABYLON.
WE WONDER,-AND SOME HUNTER MAY EXPRESS
WONDER LIKE OURS, WHEN THRO' THE WILDERNESS
WHERE LONDON STOOD, HOLDING THE WOLF IN CHACE,
HE MEETS SOME FRAGMENT HUGE, AND STOPS TO GUESS
WHAT POWERFUL BUT UNRECORDED RACE
ONCE DWELT IN THAT ANNIHILATED PLACE.
-HORACE SMITH
(WRITTEN IN COMPETITION WITH
PERCY BYSSHE SHELLEY)

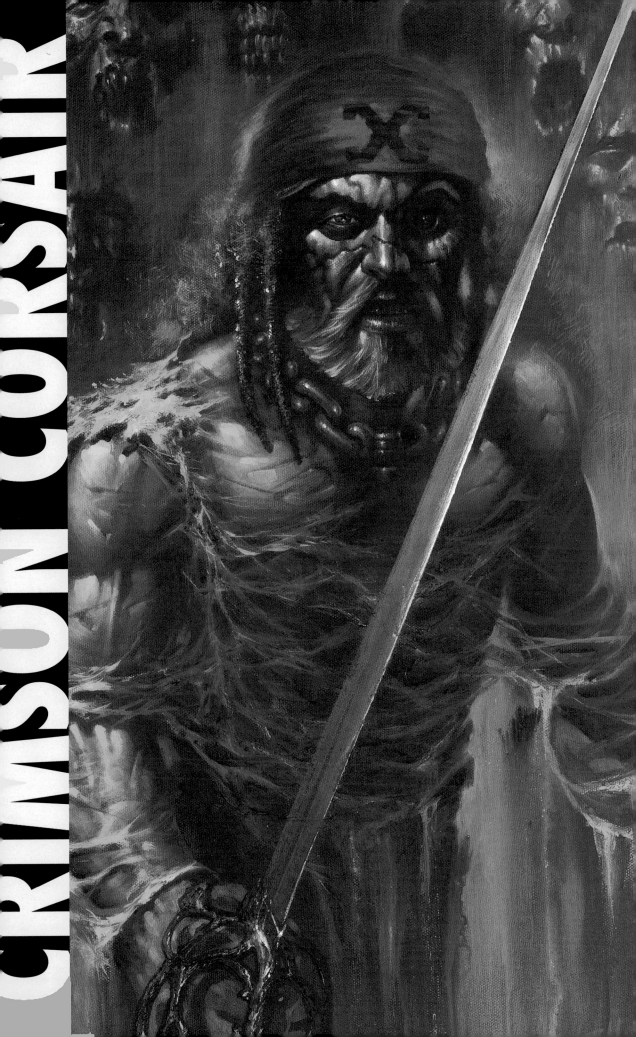

CRIMSON CORSAIR

CRIMSON CORSAIR

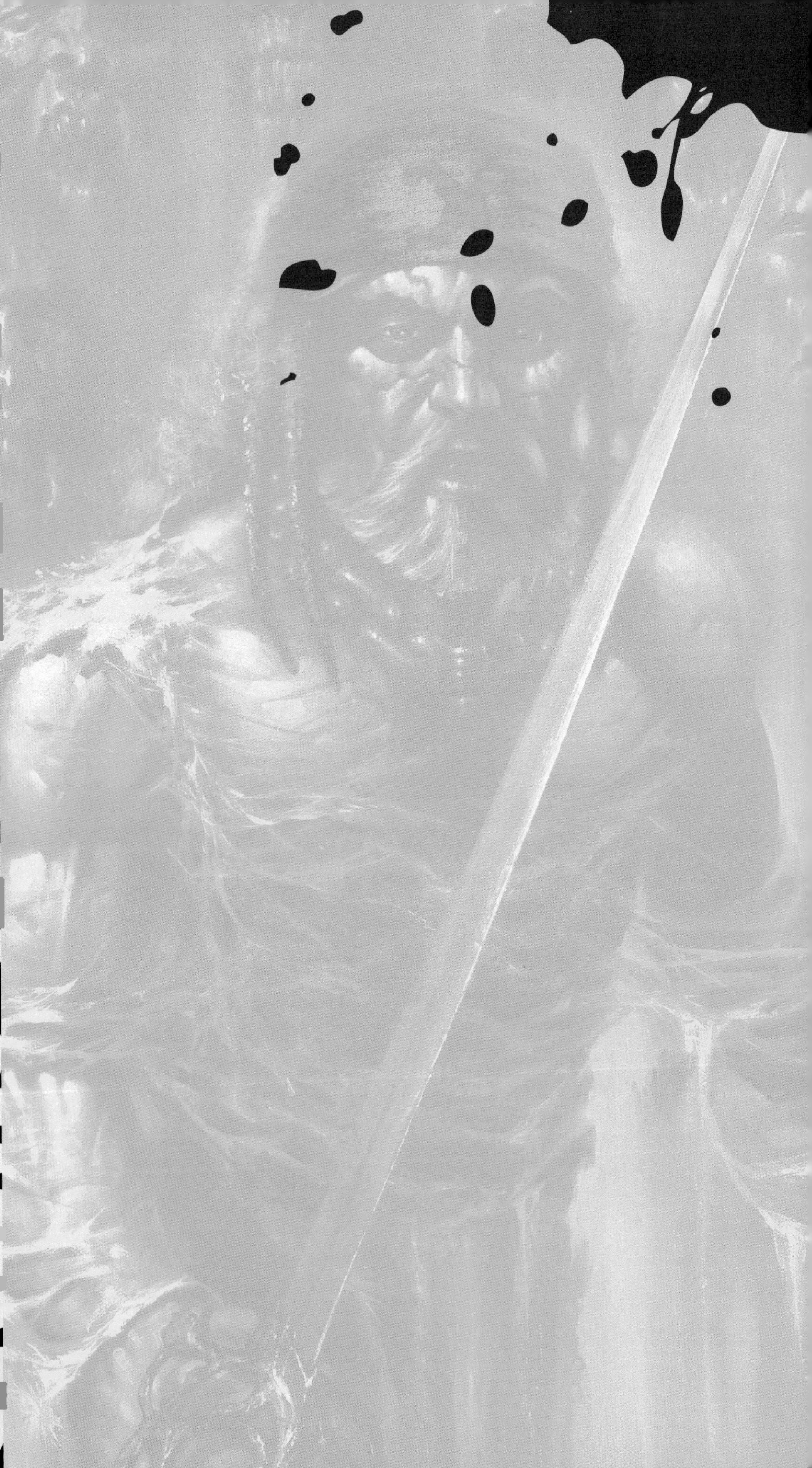

"OBLIVION BECKONED, AND I WAS COMPELLED TO COMPLY."

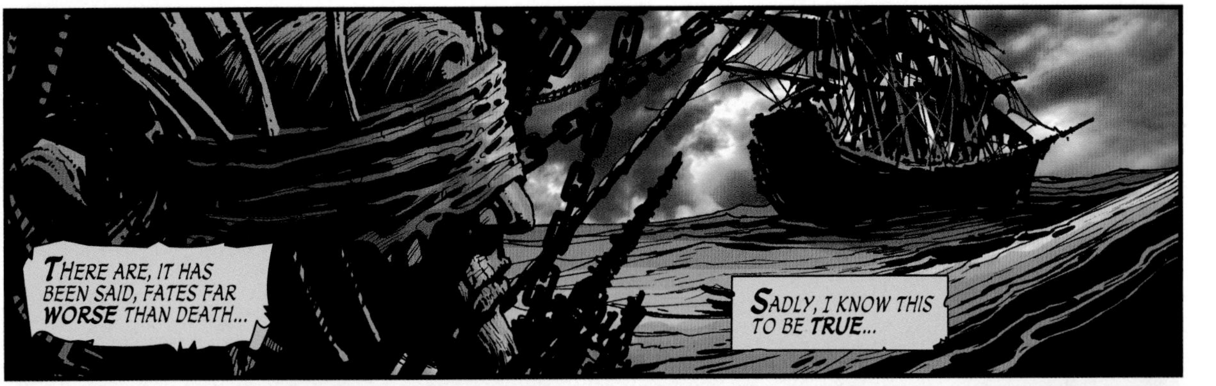
THERE ARE, IT HAS BEEN SAID, FATES FAR WORSE THAN DEATH...
SADLY, I KNOW THIS TO BE TRUE...

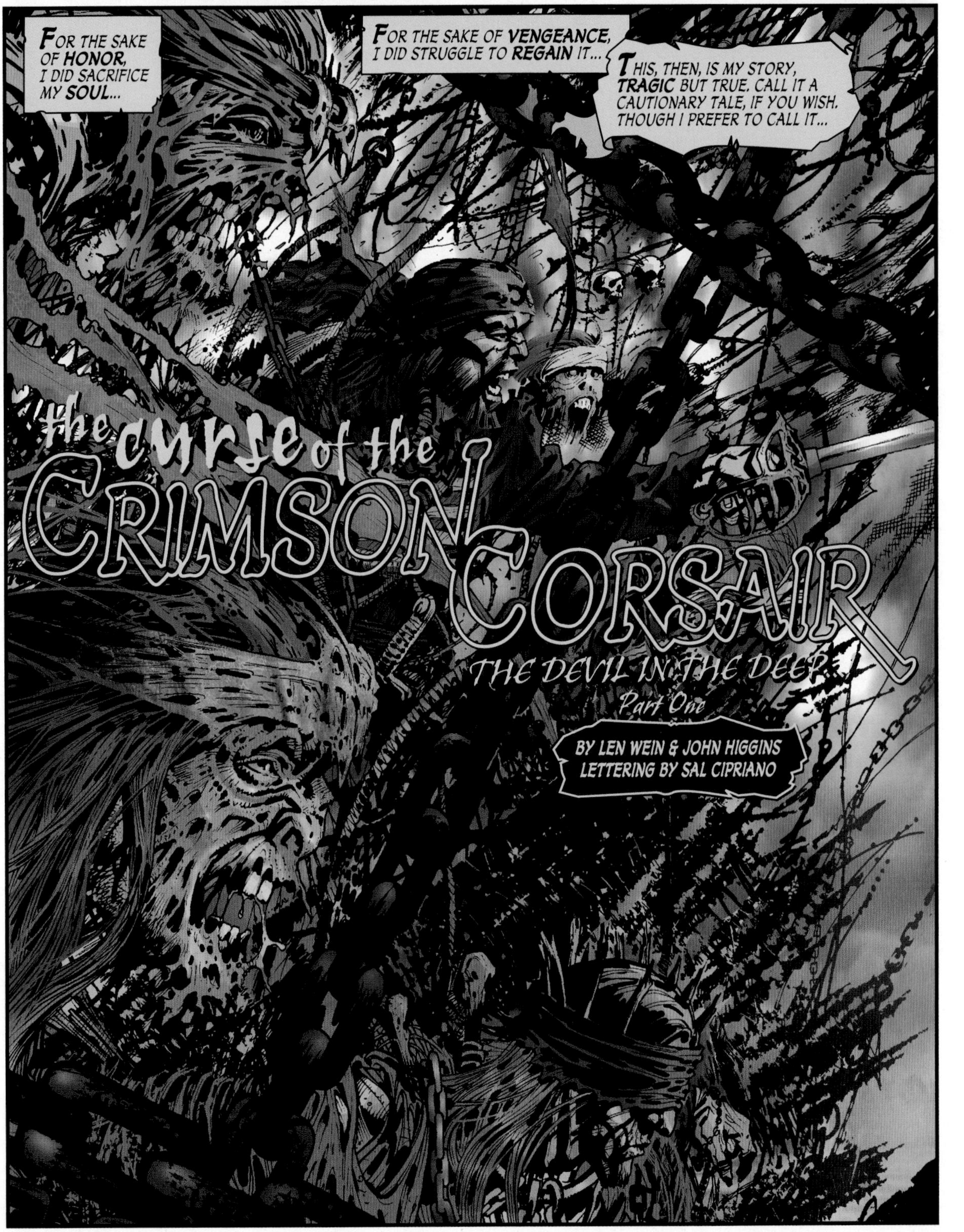
FOR THE SAKE OF HONOR, I DID SACRIFICE MY SOUL...
FOR THE SAKE OF VENGEANCE, I DID STRUGGLE TO REGAIN IT...
THIS, THEN, IS MY STORY, TRAGIC BUT TRUE. CALL IT A CAUTIONARY TALE, IF YOU WISH. THOUGH I PREFER TO CALL IT...
the curse of the CRIMSON CORSAIR
THE DEVIL IN THE DEEP
Part One
BY LEN WEIN & JOHN HIGGINS
LETTERING BY SAL CIPRIANO

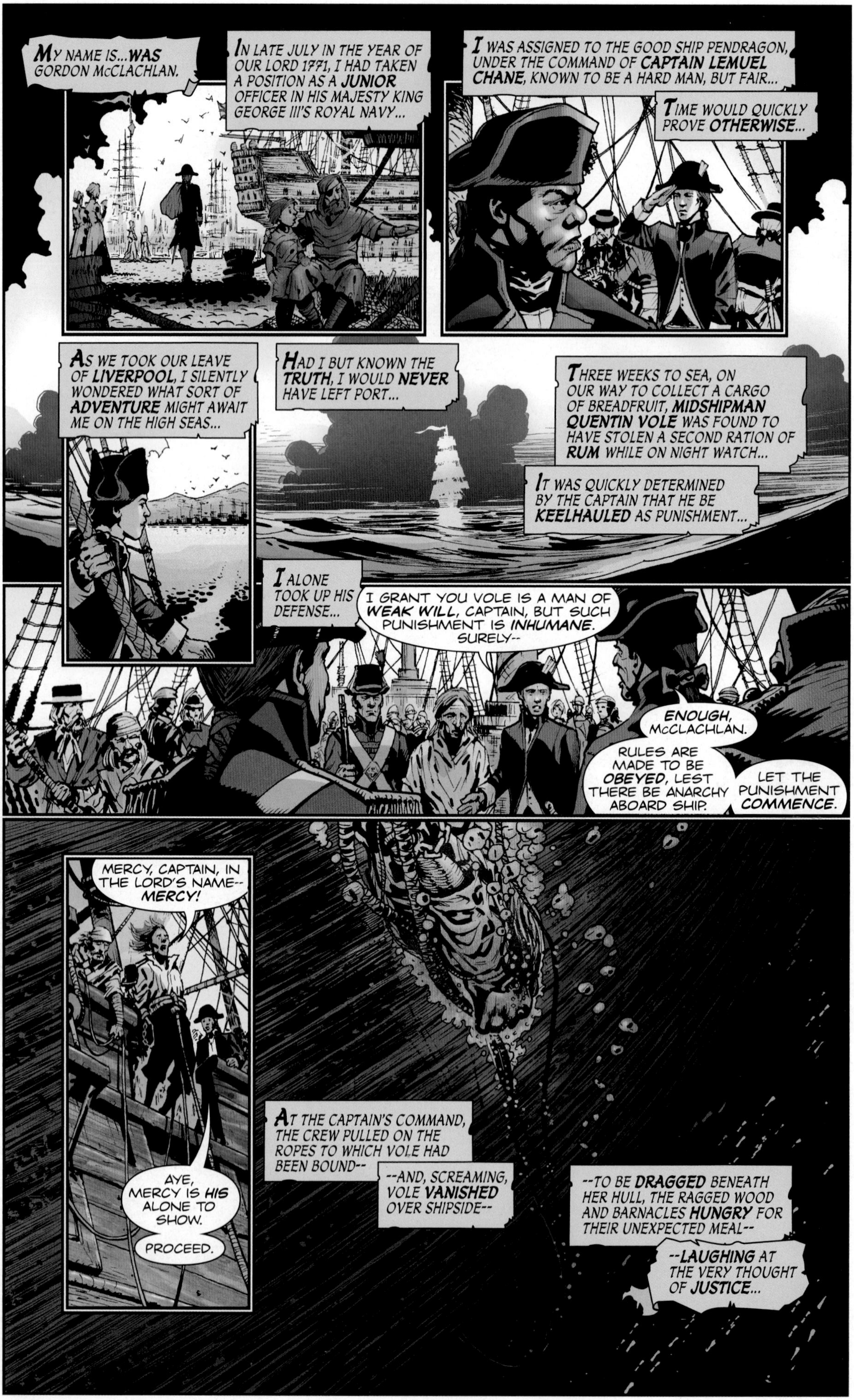

MY NAME IS...WAS GORDON McCLACHLAN.
IN LATE JULY IN THE YEAR OF OUR LORD 1771, I HAD TAKEN A POSITION AS A JUNIOR OFFICER IN HIS MAJESTY KING GEORGE III'S ROYAL NAVY...
I WAS ASSIGNED TO THE GOOD SHIP PENDRAGON, UNDER THE COMMAND OF CAPTAIN LEMUEL CHANE, KNOWN TO BE A HARD MAN, BUT FAIR...
TIME WOULD QUICKLY PROVE OTHERWISE...
AS WE TOOK OUR LEAVE OF LIVERPOOL, I SILENTLY WONDERED WHAT SORT OF ADVENTURE MIGHT AWAIT ME ON THE HIGH SEAS...
HAD I BUT KNOWN THE TRUTH, I WOULD NEVER HAVE LEFT PORT...
THREE WEEKS TO SEA, ON OUR WAY TO COLLECT A CARGO OF BREADFRUIT, MIDSHIPMAN QUENTIN VOLE WAS FOUND TO HAVE STOLEN A SECOND RATION OF RUM WHILE ON NIGHT WATCH...
IT WAS QUICKLY DETERMINED BY THE CAPTAIN THAT HE BE KEELHAULED AS PUNISHMENT...
I ALONE TOOK UP HIS DEFENSE...
I GRANT YOU VOLE IS A MAN OF WEAK WILL, CAPTAIN, BUT SUCH PUNISHMENT IS INHUMANE. SURELY--
ENOUGH, McCLACHLAN.
RULES ARE MADE TO BE OBEYED, LEST THERE BE ANARCHY ABOARD SHIP.
LET THE PUNISHMENT COMMENCE.
MERCY, CAPTAIN, IN THE LORD'S NAME-- MERCY!
AYE, MERCY IS HIS ALONE TO SHOW.
PROCEED.
AT THE CAPTAIN'S COMMAND, THE CREW PULLED ON THE ROPES TO WHICH VOLE HAD BEEN BOUND--
--AND, SCREAMING, VOLE VANISHED OVER SHIPSIDE--
--TO BE DRAGGED BENEATH HER HULL, THE RAGGED WOOD AND BARNACLES HUNGRY FOR THEIR UNEXPECTED MEAL--
--LAUGHING AT THE VERY THOUGHT OF JUSTICE...

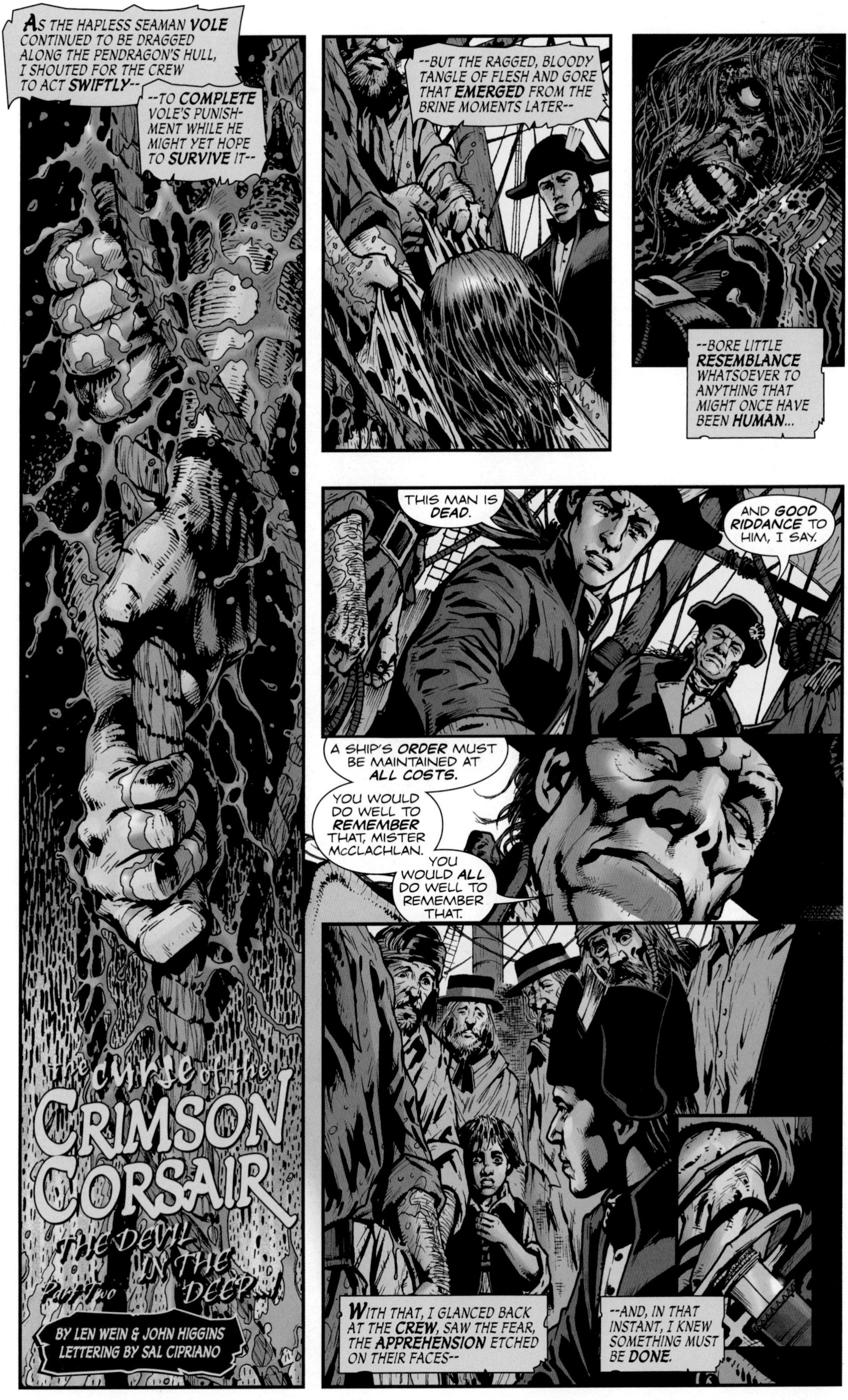

AS THE HAPLESS SEAMAN VOLE CONTINUED TO BE DRAGGED ALONG THE PENDRAGON'S HULL, I SHOUTED FOR THE CREW TO ACT SWIFTLY--
--TO COMPLETE VOLE'S PUNISHMENT WHILE HE MIGHT YET HOPE TO SURVIVE IT--
the curse of the CRIMSON CORSAIR
THE DEVIL IN THE DEEP
Part Two
BY LEN WEIN & JOHN HIGGINS
LETTERING BY SAL CIPRIANO
--BUT THE RAGGED, BLOODY TANGLE OF FLESH AND GORE THAT EMERGED FROM THE BRINE MOMENTS LATER--
--BORE LITTLE RESEMBLANCE WHATSOEVER TO ANYTHING THAT MIGHT ONCE HAVE BEEN HUMAN...
THIS MAN IS DEAD.
AND GOOD RIDDANCE TO HIM, I SAY.
A SHIP'S ORDER MUST BE MAINTAINED AT ALL COSTS.
YOU WOULD DO WELL TO REMEMBER THAT, MISTER McCLACHLAN.
YOU WOULD ALL DO WELL TO REMEMBER THAT.
WITH THAT, I GLANCED BACK AT THE CREW, SAW THE FEAR, THE APPREHENSION ETCHED ON THEIR FACES--
--AND, IN THAT INSTANT, I KNEW SOMETHING MUST BE DONE.

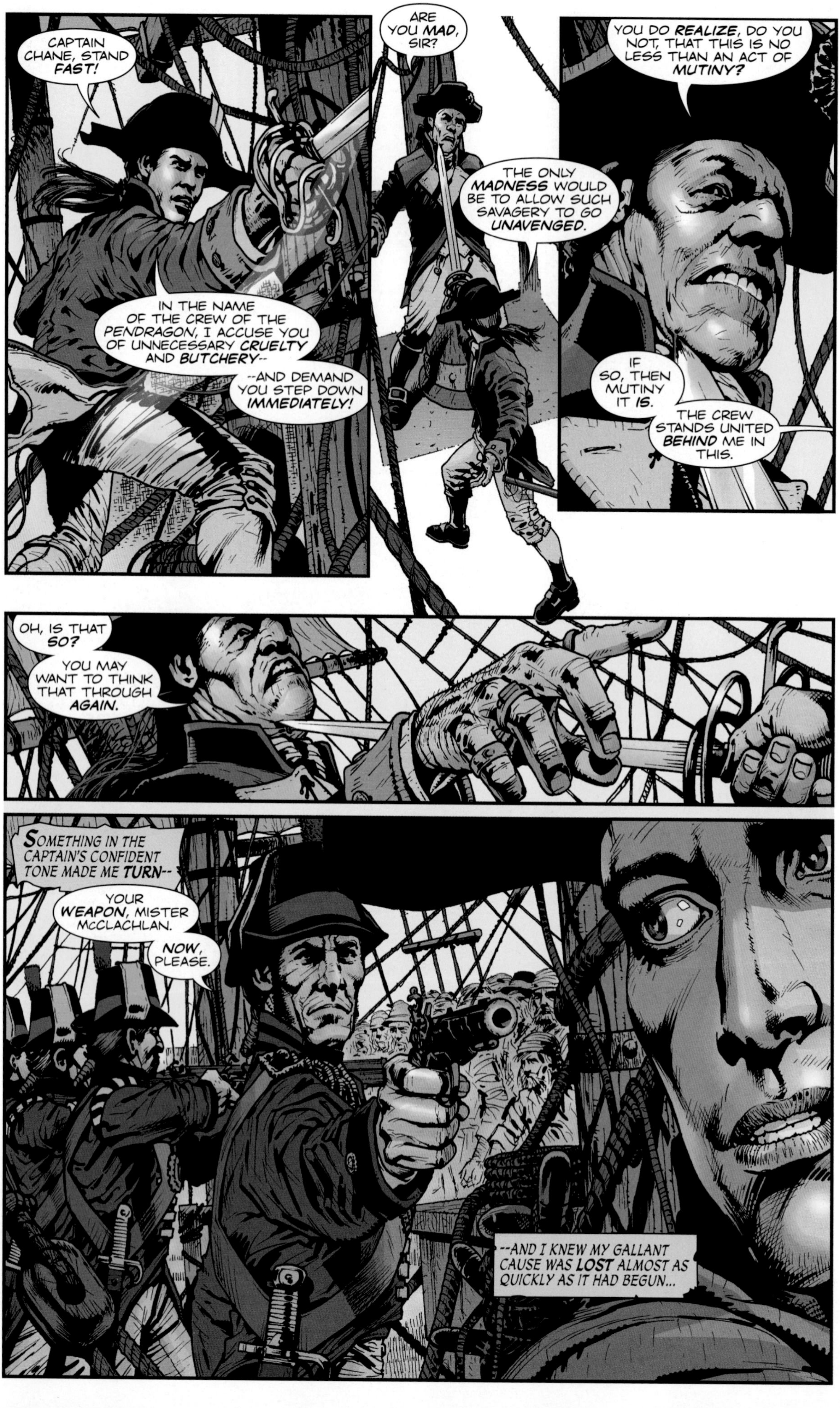
CAPTAIN CHANE, STAND FAST!
ARE YOU MAD, SIR?
YOU DO REALIZE, DO YOU NOT, THAT THIS IS NO LESS THAN AN ACT OF MUTINY?
THE ONLY MADNESS WOULD BE TO ALLOW SUCH SAVAGERY TO GO UNAVENGED.
IN THE NAME OF THE CREW OF THE PENDRAGON, I ACCUSE YOU OF UNNECESSARY CRUELTY AND BUTCHERY--
--AND DEMAND YOU STEP DOWN IMMEDIATELY!
IF SO, THEN MUTINY IT IS.
THE CREW STANDS UNITED BEHIND ME IN THIS.
OH, IS THAT SO?
YOU MAY WANT TO THINK THAT THROUGH AGAIN.
SOMETHING IN THE CAPTAIN'S CONFIDENT TONE MADE ME TURN--
YOUR WEAPON, MISTER McCLACHLAN.
NOW, PLEASE.
--AND I KNEW MY GALLANT CAUSE WAS LOST ALMOST AS QUICKLY AS IT HAD BEGUN...

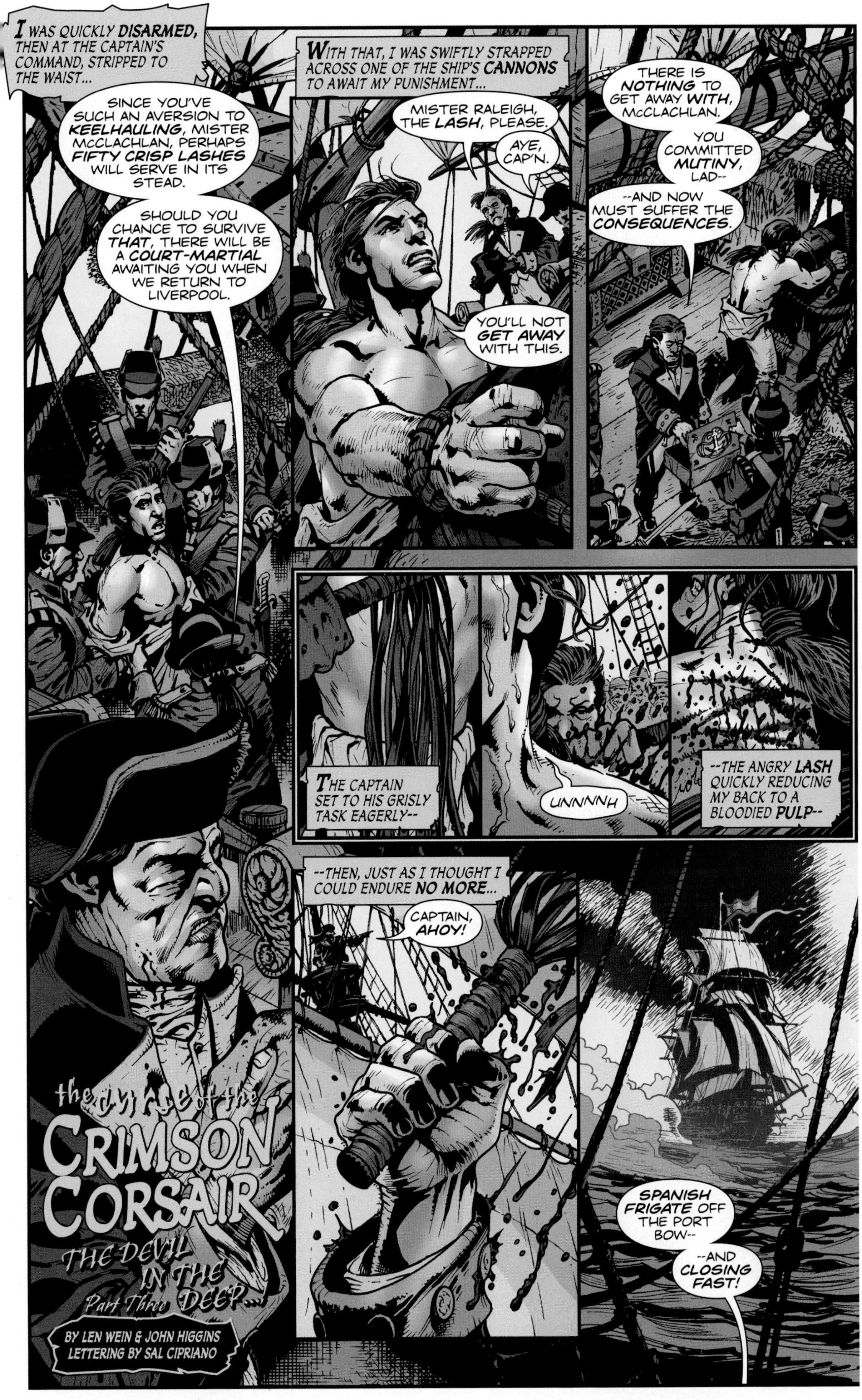
I WAS QUICKLY DISARMED, THEN AT THE CAPTAIN'S COMMAND, STRIPPED TO THE WAIST...
SINCE YOU'VE SUCH AN AVERSION TO KEELHAULING, MISTER McCLACHLAN, PERHAPS FIFTY CRISP LASHES WILL SERVE IN ITS STEAD.
SHOULD YOU CHANCE TO SURVIVE THAT, THERE WILL BE A COURT-MARTIAL AWAITING YOU WHEN WE RETURN TO LIVERPOOL.
WITH THAT, I WAS SWIFTLY STRAPPED ACROSS ONE OF THE SHIP'S CANNONS TO AWAIT MY PUNISHMENT...
MISTER RALEIGH, THE LASH, PLEASE.
AYE, CAP'N.
YOU'LL NOT GET AWAY WITH THIS.
THERE IS NOTHING TO GET AWAY WITH, McCLACHLAN.
YOU COMMITTED MUTINY, LAD--
--AND NOW MUST SUFFER THE CONSEQUENCES.
THE CAPTAIN SET TO HIS GRISLY TASK EAGERLY--
UNNNNH
--THE ANGRY LASH QUICKLY REDUCING MY BACK TO A BLOODIED PULP--
the curse of the
CRIMSON CORSAIR
THE DEVIL IN THE DEEP...
Part Three
BY LEN WEIN & JOHN HIGGINS
LETTERING BY SAL CIPRIANO
--THEN, JUST AS I THOUGHT I COULD ENDURE NO MORE...
CAPTAIN, AHOY!
SPANISH FRIGATE OFF THE PORT BOW--
--AND CLOSING FAST!

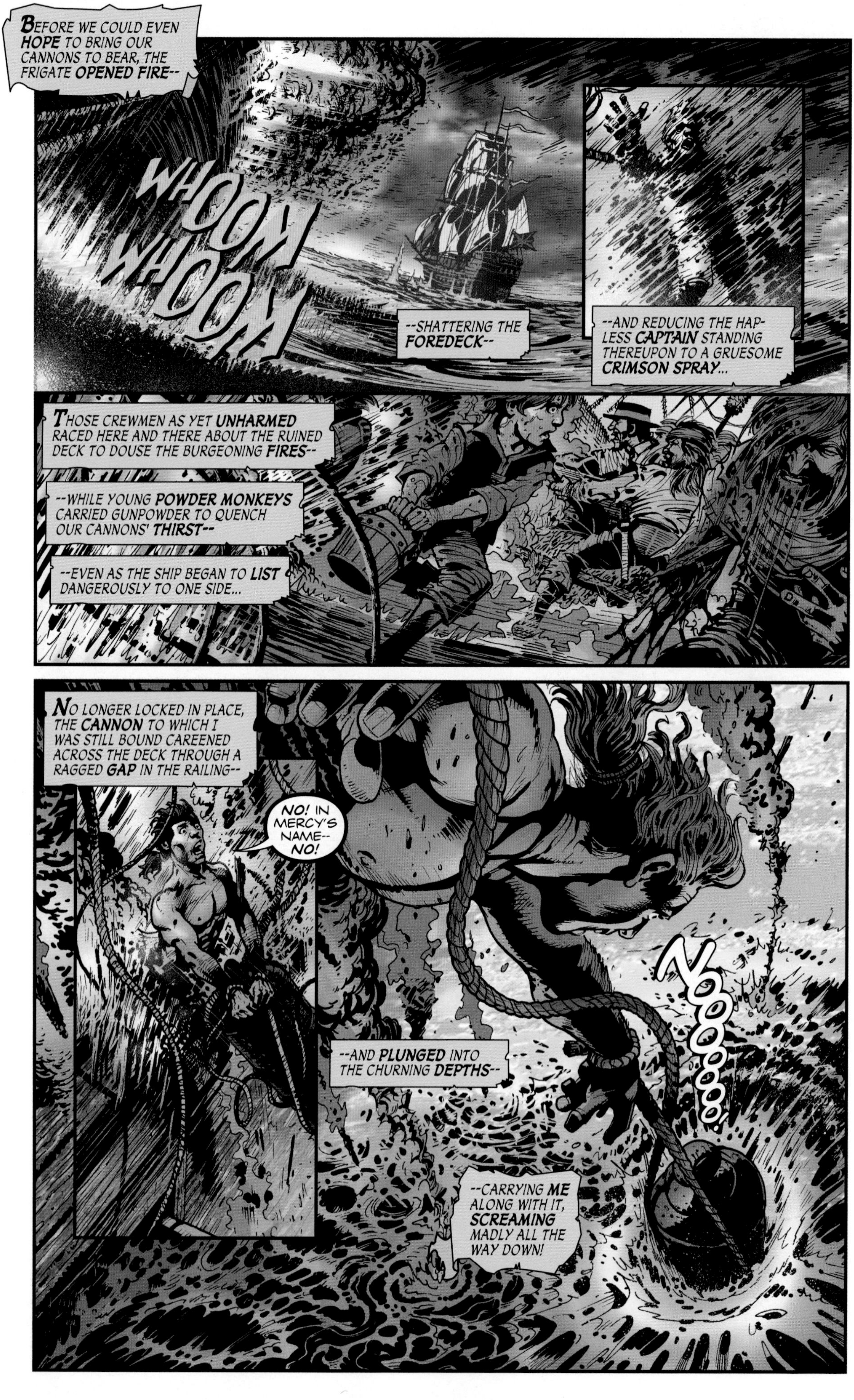
BEFORE WE COULD EVEN HOPE TO BRING OUR CANNONS TO BEAR, THE FRIGATE OPENED FIRE--
WHOOM WHOOM
--SHATTERING THE FOREDECK--
--AND REDUCING THE HAPLESS CAPTAIN STANDING THEREUPON TO A GRUESOME CRIMSON SPRAY...
THOSE CREWMEN AS YET UNHARMED RACED HERE AND THERE ABOUT THE RUINED DECK TO DOUSE THE BURGEONING FIRES--
--WHILE YOUNG POWDER MONKEYS CARRIED GUNPOWDER TO QUENCH OUR CANNONS' THIRST--
--EVEN AS THE SHIP BEGAN TO LIST DANGEROUSLY TO ONE SIDE...
NO LONGER LOCKED IN PLACE, THE CANNON TO WHICH I WAS STILL BOUND CAREENED ACROSS THE DECK THROUGH A RAGGED GAP IN THE RAILING--
NO! IN MERCY'S NAME-- NO!
--AND PLUNGED INTO THE CHURNING DEPTHS--
NOOOOOO!
--CARRYING ME ALONG WITH IT, SCREAMING MADLY ALL THE WAY DOWN!

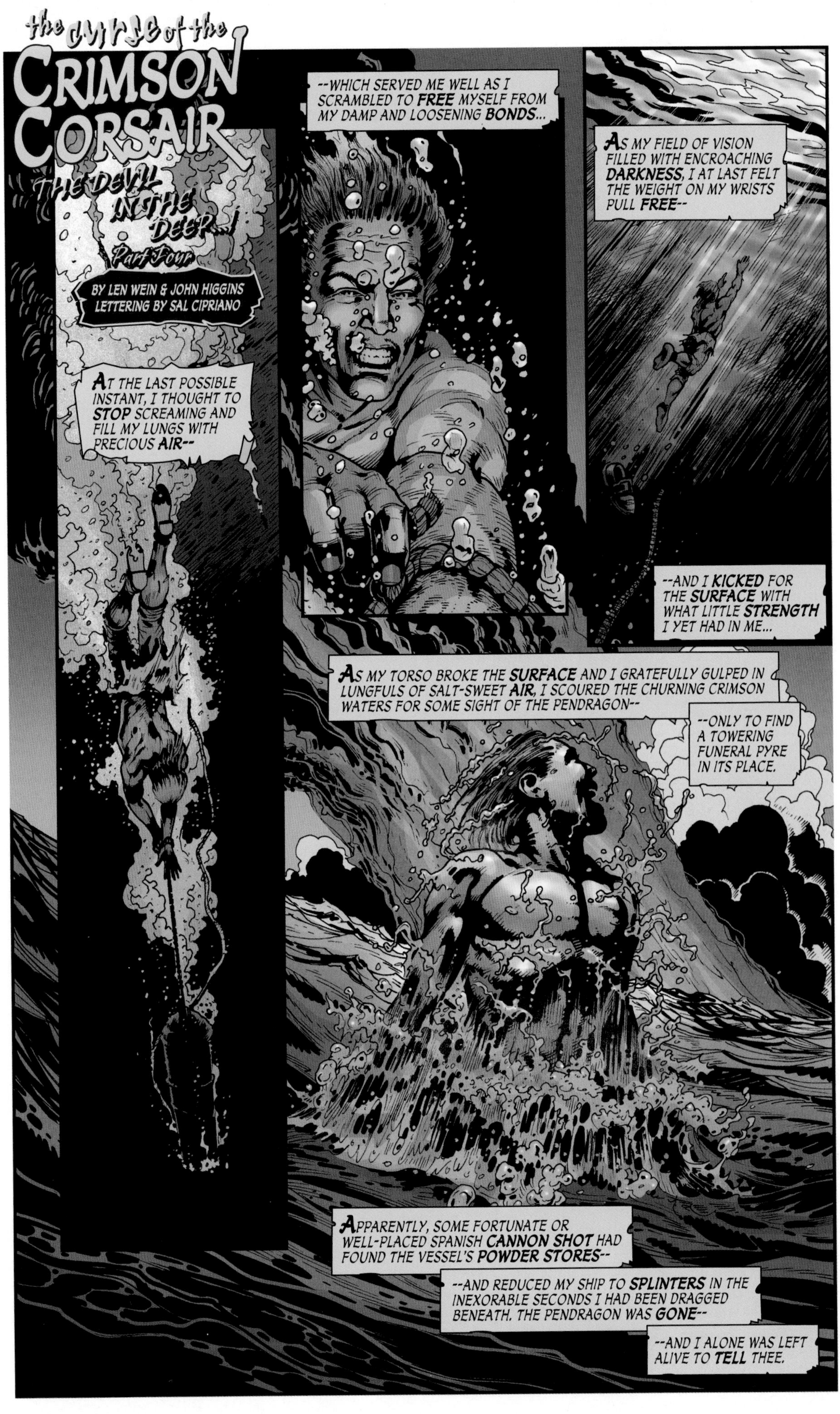
the curse of the
CRIMSON CORSAIR
THE DEVIL IN THE DEEP...!
Part Four
BY LEN WEIN & JOHN HIGGINS
LETTERING BY SAL CIPRIANO
AT THE LAST POSSIBLE INSTANT, I THOUGHT TO STOP SCREAMING AND FILL MY LUNGS WITH PRECIOUS AIR--
--WHICH SERVED ME WELL AS I SCRAMBLED TO FREE MYSELF FROM MY DAMP AND LOOSENING BONDS...
AS MY FIELD OF VISION FILLED WITH ENCROACHING DARKNESS, I AT LAST FELT THE WEIGHT ON MY WRISTS PULL FREE--
--AND I KICKED FOR THE SURFACE WITH WHAT LITTLE STRENGTH I YET HAD IN ME...
AS MY TORSO BROKE THE SURFACE AND I GRATEFULLY GULPED IN LUNGFULS OF SALT-SWEET AIR, I SCOURED THE CHURNING CRIMSON WATERS FOR SOME SIGHT OF THE PENDRAGON--
--ONLY TO FIND A TOWERING FUNERAL PYRE IN ITS PLACE.
APPARENTLY, SOME FORTUNATE OR WELL-PLACED SPANISH CANNON SHOT HAD FOUND THE VESSEL'S POWDER STORES--
--AND REDUCED MY SHIP TO SPLINTERS IN THE INEXORABLE SECONDS I HAD BEEN DRAGGED BENEATH. THE PENDRAGON WAS GONE--
--AND I ALONE WAS LEFT ALIVE TO TELL THEE.

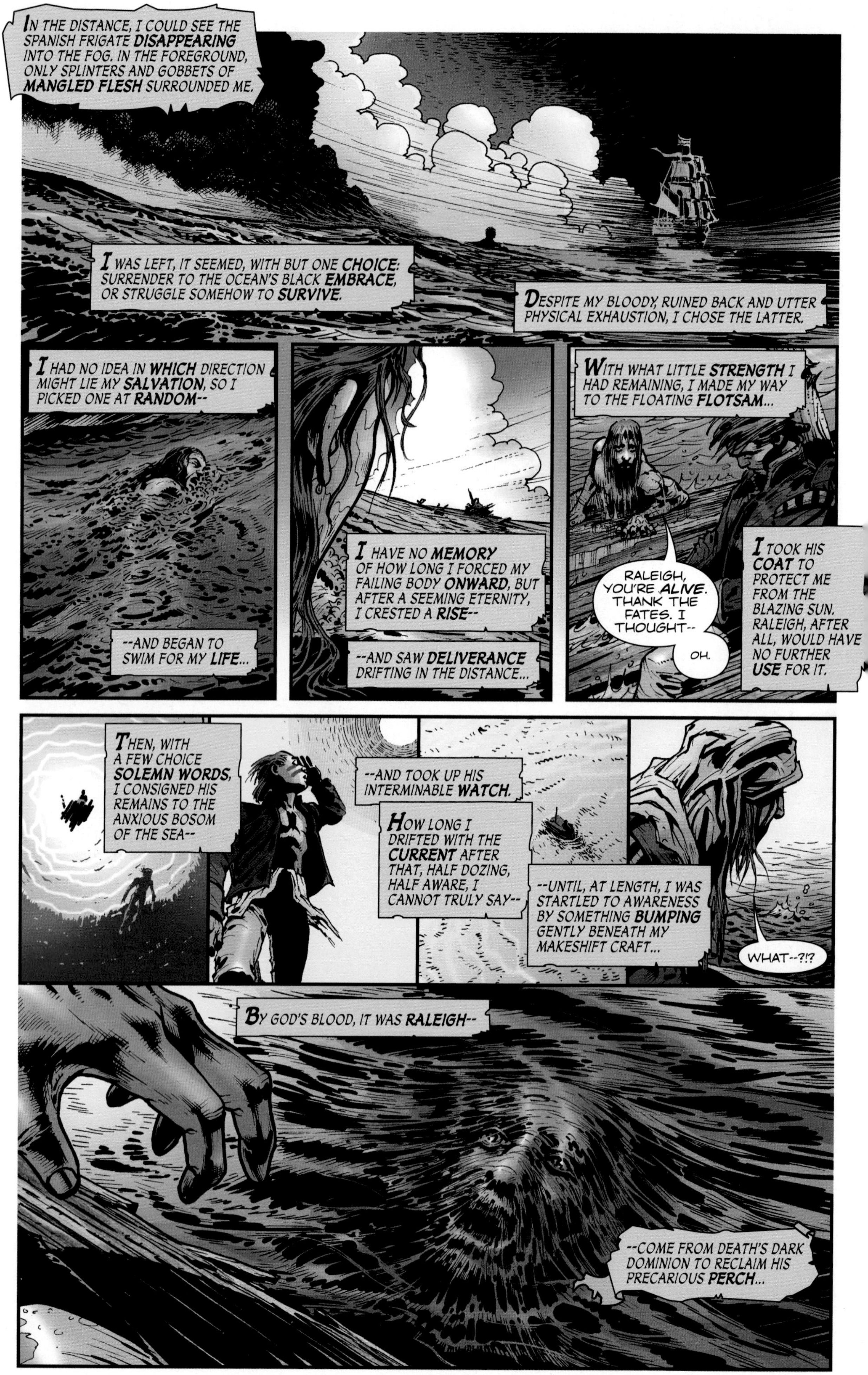
IN THE DISTANCE, I COULD SEE THE SPANISH FRIGATE DISAPPEARING INTO THE FOG. IN THE FOREGROUND, ONLY SPLINTERS AND GOBBETS OF MANGLED FLESH SURROUNDED ME.
I WAS LEFT, IT SEEMED, WITH BUT ONE CHOICE: SURRENDER TO THE OCEAN'S BLACK EMBRACE, OR STRUGGLE SOMEHOW TO SURVIVE.
DESPITE MY BLOODY, RUINED BACK AND UTTER PHYSICAL EXHAUSTION, I CHOSE THE LATTER.
I HAD NO IDEA IN WHICH DIRECTION MIGHT LIE MY SALVATION, SO I PICKED ONE AT RANDOM--
--AND BEGAN TO SWIM FOR MY LIFE...
I HAVE NO MEMORY OF HOW LONG I FORCED MY FAILING BODY ONWARD, BUT AFTER A SEEMING ETERNITY, I CRESTED A RISE--
--AND SAW DELIVERANCE DRIFTING IN THE DISTANCE...
WITH WHAT LITTLE STRENGTH I HAD REMAINING, I MADE MY WAY TO THE FLOATING FLOTSAM...
RALEIGH, YOU'RE ALIVE. THANK THE FATES. I THOUGHT--
OH.
I TOOK HIS COAT TO PROTECT ME FROM THE BLAZING SUN. RALEIGH, AFTER ALL, WOULD HAVE NO FURTHER USE FOR IT.
THEN, WITH A FEW CHOICE SOLEMN WORDS, I CONSIGNED HIS REMAINS TO THE ANXIOUS BOSOM OF THE SEA--
--AND TOOK UP HIS INTERMINABLE WATCH.
HOW LONG I DRIFTED WITH THE CURRENT AFTER THAT, HALF DOZING, HALF AWARE, I CANNOT TRULY SAY--
--UNTIL, AT LENGTH, I WAS STARTLED TO AWARENESS BY SOMETHING BUMPING GENTLY BENEATH MY MAKESHIFT CRAFT...
WHAT--?!?
BY GOD'S BLOOD, IT WAS RALEIGH--
--COME FROM DEATH'S DARK DOMINION TO RECLAIM HIS PRECARIOUS PERCH...

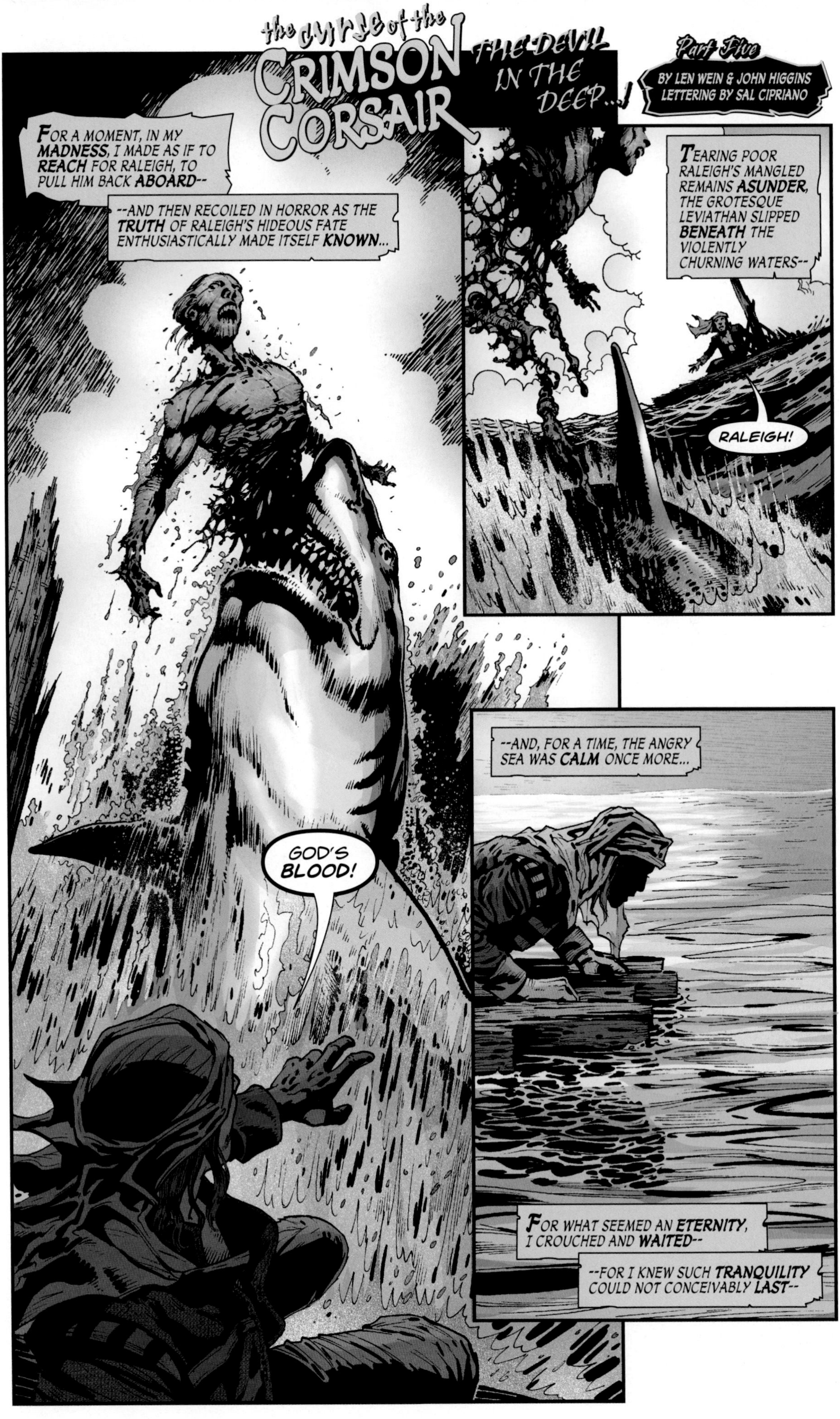
the curse of the CRIMSON CORSAIR
THE DEVIL IN THE DEEP...!
Part Five
BY LEN WEIN & JOHN HIGGINS
LETTERING BY SAL CIPRIANO
FOR A MOMENT, IN MY MADNESS, I MADE AS IF TO REACH FOR RALEIGH, TO PULL HIM BACK ABOARD--
--AND THEN RECOILED IN HORROR AS THE TRUTH OF RALEIGH'S HIDEOUS FATE ENTHUSIASTICALLY MADE ITSELF KNOWN...
GOD'S BLOOD!
TEARING POOR RALEIGH'S MANGLED REMAINS ASUNDER, THE GROTESQUE LEVIATHAN SLIPPED BENEATH THE VIOLENTLY CHURNING WATERS--
RALEIGH!
--AND, FOR A TIME, THE ANGRY SEA WAS CALM ONCE MORE...
FOR WHAT SEEMED AN ETERNITY, I CROUCHED AND WAITED--
--FOR I KNEW SUCH TRANQUILITY COULD NOT CONCEIVABLY LAST--

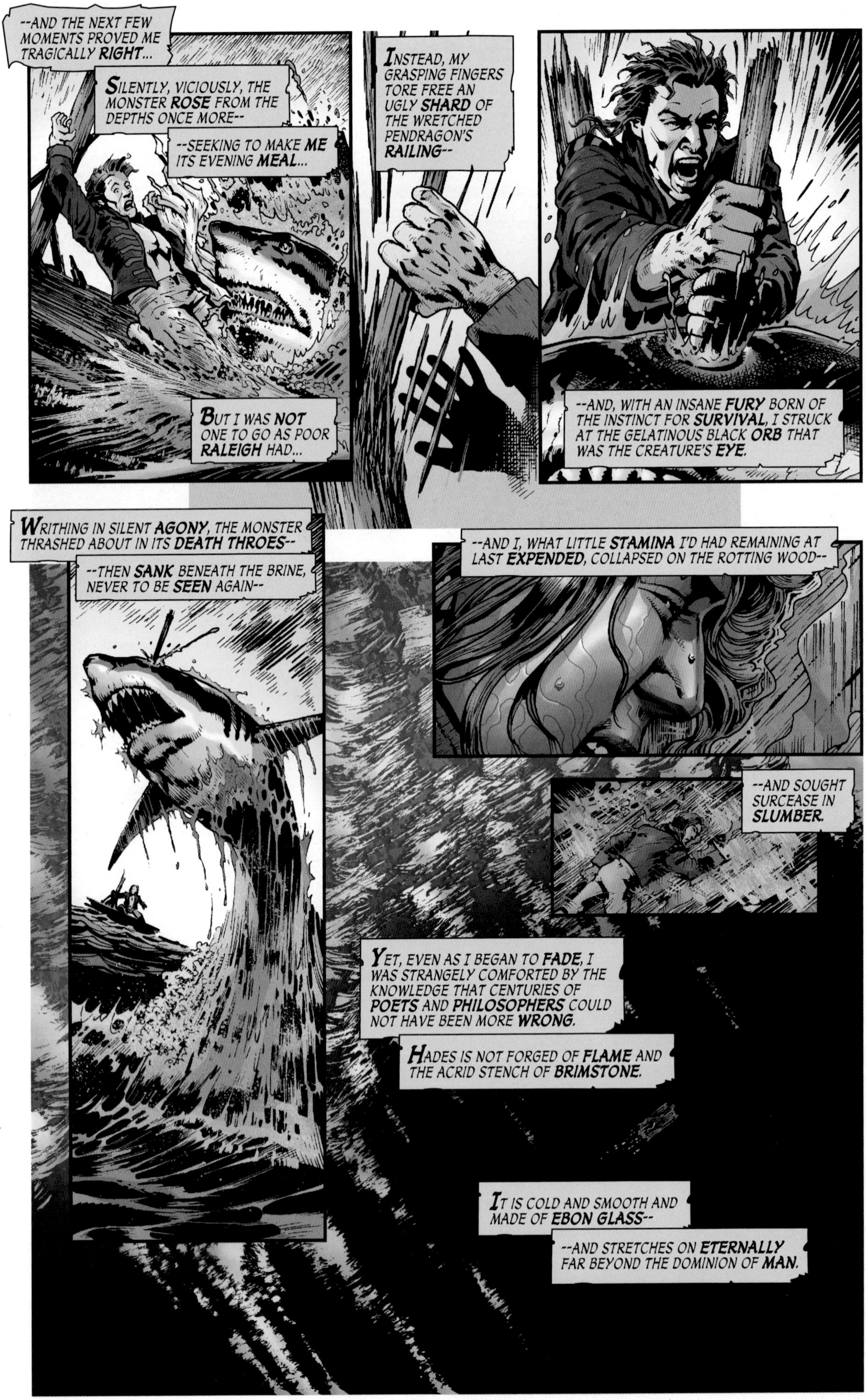
--AND THE NEXT FEW MOMENTS PROVED ME TRAGICALLY RIGHT...
SILENTLY, VICIOUSLY, THE MONSTER ROSE FROM THE DEPTHS ONCE MORE--
--SEEKING TO MAKE ME ITS EVENING MEAL...
BUT I WAS NOT ONE TO GO AS POOR RALEIGH HAD...
INSTEAD, MY GRASPING FINGERS TORE FREE AN UGLY SHARD OF THE WRETCHED PENDRAGON'S RAILING--
--AND, WITH AN INSANE FURY BORN OF THE INSTINCT FOR SURVIVAL, I STRUCK AT THE GELATINOUS BLACK ORB THAT WAS THE CREATURE'S EYE.
WRITHING IN SILENT AGONY, THE MONSTER THRASHED ABOUT IN ITS DEATH THROES--
--THEN SANK BENEATH THE BRINE, NEVER TO BE SEEN AGAIN--
--AND I, WHAT LITTLE STAMINA I'D HAD REMAINING AT LAST EXPENDED, COLLAPSED ON THE ROTTING WOOD--
--AND SOUGHT SURCEASE IN SLUMBER.
YET, EVEN AS I BEGAN TO FADE, I WAS STRANGELY COMFORTED BY THE KNOWLEDGE THAT CENTURIES OF POETS AND PHILOSOPHERS COULD NOT HAVE BEEN MORE WRONG.
HADES IS NOT FORGED OF FLAME AND THE ACRID STENCH OF BRIMSTONE.
IT IS COLD AND SMOOTH AND MADE OF EBON GLASS--
--AND STRETCHES ON ETERNALLY FAR BEYOND THE DOMINION OF MAN.

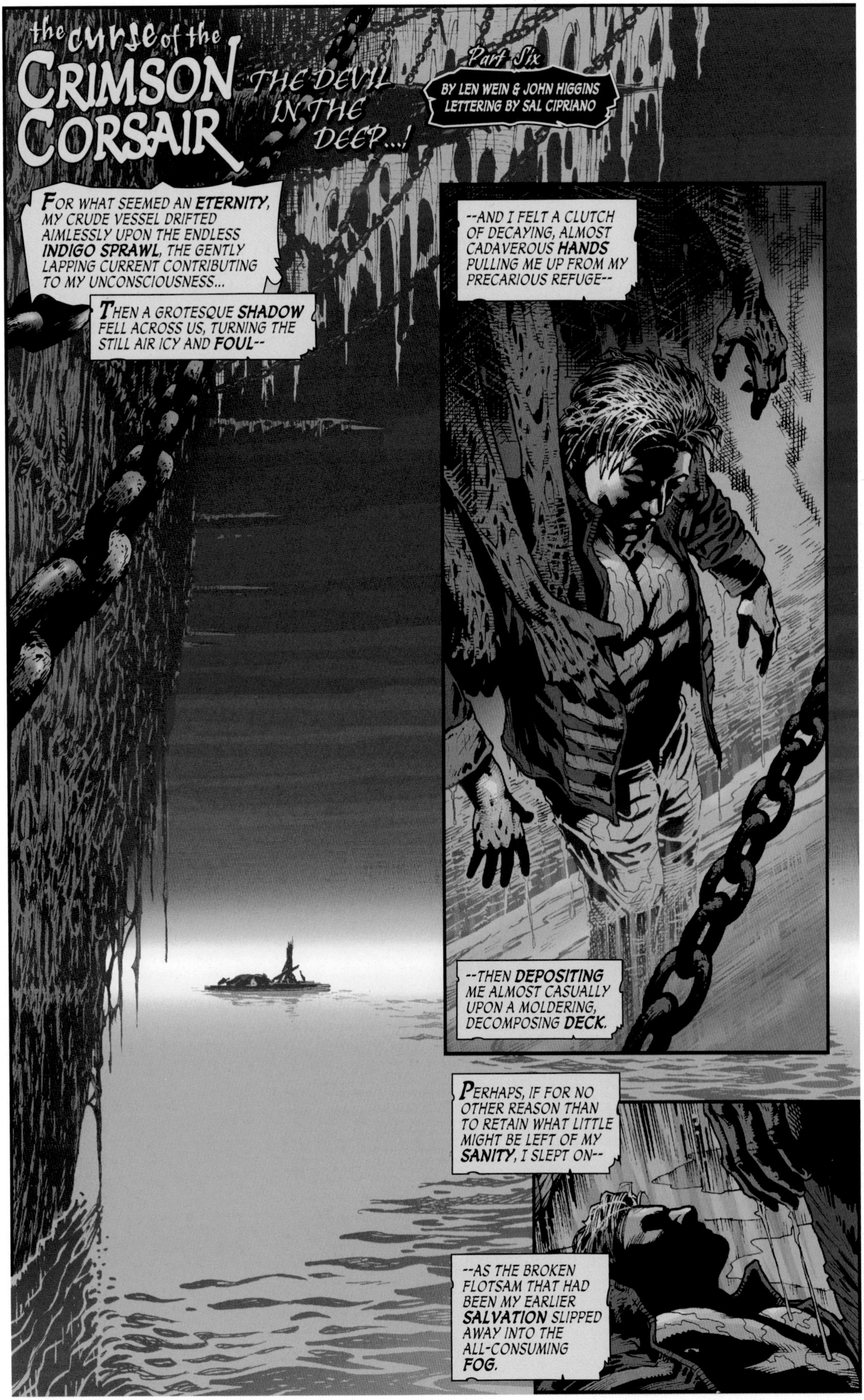
the curse of the
CRIMSON CORSAIR
THE DEVIL IN THE DEEP...!
Part Six
BY LEN WEIN & JOHN HIGGINS
LETTERING BY SAL CIPRIANO
FOR WHAT SEEMED AN ETERNITY, MY CRUDE VESSEL DRIFTED AIMLESSLY UPON THE ENDLESS INDIGO SPRAWL, THE GENTLY LAPPING CURRENT CONTRIBUTING TO MY UNCONSCIOUSNESS...
THEN A GROTESQUE SHADOW FELL ACROSS US, TURNING THE STILL AIR ICY AND FOUL--
--AND I FELT A CLUTCH OF DECAYING, ALMOST CADAVEROUS HANDS PULLING ME UP FROM MY PRECARIOUS REFUGE--
--THEN DEPOSITING ME ALMOST CASUALLY UPON A MOLDERING, DECOMPOSING DECK.
PERHAPS, IF FOR NO OTHER REASON THAN TO RETAIN WHAT LITTLE MIGHT BE LEFT OF MY SANITY, I SLEPT ON--
--AS THE BROKEN FLOTSAM THAT HAD BEEN MY EARLIER SALVATION SLIPPED AWAY INTO THE ALL-CONSUMING FOG.

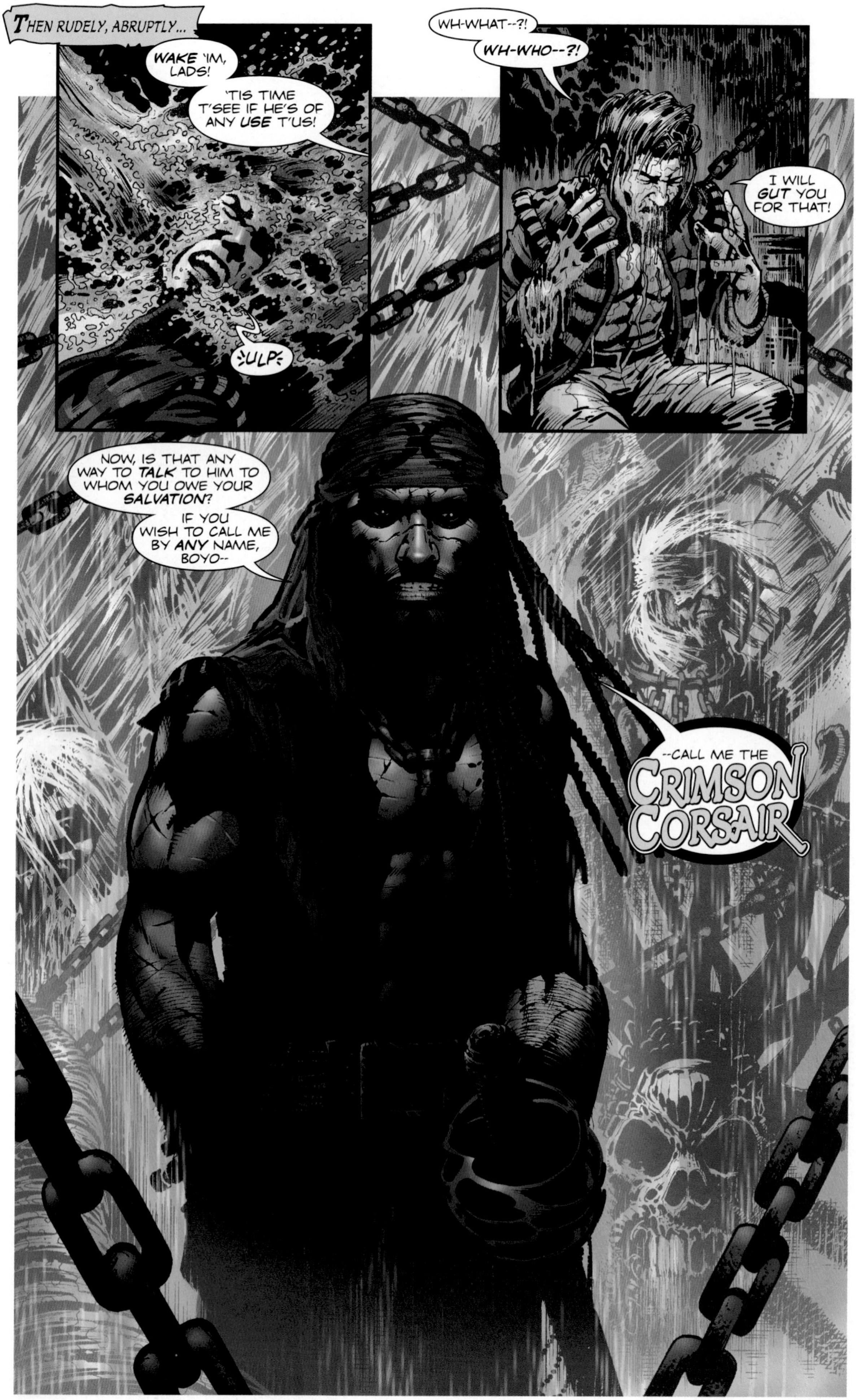
THEN RUDELY, ABRUPTLY...
WAKE 'IM, LADS!
'TIS TIME T'SEE IF HE'S OF ANY USE T'US!
ULP
WH-WHAT--?!
WH-WHO--?!
I WILL GUT YOU FOR THAT!
NOW, IS THAT ANY WAY TO TALK TO HIM TO WHOM YOU OWE YOUR SALVATION?
IF YOU WISH TO CALL ME BY ANY NAME, BOYO--
--CALL ME THE CRIMSON CORSAIR

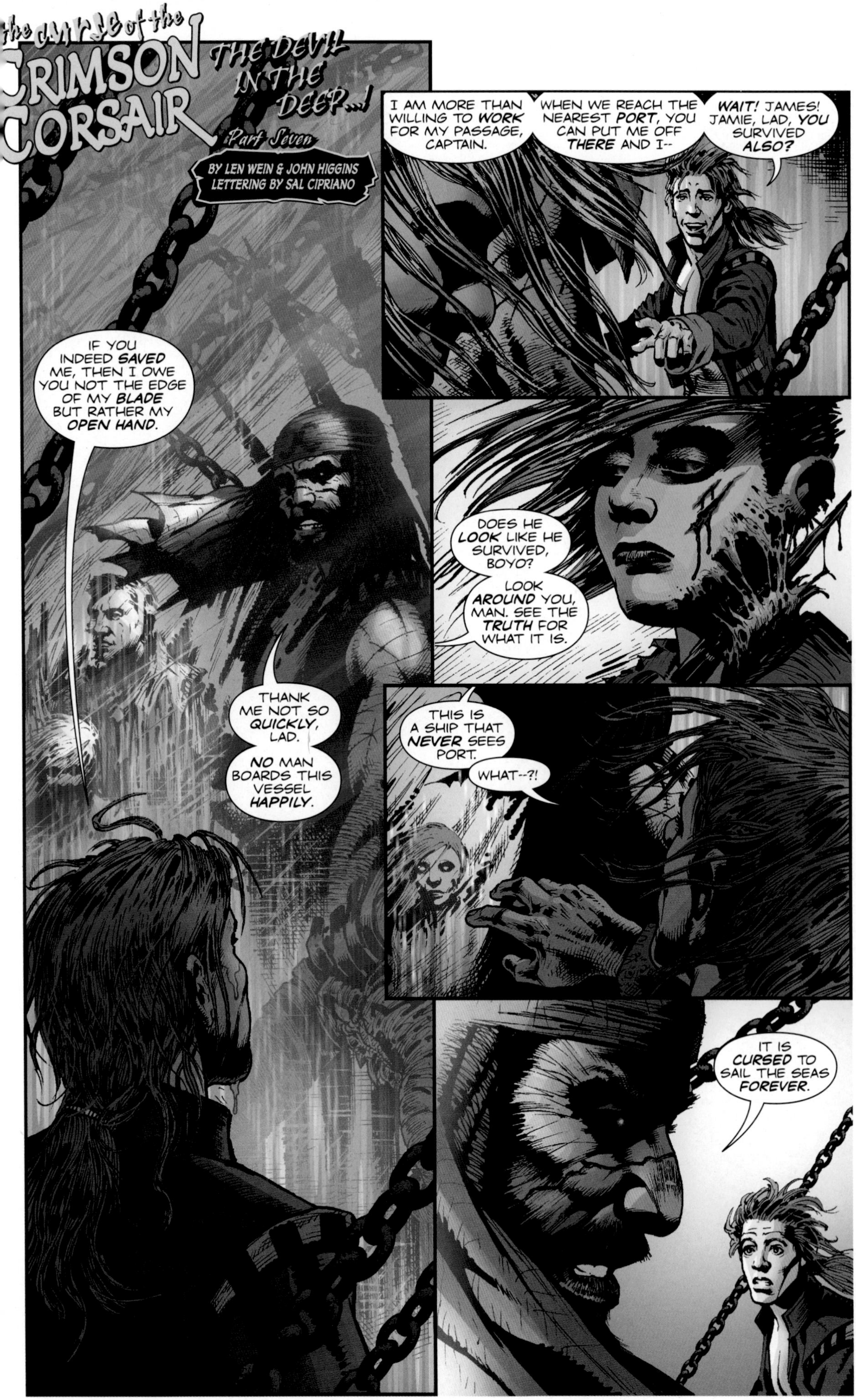
the curse of the
CRIMSON CORSAIR
THE DEVIL IN THE DEEP...!
Part Seven
BY LEN WEIN & JOHN HIGGINS
LETTERING BY SAL CIPRIANO
IF YOU INDEED SAVED ME, THEN I OWE YOU NOT THE EDGE OF MY BLADE BUT RATHER MY OPEN HAND.
THANK ME NOT SO QUICKLY, LAD.
NO MAN BOARDS THIS VESSEL HAPPILY.
I AM MORE THAN WILLING TO WORK FOR MY PASSAGE, CAPTAIN.
WHEN WE REACH THE NEAREST PORT, YOU CAN PUT ME OFF THERE AND I--
WAIT! JAMES! JAMIE, LAD, YOU SURVIVED ALSO?
DOES HE LOOK LIKE HE SURVIVED, BOYO?
LOOK AROUND YOU, MAN. SEE THE TRUTH FOR WHAT IT IS.
THIS IS A SHIP THAT NEVER SEES PORT.
WHAT--?!
IT IS CURSED TO SAIL THE SEAS FOREVER.

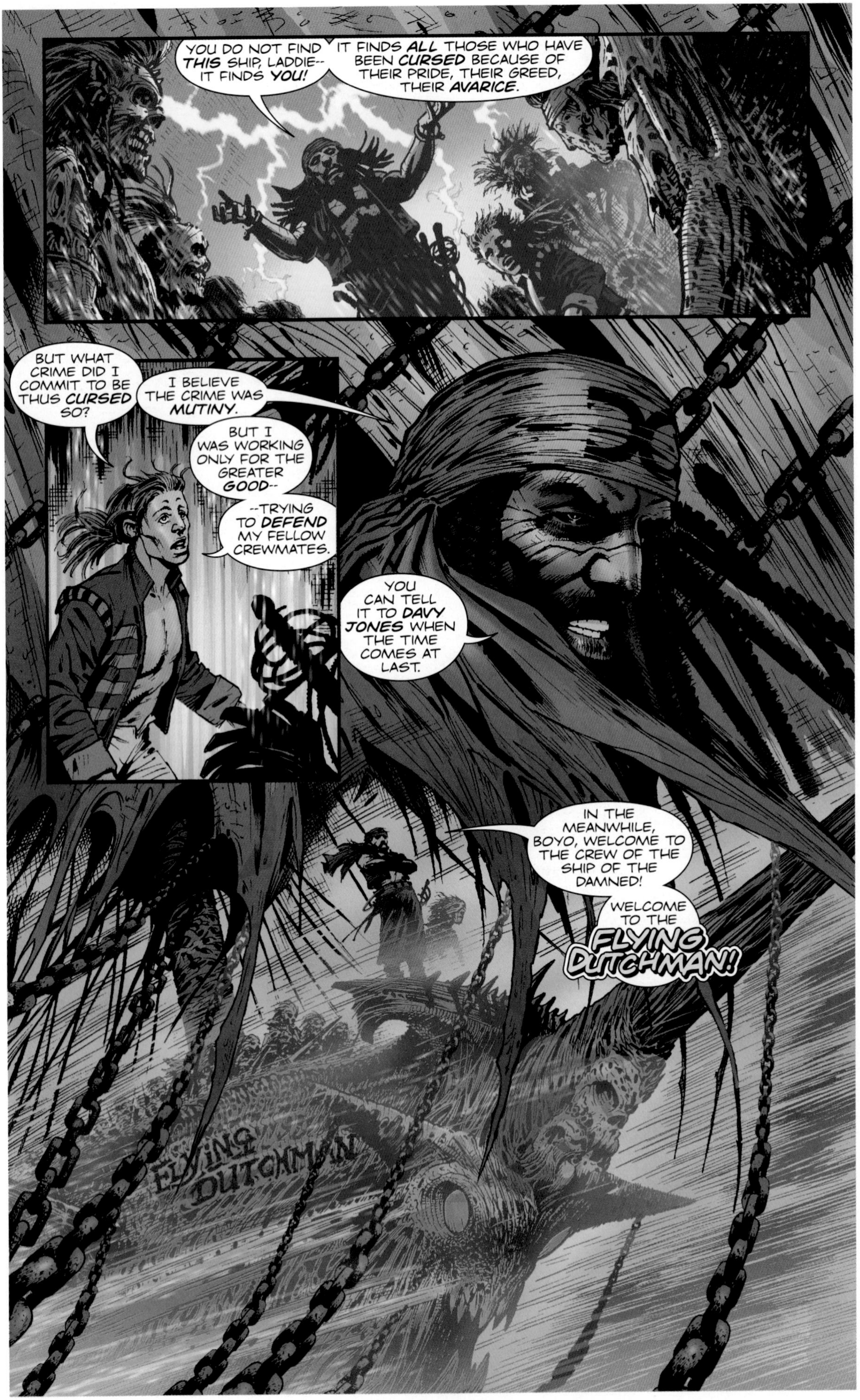

YOU DO NOT FIND THIS SHIP, LADDIE--IT FINDS YOU!
IT FINDS ALL THOSE WHO HAVE BEEN CURSED BECAUSE OF THEIR PRIDE, THEIR GREED, THEIR AVARICE.
BUT WHAT CRIME DID I COMMIT TO BE THUS CURSED SO?
I BELIEVE THE CRIME WAS MUTINY.
BUT I WAS WORKING ONLY FOR THE GREATER GOOD--
--TRYING TO DEFEND MY FELLOW CREWMATES.
YOU CAN TELL IT TO DAVY JONES WHEN THE TIME COMES AT LAST.
IN THE MEANWHILE, BOYO, WELCOME TO THE CREW OF THE SHIP OF THE DAMNED!
WELCOME TO THE FLYING DUTCHMAN!
FLYING DUTCHMAN

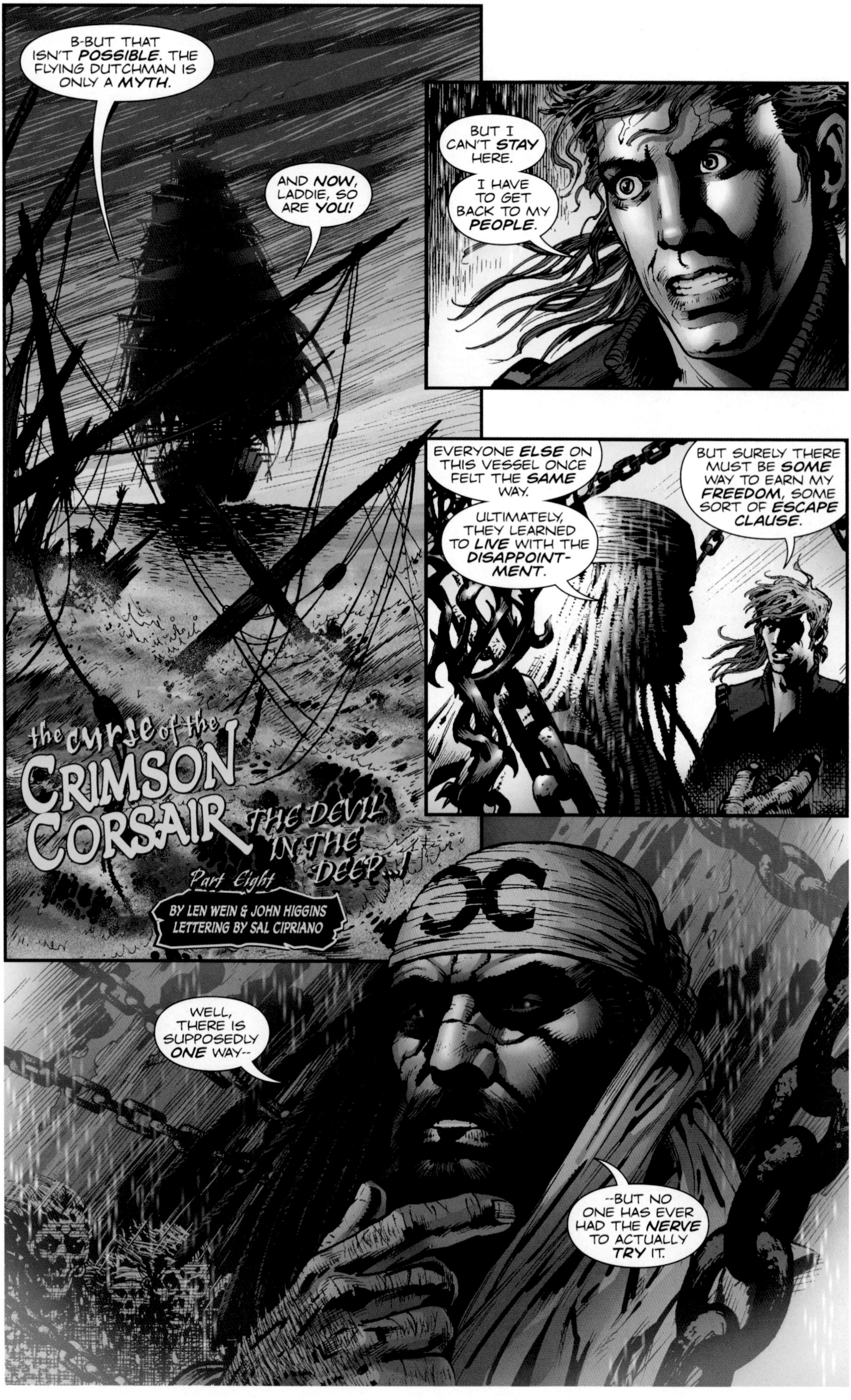
B-BUT THAT ISN'T POSSIBLE. THE FLYING DUTCHMAN IS ONLY A MYTH.
AND NOW, LADDIE, SO ARE YOU!
BUT I CAN'T STAY HERE.
I HAVE TO GET BACK TO MY PEOPLE.
the curse of the CRIMSON CORSAIR
THE DEVIL IN THE DEEP...!
Part Eight
BY LEN WEIN & JOHN HIGGINS
LETTERING BY SAL CIPRIANO
EVERYONE ELSE ON THIS VESSEL ONCE FELT THE SAME WAY.
ULTIMATELY, THEY LEARNED TO LIVE WITH THE DISAPPOINT-MENT.
BUT SURELY THERE MUST BE SOME WAY TO EARN MY FREEDOM, SOME SORT OF ESCAPE CLAUSE.
WELL, THERE IS SUPPOSEDLY ONE WAY--
--BUT NO ONE HAS EVER HAD THE NERVE TO ACTUALLY TRY IT.

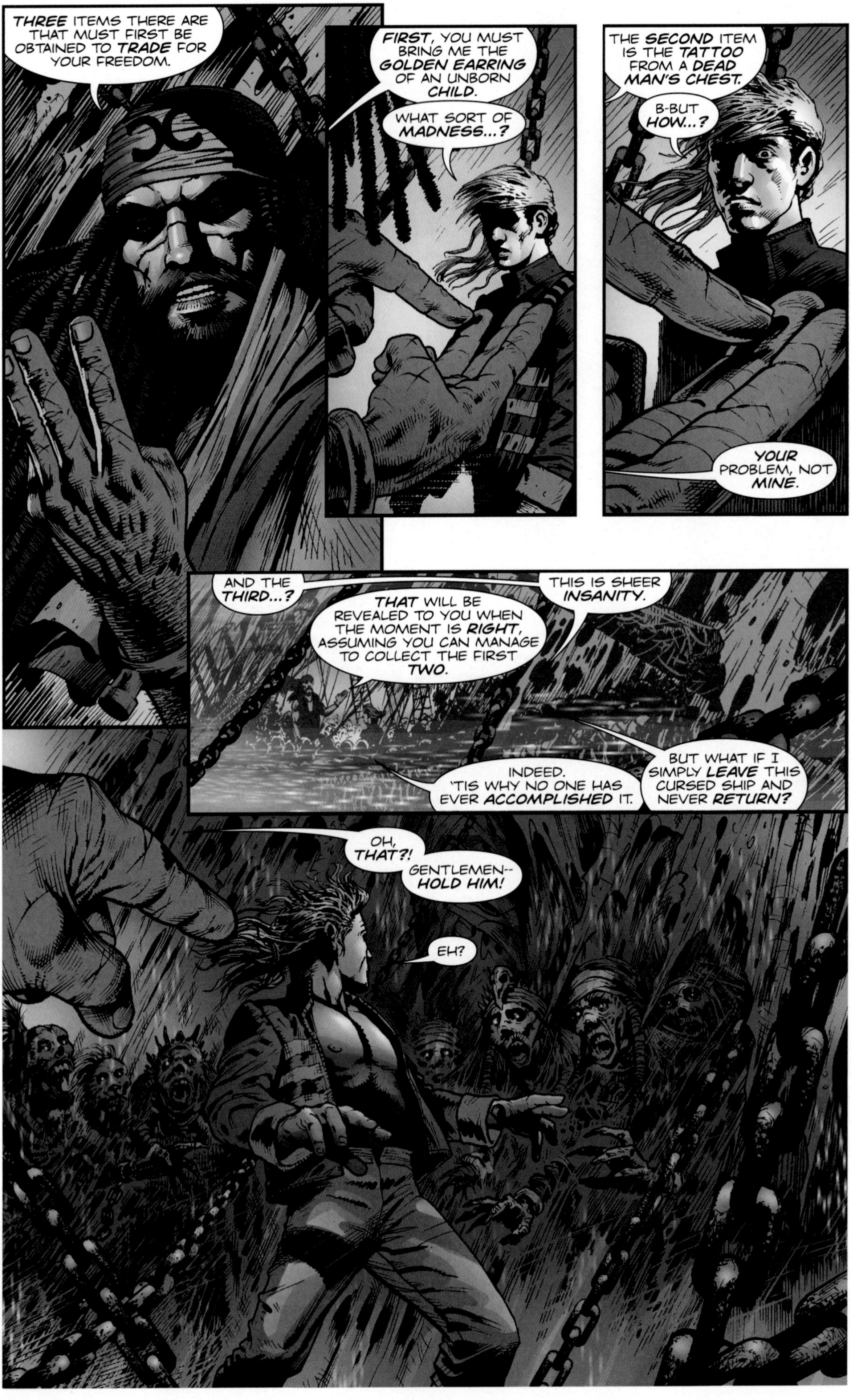
THREE ITEMS THERE ARE THAT MUST FIRST BE OBTAINED TO TRADE FOR YOUR FREEDOM.
FIRST, YOU MUST BRING ME THE GOLDEN EARRING OF AN UNBORN CHILD.
WHAT SORT OF MADNESS...?
THE SECOND ITEM IS THE TATTOO FROM A DEAD MAN'S CHEST.
B-BUT HOW...?
YOUR PROBLEM, NOT MINE.
AND THE THIRD...?
THAT WILL BE REVEALED TO YOU WHEN THE MOMENT IS RIGHT, ASSUMING YOU CAN MANAGE TO COLLECT THE FIRST TWO.
THIS IS SHEER INSANITY.
INDEED. 'TIS WHY NO ONE HAS EVER ACCOMPLISHED IT.
BUT WHAT IF I SIMPLY LEAVE THIS CURSED SHIP AND NEVER RETURN?
OH, THAT?! GENTLEMEN-- HOLD HIM!
EH?

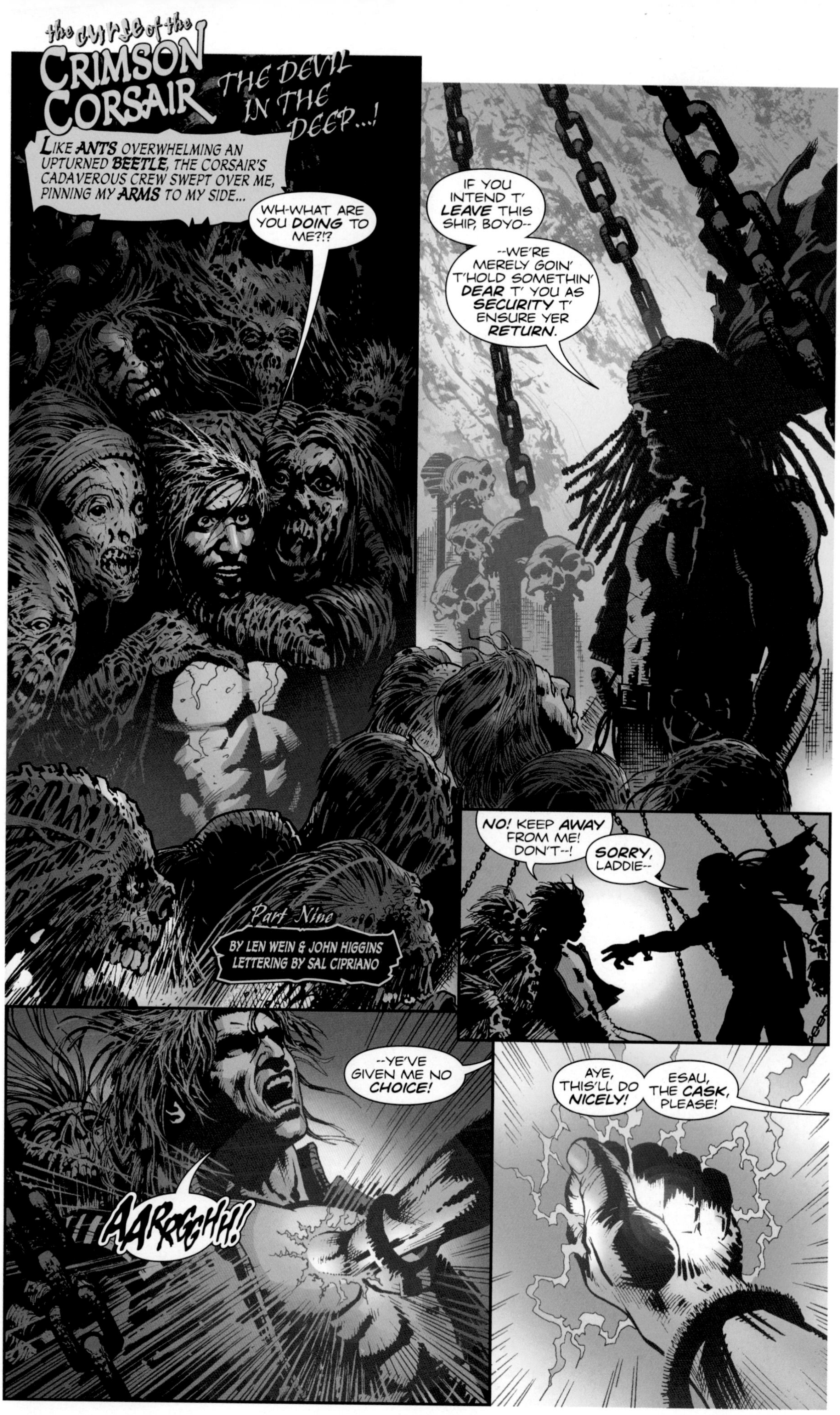
the curse of the
CRIMSON CORSAIR
THE DEVIL IN THE DEEP...!
LIKE ANTS OVERWHELMING AN UPTURNED BEETLE, THE CORSAIR'S CADAVEROUS CREW SWEPT OVER ME, PINNING MY ARMS TO MY SIDE...
WH-WHAT ARE YOU DOING TO ME?!?
IF YOU INTEND T' LEAVE THIS SHIP, BOYO--
--WE'RE MERELY GOIN' T'HOLD SOMETHIN' DEAR T' YOU AS SECURITY T' ENSURE YER RETURN.
Part Nine
BY LEN WEIN & JOHN HIGGINS
LETTERING BY SAL CIPRIANO
NO! KEEP AWAY FROM ME! DON'T--!
SORRY, LADDIE--
--YE'VE GIVEN ME NO CHOICE!
AARRGGHH!
AYE, THIS'LL DO NICELY!
ESAU, THE CASK, PLEASE!

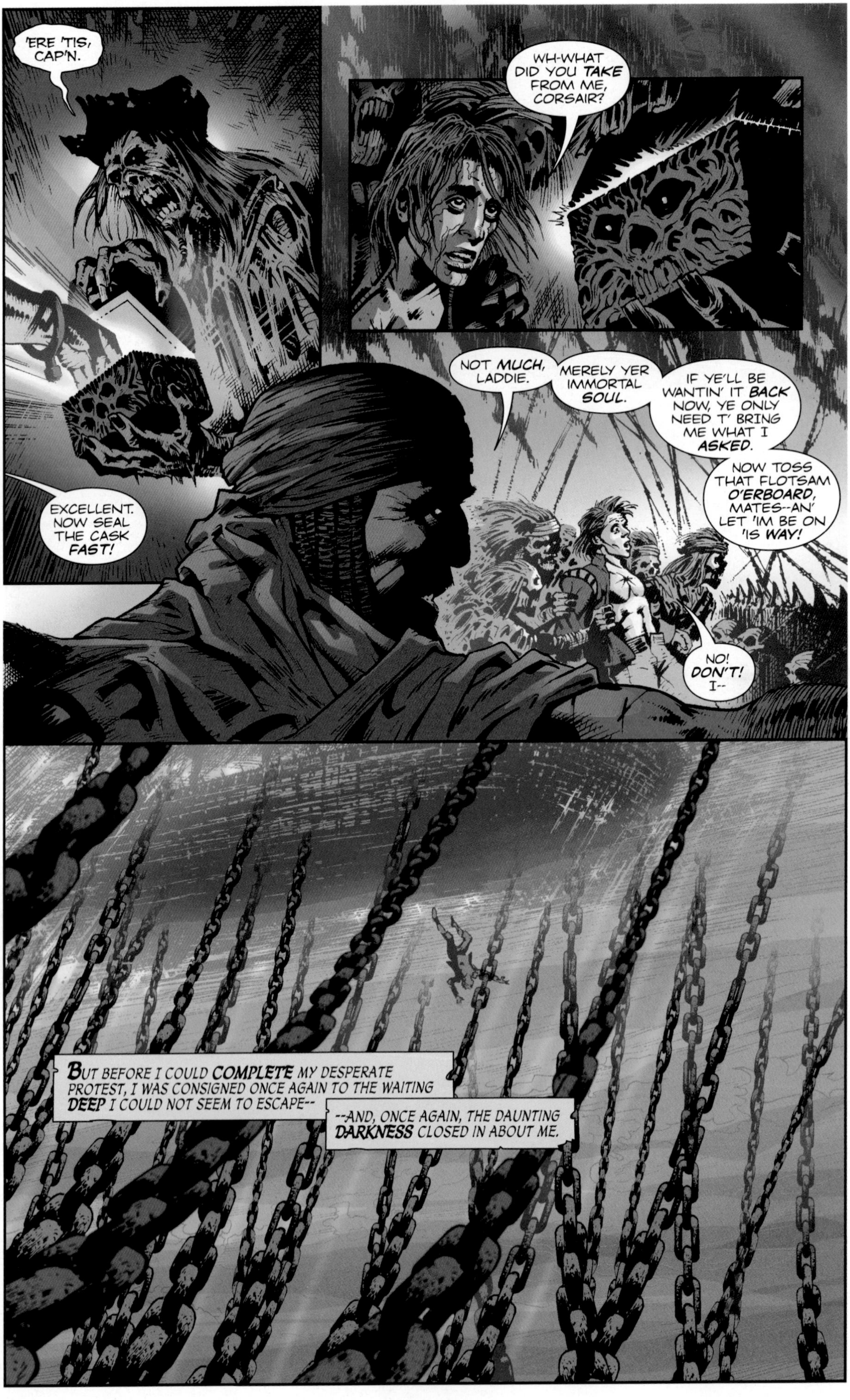
'ERE 'TIS, CAP'N.
WH-WHAT DID YOU TAKE FROM ME, CORSAIR?
EXCELLENT. NOW SEAL THE CASK FAST!
NOT MUCH, LADDIE.
MERELY YER IMMORTAL SOUL.
IF YE'LL BE WANTIN' IT BACK NOW, YE ONLY NEED T' BRING ME WHAT I ASKED.
NOW TOSS THAT FLOTSAM O'ERBOARD, MATES--AN' LET 'IM BE ON 'IS WAY!
NO! DON'T! I--
BUT BEFORE I COULD COMPLETE MY DESPERATE PROTEST, I WAS CONSIGNED ONCE AGAIN TO THE WAITING DEEP I COULD NOT SEEM TO ESCAPE--
--AND, ONCE AGAIN, THE DAUNTING DARKNESS CLOSED IN ABOUT ME.

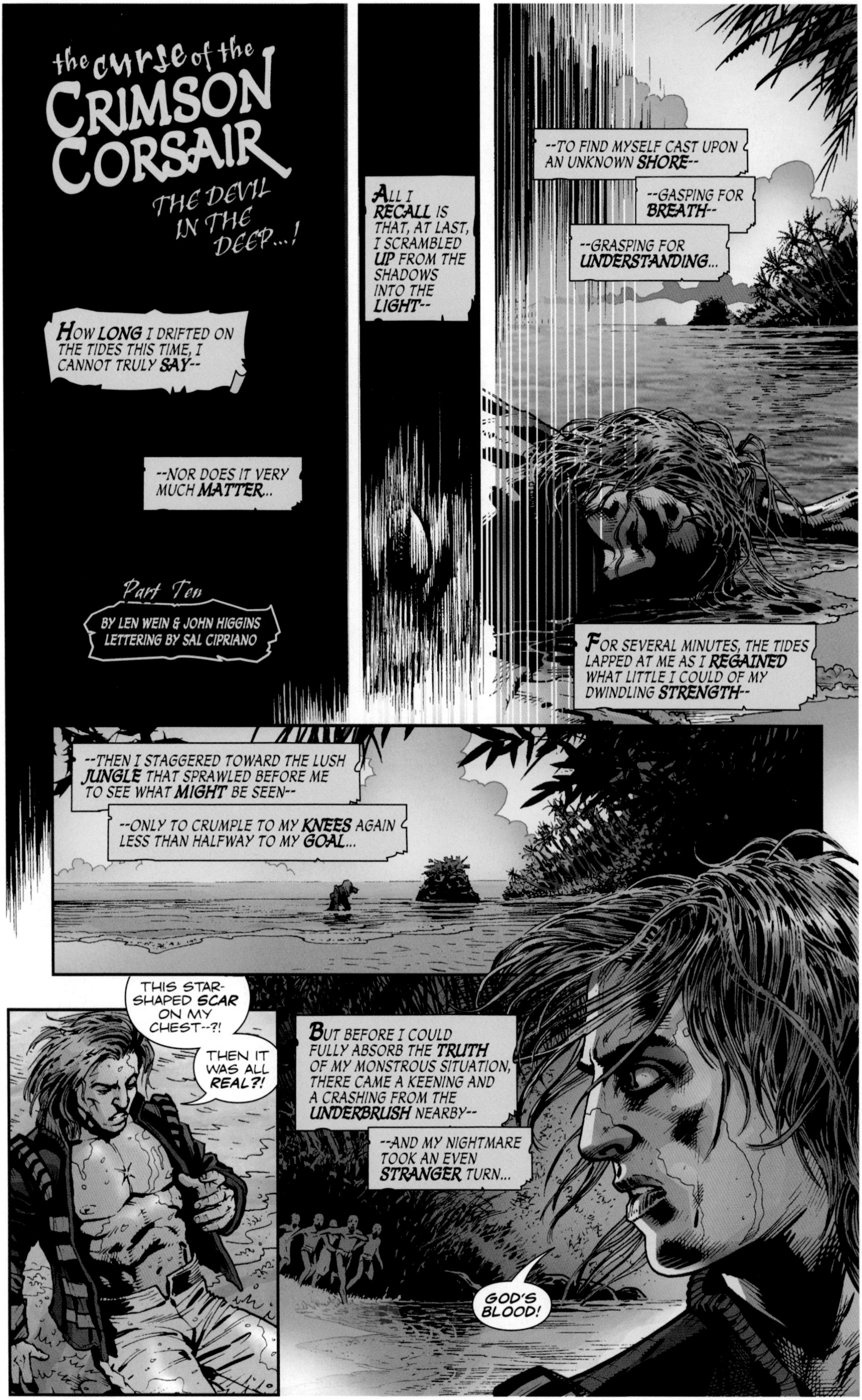

the curse of the
CRIMSON CORSAIR
THE DEVIL IN THE DEEP...!
HOW LONG I DRIFTED ON THE TIDES THIS TIME, I CANNOT TRULY SAY--
--NOR DOES IT VERY MUCH MATTER...
Part Ten
BY LEN WEIN & JOHN HIGGINS
LETTERING BY SAL CIPRIANO
ALL I RECALL IS THAT, AT LAST, I SCRAMBLED UP FROM THE SHADOWS INTO THE LIGHT--
--TO FIND MYSELF CAST UPON AN UNKNOWN SHORE--
--GASPING FOR BREATH--
--GRASPING FOR UNDERSTANDING...
FOR SEVERAL MINUTES, THE TIDES LAPPED AT ME AS I REGAINED WHAT LITTLE I COULD OF MY DWINDLING STRENGTH--
--THEN I STAGGERED TOWARD THE LUSH JUNGLE THAT SPRAWLED BEFORE ME TO SEE WHAT MIGHT BE SEEN--
--ONLY TO CRUMPLE TO MY KNEES AGAIN LESS THAN HALFWAY TO MY GOAL...
THIS STAR-SHAPED SCAR ON MY CHEST--?!
THEN IT WAS ALL REAL?!
BUT BEFORE I COULD FULLY ABSORB THE TRUTH OF MY MONSTROUS SITUATION, THERE CAME A KEENING AND A CRASHING FROM THE UNDERBRUSH NEARBY--
--AND MY NIGHTMARE TOOK AN EVEN STRANGER TURN...
GOD'S BLOOD!

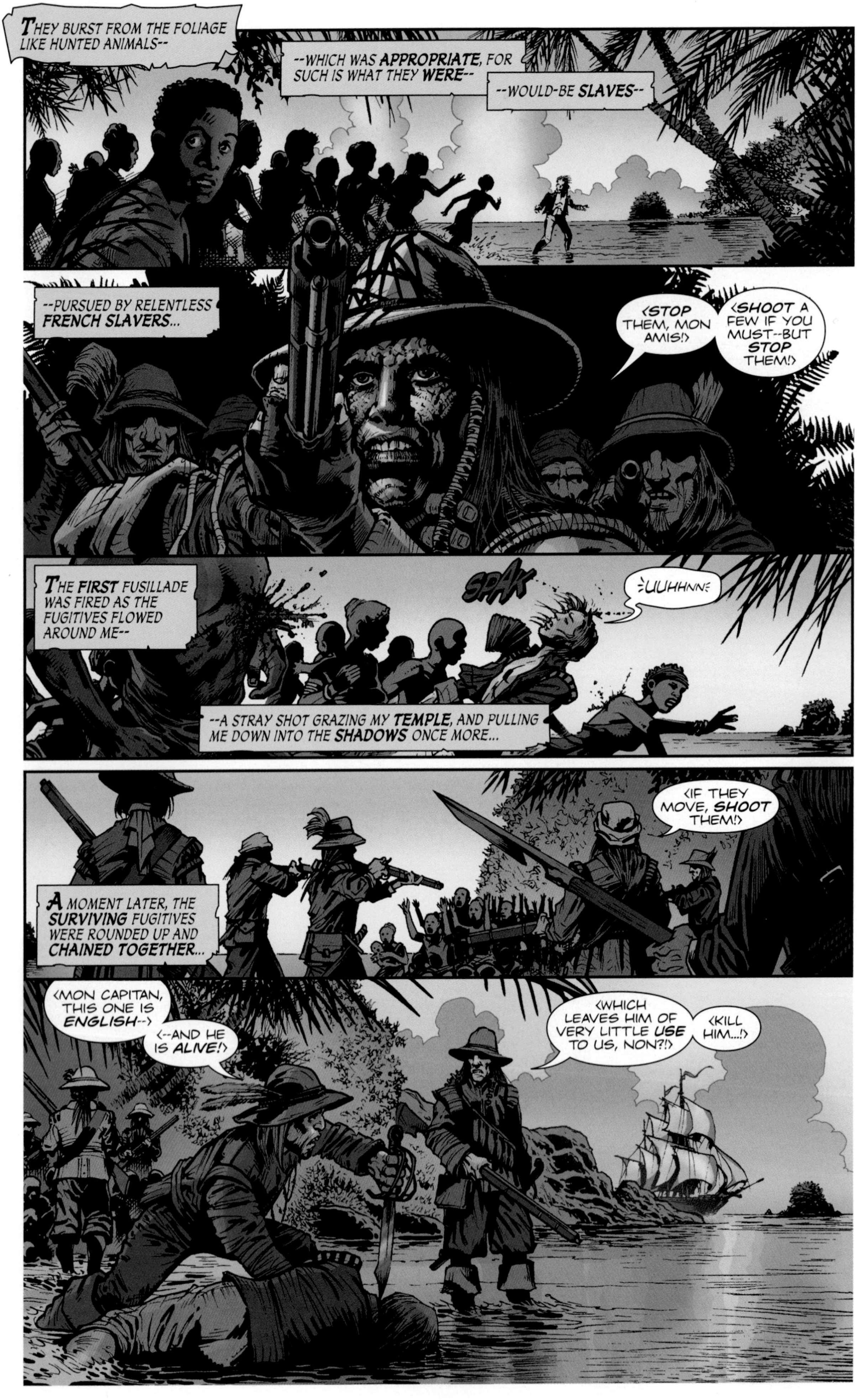
THEY BURST FROM THE FOLIAGE LIKE HUNTED ANIMALS--
--WHICH WAS APPROPRIATE, FOR SUCH IS WHAT THEY WERE--
--WOULD-BE SLAVES--
--PURSUED BY RELENTLESS FRENCH SLAVERS...
‹STOP THEM, MON AMIS!›
‹SHOOT A FEW IF YOU MUST--BUT STOP THEM!›
THE FIRST FUSILLADE WAS FIRED AS THE FUGITIVES FLOWED AROUND ME--
SPAK
UUHHNN
--A STRAY SHOT GRAZING MY TEMPLE, AND PULLING ME DOWN INTO THE SHADOWS ONCE MORE...
‹IF THEY MOVE, SHOOT THEM!›
A MOMENT LATER, THE SURVIVING FUGITIVES WERE ROUNDED UP AND CHAINED TOGETHER...
‹MON CAPITAN, THIS ONE IS ENGLISH--›
‹--AND HE IS ALIVE!›
‹WHICH LEAVES HIM OF VERY LITTLE USE TO US, NON?!›
‹KILL HIM...!›

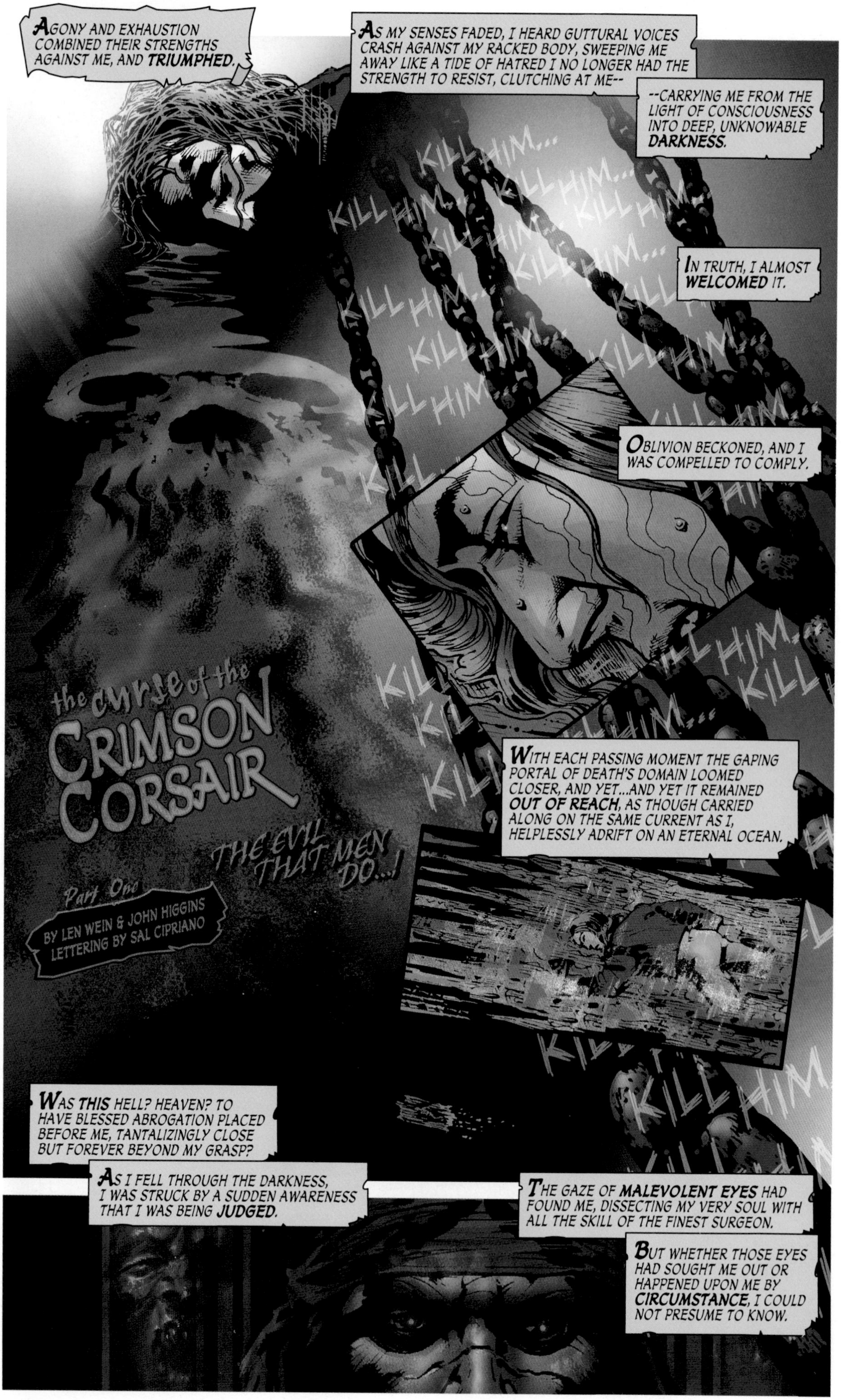
AGONY AND EXHAUSTION COMBINED THEIR STRENGTHS AGAINST ME, AND **TRIUMPHED**.
AS MY SENSES FADED, I HEARD GUTTURAL VOICES CRASH AGAINST MY RACKED BODY, SWEEPING ME AWAY LIKE A TIDE OF HATRED I NO LONGER HAD THE STRENGTH TO RESIST, CLUTCHING AT ME--
--CARRYING ME FROM THE LIGHT OF CONSCIOUSNESS INTO DEEP, UNKNOWABLE **DARKNESS**.
KILL HIM... KILL HIM... KILL HIM...
IN TRUTH, I ALMOST **WELCOMED** IT.
OBLIVION BECKONED, AND I WAS COMPELLED TO COMPLY.
the curse of the CRIMSON CORSAIR
THE EVIL THAT MEN DO...!
Part One
BY LEN WEIN & JOHN HIGGINS
LETTERING BY SAL CIPRIANO
WITH EACH PASSING MOMENT THE GAPING PORTAL OF DEATH'S DOMAIN LOOMED CLOSER, AND YET...AND YET IT REMAINED **OUT OF REACH**, AS THOUGH CARRIED ALONG ON THE SAME CURRENT AS I, HELPLESSLY ADRIFT ON AN ETERNAL OCEAN.
WAS **THIS** HELL? HEAVEN? TO HAVE BLESSED ABROGATION PLACED BEFORE ME, TANTALIZINGLY CLOSE BUT FOREVER BEYOND MY GRASP?
AS I FELL THROUGH THE DARKNESS, I WAS STRUCK BY A SUDDEN AWARENESS THAT I WAS BEING **JUDGED**.
THE GAZE OF **MALEVOLENT EYES** HAD FOUND ME, DISSECTING MY VERY SOUL WITH ALL THE SKILL OF THE FINEST SURGEON.
BUT WHETHER THOSE EYES HAD SOUGHT ME OUT OR HAPPENED UPON ME BY **CIRCUMSTANCE**, I COULD NOT PRESUME TO KNOW.

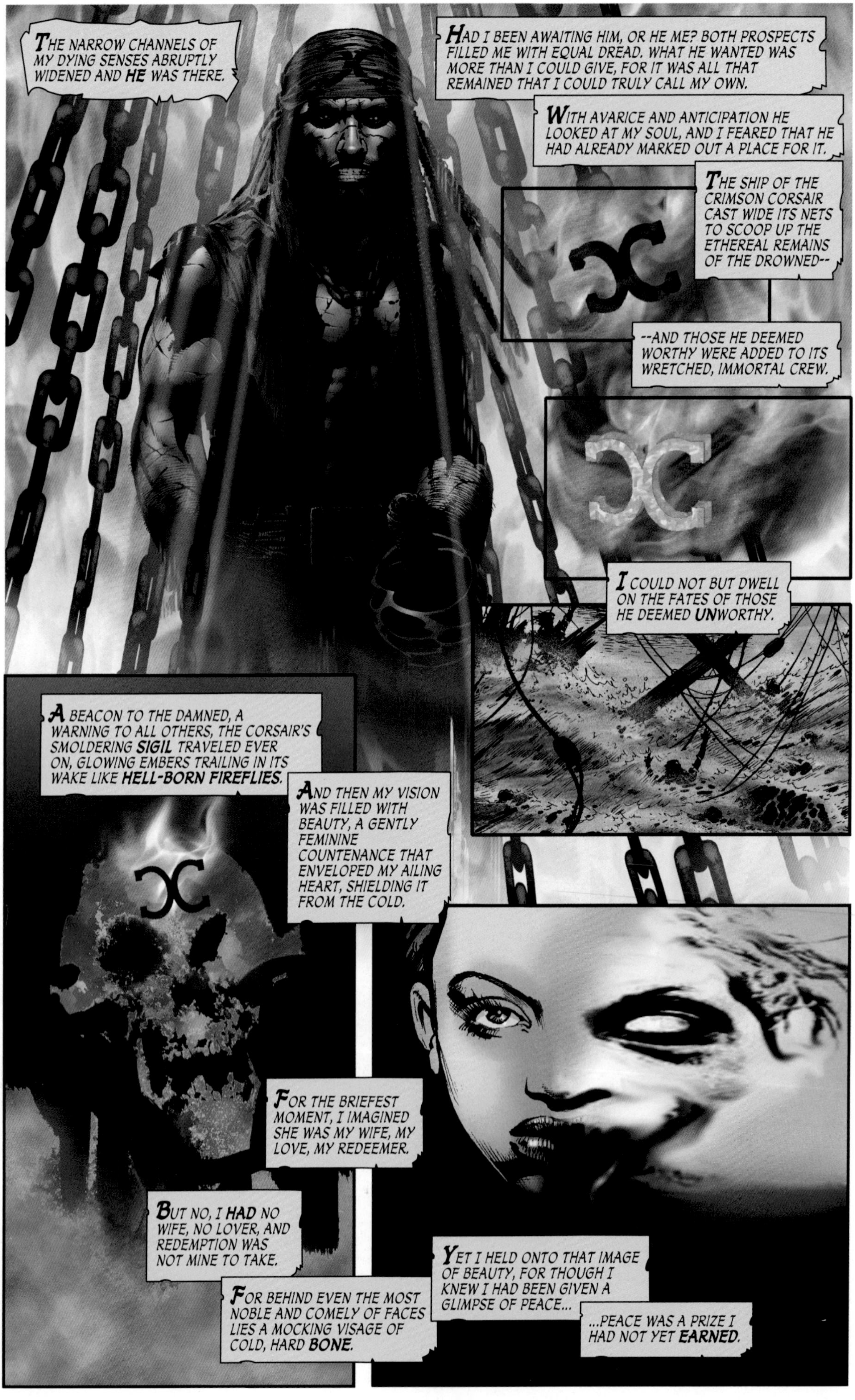
THE NARROW CHANNELS OF MY DYING SENSES ABRUPTLY WIDENED AND HE WAS THERE.
HAD I BEEN AWAITING HIM, OR HE ME? BOTH PROSPECTS FILLED ME WITH EQUAL DREAD. WHAT HE WANTED WAS MORE THAN I COULD GIVE, FOR IT WAS ALL THAT REMAINED THAT I COULD TRULY CALL MY OWN.
WITH AVARICE AND ANTICIPATION HE LOOKED AT MY SOUL, AND I FEARED THAT HE HAD ALREADY MARKED OUT A PLACE FOR IT.
THE SHIP OF THE CRIMSON CORSAIR CAST WIDE ITS NETS TO SCOOP UP THE ETHEREAL REMAINS OF THE DROWNED--
--AND THOSE HE DEEMED WORTHY WERE ADDED TO ITS WRETCHED, IMMORTAL CREW.
I COULD NOT BUT DWELL ON THE FATES OF THOSE HE DEEMED UNWORTHY.
A BEACON TO THE DAMNED, A WARNING TO ALL OTHERS, THE CORSAIR'S SMOLDERING SIGIL TRAVELED EVER ON, GLOWING EMBERS TRAILING IN ITS WAKE LIKE HELL-BORN FIREFLIES.
AND THEN MY VISION WAS FILLED WITH BEAUTY, A GENTLY FEMININE COUNTENANCE THAT ENVELOPED MY AILING HEART, SHIELDING IT FROM THE COLD.
FOR THE BRIEFEST MOMENT, I IMAGINED SHE WAS MY WIFE, MY LOVE, MY REDEEMER.
BUT NO, I HAD NO WIFE, NO LOVER, AND REDEMPTION WAS NOT MINE TO TAKE.
FOR BEHIND EVEN THE MOST NOBLE AND COMELY OF FACES LIES A MOCKING VISAGE OF COLD, HARD BONE.
YET I HELD ONTO THAT IMAGE OF BEAUTY, FOR THOUGH I KNEW I HAD BEEN GIVEN A GLIMPSE OF PEACE...
...PEACE WAS A PRIZE I HAD NOT YET EARNED.

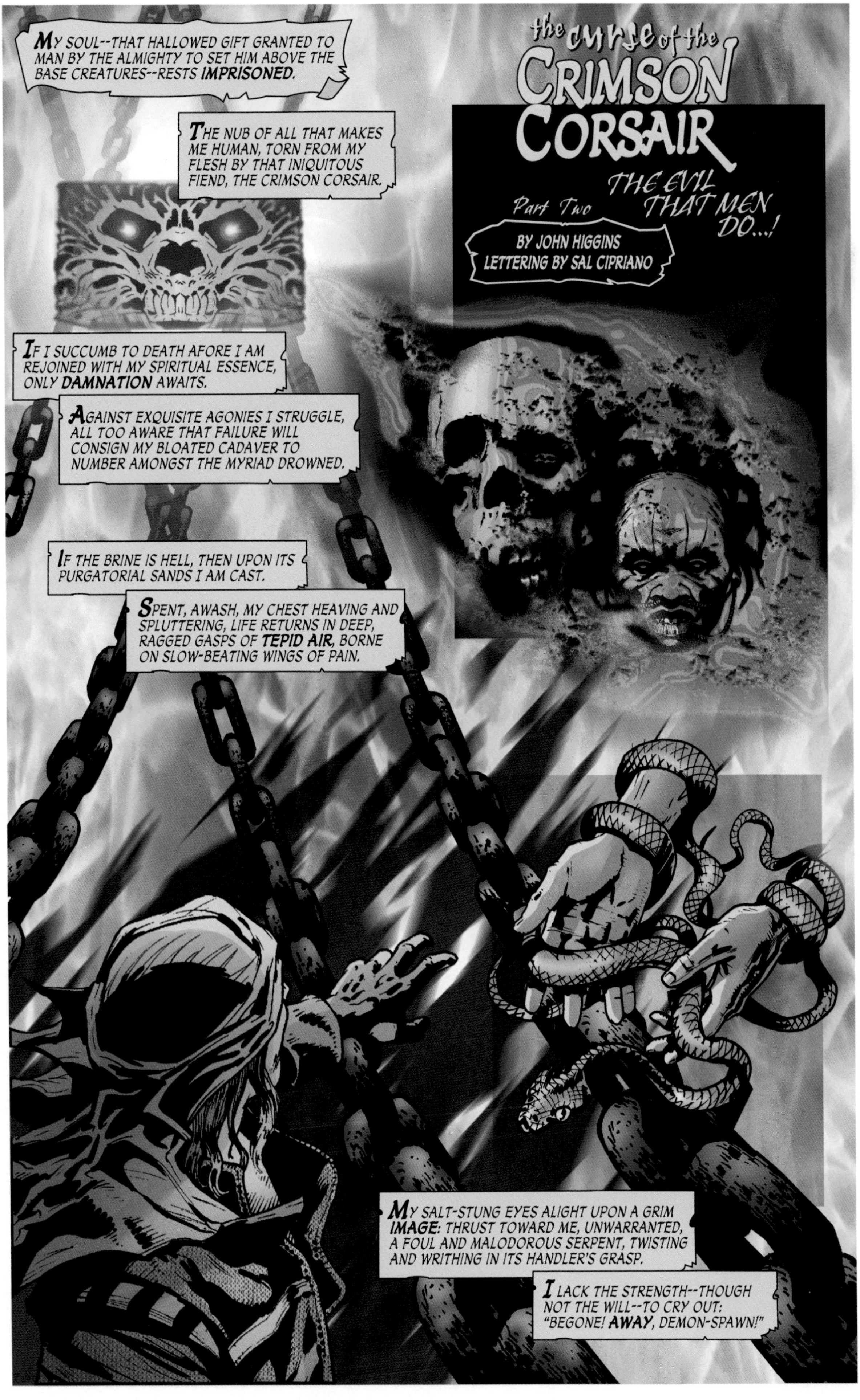
MY SOUL--THAT HALLOWED GIFT GRANTED TO MAN BY THE ALMIGHTY TO SET HIM ABOVE THE BASE CREATURES--RESTS IMPRISONED.
THE NUB OF ALL THAT MAKES ME HUMAN, TORN FROM MY FLESH BY THAT INIQUITOUS FIEND, THE CRIMSON CORSAIR.
the curse of the CRIMSON CORSAIR
Part Two
THE EVIL THAT MEN DO...!
BY JOHN HIGGINS
LETTERING BY SAL CIPRIANO
IF I SUCCUMB TO DEATH AFORE I AM REJOINED WITH MY SPIRITUAL ESSENCE, ONLY DAMNATION AWAITS.
AGAINST EXQUISITE AGONIES I STRUGGLE, ALL TOO AWARE THAT FAILURE WILL CONSIGN MY BLOATED CADAVER TO NUMBER AMONGST THE MYRIAD DROWNED.
IF THE BRINE IS HELL, THEN UPON ITS PURGATORIAL SANDS I AM CAST.
SPENT, AWASH, MY CHEST HEAVING AND SPLUTTERING, LIFE RETURNS IN DEEP, RAGGED GASPS OF TEPID AIR, BORNE ON SLOW-BEATING WINGS OF PAIN.
MY SALT-STUNG EYES ALIGHT UPON A GRIM IMAGE: THRUST TOWARD ME, UNWARRANTED, A FOUL AND MALODOROUS SERPENT, TWISTING AND WRITHING IN ITS HANDLER'S GRASP.
I LACK THE STRENGTH--THOUGH NOT THE WILL--TO CRY OUT: "BEGONE! AWAY, DEMON-SPAWN!"

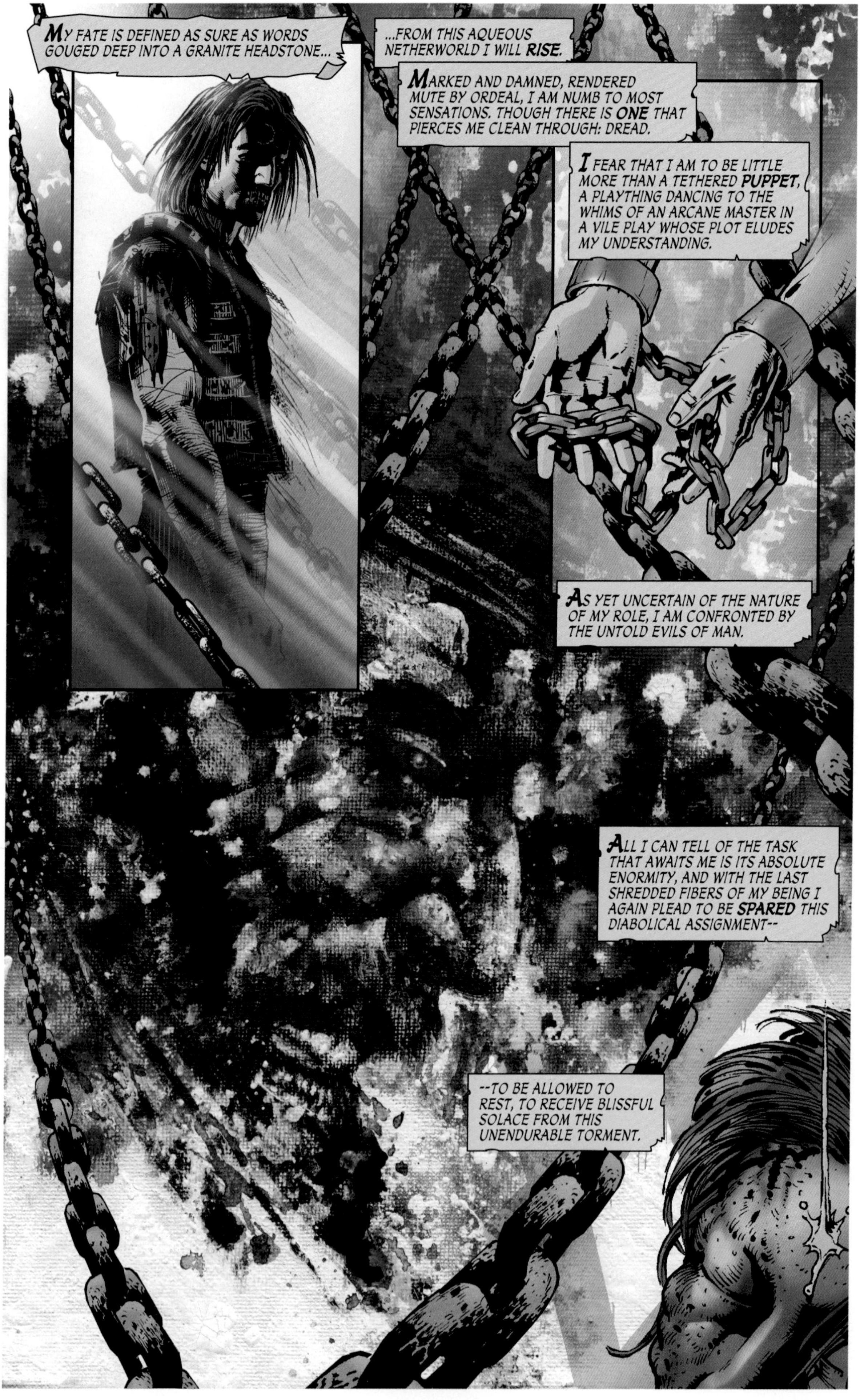
MY FATE IS DEFINED AS SURE AS WORDS GOUGED DEEP INTO A GRANITE HEADSTONE...
...FROM THIS AQUEOUS NETHERWORLD I WILL RISE.
MARKED AND DAMNED, RENDERED MUTE BY ORDEAL, I AM NUMB TO MOST SENSATIONS. THOUGH THERE IS ONE THAT PIERCES ME CLEAN THROUGH: DREAD.
I FEAR THAT I AM TO BE LITTLE MORE THAN A TETHERED PUPPET, A PLAYTHING DANCING TO THE WHIMS OF AN ARCANE MASTER IN A VILE PLAY WHOSE PLOT ELUDES MY UNDERSTANDING.
AS YET UNCERTAIN OF THE NATURE OF MY ROLE, I AM CONFRONTED BY THE UNTOLD EVILS OF MAN.
ALL I CAN TELL OF THE TASK THAT AWAITS ME IS ITS ABSOLUTE ENORMITY, AND WITH THE LAST SHREDDED FIBERS OF MY BEING I AGAIN PLEAD TO BE SPARED THIS DIABOLICAL ASSIGNMENT--
--TO BE ALLOWED TO REST, TO RECEIVE BLISSFUL SOLACE FROM THIS UNENDURABLE TORMENT.

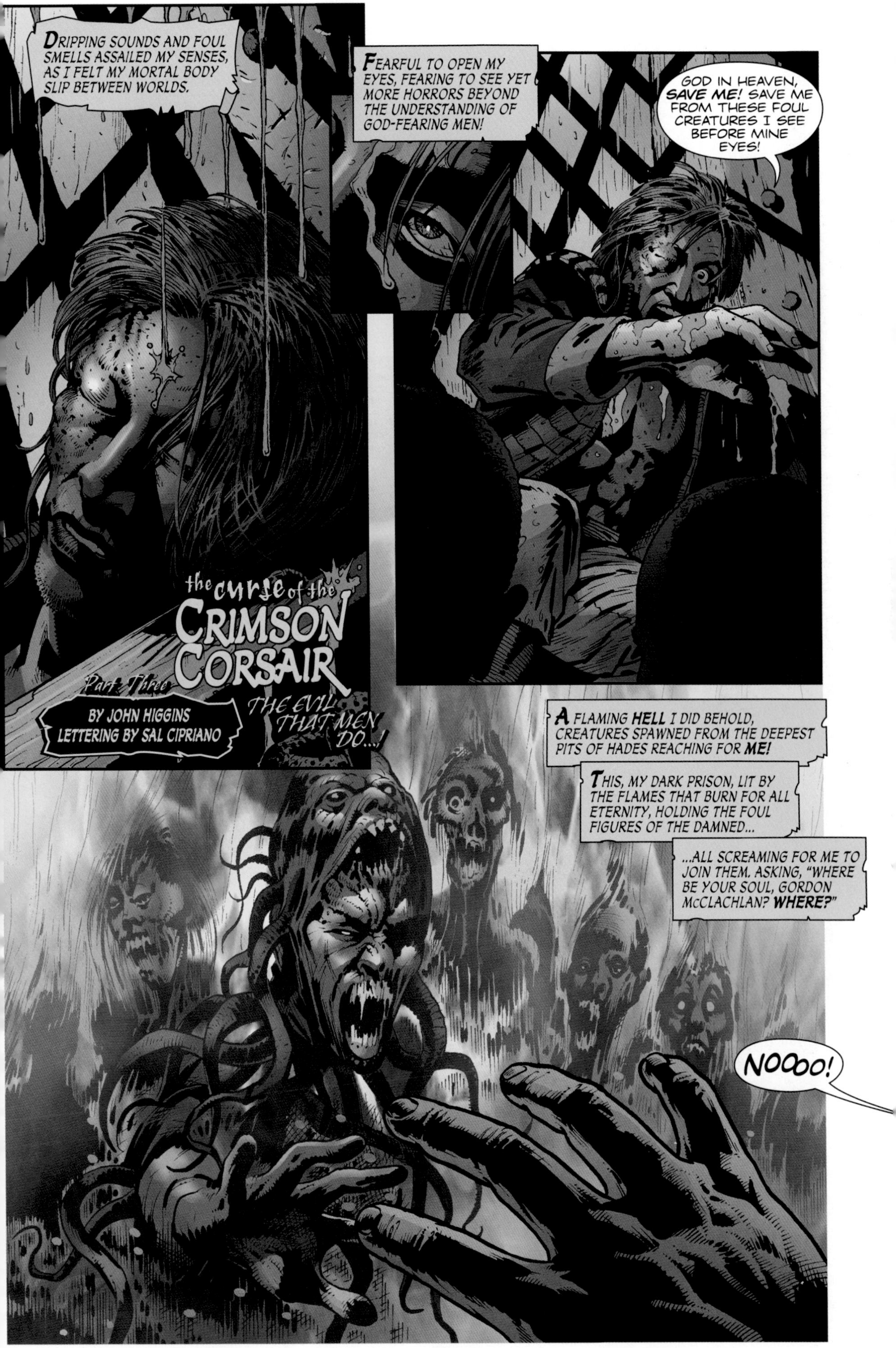
DRIPPING SOUNDS AND FOUL SMELLS ASSAILED MY SENSES, AS I FELT MY MORTAL BODY SLIP BETWEEN WORLDS.
the curse of the CRIMSON CORSAIR
Part Three
BY JOHN HIGGINS
LETTERING BY SAL CIPRIANO
THE EVIL THAT MEN DO...!
FEARFUL TO OPEN MY EYES, FEARING TO SEE YET MORE HORRORS BEYOND THE UNDERSTANDING OF GOD-FEARING MEN!
GOD IN HEAVEN, SAVE ME! SAVE ME FROM THESE FOUL CREATURES I SEE BEFORE MINE EYES!
A FLAMING HELL I DID BEHOLD, CREATURES SPAWNED FROM THE DEEPEST PITS OF HADES REACHING FOR ME!
THIS, MY DARK PRISON, LIT BY THE FLAMES THAT BURN FOR ALL ETERNITY, HOLDING THE FOUL FIGURES OF THE DAMNED...
...ALL SCREAMING FOR ME TO JOIN THEM. ASKING, "WHERE BE YOUR SOUL, GORDON McCLACHLAN? WHERE?"
NOOOO!

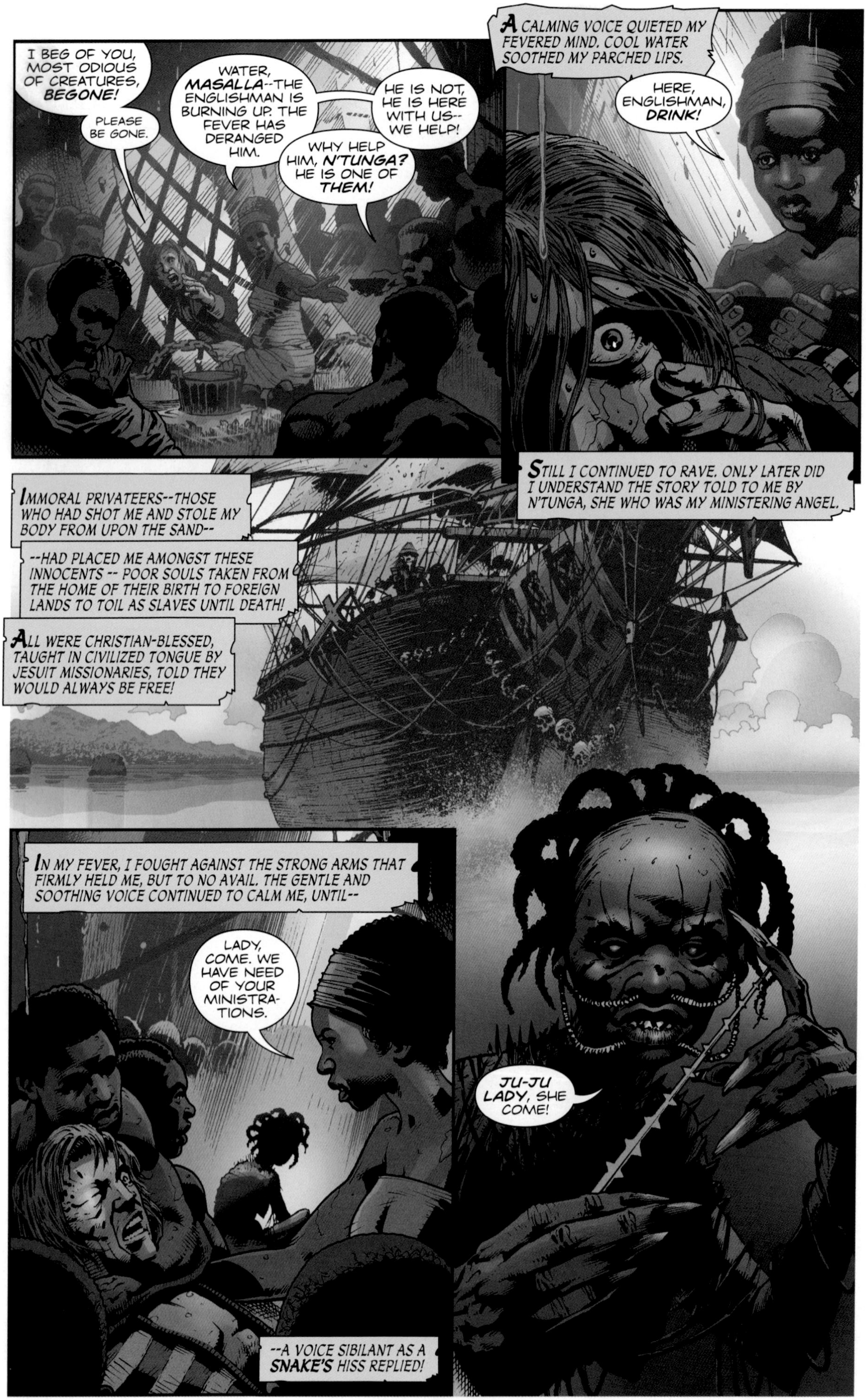
I BEG OF YOU, MOST ODIOUS OF CREATURES, BEGONE!
PLEASE BE GONE.
WATER, MASALLA--THE ENGLISHMAN IS BURNING UP. THE FEVER HAS DERANGED HIM.
HE IS NOT, HE IS HERE WITH US-- WE HELP!
WHY HELP HIM, N'TUNGA? HE IS ONE OF THEM!
A CALMING VOICE QUIETED MY FEVERED MIND. COOL WATER SOOTHED MY PARCHED LIPS.
HERE, ENGLISHMAN, DRINK!
STILL I CONTINUED TO RAVE. ONLY LATER DID I UNDERSTAND THE STORY TOLD TO ME BY N'TUNGA, SHE WHO WAS MY MINISTERING ANGEL.
IMMORAL PRIVATEERS--THOSE WHO HAD SHOT ME AND STOLE MY BODY FROM UPON THE SAND--
--HAD PLACED ME AMONGST THESE INNOCENTS -- POOR SOULS TAKEN FROM THE HOME OF THEIR BIRTH TO FOREIGN LANDS TO TOIL AS SLAVES UNTIL DEATH!
ALL WERE CHRISTIAN-BLESSED, TAUGHT IN CIVILIZED TONGUE BY JESUIT MISSIONARIES, TOLD THEY WOULD ALWAYS BE FREE!
IN MY FEVER, I FOUGHT AGAINST THE STRONG ARMS THAT FIRMLY HELD ME, BUT TO NO AVAIL. THE GENTLE AND SOOTHING VOICE CONTINUED TO CALM ME, UNTIL--
LADY, COME. WE HAVE NEED OF YOUR MINISTRATIONS.
JU-JU LADY, SHE COME!
--A VOICE SIBILANT AS A SNAKE'S HISS REPLIED!

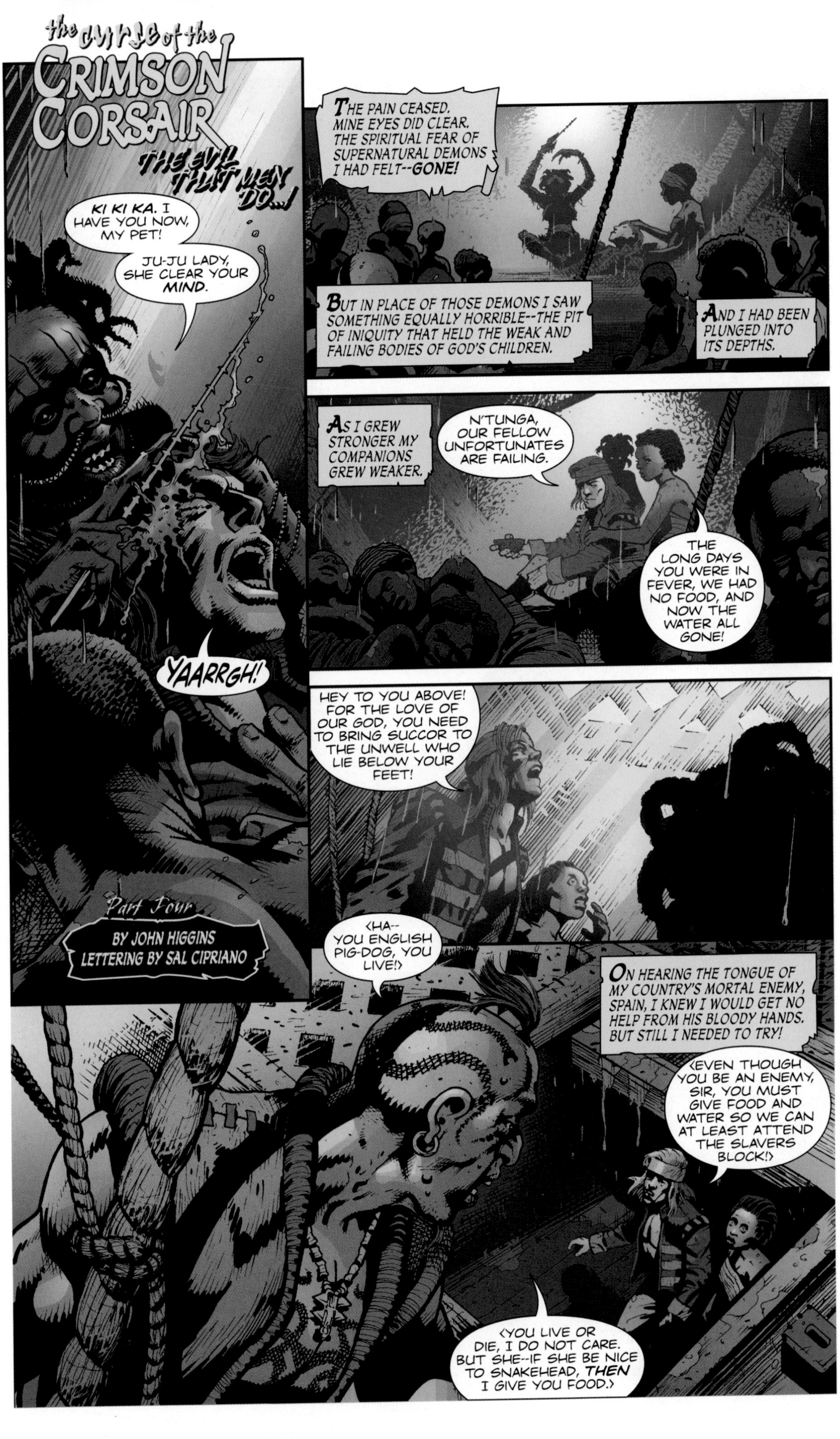

the curse of the
CRIMSON CORSAIR
THE EVIL THAT MEN DO...!
KI KI KA. I HAVE YOU NOW, MY PET!
JU-JU LADY, SHE CLEAR YOUR MIND.
YAARRGH!
Part Four
BY JOHN HIGGINS
LETTERING BY SAL CIPRIANO
THE PAIN CEASED. MINE EYES DID CLEAR. THE SPIRITUAL FEAR OF SUPERNATURAL DEMONS I HAD FELT--GONE!
BUT IN PLACE OF THOSE DEMONS I SAW SOMETHING EQUALLY HORRIBLE--THE PIT OF INIQUITY THAT HELD THE WEAK AND FAILING BODIES OF GOD'S CHILDREN.
AND I HAD BEEN PLUNGED INTO ITS DEPTHS.
AS I GREW STRONGER MY COMPANIONS GREW WEAKER.
N'TUNGA, OUR FELLOW UNFORTUNATES ARE FAILING.
THE LONG DAYS YOU WERE IN FEVER, WE HAD NO FOOD, AND NOW THE WATER ALL GONE!
HEY TO YOU ABOVE! FOR THE LOVE OF OUR GOD, YOU NEED TO BRING SUCCOR TO THE UNWELL WHO LIE BELOW YOUR FEET!
<HA-- YOU ENGLISH PIG-DOG, YOU LIVE!>
ON HEARING THE TONGUE OF MY COUNTRY'S MORTAL ENEMY, SPAIN, I KNEW I WOULD GET NO HELP FROM HIS BLOODY HANDS. BUT STILL I NEEDED TO TRY!
<EVEN THOUGH YOU BE AN ENEMY, SIR, YOU MUST GIVE FOOD AND WATER SO WE CAN AT LEAST ATTEND THE SLAVERS BLOCK!>
<YOU LIVE OR DIE, I DO NOT CARE. BUT SHE--IF SHE BE NICE TO SNAKEHEAD, THEN I GIVE YOU FOOD.>

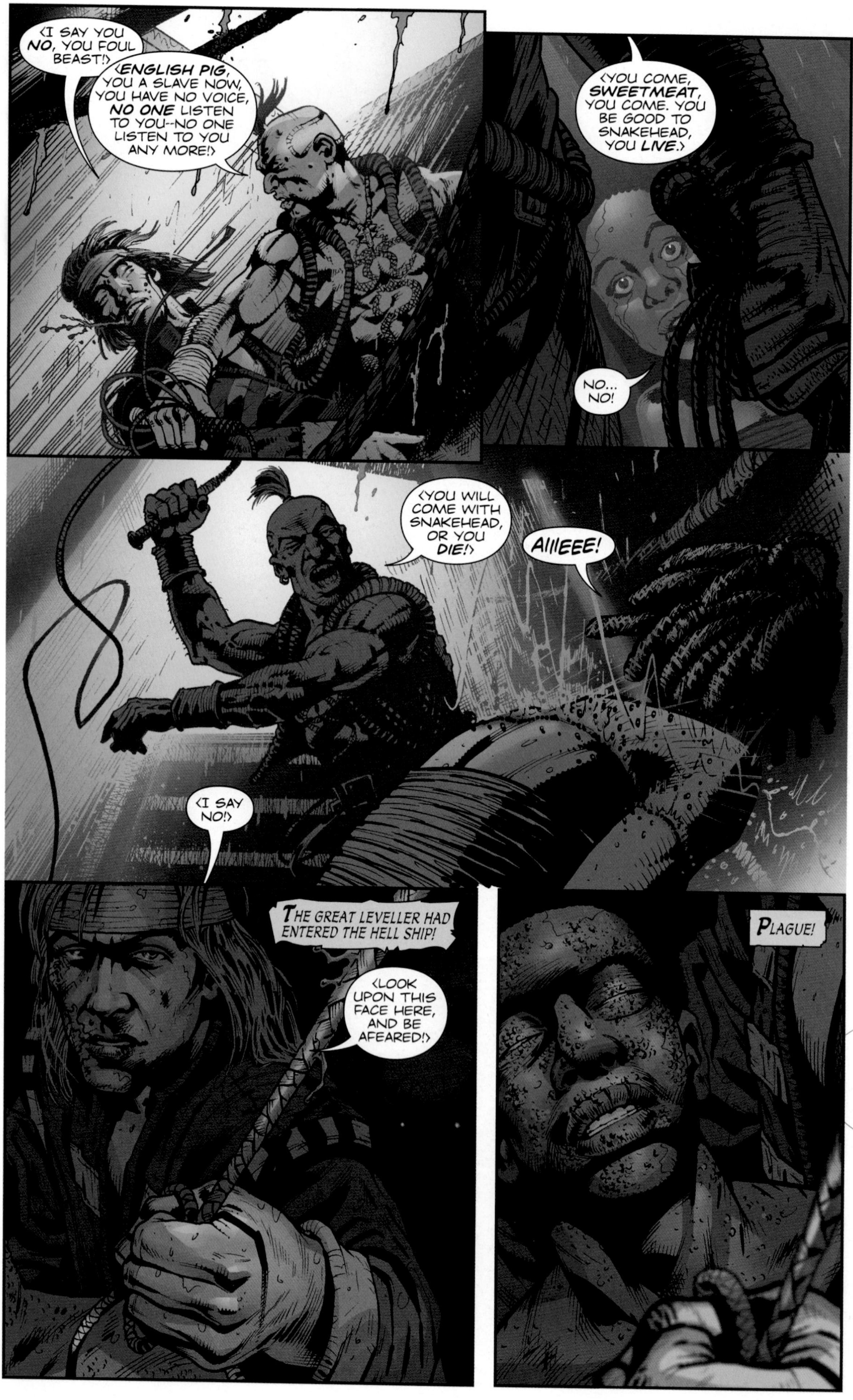
<I SAY YOU NO, YOU FOUL BEAST!>
<ENGLISH PIG, YOU A SLAVE NOW, YOU HAVE NO VOICE, NO ONE LISTEN TO YOU--NO ONE LISTEN TO YOU ANY MORE!>
<YOU COME, SWEETMEAT, YOU COME. YOU BE GOOD TO SNAKEHEAD, YOU LIVE.>
NO... NO!
<YOU WILL COME WITH SNAKEHEAD, OR YOU DIE!>
AIIIEEE!
<I SAY NO!>
THE GREAT LEVELLER HAD ENTERED THE HELL SHIP!
<LOOK UPON THIS FACE HERE, AND BE AFEARED!>
PLAGUE!

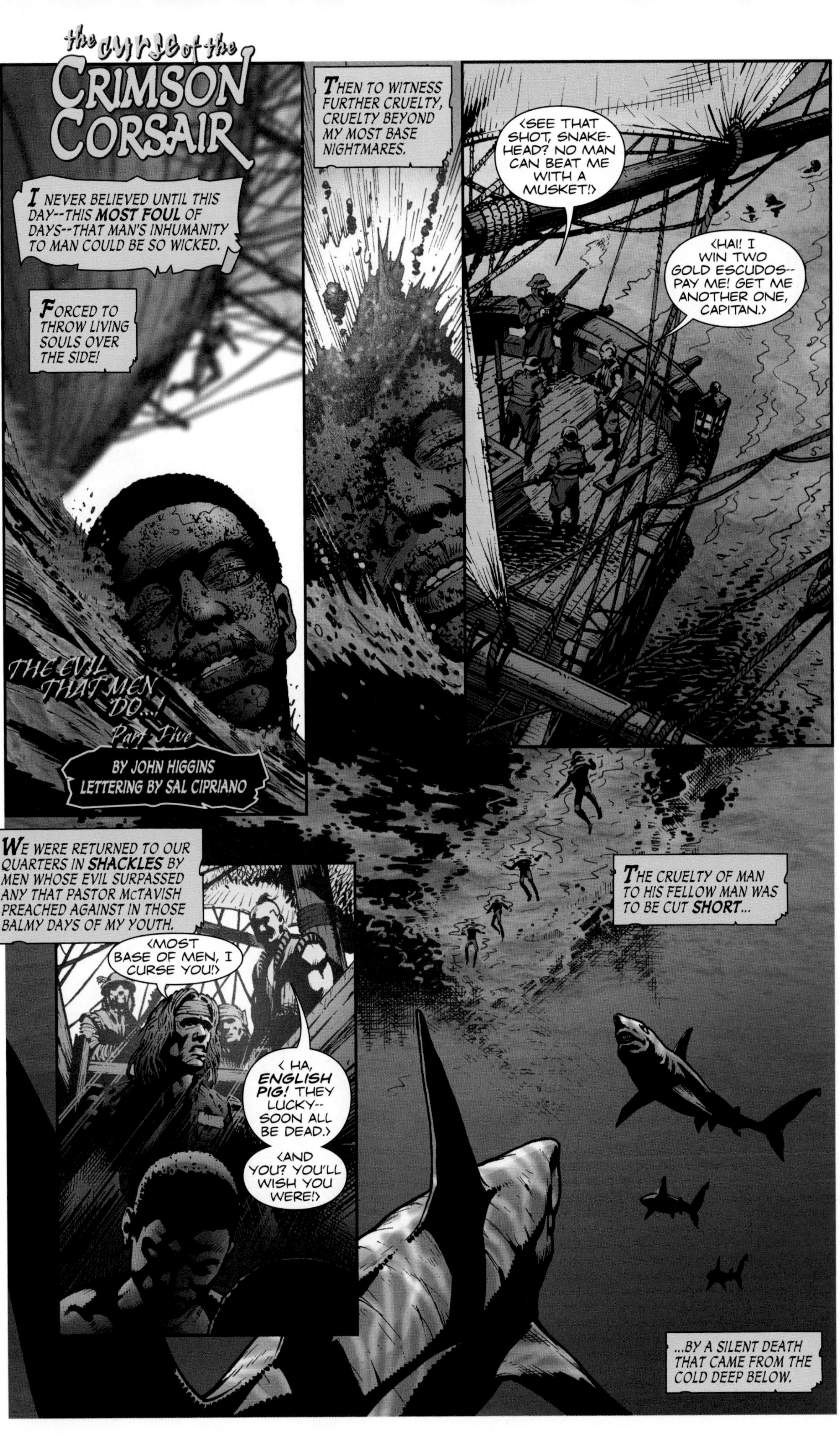
the curse of the
CRIMSON CORSAIR
I NEVER BELIEVED UNTIL THIS DAY--THIS MOST FOUL OF DAYS--THAT MAN'S INHUMANITY TO MAN COULD BE SO WICKED.
FORCED TO THROW LIVING SOULS OVER THE SIDE!
THE EVIL THAT MEN DO...!
Part Five
BY JOHN HIGGINS
LETTERING BY SAL CIPRIANO
THEN TO WITNESS FURTHER CRUELTY, CRUELTY BEYOND MY MOST BASE NIGHTMARES.
<SEE THAT SHOT, SNAKE-HEAD? NO MAN CAN BEAT ME WITH A MUSKET!>
<HAI! I WIN TWO GOLD ESCUDOS--PAY ME! GET ME ANOTHER ONE, CAPITAN.>
WE WERE RETURNED TO OUR QUARTERS IN SHACKLES BY MEN WHOSE EVIL SURPASSED ANY THAT PASTOR McTAVISH PREACHED AGAINST IN THOSE BALMY DAYS OF MY YOUTH.
<MOST BASE OF MEN, I CURSE YOU!>
<HA, ENGLISH PIG! THEY LUCKY--SOON ALL BE DEAD.>
<AND YOU? YOU'LL WISH YOU WERE!>
THE CRUELTY OF MAN TO HIS FELLOW MAN WAS TO BE CUT SHORT...
...BY A SILENT DEATH THAT CAME FROM THE COLD DEEP BELOW.

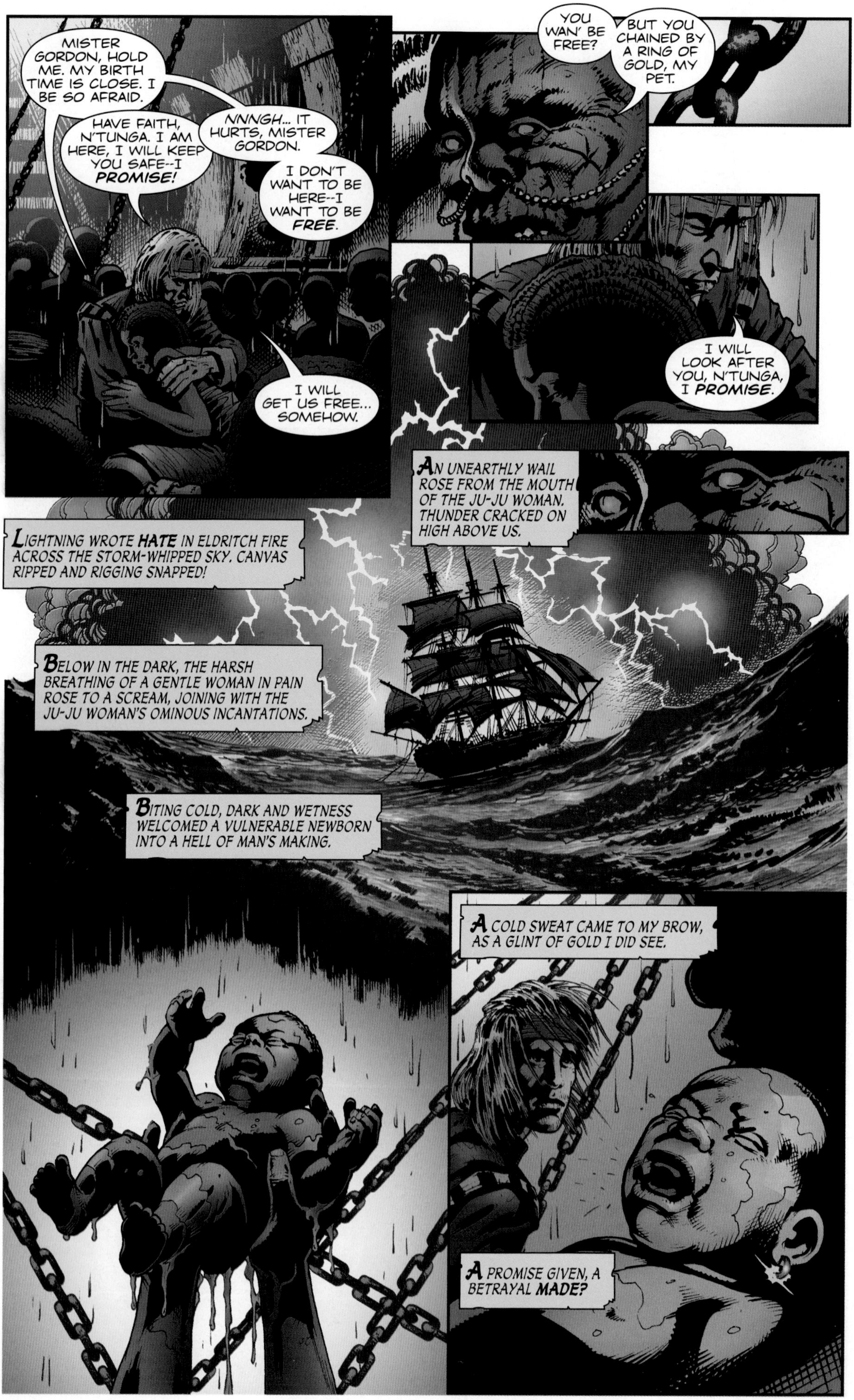
MISTER GORDON, HOLD ME. MY BIRTH TIME IS CLOSE. I BE SO AFRAID.
HAVE FAITH, N'TUNGA. I AM HERE, I WILL KEEP YOU SAFE--I PROMISE!
NNNGH... IT HURTS, MISTER GORDON.
I DON'T WANT TO BE HERE--I WANT TO BE FREE.
I WILL GET US FREE... SOMEHOW.
YOU WAN' BE FREE?
BUT YOU CHAINED BY A RING OF GOLD, MY PET.
I WILL LOOK AFTER YOU, N'TUNGA, I PROMISE.
AN UNEARTHLY WAIL ROSE FROM THE MOUTH OF THE JU-JU WOMAN. THUNDER CRACKED ON HIGH ABOVE US.
LIGHTNING WROTE HATE IN ELDRITCH FIRE ACROSS THE STORM-WHIPPED SKY. CANVAS RIPPED AND RIGGING SNAPPED!
BELOW IN THE DARK, THE HARSH BREATHING OF A GENTLE WOMAN IN PAIN ROSE TO A SCREAM, JOINING WITH THE JU-JU WOMAN'S OMINOUS INCANTATIONS.
BITING COLD, DARK AND WETNESS WELCOMED A VULNERABLE NEWBORN INTO A HELL OF MAN'S MAKING.
A COLD SWEAT CAME TO MY BROW, AS A GLINT OF GOLD I DID SEE.
A PROMISE GIVEN, A BETRAYAL MADE?

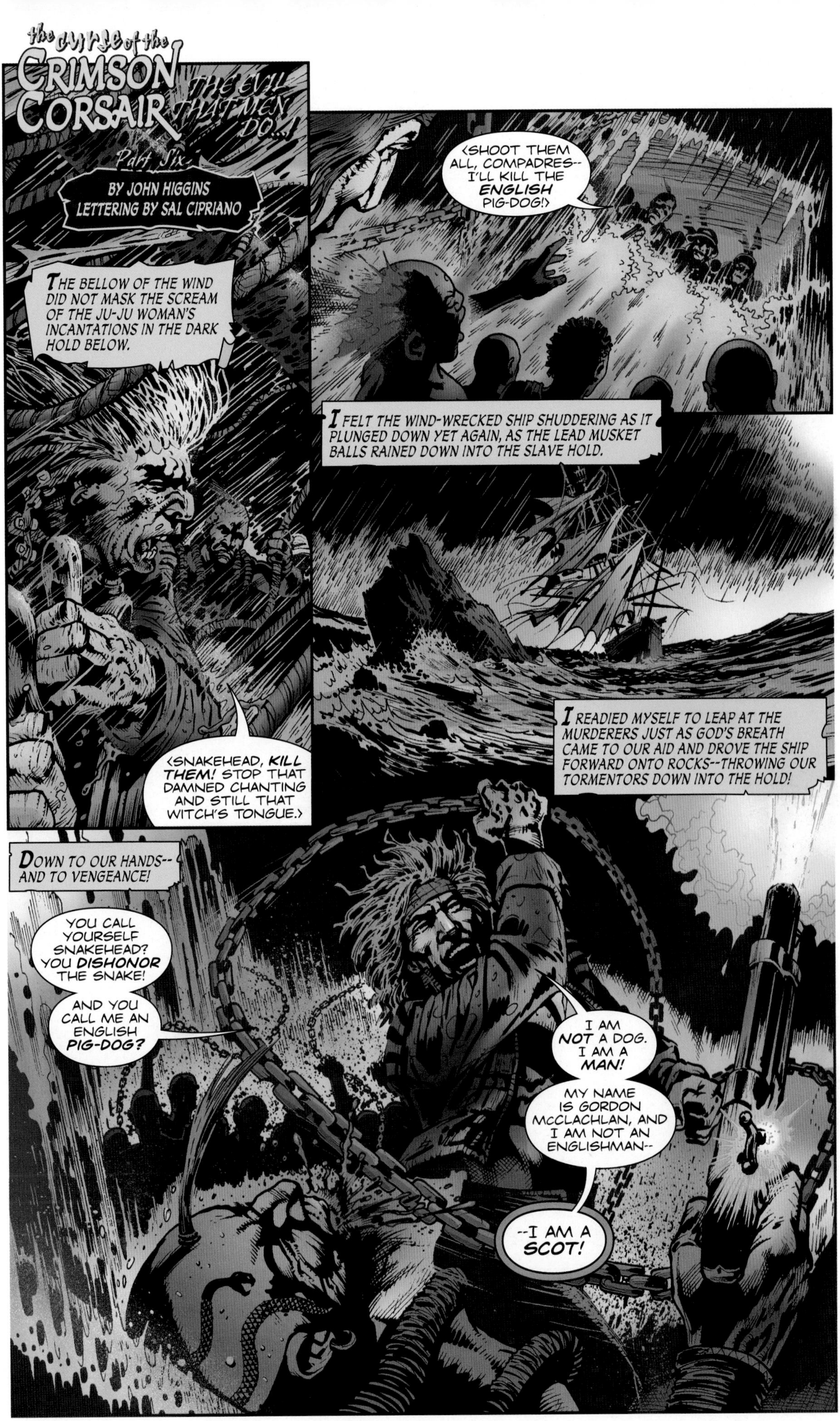
the curse of the
CRIMSON CORSAIR
THE EVIL THAT MEN DO...!
Part Six
BY JOHN HIGGINS
LETTERING BY SAL CIPRIANO
THE BELLOW OF THE WIND DID NOT MASK THE SCREAM OF THE JU-JU WOMAN'S INCANTATIONS IN THE DARK HOLD BELOW.
<SHOOT THEM ALL, COMPADRES-- I'LL KILL THE ENGLISH PIG-DOG!>
<SNAKEHEAD, KILL THEM! STOP THAT DAMNED CHANTING AND STILL THAT WITCH'S TONGUE.>
I FELT THE WIND-WRECKED SHIP SHUDDERING AS IT PLUNGED DOWN YET AGAIN, AS THE LEAD MUSKET BALLS RAINED DOWN INTO THE SLAVE HOLD.
I READIED MYSELF TO LEAP AT THE MURDERERS JUST AS GOD'S BREATH CAME TO OUR AID AND DROVE THE SHIP FORWARD ONTO ROCKS--THROWING OUR TORMENTORS DOWN INTO THE HOLD!
DOWN TO OUR HANDS-- AND TO VENGEANCE!
YOU CALL YOURSELF SNAKEHEAD? YOU DISHONOR THE SNAKE!
AND YOU CALL ME AN ENGLISH PIG-DOG?
I AM NOT A DOG. I AM A MAN!
MY NAME IS GORDON McCLACHLAN, AND I AM NOT AN ENGLISHMAN--
--I AM A SCOT!

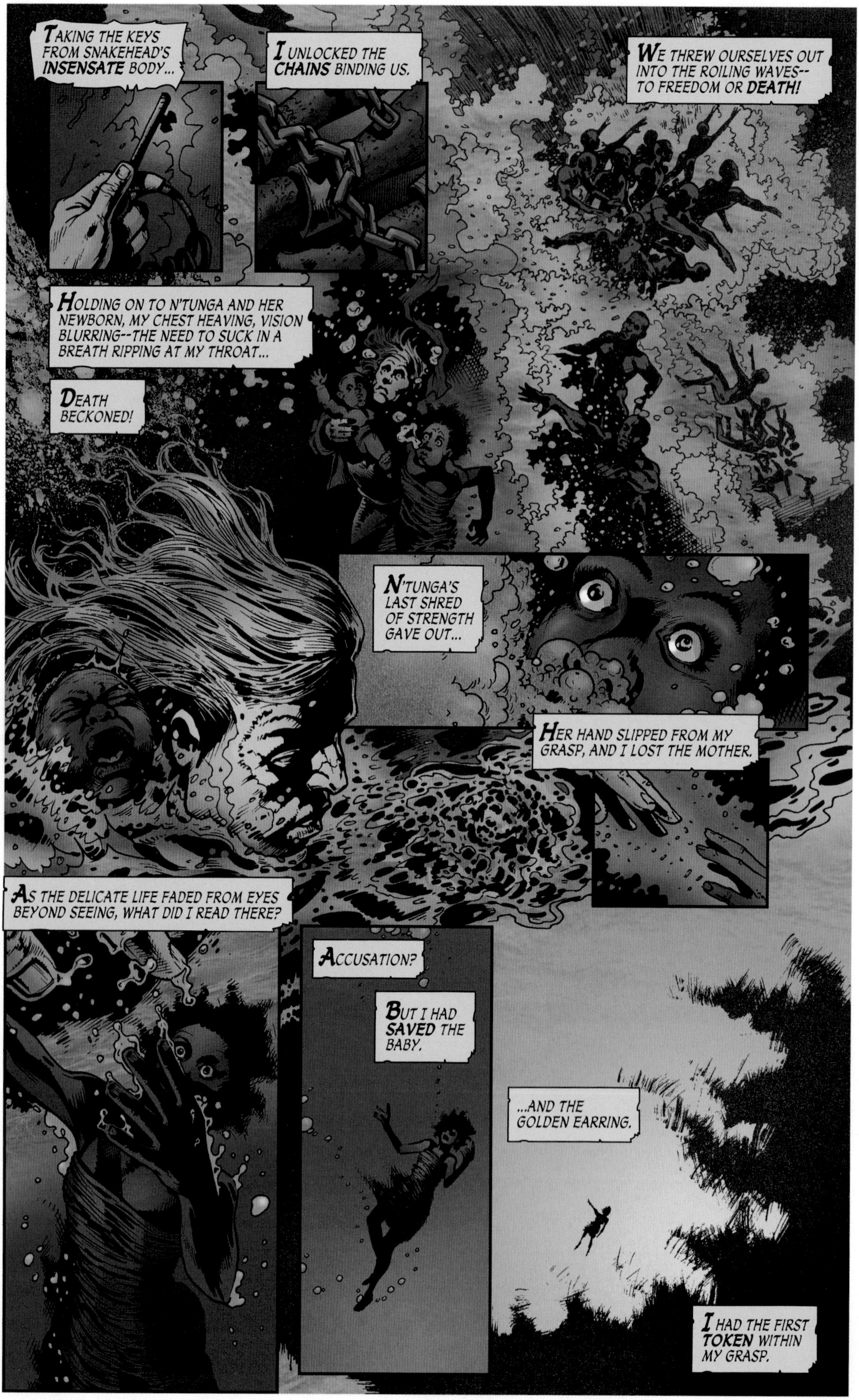
TAKING THE KEYS FROM SNAKEHEAD'S INSENSATE BODY...
I UNLOCKED THE CHAINS BINDING US.
WE THREW OURSELVES OUT INTO THE ROILING WAVES-- TO FREEDOM OR DEATH!
HOLDING ON TO N'TUNGA AND HER NEWBORN, MY CHEST HEAVING, VISION BLURRING--THE NEED TO SUCK IN A BREATH RIPPING AT MY THROAT...
DEATH BECKONED!
N'TUNGA'S LAST SHRED OF STRENGTH GAVE OUT...
HER HAND SLIPPED FROM MY GRASP, AND I LOST THE MOTHER.
AS THE DELICATE LIFE FADED FROM EYES BEYOND SEEING, WHAT DID I READ THERE?
ACCUSATION?
BUT I HAD SAVED THE BABY.
...AND THE GOLDEN EARRING.
I HAD THE FIRST TOKEN WITHIN MY GRASP.

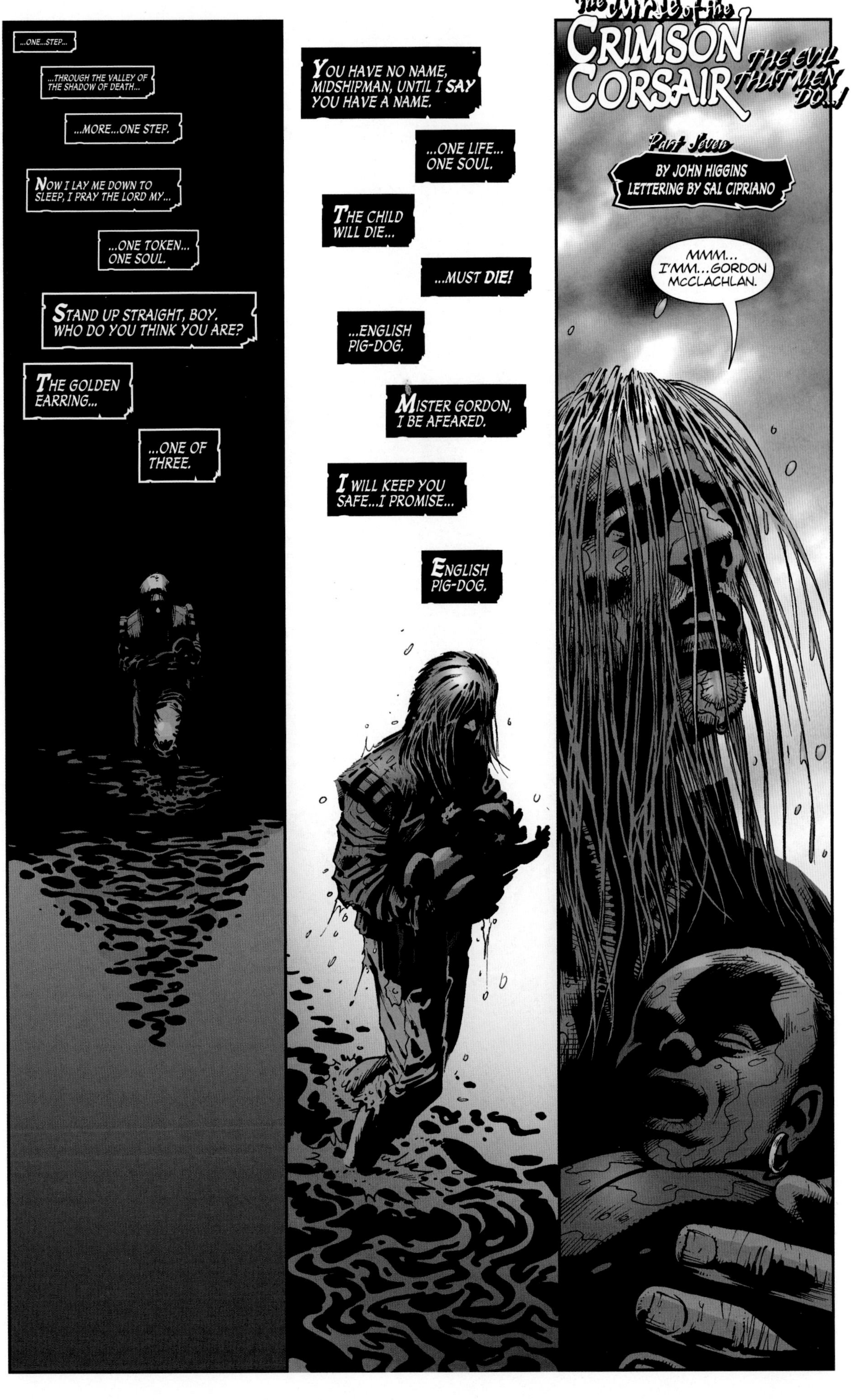
...ONE...STEP...
...THROUGH THE VALLEY OF THE SHADOW OF DEATH...
...MORE...ONE STEP.
NOW I LAY ME DOWN TO SLEEP, I PRAY THE LORD MY...
...ONE TOKEN... ONE SOUL.
STAND UP STRAIGHT, BOY. WHO DO YOU THINK YOU ARE?
THE GOLDEN EARRING...
...ONE OF THREE.
YOU HAVE NO NAME, MIDSHIPMAN, UNTIL I SAY YOU HAVE A NAME.
...ONE LIFE... ONE SOUL.
THE CHILD WILL DIE...
...MUST DIE!
...ENGLISH PIG-DOG.
MISTER GORDON, I BE AFEARED.
I WILL KEEP YOU SAFE...I PROMISE...
ENGLISH PIG-DOG.
the curse of the
CRIMSON CORSAIR
THE EVIL THAT MEN DO...!
Part Seven
BY JOHN HIGGINS
LETTERING BY SAL CIPRIANO
MMM... I'MM...GORDON McCLACHLAN.

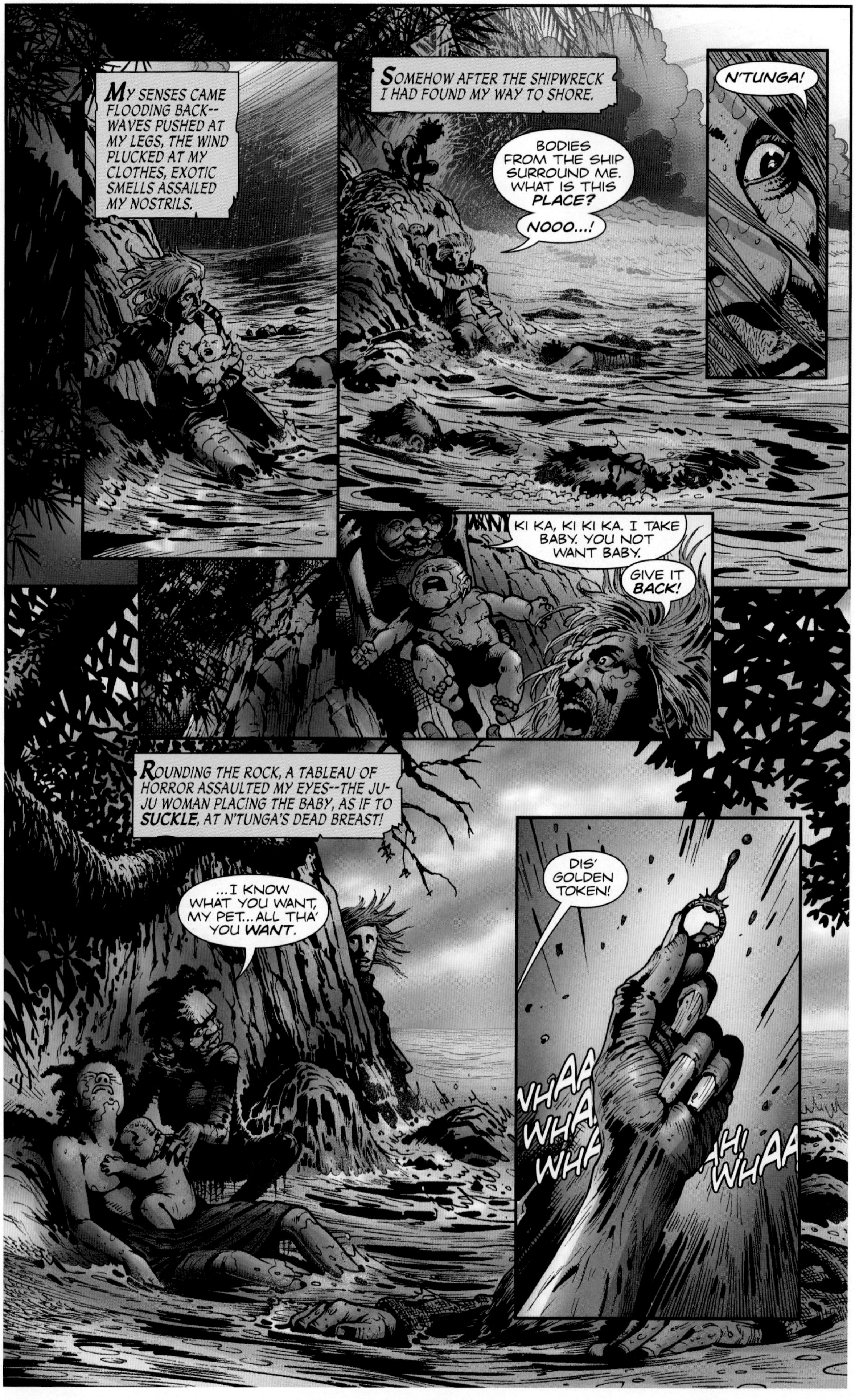
MY SENSES CAME FLOODING BACK--WAVES PUSHED AT MY LEGS, THE WIND PLUCKED AT MY CLOTHES, EXOTIC SMELLS ASSAILED MY NOSTRILS.
SOMEHOW AFTER THE SHIPWRECK I HAD FOUND MY WAY TO SHORE.
BODIES FROM THE SHIP SURROUND ME. WHAT IS THIS PLACE?
NOOO...!
N'TUNGA!
KI KA, KI KI KA. I TAKE BABY. YOU NOT WANT BABY.
GIVE IT BACK!
ROUNDING THE ROCK, A TABLEAU OF HORROR ASSAULTED MY EYES--THE JU-JU WOMAN PLACING THE BABY, AS IF TO SUCKLE, AT N'TUNGA'S DEAD BREAST!
...I KNOW WHAT YOU WANT, MY PET...ALL THA' YOU WANT.
DIS' GOLDEN TOKEN!
WHAA
WHAA
WHAA

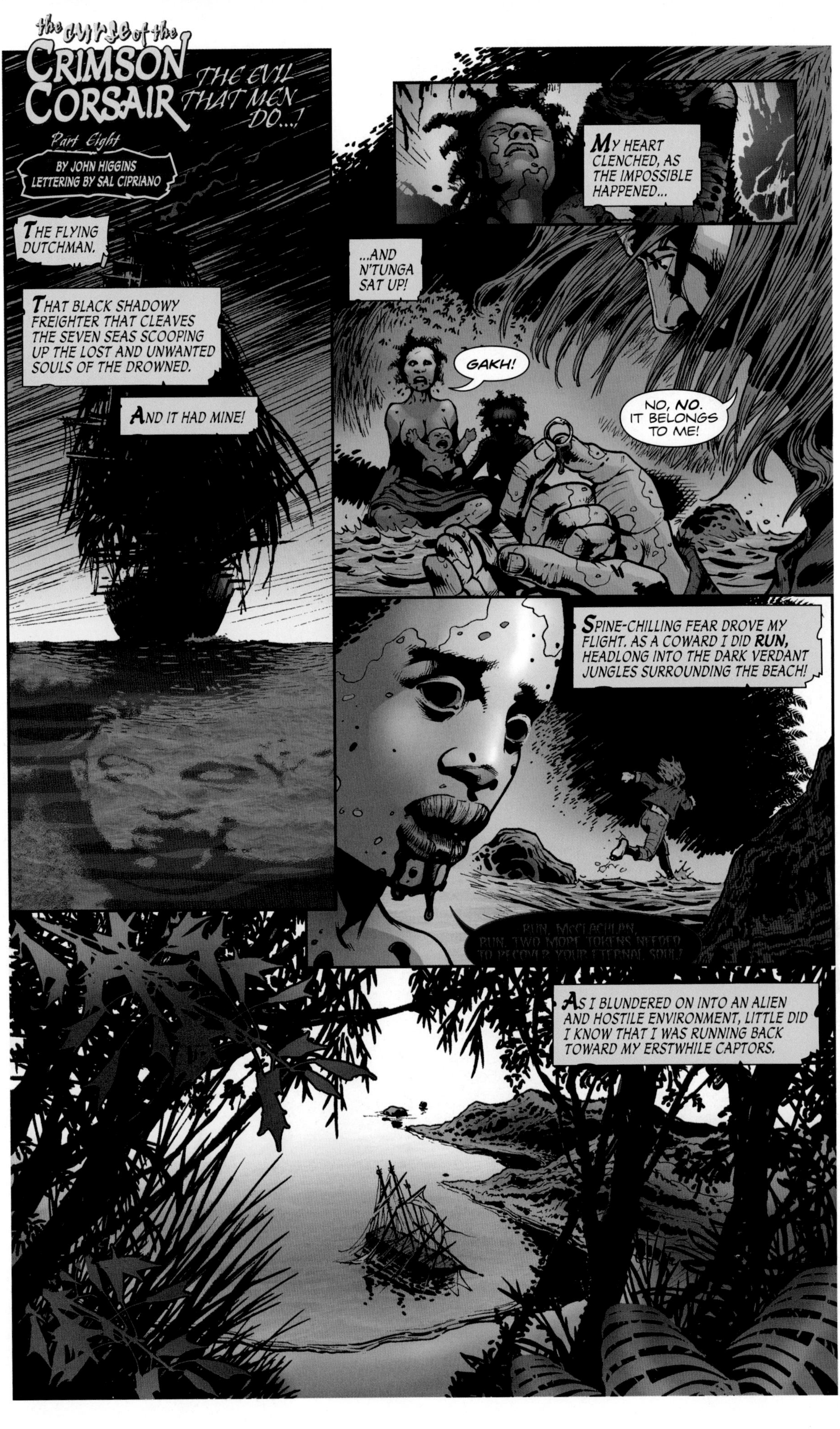
the curse of the CRIMSON CORSAIR
THE EVIL THAT MEN DO...!
Part Eight
BY JOHN HIGGINS
LETTERING BY SAL CIPRIANO
THE FLYING DUTCHMAN.
THAT BLACK SHADOWY FREIGHTER THAT CLEAVES THE SEVEN SEAS SCOOPING UP THE LOST AND UNWANTED SOULS OF THE DROWNED.
AND IT HAD MINE!
MY HEART CLENCHED, AS THE IMPOSSIBLE HAPPENED...
...AND N'TUNGA SAT UP!
GAKH!
NO, NO. IT BELONGS TO ME!
SPINE-CHILLING FEAR DROVE MY FLIGHT. AS A COWARD I DID RUN, HEADLONG INTO THE DARK VERDANT JUNGLES SURROUNDING THE BEACH!
RUN, McCLACHLAN, RUN. TWO MORE TOKENS NEEDED TO RECOVER YOUR ETERNAL SOUL!
AS I BLUNDERED ON INTO AN ALIEN AND HOSTILE ENVIRONMENT, LITTLE DID I KNOW THAT I WAS RUNNING BACK TOWARD MY ERSTWHILE CAPTORS.

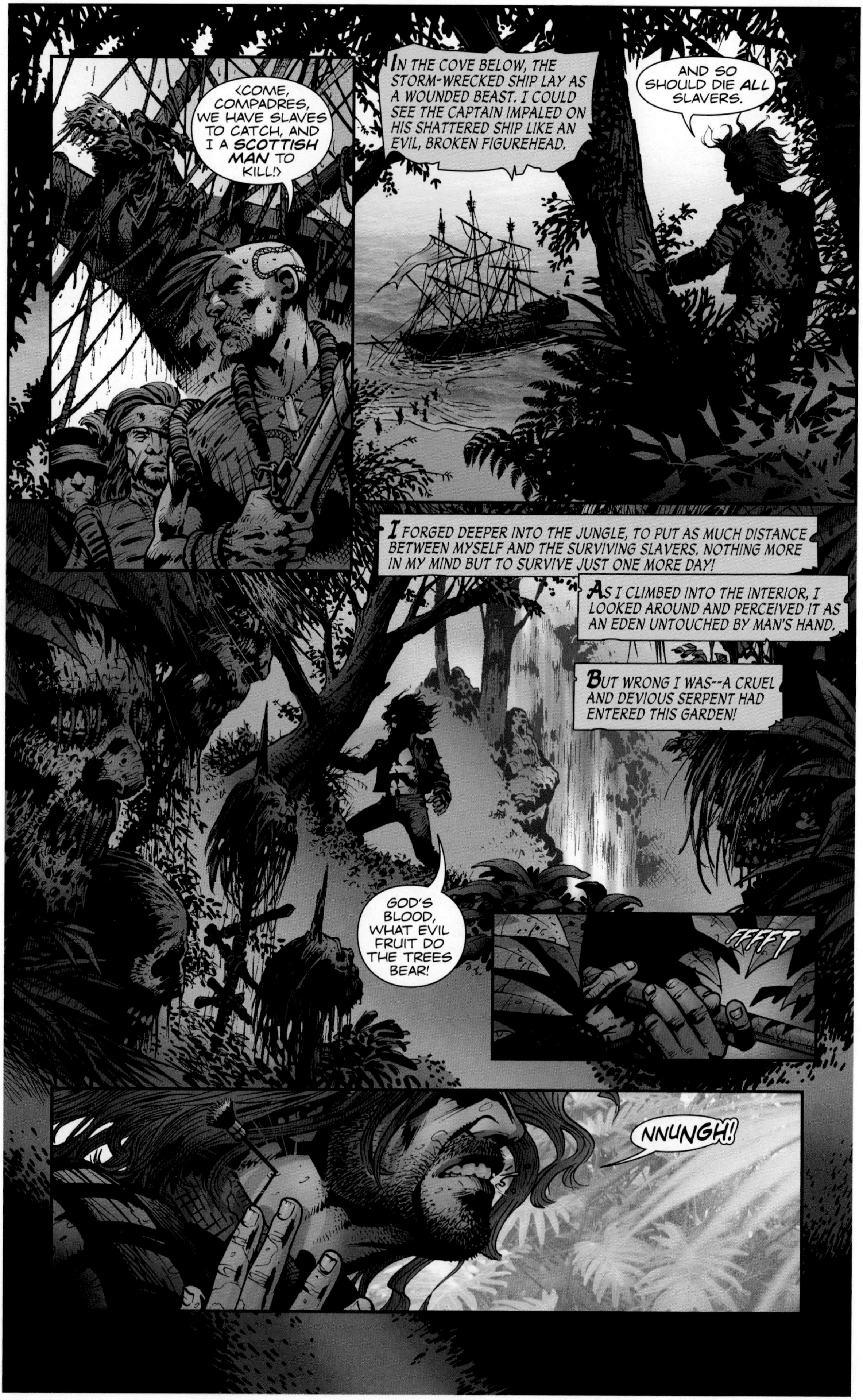

<COME, COMPADRES, WE HAVE SLAVES TO CATCH, AND I A SCOTTISH MAN TO KILL!>
IN THE COVE BELOW, THE STORM-WRECKED SHIP LAY AS A WOUNDED BEAST. I COULD SEE THE CAPTAIN IMPALED ON HIS SHATTERED SHIP LIKE AN EVIL, BROKEN FIGUREHEAD.
AND SO SHOULD DIE ALL SLAVERS.
I FORGED DEEPER INTO THE JUNGLE, TO PUT AS MUCH DISTANCE BETWEEN MYSELF AND THE SURVIVING SLAVERS. NOTHING MORE IN MY MIND BUT TO SURVIVE JUST ONE MORE DAY!
AS I CLIMBED INTO THE INTERIOR, I LOOKED AROUND AND PERCEIVED IT AS AN EDEN UNTOUCHED BY MAN'S HAND.
BUT WRONG I WAS--A CRUEL AND DEVIOUS SERPENT HAD ENTERED THIS GARDEN!
GOD'S BLOOD, WHAT EVIL FRUIT DO THE TREES BEAR!
FFFFT
NNUNGH!

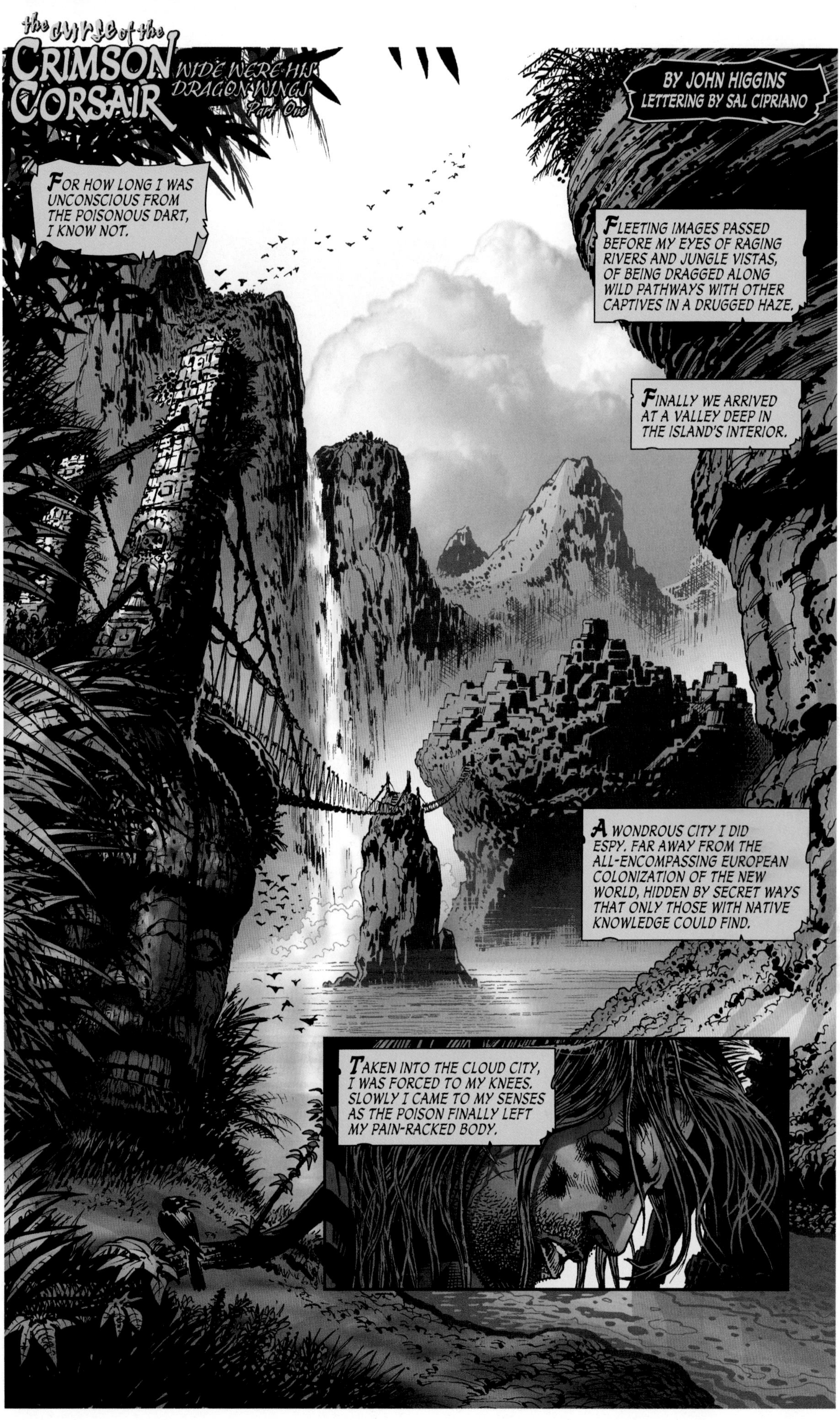
the Curse of the Crimson Corsair
WIDE WERE HIS DRAGON WINGS Part One
BY JOHN HIGGINS
LETTERING BY SAL CIPRIANO
FOR HOW LONG I WAS UNCONSCIOUS FROM THE POISONOUS DART, I KNOW NOT.
FLEETING IMAGES PASSED BEFORE MY EYES OF RAGING RIVERS AND JUNGLE VISTAS, OF BEING DRAGGED ALONG WILD PATHWAYS WITH OTHER CAPTIVES IN A DRUGGED HAZE.
FINALLY WE ARRIVED AT A VALLEY DEEP IN THE ISLAND'S INTERIOR.
A WONDROUS CITY I DID ESPY. FAR AWAY FROM THE ALL-ENCOMPASSING EUROPEAN COLONIZATION OF THE NEW WORLD, HIDDEN BY SECRET WAYS THAT ONLY THOSE WITH NATIVE KNOWLEDGE COULD FIND.
TAKEN INTO THE CLOUD CITY, I WAS FORCED TO MY KNEES. SLOWLY I CAME TO MY SENSES AS THE POISON FINALLY LEFT MY PAIN-RACKED BODY.

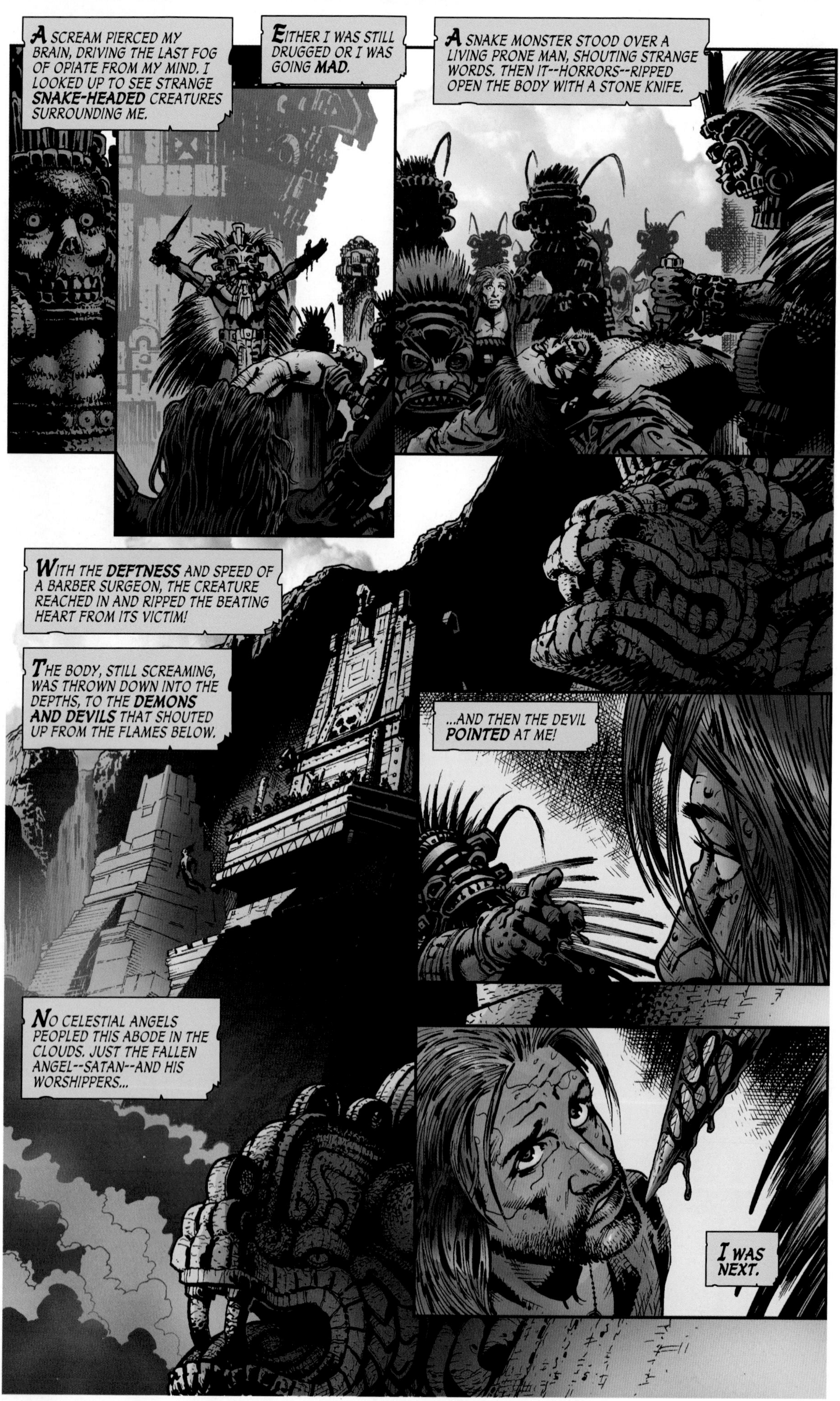
A SCREAM PIERCED MY BRAIN, DRIVING THE LAST FOG OF OPIATE FROM MY MIND. I LOOKED UP TO SEE STRANGE **SNAKE-HEADED** CREATURES SURROUNDING ME.
EITHER I WAS STILL DRUGGED OR I WAS GOING **MAD**.
A SNAKE MONSTER STOOD OVER A LIVING PRONE MAN, SHOUTING STRANGE WORDS. THEN IT--HORRORS--RIPPED OPEN THE BODY WITH A STONE KNIFE.
WITH THE **DEFTNESS** AND SPEED OF A BARBER SURGEON, THE CREATURE REACHED IN AND RIPPED THE BEATING HEART FROM ITS VICTIM!
THE BODY, STILL SCREAMING, WAS THROWN DOWN INTO THE DEPTHS, TO THE **DEMONS AND DEVILS** THAT SHOUTED UP FROM THE FLAMES BELOW.
...AND THEN THE DEVIL **POINTED** AT ME!
NO CELESTIAL ANGELS PEOPLED THIS ABODE IN THE CLOUDS. JUST THE FALLEN ANGEL--SATAN--AND HIS WORSHIPPERS...
I WAS NEXT.

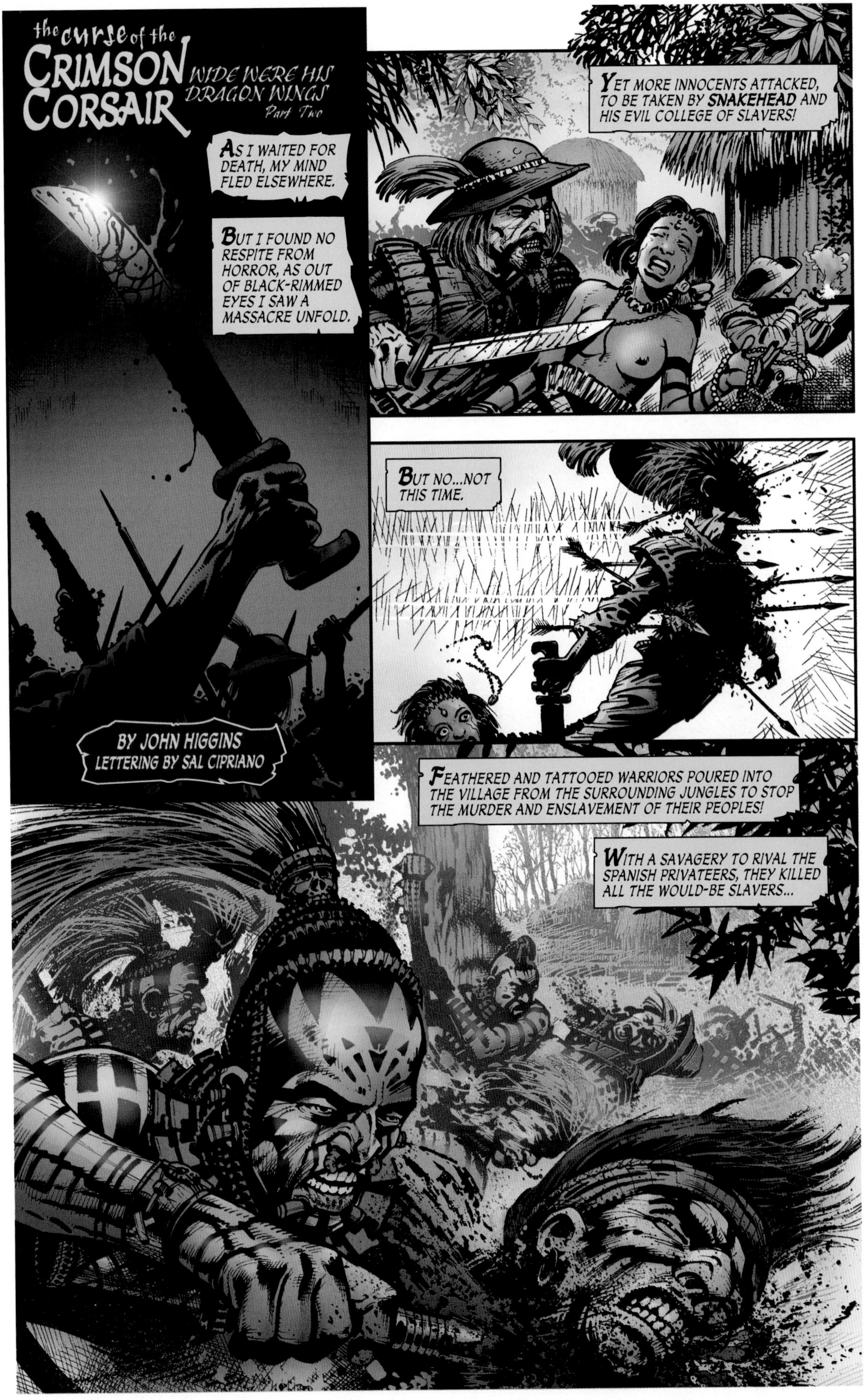
the curse of the
CRIMSON CORSAIR
WIDE WERE HIS DRAGON WINGS
Part Two
AS I WAITED FOR DEATH, MY MIND FLED ELSEWHERE.
BUT I FOUND NO RESPITE FROM HORROR, AS OUT OF BLACK-RIMMED EYES I SAW A MASSACRE UNFOLD.
BY JOHN HIGGINS
LETTERING BY SAL CIPRIANO
YET MORE INNOCENTS ATTACKED, TO BE TAKEN BY SNAKEHEAD AND HIS EVIL COLLEGE OF SLAVERS!
BUT NO...NOT THIS TIME.
FEATHERED AND TATTOOED WARRIORS POURED INTO THE VILLAGE FROM THE SURROUNDING JUNGLES TO STOP THE MURDER AND ENSLAVEMENT OF THEIR PEOPLES!
WITH A SAVAGERY TO RIVAL THE SPANISH PRIVATEERS, THEY KILLED ALL THE WOULD-BE SLAVERS...

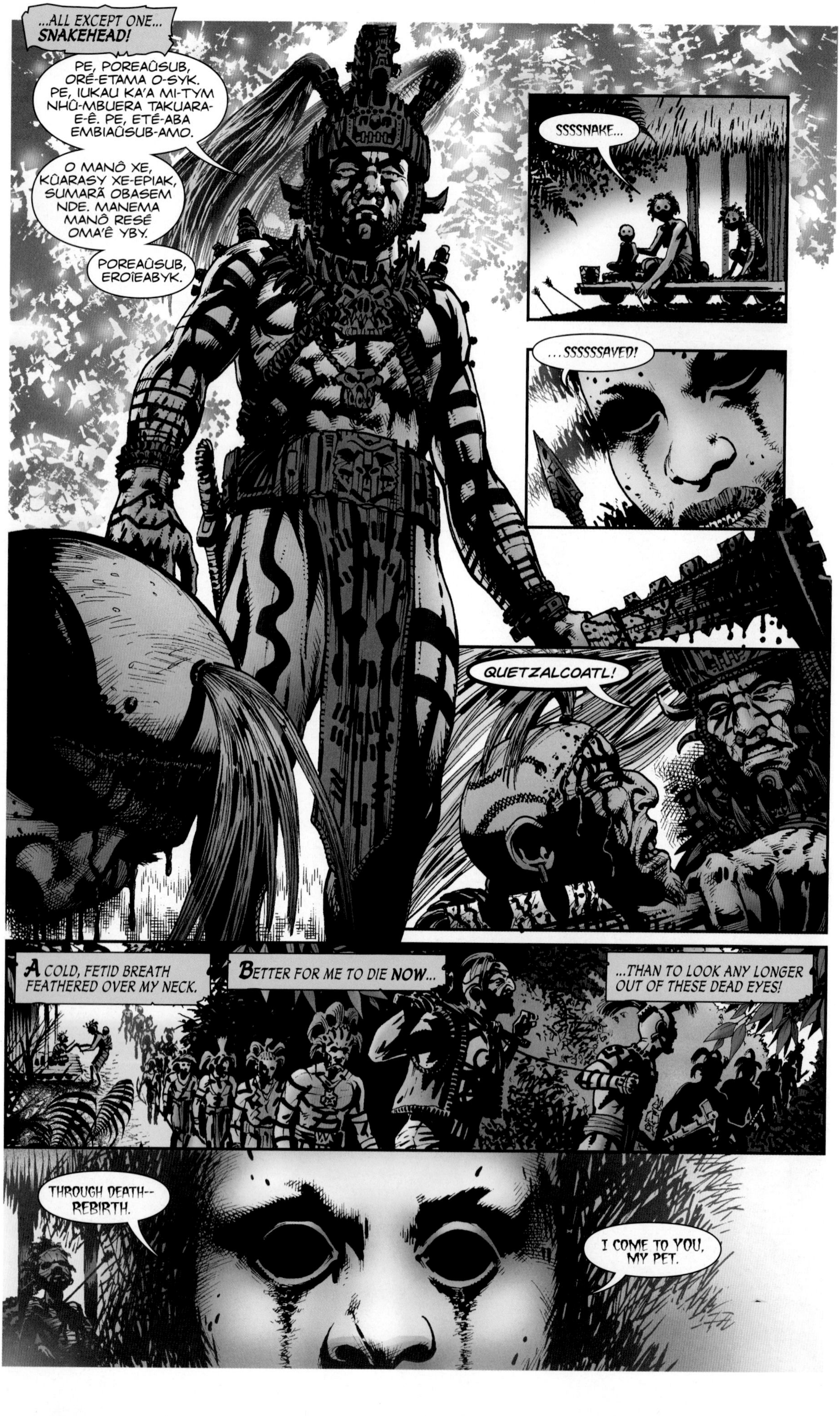

...ALL EXCEPT ONE... SNAKEHEAD!
PE, POREAÛSUB, ORÉ-ETAMA O-SYK. PE, IUKAU KA'A MI-TYM NHÛ-MBUERA TAKUARA-E-Ê. PE, ETÉ-ABA EMBIAÛSUB-AMO.
O MANÔ XE, KÛARASY XE-EPIAK, SUMARÃ OBASEM NDE. MANEMA MANÔ RESÉ OMA'Ê YBY.
POREAÛSUB, EROÎEABYK.
SSSSNAKE...
...SSSSSSAVED!
QUETZALCOATL!
A COLD, FETID BREATH FEATHERED OVER MY NECK.
BETTER FOR ME TO DIE NOW...
...THAN TO LOOK ANY LONGER OUT OF THESE DEAD EYES!
THROUGH DEATH-- REBIRTH.
I COME TO YOU, MY PET.

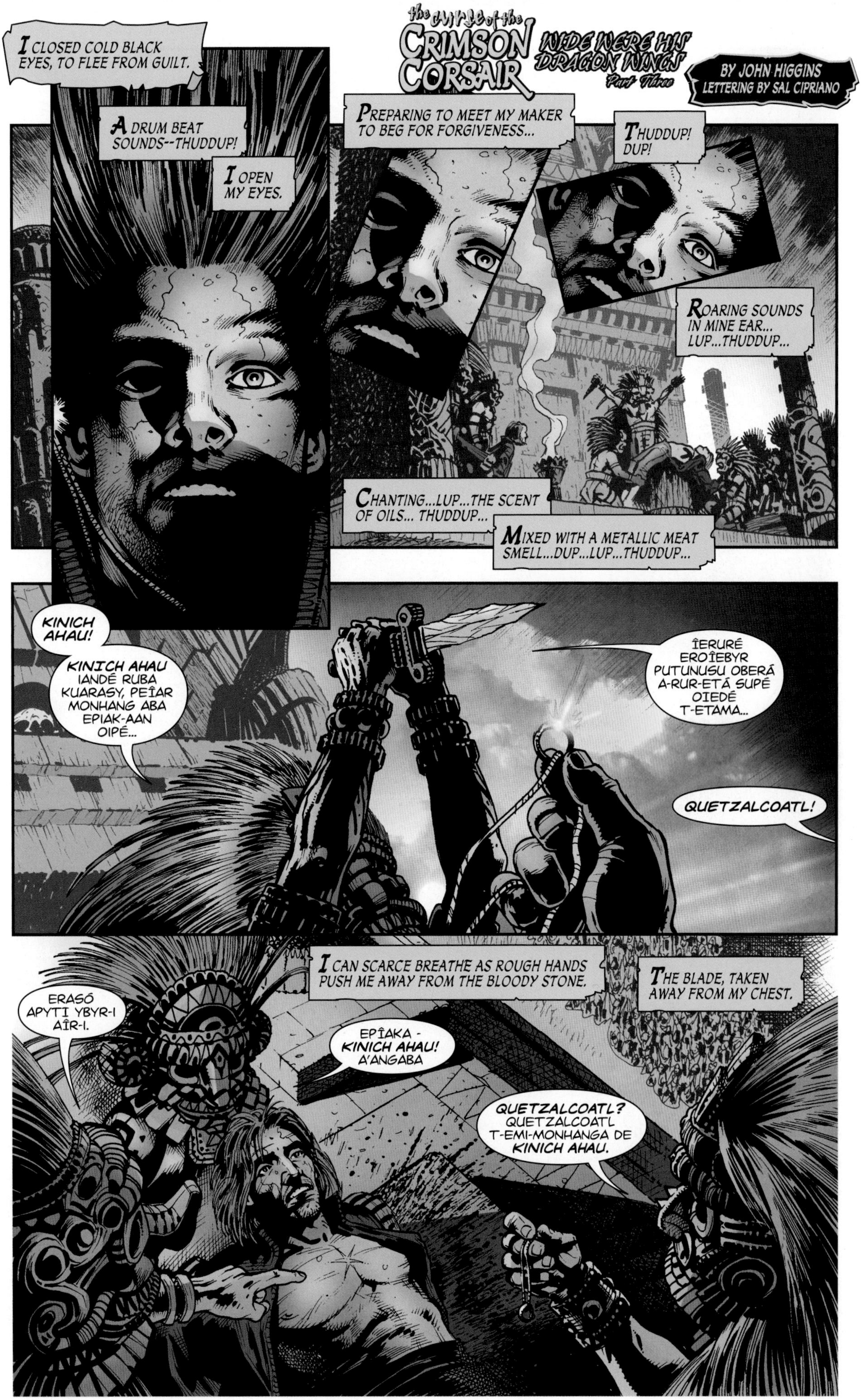
the curse of the
CRIMSON CORSAIR
WIDE WERE HIS DRAGON WINGS
Part Three
BY JOHN HIGGINS
LETTERING BY SAL CIPRIANO
I CLOSED COLD BLACK EYES, TO FLEE FROM GUILT.
A DRUM BEAT SOUNDS--THUDDUP!
I OPEN MY EYES.
PREPARING TO MEET MY MAKER TO BEG FOR FORGIVENESS...
THUDDUP! DUP!
ROARING SOUNDS IN MINE EAR... LUP...THUDDUP...
CHANTING...LUP...THE SCENT OF OILS... THUDDUP...
MIXED WITH A METALLIC MEAT SMELL...DUP...LUP...THUDDUP...
KINICH AHAU!
KINICH AHAU IANDÉ RUBA KUARASY, PEÎAR MONHANG ABA EPIAK-AAN OIPÉ...
ÎERURÉ EROÎEBYR PUTUNUSU OBERÁ A-RUR-ETÁ SUPÉ OIEDÉ T-ETAMA...
QUETZALCOATL!
I CAN SCARCE BREATHE AS ROUGH HANDS PUSH ME AWAY FROM THE BLOODY STONE.
THE BLADE, TAKEN AWAY FROM MY CHEST.
ERASÓ APYTI YBYR-I AÎR-I.
EPÎAKA - KINICH AHAU! A'ANGABA
QUETZALCOATL? QUETZALCOATL T-EMI-MONHANGA DE KINICH AHAU.

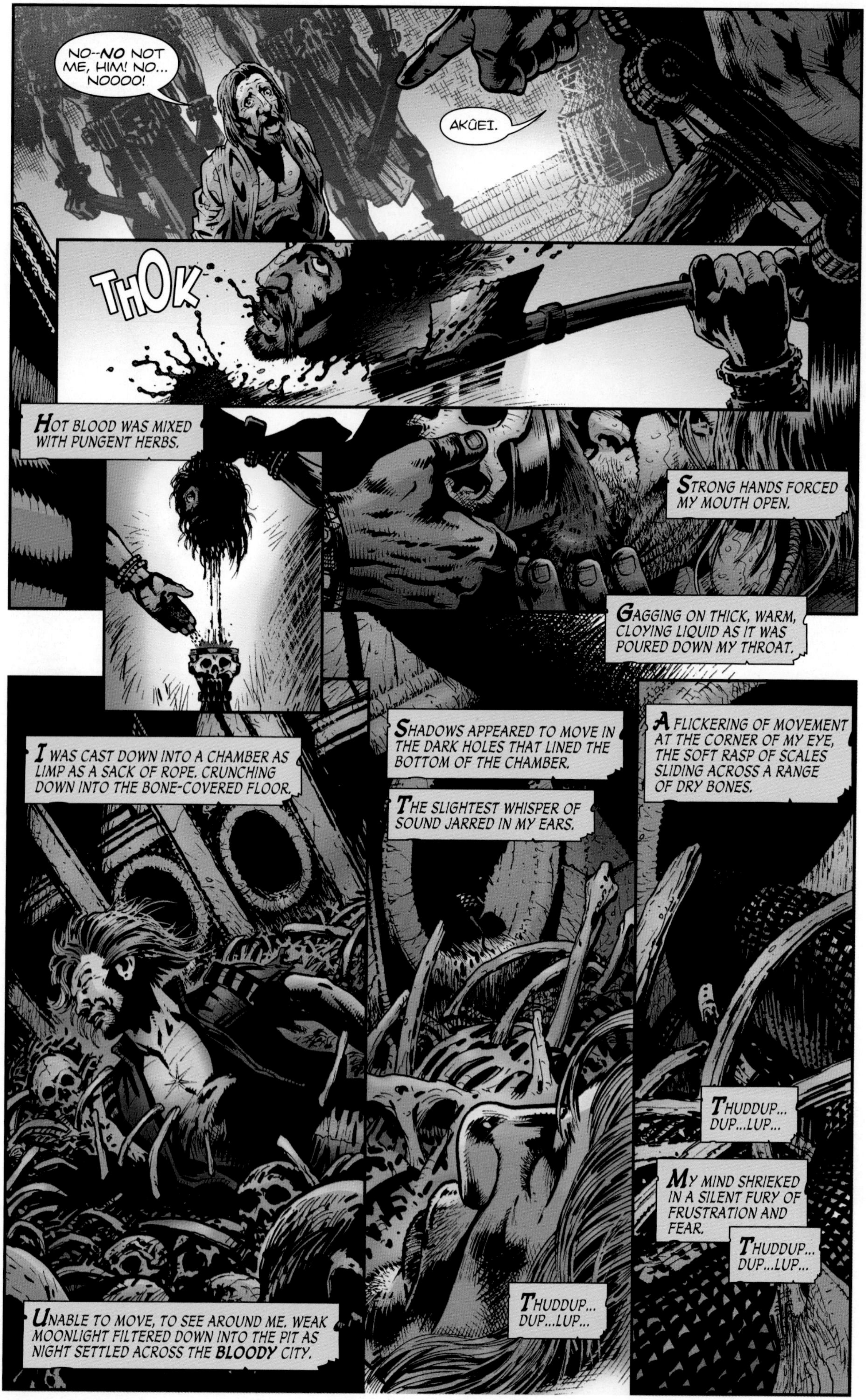
NO--NO NOT ME, HIM! NO... NOOOO!
AKÛEI.
THOK
HOT BLOOD WAS MIXED WITH PUNGENT HERBS.
STRONG HANDS FORCED MY MOUTH OPEN.
GAGGING ON THICK, WARM, CLOYING LIQUID AS IT WAS POURED DOWN MY THROAT.
I WAS CAST DOWN INTO A CHAMBER AS LIMP AS A SACK OF ROPE, CRUNCHING DOWN INTO THE BONE-COVERED FLOOR.
UNABLE TO MOVE, TO SEE AROUND ME. WEAK MOONLIGHT FILTERED DOWN INTO THE PIT AS NIGHT SETTLED ACROSS THE BLOODY CITY.
SHADOWS APPEARED TO MOVE IN THE DARK HOLES THAT LINED THE BOTTOM OF THE CHAMBER.
THE SLIGHTEST WHISPER OF SOUND JARRED IN MY EARS.
THUDDUP... DUP...LUP...
A FLICKERING OF MOVEMENT AT THE CORNER OF MY EYE, THE SOFT RASP OF SCALES SLIDING ACROSS A RANGE OF DRY BONES.
THUDDUP... DUP...LUP...
MY MIND SHRIEKED IN A SILENT FURY OF FRUSTRATION AND FEAR.
THUDDUP... DUP...LUP...

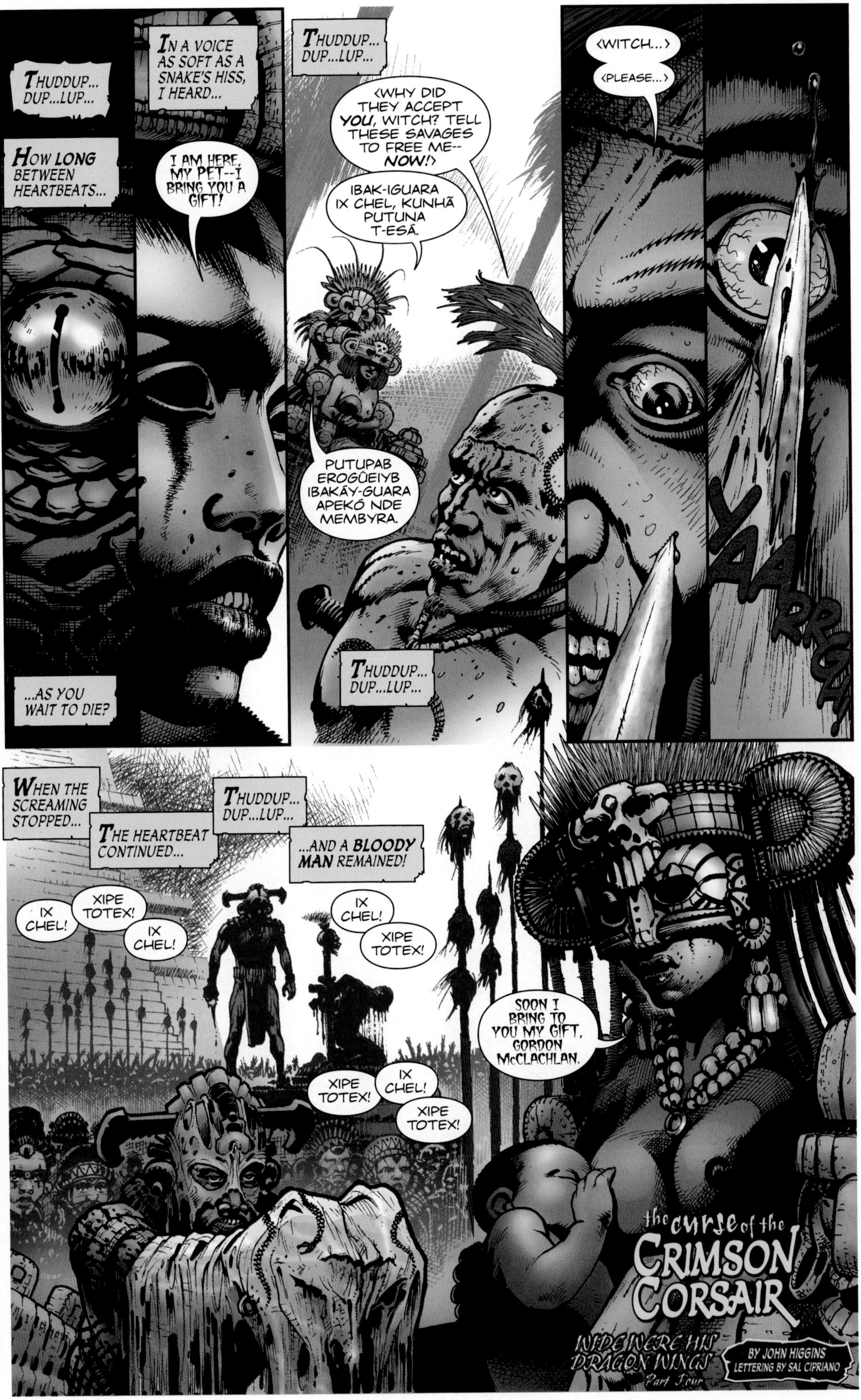
THUDDUP... DUP...LUP...
HOW LONG BETWEEN HEARTBEATS...
IN A VOICE AS SOFT AS A SNAKE'S HISS, I HEARD...
I AM HERE, MY PET--I BRING YOU A GIFT!
...AS YOU WAIT TO DIE?
THUDDUP... DUP...LUP...
‹WHY DID THEY ACCEPT YOU, WITCH? TELL THESE SAVAGES TO FREE ME--NOW!›
IBAK-IGUARA IX CHEL, KUNHÃ PUTUNA T-ESÃ.
PUTUPAB EROGÛEIYB IBAKÃY-GUARA APEKÓ NDE MEMBYRA.
THUDDUP... DUP...LUP...
‹WITCH...›
‹PLEASE...›
YAARRGH!
WHEN THE SCREAMING STOPPED...
THE HEARTBEAT CONTINUED...
THUDDUP... DUP...LUP...
...AND A BLOODY MAN REMAINED!
IX CHEL!
XIPE TOTEX!
IX CHEL!
IX CHEL!
XIPE TOTEX!
SOON I BRING TO YOU MY GIFT, GORDON McCLACHLAN.
XIPE TOTEX!
IX CHEL!
XIPE TOTEX!
the curse of the CRIMSON CORSAIR
WIDE WERE HIS DRAGON WINGS Part Four
BY JOHN HIGGINS
LETTERING BY SAL CIPRIANO

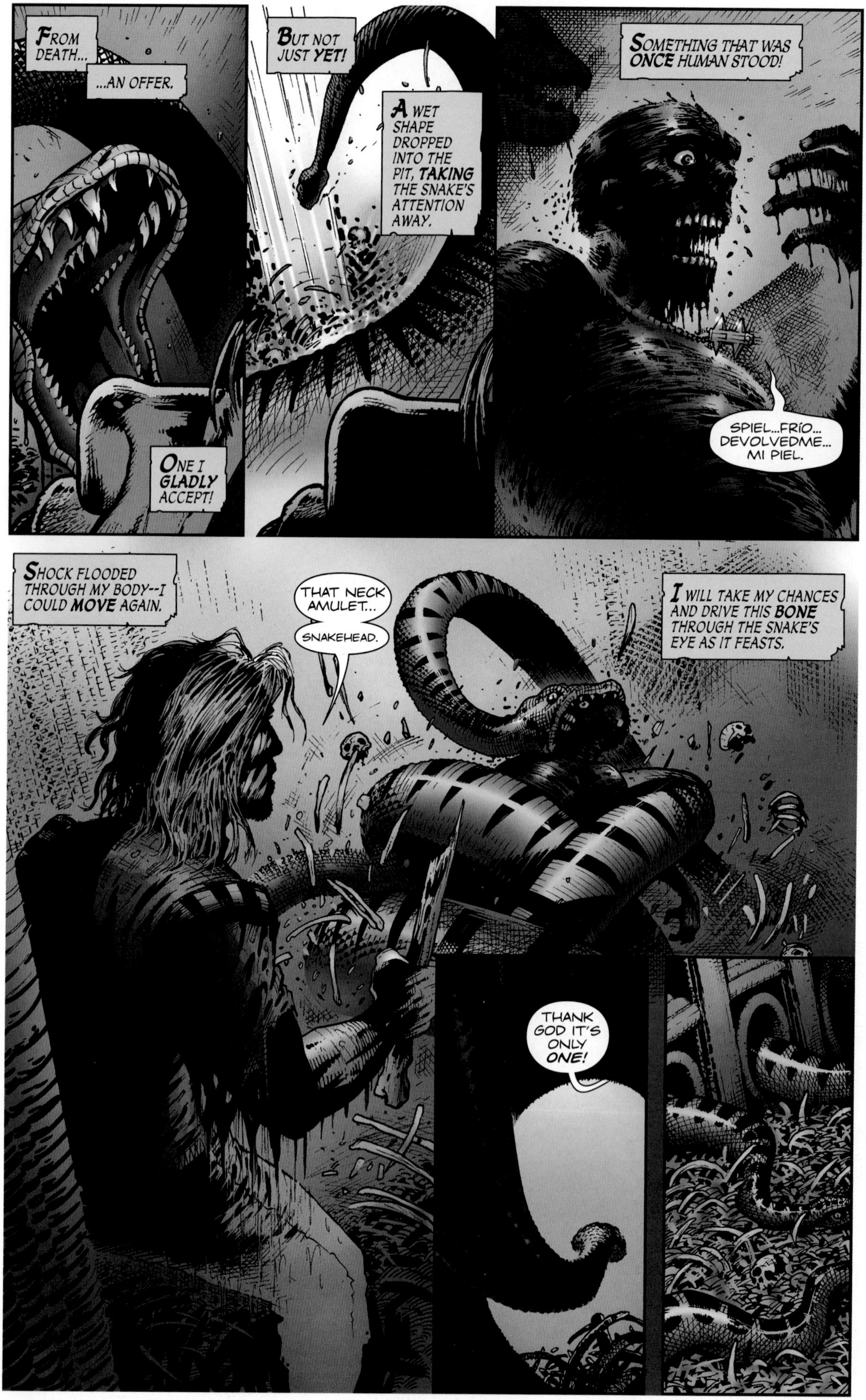
FROM DEATH...
...AN OFFER.
ONE I GLADLY ACCEPT!
BUT NOT JUST YET!
A WET SHAPE DROPPED INTO THE PIT, TAKING THE SNAKE'S ATTENTION AWAY.
SOMETHING THAT WAS ONCE HUMAN STOOD!
SPIEL...FRÍO... DEVOLVEDME... MI PIEL.
SHOCK FLOODED THROUGH MY BODY--I COULD MOVE AGAIN.
THAT NECK AMULET...
SNAKEHEAD.
I WILL TAKE MY CHANCES AND DRIVE THIS BONE THROUGH THE SNAKE'S EYE AS IT FEASTS.
THANK GOD IT'S ONLY ONE!

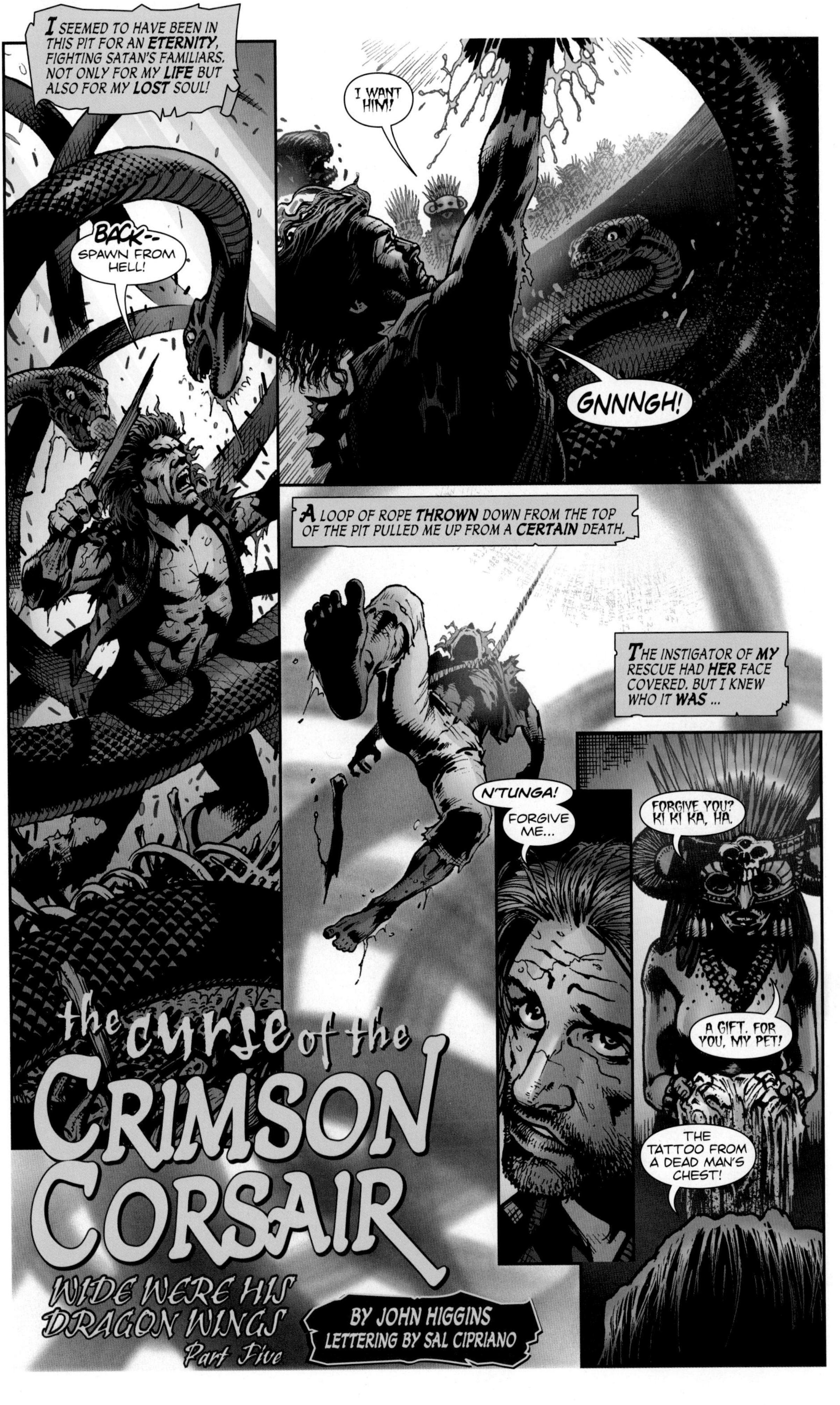
I SEEMED TO HAVE BEEN IN THIS PIT FOR AN ETERNITY, FIGHTING SATAN'S FAMILIARS. NOT ONLY FOR MY LIFE BUT ALSO FOR MY LOST SOUL!
BACK-- SPAWN FROM HELL!
I WANT HIM!
GNNNGH!
A LOOP OF ROPE THROWN DOWN FROM THE TOP OF THE PIT PULLED ME UP FROM A CERTAIN DEATH.
THE INSTIGATOR OF MY RESCUE HAD HER FACE COVERED. BUT I KNEW WHO IT WAS ...
N'TUNGA! FORGIVE ME...
FORGIVE YOU? KI KI KA, HA.
A GIFT. FOR YOU, MY PET!
THE TATTOO FROM A DEAD MAN'S CHEST!
the curse of the
CRIMSON CORSAIR
WIDE WERE HIS DRAGON WINGS
Part Five
BY JOHN HIGGINS
LETTERING BY SAL CIPRIANO

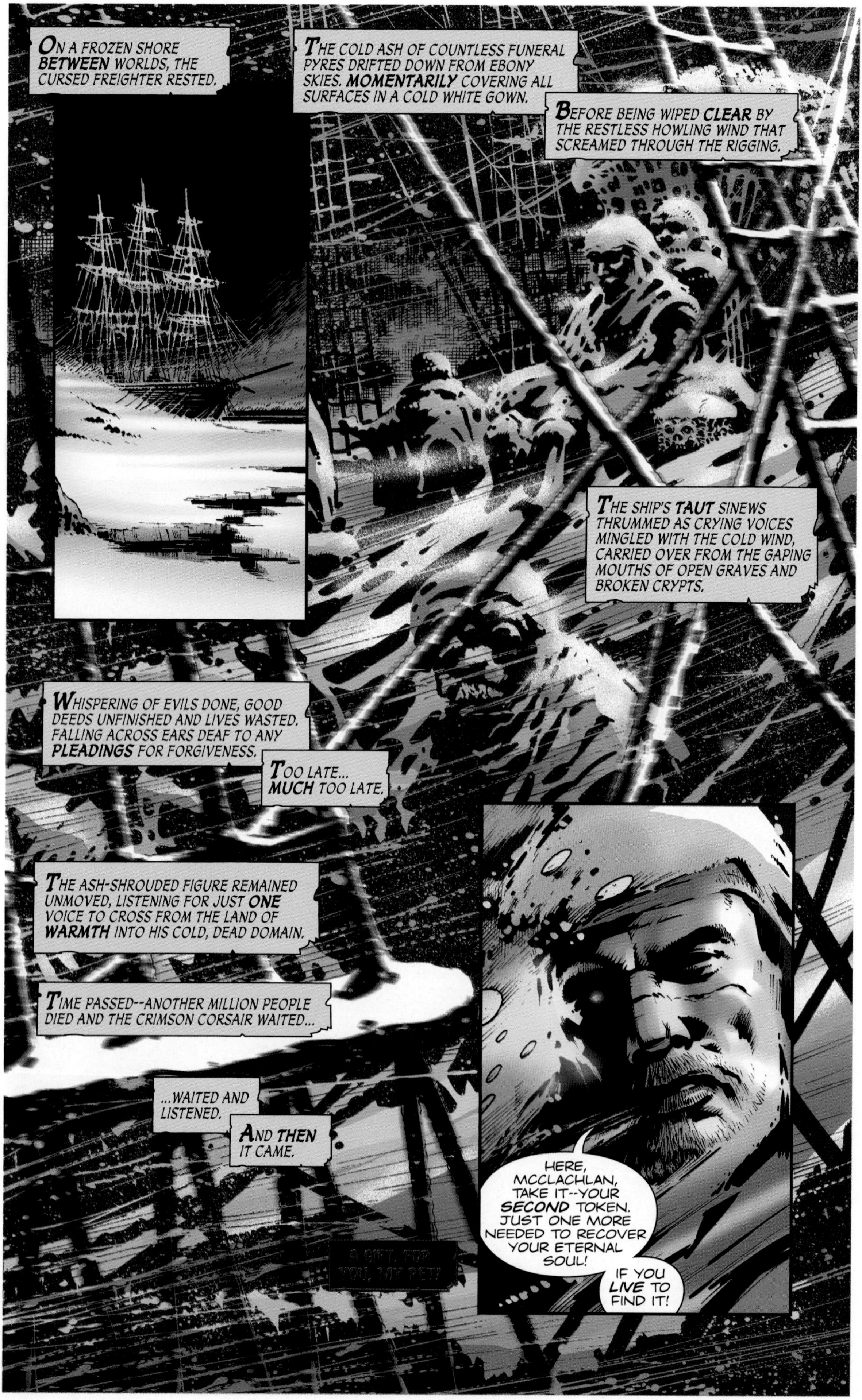

ON A FROZEN SHORE BETWEEN WORLDS, THE CURSED FREIGHTER RESTED.
THE COLD ASH OF COUNTLESS FUNERAL PYRES DRIFTED DOWN FROM EBONY SKIES. MOMENTARILY COVERING ALL SURFACES IN A COLD WHITE GOWN.
BEFORE BEING WIPED CLEAR BY THE RESTLESS HOWLING WIND THAT SCREAMED THROUGH THE RIGGING.
THE SHIP'S TAUT SINEWS THRUMMED AS CRYING VOICES MINGLED WITH THE COLD WIND, CARRIED OVER FROM THE GAPING MOUTHS OF OPEN GRAVES AND BROKEN CRYPTS.
WHISPERING OF EVILS DONE, GOOD DEEDS UNFINISHED AND LIVES WASTED. FALLING ACROSS EARS DEAF TO ANY PLEADINGS FOR FORGIVENESS.
TOO LATE... MUCH TOO LATE.
THE ASH-SHROUDED FIGURE REMAINED UNMOVED, LISTENING FOR JUST ONE VOICE TO CROSS FROM THE LAND OF WARMTH INTO HIS COLD, DEAD DOMAIN.
TIME PASSED--ANOTHER MILLION PEOPLE DIED AND THE CRIMSON CORSAIR WAITED...
...WAITED AND LISTENED.
AND THEN IT CAME.
HERE, MCCLACHLAN, TAKE IT--YOUR SECOND TOKEN. JUST ONE MORE NEEDED TO RECOVER YOUR ETERNAL SOUL!
IF YOU LIVE TO FIND IT!
A GIFT, FOR YOU, MY PET?

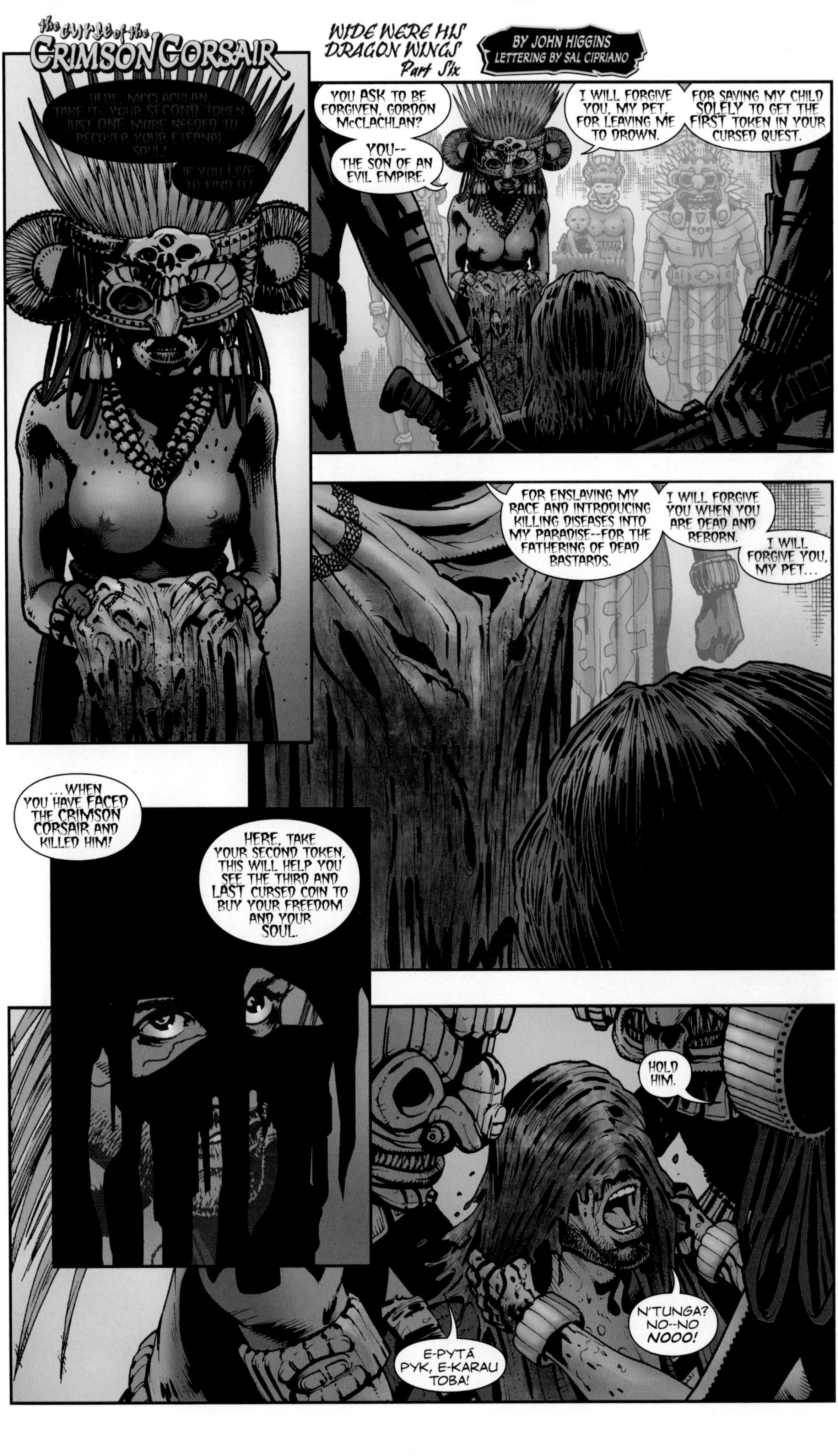
the curse of the
CRIMSON CORSAIR
WIDE WERE HIS DRAGON WINGS
Part Six
BY JOHN HIGGINS
LETTERING BY SAL CIPRIANO
HERE, MCCLACHLAN, TAKE IT--YOUR SECOND TOKEN. JUST ONE MORE NEEDED TO RECOVER YOUR ETERNAL SOUL!
IF YOU LIVE TO FIND IT!
YOU ASK TO BE FORGIVEN, GORDON McCLACHLAN?
YOU-- THE SON OF AN EVIL EMPIRE.
I WILL FORGIVE YOU, MY PET, FOR LEAVING ME TO DROWN.
FOR SAVING MY CHILD SOLELY TO GET THE FIRST TOKEN IN YOUR CURSED QUEST.
FOR ENSLAVING MY RACE AND INTRODUCING KILLING DISEASES INTO MY PARADISE--FOR THE FATHERING OF DEAD BASTARDS.
I WILL FORGIVE YOU WHEN YOU ARE DEAD AND REBORN.
I WILL FORGIVE YOU, MY PET...
...WHEN YOU HAVE FACED THE CRIMSON CORSAIR AND KILLED HIM!
HERE, TAKE YOUR SECOND TOKEN, THIS WILL HELP YOU SEE THE THIRD AND LAST CURSED COIN TO BUY YOUR FREEDOM AND YOUR SOUL.
HOLD HIM.
N'TUNGA? NO--NO NOOO!
E-PYTÁ PYK, E-KARAU TOBA!

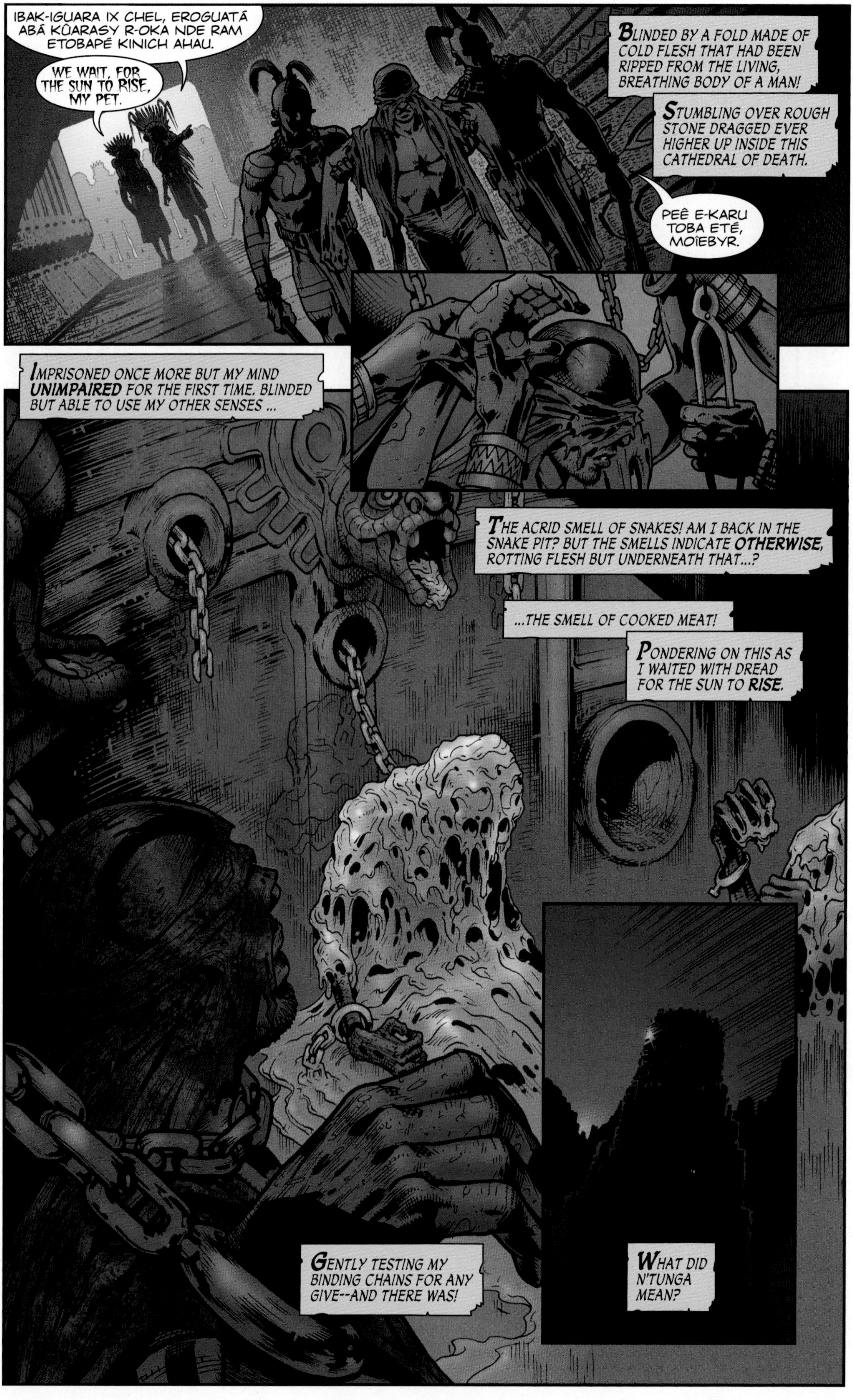

IBAK-IGUARA IX CHEL, EROGUATÃ ABÃ KÛARASY R-OKA NDE RAM ETOBAPÉ KINICH AHAU.
WE WAIT, FOR THE SUN TO RISE, MY PET.
BLINDED BY A FOLD MADE OF COLD FLESH THAT HAD BEEN RIPPED FROM THE LIVING, BREATHING BODY OF A MAN!
STUMBLING OVER ROUGH STONE DRAGGED EVER HIGHER UP INSIDE THIS CATHEDRAL OF DEATH.
PEÊ E-KARU TOBA ETÉ, MOÏEBYR.
IMPRISONED ONCE MORE BUT MY MIND UNIMPAIRED FOR THE FIRST TIME. BLINDED BUT ABLE TO USE MY OTHER SENSES ...
THE ACRID SMELL OF SNAKES! AM I BACK IN THE SNAKE PIT? BUT THE SMELLS INDICATE OTHERWISE, ROTTING FLESH BUT UNDERNEATH THAT...?
...THE SMELL OF COOKED MEAT!
PONDERING ON THIS AS I WAITED WITH DREAD FOR THE SUN TO RISE.
GENTLY TESTING MY BINDING CHAINS FOR ANY GIVE--AND THERE WAS!
WHAT DID N'TUNGA MEAN?

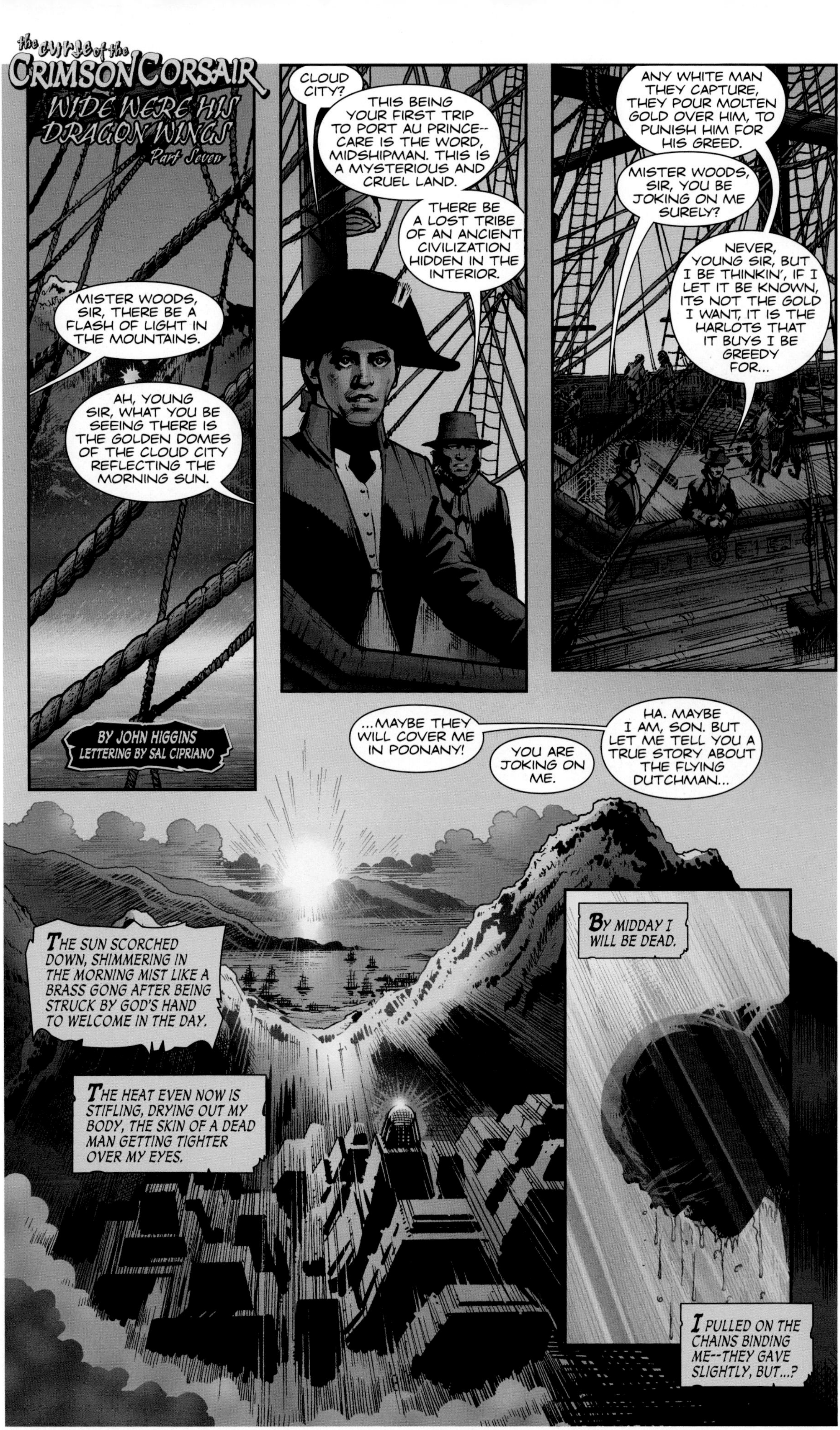
the curse of the
CRIMSON CORSAIR
WIDE WERE HIS DRAGON WINGS
Part Seven
MISTER WOODS, SIR, THERE BE A FLASH OF LIGHT IN THE MOUNTAINS.
AH, YOUNG SIR, WHAT YOU BE SEEING THERE IS THE GOLDEN DOMES OF THE CLOUD CITY REFLECTING THE MORNING SUN.
BY JOHN HIGGINS
LETTERING BY SAL CIPRIANO
CLOUD CITY?
THIS BEING YOUR FIRST TRIP TO PORT AU PRINCE-- CARE IS THE WORD, MIDSHIPMAN. THIS IS A MYSTERIOUS AND CRUEL LAND.
THERE BE A LOST TRIBE OF AN ANCIENT CIVILIZATION HIDDEN IN THE INTERIOR.
ANY WHITE MAN THEY CAPTURE, THEY POUR MOLTEN GOLD OVER HIM, TO PUNISH HIM FOR HIS GREED.
MISTER WOODS, SIR, YOU BE JOKING ON ME SURELY?
NEVER, YOUNG SIR, BUT I BE THINKIN', IF I LET IT BE KNOWN, ITS NOT THE GOLD I WANT, IT IS THE HARLOTS THAT IT BUYS I BE GREEDY FOR...
...MAYBE THEY WILL COVER ME IN POONANY!
YOU ARE JOKING ON ME.
HA. MAYBE I AM, SON. BUT LET ME TELL YOU A TRUE STORY ABOUT THE FLYING DUTCHMAN...
THE SUN SCORCHED DOWN, SHIMMERING IN THE MORNING MIST LIKE A BRASS GONG AFTER BEING STRUCK BY GOD'S HAND TO WELCOME IN THE DAY.
THE HEAT EVEN NOW IS STIFLING, DRYING OUT MY BODY, THE SKIN OF A DEAD MAN GETTING TIGHTER OVER MY EYES.
BY MIDDAY I WILL BE DEAD.
I PULLED ON THE CHAINS BINDING ME--THEY GAVE SLIGHTLY, BUT...?

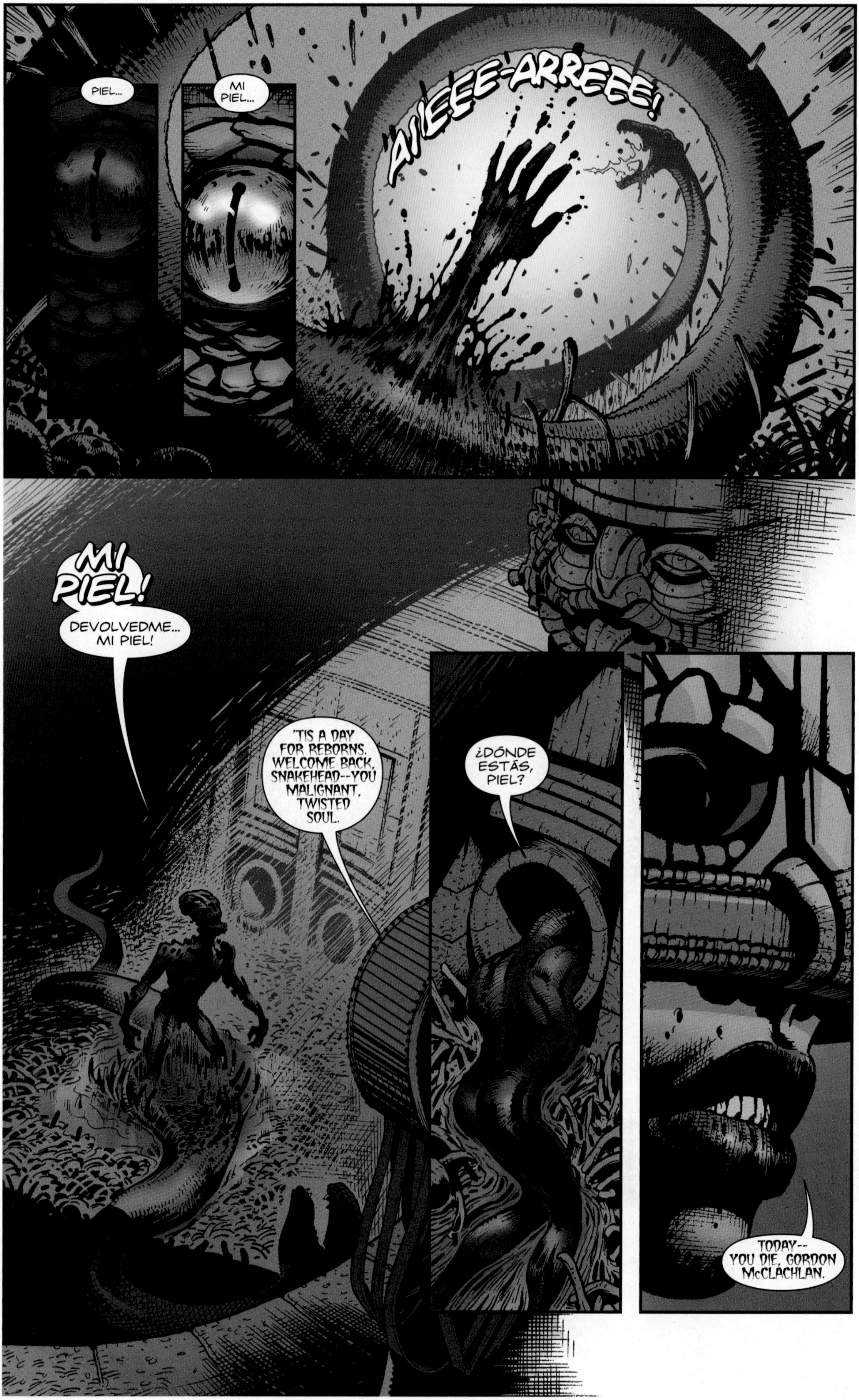
PIEL...
MI PIEL...
AIIEEEE-ARREEEE!
MI PIEL!
DEVOLVEDME... MI PIEL!
'TIS A DAY FOR REBORNS. WELCOME BACK, SNAKEHEAD--YOU MALIGNANT, TWISTED SOUL.
¿DÓNDE ESTÁS, PIEL?
TODAY-- YOU DIE, GORDON McCLACHLAN.

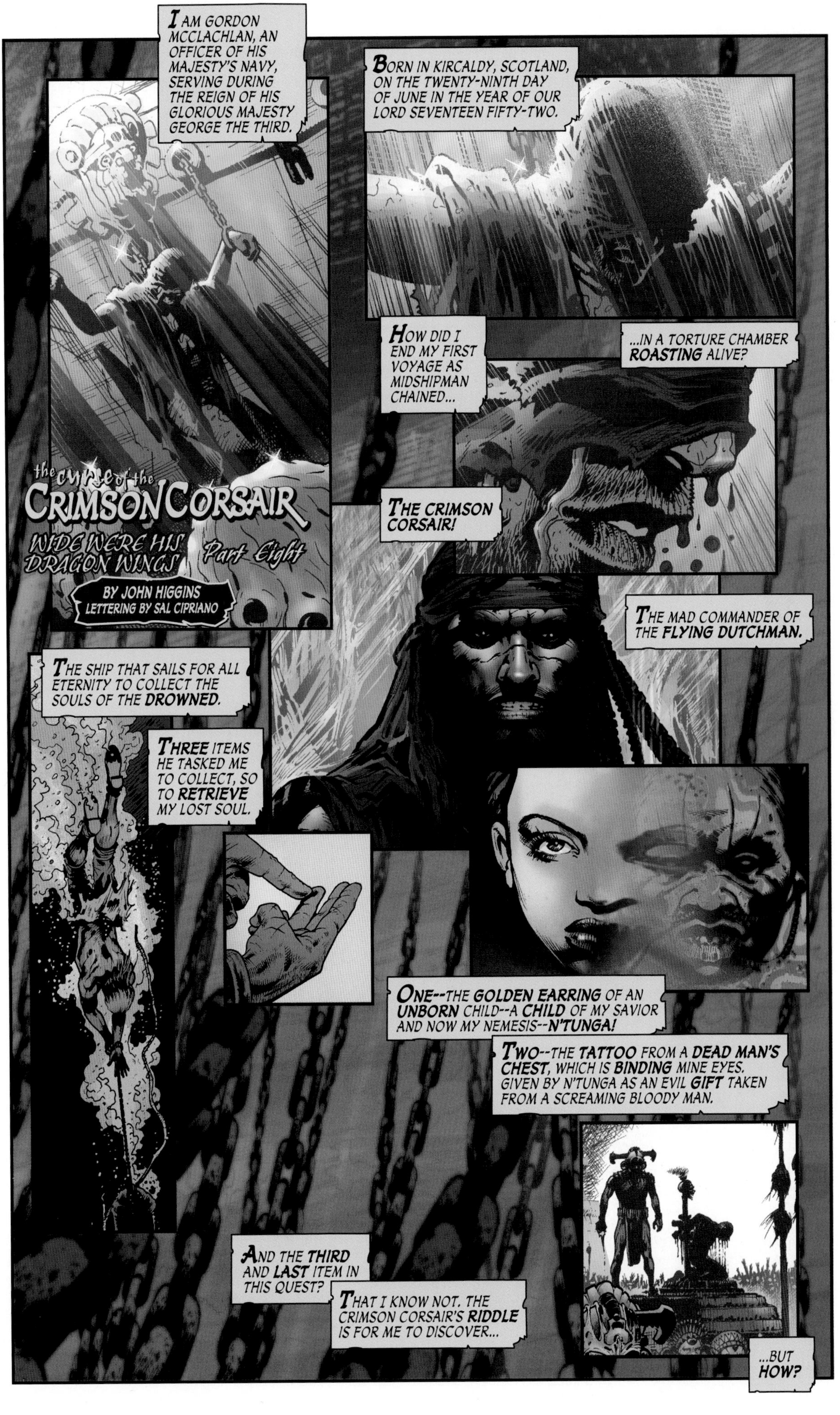

I AM GORDON MCCLACHLAN, AN OFFICER OF HIS MAJESTY'S NAVY, SERVING DURING THE REIGN OF HIS GLORIOUS MAJESTY GEORGE THE THIRD.
BORN IN KIRCALDY, SCOTLAND, ON THE TWENTY-NINTH DAY OF JUNE IN THE YEAR OF OUR LORD SEVENTEEN FIFTY-TWO.
HOW DID I END MY FIRST VOYAGE AS MIDSHIPMAN CHAINED...
...IN A TORTURE CHAMBER ROASTING ALIVE?
the curse of the CRIMSON CORSAIR
WIDE WERE HIS DRAGON WINGS Part Eight
BY JOHN HIGGINS
LETTERING BY SAL CIPRIANO
THE CRIMSON CORSAIR!
THE MAD COMMANDER OF THE FLYING DUTCHMAN.
THE SHIP THAT SAILS FOR ALL ETERNITY TO COLLECT THE SOULS OF THE DROWNED.
THREE ITEMS HE TASKED ME TO COLLECT, SO TO RETRIEVE MY LOST SOUL.
ONE--THE GOLDEN EARRING OF AN UNBORN CHILD--A CHILD OF MY SAVIOR AND NOW MY NEMESIS--N'TUNGA!
TWO--THE TATTOO FROM A DEAD MAN'S CHEST, WHICH IS BINDING MINE EYES. GIVEN BY N'TUNGA AS AN EVIL GIFT TAKEN FROM A SCREAMING BLOODY MAN.
AND THE THIRD AND LAST ITEM IN THIS QUEST?
THAT I KNOW NOT. THE CRIMSON CORSAIR'S RIDDLE IS FOR ME TO DISCOVER...
...BUT HOW?

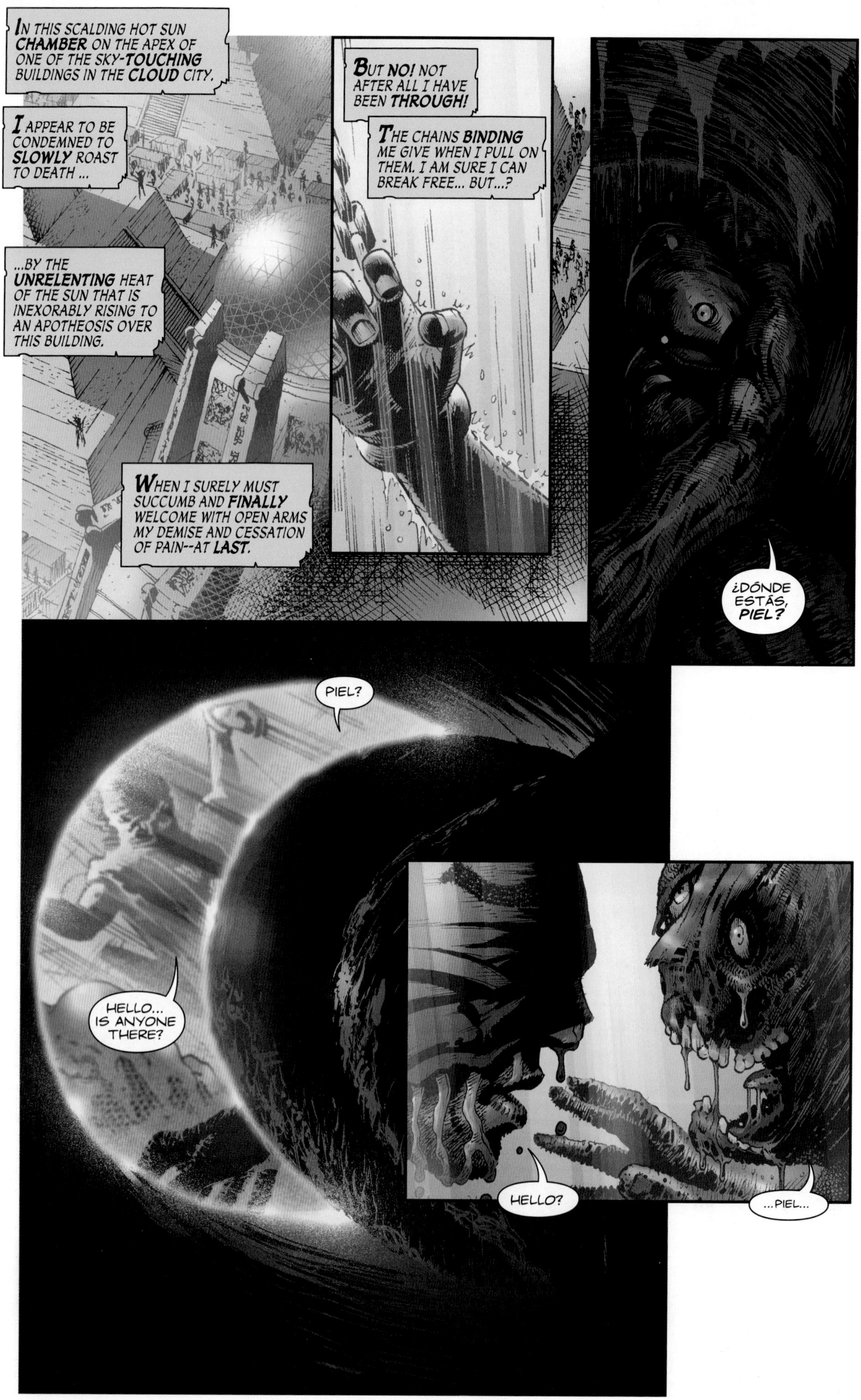
IN THIS SCALDING HOT SUN CHAMBER ON THE APEX OF ONE OF THE SKY-TOUCHING BUILDINGS IN THE CLOUD CITY.
I APPEAR TO BE CONDEMNED TO SLOWLY ROAST TO DEATH ...
...BY THE UNRELENTING HEAT OF THE SUN THAT IS INEXORABLY RISING TO AN APOTHEOSIS OVER THIS BUILDING.
WHEN I SURELY MUST SUCCUMB AND FINALLY WELCOME WITH OPEN ARMS MY DEMISE AND CESSATION OF PAIN--AT LAST.
BUT NO! NOT AFTER ALL I HAVE BEEN THROUGH!
THE CHAINS BINDING ME GIVE WHEN I PULL ON THEM. I AM SURE I CAN BREAK FREE... BUT...?
¿DÓNDE ESTÁS, PIEL?
PIEL?
HELLO... IS ANYONE THERE?
HELLO?
...PIEL...

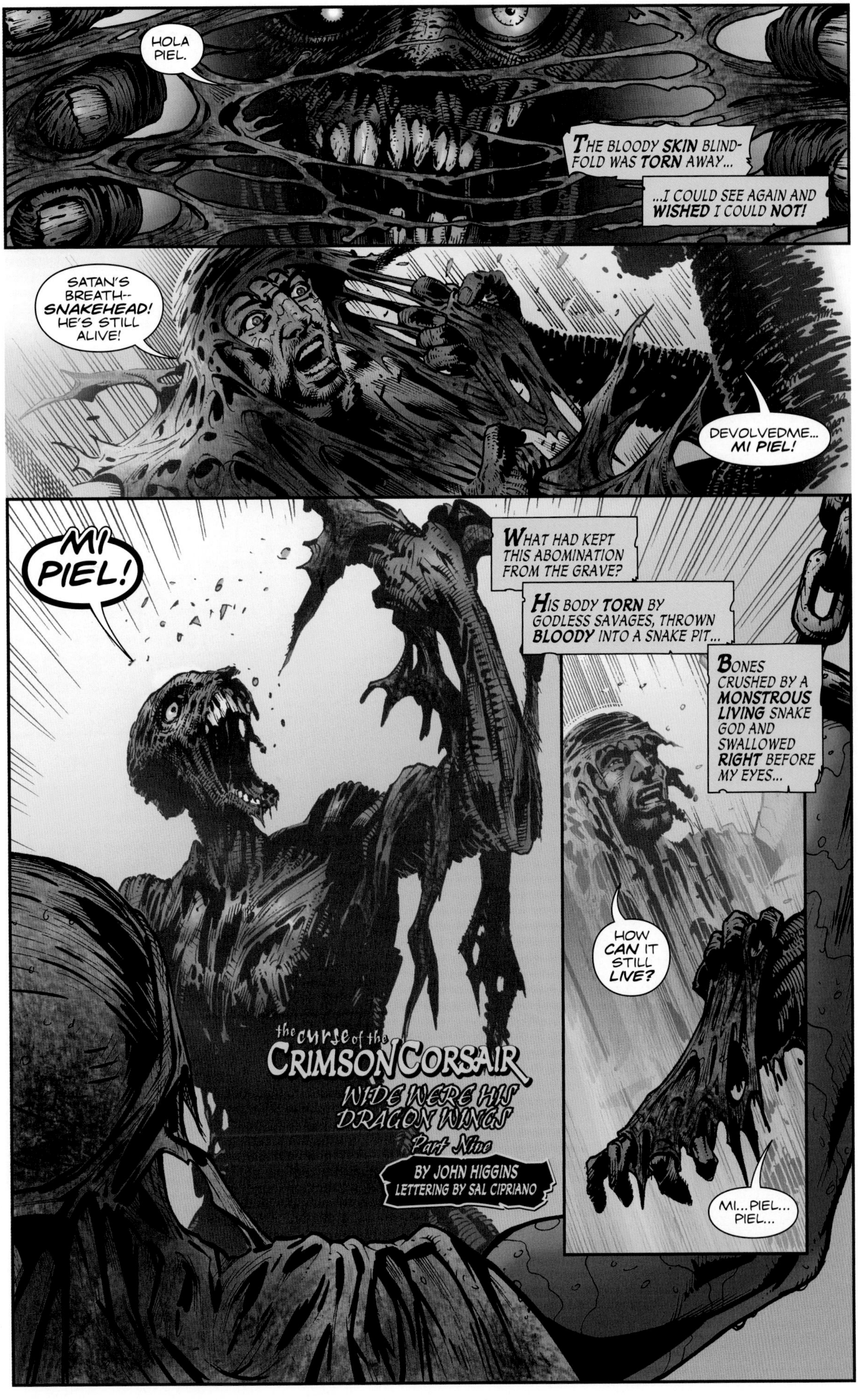
HOLA PIEL.
THE BLOODY SKIN BLIND-FOLD WAS TORN AWAY...
...I COULD SEE AGAIN AND WISHED I COULD NOT!
SATAN'S BREATH-- SNAKEHEAD! HE'S STILL ALIVE!
DEVOLVEDME... MI PIEL!
MI PIEL!
WHAT HAD KEPT THIS ABOMINATION FROM THE GRAVE?
HIS BODY TORN BY GODLESS SAVAGES, THROWN BLOODY INTO A SNAKE PIT...
BONES CRUSHED BY A MONSTROUS LIVING SNAKE GOD AND SWALLOWED RIGHT BEFORE MY EYES...
HOW CAN IT STILL LIVE?
the curse of the CRIMSON CORSAIR
WIDE WERE HIS DRAGON WINGS
Part Nine
BY JOHN HIGGINS
LETTERING BY SAL CIPRIANO
MI...PIEL... PIEL...

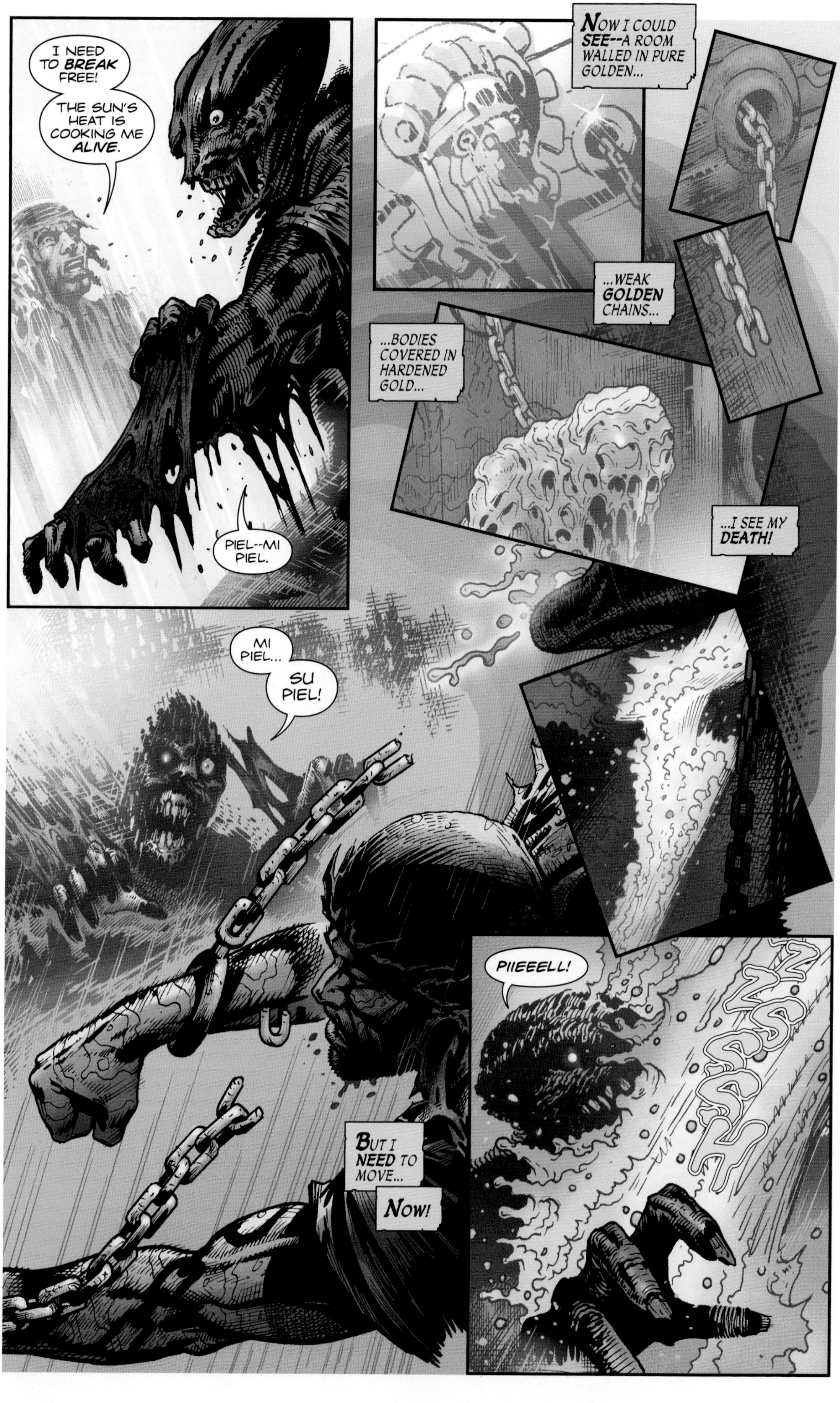
I NEED TO BREAK FREE!
THE SUN'S HEAT IS COOKING ME ALIVE.
PIEL--MI PIEL.
NOW I COULD SEE--A ROOM WALLED IN PURE GOLDEN...
...WEAK GOLDEN CHAINS...
...BODIES COVERED IN HARDENED GOLD...
...I SEE MY DEATH!
MI PIEL...
SU PIEL!
BUT I NEED TO MOVE...
NOW!
PIIEEELL!
ZZSSSH

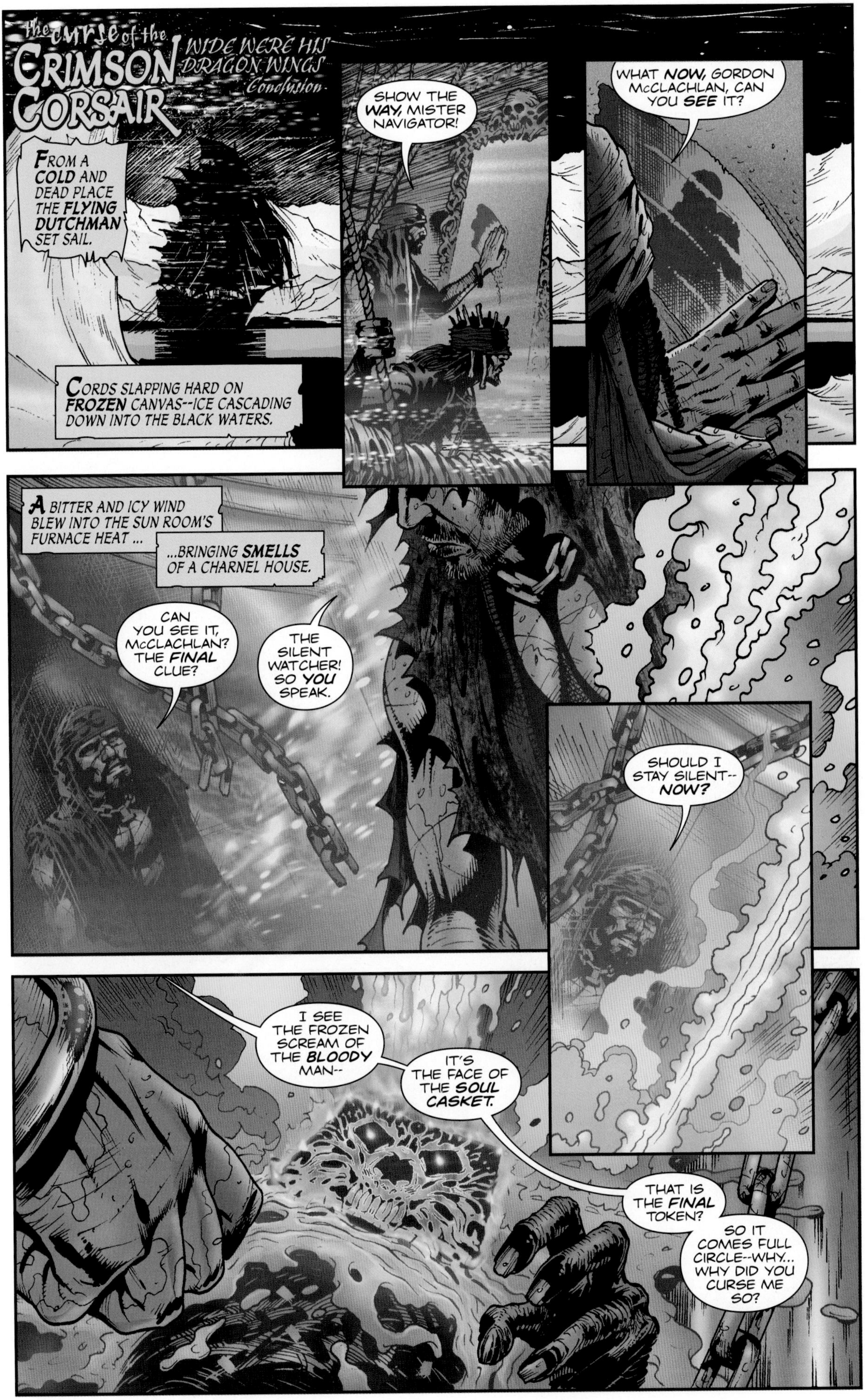

the curse of the CRIMSON CORSAIR
WIDE WERE HIS DRAGON WINGS
Conclusion
FROM A COLD AND DEAD PLACE THE FLYING DUTCHMAN SET SAIL.
CORDS SLAPPING HARD ON FROZEN CANVAS--ICE CASCADING DOWN INTO THE BLACK WATERS.
SHOW THE WAY, MISTER NAVIGATOR!
WHAT NOW, GORDON McCLACHLAN, CAN YOU SEE IT?
A BITTER AND ICY WIND BLEW INTO THE SUN ROOM'S FURNACE HEAT ...
...BRINGING SMELLS OF A CHARNEL HOUSE.
CAN YOU SEE IT, McCLACHLAN? THE FINAL CLUE?
THE SILENT WATCHER! SO YOU SPEAK.
SHOULD I STAY SILENT-- NOW?
I SEE THE FROZEN SCREAM OF THE BLOODY MAN--
IT'S THE FACE OF THE SOUL CASKET.
THAT IS THE FINAL TOKEN?
SO IT COMES FULL CIRCLE--WHY... WHY DID YOU CURSE ME SO?

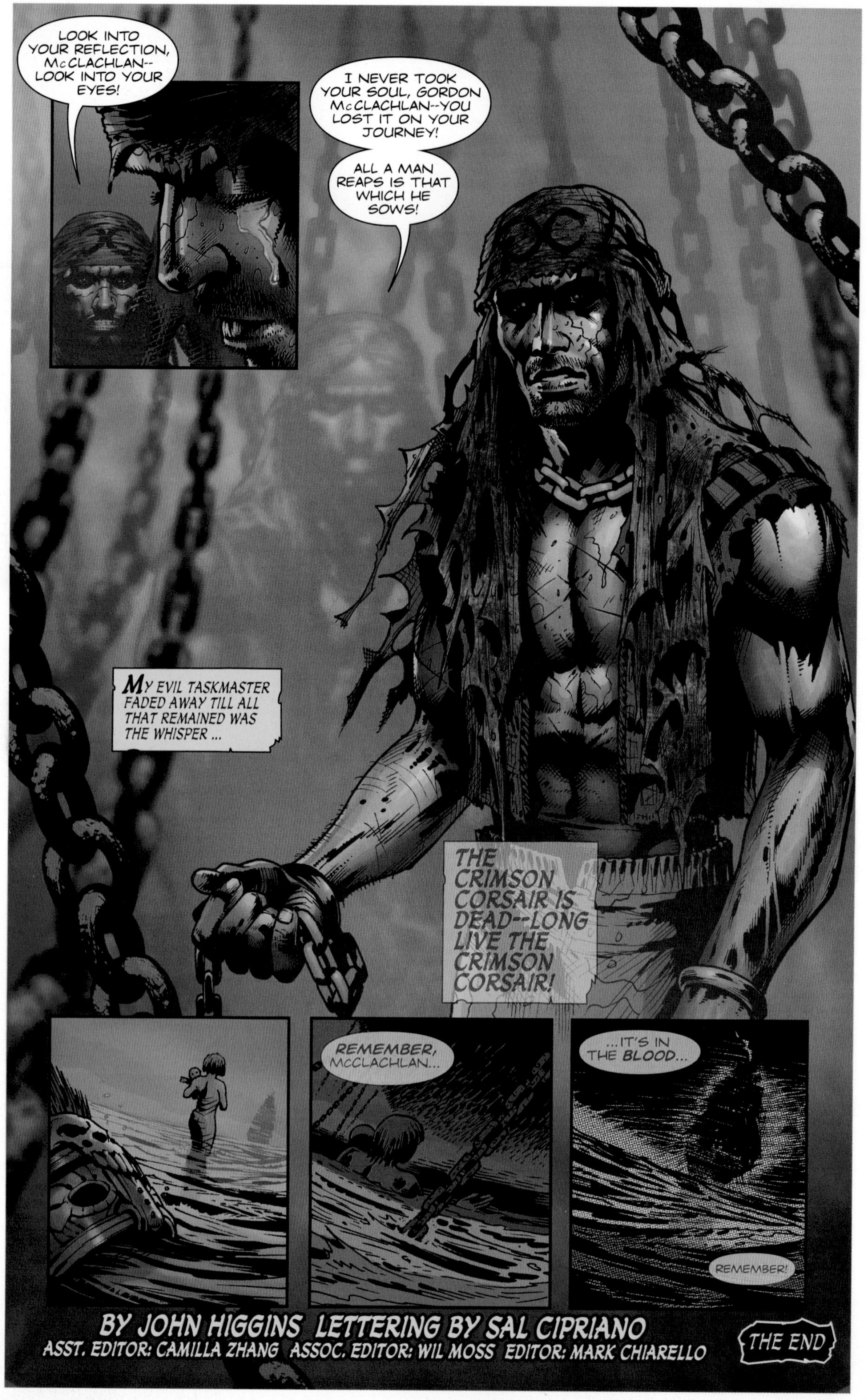
LOOK INTO YOUR REFLECTION, McCLACHLAN-- LOOK INTO YOUR EYES!
I NEVER TOOK YOUR SOUL, GORDON McCLACHLAN--YOU LOST IT ON YOUR JOURNEY!
ALL A MAN REAPS IS THAT WHICH HE SOWS!
MY EVIL TASKMASTER FADED AWAY TILL ALL THAT REMAINED WAS THE WHISPER ...
THE CRIMSON CORSAIR IS DEAD--LONG LIVE THE CRIMSON CORSAIR!
REMEMBER, McCLACHLAN...
...IT'S IN THE BLOOD...
REMEMBER!
BY JOHN HIGGINS LETTERING BY SAL CIPRIANO
ASST. EDITOR: CAMILLA ZHANG ASSOC. EDITOR: WIL MOSS EDITOR: MARK CHIARELLO
THE END

DOLLAR BILL

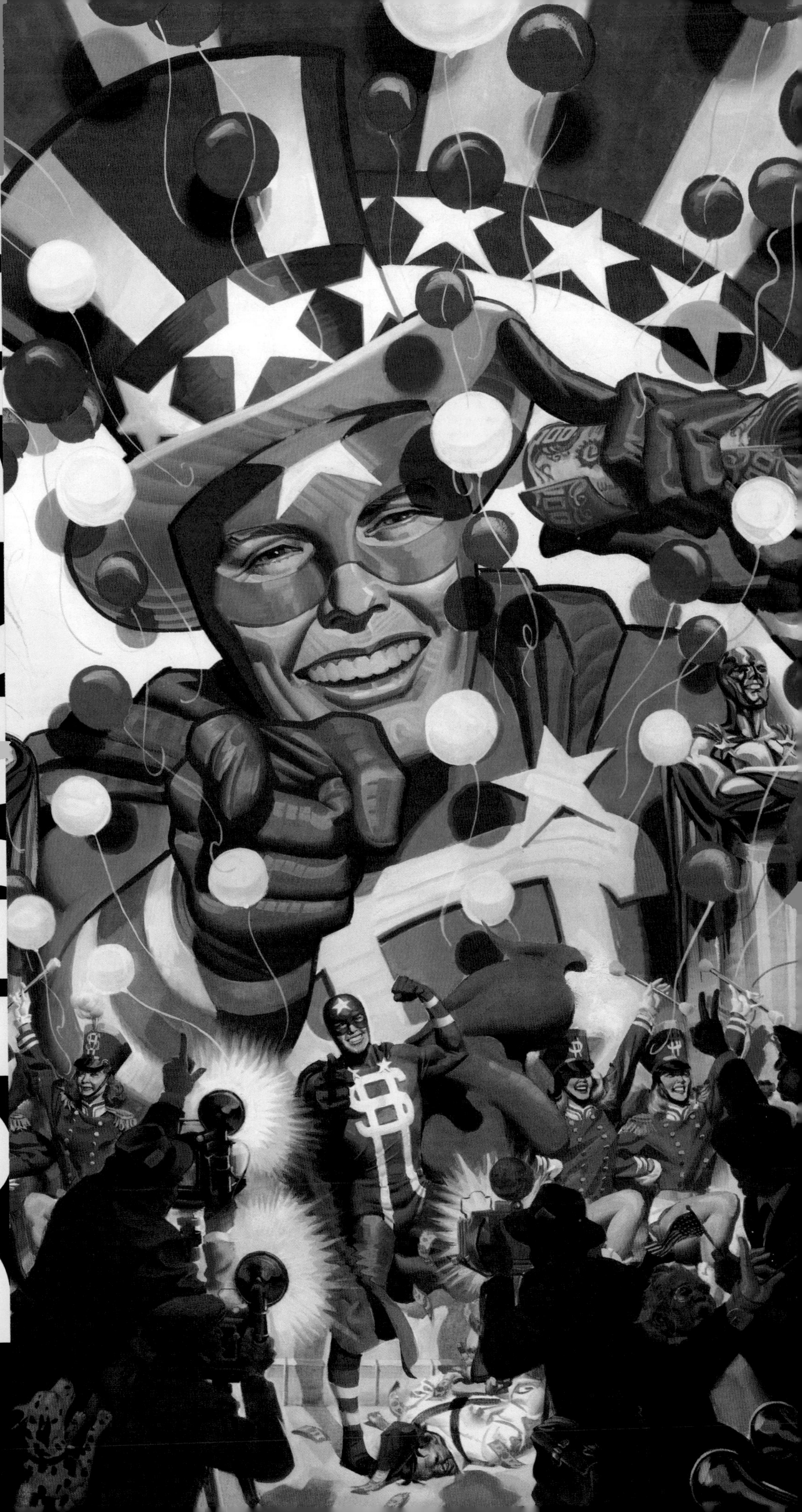

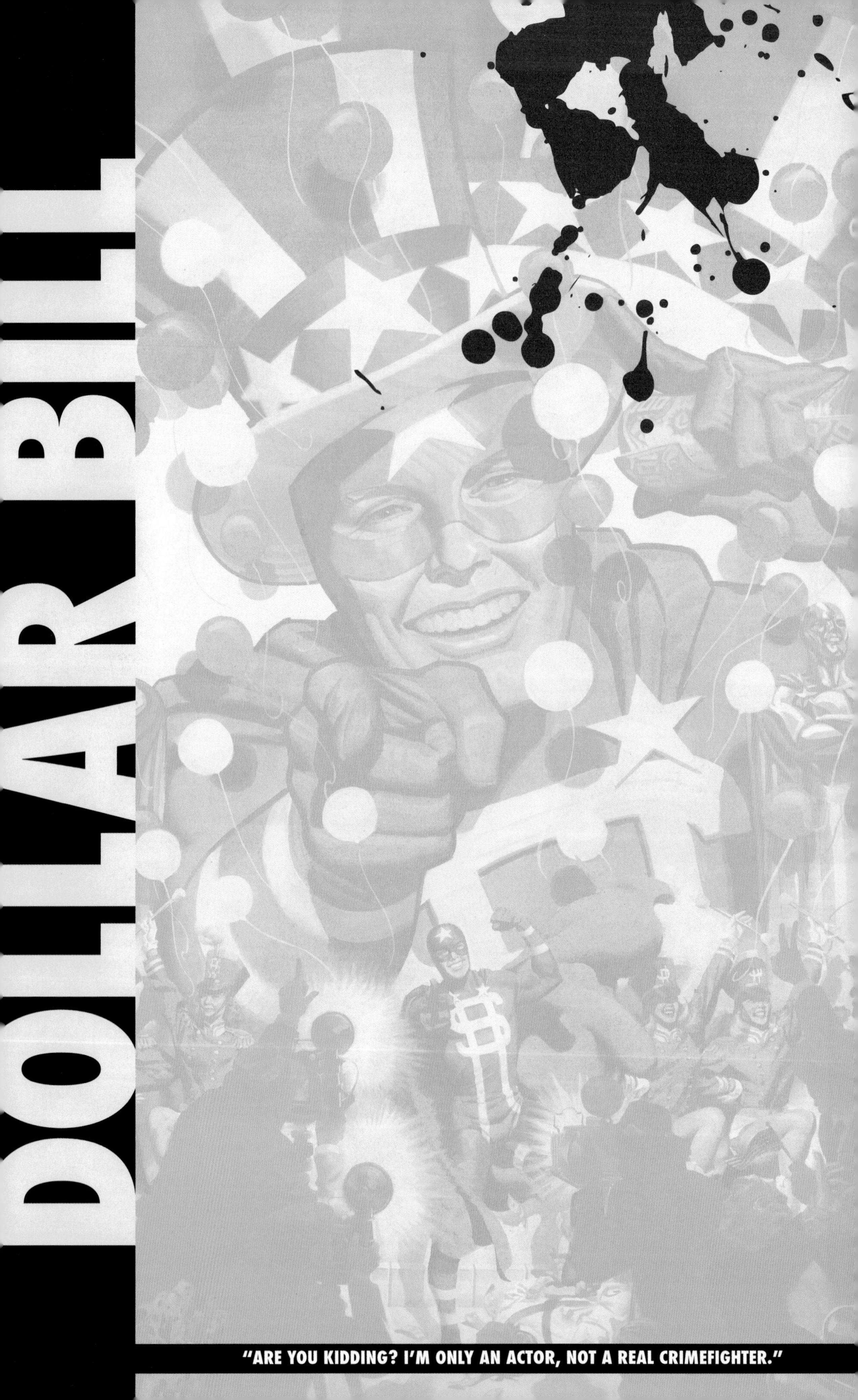
DOLLAR BILL
"ARE YOU KIDDING? I'M ONLY AN ACTOR, NOT A REAL CRIMEFIGHTER."

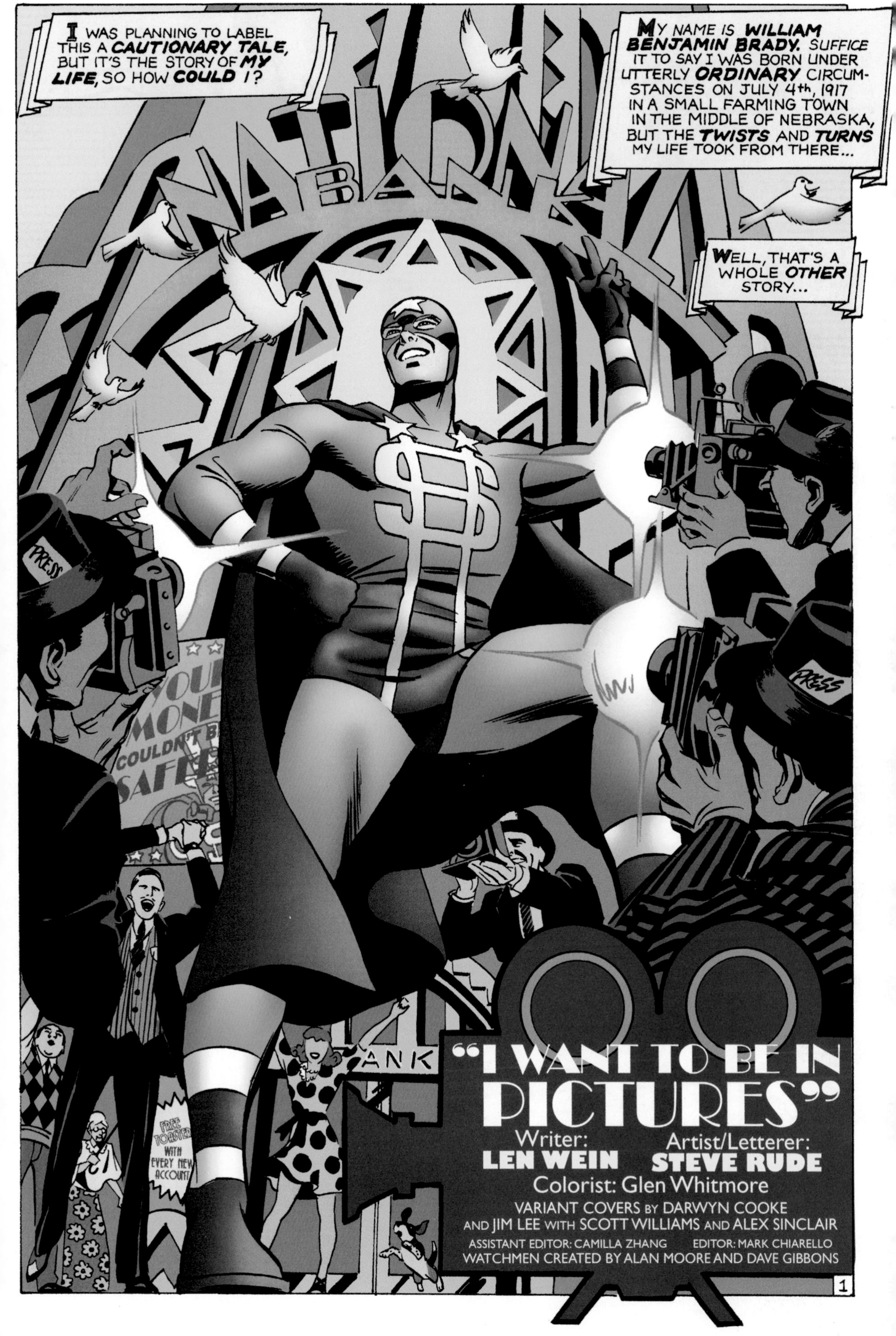
I WAS PLANNING TO LABEL THIS A CAUTIONARY TALE, BUT IT'S THE STORY OF MY LIFE, SO HOW COULD I?
MY NAME IS WILLIAM BENJAMIN BRADY. SUFFICE IT TO SAY I WAS BORN UNDER UTTERLY ORDINARY CIRCUMSTANCES ON JULY 4th, 1917 IN A SMALL FARMING TOWN IN THE MIDDLE OF NEBRASKA, BUT THE TWISTS AND TURNS MY LIFE TOOK FROM THERE...
WELL, THAT'S A WHOLE OTHER STORY...
PRESS
PRESS
FREE TOASTER WITH EVERY NEW ACCOUNT
"I WANT TO BE IN PICTURES"
Writer: LEN WEIN
Artist/Letterer: STEVE RUDE
Colorist: Glen Whitmore
VARIANT COVERS BY DARWYN COOKE AND JIM LEE WITH SCOTT WILLIAMS AND ALEX SINCLAIR
ASSISTANT EDITOR: CAMILLA ZHANG
EDITOR: MARK CHIARELLO
WATCHMEN CREATED BY ALAN MOORE AND DAVE GIBBONS
1

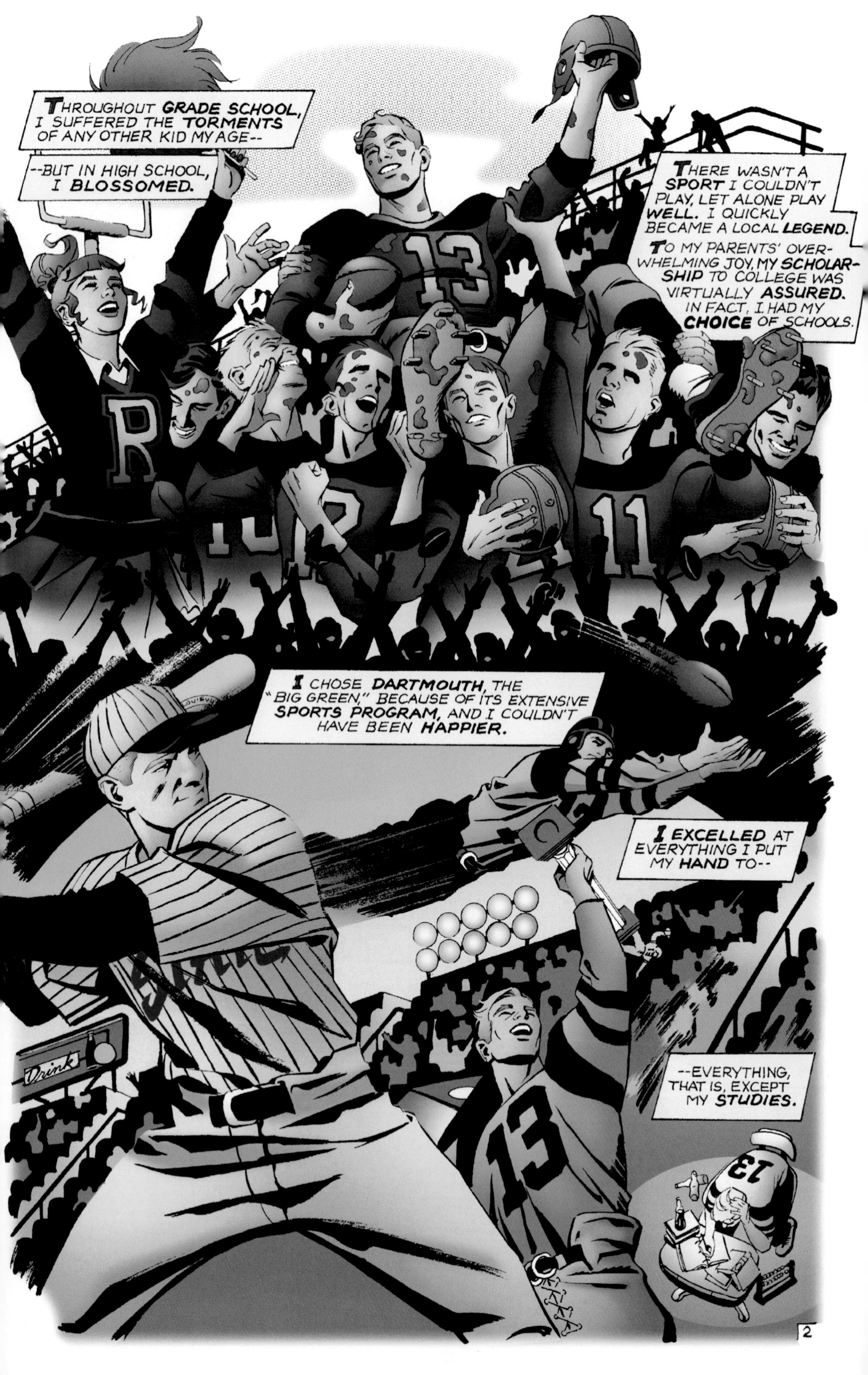
THROUGHOUT GRADE SCHOOL, I SUFFERED THE TORMENTS OF ANY OTHER KID MY AGE--
--BUT IN HIGH SCHOOL, I BLOSSOMED.
THERE WASN'T A SPORT I COULDN'T PLAY, LET ALONE PLAY WELL. I QUICKLY BECAME A LOCAL LEGEND.
TO MY PARENTS' OVERWHELMING JOY, MY SCHOLARSHIP TO COLLEGE WAS VIRTUALLY ASSURED. IN FACT, I HAD MY CHOICE OF SCHOOLS.
I CHOSE DARTMOUTH, THE "BIG GREEN," BECAUSE OF ITS EXTENSIVE SPORTS PROGRAM, AND I COULDN'T HAVE BEEN HAPPIER.
I EXCELLED AT EVERYTHING I PUT MY HAND TO--
--EVERYTHING, THAT IS, EXCEPT MY STUDIES.
Drink

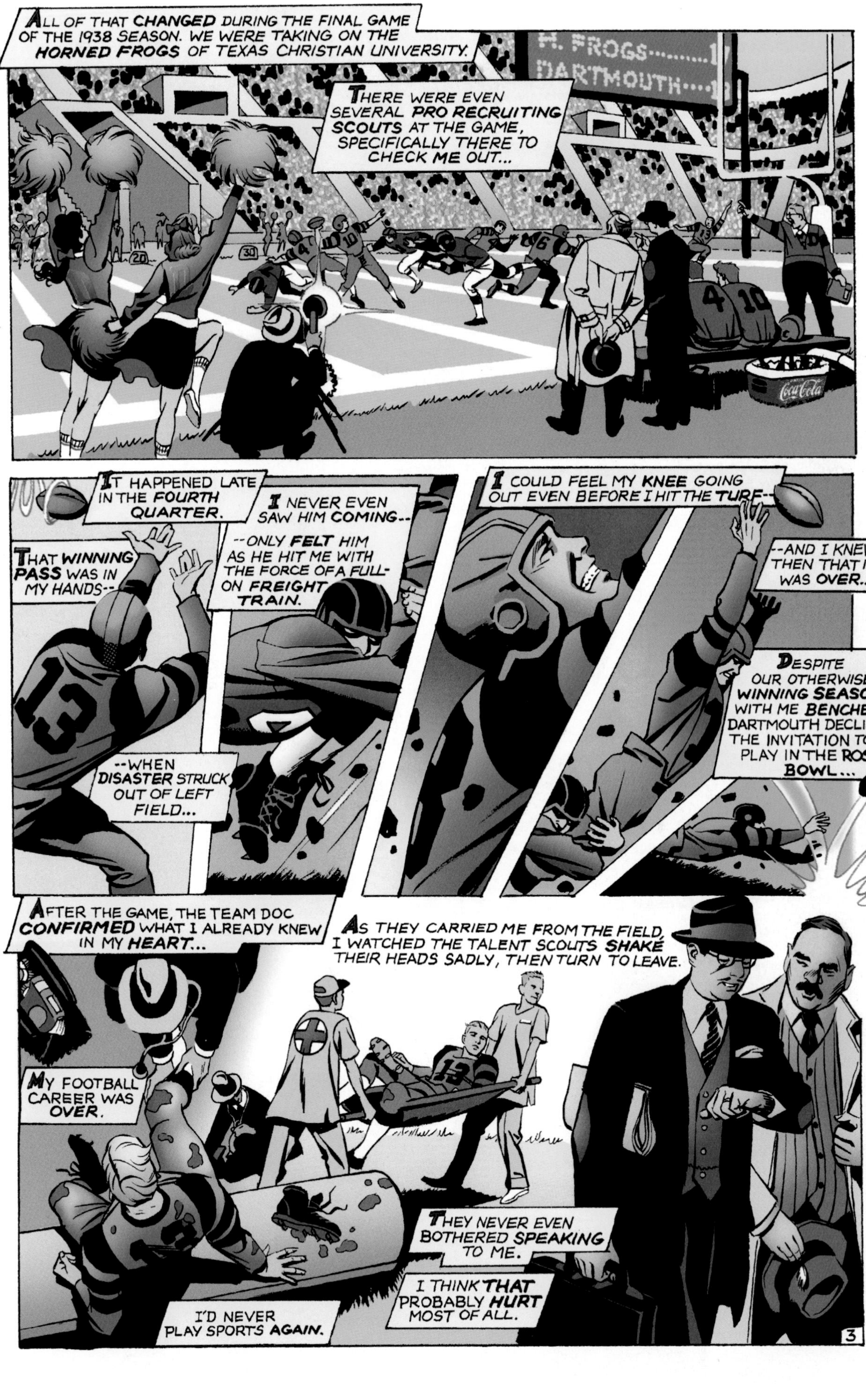

ALL OF THAT CHANGED DURING THE FINAL GAME OF THE 1938 SEASON. WE WERE TAKING ON THE HORNED FROGS OF TEXAS CHRISTIAN UNIVERSITY.
H. FROGS
DARTMOUTH
THERE WERE EVEN SEVERAL PRO RECRUITING SCOUTS AT THE GAME, SPECIFICALLY THERE TO CHECK ME OUT...
Coca-Cola
IT HAPPENED LATE IN THE FOURTH QUARTER.
THAT WINNING PASS WAS IN MY HANDS--
--WHEN DISASTER STRUCK OUT OF LEFT FIELD...
I NEVER EVEN SAW HIM COMING--
--ONLY FELT HIM AS HE HIT ME WITH THE FORCE OF A FULL-ON FREIGHT TRAIN.
I COULD FEEL MY KNEE GOING OUT EVEN BEFORE I HIT THE TURF--
--AND I KNEW THEN THAT IT WAS OVER...
DESPITE OUR OTHERWISE WINNING SEASON, WITH ME BENCHED, DARTMOUTH DECLINED THE INVITATION TO PLAY IN THE ROSE BOWL...
AFTER THE GAME, THE TEAM DOC CONFIRMED WHAT I ALREADY KNEW IN MY HEART...
MY FOOTBALL CAREER WAS OVER.
I'D NEVER PLAY SPORTS AGAIN.
AS THEY CARRIED ME FROM THE FIELD, I WATCHED THE TALENT SCOUTS SHAKE THEIR HEADS SADLY, THEN TURN TO LEAVE.
THEY NEVER EVEN BOTHERED SPEAKING TO ME.
I THINK THAT PROBABLY HURT MOST OF ALL.

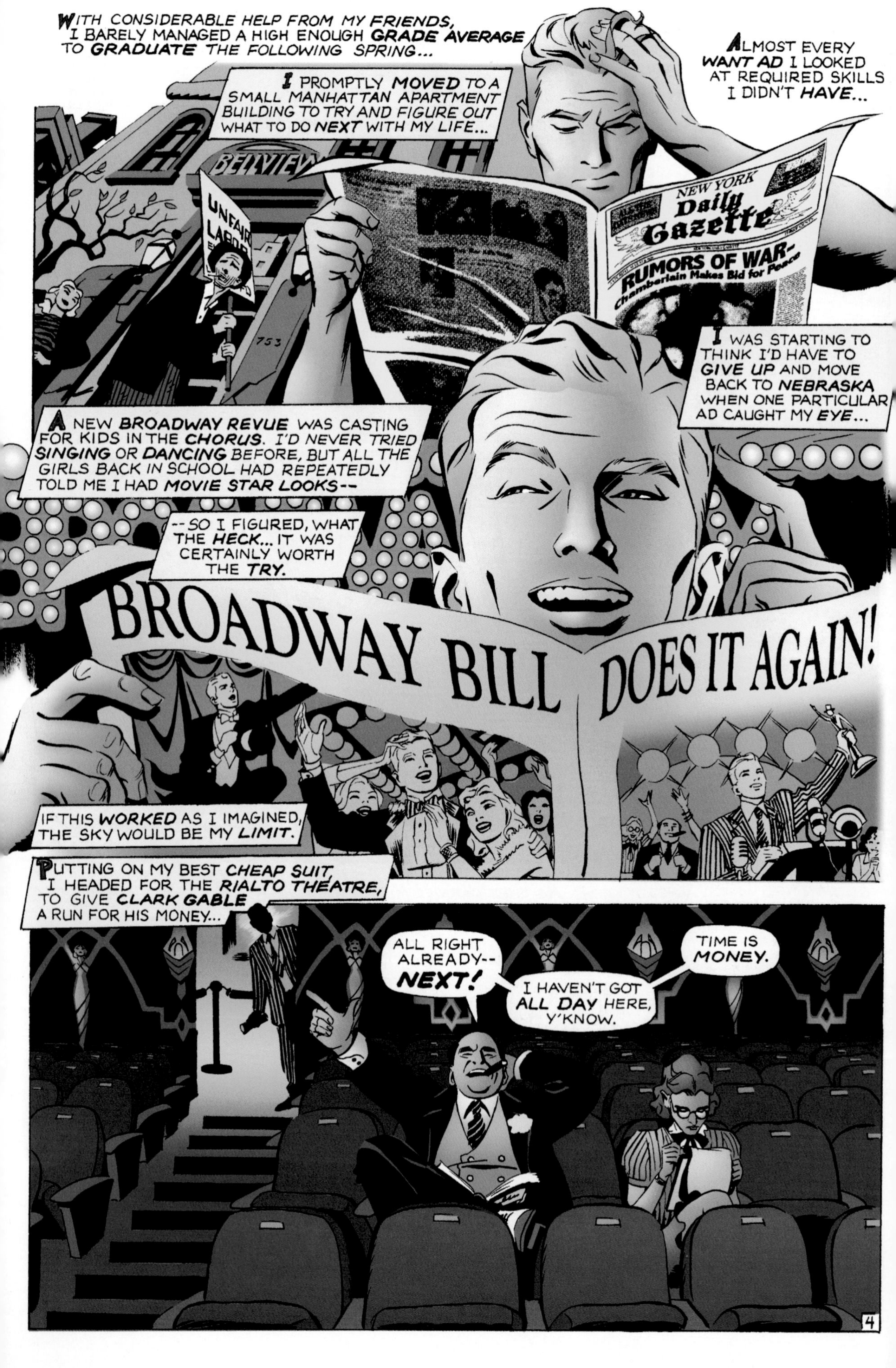
WITH CONSIDERABLE HELP FROM MY FRIENDS, I BARELY MANAGED A HIGH ENOUGH GRADE AVERAGE TO GRADUATE THE FOLLOWING SPRING...
I PROMPTLY MOVED TO A SMALL MANHATTAN APARTMENT BUILDING TO TRY AND FIGURE OUT WHAT TO DO NEXT WITH MY LIFE...
ALMOST EVERY WANT AD I LOOKED AT REQUIRED SKILLS I DIDN'T HAVE...
BELLVIEW
UNFAIR LABOR
NEW YORK Daily Gazette
RUMORS OF WAR-
Chamberlain Makes Bid for Peace
I WAS STARTING TO THINK I'D HAVE TO GIVE UP AND MOVE BACK TO NEBRASKA WHEN ONE PARTICULAR AD CAUGHT MY EYE...
A NEW BROADWAY REVUE WAS CASTING FOR KIDS IN THE CHORUS. I'D NEVER TRIED SINGING OR DANCING BEFORE, BUT ALL THE GIRLS BACK IN SCHOOL HAD REPEATEDLY TOLD ME I HAD MOVIE STAR LOOKS--
--SO I FIGURED, WHAT THE HECK... IT WAS CERTAINLY WORTH THE TRY.
BROADWAY BILL DOES IT AGAIN!
IF THIS WORKED AS I IMAGINED, THE SKY WOULD BE MY LIMIT.
PUTTING ON MY BEST CHEAP SUIT, I HEADED FOR THE RIALTO THEATRE, TO GIVE CLARK GABLE A RUN FOR HIS MONEY...
ALL RIGHT ALREADY-- NEXT!
I HAVEN'T GOT ALL DAY HERE, Y'KNOW.
TIME IS MONEY.

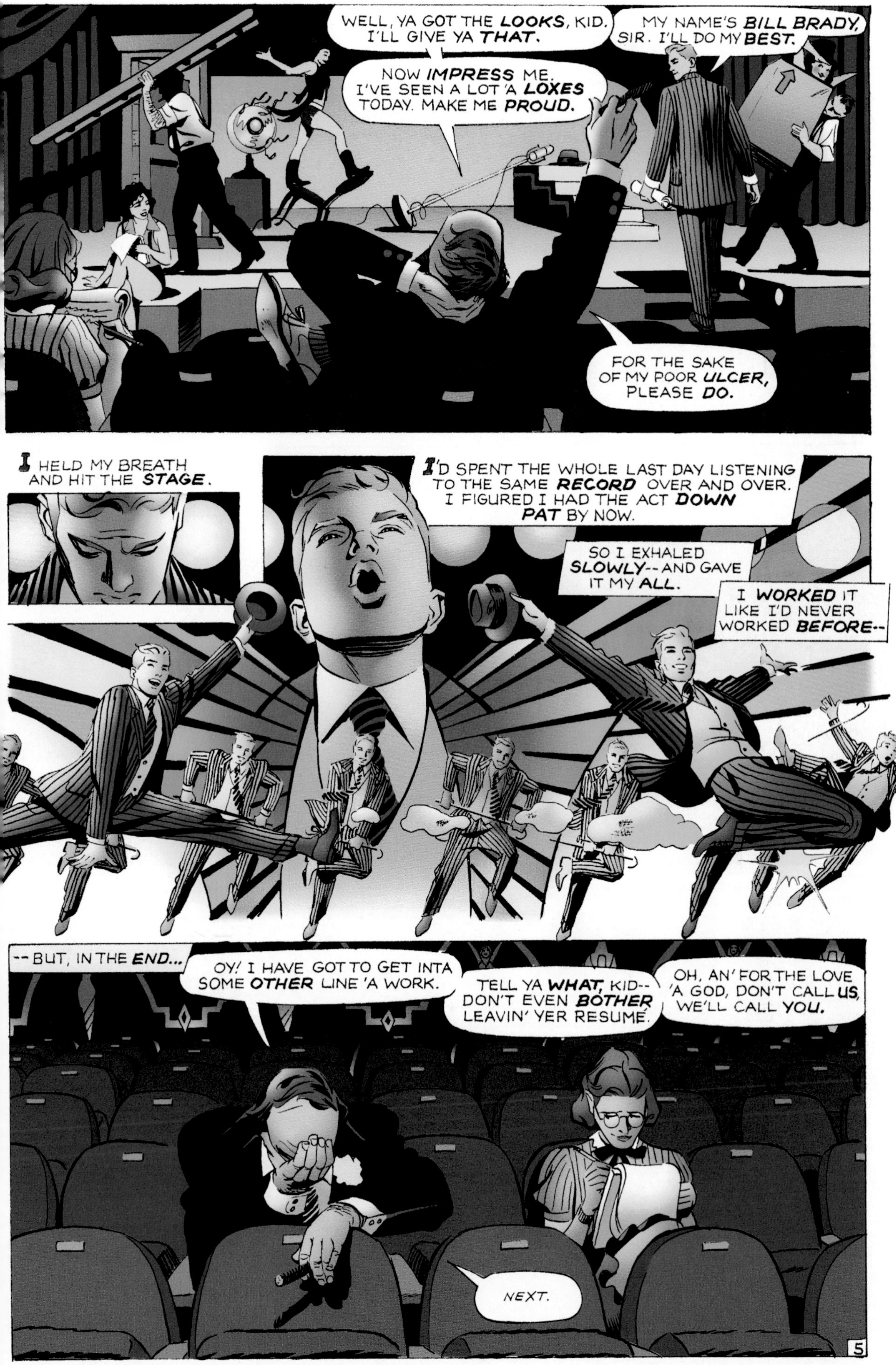
WELL, YA GOT THE LOOKS, KID. I'LL GIVE YA THAT.
NOW IMPRESS ME. I'VE SEEN A LOT 'A LOXES TODAY. MAKE ME PROUD.
MY NAME'S BILL BRADY, SIR. I'LL DO MY BEST.
FOR THE SAKE OF MY POOR ULCER, PLEASE DO.
I HELD MY BREATH AND HIT THE STAGE.
I'D SPENT THE WHOLE LAST DAY LISTENING TO THE SAME RECORD OVER AND OVER. I FIGURED I HAD THE ACT DOWN PAT BY NOW.
SO I EXHALED SLOWLY-- AND GAVE IT MY ALL.
I WORKED IT LIKE I'D NEVER WORKED BEFORE--
-- BUT, IN THE END...
OY! I HAVE GOT TO GET INTA SOME OTHER LINE 'A WORK.
TELL YA WHAT, KID-- DON'T EVEN BOTHER LEAVIN' YER RESUME.
OH, AN' FOR THE LOVE 'A GOD, DON'T CALL US, WE'LL CALL YOU.
NEXT.

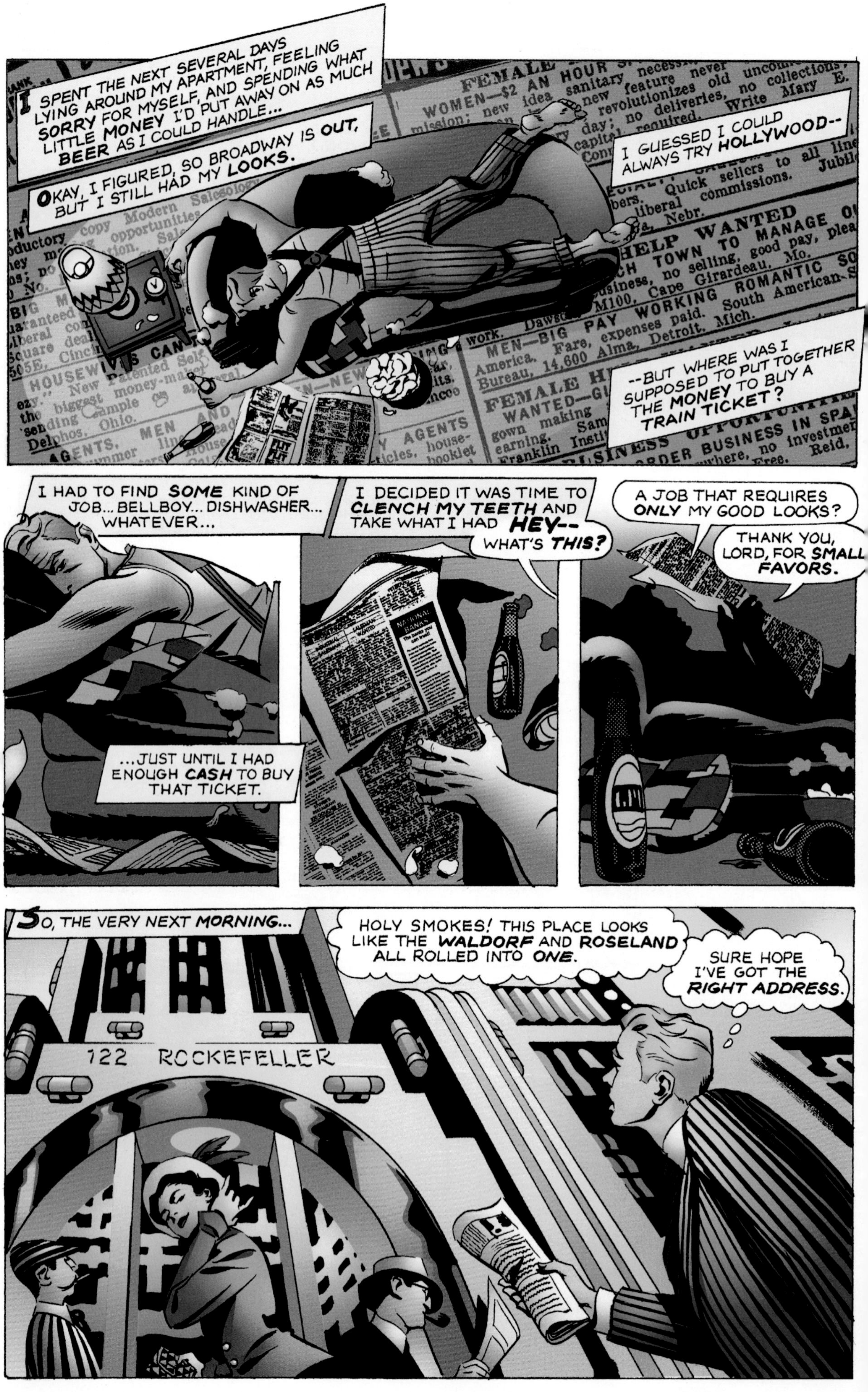
I SPENT THE NEXT SEVERAL DAYS LYING AROUND MY APARTMENT, FEELING SORRY FOR MYSELF, AND SPENDING WHAT LITTLE MONEY I'D PUT AWAY ON AS MUCH BEER AS I COULD HANDLE...
OKAY, I FIGURED, SO BROADWAY IS OUT, BUT I STILL HAD MY LOOKS.
I GUESSED I COULD ALWAYS TRY HOLLYWOOD--
--BUT WHERE WAS I SUPPOSED TO PUT TOGETHER THE MONEY TO BUY A TRAIN TICKET?
I HAD TO FIND SOME KIND OF JOB... BELLBOY... DISHWASHER... WHATEVER...
...JUST UNTIL I HAD ENOUGH CASH TO BUY THAT TICKET.
I DECIDED IT WAS TIME TO CLENCH MY TEETH AND TAKE WHAT I HAD HEY--
WHAT'S THIS?
A JOB THAT REQUIRES ONLY MY GOOD LOOKS?
THANK YOU, LORD, FOR SMALL FAVORS.
SO, THE VERY NEXT MORNING...
HOLY SMOKES! THIS PLACE LOOKS LIKE THE WALDORF AND ROSELAND ALL ROLLED INTO ONE.
SURE HOPE I'VE GOT THE RIGHT ADDRESS.
122 ROCKEFELLER

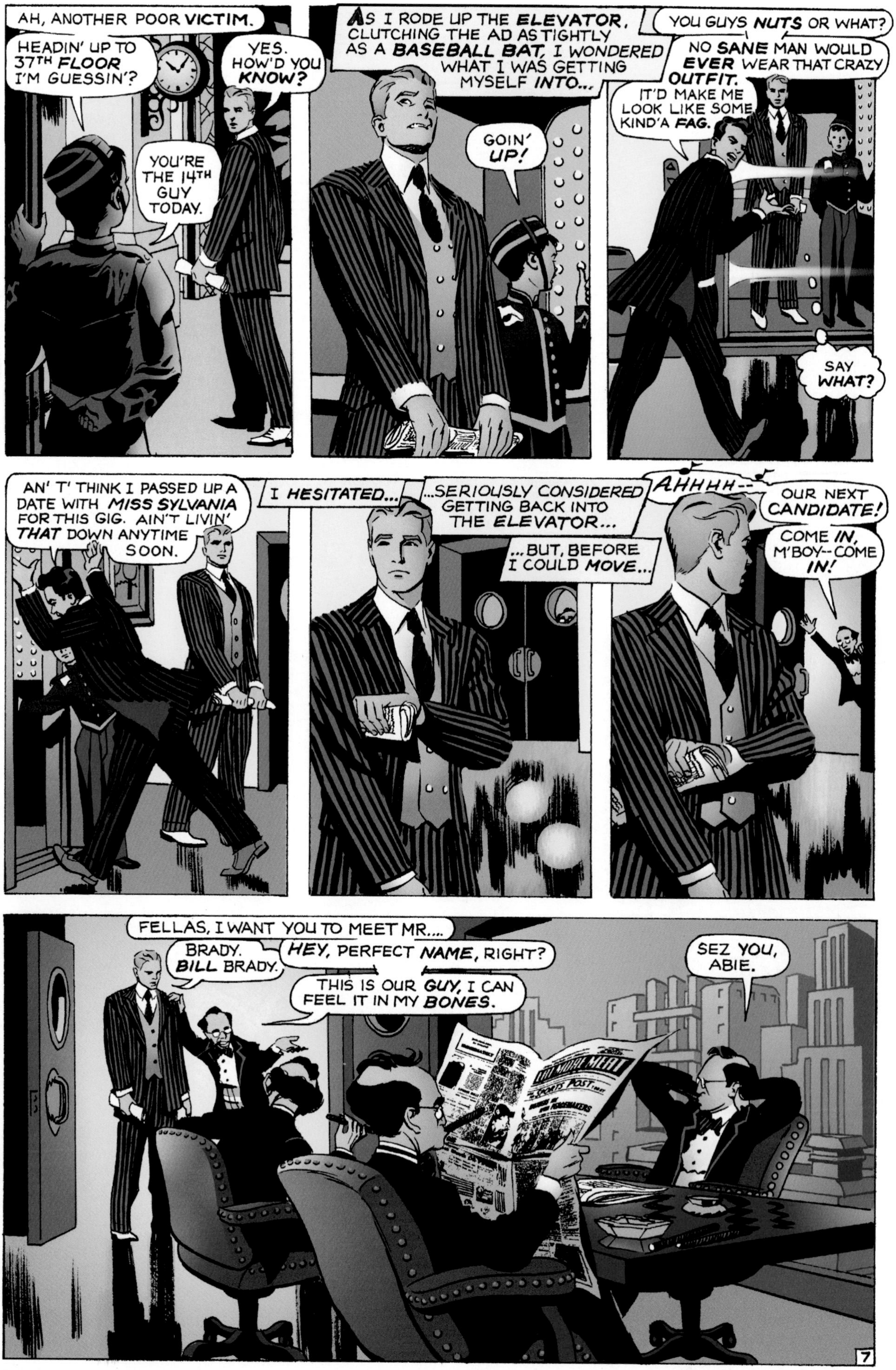
AH, ANOTHER POOR VICTIM.
HEADIN' UP TO 37TH FLOOR I'M GUESSIN'?
YES. HOW'D YOU KNOW?
YOU'RE THE 14TH GUY TODAY.
AS I RODE UP THE ELEVATOR, CLUTCHING THE AD AS TIGHTLY AS A BASEBALL BAT, I WONDERED WHAT I WAS GETTING MYSELF INTO...
GOIN' UP!
YOU GUYS NUTS OR WHAT?
NO SANE MAN WOULD EVER WEAR THAT CRAZY OUTFIT.
IT'D MAKE ME LOOK LIKE SOME KIND'A FAG.
SAY WHAT?
AN' T' THINK I PASSED UP A DATE WITH MISS SYLVANIA FOR THIS GIG. AIN'T LIVIN' THAT DOWN ANYTIME SOON.
I HESITATED...
...SERIOUSLY CONSIDERED GETTING BACK INTO THE ELEVATOR...
...BUT, BEFORE I COULD MOVE...
AHHHH--
OUR NEXT CANDIDATE!
COME IN, M'BOY--COME IN!
FELLAS, I WANT YOU TO MEET MR....
BRADY. BILL BRADY.
HEY, PERFECT NAME, RIGHT?
THIS IS OUR GUY, I CAN FEEL IT IN MY BONES.
SEZ YOU, ABIE.
SPORTS POST

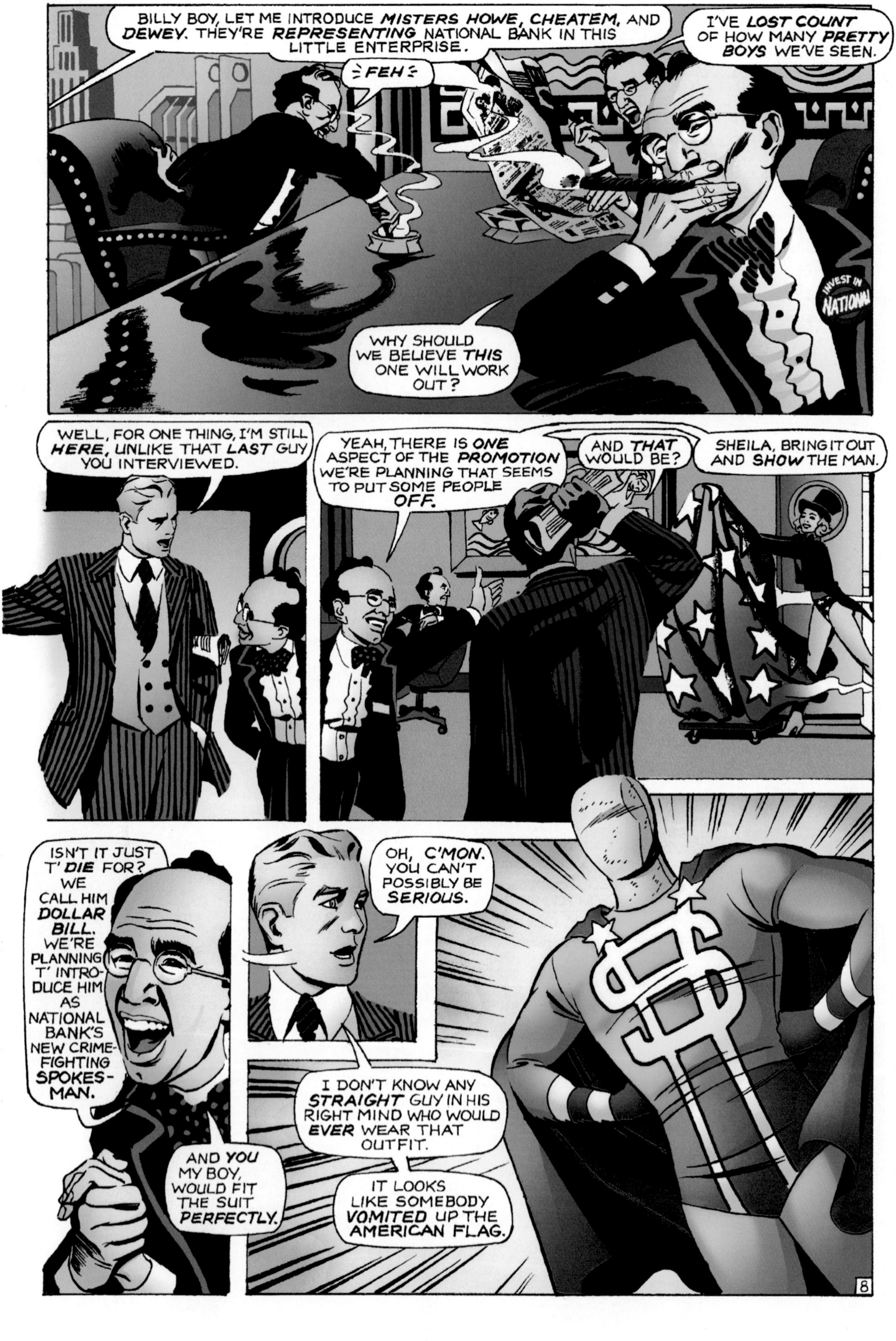
BILLY BOY, LET ME INTRODUCE MISTERS HOWE, CHEATEM, AND DEWEY. THEY'RE REPRESENTING NATIONAL BANK IN THIS LITTLE ENTERPRISE.
FEH
I'VE LOST COUNT OF HOW MANY PRETTY BOYS WE'VE SEEN.
INVEST IN NATIONAL
WHY SHOULD WE BELIEVE THIS ONE WILL WORK OUT?
WELL, FOR ONE THING, I'M STILL HERE, UNLIKE THAT LAST GUY YOU INTERVIEWED.
YEAH, THERE IS ONE ASPECT OF THE PROMOTION WE'RE PLANNING THAT SEEMS TO PUT SOME PEOPLE OFF.
AND THAT WOULD BE?
SHEILA, BRING IT OUT AND SHOW THE MAN.
ISN'T IT JUST T' DIE FOR? WE CALL HIM DOLLAR BILL. WE'RE PLANNING T' INTRODUCE HIM AS NATIONAL BANK'S NEW CRIME-FIGHTING SPOKESMAN.
AND YOU MY BOY, WOULD FIT THE SUIT PERFECTLY.
OH, C'MON. YOU CAN'T POSSIBLY BE SERIOUS.
I DON'T KNOW ANY STRAIGHT GUY IN HIS RIGHT MIND WHO WOULD EVER WEAR THAT OUTFIT.
IT LOOKS LIKE SOMEBODY VOMITED UP THE AMERICAN FLAG.

WE PUT A LOT OF EFFORT INTO *DESIGNING* THAT OUTFIT, SON.

TEST AUDIENCES JUST *LOVE* IT.

WELL, CAN YOU AT LEAST GET RID OF THE *CAPE?* IT'S BOUND TO RESTRICT MY *MOVEMENTS.*

CAPE WAS THE PART THEY LIKED *BEST.*

IT STAYS.

BESIDES, HAVE YOU *SEEN* THE *PAPERS* LATELY?

THERE'S A *COSTUMED VIGILANTE* RUNNING AROUND IN *BARE* ARMS AND LEGS.

AIN'T NOBODY CALLED *HIM* A QUEER.

AND THERE'S *MORE* OF THESE NUTJOBS GOING PUBLIC EVERY *DAY.*

WE'D HAVE TO BE NUTS *OURSELVES* NOT TO *CASH IN* ON THE CRAZE.

SO WHAT EXACTLY IS THE *POINT* OF ALL THIS? I MEAN, WHAT IS IT YOU EXPECT ME TO *DO?*

AS OFFICIAL SPOKESMAN FOR THE *NATIONAL BANK COMPANY,* WE EXPECT YOU TO MAKE DOLLAR BILL AS *FAMILIAR* A NAME AS, SAY, *UNCLE SAM.*

AND YOU WANT ME TO *DO* ALL THIS WITHOUT MAKING AN ABSOLUTE *FOOL* OF MYSELF?

GUESS THAT ALL DEPENDS ON HOW GOOD AN *ACTOR* YOU ARE.

SO, KID, WHADDYA SAY?

*F*OR A MOMENT, I JUST *STOOD* THERE, BITING MY *LIP,* CONSIDERING MY *OPTIONS*--

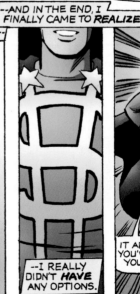

--AND IN THE END, I FINALLY CAME TO *REALIZE*--

--I REALLY DIDN'T *HAVE* ANY OPTIONS.

CONGRATULATIONS, GENTLEMEN...

IT APPEARS YOU'VE FOUND YOUR *MAN.*

SAY HELLO TO *DOLLAR BILL!*

9

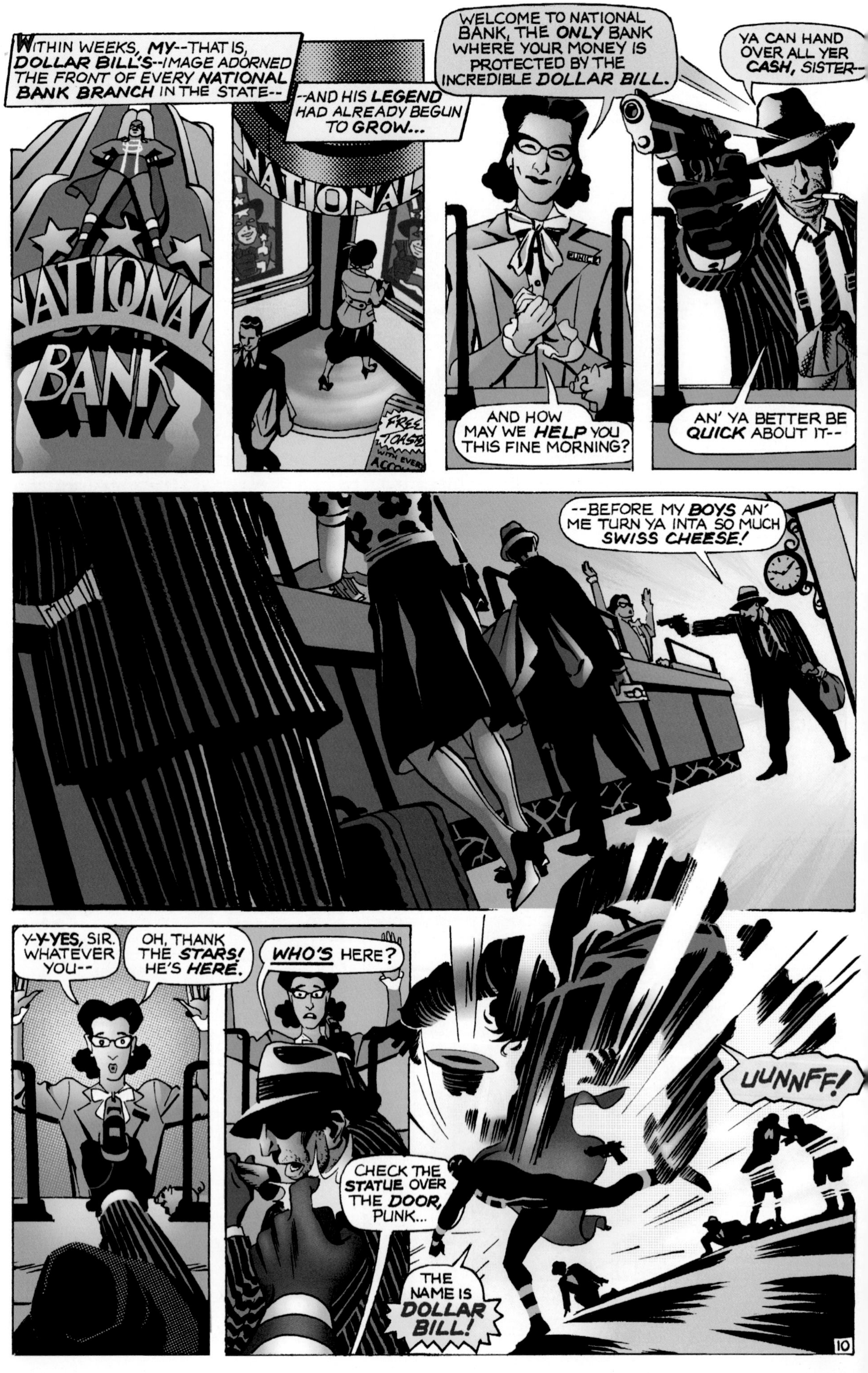
WITHIN WEEKS, MY--THAT IS, DOLLAR BILL'S--IMAGE ADORNED THE FRONT OF EVERY NATIONAL BANK BRANCH IN THE STATE--
NATIONAL BANK
--AND HIS LEGEND HAD ALREADY BEGUN TO GROW...
NATIONAL
FREE TOASTER WITH EVERY
WELCOME TO NATIONAL BANK, THE ONLY BANK WHERE YOUR MONEY IS PROTECTED BY THE INCREDIBLE DOLLAR BILL.
AND HOW MAY WE HELP YOU THIS FINE MORNING?
YA CAN HAND OVER ALL YER CASH, SISTER--
AN' YA BETTER BE QUICK ABOUT IT--
--BEFORE MY BOYS AN' ME TURN YA INTA SO MUCH SWISS CHEESE!
Y-Y-YES, SIR. WHATEVER YOU--
OH, THANK THE STARS! HE'S HERE.
WHO'S HERE?
CHECK THE STATUE OVER THE DOOR, PUNK...
THE NAME IS DOLLAR BILL!
UUNNFF!

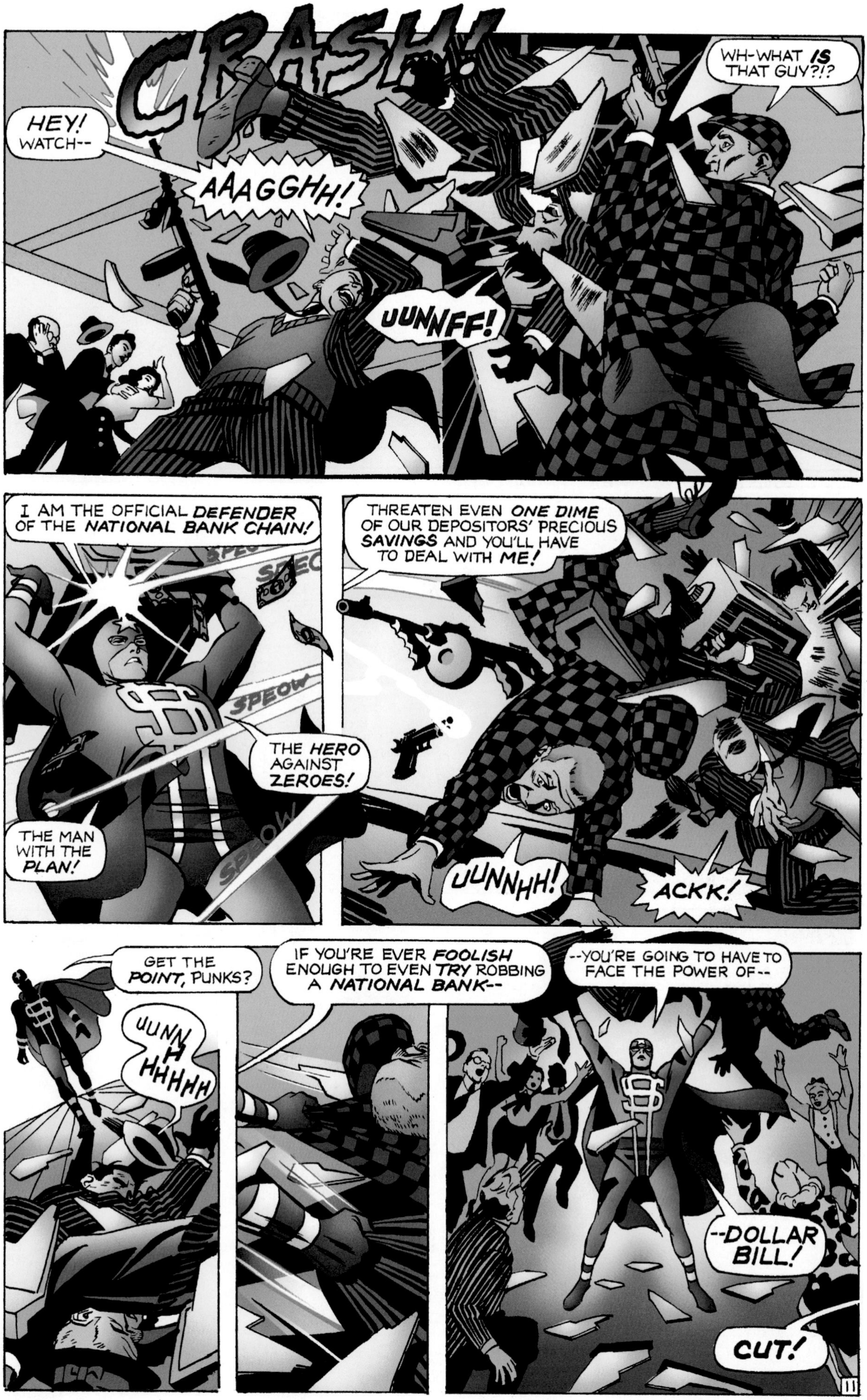
CRASH!
HEY! WATCH--
AAAGGHH!
WH-WHAT IS THAT GUY?!?
UUNNFF!
I AM THE OFFICIAL DEFENDER OF THE NATIONAL BANK CHAIN!
SPEOW
SPEOW
THE HERO AGAINST ZEROES!
THE MAN WITH THE PLAN!
SPEOW
THREATEN EVEN ONE DIME OF OUR DEPOSITORS' PRECIOUS SAVINGS AND YOU'LL HAVE TO DEAL WITH ME!
UUNHH!
ACKK!
GET THE POINT, PUNKS?
UUNN H HHHHH
IF YOU'RE EVER FOOLISH ENOUGH TO EVEN TRY ROBBING A NATIONAL BANK--
--YOU'RE GOING TO HAVE TO FACE THE POWER OF--
--DOLLAR BILL!
CUT!

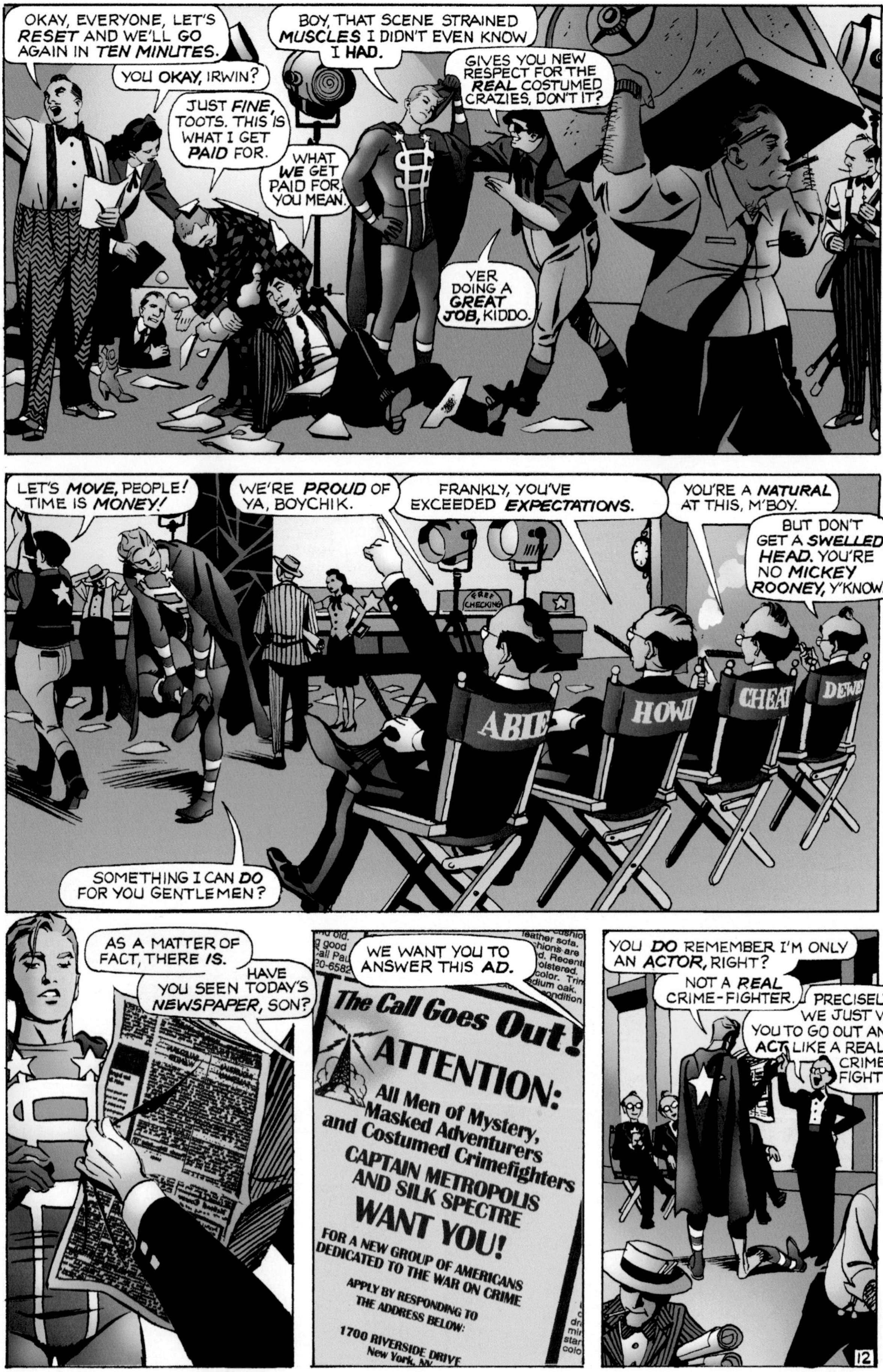
OKAY, EVERYONE, LET'S RESET AND WE'LL GO AGAIN IN TEN MINUTES.
YOU OKAY, IRWIN?
JUST FINE, TOOTS. THIS IS WHAT I GET PAID FOR.
WHAT WE GET PAID FOR, YOU MEAN.
BOY, THAT SCENE STRAINED MUSCLES I DIDN'T EVEN KNOW I HAD.
GIVES YOU NEW RESPECT FOR THE REAL COSTUMED CRAZIES, DON'T IT?
YER DOING A GREAT JOB, KIDDO.
LET'S MOVE, PEOPLE! TIME IS MONEY!
WE'RE PROUD OF YA, BOYCHIK.
FRANKLY, YOU'VE EXCEEDED EXPECTATIONS.
YOU'RE A NATURAL AT THIS, M'BOY.
BUT DON'T GET A SWELLED HEAD. YOU'RE NO MICKEY ROONEY, Y'KNOW.
FREE CHECKING
ABIE
HOWI
CHEAT
DEWE
SOMETHING I CAN DO FOR YOU GENTLEMEN?
AS A MATTER OF FACT, THERE IS.
HAVE YOU SEEN TODAY'S NEWSPAPER, SON?
WE WANT YOU TO ANSWER THIS AD.
The Call Goes Out!
ATTENTION:
All Men of Mystery, Masked Adventurers and Costumed Crimefighters
CAPTAIN METROPOLIS AND SILK SPECTRE
WANT YOU!
FOR A NEW GROUP OF AMERICANS DEDICATED TO THE WAR ON CRIME
APPLY BY RESPONDING TO THE ADDRESS BELOW:
1700 RIVERSIDE DRIVE
New York, NY
YOU DO REMEMBER I'M ONLY AN ACTOR, RIGHT?
NOT A REAL CRIME-FIGHTER.
PRECISELY. WE JUST WA YOU TO GO OUT AND ACT LIKE A REAL CRIME-FIGHTER
12

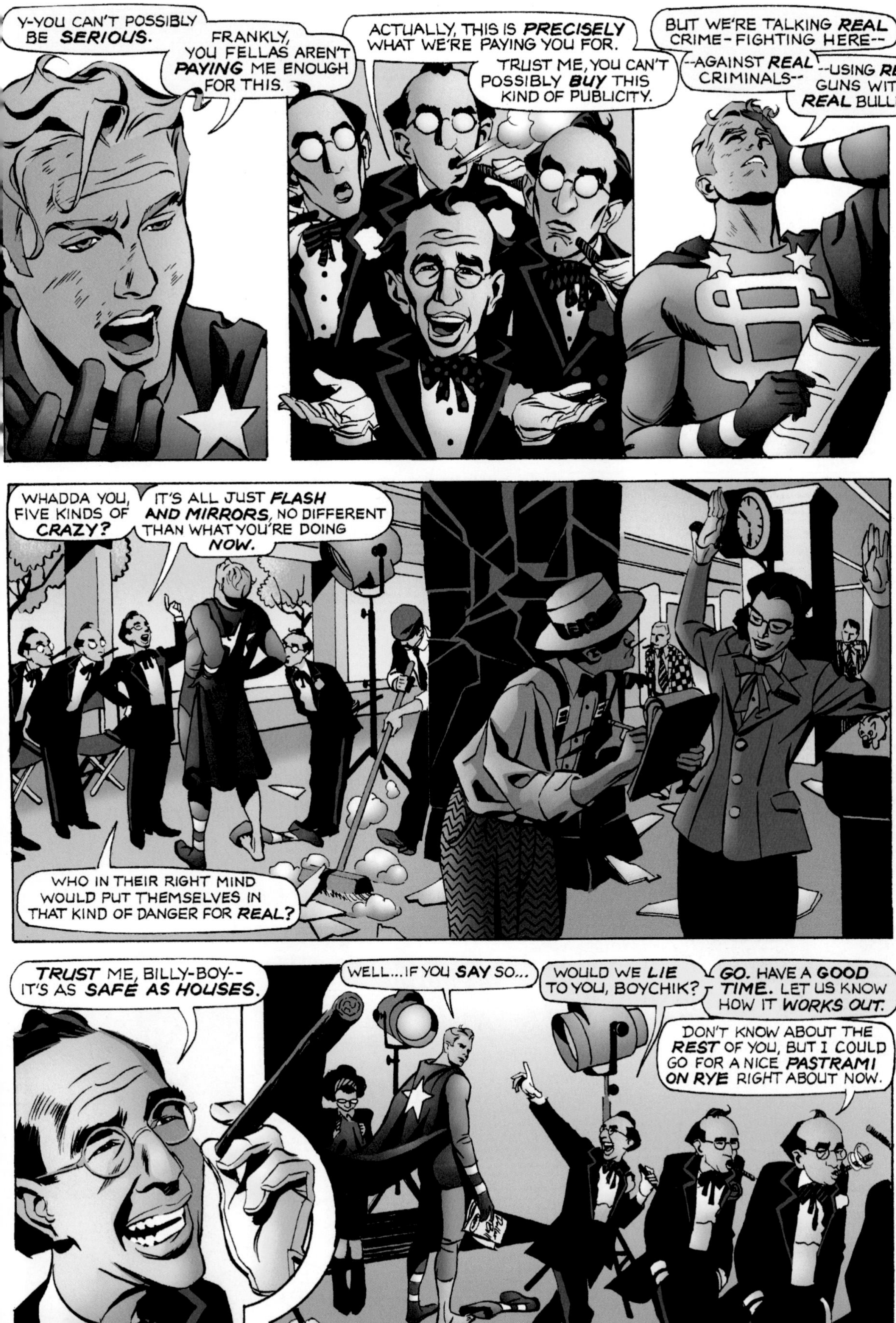
Y-YOU CAN'T POSSIBLY BE SERIOUS.
FRANKLY, YOU FELLAS AREN'T PAYING ME ENOUGH FOR THIS.
ACTUALLY, THIS IS PRECISELY WHAT WE'RE PAYING YOU FOR.
TRUST ME, YOU CAN'T POSSIBLY BUY THIS KIND OF PUBLICITY.
BUT WE'RE TALKING REAL CRIME-FIGHTING HERE--
--AGAINST REAL CRIMINALS--
--USING REAL GUNS WITH REAL BULLETS.
WHADDA YOU, FIVE KINDS OF CRAZY?
IT'S ALL JUST FLASH AND MIRRORS, NO DIFFERENT THAN WHAT YOU'RE DOING NOW.
WHO IN THEIR RIGHT MIND WOULD PUT THEMSELVES IN THAT KIND OF DANGER FOR REAL?
TRUST ME, BILLY-BOY-- IT'S AS SAFE AS HOUSES.
WELL... IF YOU SAY SO...
WOULD WE LIE TO YOU, BOYCHIK?
GO. HAVE A GOOD TIME. LET US KNOW HOW IT WORKS OUT.
DON'T KNOW ABOUT THE REST OF YOU, BUT I COULD GO FOR A NICE PASTRAMI ON RYE RIGHT ABOUT NOW.
13

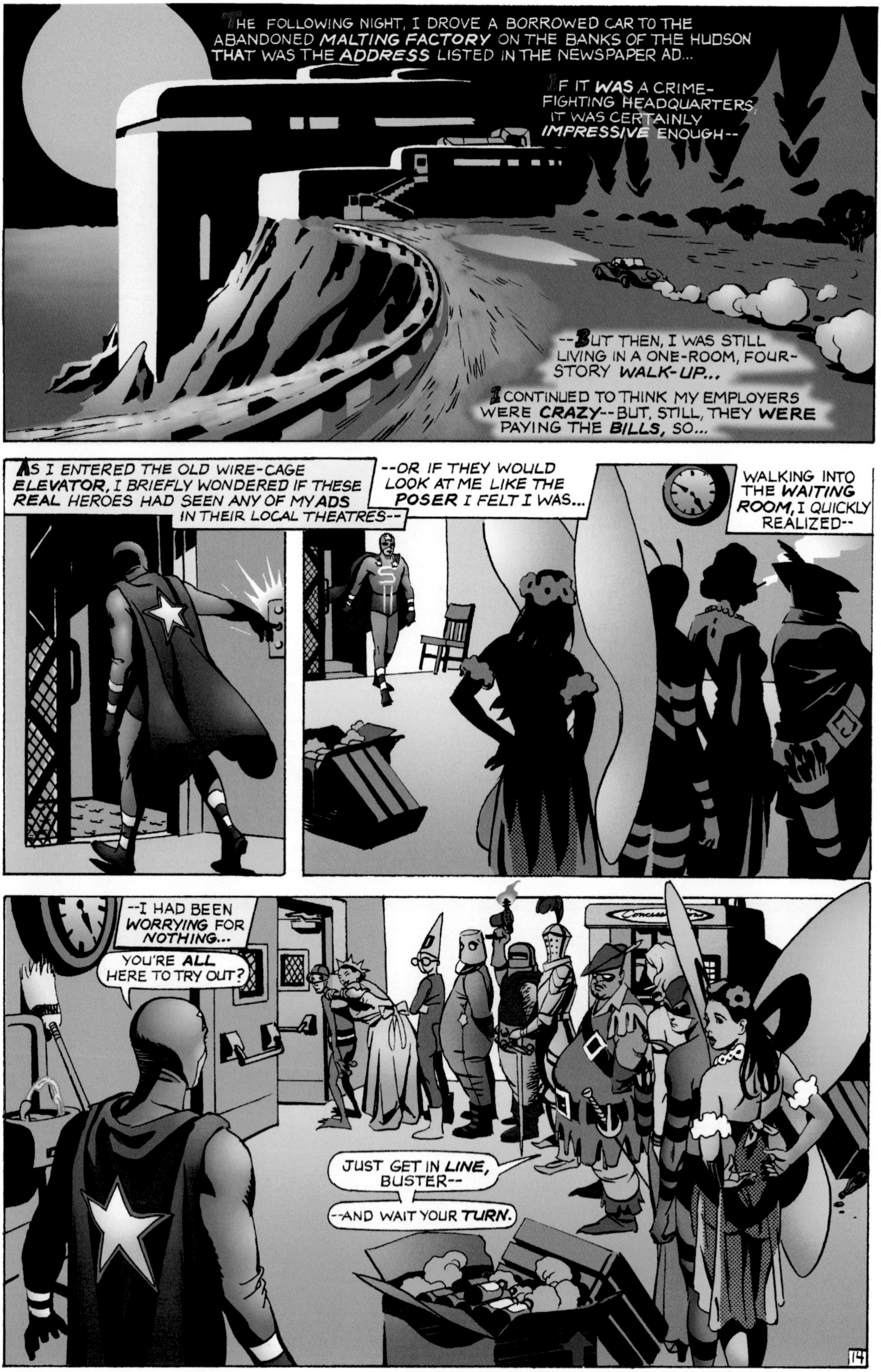
THE FOLLOWING NIGHT, I DROVE A BORROWED CAR TO THE ABANDONED MALTING FACTORY ON THE BANKS OF THE HUDSON THAT WAS THE ADDRESS LISTED IN THE NEWSPAPER AD...
IF IT WAS A CRIME-FIGHTING HEADQUARTERS, IT WAS CERTAINLY IMPRESSIVE ENOUGH--
--BUT THEN, I WAS STILL LIVING IN A ONE-ROOM, FOUR-STORY WALK-UP...
I CONTINUED TO THINK MY EMPLOYERS WERE CRAZY--BUT, STILL, THEY WERE PAYING THE BILLS, SO...
AS I ENTERED THE OLD WIRE-CAGE ELEVATOR, I BRIEFLY WONDERED IF THESE REAL HEROES HAD SEEN ANY OF MY ADS IN THEIR LOCAL THEATRES--
--OR IF THEY WOULD LOOK AT ME LIKE THE POSER I FELT I WAS...
WALKING INTO THE WAITING ROOM, I QUICKLY REALIZED--
--I HAD BEEN WORRYING FOR NOTHING...
YOU'RE ALL HERE TO TRY OUT?
JUST GET IN LINE, BUSTER--
--AND WAIT YOUR TURN.
14

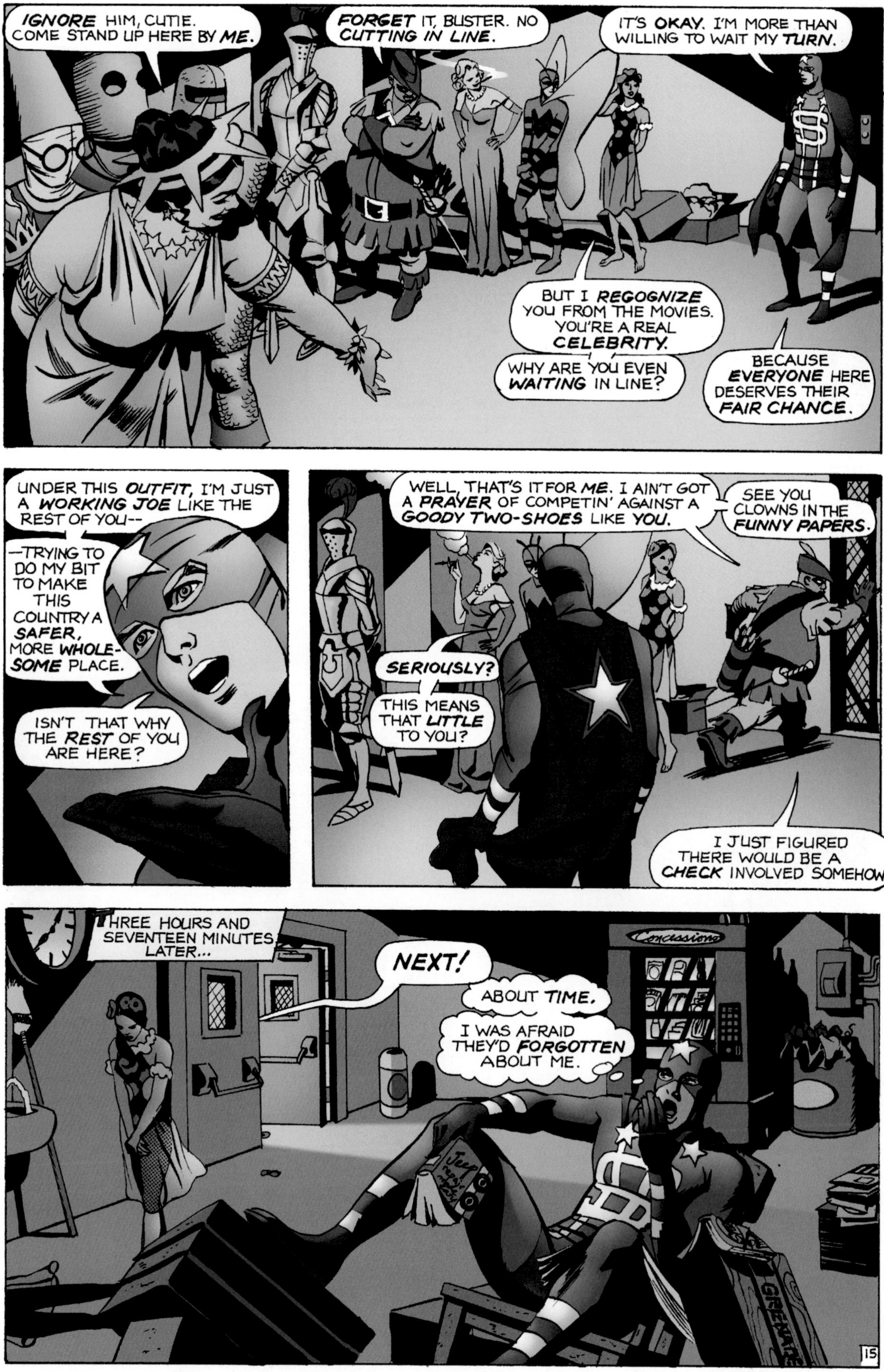
IGNORE HIM, CUTIE. COME STAND UP HERE BY ME.
FORGET IT, BUSTER. NO CUTTING IN LINE.
IT'S OKAY. I'M MORE THAN WILLING TO WAIT MY TURN.
BUT I REGOGNIZE YOU FROM THE MOVIES. YOU'RE A REAL CELEBRITY.
WHY ARE YOU EVEN WAITING IN LINE?
BECAUSE EVERYONE HERE DESERVES THEIR FAIR CHANCE.
UNDER THIS OUTFIT, I'M JUST A WORKING JOE LIKE THE REST OF YOU--
--TRYING TO DO MY BIT TO MAKE THIS COUNTRY A SAFER, MORE WHOLESOME PLACE.
ISN'T THAT WHY THE REST OF YOU ARE HERE?
WELL, THAT'S IT FOR ME. I AIN'T GOT A PRAYER OF COMPETIN' AGAINST A GOODY TWO-SHOES LIKE YOU.
SEE YOU CLOWNS IN THE FUNNY PAPERS.
SERIOUSLY?
THIS MEANS THAT LITTLE TO YOU?
I JUST FIGURED THERE WOULD BE A CHECK INVOLVED SOMEHOW.
THREE HOURS AND SEVENTEEN MINUTES LATER...
Concessions
NEXT!
ABOUT TIME.
I WAS AFRAID THEY'D FORGOTTEN ABOUT ME.

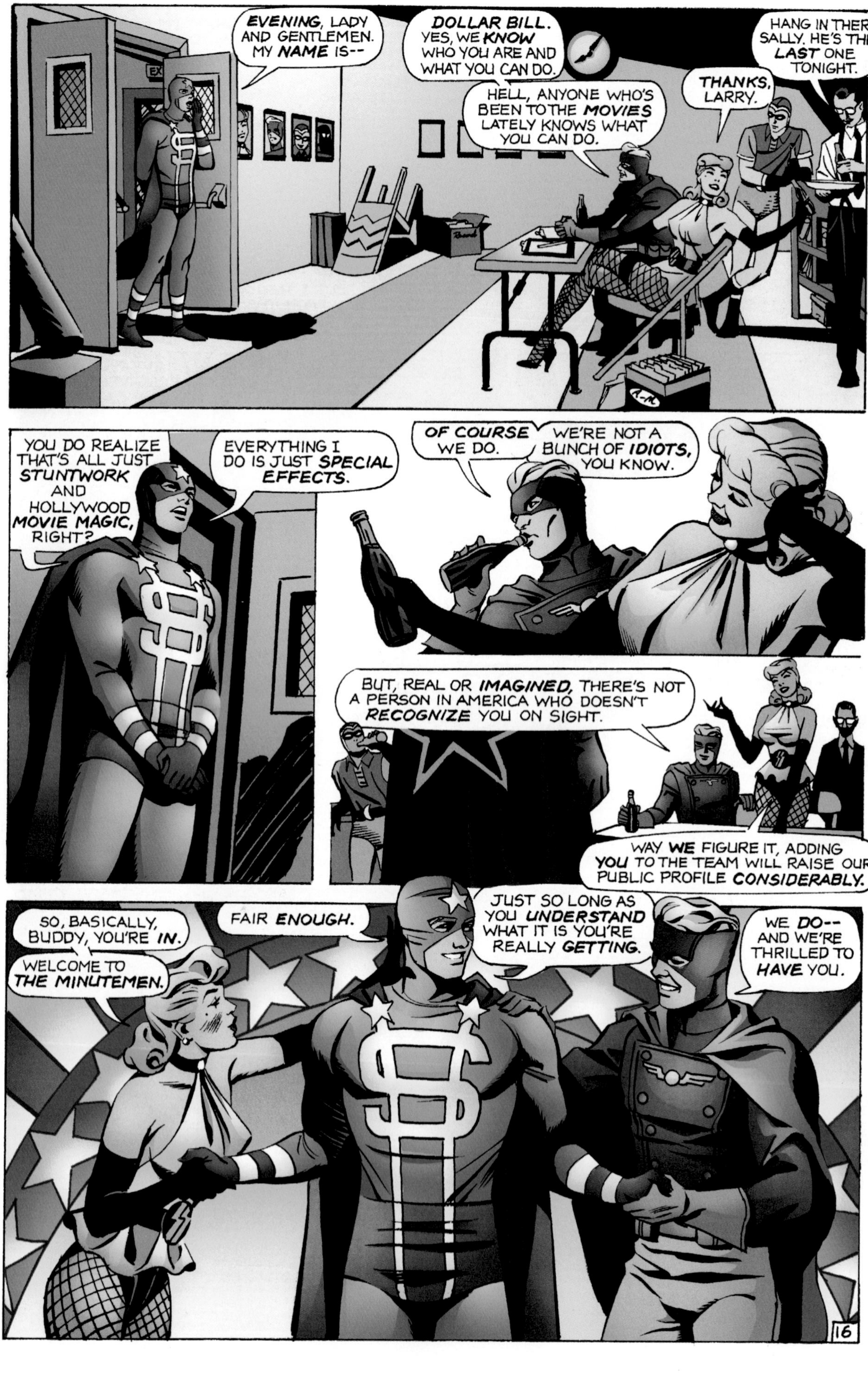
EVENING, LADY AND GENTLEMEN. MY NAME IS--
DOLLAR BILL. YES, WE KNOW WHO YOU ARE AND WHAT YOU CAN DO.
HELL, ANYONE WHO'S BEEN TO THE MOVIES LATELY KNOWS WHAT YOU CAN DO.
HANG IN THERE, SALLY. HE'S THE LAST ONE TONIGHT.
THANKS, LARRY.
YOU DO REALIZE THAT'S ALL JUST STUNTWORK AND HOLLYWOOD MOVIE MAGIC, RIGHT?
EVERYTHING I DO IS JUST SPECIAL EFFECTS.
OF COURSE WE DO.
WE'RE NOT A BUNCH OF IDIOTS, YOU KNOW.
BUT, REAL OR IMAGINED, THERE'S NOT A PERSON IN AMERICA WHO DOESN'T RECOGNIZE YOU ON SIGHT.
WAY WE FIGURE IT, ADDING YOU TO THE TEAM WILL RAISE OUR PUBLIC PROFILE CONSIDERABLY.
SO, BASICALLY, BUDDY, YOU'RE IN.
WELCOME TO THE MINUTEMEN.
FAIR ENOUGH.
JUST SO LONG AS YOU UNDERSTAND WHAT IT IS YOU'RE REALLY GETTING.
WE DO-- AND WE'RE THRILLED TO HAVE YOU.

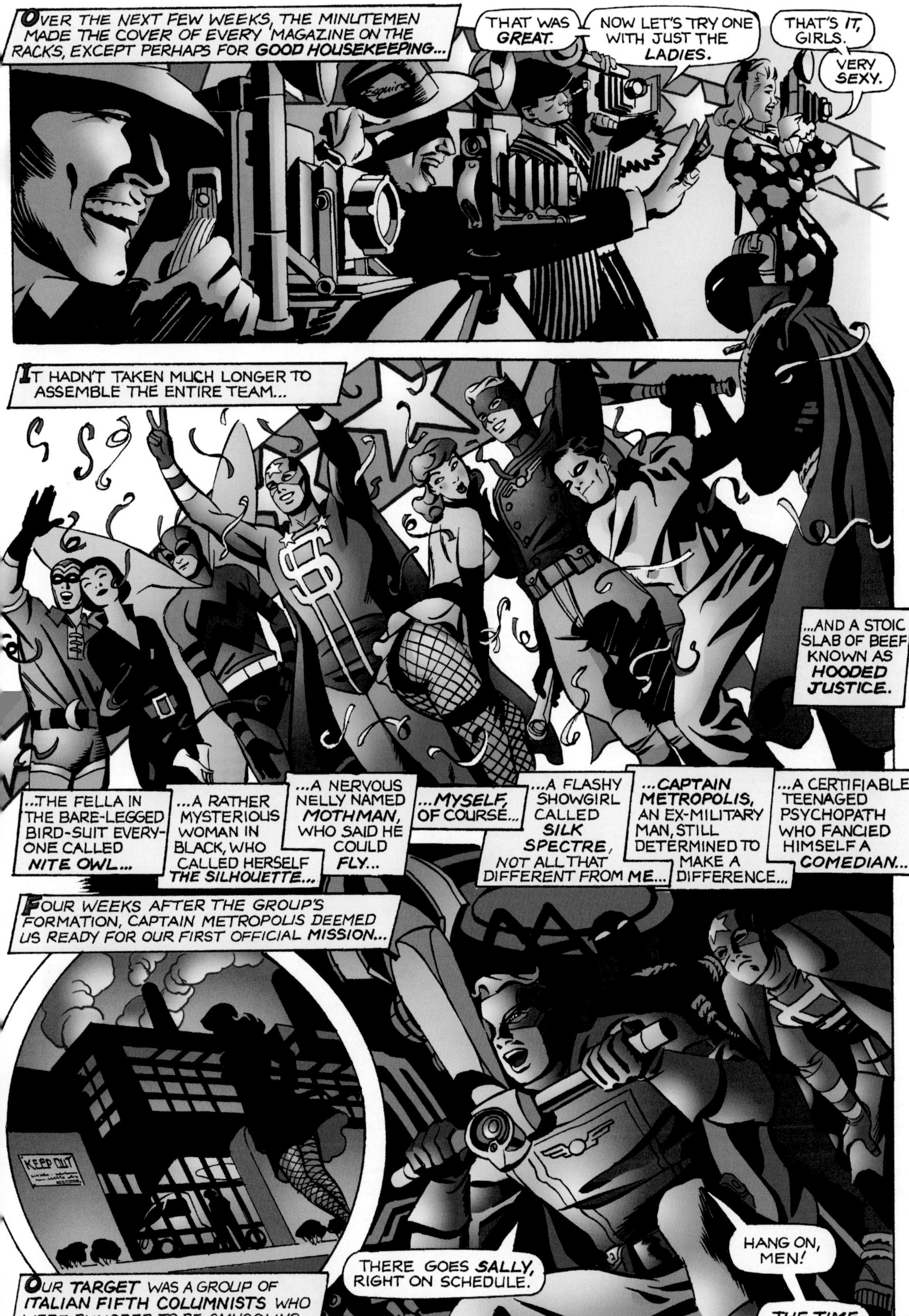
OVER THE NEXT FEW WEEKS, THE MINUTEMEN MADE THE COVER OF EVERY MAGAZINE ON THE RACKS, EXCEPT PERHAPS FOR GOOD HOUSEKEEPING...
THAT WAS GREAT.
NOW LET'S TRY ONE WITH JUST THE LADIES.
THAT'S IT, GIRLS.
VERY SEXY.
IT HADN'T TAKEN MUCH LONGER TO ASSEMBLE THE ENTIRE TEAM...
...AND A STOIC SLAB OF BEEF KNOWN AS HOODED JUSTICE.
...THE FELLA IN THE BARE-LEGGED BIRD-SUIT EVERY-ONE CALLED NITE OWL...
...A RATHER MYSTERIOUS WOMAN IN BLACK, WHO CALLED HERSELF THE SILHOUETTE...
...A NERVOUS NELLY NAMED MOTHMAN, WHO SAID HE COULD FLY...
...MYSELF, OF COURSE...
...A FLASHY SHOWGIRL CALLED SILK SPECTRE, NOT ALL THAT DIFFERENT FROM ME...
...CAPTAIN METROPOLIS, AN EX-MILITARY MAN, STILL DETERMINED TO MAKE A DIFFERENCE...
...A CERTIFIABLE TEENAGED PSYCHOPATH WHO FANCIED HIMSELF A COMEDIAN...
FOUR WEEKS AFTER THE GROUP'S FORMATION, CAPTAIN METROPOLIS DEEMED US READY FOR OUR FIRST OFFICIAL MISSION...
KEEP OUT
OUR TARGET WAS A GROUP OF ITALIAN FIFTH COLUMNISTS WHO WERE RUMORED TO BE SMUGGLING WEAPONS INTO NEW YORK HARBOR...
THERE GOES SALLY, RIGHT ON SCHEDULE.
HANG ON, MEN!
THE TIME IS NIGH!

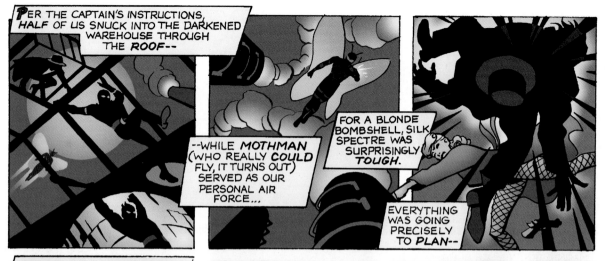

PER THE CAPTAIN'S INSTRUCTIONS, *HALF* OF US SNUCK INTO THE DARKENED WAREHOUSE THROUGH THE *ROOF*--

--WHILE *MOTHMAN* (WHO REALLY *COULD* FLY, IT TURNS OUT) SERVED AS OUR PERSONAL AIR FORCE...

FOR A BLONDE BOMBSHELL, SILK SPECTRE WAS SURPRISINGLY *TOUGH*.

EVERYTHING WAS GOING PRECISELY TO *PLAN*--

--WITH ONE SMALL *EXCEPTION:*

SPUK

UNFORTUNATELY, CAPTAIN METROPOLIS HAD FAILED TO *VERIFY* HIS INFORMATION.

WHAT THE GOOD CAPTAIN HAD *ASSUMED* TO BE A WAREHOUSE FULL OF *MUNITIONS*--

SPOK

SPUK

--WAS *INSTEAD* A WAREHOUSE FILLED WITH ILLEGAL *FIREWORKS*--

POK

KLUK

PUK

FLAMMABLE

--WHICH DID NOT RESPOND *WELL* TO A SPARKING *SMOKE GRENADE* DROPPED IN AMONG THEM.

NOT *VERY* WELL AT ALL.

18

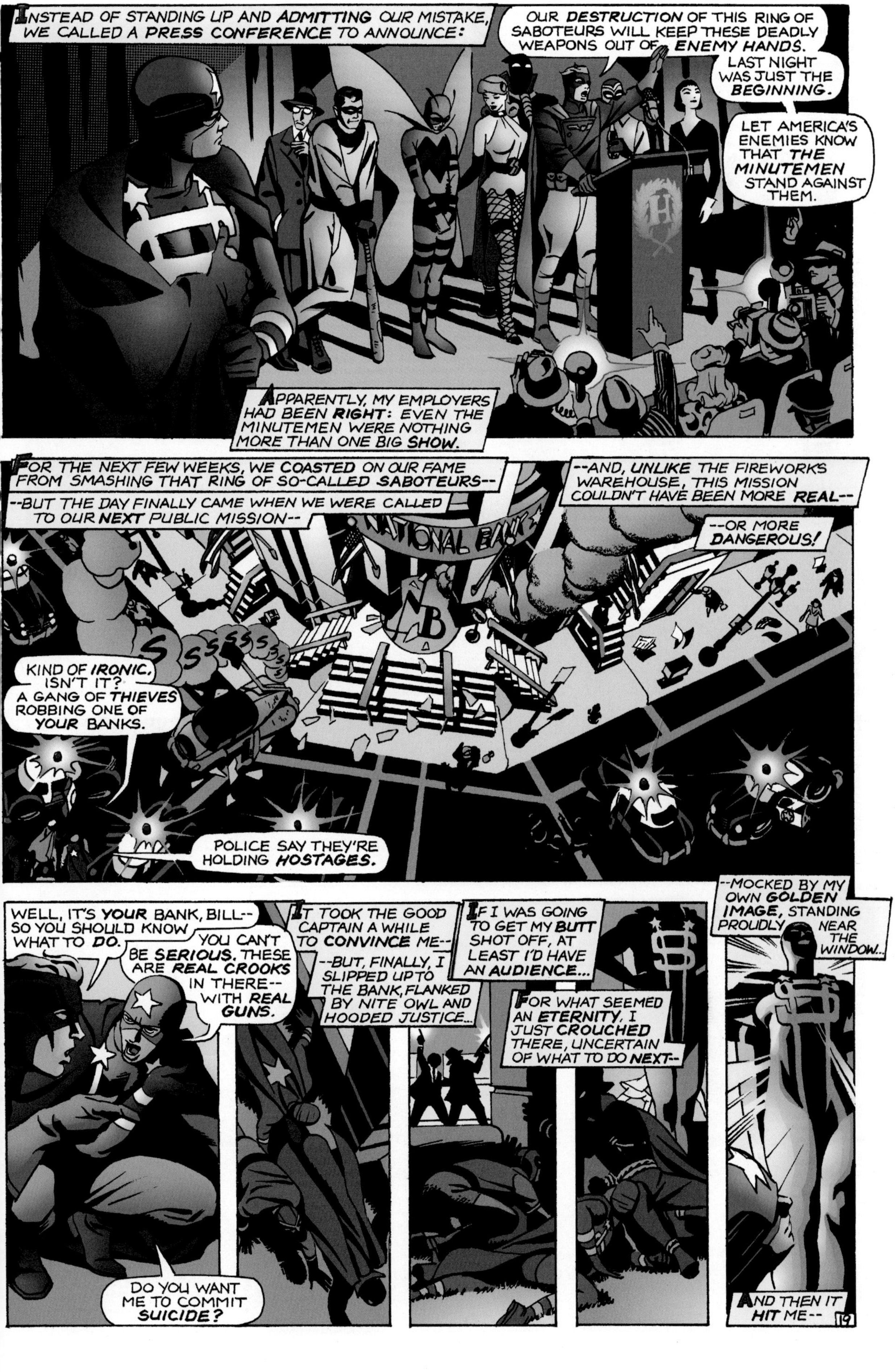
INSTEAD OF STANDING UP AND ADMITTING OUR MISTAKE, WE CALLED A PRESS CONFERENCE TO ANNOUNCE:
OUR DESTRUCTION OF THIS RING OF SABOTEURS WILL KEEP THESE DEADLY WEAPONS OUT OF ENEMY HANDS.
LAST NIGHT WAS JUST THE BEGINNING.
LET AMERICA'S ENEMIES KNOW THAT THE MINUTEMEN STAND AGAINST THEM.
APPARENTLY, MY EMPLOYERS HAD BEEN RIGHT: EVEN THE MINUTEMEN WERE NOTHING MORE THAN ONE BIG SHOW.
FOR THE NEXT FEW WEEKS, WE COASTED ON OUR FAME FROM SMASHING THAT RING OF SO-CALLED SABOTEURS--
--BUT THE DAY FINALLY CAME WHEN WE WERE CALLED TO OUR NEXT PUBLIC MISSION--
--AND, UNLIKE THE FIREWORKS WAREHOUSE, THIS MISSION COULDN'T HAVE BEEN MORE REAL--
--OR MORE DANGEROUS!
NATIONAL BANK
SSSSSSSS
KIND OF IRONIC, ISN'T IT? A GANG OF THIEVES ROBBING ONE OF YOUR BANKS.
POLICE SAY THEY'RE HOLDING HOSTAGES.
WELL, IT'S YOUR BANK, BILL-- SO YOU SHOULD KNOW WHAT TO DO.
YOU CAN'T BE SERIOUS. THESE ARE REAL CROOKS IN THERE-- WITH REAL GUNS.
DO YOU WANT ME TO COMMIT SUICIDE?
IT TOOK THE GOOD CAPTAIN A WHILE TO CONVINCE ME--
--BUT, FINALLY, I SLIPPED UP TO THE BANK, FLANKED BY NITE OWL AND HOODED JUSTICE...
IF I WAS GOING TO GET MY BUTT SHOT OFF, AT LEAST I'D HAVE AN AUDIENCE...
FOR WHAT SEEMED AN ETERNITY, I JUST CROUCHED THERE, UNCERTAIN OF WHAT TO DO NEXT--
--MOCKED BY MY OWN GOLDEN IMAGE, STANDING PROUDLY NEAR THE WINDOW...
AND THEN IT HIT ME--

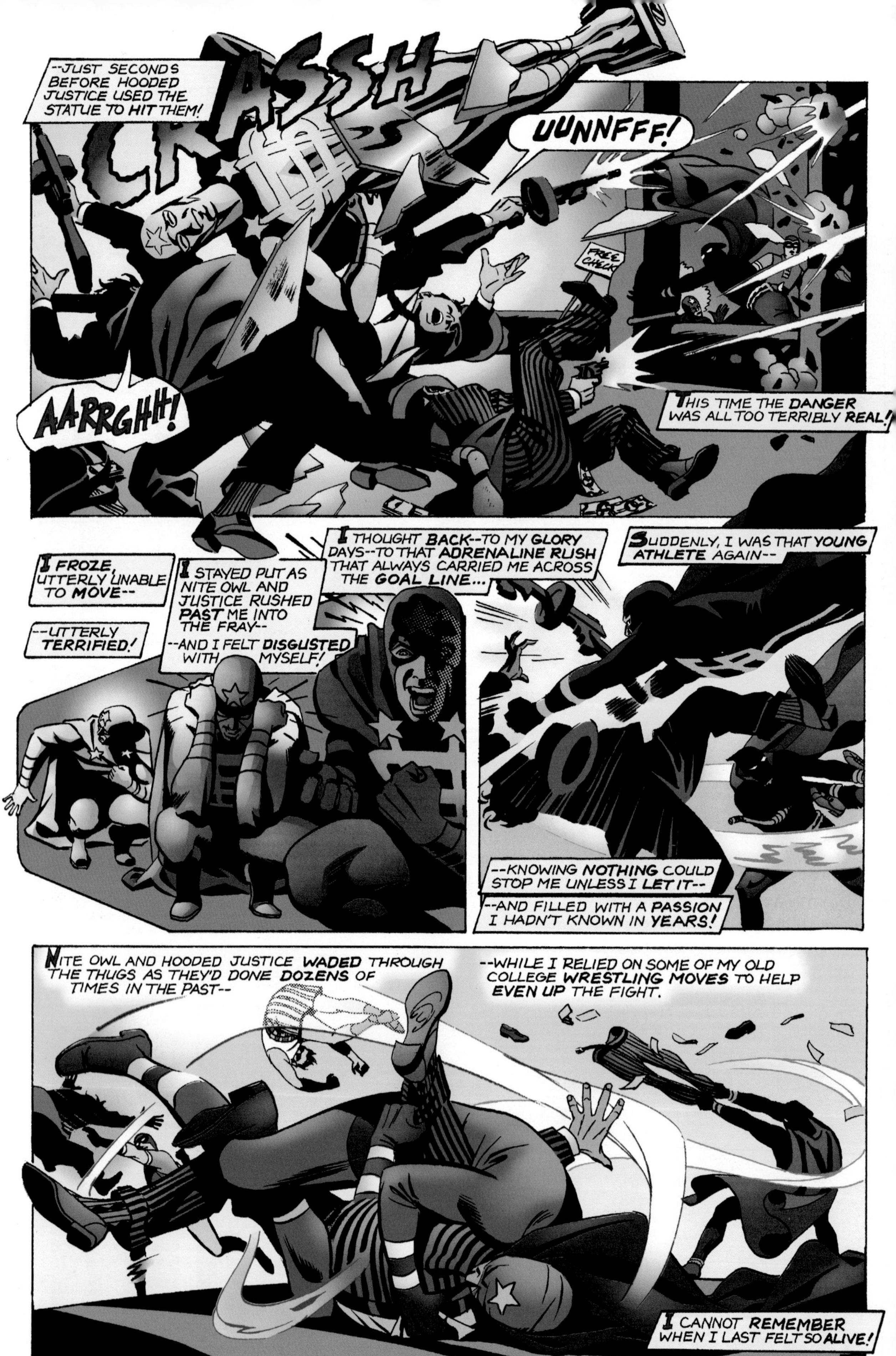

--JUST SECONDS BEFORE HOODED JUSTICE USED THE STATUE TO HIT THEM!
CRASSH
UUNNFFF!
AARRGHH!
THIS TIME THE DANGER WAS ALL TOO TERRIBLY REAL!
I FROZE, UTTERLY UNABLE TO MOVE--
--UTTERLY TERRIFIED!
I STAYED PUT AS NITE OWL AND JUSTICE RUSHED PAST ME INTO THE FRAY--
--AND I FELT DISGUSTED WITH MYSELF!
I THOUGHT BACK--TO MY GLORY DAYS--TO THAT ADRENALINE RUSH THAT ALWAYS CARRIED ME ACROSS THE GOAL LINE...
SUDDENLY, I WAS THAT YOUNG ATHLETE AGAIN--
--KNOWING NOTHING COULD STOP ME UNLESS I LET IT--
--AND FILLED WITH A PASSION I HADN'T KNOWN IN YEARS!
NITE OWL AND HOODED JUSTICE WADED THROUGH THE THUGS AS THEY'D DONE DOZENS OF TIMES IN THE PAST--
--WHILE I RELIED ON SOME OF MY OLD COLLEGE WRESTLING MOVES TO HELP EVEN UP THE FIGHT.
I CANNOT REMEMBER WHEN I LAST FELT SO ALIVE!

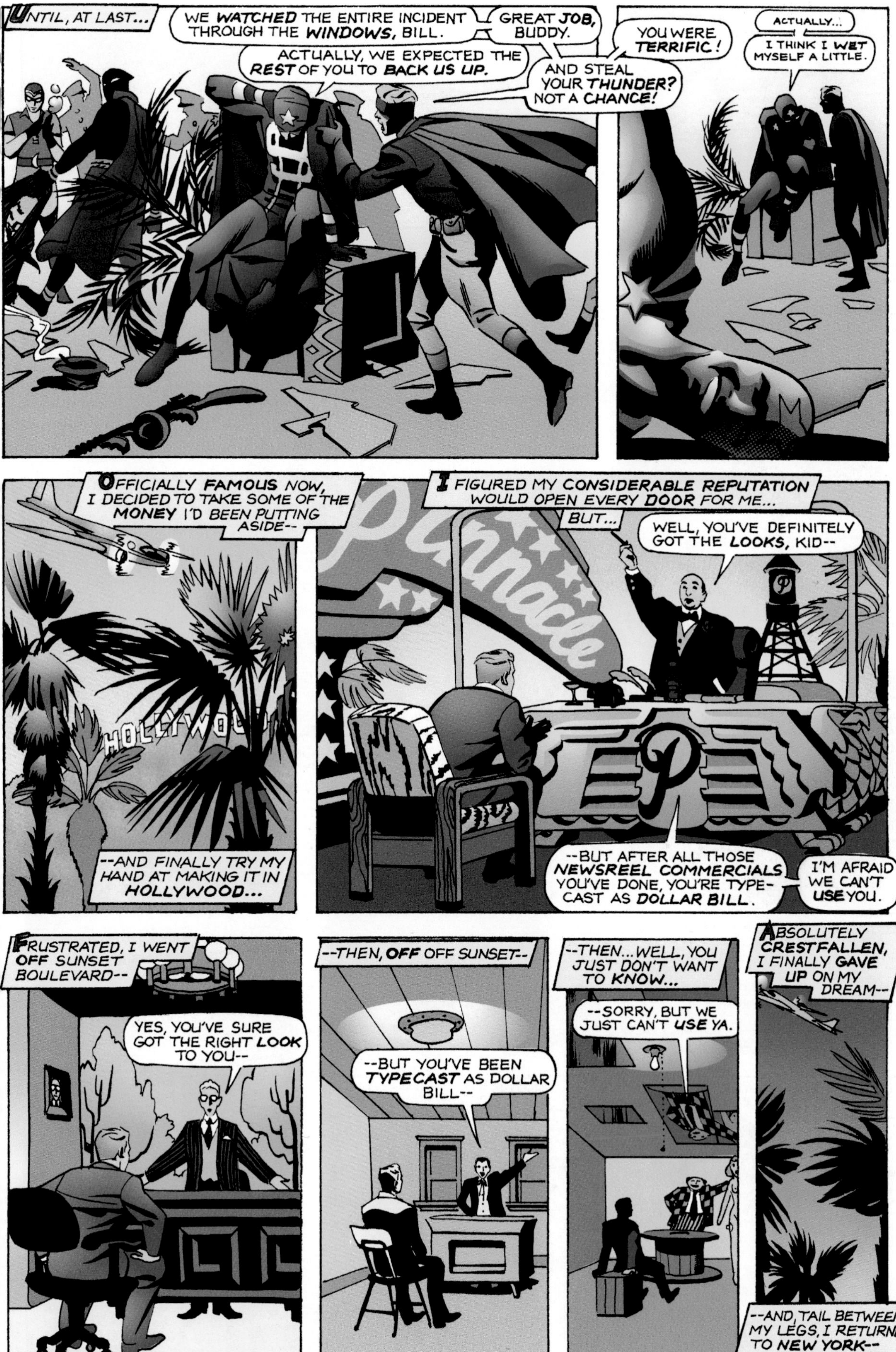
UNTIL, AT LAST...
WE WATCHED THE ENTIRE INCIDENT THROUGH THE WINDOWS, BILL.
GREAT JOB, BUDDY.
ACTUALLY, WE EXPECTED THE REST OF YOU TO BACK US UP.
YOU WERE TERRIFIC!
AND STEAL YOUR THUNDER? NOT A CHANCE!
ACTUALLY...
I THINK I WET MYSELF A LITTLE.
OFFICIALLY FAMOUS NOW, I DECIDED TO TAKE SOME OF THE MONEY I'D BEEN PUTTING ASIDE--
HOLLYWOOD
--AND FINALLY TRY MY HAND AT MAKING IT IN HOLLYWOOD...
I FIGURED MY CONSIDERABLE REPUTATION WOULD OPEN EVERY DOOR FOR ME...
BUT...
Pinnacle
WELL, YOU'VE DEFINITELY GOT THE LOOKS, KID--
--BUT AFTER ALL THOSE NEWSREEL COMMERCIALS YOU'VE DONE, YOU'RE TYPE-CAST AS DOLLAR BILL.
I'M AFRAID WE CAN'T USE YOU.
FRUSTRATED, I WENT OFF SUNSET BOULEVARD--
YES, YOU'VE SURE GOT THE RIGHT LOOK TO YOU--
--THEN, OFF OFF SUNSET--
--BUT YOU'VE BEEN TYPECAST AS DOLLAR BILL--
--THEN...WELL, YOU JUST DON'T WANT TO KNOW...
--SORRY, BUT WE JUST CAN'T USE YA.
ABSOLUTELY CRESTFALLEN, I FINALLY GAVE UP ON MY DREAM--
--AND, TAIL BETWEEN MY LEGS, I RETURNED TO NEW YORK--

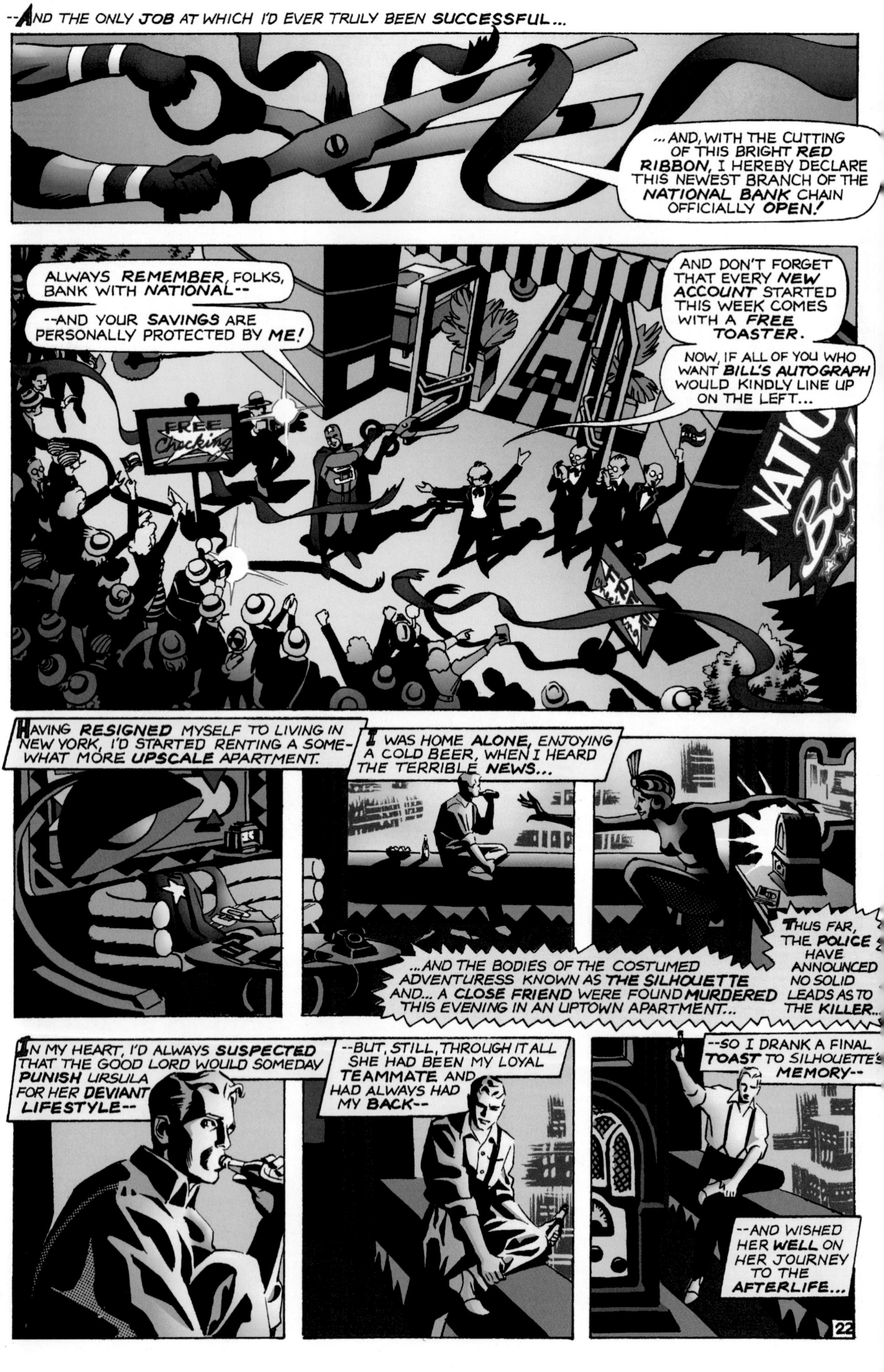

--AND THE ONLY JOB AT WHICH I'D EVER TRULY BEEN SUCCESSFUL...
...AND, WITH THE CUTTING OF THIS BRIGHT RED RIBBON, I HEREBY DECLARE THIS NEWEST BRANCH OF THE NATIONAL BANK CHAIN OFFICIALLY OPEN!
ALWAYS REMEMBER, FOLKS, BANK WITH NATIONAL--
--AND YOUR SAVINGS ARE PERSONALLY PROTECTED BY ME!
AND DON'T FORGET THAT EVERY NEW ACCOUNT STARTED THIS WEEK COMES WITH A FREE TOASTER.
NOW, IF ALL OF YOU WHO WANT BILL'S AUTOGRAPH WOULD KINDLY LINE UP ON THE LEFT...
FREE Checking
HAVING RESIGNED MYSELF TO LIVING IN NEW YORK, I'D STARTED RENTING A SOMEWHAT MORE UPSCALE APARTMENT.
I WAS HOME ALONE, ENJOYING A COLD BEER, WHEN I HEARD THE TERRIBLE NEWS...
...AND THE BODIES OF THE COSTUMED ADVENTURESS KNOWN AS THE SILHOUETTE AND... A CLOSE FRIEND WERE FOUND MURDERED THIS EVENING IN AN UPTOWN APARTMENT...
THUS FAR, THE POLICE HAVE ANNOUNCED NO SOLID LEADS AS TO THE KILLER...
IN MY HEART, I'D ALWAYS SUSPECTED THAT THE GOOD LORD WOULD SOMEDAY PUNISH URSULA FOR HER DEVIANT LIFESTYLE--
--BUT, STILL, THROUGH IT ALL SHE HAD BEEN MY LOYAL TEAMMATE AND HAD ALWAYS HAD MY BACK--
--SO I DRANK A FINAL TOAST TO SILHOUETTE'S MEMORY--
--AND WISHED HER WELL ON HER JOURNEY TO THE AFTERLIFE...
22

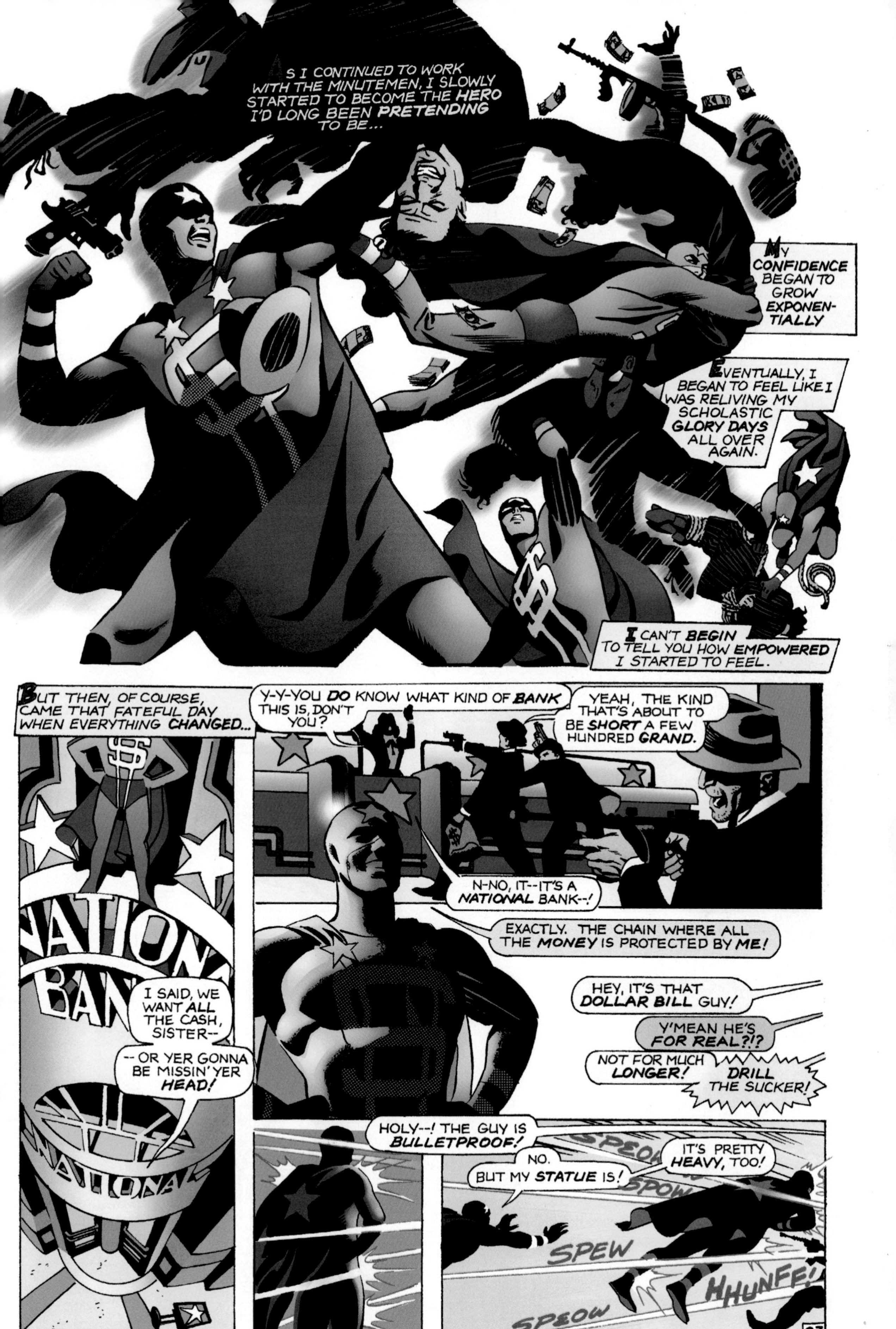
AS I CONTINUED TO WORK WITH THE MINUTEMEN, I SLOWLY STARTED TO BECOME THE HERO I'D LONG BEEN PRETENDING TO BE...
MY CONFIDENCE BEGAN TO GROW EXPONENTIALLY
EVENTUALLY, I BEGAN TO FEEL LIKE I WAS RELIVING MY SCHOLASTIC GLORY DAYS ALL OVER AGAIN.
I CAN'T BEGIN TO TELL YOU HOW EMPOWERED I STARTED TO FEEL.
BUT THEN, OF COURSE, CAME THAT FATEFUL DAY WHEN EVERYTHING CHANGED...
NATIONAL BANK
I SAID, WE WANT ALL THE CASH, SISTER--
-- OR YER GONNA BE MISSIN' YER HEAD!
NATIONAL
Y-Y-YOU DO KNOW WHAT KIND OF BANK THIS IS, DON'T YOU?
YEAH, THE KIND THAT'S ABOUT TO BE SHORT A FEW HUNDRED GRAND.
N-NO, IT--IT'S A NATIONAL BANK--!
EXACTLY. THE CHAIN WHERE ALL THE MONEY IS PROTECTED BY ME!
HEY, IT'S THAT DOLLAR BILL GUY!
Y'MEAN HE'S FOR REAL?!?
NOT FOR MUCH LONGER!
DRILL THE SUCKER!
HOLY--! THE GUY IS BULLETPROOF!
NO. BUT MY STATUE IS!
IT'S PRETTY HEAVY, TOO!
SPEOW
SPOW
SPEW
HHUNFF!
SPEOW

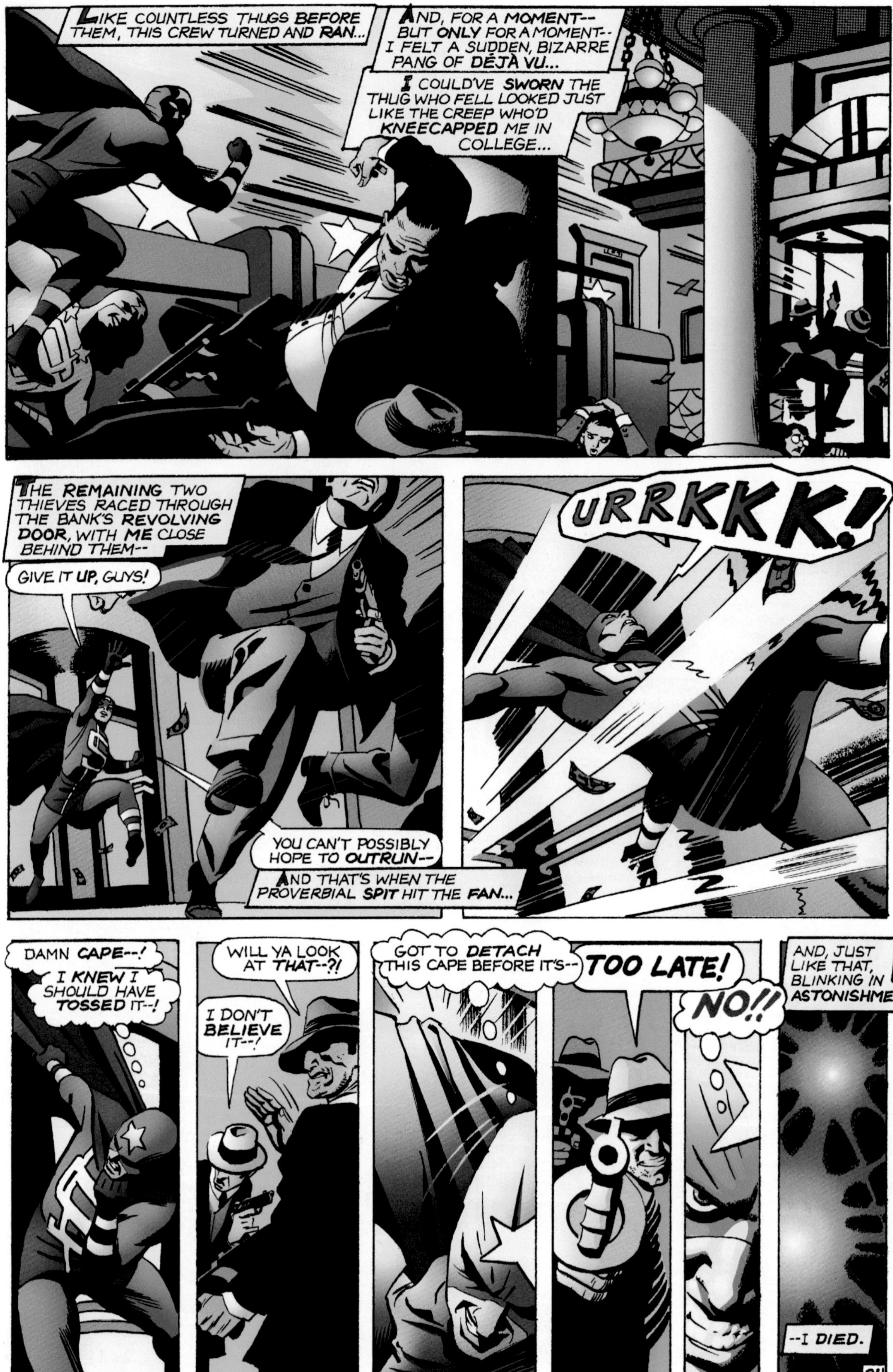
LIKE COUNTLESS THUGS BEFORE THEM, THIS CREW TURNED AND RAN...
AND, FOR A MOMENT-- BUT ONLY FOR A MOMENT-- I FELT A SUDDEN, BIZARRE PANG OF DÉJÀ VU...
I COULD'VE SWORN THE THUG WHO FELL LOOKED JUST LIKE THE CREEP WHO'D KNEECAPPED ME IN COLLEGE...
THE REMAINING TWO THIEVES RACED THROUGH THE BANK'S REVOLVING DOOR, WITH ME CLOSE BEHIND THEM--
GIVE IT UP, GUYS!
YOU CAN'T POSSIBLY HOPE TO OUTRUN--
AND THAT'S WHEN THE PROVERBIAL SPIT HIT THE FAN...
URRKKK!
DAMN CAPE--!
I KNEW I SHOULD HAVE TOSSED IT--!
WILL YA LOOK AT THAT--?!
I DON'T BELIEVE IT--!
GOT TO DETACH THIS CAPE BEFORE IT'S--
TOO LATE!
NO!!
AND, JUST LIKE THAT, BLINKING IN ASTONISHMENT--
--I DIED.

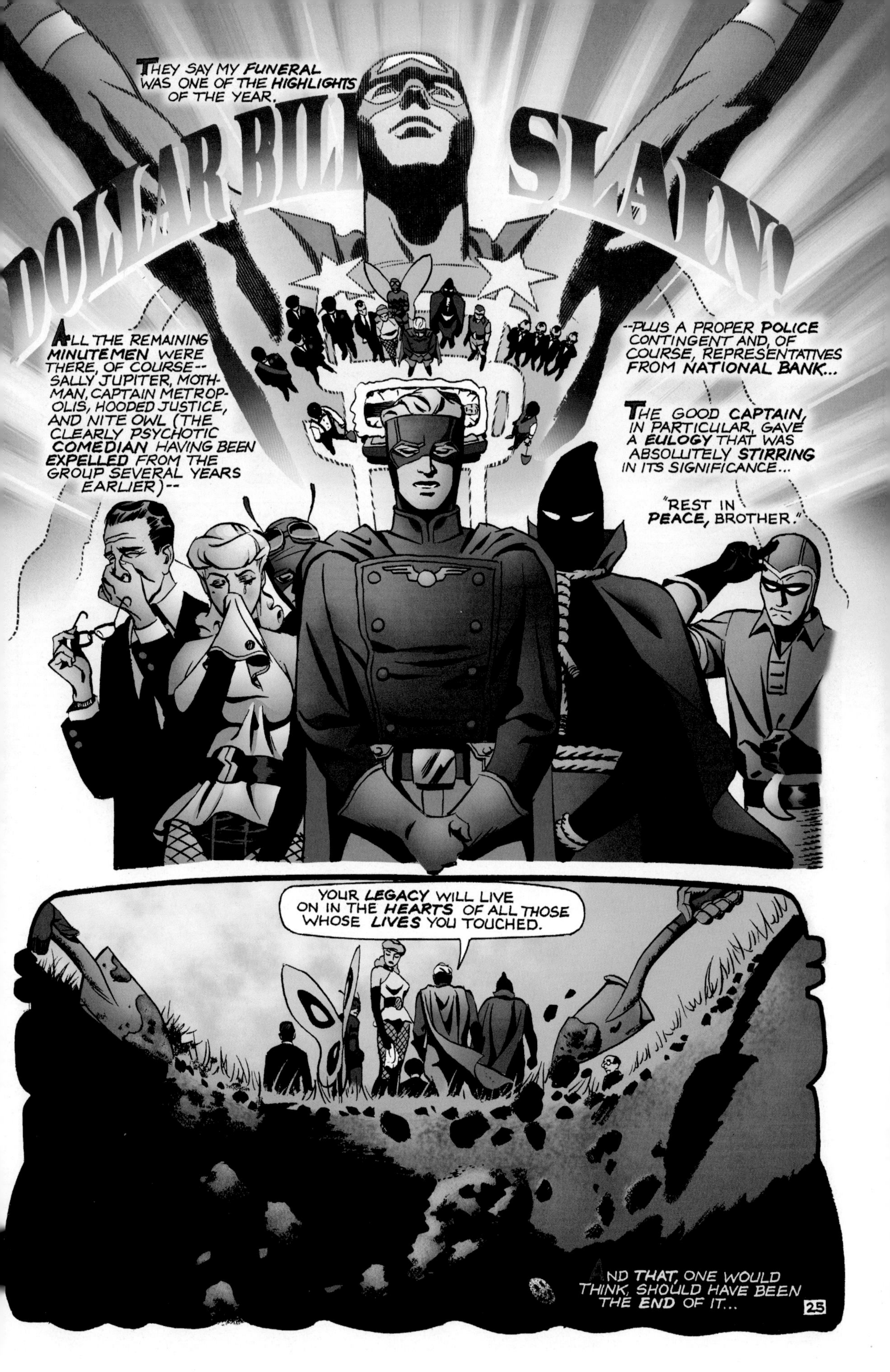

THEY SAY MY FUNERAL WAS ONE OF THE HIGHLIGHTS OF THE YEAR.
DOLLAR BILL SLAIN!
ALL THE REMAINING MINUTEMEN WERE THERE, OF COURSE-- SALLY JUPITER, MOTHMAN, CAPTAIN METROPOLIS, HOODED JUSTICE, AND NITE OWL (THE CLEARLY PSYCHOTIC COMEDIAN HAVING BEEN EXPELLED FROM THE GROUP SEVERAL YEARS EARLIER)--
--PLUS A PROPER POLICE CONTINGENT AND, OF COURSE, REPRESENTATIVES FROM NATIONAL BANK...
THE GOOD CAPTAIN, IN PARTICULAR, GAVE A EULOGY THAT WAS ABSOLUTELY STIRRING IN ITS SIGNIFICANCE...
"REST IN PEACE, BROTHER."
YOUR LEGACY WILL LIVE ON IN THE HEARTS OF ALL THOSE WHOSE LIVES YOU TOUCHED.
AND THAT, ONE WOULD THINK, SHOULD HAVE BEEN THE END OF IT...

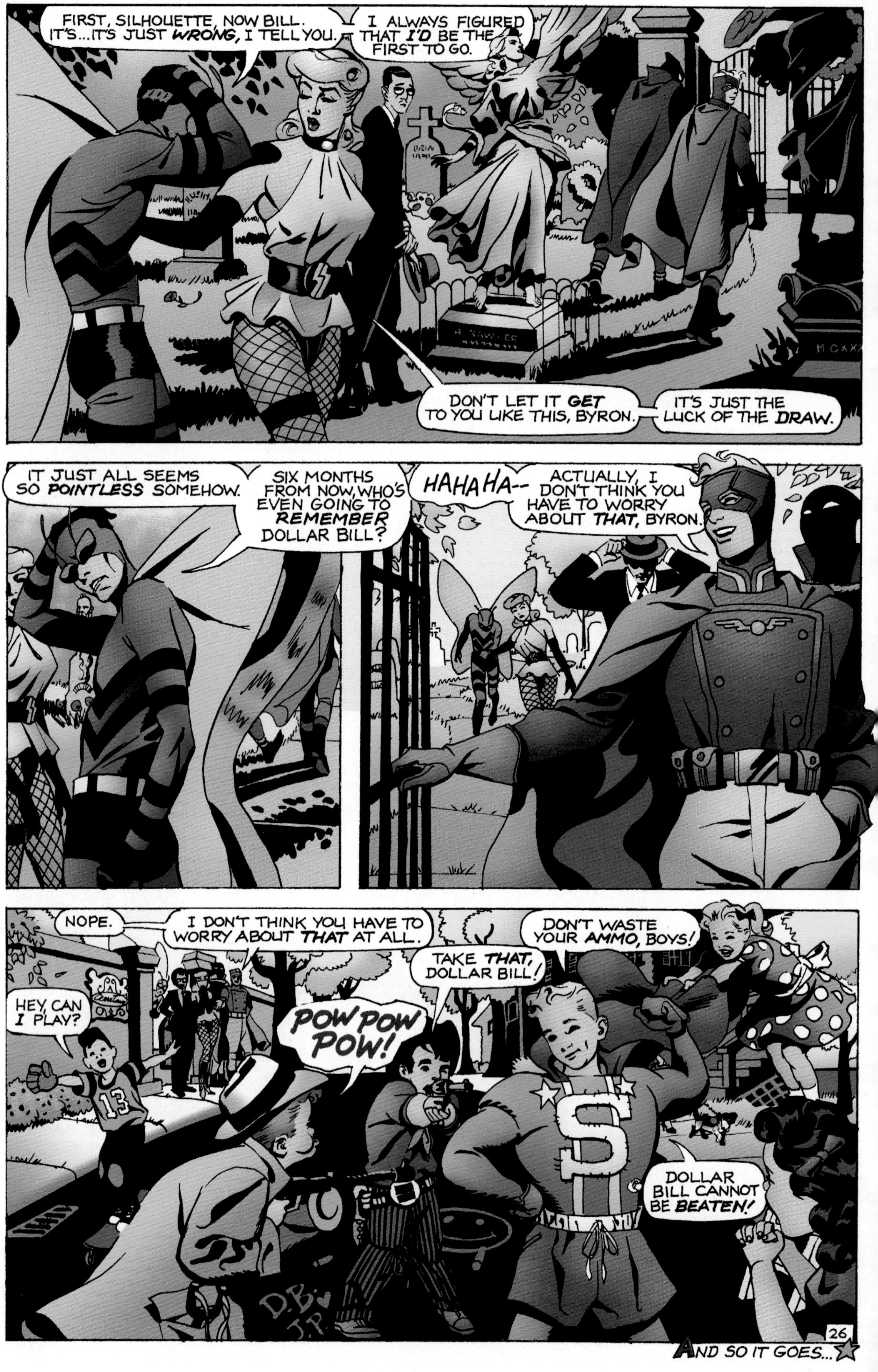
FIRST, SILHOUETTE, NOW BILL. IT'S...IT'S JUST WRONG, I TELL YOU.
I ALWAYS FIGURED THAT I'D BE THE FIRST TO GO.
DON'T LET IT GET TO YOU LIKE THIS, BYRON.
IT'S JUST THE LUCK OF THE DRAW.
IT JUST ALL SEEMS SO POINTLESS SOMEHOW.
SIX MONTHS FROM NOW, WHO'S EVEN GOING TO REMEMBER DOLLAR BILL?
HAHAHA--
ACTUALLY, I DON'T THINK YOU HAVE TO WORRY ABOUT THAT, BYRON.
NOPE.
I DON'T THINK YOU HAVE TO WORRY ABOUT THAT AT ALL.
DON'T WASTE YOUR AMMO, BOYS!
TAKE THAT, DOLLAR BILL!
HEY, CAN I PLAY?
POW POW POW!
13
DOLLAR BILL CANNOT BE BEATEN!

AND SO IT GOES...

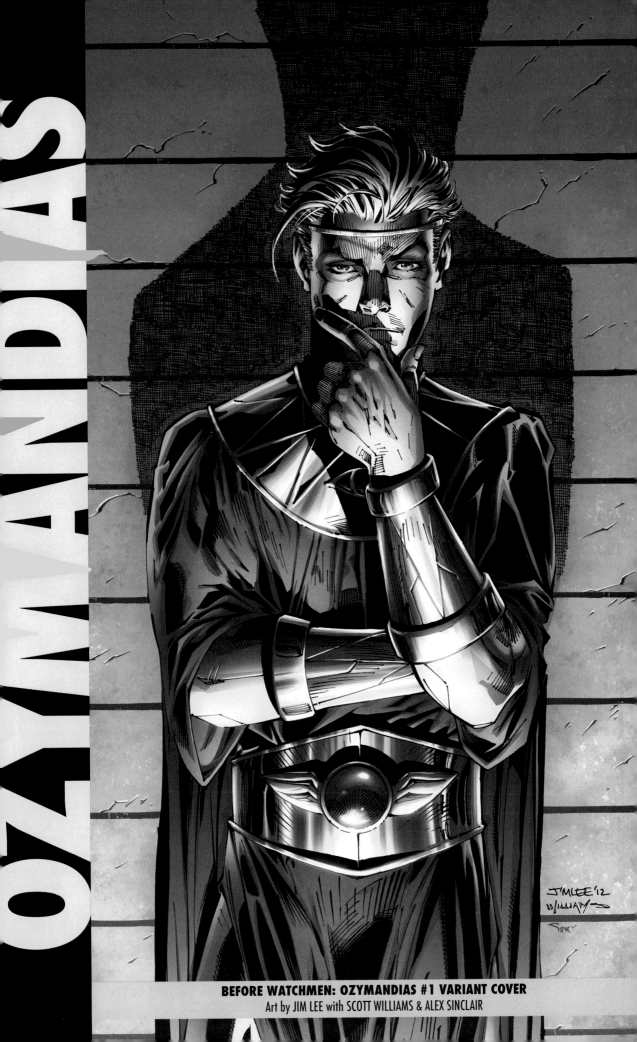

BEFORE WATCHMEN: OZYMANDIAS #1 VARIANT COVER
Art by JIM LEE with SCOTT WILLIAMS & ALEX SINCLAIR

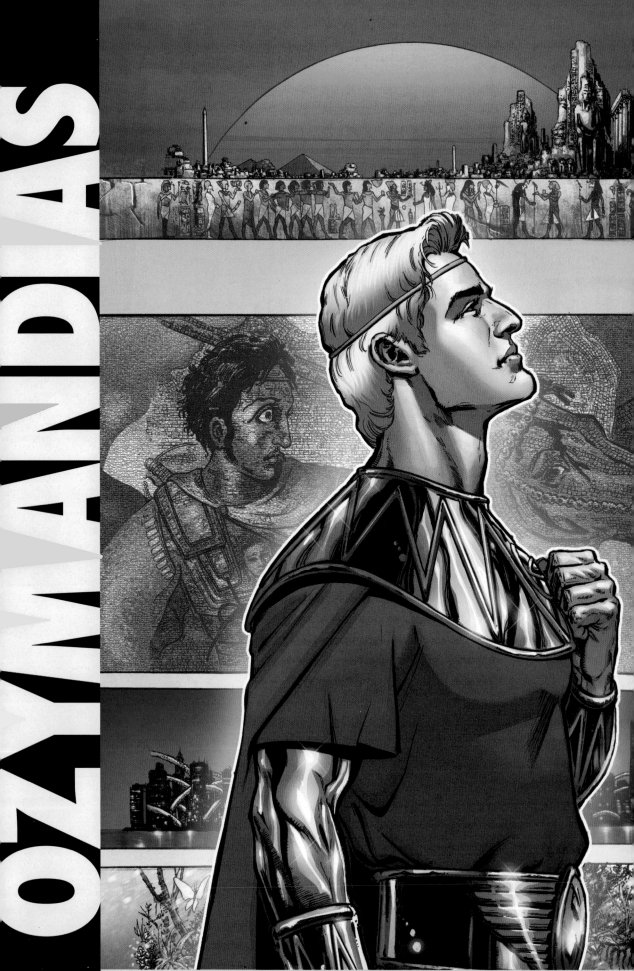

BEFORE WATCHMEN: OZYMANDIAS #1 VARIANT COVER
Art by PHIL JIMENEZ with ROMULO FAJARDO, JR.

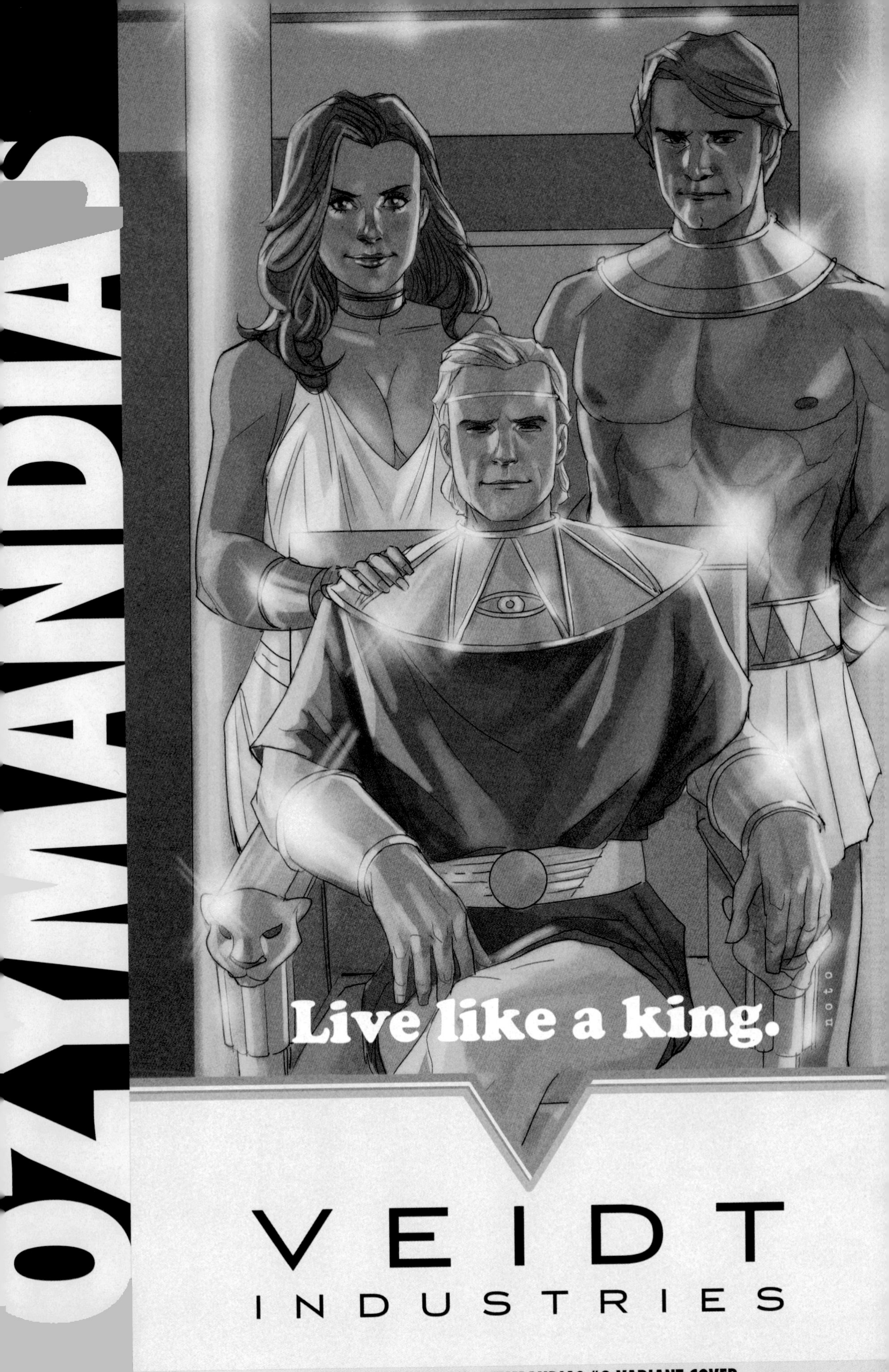
OZYMANDIAS
Live like a king.
VEIDT
INDUSTRIES

BEFORE WATCHMEN: OZYMANDIAS #2 VARIANT COVER
Art by PHIL NOTO

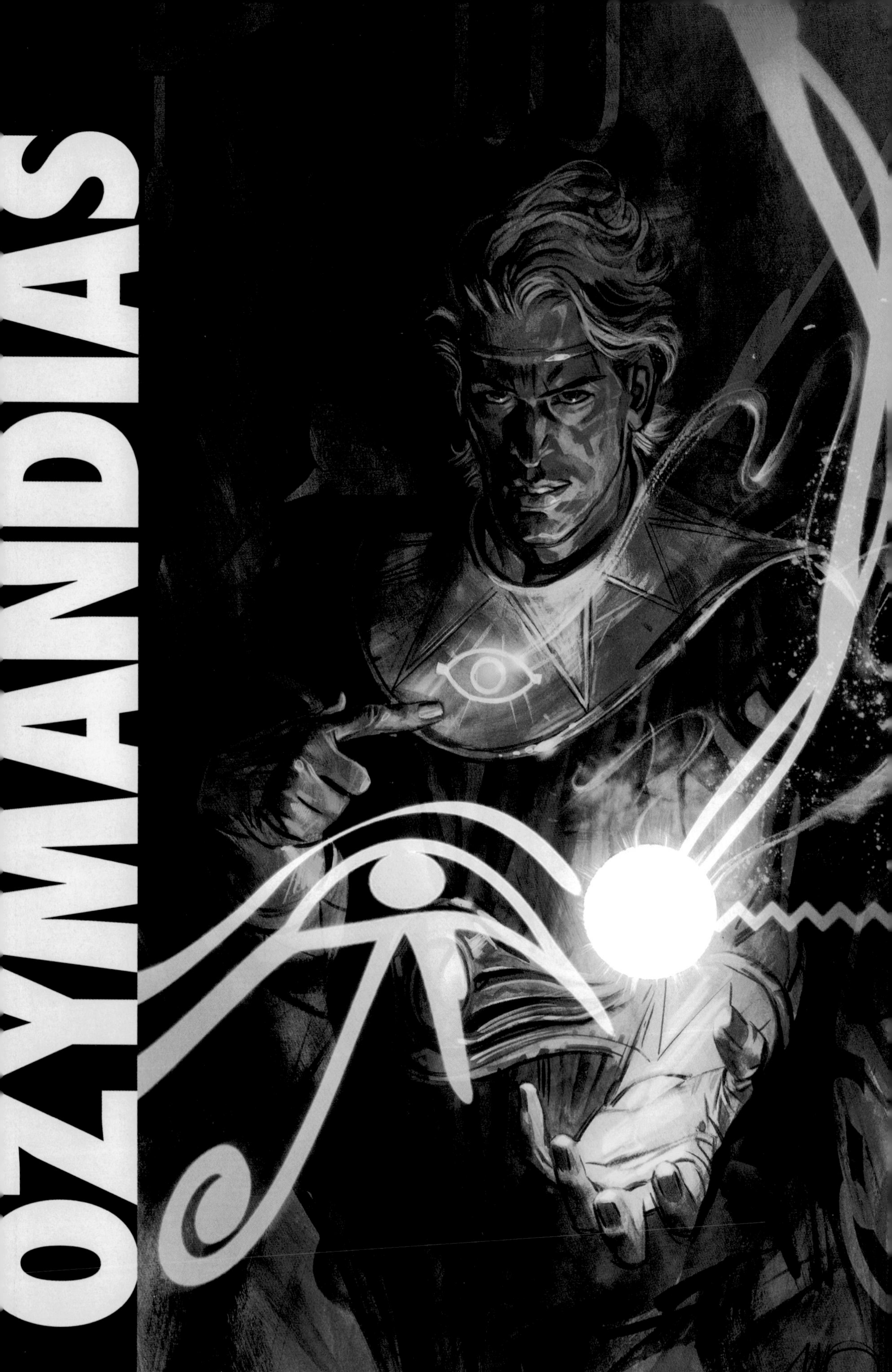
OZYMANDIAS

BEFORE WATCHMEN: OZYMANDIAS #3 VARIANT COVER
Art by MASSIMO CARNEVALE

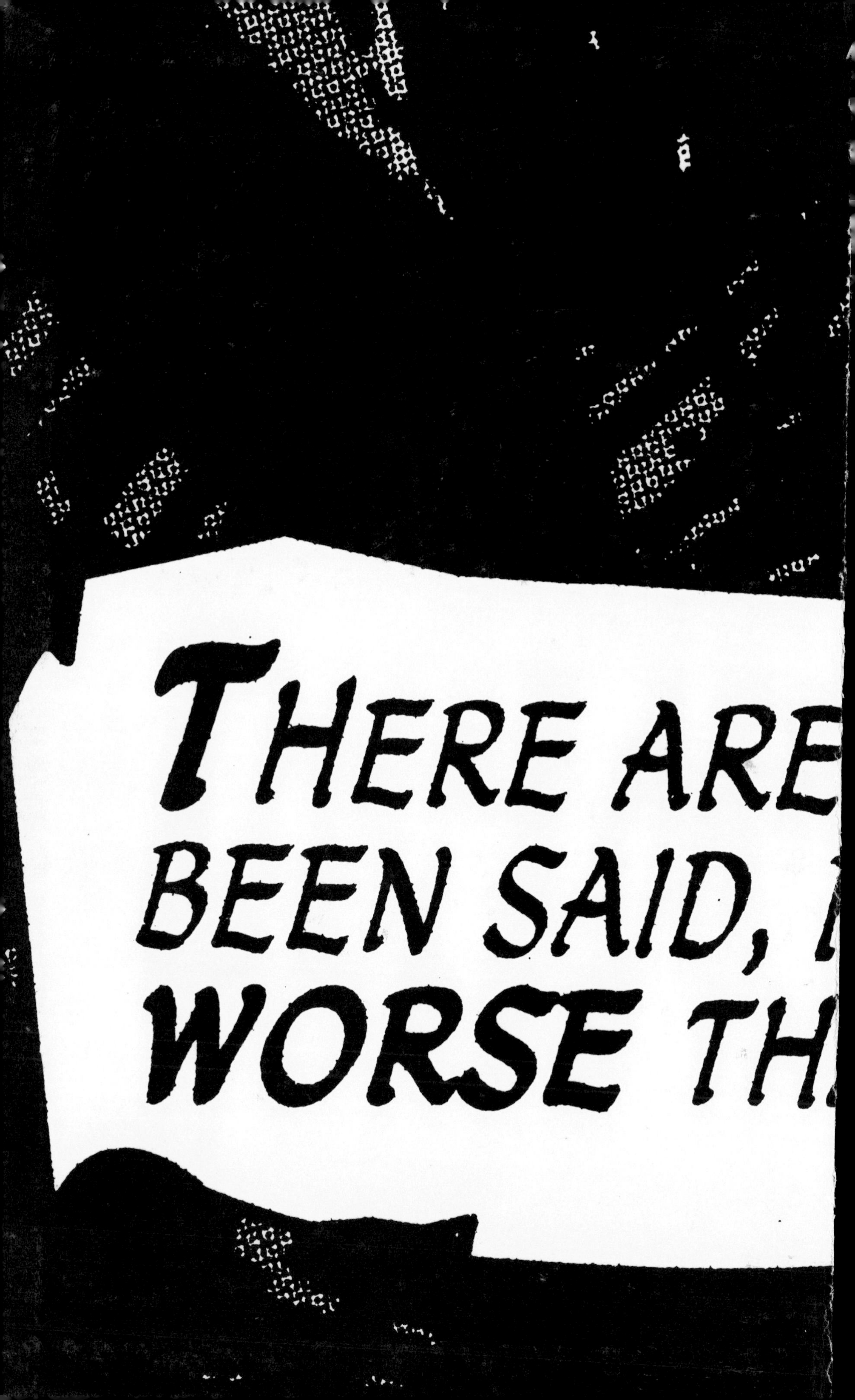
THERE ARE
BEEN SAID,
WORSE TH

BIOGRAPHIES

LEN WEIN Veteran comics writer and editor Len Wein is the creator of such memorable characters as Wolverine, the New X-Men, the Human Target and Lucius Fox, as well as the co-creator (with Bernie Wrightson) of the Swamp Thing. In his long and prolific career he has written for hundreds of titles, encompassing nearly every significant character in the medium. He has also built a successful career in TV animation, scripting such hit series as *X-Men*, *Spider-Man* and *Batman: The Animated Series*.

JAE LEE Jae Lee is a Korean-American comic book artist who has worked on such titles as *Hellshock*, *The Inhumans*, and Stephen King's *The Dark Tower: Gunslinger Born*. He got his start at Marvel Comics illustrating a Beast story arc in the *Marvel Comics Presents* title. Jae's first major comic book project was a 13-issue story arc on *Namor the Sub-Mariner*, written by one of his biggest artistic influences, the legendary John Byrne. The success of the title led to his Eisner Award-winning work on *The Inhumans* with Paul Jenkins. At DC, Lee has lent his inimitable style to BATMAN: JEKYLL & HYDE and will be the ongoing artist on the new BATMAN/SUPERMAN series.

JOHN HIGGINS Although John Higgins is perhaps best known for his award-winning coloring on *Watchmen*, he has also worked on a huge variety of titles for most of the major comic-book publishers, bringing his skills as an artist and sometimes writer to characters ranging from the 18th century bounty hunter Jonah Hex all the way to the 21st century's ultimate lawman Judge Dredd... and pretty much every other major comic character in between.

John also created *Razorjack* — which he wrote, illustrated and initially published — as a personal project that gave him the opportunity to express his darkest fears and to shine a light into the deepest recesses of his mind. He feels that this experience helped shape the twisted mindset required for the Crimson Corsair and guide its hero, poor Gordon McClachlan, through many trials, terrors and tribulations in his quest to regain control of his immortal soul.

STEVE RUDE, nicknamed "The Dude," is a multiple award-winning artist who is best known for his work on the offbeat science fiction title *Nexus*, on which he and co-creator Mike Baron have been collaborating since 1981. Rude considers comics legend Jack "King" Kirby one of his biggest influences, and Rude's style meshes Kirby's streamlined dynamism with his own polished style and attention to detail.

Some of Rude's other credits include MISTER MIRACLE SPECIAL, LEGENDS OF THE DC UNIVERSE, HULK VS. SUPERMAN, *Captain America: What Price Glory?*, and *Space Ghost*. In 1997, he co-created The Moth with Gary Martin under his own Rude Dude Productions. He is currently drawing the further adventures of Nexus under the *Dark Horse Presents* title.

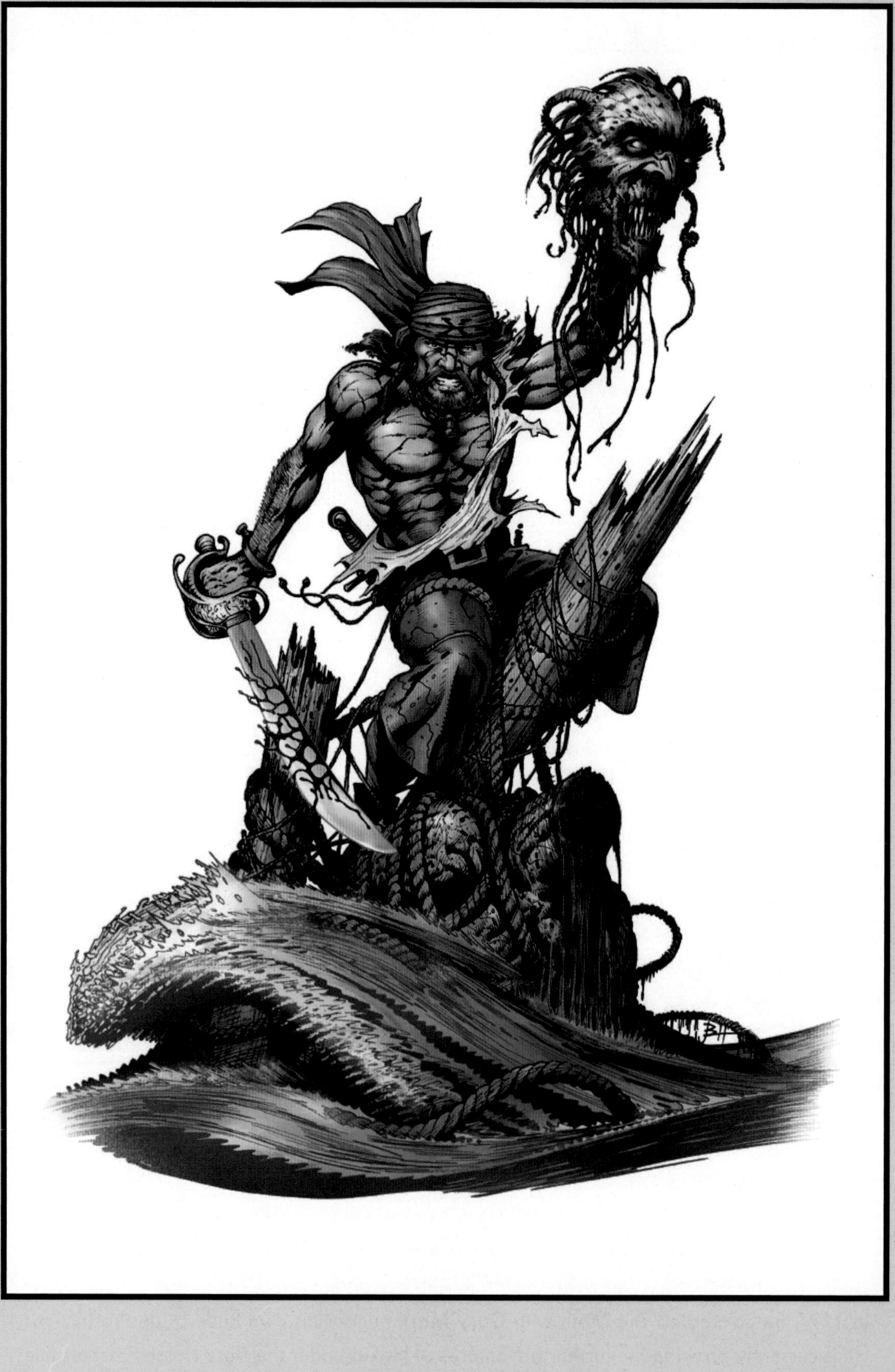

CRIMSON CORSAIR ART BY JOHN HIGGINS

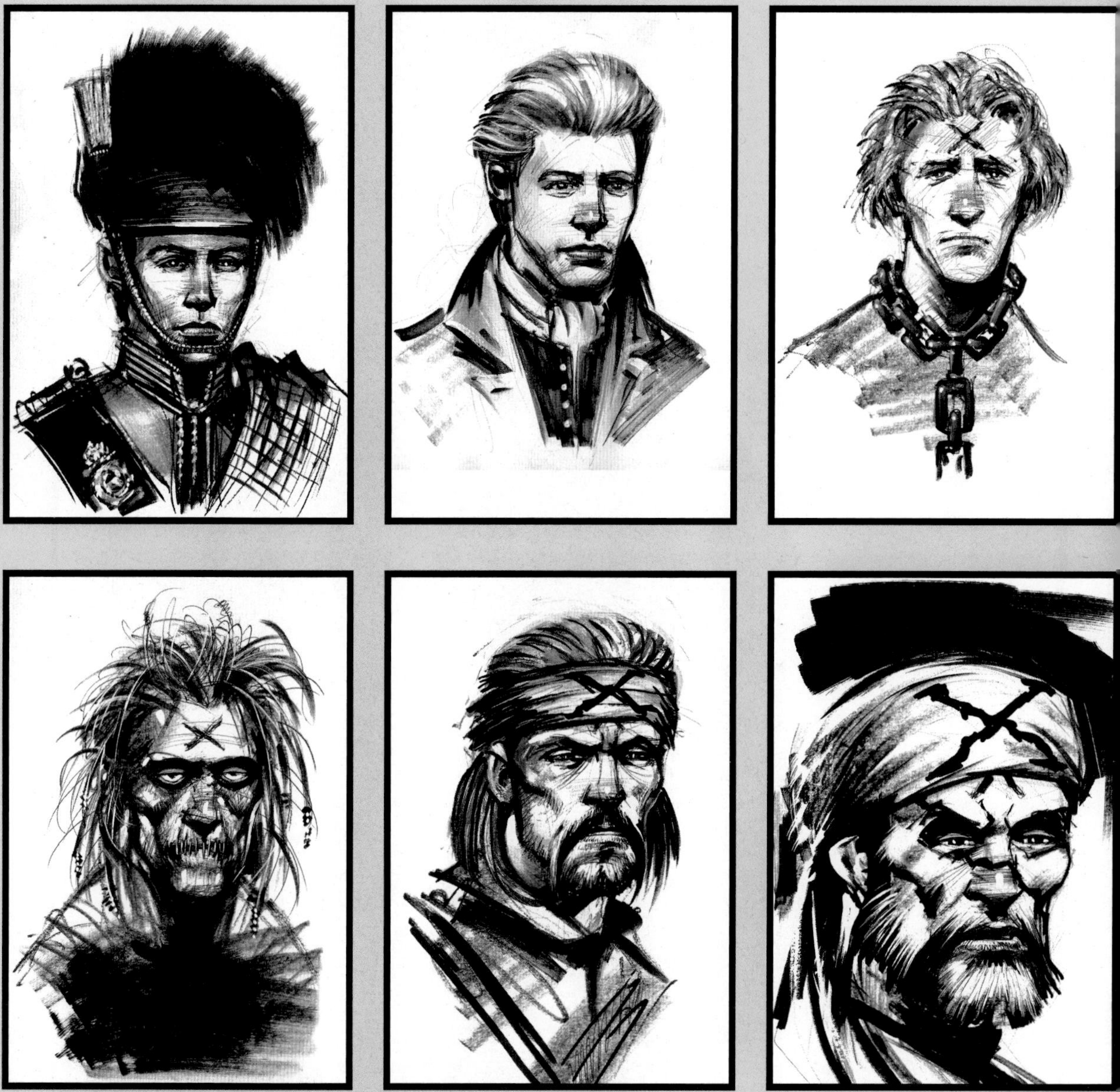

CRIMSON CORSAIR CHARACTER SKETCHES BY JOHN HIGGINS

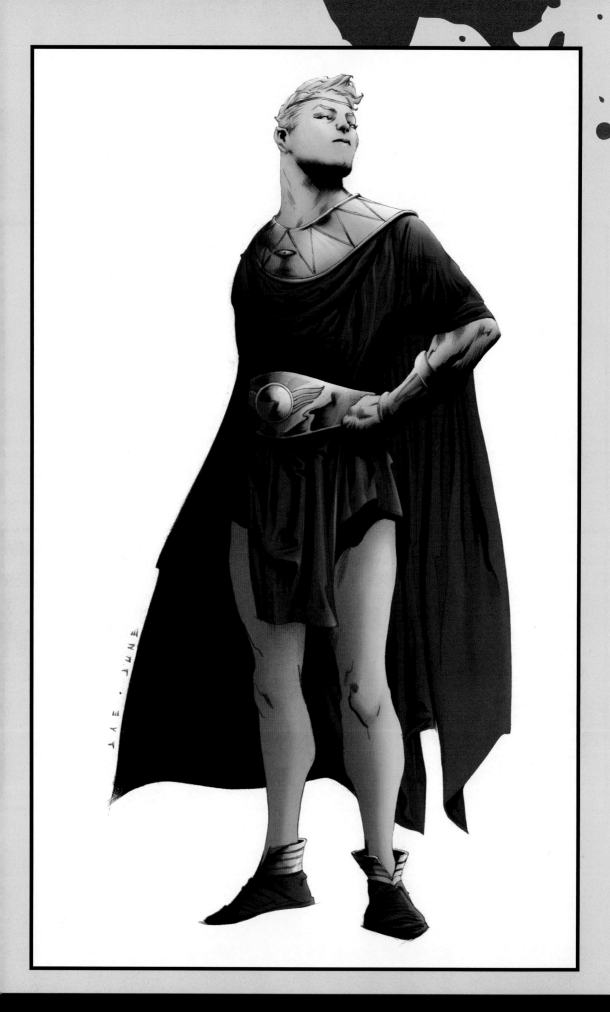

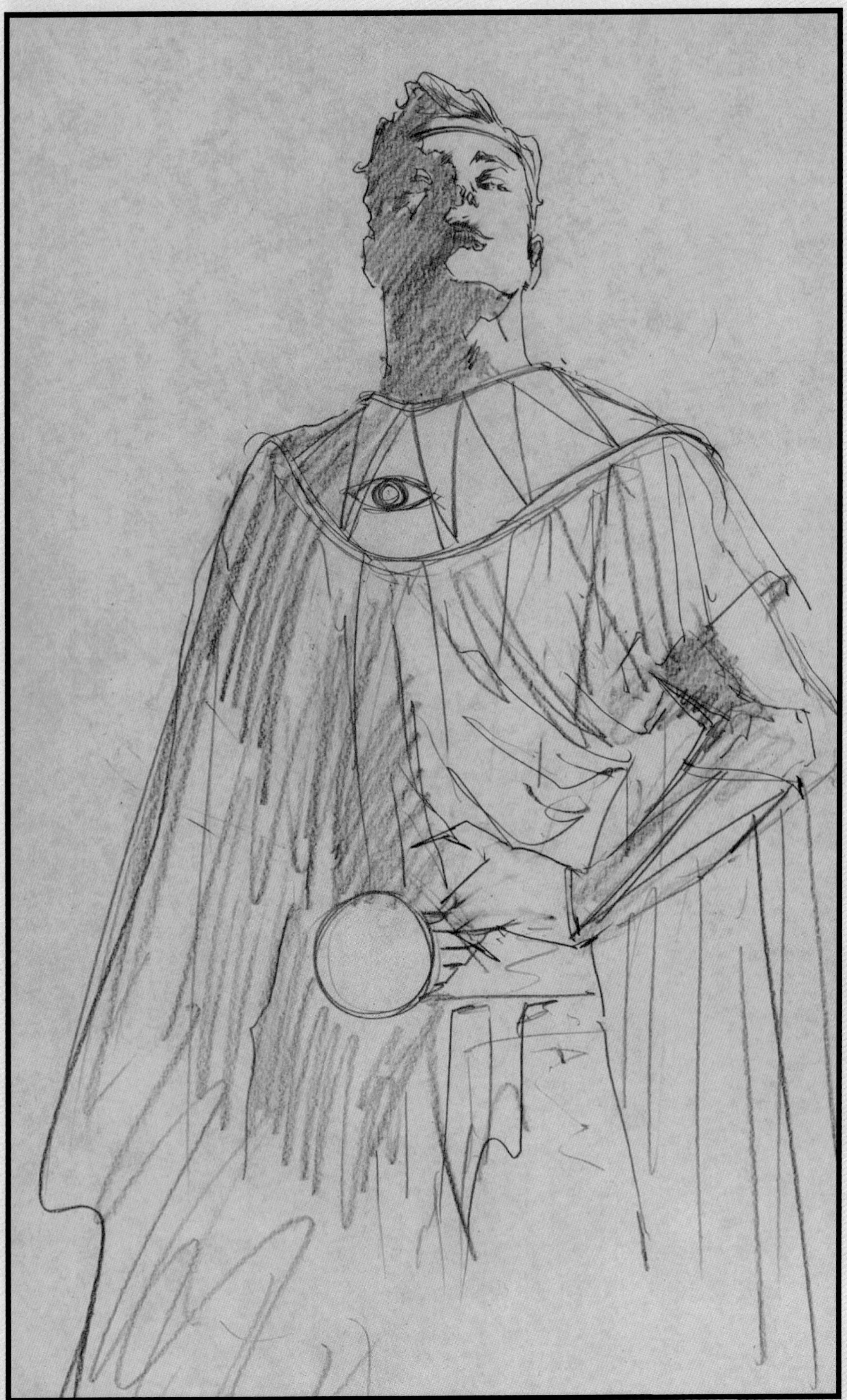

OZYMANDIAS SKETCHES BY JAE LEE

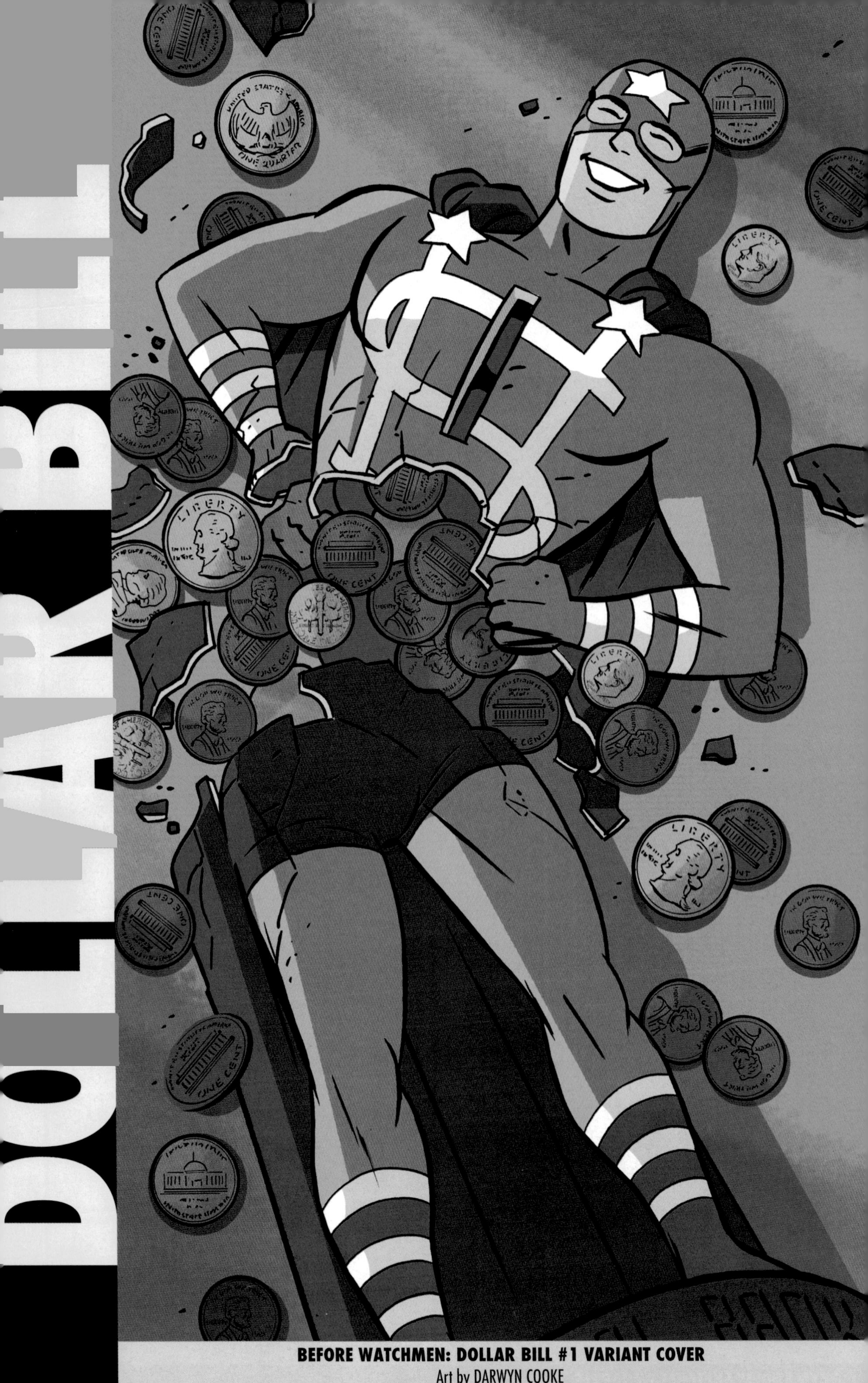
DOLLAR BILL

BEFORE WATCHMEN: DOLLAR BILL #1 VARIANT COVER
Art by DARWYN COOKE

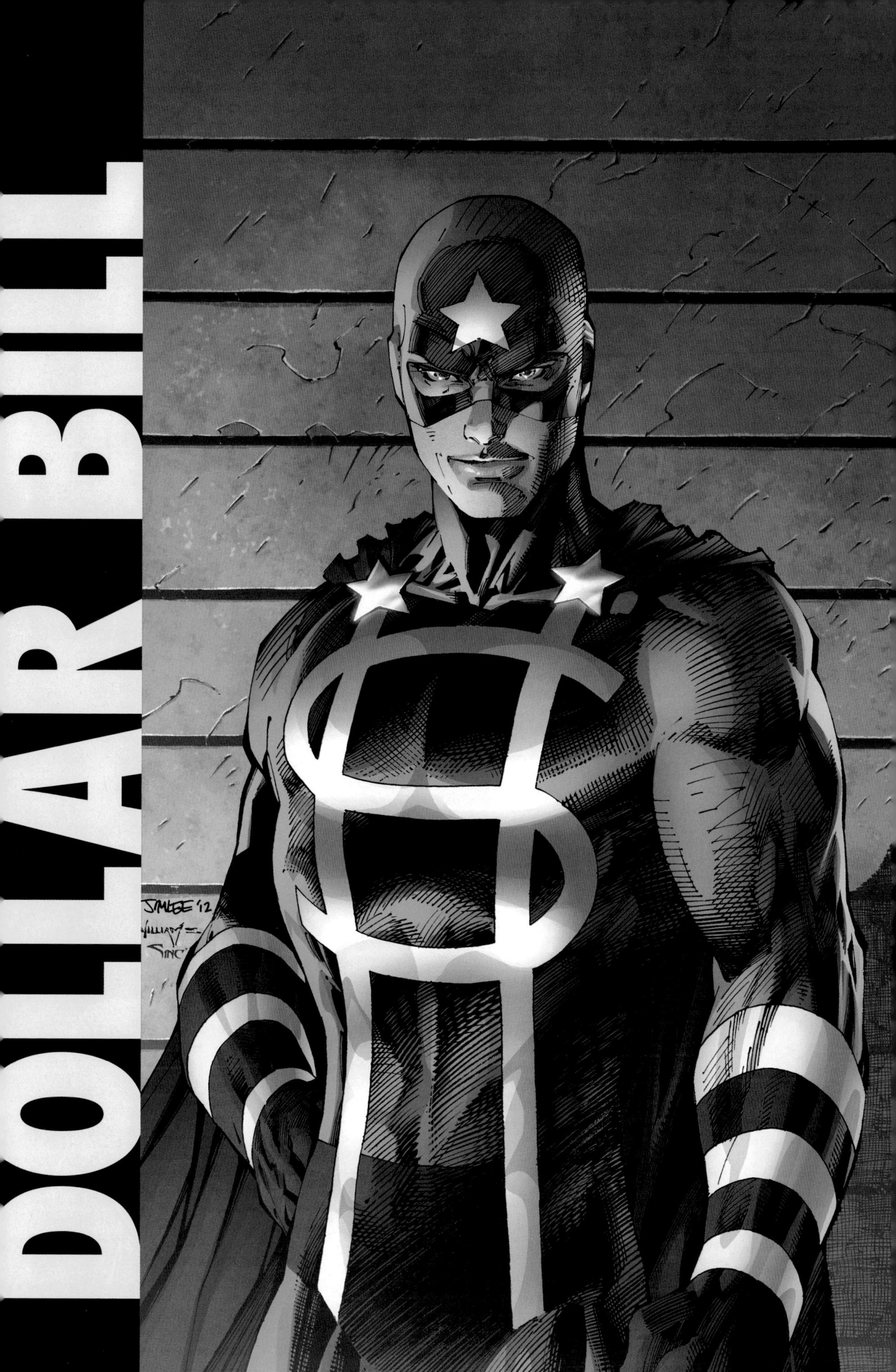
DOLLAR BILL

BEFORE WATCHMEN: DOLLAR BILL #1 VARIANT COVER
Art by JIM LEE with SCOTT WILLIAMS & ALEX SINCLAIR

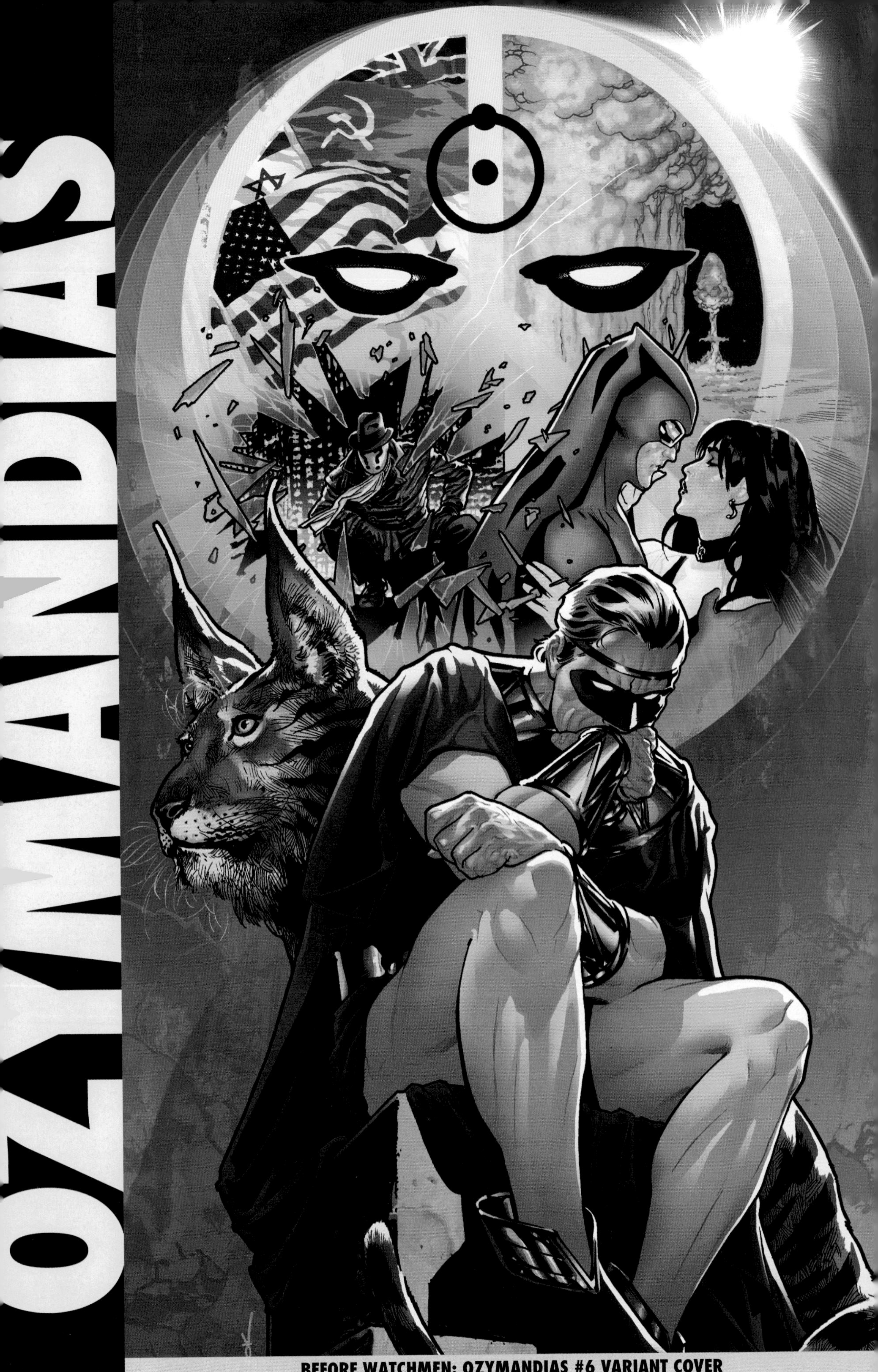
OZYMANDIAS

BEFORE WATCHMEN: OZYMANDIAS #6 VARIANT COVER
Art by RYAN SOOK

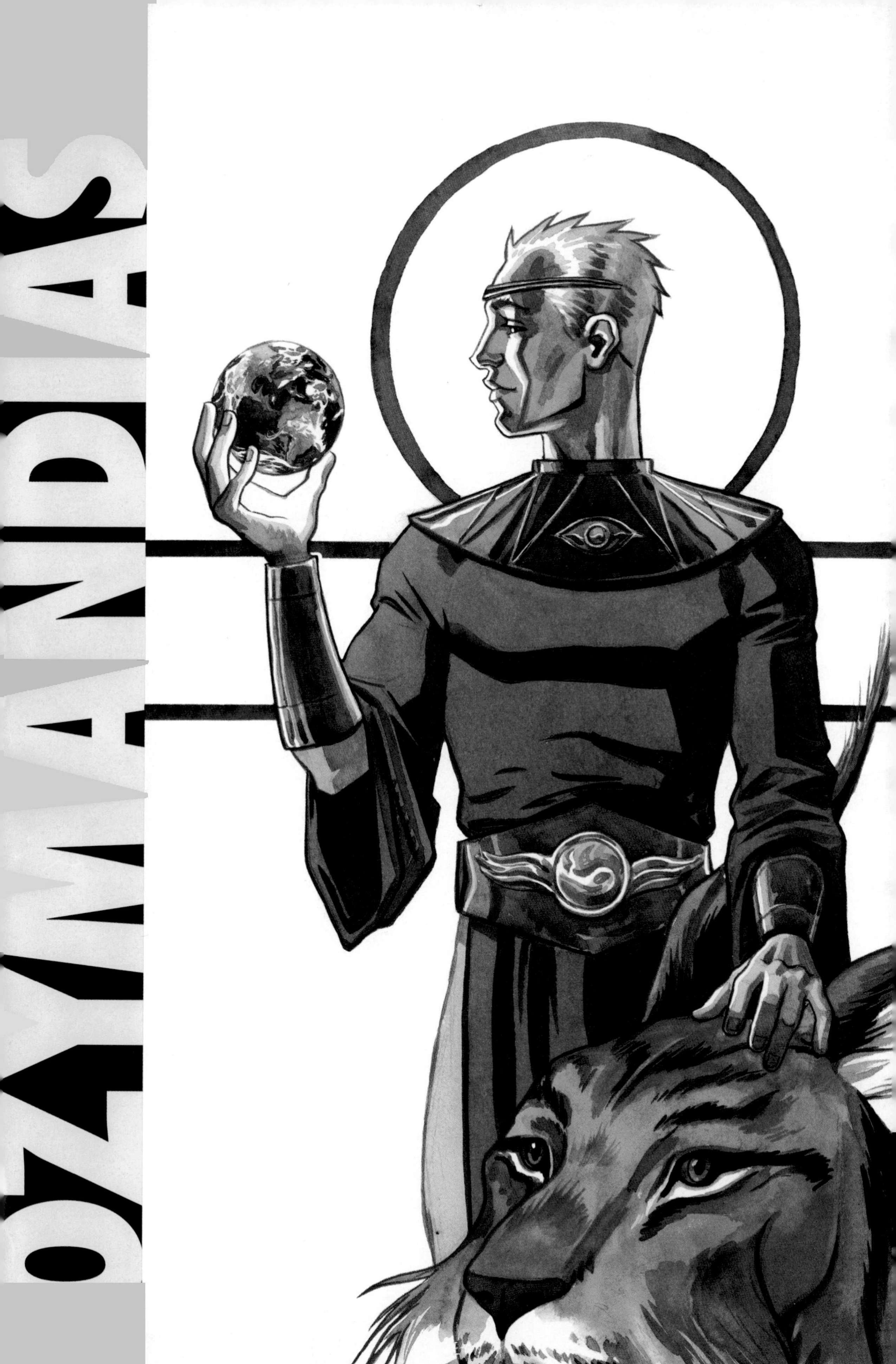
OZYMANDIAS

BEFORE WATCHMEN: OZYMANDIAS #5 VARIANT COVER
Art by JILL THOMPSON

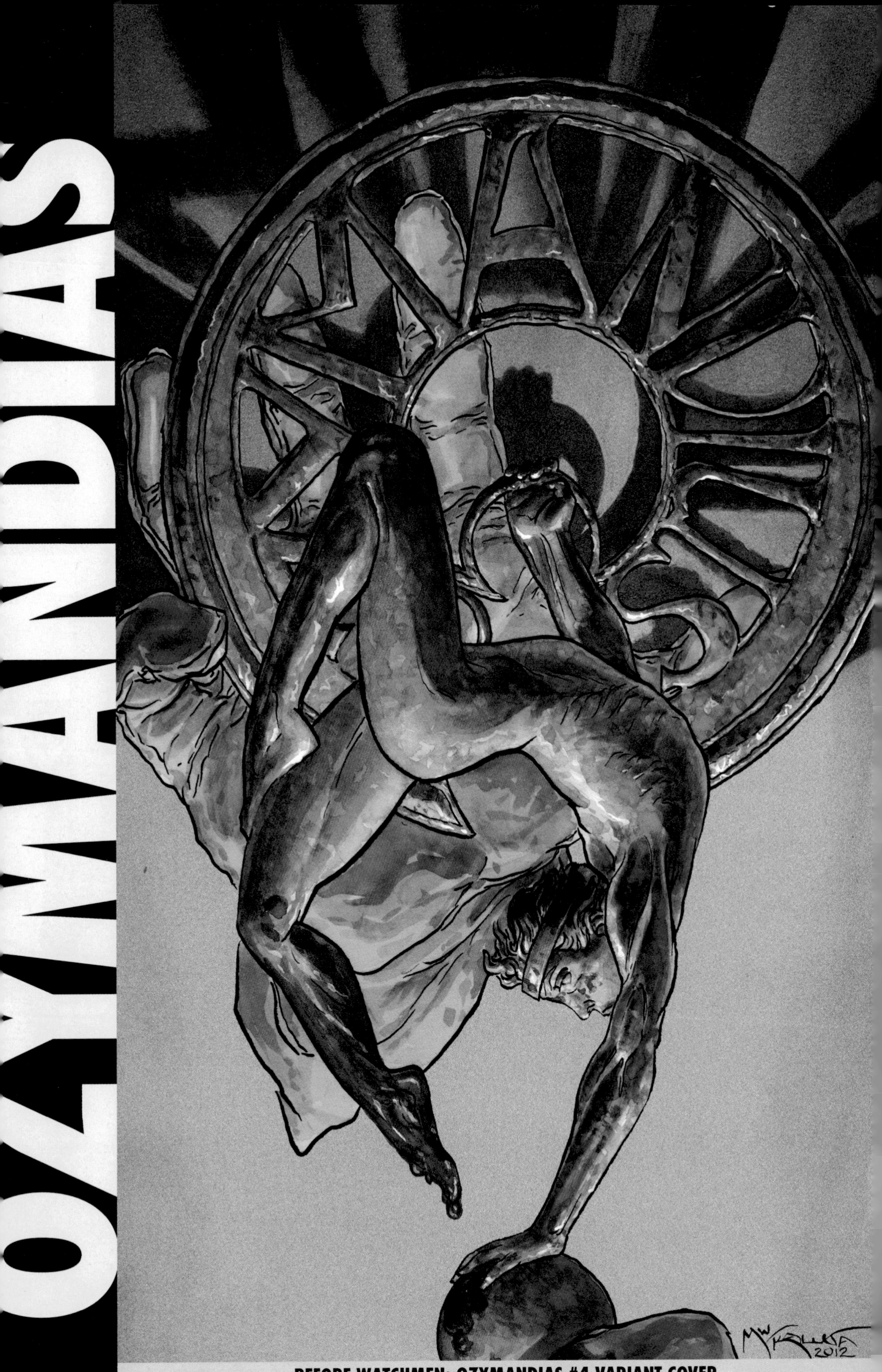
OZYMANDIAS

BEFORE WATCHMEN: OZYMANDIAS #4 VARIANT COVER

Art by MICHAEL WM. KALUTA